Tableau at Work

With data and AI increasingly at the forefront of business today, you have a significant advantage when you can manage data, and uncover and communicate data insights effectively. By thoroughly cataloging, indexing, and cross-referencing material, this book flattens the steep Tableau learning curve, starting you on your data journey and serving as a comprehensive reference and study guide.

- Where do I start with Tableau?
- How do I prepare and connect to data files that are constantly changing?
- How do I share Tableau files with co-workers, and what is tall data?
- How do I test whether the calculations and aggregations are correct?
- How can I create vibrant charts with sorting, color, axis labels, annotations, mark labels, trend lines, tooltips, or reference lines?

The book includes over 60 worksheets and guides to deliver 40 quality charts and dashboards. In addition, there are another 60 focused and on-point examples, covering everything from context filters and weighted average calculations to transparent shapes and colors with placeholder fields. Similarly, nine step-by-step dashboard guides illustrate parameters, containers, buttons, actions, and more. With over 800 diagrams and images, clear explanations are provided for concepts including: Measures and Dimensions; Discrete vs. Continuous; Aggregation; Joins, Blends, and Relationships; Order of Operations; Mark Types and Color, Size, Text, Detail, and Tooltip Tiles; Actions, Sets, Links, Highlighting, and Parameters; Reference Lines and Trend Lines; Dashboard Layout, Containers, Filtering, and Interactivity.

Tableau at Work is the perfect book for anyone who wants a comprehensive guide and reference to Tableau, from beginners and novices all the way to advanced and professional users. Many of the Tableau workbooks can be downloaded from the author's Tableau Public profile and for more information you can also visit the author's website (www.TableauAtWork.com).

Tableau at Work

Cathy Young

CRC Press
Taylor & Francis Group
Boca Raton New York London

CRC Press is an imprint of the
Taylor & Francis Group, an **informa** business

Designed cover image: Shutterstock image 516643384

First edition published 2025
by CRC Press
2385 NW Executive Center Drive, Suite 320, Boca Raton FL 33431

and by CRC Press
4 Park Square, Milton Park, Abingdon, Oxon, OX14 4RN

CRC Press is an imprint of Taylor & Francis Group, LLC

© 2025 Cathy Young

ISBN: 978-1-032-93564-5 (hbk)
ISBN: 978-1-032-93418-1 (pbk)
ISBN: 978-1-003-56645-8 (ebk)

DOI: 10.1201/9781003566458

Typeset in Palatino
by SPi Technologies India Pvt Ltd (Straive)

My "twenty seconds of insane courage*" is sharing this book with you. As Benjamin Mee said in We Bought a Zoo, I hope that "something great will come of it*" for both of us. I want to thank the incredible #datafam ambassadors who take the time to share their knowledge, like Tableau Tim, Andy Kriebel, Ryan Sleeper, Zak Geis, Kevin Flerlage, Priyah Padham, Craig Heard, Will Perkins, and many more. I appreciate your Tableau Public files, LinkedIn chats, YouTube videos, and how you all share your expertise! Special thanks to Dawn Harrington for her great tech tips and Scott Eaton, who introduced me to my favorite companion tool, RapidDox. This book is dedicated to my family, whose support and feedback were essential. To my husband, thank you for your boundless patience. And to Mickey, my cherished friend, thank you for your keen eye and enduring friendship. Your willingness to proofread the final copy was a gift. I am so fortunate to have a friend who understands me so well.

Tell me, and I forget. Teach me, and I remember. Involve me, and I learn. – Benjamin Franklin

*"We Bought a Zoo Quotes." Quotes.net. STANDS4 LLC, 2024. Web. 2 Sep. 2024. https://www.quotes.net/mquote/1132849.

Contents

Author Biography

As an award-winning author who has published books on Python, Tableau, Apple devices, and smart home technology, Cathy Young enjoys learning new technology and organizing her notes to solidify new knowledge. Her book *Apple Watch Series 4: Telling Time & So Much More* is the eLit Awards 2019 Silver Medal Winner.

Introduction

Welcome to the world of Tableau. And thank you for picking up my book. Assuming you picked it up on purpose (i.e., you didn't confuse it with a book on French furniture or cooking), you might have found yourself, as I did, needing to learn Tableau on the job – maybe to complete a special project. Big deal, right? If you are at all like I am, you have mastered plenty of software applications on the fly by playing around with them for a bit. So, I will start with a gentle warning: Tableau is unlike Excel, Cognos, Illustrator, InDesign, Corel Draw, or any other consumer-level applications. It just isn't. From one data analyst and software nerd to perhaps another, Tableau is a bear to learn. Prepare to be challenged and frustrated for a while. It will make sense eventually, but you'll probably have to work at it. Let me help. There are 50 step-by-step guides to create 40 chart types at a glance and over 60 detailed examples of everything from context filters and weighted average calculations to transparent shapes and colors with placeholder fields. Similarly, the dashboard chapter has nine step-by-step dashboards illustrating parameters, containers, buttons, actions, and more. With over 800 diagrams and images, the clear explanations delve deeper into concepts like these:

- Measures and Dimensions
- Discrete and Continuous
- Aggregation
- Joins, Blends, and Relationships
- Filter Order of Operations
- Mark Types and Color, Size, Text, Detail, and Tooltips
- Actions with Filters, Sets, Links, Highlighting, and Parameters
- Reference Lines and Trend Lines
- Dashboard Layout, Containers, Filtering, Interactivity, and Stories

I have been very intentional in making this book as simple as possible. However, there is a limit to how simple such a complex topic can be. So, be patient with yourself (and with me). Don't be surprised if you must read and re-read some parts two or three times. The weeds can be thick at times. I encourage you to have Tableau open and follow along as you read. Getting through the book will take longer, but I believe this approach will ultimately save you time.

The world of Tableau has new terminology to learn and requires a lot of searching to figure out how things work. The learning curve, as I suggested, can be steep. Even with the free Tableau videos, virtual classes, and studying the certification syllabus, I easily spent two years at it before things gelled and finally made sense to me. That period of my Tableau journey was difficult. Was it worth it? Absolutely. Am I still learning? Yep.

Since a lot goes on "under the hood" in Tableau, I was concerned I would inadvertently create an incorrect visualization (a term that will become clear soon enough). So, my priority was figuring out how to test and validate. I spent a good bit of time organizing and refining my notes. I researched details until I was confident I understood how things worked.

Looking back, I am amused to find that I flagged items for research that now seem obvious. While my original nomenclature was sometimes wrong, I realized that all that knowledge was valuable in bridging the gap between common terminology and Tableau lingo. I incorporated my knowledge into a vast, cross-referenced, indexed knowledge base. Today, I can use that perspective to help you avoid pitfalls and remove some of the frustration from your Tableau journey.

Tableau skills are not limited to developers. As a data ambassador, I regularly work with my business partners to explore their data. Our partnership means we can uncover new insights and quickly answer questions in real time. Data analytics skills are the new email; we must climb this mountain to succeed in the future.

Before you join me on this fascinating journey to "#datafam" independence, let's browse through this gallery of step-by-step visualizations we will explore together. I included the topic and page numbers for quick reference.

Additional Information

Tableau Public: https://public.tableau.com/app/profile/cathy.y7960/vizzes

Tableau Reference: https://www.tableau.com/data-insights/reference-library/visual-analytics

DOI: 10.1201/9781003566458-1

YouTube Channel: https://www.youtube.com/
@TableauAtWork/videos

LinkedIn: https://www.linkedin.com/groups/
13004387/ Author Page: http://amazon.
com/author/cathyryoung

See Figure 6.8, Dual Axes Area and Line on page 106
See Figure 8.44, Area Chart, Click Data Points to
Sort with a Set, page 187

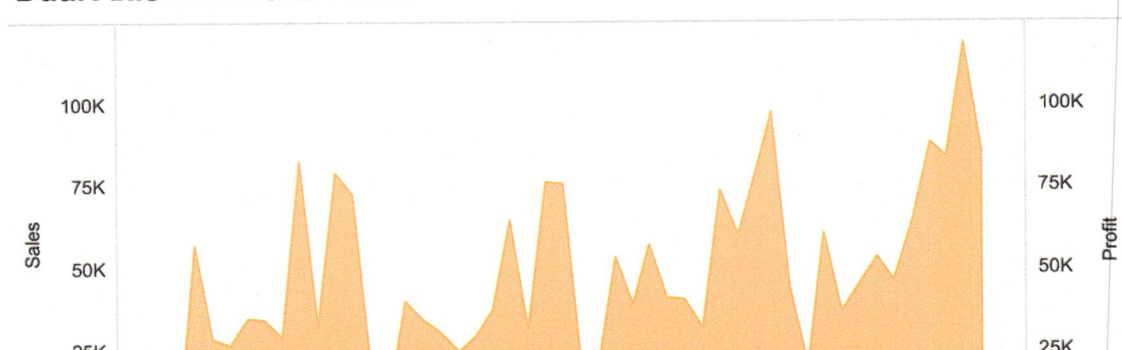

FIGURE 1

A dual-axis chart.

This chart employs a dual-axis format to present both sales and profit data. Sales are represented using an area chart, while profit is depicted using a line chart. Color-coding within the chart title serves as a direct visual cue, associating each variable with its corresponding chart type, thereby eliminating the need for a separate legend.

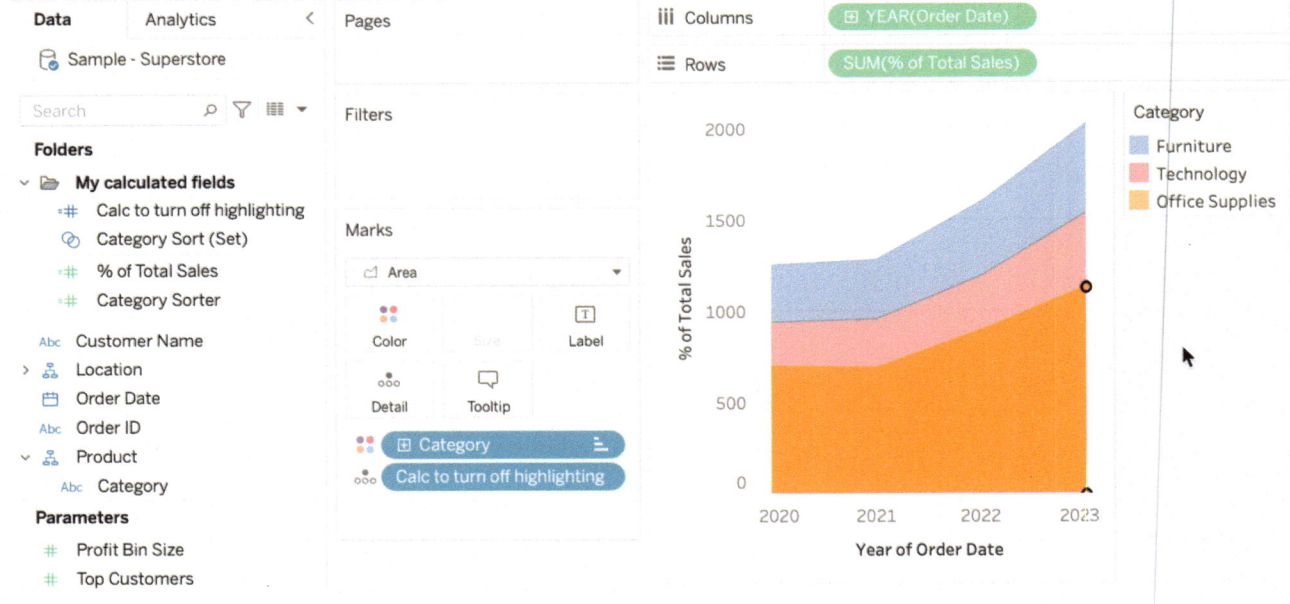

FIGURE 2

The Calculated Field % of Total Sales.

Area charts, which shade the area beneath the line, effectively visualize how parts contribute to a whole and change over time. They are particularly useful for showing composition. As this chart demonstrates, furniture sales are the highest, while office supplies have the lowest. For time-series data, a horizontal axis and continuous data are essential.

See Figure 13.30 Annotations, Annotate the Area Chart, page 302

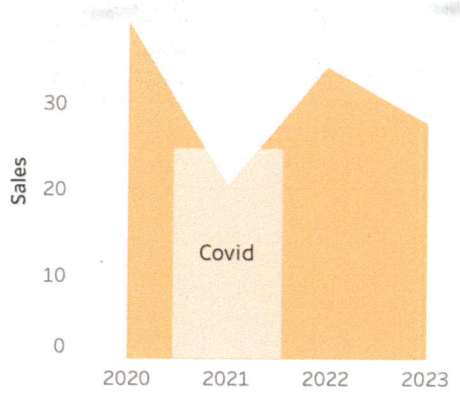

FIGURE 3
Annotate an Area.

A shaded annotation on this area chart marks the timeline of the COVID-19 pandemic. In Tableau, annotations can be added to marks, points, or areas, and customized through resizing, formatting, and repositioning.

See Figure 7.76, Match Label Colors to Bar Colors, page 145

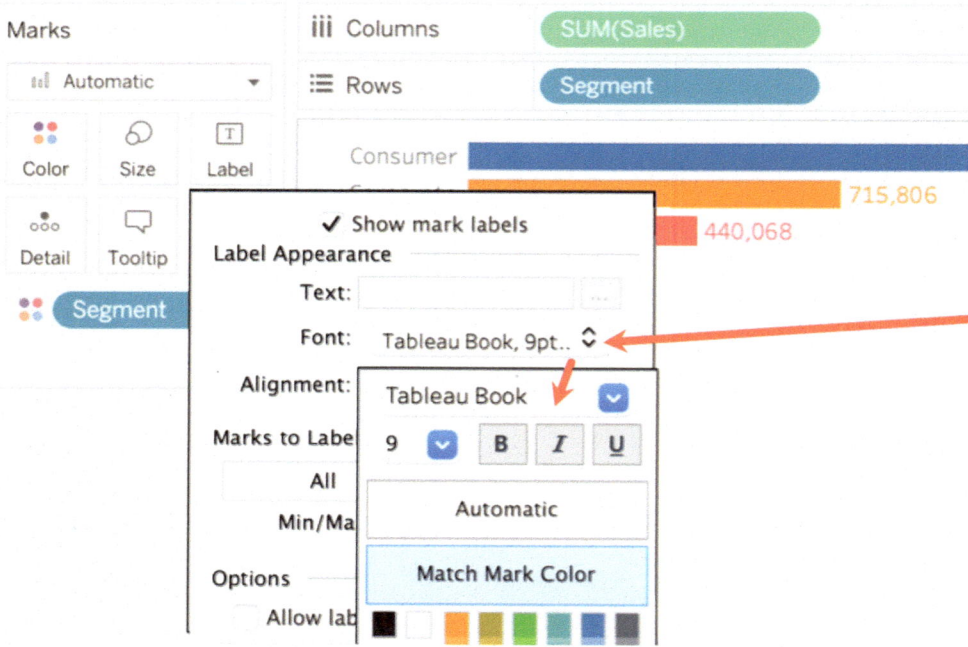

FIGURE 4
Match Mark Color.

In this horizontal bar chart, color highlights each segment, and the mark labels mirror these colors, thanks to the "Show mark labels" option and matching font color setting on the Marks card.

See Figure 8.55, Hover to Choose a Field for Sorting, page 182

FIGURE 5

The **Edit Parameter** Dialog Window.

This dashboard features two worksheets. The top worksheet displays Sales, Price, and Quantity using the Measure Names field. A horizontal bar chart below presents the same three measures, and a parameter allows users to dynamically sort this chart by any of the measures.

See Figure 11.39, Fixed LOD Example, page 242

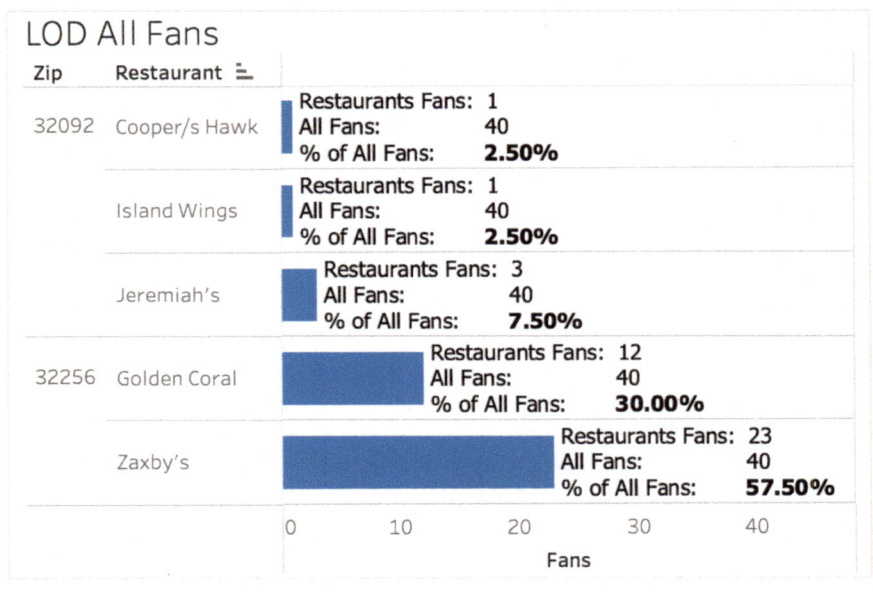

FIGURE 6

Chart with LoDs for All Fans.

This horizontal bar chart displays three values for each restaurant using labels on the Marks card: the restaurant's individual fan count, the total fan count across all restaurants, and the restaurant's percentage of that total.

See Figure 13.23, Custom Color and Shape Legend (Yellow Diamond), page 300

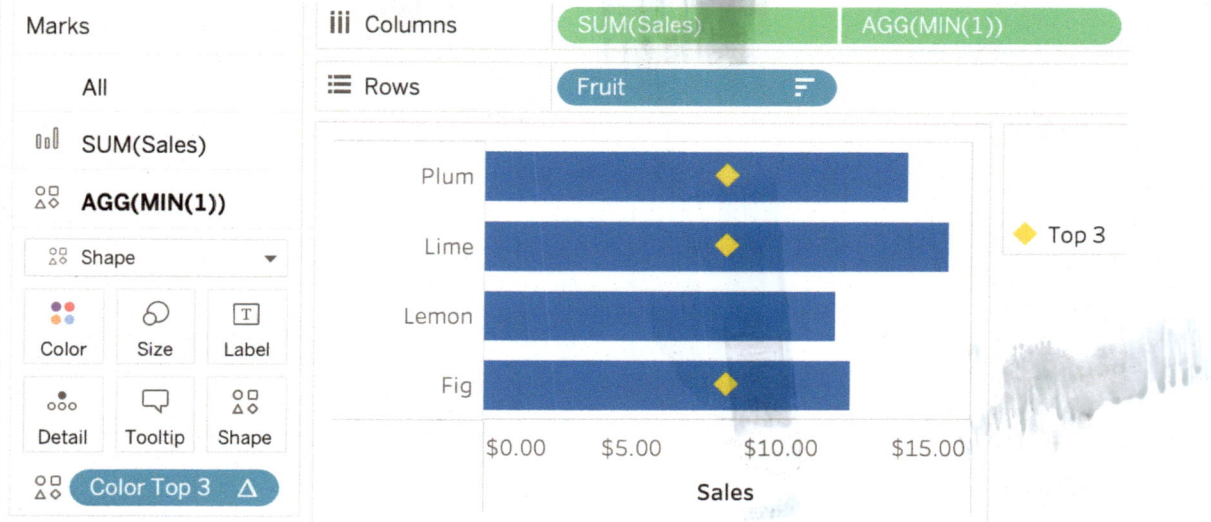

FIGURE 7
A bar chart with yellow diamonds.

This dual-axis horizontal bar chart uses a placeholder measure to highlight the top three sales performers with yellow diamond markers.

See Figure 7.36, Box and Whisker, page 128

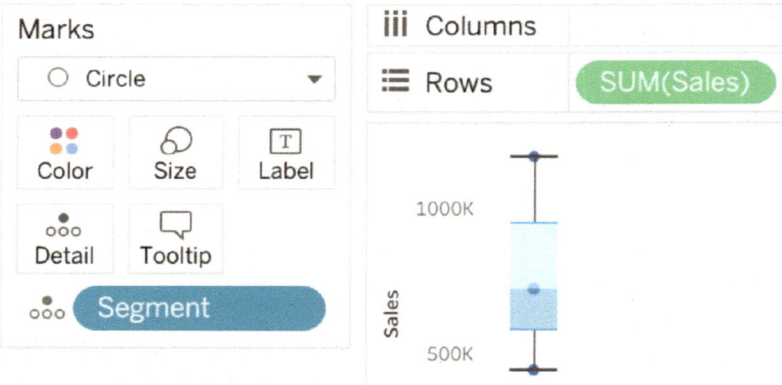

FIGURE 8
The Circle Mark type.

This box and whisker plot, which uses circular marks and a distribution band, effectively visualizes data distribution. It can be created manually by following the steps in Chapter 7, or automatically using Tableau's "Show Me" feature.

See Figure 7.104, Bullet Graph with Reference Line and Distribution Band, page 153

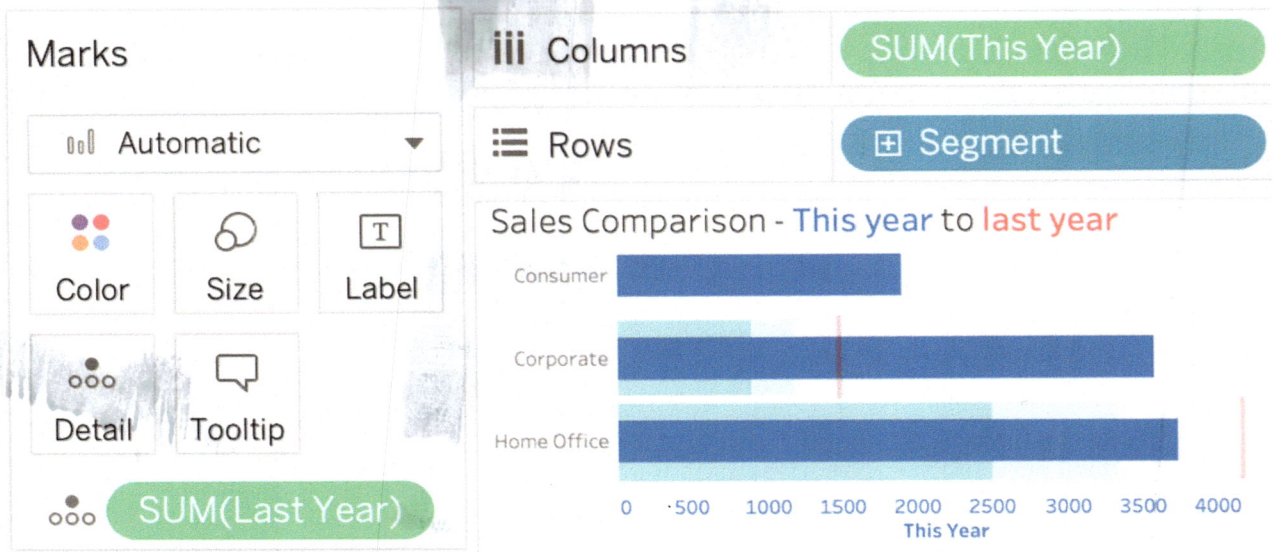

FIGURE 9
The Title with matching colors.

This bullet graph effectively compares current sales to last year's performance. It uses a reference line to represent last year's sales figure and a distribution band to visualize 60% and 80% of that total. The title's color coding matches the two sales metrics. Bullet graphs are ideal for comparing a single metric against a target value or range, such as comparing actual results against a forecast.

See Figure 10.22, Bump Chart, page 217

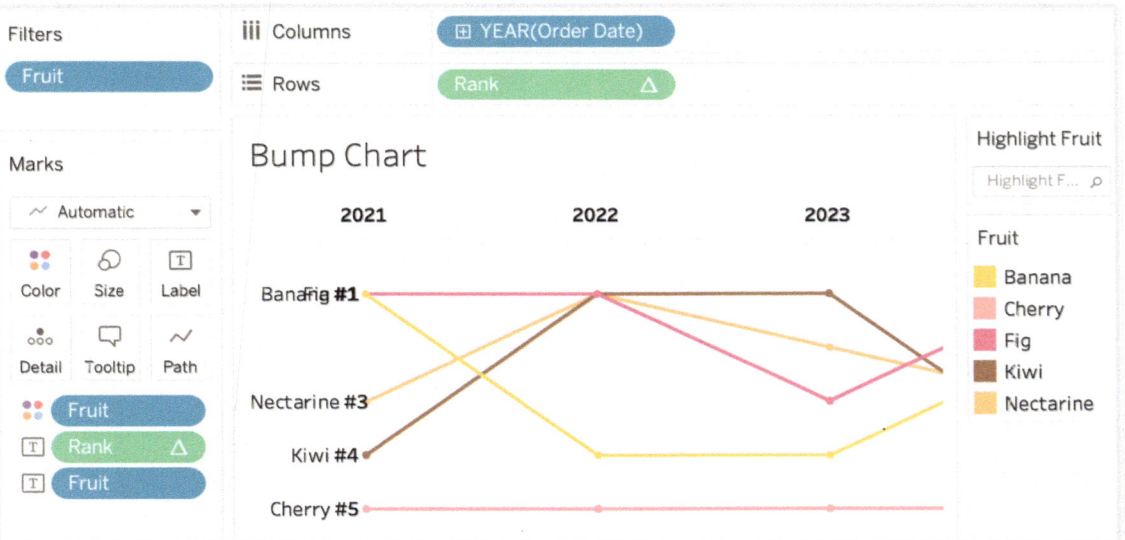

FIGURE 10
A Bump chart.

This bump chart visualizes the change in sales ranking over time.

See Figure 7.27, Packed Bubbles, page 125

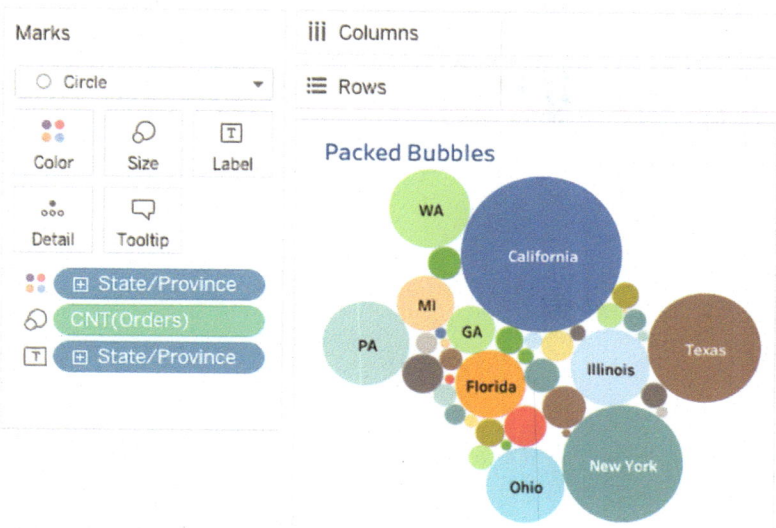

FIGURE 11

Circle Marks – packed bubbles.

This packed bubble chart uses size to represent the number of orders from each state, with color used to identify the individual states. Note that circular marks like these are also used in word cloud charts.

See Figure 7.77, Opacity, page 145

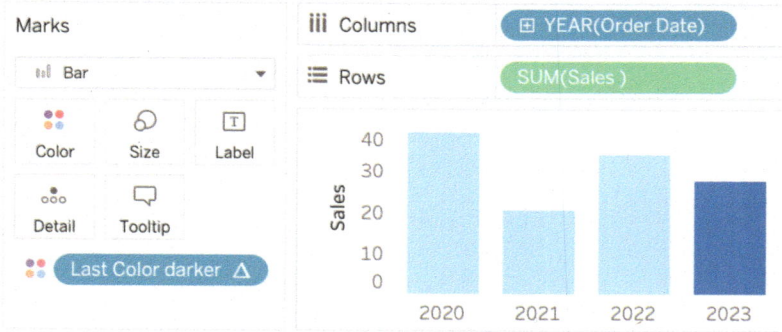

FIGURE 12

Opacity.

This vertical bar chart uses a table calculation to conditionally format the last bar with a distinct color.

See Figure 15.19, Drill Down with a Set Action, page 362

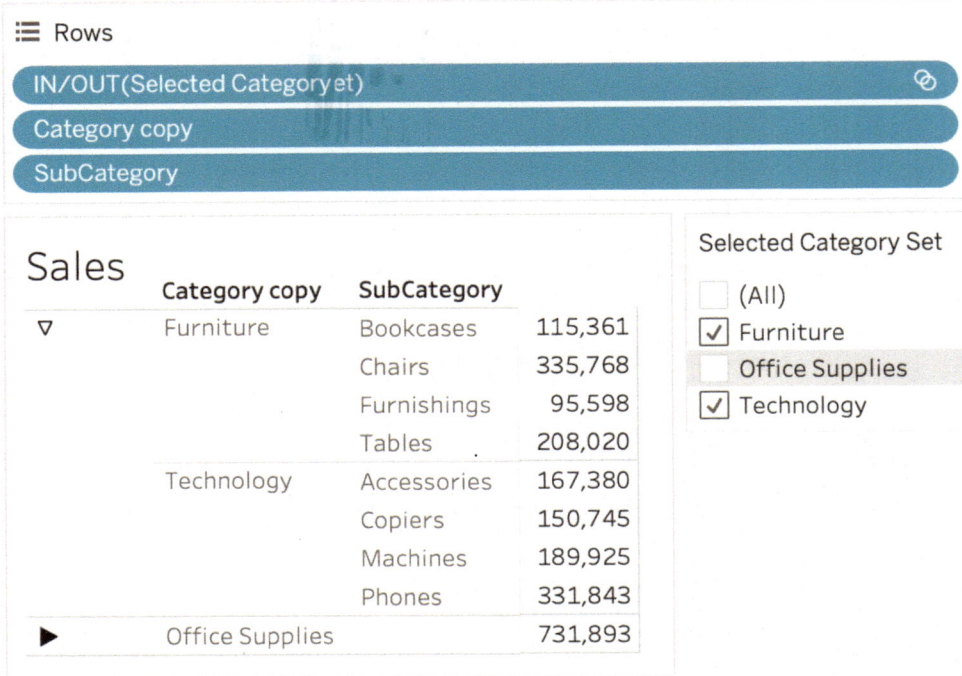

FIGURE 13

The Set Control on the right side of the view.

This text-based chart uses a set to enable drill-down functionality for sub-categories. Down arrows on the left indicate the Furniture and Technology categories have further sub-categories that can be expanded, while the right arrow next to Office Supplies shows that its sub-categories are currently hidden.

See Figure 7.62, Density Mark, page 139

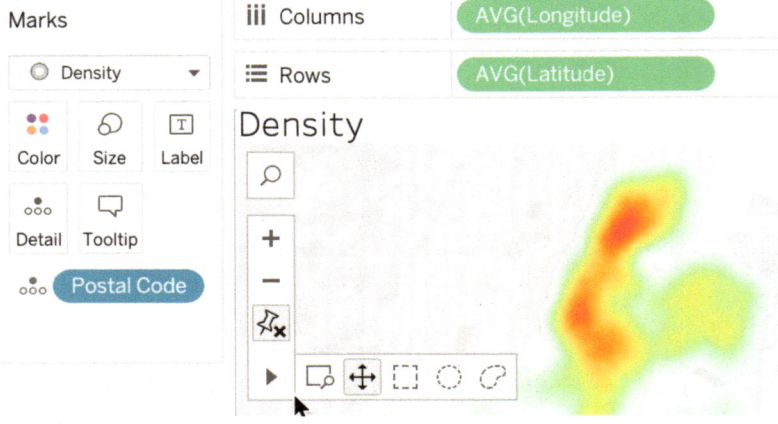

FIGURE 14

A density map.

This density chart uses a diverging color palette to highlight areas with the highest concentration of data points. Heat maps like this are particularly useful for visualizing large datasets where overlapping data points on a map can obscure patterns.

See Figure 6.22, Donut Chart, page 112

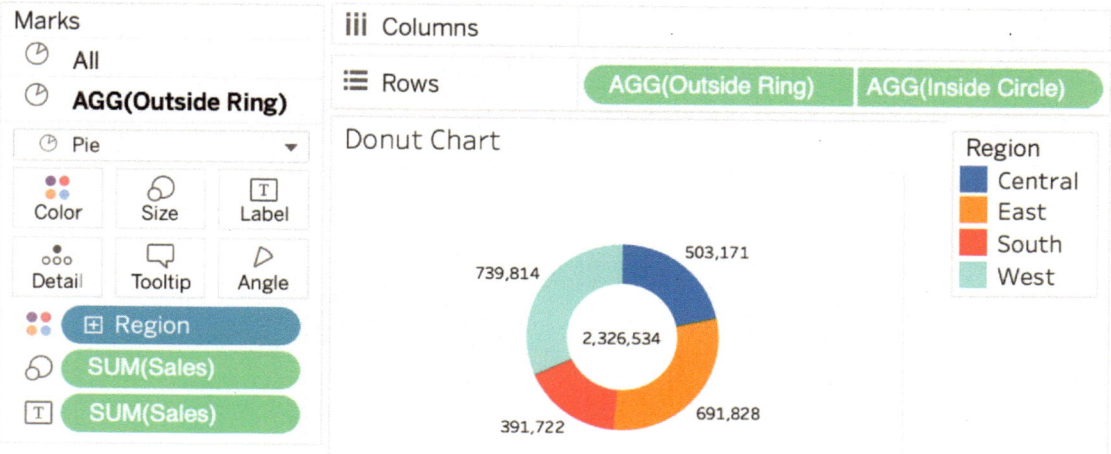

FIGURE 15
The Donut chart.

This donut chart effectively visualizes part-to-whole relationships. The color-coded segments represent each part, with their labels displayed around the outer edge, while the center of the donut shows the total for all segments.

See Figure 7.61, Dumbbell Chart, page 138

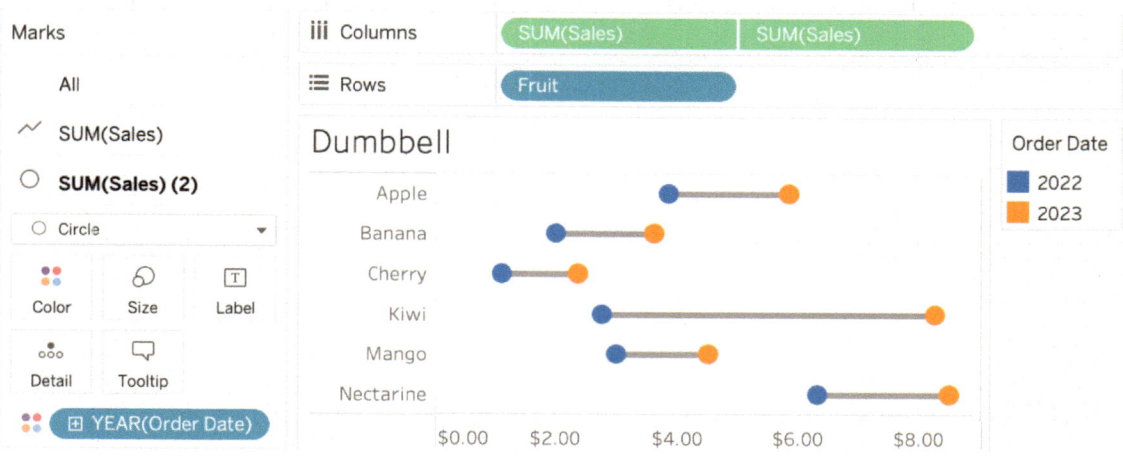

FIGURE 16
A Dumbbell chart.

Dumbbell charts effectively visualize the change between two data points, using circles to represent the values and a line to connect them.

See Figure 7.39, Gantt Bar Marks, page 131

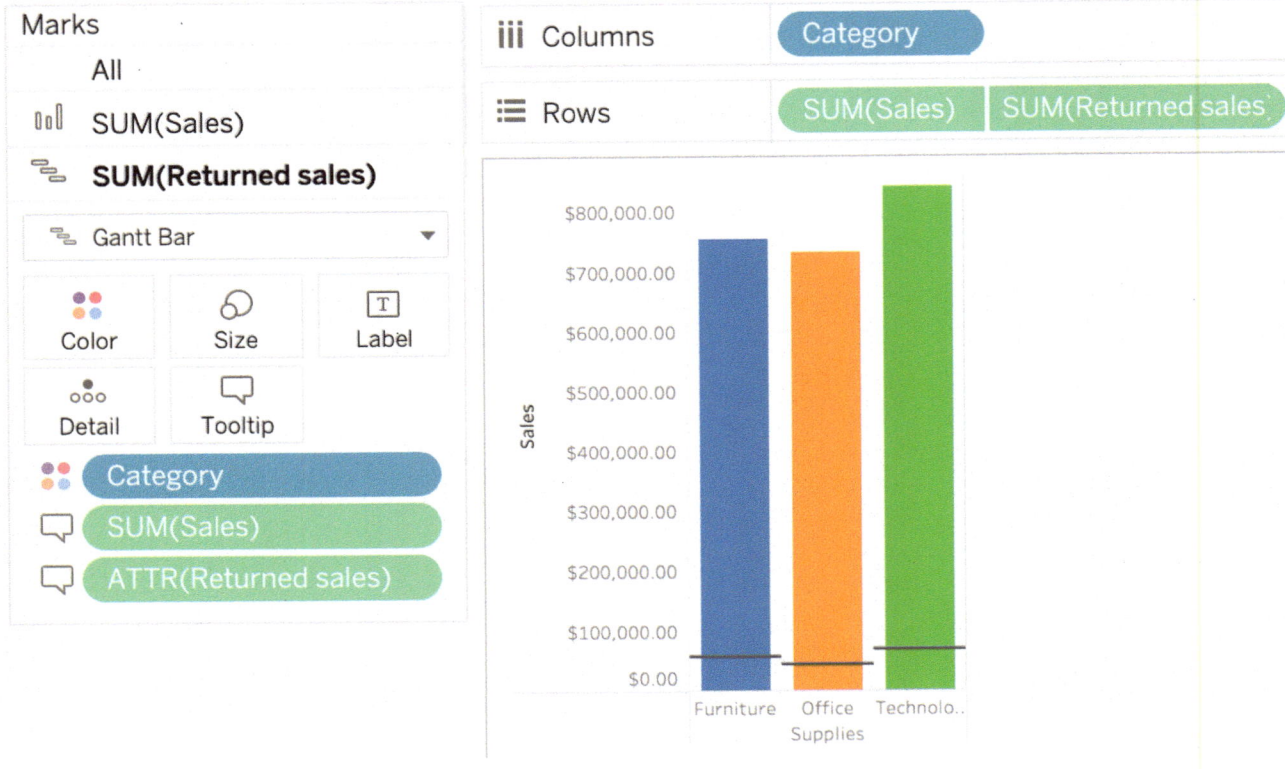

FIGURE 17
Gantt Bar Chart.

This dual-axis chart combines a Gantt bar chart with a vertical bar chart. The Gantt bars represent returned sales amounts.

See Figure 9.29, Time Duration for Gantt Bar, Waterfall, and Resume, page 204

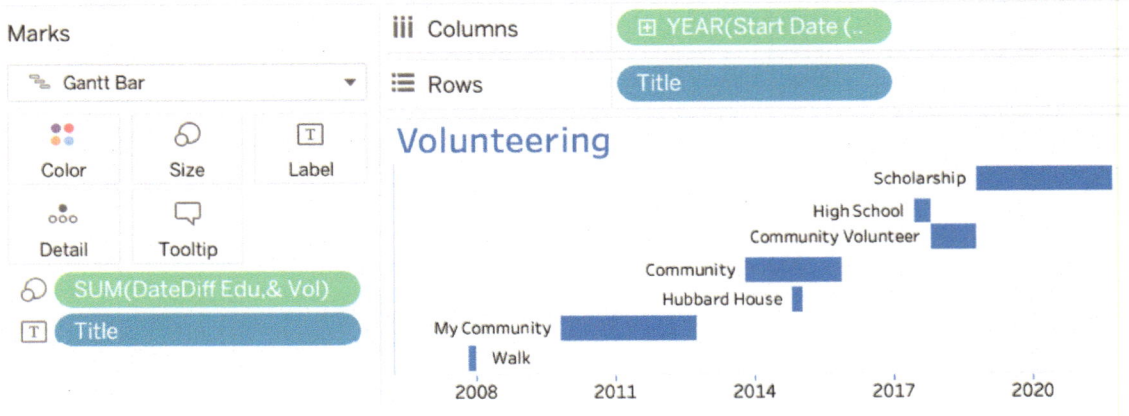

FIGURE 18
Gantt Bars with duration.

While Gantt charts are commonly used for project management to visualize timelines, this example demonstrates their application in showing the date ranges of various volunteer events.

See Figure 7.73, Color Property, Highlight Table – Include Totals in Color, page 153

See Figure 7.24, Histogram, page 124

FIGURE 19

A highlight table.

This highlight table uses square marks and the same measure on both the Color and Text tiles to highlight key values within the text table.

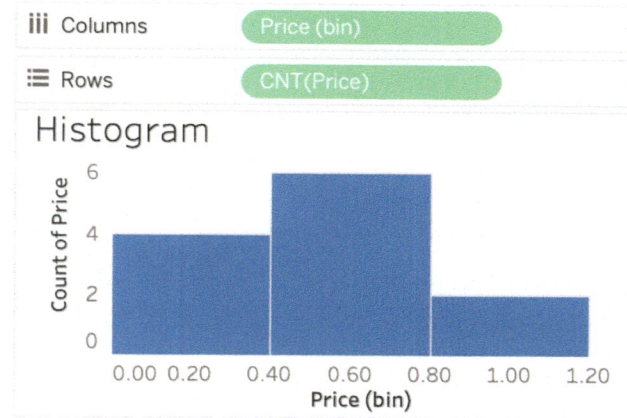

FIGURE 20

Histogram.

This histogram uses bins to group data points based on value ranges along an axis. In this example, the central bin shows that the majority of item prices fall between $0.40 and $0.80.

See Figure 14.97, KPIs and BANs, page 352

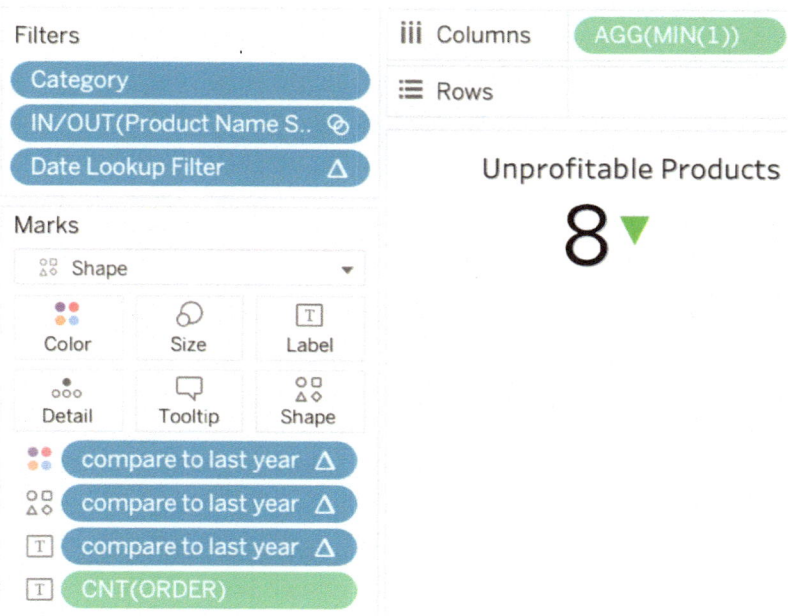

FIGURE 21

The Filters shelf with the date lookup Filter field.

Key Performance Indicators (KPIs) are often prominently displayed on dashboards as large, easily readable numbers. Trend arrows are commonly used to indicate whether the KPI is trending upwards or downwards.

See Figure 6.2, Line Charts, Blended Axis, page 103

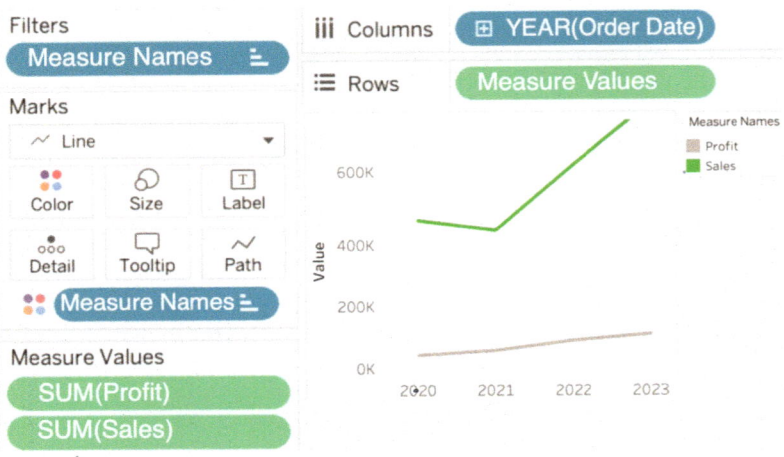

FIGURE 22
Blended chart.

This view displays two measures, Profit (green) and Sales (gray), on a single blended axis, resulting in two distinct lines.

See Figure 6.6, A Continuous Date Axis, page 105

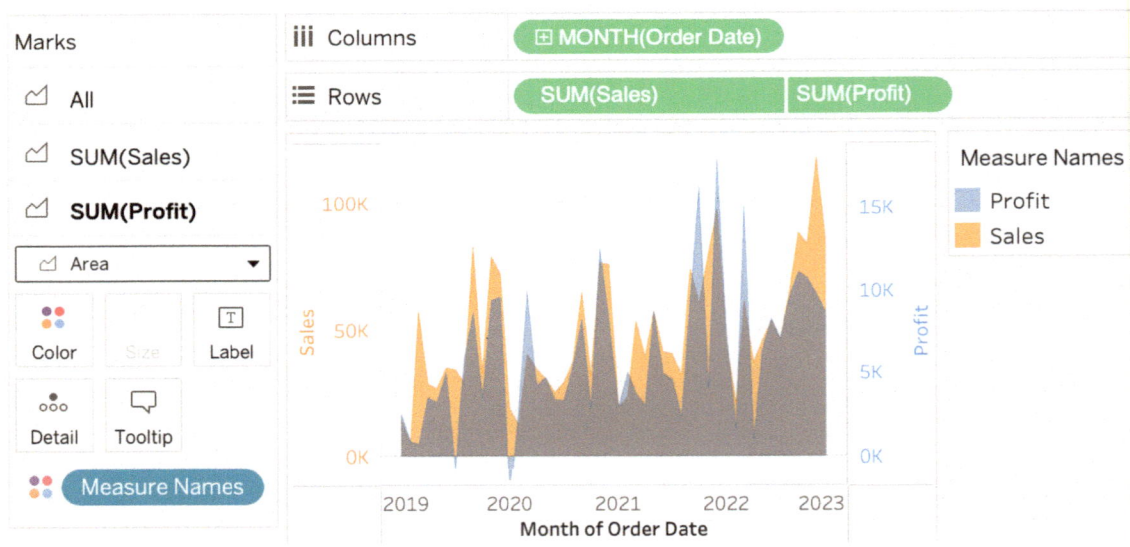

FIGURE 23
The worksheet with a continuous measure date.

This dual-axis area chart displays both Profit and Sales. Each measure has its own axis, color-coded to match the corresponding area, and each axis spans a different range. Tableau supports up to four layered axes in a single view, with two on the Columns shelf and two on the Rows shelf.

See Figure 1.33, Maps, Show, Hide, and Format Legends, page 35

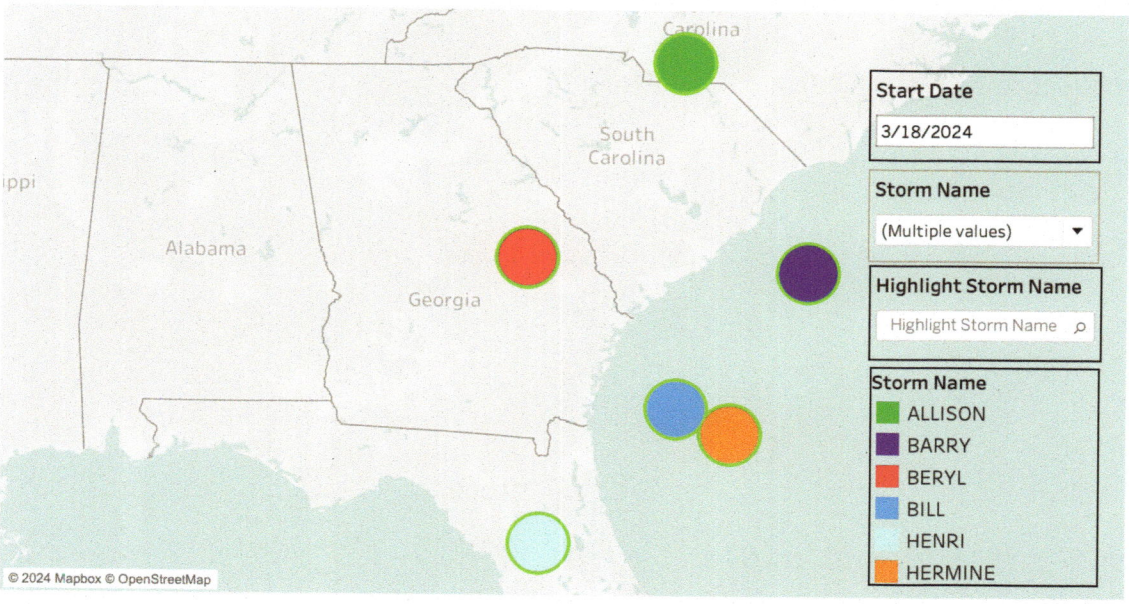

FIGURE 24

Map Legends and Controls.

Tableau map legends are designed to be transparent, so the underlying map remains visible.

See Figure 7.70, Maps, Halo, *page 143*

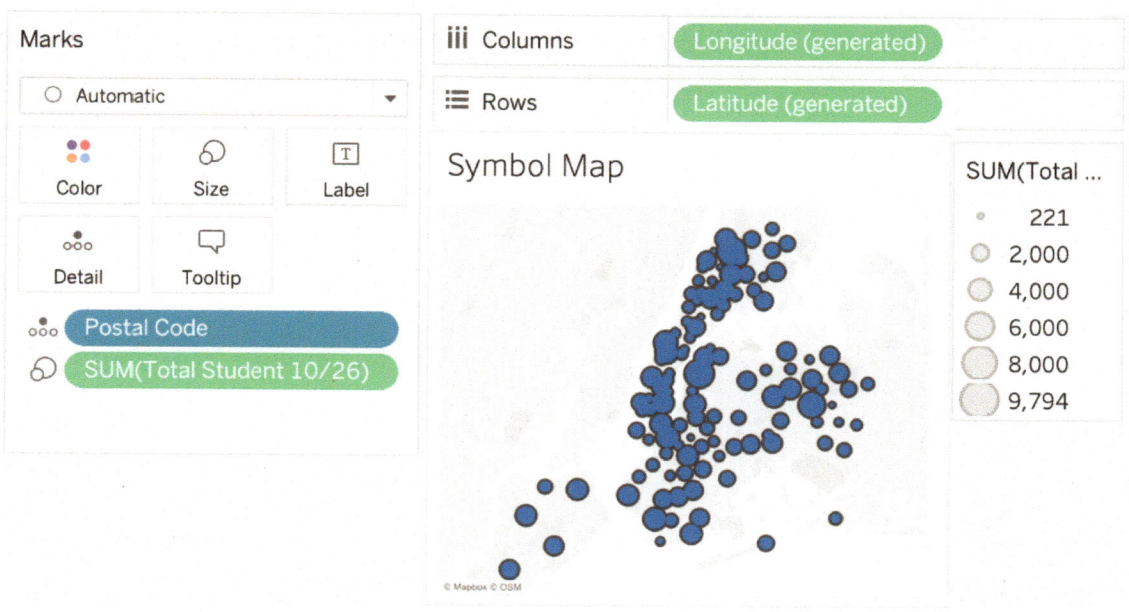

FIGURE 25

The Halo setting on a Map chart.

A halo effect around the markers in this symbol map improves the visibility of overlapping points.

See Figure 7.64, Formatting and Transparent Backgrounds, page 140

Storm

FIGURE 26
A Map chart.

This map features a satellite image as its background. The Storm Names filter control has a transparent background.

See Figure 6.10, Multiple Charts in One View, page 106

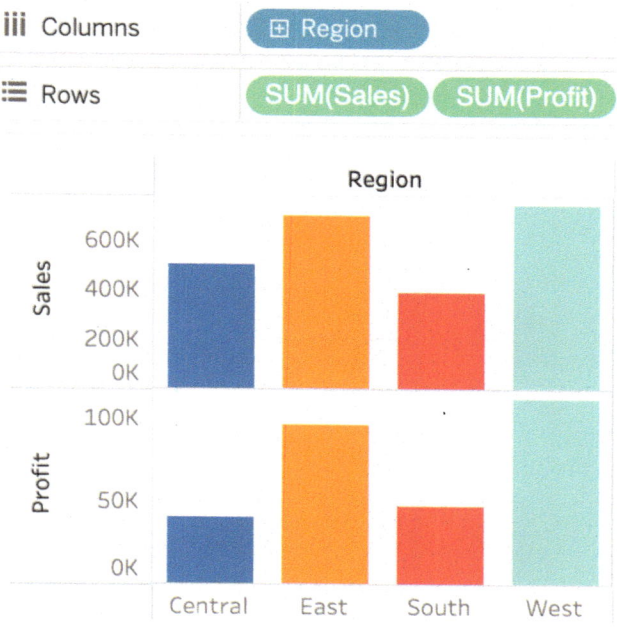

FIGURE 27

Multiple charts in one pane.

The Sales and Profit measures are visualized in two panes within this view.

See Figure 6.11, Multiple Panes in One View, page 107

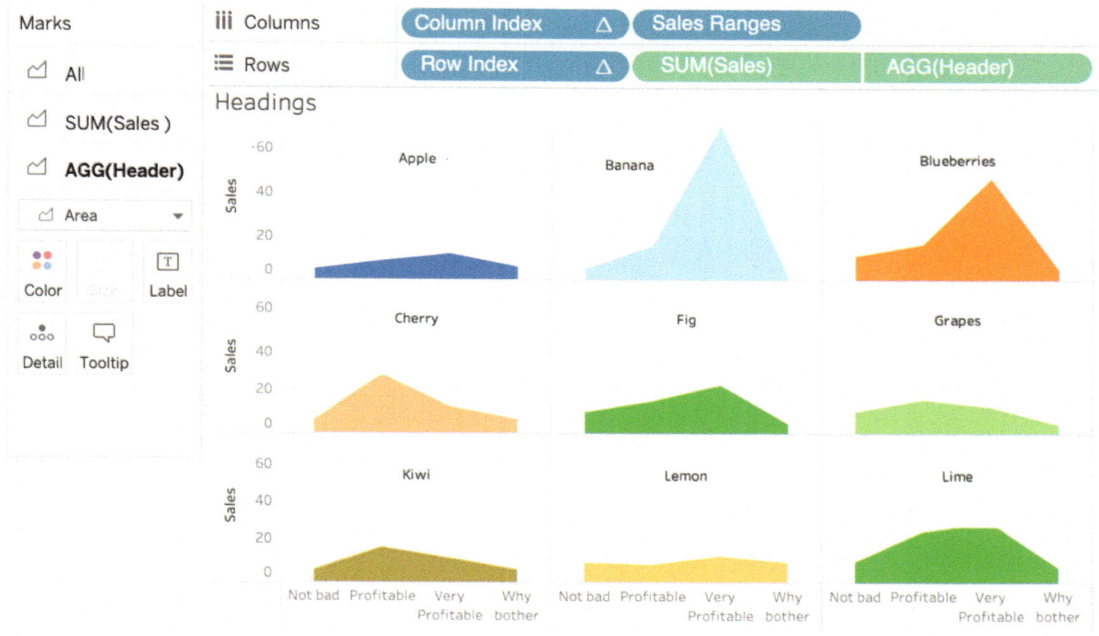

FIGURE 28

A small multiples view.

Column and row indexes divide the Sales measure into nine panes in this view.

See Figure 10.9, Pareto on page 213

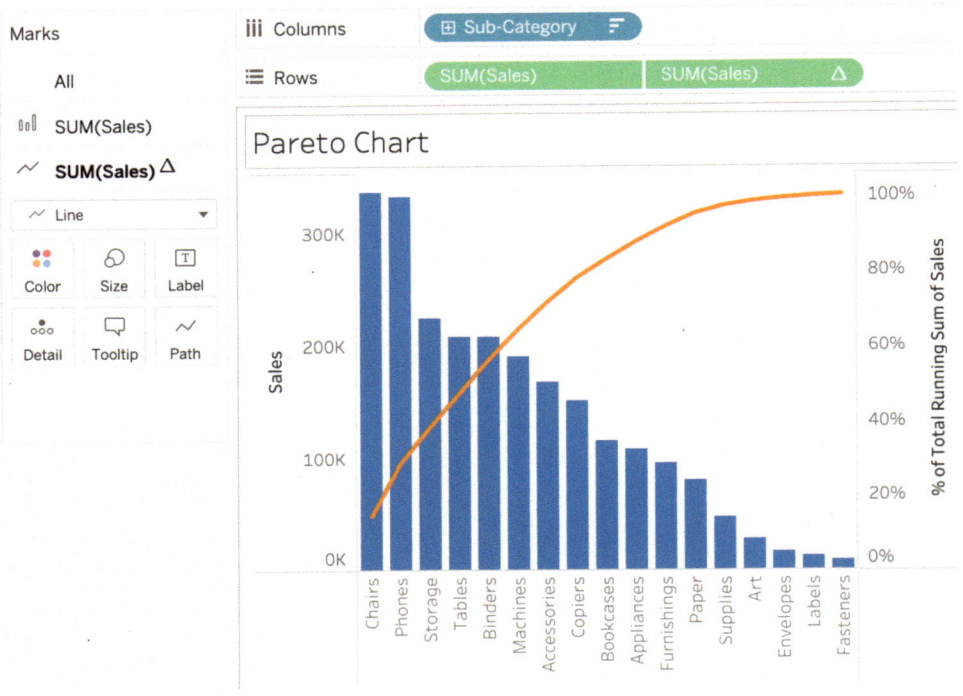

FIGURE 29
The Pareto chart.

A Pareto chart combines descending vertical bars representing individual values with an ascending line showing their cumulative total, ranging from 0% to 100%. This visualization highlights the Pareto principle, which suggests that roughly 80% of effects come from 20% of the causes.

See Figure 8.30, Filter the View, Not the Underlying Data, page 170

Filter a View, Not the Underlying Data

Average		Moving Average		Filtered Moving Average	
February 2020	2.30	February 2020	2.30	February 2023	3.23
August 2020	3.00	August 2020	2.65	March 2023	3.23
May 2021	0.10	May 2021	1.80	April 2023	2.57
June 2021	0.40	June 2021	1.17	May 2023	1.73
April 2022	0.60	April 2022	0.37	Grand Total	1.86
June 2022	0.30	June 2022	0.43		
July 2022	1.40	July 2022	0.77		
October 2022	4.00	October 2022	1.90		
December 2022	3.00	December 2022	2.80		
February 2023	2.70	February 2023	3.23		
March 2023	4.00	March 2023	3.23		
April 2023	1.00	April 2023	2.57		
May 2023	0.20	May 2023	1.73		
Grand Total	1.86	Grand Total	1.86		

FIGURE 30
Three Charts.

This dashboard includes three text tables showing an average, a moving average, and a filtered moving average. A table calculation filters the displayed dates to 2023 without affecting the underlying data used for the moving average calculations.

See Figure 7.72, Color Positive and Negative Numbers, page 144

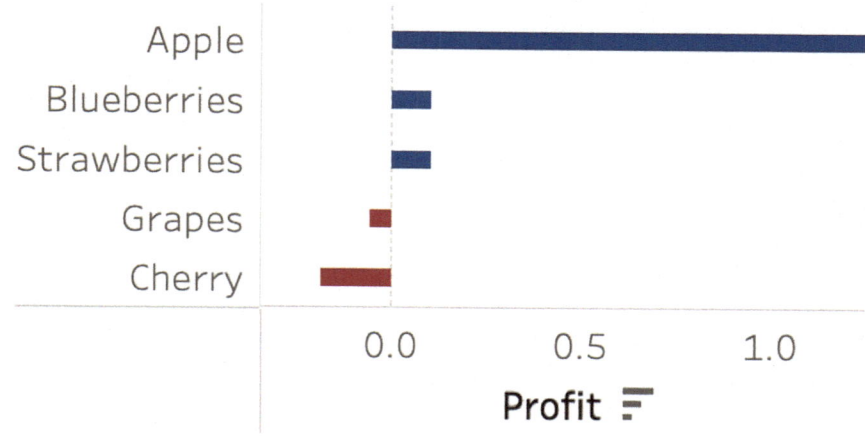

FIGURE 31
Positive and negative marks.

This horizontal bar chart uses red for negative values (left) and blue for positive values (right).

See Figure 15.42, Positive and Negative Values, Switch Between Measures, page 370

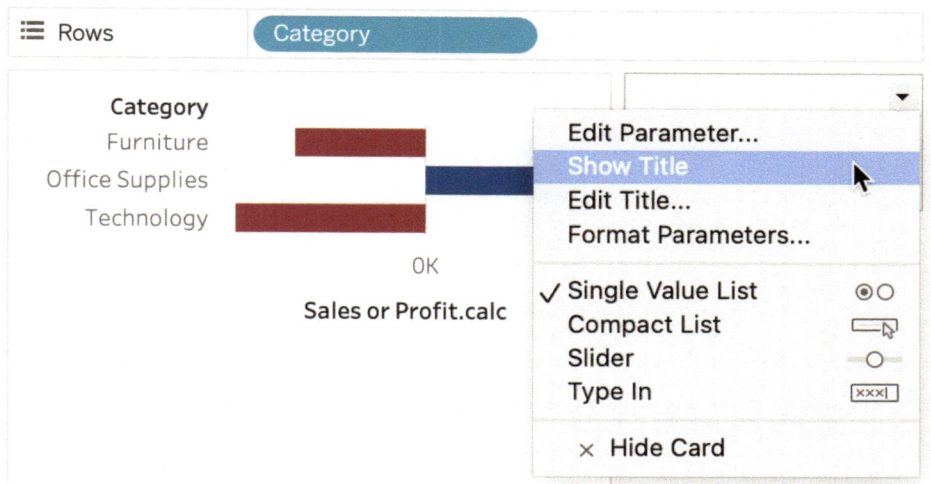

FIGURE 32
The Parameter Control context menu.

This interactive chart allows users to toggle between displaying 'Sales' and 'Profit' data using a parameter control. The same control also offers the option to show or edit the chart title. When 'Profit' is selected, a stepped color scheme dynamically highlights positive and negative values, providing a clear visual representation of profitability.

See Figure 9.31 A Resume Combining a Waterfall Chart, Time Duration, and Gantt Bar on page 205

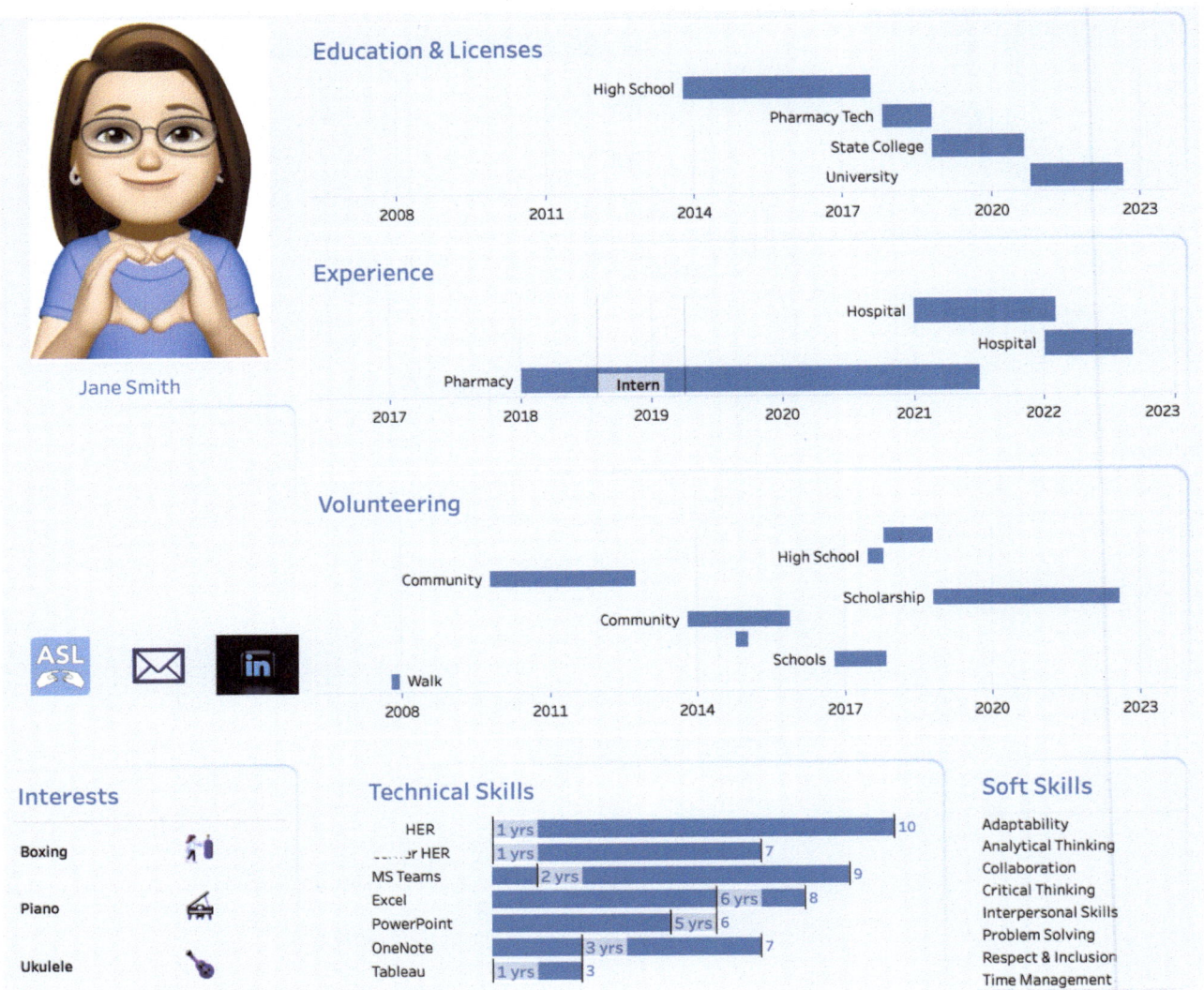

FIGURE 33

A resume combining a Waterfall chart, Time Duration, and Gantt Bar.

Breaking from traditional resume formats, this re-imagined version leverages the power of data visualization, using a waterfall and Gantt charts to showcase a linear timeline of career progression.

See Figure 7.59, Scatter Plot on page 138

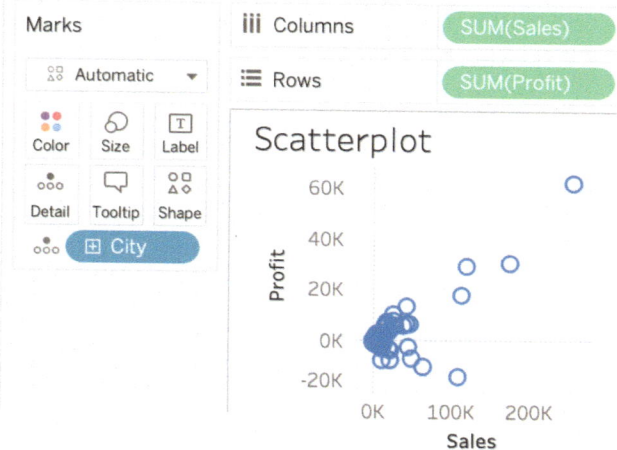

FIGURE 34
A Scatter Plot.

A scatter plot visualizes the relationship between sales and profit. In this example, the majority of data points cluster at the lower end of both axes, suggesting a concentration of low sales and low profit.

See Figure 7.50, Call Attention to Marks with Invisible Shapes on page 135

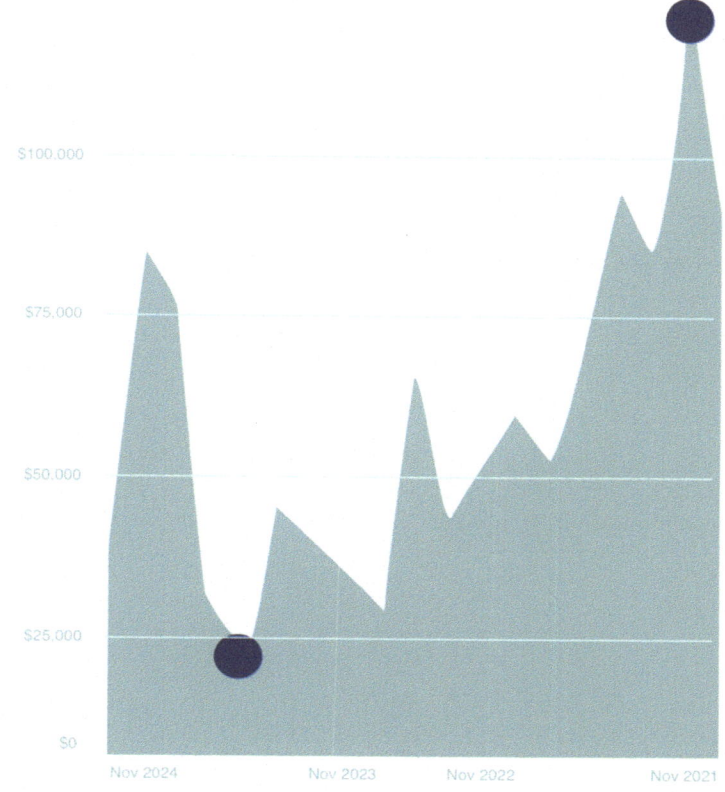

FIGURE 35
Minimum and maximum marks.

This area chart's color scheme is driven by a placeholder field. The minimum and maximum values are assigned specific colors, while all other values are assigned a transparent color. This approach emphasizes the extreme data points within the area.

See Figure 12.63, Shape Chart, Arrows Comparing Two Values on page 282

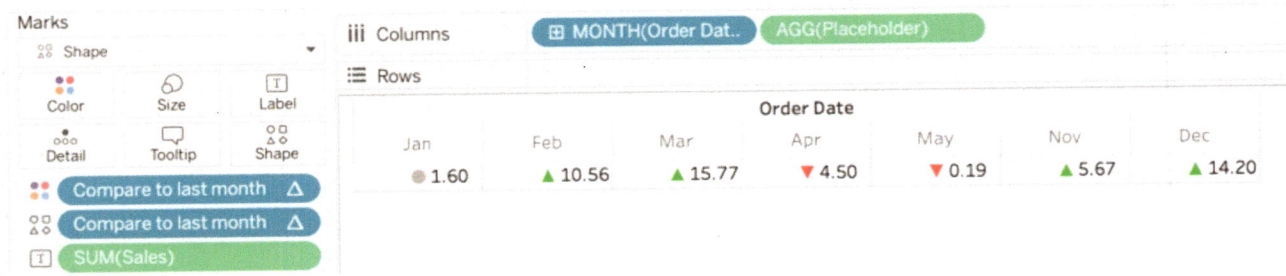

FIGURE 36
Move marks to the front.

This shape chart visually compares current sales to last month's figures by using up and down arrows and color-coding. The actual sales values are displayed via the Label tile on the Marks card.

See Figure 7.60, Side-by-Side Circles on page 138

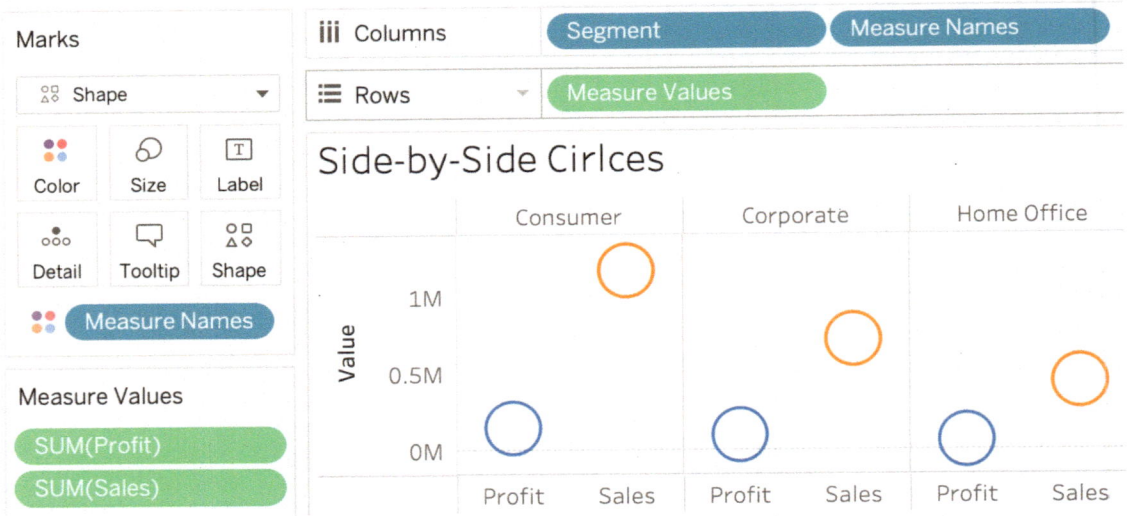

FIGURE 37
Side-by-side circles.

Side-by-side circle charts enhance analysis by providing a more granular view of the data.

See Figure 10.21, Slope Chart with Rank on page 217

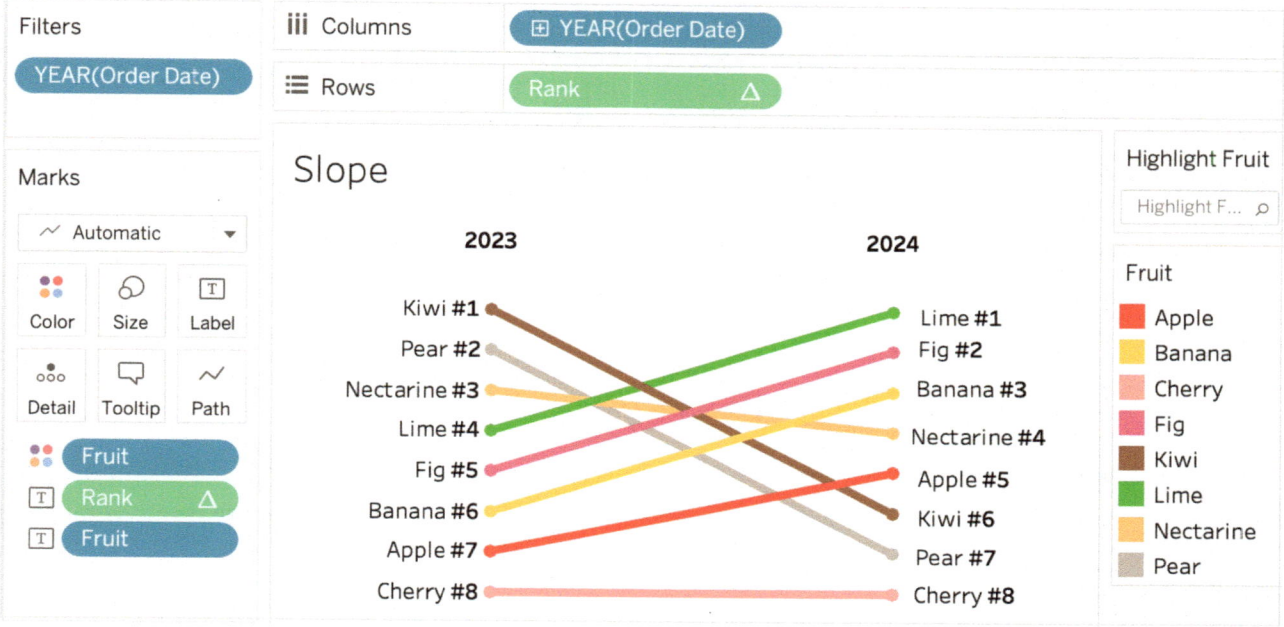

FIGURE 38
A Slope chart.

This slope chart visualizes sales trends for several fruits. Limes, figs, bananas, and apples all show positive sales growth. In contrast, kiwis, pears, and nectarines experienced declining sales. Cherry sales remained unchanged.

See Figure 7.30, Spark Lines on page 126

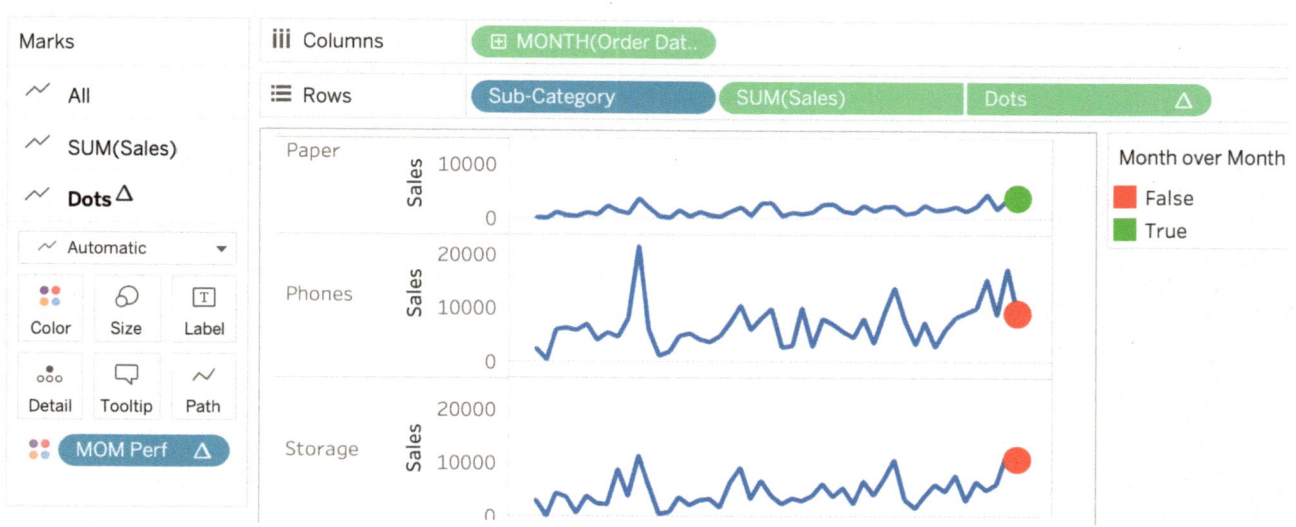

FIGURE 39
The Sparkline chart.

Sparklines offer a clear and compact way to visualize data trends. These small charts, often displayed without axes, combine two measures to quickly communicate whether data is trending upwards or downwards, as commonly seen with stock market prices.

See Figure 5.6, Stacked Bars on page 91

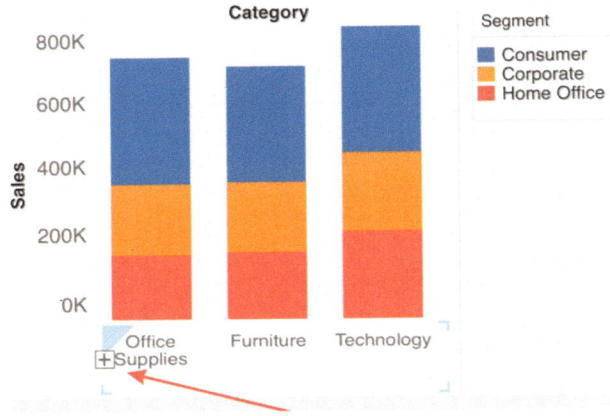

FIGURE 40
The Plus Symbol for a Hierarchy.

This stacked bar chart uses color to represent multiple segments within each bar. A small plus symbol indicates the presence of a hierarchy, which can be expanded for more detail.

See Figure 8.70, Sorting Segments within a Stacked Bar on page 188

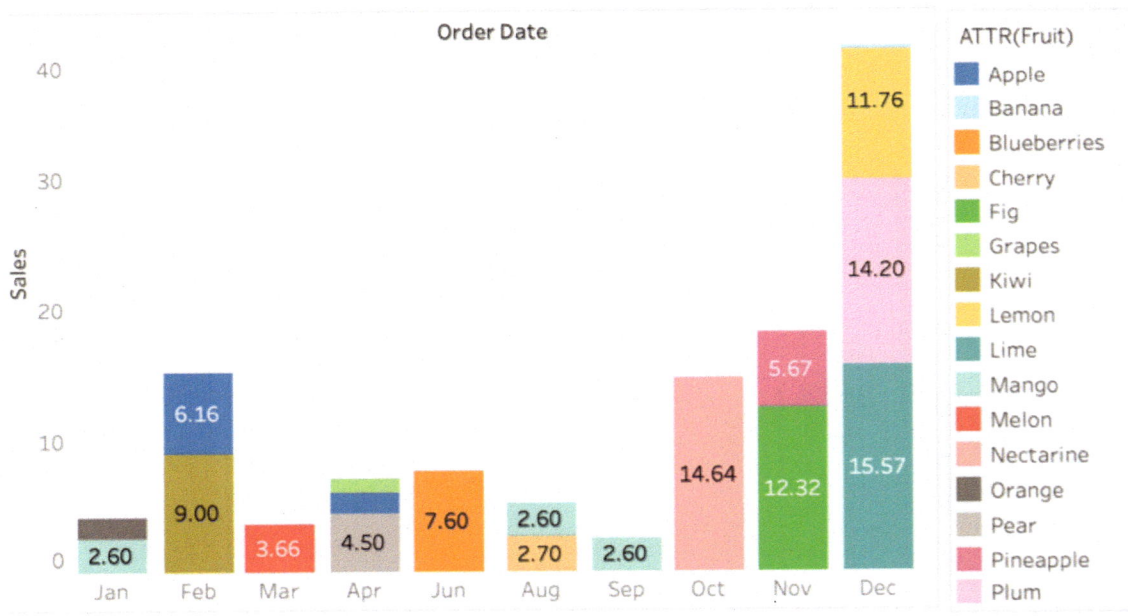

FIGURE 41
The Marks Card.

This stacked bar chart arranges segments within each month in descending order of size, placing the largest segment at the bottom for easy comparison.

See Figure 10.26, Text Table, Compute Using on page 220

Compute Using: Table Down Then Across

			2020	2021	2022	2023
Q1	Jan	Mango				96.31
		Orange			61.18	
	Feb	Apple				102.47
		Kiwi			70.18	
	Mar	Melon			73.84	
Q2	Apr	Apple				104.01
		Grapes		40.22		
		Pear				108.51
	Jun	Blueberries		47.82		
Q3	Aug	Cherry	1.35			109.86
		Mango				112.46
	Sep	Mango	3.95			
Q4	Oct	Nectarine	11.27			119.78
	Nov	Fig	23.59			
		Pineapple			79.51	
	Dec	Banana				121.39
		Lemon		59.58		
		Lime	39.16			
		Plum			93.71	

			2020	2021	2022	2023
Q1	Jan	Mango				2.60
		Orange			1.60	
	Feb	Apple				6.16
		Kiwi			9.00	
	Mar	Melon			3.66	
Q2	Apr	Apple				1.54
		Grapes		1.06		
		Pear				4.50
	Jun	Blueberries		7.60		
Q3	Aug	Cherry	1.35			1.35
		Mango				2.60
	Sep	Mango	2.60			
Q4	Oct	Nectarine	7.32			7.32
	Nov	Fig	12.32			
		Pineapple			5.67	
	Dec	Banana				1.61
		Lemon		11.76		
		Lime	15.57			
		Plum			14.20	

FIGURE 42

Compute using: table down, then across.

These side-by-side text tables demonstrate the computation of a table calculation. The table on the right displays the original data, while the table on the left shows the results of a calculation computed across the entire table (down then across).

See Figure 11.54, Text Table – *Weighted Average on page 249*

FIGURE 43
The finished dashboard.

This chart utilizes a calculated field, incorporating a level of detail (LOD) expression, to compute and display a weighted average. The LOD expression calculates the average of averages.

See Figure 7.49, Timeline Chart – Shape Marks on page 135

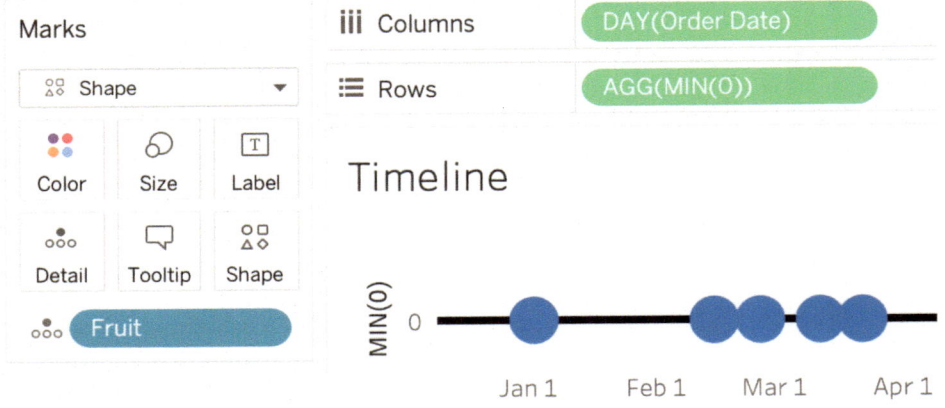

FIGURE 44
A Timeline chart.

This timeline chart effectively communicates the timing of events or milestones through the use of shapes plotted along a timeline.

See Figure 7.68, Treemap, Ch 5, Diverging Color Palette on page 142

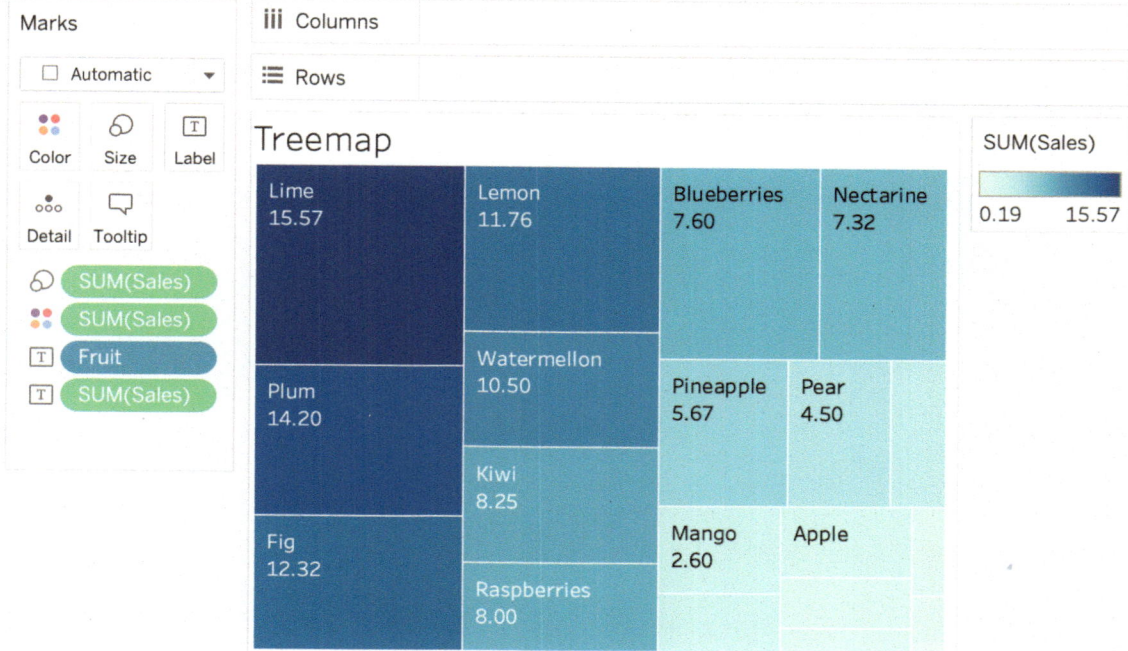

FIGURE 45

A Treemap chart.

Treemaps employ a space-filling, hierarchical layout using nested rectangles. The area and color of each rectangle are mapped to data attributes, facilitating the identification of patterns and relationships within the categorical data.

See Figure 9.30, Time Duration for Gantt Bar and Waterfall (Resume) on page 205

FIGURE 46

Waterfall chart.

Waterfall charts visualize how a value changes incrementally over time.

See Figure 7.31, Word Clouds With Circle Marks on page 126

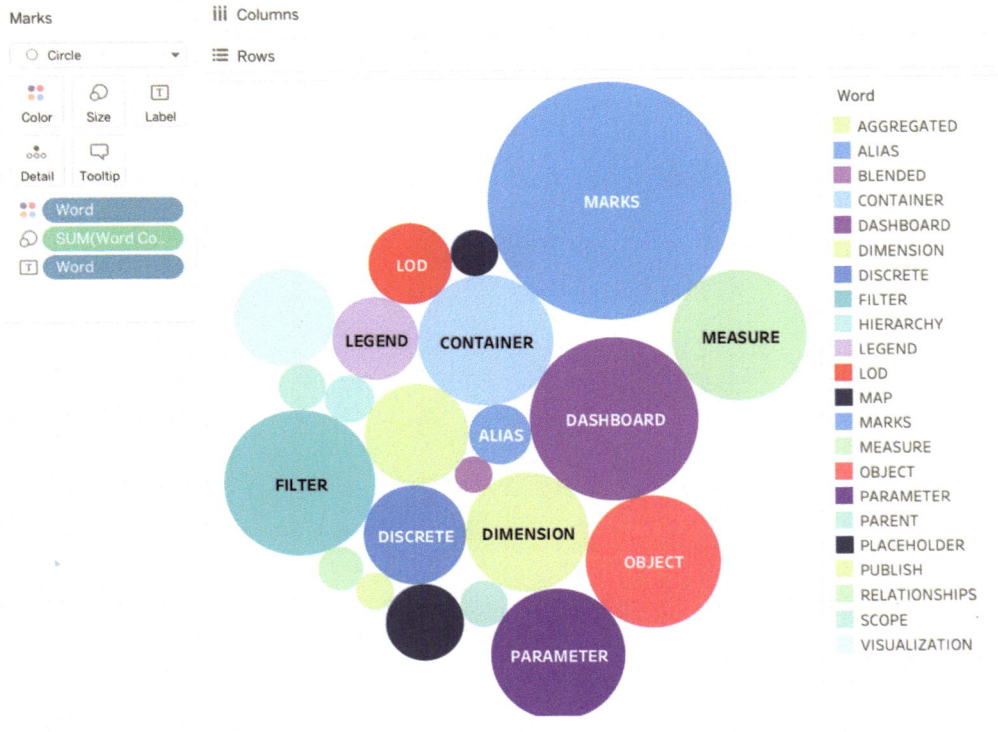

FIGURE 47

Word Clouds.

This variation of a packed bubble chart, known as a word cloud, visually represents word frequency. Larger circles indicate more frequent words.

See Figure 7.23, Rounded End for Bar Charts on page 123

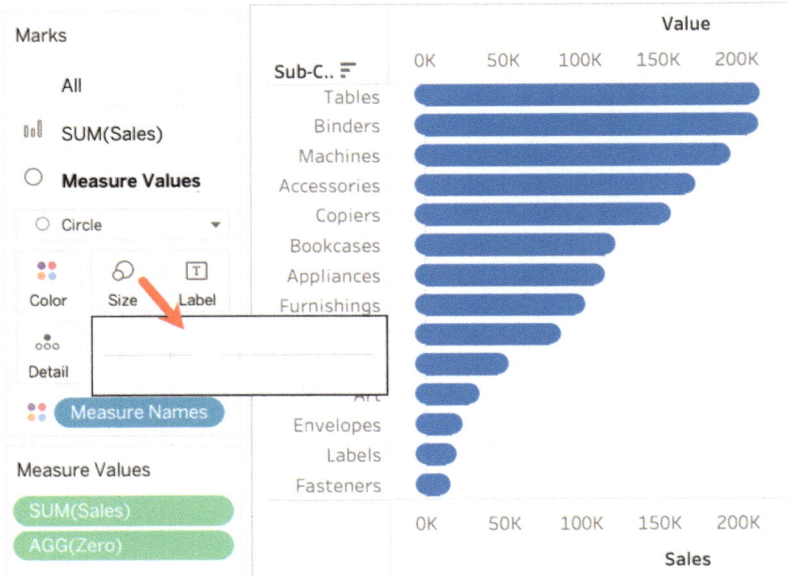

FIGURE 48

The **Measure Values** Layer in the **Marks** card.

This bar chart uses a placeholder field with circle marks to create rounded bar ends. The circles are sized to visually achieve the rounding effect.

See Figure 7.81, Call Attention to the Difference with Color on page 147

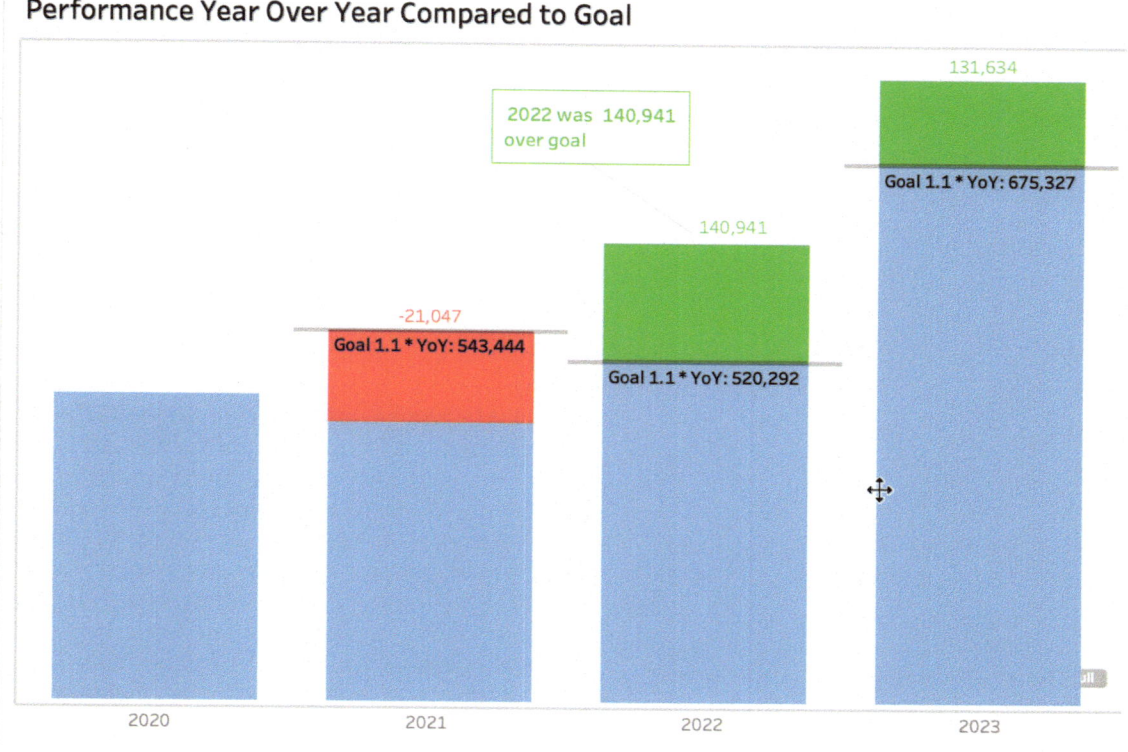

FIGURE 49

Dashboard Showing the Difference between Sales and Goals.

This dashboard uses two worksheets and a reference line to visualize performance against a goal. Background bars are color-coded red for below goal and green for above goal.

See Figure 8.70, Sorting Segments within a Stacked Bar on page 188

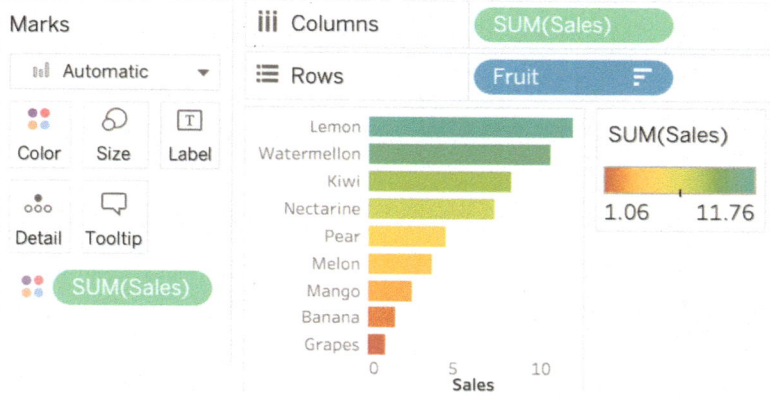

FIGURE 50

The Marks Card.

This bar chart uses a diverging color palette (red to green) to represent the continuous 'Sales' field, with red indicating lower sales and green indicating higher sales.

1

The Tableau Workspace

In this topic, we discuss

Start Page

The Toolbar

The Sidebar

The Data pane

The Analytics pane

Cards, Shelves, Controls, and Legends

Select Marks

Working with Fields

The Status Bar and Sheet Tabs Menus

Menus

Tableau is a software application that creates worksheets (charts), dashboards, and stories in a Tableau workbook. Tableau refers to the view as a visualization or "viz." When creating a visualization,

dashboard, or story, you add objects to the "view." The beginning of Chapter 12 has several diagrams of various view objects such as field labels, headers, marks, panes, y-axis, legends, and annotations.

A "mark" refers to a data point and the type of chart – a bar, line, square, etc. Data points can be dots, lines, or bars on a chart, representing a single row of data or aggregated rows of data. Dashboards might have several charts, added text, or interactive elements. Together, these visualizations tell a story. A story represents a linear view of charts and dashboards. An advantage of stories is that changes, such as filtering, do not affect the original worksheet or dashboard.

Visualizations are interactive when uploaded to a Tableau server or viewed within Tableau Desktop. I have grouped interactive features in Chapter 15 because unless your audience has Tableau Desktop, Tableau Public, or a Tableau server, features such as highlighting, parameters, actions, tooltips, and hierarchies do not apply.

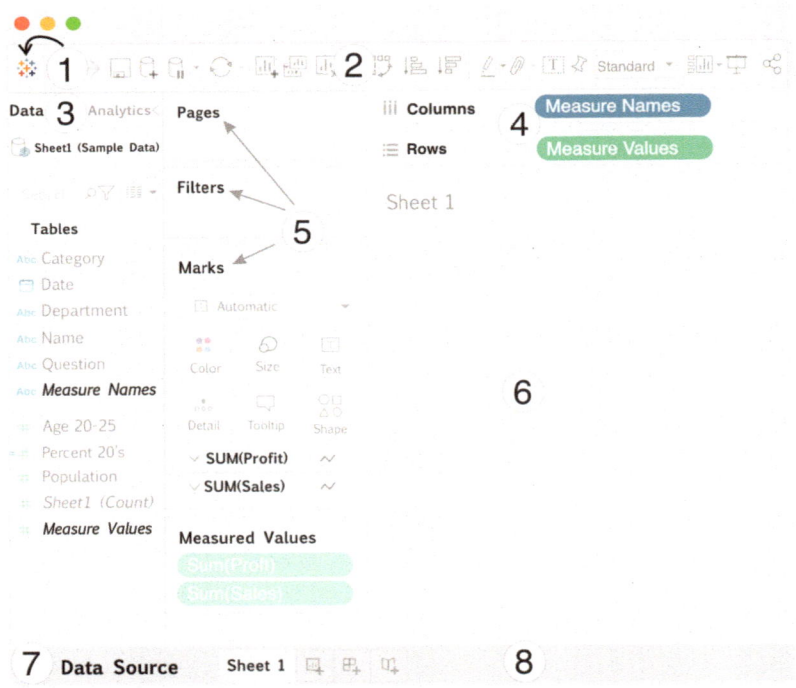

FIGURE 1.1

The Workspace

1. Start Page, 2. Toolbar, 3. Side Bar, 4. Columns Shelf and Rows Shelf, 5. Pages Shelf, Filters Shelf, and Marks Card, 6. Canvas, 7. Data Source, 8. Tabs

DOI: 10.1201/9781003566458-2

Tableau uses icons and visual clues to guide users as they navigate the workspace. In Figure 1.1, we will explore the Tableau workspace.

1.1 The Start Page

When you open a file, the **Start** page icon is on the far left in the toolbar at the top of the workspace. The first time you launch Tableau, the <u>Start page</u> is displayed, as shown in Figure 1.2. The **Start** page below has three panels:

- Left: Blue Connect Pane
- Middle: Samples and Recent Projects
- Right: Discover Training and News

Before creating a chart or visualization, we must connect to external data. Tableau does not allow you to enter data directly into a chart. While we look at data connections in detail in the next chapter, let's briefly examine connecting to a data source.

1.1.1 Connect to a Data Source

Use the blue **Connect** pane to connect to a data source. After you select a data source, Tableau opens the **Data Source** page, where you can connect to a table. At any time, in the left corner of the bottom tab bar, you can click "Data Source" to open the **Data Source** page.

1. Use the blue **Connect** pane on the left side of the **Start** page to create a connection. To

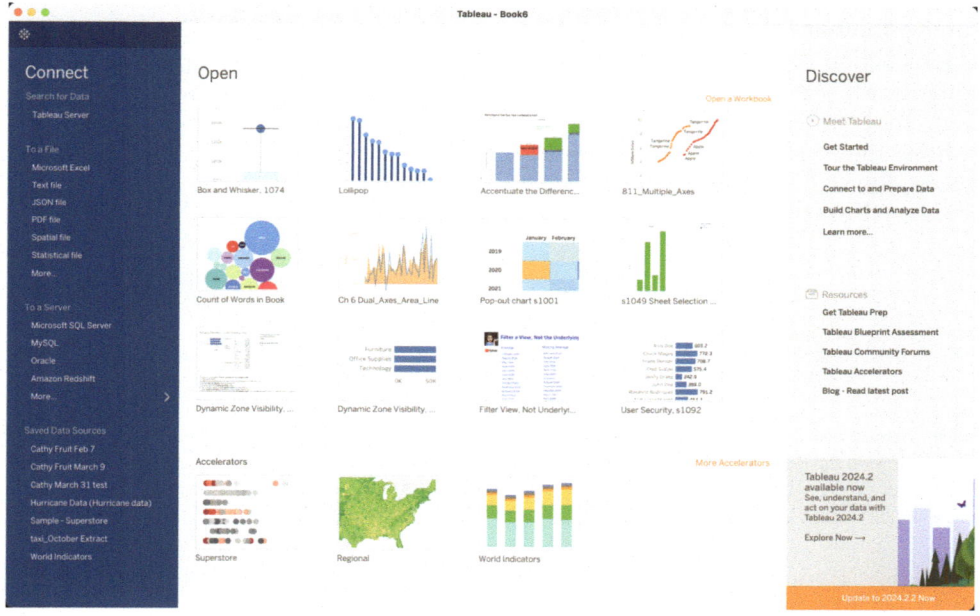

FIGURE 1.2
The Start page.

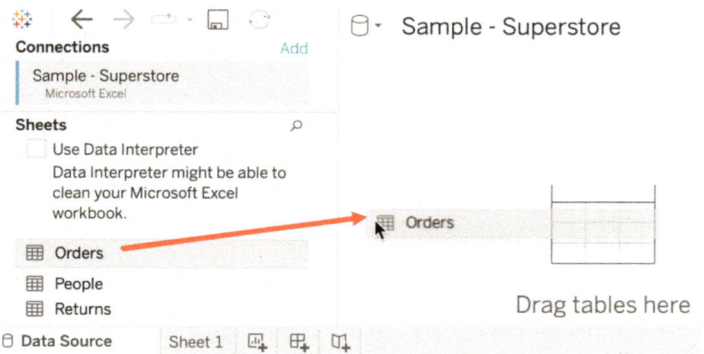

FIGURE 1.3
Drag orders onto the canvas.

connect to an Excel file, select Microsoft Excel and browse to your Excel file location. After creating the data source connection to your Excel file, Tableau opens the **Data Source** page (Figure 1.3).

2. Now, you can drag the "Orders" worksheet onto the canvas. In the previous image, the Excel workbook is called "Sample – Superstore." The file has three worksheets: Orders, People, and Returns (Figures 1.3).

1.2 The Toolbar

The **Toolbar** at the top of the screen has shortcut buttons for many common tasks and additional functionality. The **Start** page button is on the far left. Let's look at the left half of the **Toolbar** first shown in Figure 1.6. To undo a previous action, use the "Undo" arrow. If you change your mind, use "Redo" to return your action. The save tool saves your workbook. The **Toolbar** below shows the other tools (Figures 1.6–1.25).

Figure 1.14 shows the right side of the **Toolbar**. The "Show Me" tool is on the far right.

FIGURE 1.4

Tip: *For a quick analysis, create a new Tableau worksheet. Copy data from an Excel file and select Paste from the File menu of the new Tableau worksheet, as shown in Figure 1.5.*

FIGURE 1.6
The left side of the Toolbar.

FIGURE 1.7
The Start page.

FIGURE 1.8
New data source.

FIGURE 1.9
Pause auto update.

FIGURE 1.10
Run update.

FIGURE 1.11
New Worksheet.

FIGURE 1.12
Duplicate.

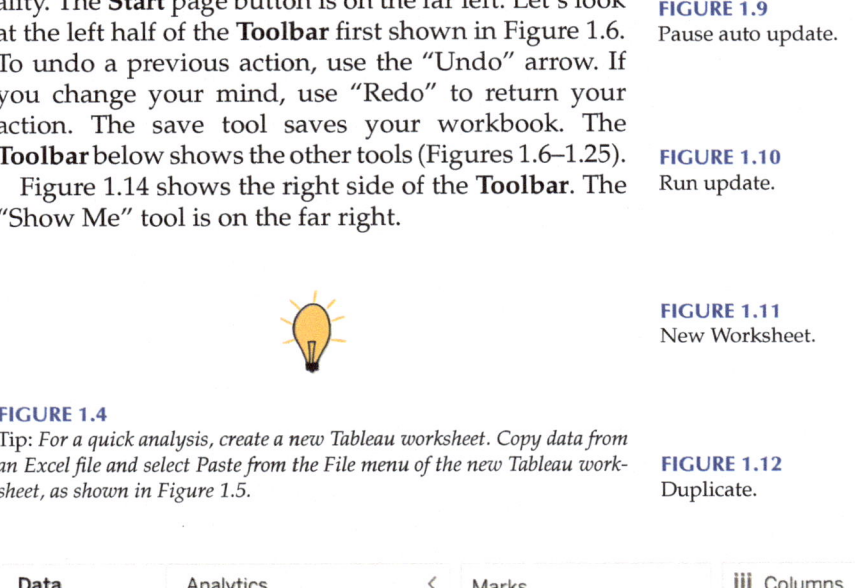
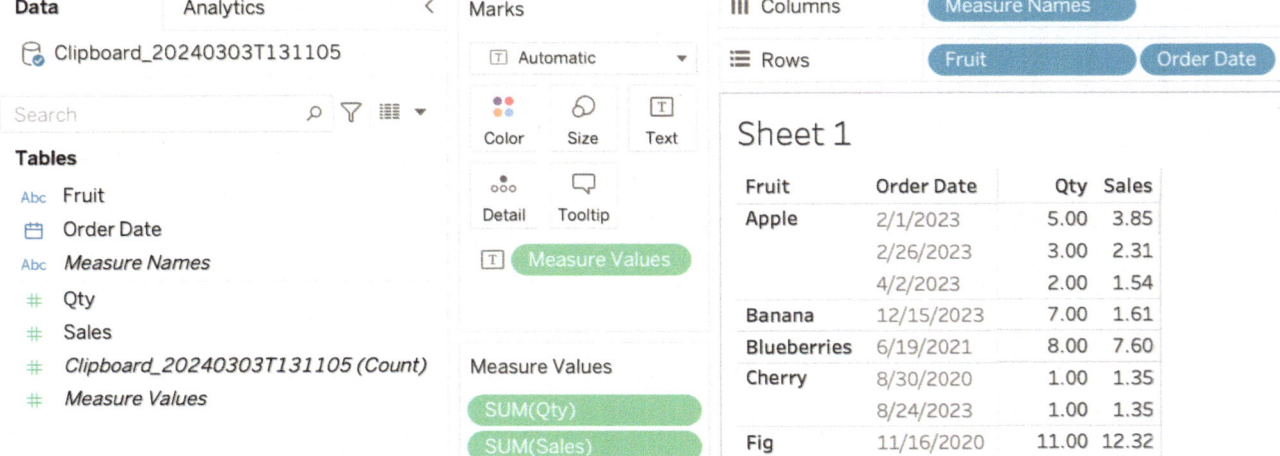

FIGURE 1.5
Clipboard data.

FIGURE 1.13
Clear Worksheet.

FIGURE 1.14
The right side of the Toolbar.

FIGURE 1.15
Swap rows and columns.

FIGURE 1.16
Sort ascending.

FIGURE 1.17
Sort descending.

FIGURE 1.18
Highlight tool.

FIGURE 1.19
Group members.

FIGURE 1.20
Show mark labels.

FIGURE 1.21
Fix axes.

Fit (Standard, Fit Width, Fit Height, Entire View)

FIGURE 1.22
Show/hide cards.

FIGURE 1.23
Presentation mode.

FIGURE 1.24
Share Workbook.

FIGURE 1.25
Show Me.

To switch between a vertical or horizontal bar chart, use the "Swap Rows and Columns" tool. If you do not see the **Toolbar**, on the **Window** menu, select "Show Toolbar."

1.2.1 The Highlight Tool

When you click to select a mark on the visualization, Tableau's default behavior highlights the mark, and all other marks are gray. To turn this behavior off, follow the steps below. "*Section 8.13 Click Data Points to Sort with a Set*" *on page 175* illustrates how to work with highlighting.

1. Select the *highlight* tool on the **Toolbar** to open the *context menu*.
2. Select the field to turn off highlighting.

1.2.2 Fit

Instead of formatting cell size or column widths, I like to use the "Fit" options, such as *Fit Width* or *Entire View*, whenever possible. Fit is especially useful for laying out dashboards, as shown in "*Section 14.6.1 Fit*" *on page 311*. The options for "Fit" include:

- Standard
- Fit Width
- Fit Height
- Entire View

The example "*Section 14.19 A Reset All Filters Button*" *on page 339* adjusts the fit to create a worksheet that acts as a button. Also, *"Section 12.15.7 Cell Size" on page 284* uses the size of a worksheet on a dashboard combined with the "Standard" fit on the dashboard to set the new column widths.

1.2.3 Show Me

If you know the fields you want in your visualization, select them in the **Data** pane and then click the "Show Me" button at the top right corner of the worksheet screen. Choose a format, and Tableau draws the visualization for you. Charts that are inappropriate for your selected fields are grayed out. The "Show Me" views use different combinations of *Mark Types* and other elements.

1.3 The Sidebar

The left **Sidebar** of a worksheet screen has two tabbed panes: the **Data** and **Analytics** panes. The left **Sidebar** of a dashboard screen has two tabbed panes: the **Dashboard** pane and the **Layout** pane. **Chapter 14** examines dashboards in detail.

1.4 The Data Pane

When viewing a worksheet, the **Data** pane is on the left side of the view. By default, it groups fields into tables and data sources. A horizontal line divides the **Data** pane, with **dimension** fields at the top and **measure** fields at the bottom, as shown in Figure 1.26. If you also have Sets, Bins, and Parameters, they are at the bottom of the **Data** pane just above *Measure Names*.

You can reorganize the **Data** pane with custom folders for fields. You can switch between grouping fields in the custom folders you create or grouping the original data source. I illustrate how to create folders in Step 4 of the step-by-step instructions "Replace a Data Source" in Chapter 2. If you inherit someone else's workbook and are unfamiliar with the data, the **Search** field and the option **Hide All Unused Fields** are quick ways to focus on critical fields. In Chapter 4, we will look at the icons representing different types of fields. Figure 1.26 shows a "Fruit Hierarchy" with a set and group.

1.4.1 Data Pane Context Menu

The top of the **Data** pane has a **Search** box, a **Filter** tool, and a **View Data** tool. Click the drop-down arrow to open the **Date** pane's *context menu* with these options:

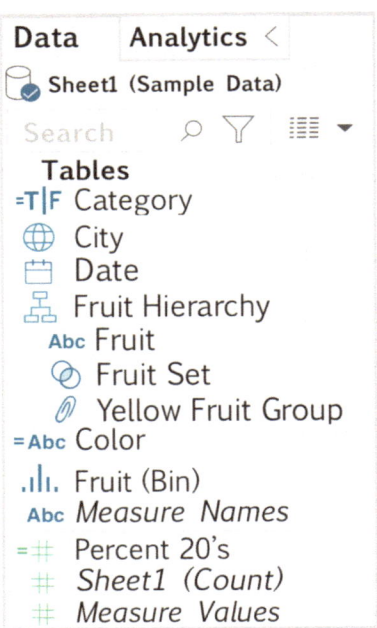

FIGURE 1.26
The Data pane.

- Create a Calculated Field
- Create Parameter
- Group by Folder
- Group by Data Source
- Sort
- Hide All Unused Fields
- Show Hidden Fields

To download the data used in a workbook, click the **View Data** tool shown in Figure 1.27.

1.4.2 Transform

You can also use split options for fields in the **Data** pane. Right-click a field name, choose "Transform," and select "Split," as shown in Figure 1.28. The *Split* option immediately creates two new fields.

The *Custom Split* option in Figure 1.29 allows you more control over how the field is split. You can choose what to split off, the separator, and the number of columns.

1.4.3 Describe

When you right-click a field name in the **Data** pane, the field's *context menu* has a choice for "Describe." If unsure whether a field is a measure or dimension, right-click the field name in the **Data** pane and select "Describe" to open the **Describe Field** window shown in Figure 1.30.

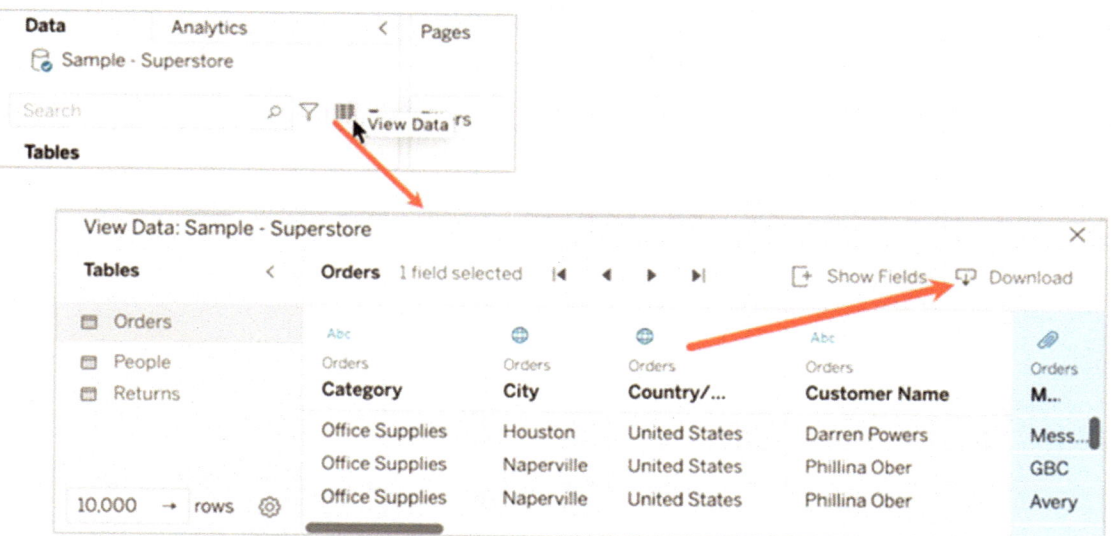

FIGURE 1.27
View Data.

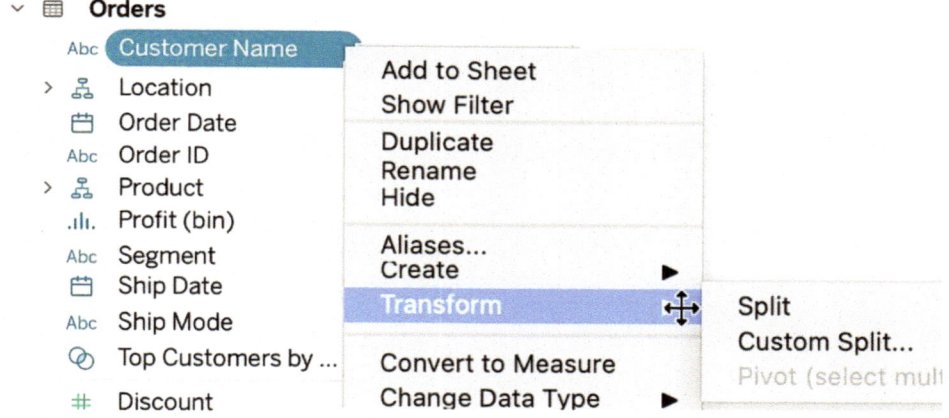

FIGURE 1.28
Transform.

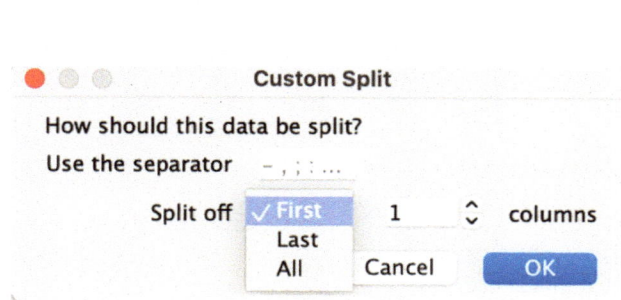

FIGURE 1.29
Custom Split.

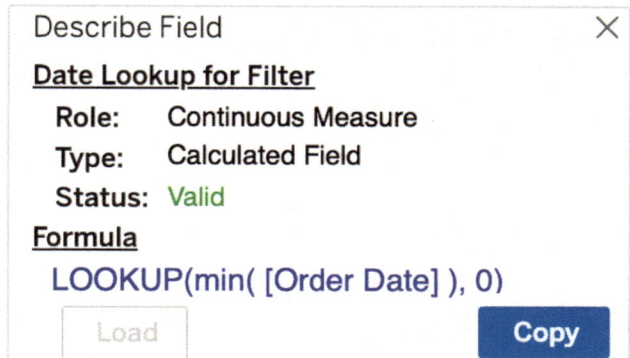

FIGURE 1.30
Describe Field window.

1.5 Analytics Pane

Depending on chart elements, different items are available in the **Analytics** pane. For example, a *Trend Line* may be grayed out depending on the fields in the view and whether they are **Discrete** or **Continuous**. This list includes some of my favorite **Analytics** pane items. **Chapter 7** demonstrates trend lines and reference lines. *"Section 11.15 Totals" on page 253* looks at totals.

- Totals
- Trend Lines
- Reference Lines

1.6 Cards, Shelves, Controls, and Legends

Tableau uses the concept of "Cards," "Shelves," "Legends," "Controls," and "Tiles." In addition to the Columns and Rows shelves, you can add fields to the *tiles* on the **Marks** card and other shelves. When you add fields to shelves or tiles, Tableau creates controls and legends for the view, including these elements:

- Caption
- Color Legend
- Columns Shelf
- Filter Shelf
- Filter Control
- Highlight Control
- Map Legend
- Marks Card

- Measure Values Shelf
- Page Control
- Pages Shelf
- Parameter Controls
- Rows Shelf
- Set Control
- Shape Legend
- Size Legend
- Summary Card
- Title

Controls and **Legends** are displayed when a corresponding **Shelf** has a value. For example, the **Page** control is shown when a field is on the **Pages** shelf. In Figure 1.31, a field is on the *Color* tile, and the **Color** legend is on the right.

1.7 Add Fields and Objects to the View

In later topics, we will use the *type of mark* to establish the kind of chart, such as a text table, bar chart, line chart, or histogram. We will also use *tiles to* encode chart marks with color, text, shapes, and other properties. You can reuse the same field on the **Filter** shelf, the *Color* tile on the **Marks** card, the **Rows** or **Columns** shelf, or other tiles and shelves. Fields on the **Rows** and **Columns** shelves control the data in the visualization and add "Headers" or "Axes" to the view. As you look through the charts in **Chapter 7**, you'll notice that not all visualizations have fields on the **Rows** or **Columns** shelves. For example, Word Clouds and Treemaps only have fields on the **Marks** card.

FIGURE 1.31
The Color legend.

Chapter 7 details the **Marks** card. In **Chapter 8**, we explore the **Filters** shelf. To display legends, select "Legends" on the **Analysis** menu and then choose the Color, Shape, or Size legend, as shown in Figure 1.32. The **Size** legend is helpful when working with scatterplots. **Chapter 15** looks at legends and parameter controls in more detail.

1.7.1 The Pages Shelf

The **Pages** shelf allows you to flip through views. If, for example, I add Year(Order Date) to the **Pages** shelf,

a "Pages" control allows me to move through the years in an animation.

1.7.2 Show, Hide, and Format Legends

Depending on the type of chart you have, you might see a color legend, shape legend, or size legend. On the **Analysis** menu, choose "Legends" to toggle the legend control display. In Figure 1.33, the map has a **Filter Control**, a **Color Legend**, a **Parameter Control**, and a **Highlight Control**. Because all these objects are transparent by default, I formatted them to add

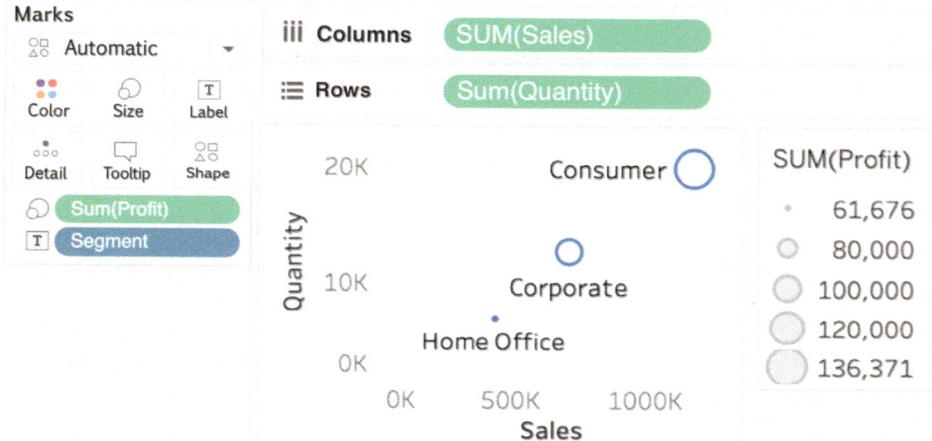

FIGURE 1.32
The Size legend.

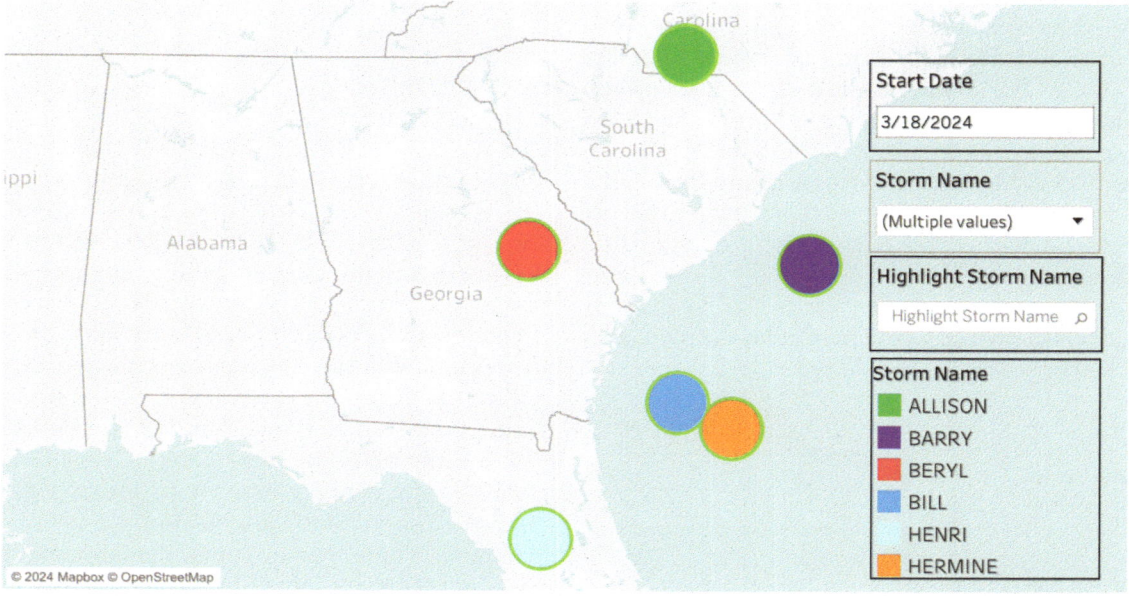

FIGURE 1.33
Map Legends and Controls.

borders. *"Section 15.3.4 Legend Highlighting" on page 366* has an example of legend highlighting. *"Section 14.8 Legend" on page 314* and *"Section 7.3.10 Color Legend From Field Values" on page 143* have examples of color legends.

1.7.3 The Columns Shelf and Rows Shelf

To create a visualization, add fields to "shelves" or "cards." In Figure 1.34, the dimension field [Region] is on the **Columns** shelf and shown as a **blue** field because it is **discrete**. The measure field [Sales] is aggregated as a "Sum" on the **Rows** shelf and shown as Sum (Sales). It is a **green** field because it is **continuous**. We look at the concepts of **discrete** and **continuous** in Chapter 3. The "Floating Container for Filters" example in **Chapter 14** illustrates headings and an axis for fields on these shelves.

If you previously closed a shelf and want to reopen it, on the **Worksheet** menu, select "Show Cards."

1.8 Select Marks

Once you add fields to the view, select data points or "marks" to create groups, sets, or filters. Marks are dots, lines, bars, etc., on the canvas. Hold down the *Control* key and click with your mouse to select marks. In MacOS, use the *Command* key.

Right-click selected marks to open the *context menu* with additional choices, or hover the mouse over marks until a tooltip opens. In the tooltip window, the paperclip icon creates groups, the Zen diagram icon creates sets, and the **Keep Only** or **Exclude** choices creates filters. For example, after you select **Keep Only**, Tableau adds the field to the **Filters** shelf with those selected marks included in the filter. When creating a group, Tableau adds the new group field to the **Data** pane. Tableau also adds the field to the *Color* tile on the **Marks** card if this is the first group for that dimension.

"Section 9.2.2 Select Marks on the View to View Data" on page 196 demonstrates how to select multiple marks in a stacked bar.

FIGURE 1.34
Discrete and continuous.

1.9 Working with Fields

1.9.1 Field Unavailable

If you are trying to use a field in a *Tooltip* or as a view object in general and it is unavailable, add it to the *Detail* tile on the **Marks** card. When showing hidden fields in the **Data** pane, the fields are grayed out. Because you can't use hidden fields in a view, unhide the field before trying to add the field to the view.

1.9.2 The Field is Missing from the Data Source Page

Not all calculated fields show on the **Data Source** page. For example, you won't see Level of Detail (LOD) fields and table calculations on a **Data Source** page.

1.9.3 Cannot Change the Order of Fields on Shelves

You cannot place measure fields to the left of "dimension fields" on the **Rows** or **Columns** shelves.

However, you can change a field to a "dimension" and reorder it from left to right.

1.9.4 Cannot Delete a Field

You cannot delete a field used on a worksheet or calculation. When you edit a calculated field, a message at the bottom of the field counts how many times it is used.

1.10 The Status Bar and Sheet Tabs

The **Status Bar** is located at the bottom of the screen. The left side shows marks, row counts, column counts, and aggregations. The right side has arrows to move between worksheets or tools like a "Show the Sheet Sorter" tool.

Each worksheet, dashboard, and story has a tab at the bottom of the screen, assuming the worksheets are not hidden. In addition to these tabs, the tab bar has a **Data Source** tab in the bottom left corner. On the far right corner of the tab bar, there are several icons for creating new items (worksheets, dashboards, or stories) and a shortcut to view all sheets in the workbook. When you right-click on a tab, the tab's *context menu* has several options, including changing the color of a tab or hiding the worksheet. I like to color code worksheets to match the corresponding dashboard.

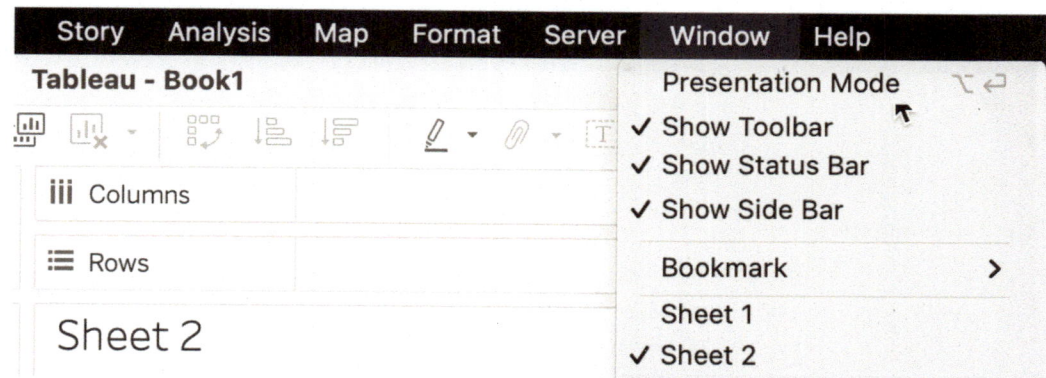

FIGURE 1.35
The Window menu.

Sheets used in dashboards or tooltips also have an "Unhide" choice.

1.10.1 Unhide Sheets

To unhide sheets used in a *Tooltip*, edit the worksheet with the tooltip. Right-click the sheet name at the bottom of the workspace and choose "Unhide All Sheets." Only sheets with embedded tooltip sheets have the "Hide All Sheets" and "Unhide All Sheets" options.

1.10.2 Copy Dashboards and Worksheets

Tableau Public is a great place to find interesting ideas and sample workbooks. Tableau's help <u>reuse workbooks</u> outlines how to handle common tasks. When copying dashboards and worksheets from one workbook to another, navigation buttons may not work properly if the worksheet in the first navigation button is missing.

1.11 Menus

While working in Tableau, we'll use menus to connect to data or servers and control dashboards, stories, maps, and worksheets. The "Workbook Locale" is automatic, but you can change that to another locale using the **File** menu.

1.11.1 The Format and Window Menus

To change formatting, right-click on the view and choose "Format" from the pop-up *context menu*. The **Format** pane dynamically changes based on where you click on the view. Another option is the **Format** menu, which allows you to go to the correct format option on the first try. **Chapter 12** looks at formatting in great detail.

Figure 1.35 shows only a few options on the **Window** menu. Still, a handy one is *Presentation Mode*, which allows you to test interactively.

1.11.2 Worksheet Menu

In addition to the option to *export* data, the **Worksheet** menu has choices to create a worksheet *action* or to *show cards*. When you display the **Summary** card, Tableau shows current values based on the level of aggregation, which is helpful when working on calculations. In Figure 1.36, "Describe Sheet…" is at the bottom of the **Worksheet** menu.

When there are fields on the view, "Describe Sheet" details the sheet aggregation, data source, field names, marks, shelves, dimensions, measures, aggregation, fields, and calculated field formulas.

1.11.2.1 Caption

To add a field comment, edit the "Caption." Right-click the field to open the field's *context menu*, select "Default Properties," and then select "Comment."

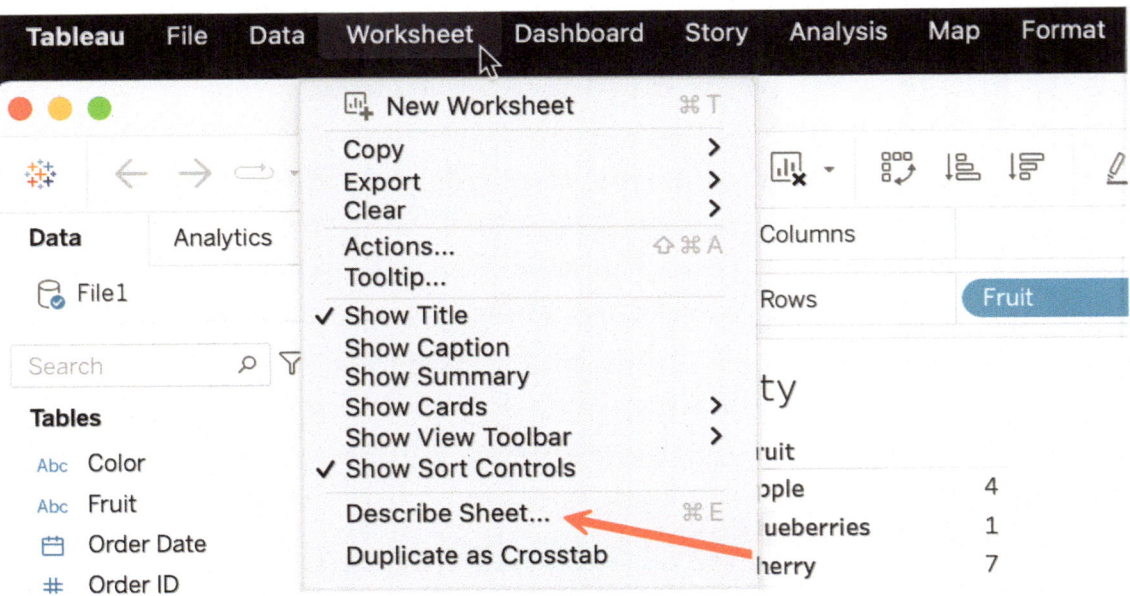

FIGURE 1.36
Worksheet menu.

2

Data Sources

In this topic, we discuss

The Start Page

The Data Source Page

Work with Data Sources Connect to a Data Source

Tableau Server Published Data Sources

Replace a Data Source

Create an Extract

To jump right into using Tableau, first connect to a data source. Because the structure of columns and rows is critical to successful visualizations, we will first look at data preparation and explore the concept of "tall data." We will also look at the type of data, especially dates, because data types are a factor in how Tableau performs. The rest of this chapter explores field default properties, combining data tables, customizing data and geographic roles, and replacing a data source.

It is worth noting that sometimes you want to add data strictly for Tableau to use internally for things like filters or calculations – similar to drop-down lists in Excel. In *"Section 14.17 Horizontal Radial Buttons to Switch Sheets" on page 328*, I use this type of data for worksheet names in parameters.

2.1 The Start Page

When you first launch Tableau Desktop, the **Start** page opens with the blue Connect pane on the left that lists available data connectors, as shown in Figure 1.2 in Chapter 1. From the **Start** page, connect to a data source. A data source can be an Excel file, a database, a *.hyper file on a Tableau server, or one of the dozens of formats supported by Tableau. After selecting your data source file (Excel, perhaps), you are taken to the **Data Source** page. Tableau's Trailhead Academy has a free module on how to Connect Your Data.

Saved Data Sources are in the bottom left corner of the **Start** page. Later in this chapter, we examine TDS (or Tableau data source) files in more detail and how to connect to the Tableau *Sample Superstore.tds* and *World Indicators.tds* saved data sources.

2.2 The Data Source Page

The **Data Source** page is where you prepare your data for analysis. If you have a worksheet open, click the **Data Source** tab at the bottom left corner of the Tableau workspace. Continuing with the previous example of an Excel file, the **Data Source** page shows the available worksheets in the Excel file in the gray pane on the left. In Figure 2.1, I added the Orders, People, and Returns worksheets to the canvas.

Connections to files, in this case, the Excel file, are at the top of the gray pane. The white area on the right side of the gray pane displays the *canvas* at the top and the **Metadata Grid** and **Data Grid** at the bottom of the screen.

2.2.1 The Context Menu

Right-click a field on the **Data Source** page or click the drop-down arrow in the top-right corner by the field name to display the field's *context menu* with these choices.

- Rename
- Copy Values
- Hide (Field)
- Aliases
- Create Calculated Field
- Create Group
- Transform (Split a Field)

2.2.1.1 Rename a Field

To rename a field in the **Data Source** pane, click the drop-down arrow in the field pane to open the field's *context menu* and choose "Rename," as shown in Figure 2.2. You can also right-click a field name in the **Data** pane of a worksheet to open a field's *context menu*.

In Figure 2.3, I renamed the field [State/Province]. The "Remote Field Name" on the right is the field name in the original data source. On the left, "Field Name" is the new name in Tableau.

DOI: 10.1201/9781003566458-3

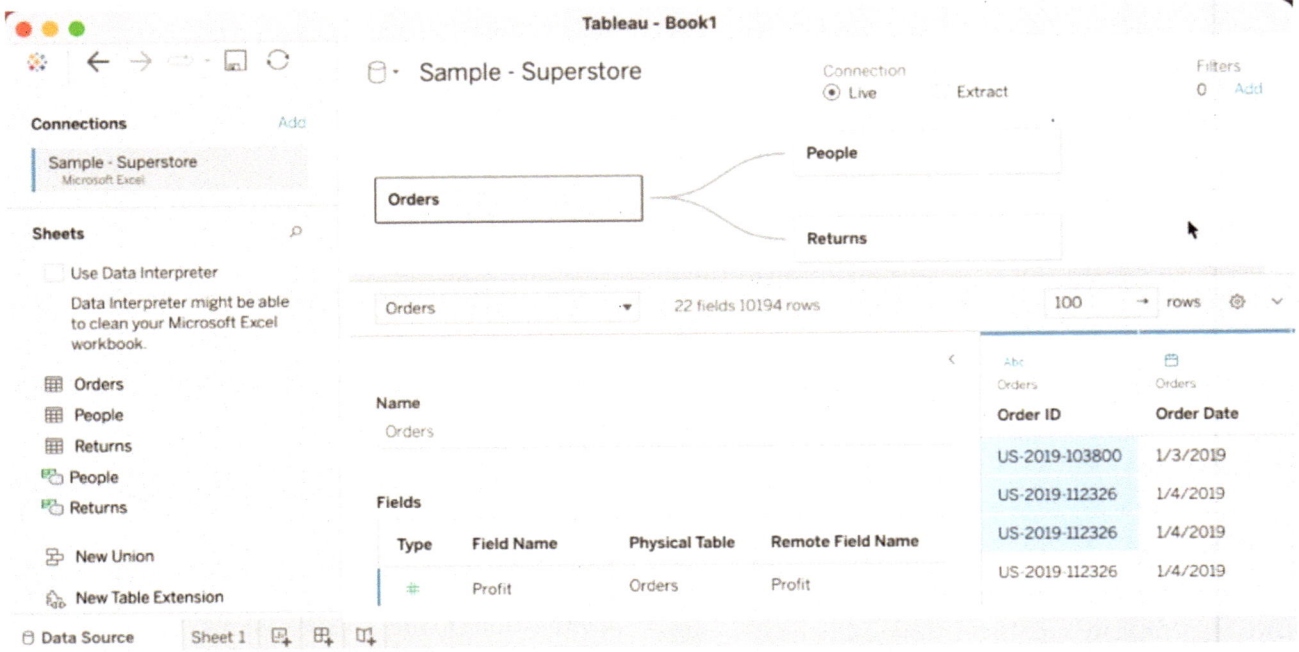

FIGURE 2.1
Data Source page.

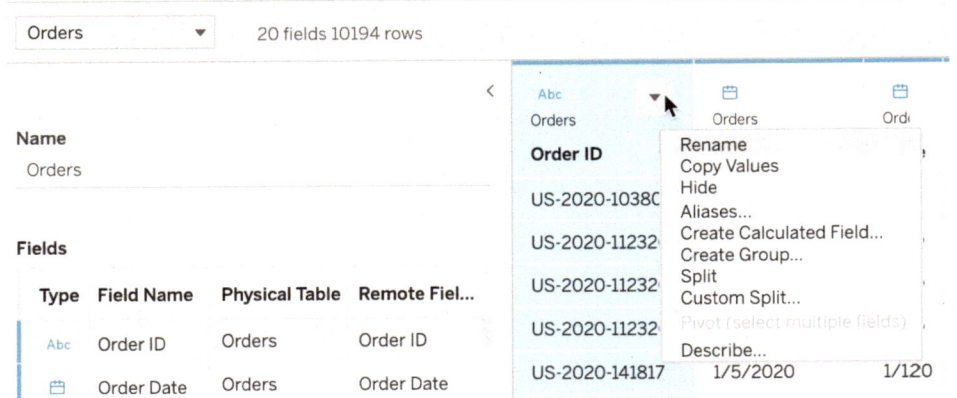

FIGURE 2.2
The Field Context Menu on the Data Source page.

2.2.1.2 Hide a Field

Click a field name to open the field's *context menu* and choose "Hide" to remove it from the list of available fields in the <u>Metadata</u> grid, **Data** grid, or a worksheet's **Data** pane. Use the gear icon on the right side of the **Data Source** page to hide all unused fields. Alternatively, at the top of a worksheet's **Data** pane, click the drop-down arrow to open the *context menu* and choose "Show Hidden Fields."

Tableau also identifies a field as unused when the field is only used to populate parameters. You cannot add a hidden field to a visualization. If you decide to unhide fields in the future, follow these steps.

- Click the gear icon on the right side of the **Data Source** page to "Show Hidden Fields." The hidden fields are light gray.

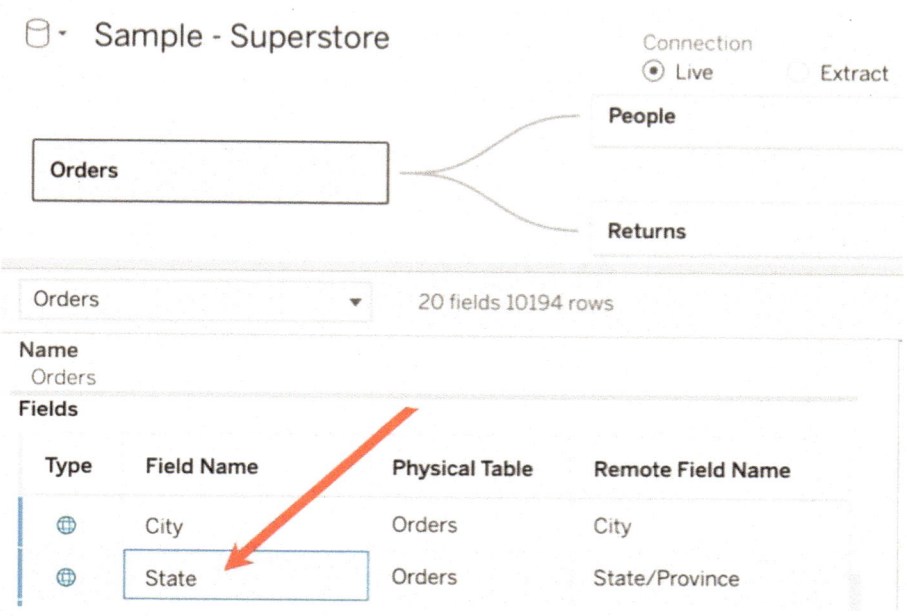

FIGURE 2.3
Remote Field Name.

FIGURE 2.4
Tip: *If you replace a data source, identify renamed fields so you can make the same changes in the new data source.*

- Alternatively, at the top of a worksheet's **Data** pane, click the drop-down arrow to open the *context menu* and choose "Show Hidden fields."
- Select the fields, right-click to open the *context menu*, and choose "Unhide."

2.2.2 Transform (Split) Strings

For some data sources, Tableau has split options to separate a string field to create new string fields. Tableau offers three ways to split a field.

1. Choose *Split* and *Custom Split* from a field's *context menu* on the **Data Source** page.
2. Select *Transform* from the field's *context menu* in the **Data** pane on a worksheet.
3. Create calculated fields with functions like SPLIT() or LEFT().

In Figure 2.6, split is an option on the pop-up field menu on the **Data Source** page, indicating this data source supports splitting strings. Use a delimiter or repeated pattern when splitting fields. The third way to split a field is a calculated field with functions. If you want the left or right part of a string, you can use the LEFT(), RIGHT(), or REGEXP_EXTRACT() functions. Tableau has several RegEx functions, also known as regular expressions. The SPLIT() function allows you to select a specific token. When you break a string into chunks of data, they are called tokens. The syntax for the SPLIT() function is shown below.

SPLIT(string, delimiter, token number)

2.2.3 Hide All Unused Fields

After you have finished creating your visualizations, open the **Data** pane *context menu* and select "Hide All Unused Fields," so that extracts are smaller, improving performance. When creating an extract, there is also an option to "Hide All Unused Fields" in the export dialog window.

FIGURE 2.5
Tip: *When using web authoring instead of Tableau Desktop, use a SPLIT() function to split fields.*

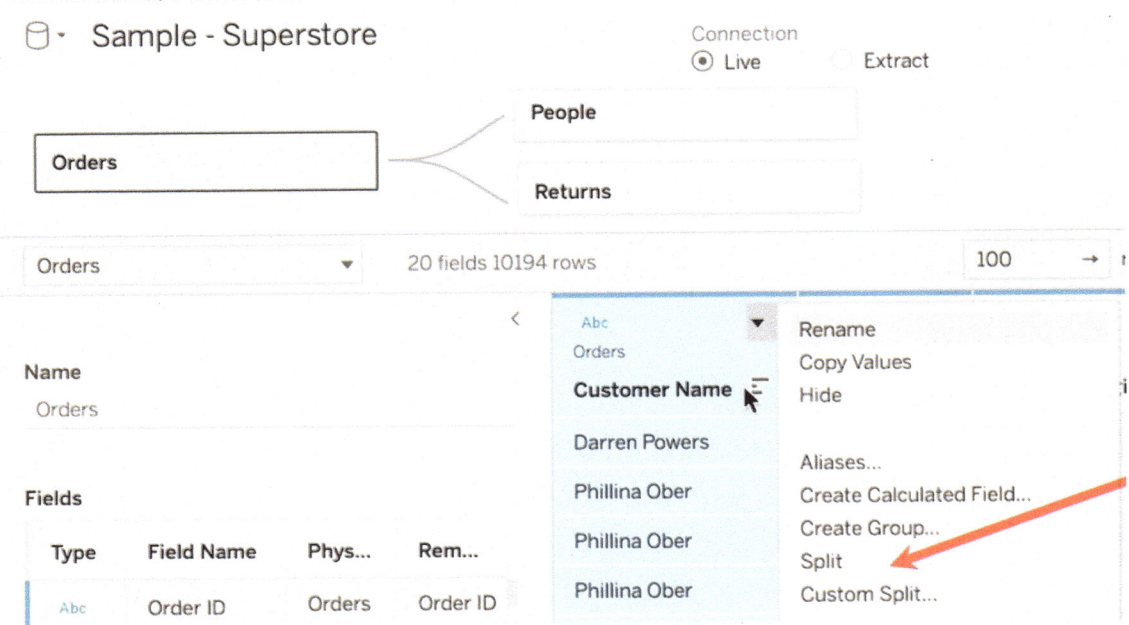

FIGURE 2.6
Split a field.

2.2.4 Create an Alias

In Tableau, you can create an alias for a field name or for members (values) in a field. Tableau <u>aliases</u> only apply to **discrete** dimensions and are not available for published data sources. Dimensions describe what, when, or who. For example, for a *Products* field with "Laptop" and "Desktop" members, you can create an alias of "CPU" for the "Desktop" member. You cannot create aliases for measures, dates, and **continuous** dimensions. We look at dimensions and measures in *"Section 3.1 Dimension Fields" on page 57 and "Section 3.2 Measure Fields" on page 57*. You cannot use an alias more than once, which can be an issue on dashboards where you combine several charts from several data sources with the same fields. One alternative to an alias is a calculated field, as shown in *"Section 13.4.2 A Heading for a Field on the Text Tile" on page 295*.

To assign an alias to a field's members, right-click the field name on the **Data Source** page, a shelf, or in the **Data** pane to open the field's *context menu* and choose "Aliases…" Figure 2.7 shows a *context menu* for a field that already has aliases. You can also assign aliases in **Legend Controls** when you right-click a member in a legend. In *"Section 15.1.8 Drill Down with a Set Action" on page 359*, I assign an ASCII symbol as an alias.

For aliases for field names, select the data source name on the **Data** menu to work with "Aliases" at the data source level or right-click the data source at the top of the **Data** pane. Alternatively, right-click the [Measure Names] field in the **Data** pane and select "Aliases."

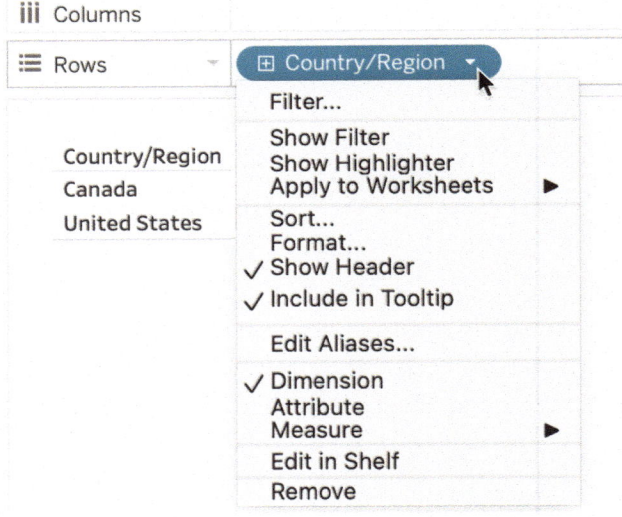

FIGURE 2.7
Edit Aliases.

2.2.5 Edit or Remove Aliases

To change an alias for members of a field, right-click the field in the **Data** pane to open the field's *context menu*. Select "Aliases" from the drop-down menu. A pop-up window opens where members with an alias are indicated with an asterisk in the "Has Alias" column.

To edit or remove aliases for field names, select the data source name on the **Data** menu to "Edit Aliases"

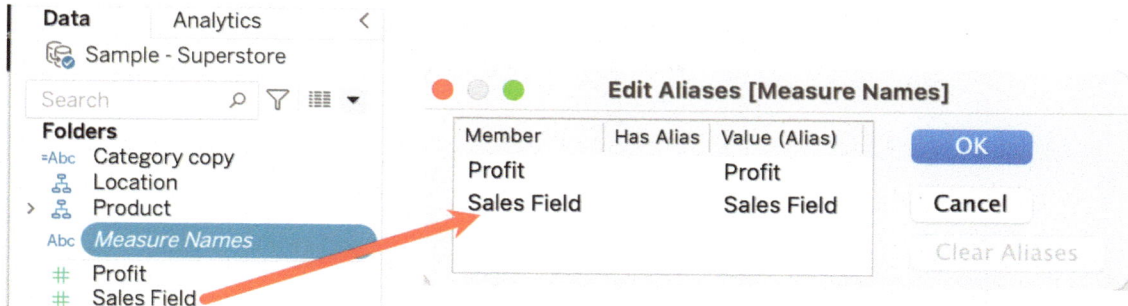

FIGURE 2.8
Edit Aliases – Measure names.

at the data source level or right-click the data source at the top of the **Data** pane. Alternatively, right-click the [Measure Names] field in the **Data** pane and select "Aliases" to edit or clear an alias. In Figure 2.8, I am creating an alias for the [Sales] field.

FIGURE 2.9
Drop-down arrow to the right of the Data Source Cylinder Icon.

2.3 Work with Data Sources

In this topic, we look at several data source actions: connect to a data source, move a data source's data file, rename a data source, remove or close a data source, and save a data source. TDS files (or Tableau data source files) do not include visualizations, dashboards, or data but do include connection information and customizations like these elements:

- Sets
- Groups
- Bins
- Hierarchies
- Data Type Changes
- Aliases and Renamed Fields
- Calculated Fields
- Default Properties

2.4 Connect to a Data Source

While you can connect to a *Data Source* from the **Start** page, you can also edit or create a new data source connection on the **Data Source** page or from a worksheet using the **Data** menu.

- On the **Data Source** page, click the drop-down arrow on the right side of the data source icon (in the white canvas area in the

top half of the page), as shown in Figure 2.9. Select "New Data Source." Note that the cylinder icon is on the left of the selected data source's name.

- On the **Data** menu, select "New Data Source." You can also connect to the *Sample Superstore* data source in the bottom left corner of the **Start** page.

2.4.1 Connect to a Saved Data Source

Saved **Data Sources** are shown in the bottom left corner of the **Start** page. Click the **Start** page icon in the top left corner of the workspace and then select the saved data source in the bottom left corner of the page in the blue area.

2.5 Tableau Server Data Source

You will need your Tableau server name and project to sign in to a Tableau server.

1. Open a browser and go to your Tableau server.
2. If you're not already logged into the Tableau server, open Tableau, and on the **Data Source** page, select "Tableau Server" at the top of the blue *Connect* pane on the left, as shown in Figure 2.10. Alternatively, on the **Server** menu, choose **Sign In…**, as shown in Figure 2.11.

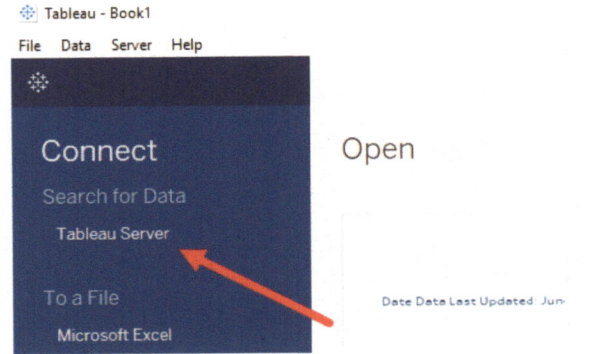

FIGURE 2.10
Connect to Tableau server.

is a point-in-time copy of the data and has the following benefits:

- Filtering (reduces load).
- Speed (stored locally to improve performance).
- For security reasons, you might want an extract that creates a silo or to limit access to only relevant information.

Figure 2.13 is a worksheet page with a live connection, as indicated by the single cylinder icon to the left of the connection name at the top of the **Data** pane.

In Figure 2.14, a small double-cylinder icon to the left of the connection name indicates this is an extract.

3. In the **Tableau Server Sign In** window, type the name of the server, as shown in Figure 2.24.

2.5.2 Data Source Extract Filters

At the top right corner of the **Data Source** page, you can create an extract filter for the data source. For example, to filter to the two most recent orders, select the [Order Date] field and click "Individual Dates and Times" at the bottom of the list, as shown in Figure 2.15. Data Source *extract filters* are not replaced when you switch data sources. For more information, see the later topic, "Change Data Source."

2.5.1 Live vs. Extract

When you first connect to an Excel file, Tableau creates a "live" connection. With a live connection, you see the latest data when you open the workbook or "refresh" the data source. There is also an option for an "extract" that creates a *.hyper file, as shown in the top-right corner of the screen in Figure 2.12. An extract

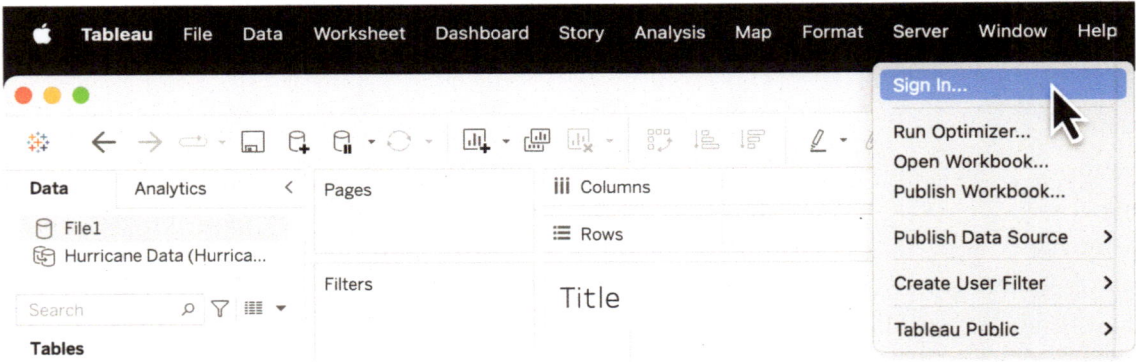

FIGURE 2.11
Server Menu, Sign In.

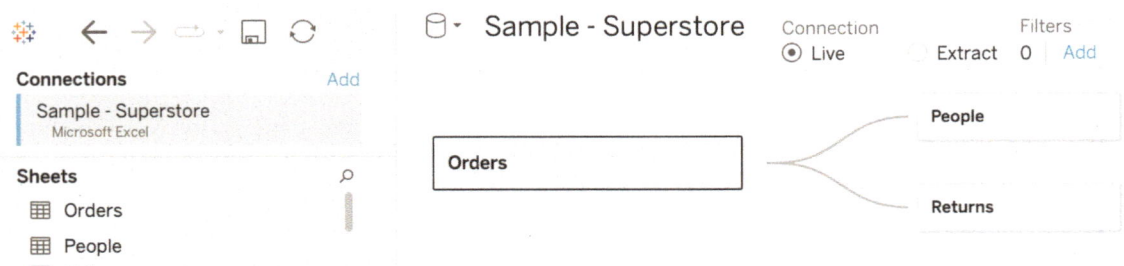

FIGURE 2.12
Connection: Live or Extract.

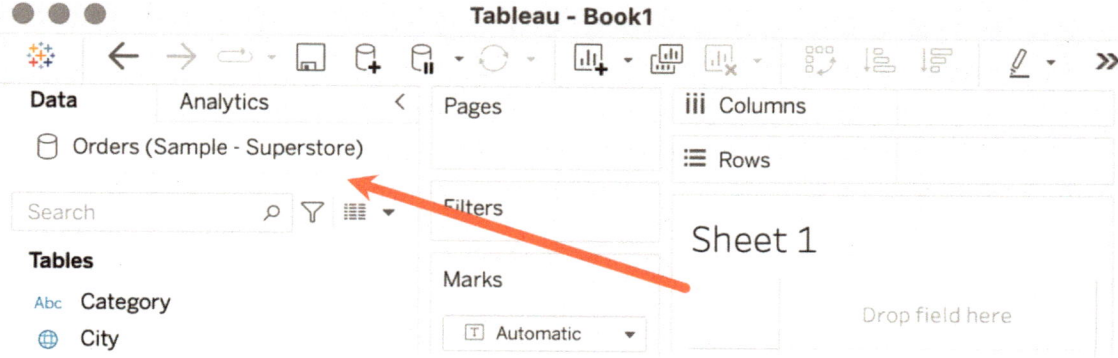

FIGURE 2.13
A live connection.

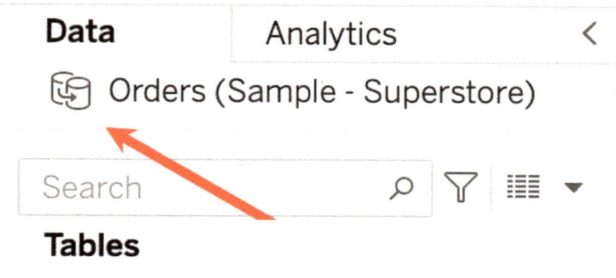

FIGURE 2.14
The double-cylinder icon.

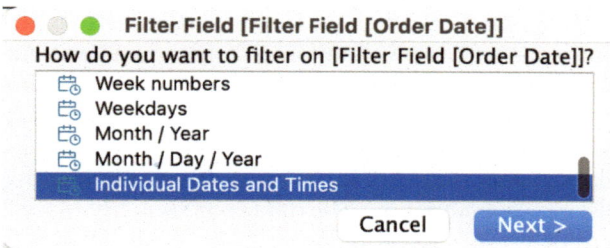

FIGURE 2.15
Extract filters.

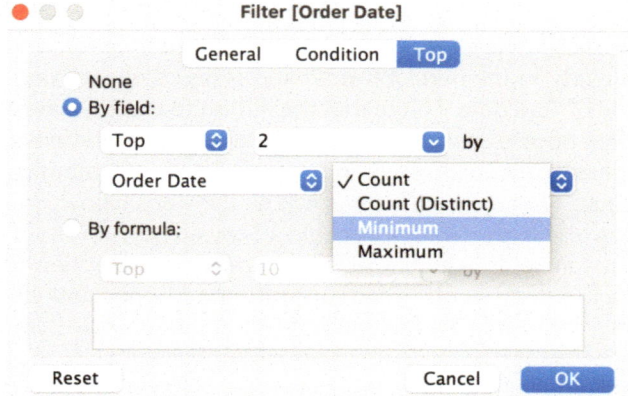

FIGURE 2.16
Filter by field.

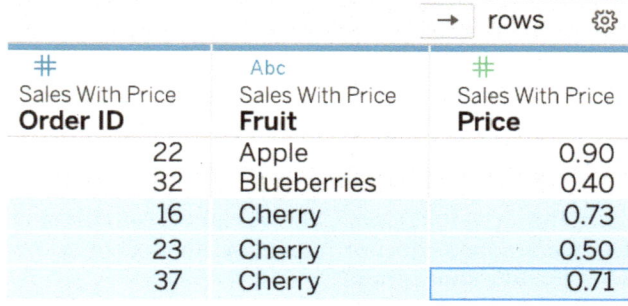

FIGURE 2.17
Data Source page with data.

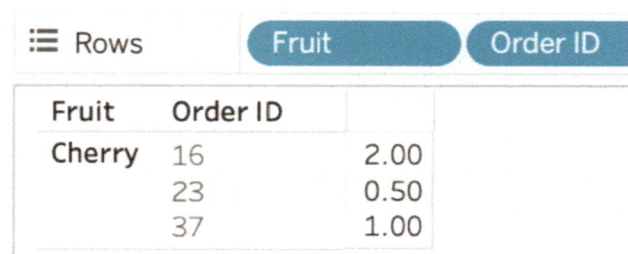

FIGURE 2.18
View values are different than the Data Source page.

In Figure 2.16, I selected the radial button "By field" and the *Top 2* values. For aggregation, I selected "Minimum." Later in this chapter, we look at aggregations like count or sum.

2.5.2.1 Refresh the Extract so the Visualization Data Matches the Data Source

When I know my data source data has changed, and I don't see the values I expect, I look at the **Data Source** page to see if the connection is live. In Figure 2.17, I created a new connection to the same **Data Source**. This live connection shows the price for cherries is 0.73, 0.50, and 0.71.

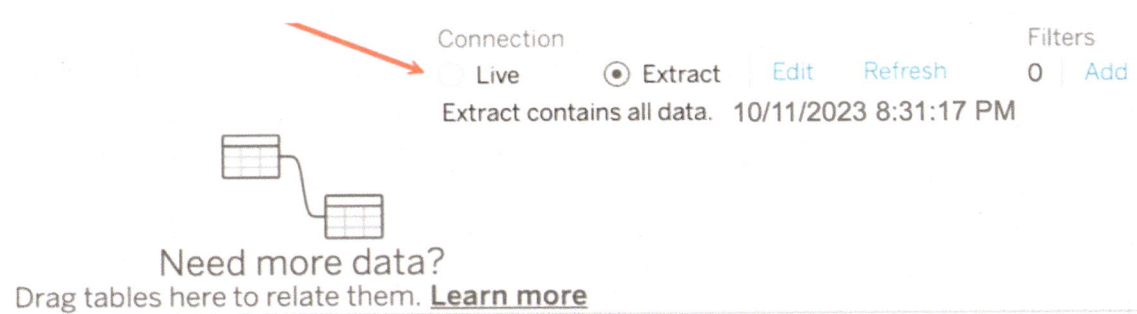

Need more data?
Drag tables here to relate them. **Learn more**

FIGURE 2.19
Extract connection.

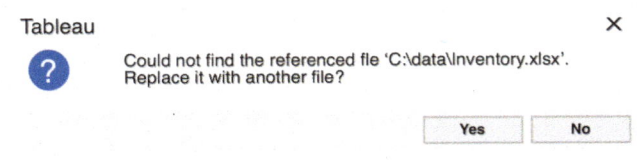

FIGURE 2.20
Error message.

On the chart in Figure 2.18, the values from the original data source do not match the new data source with the live connection.

When I look at my **Data Source** page again for the first data source, I have "Extract" selected in the top right corner of Figure 2.19, which means the data is not current. I need to "Refresh" the data extract from the **Data** menu or change the connection to "Live" to see the latest data.

2.5.3 Move a Data Source's Data File

Suppose you open a Tableau workbook but do not have access to the location of the data source file. An error similar to the one in Figure 2.20 will be displayed. The exact error message depends on how Tableau is connected to the **Data Source**. When a data source file moves to a new location, browse and reconnect to the data source file to continue working as usual. Errors also happen when you use a drive letter that is different from the original developer's. When you use a packaged data source file (*.twbx), you won't have drive letter issues. A packaged file is a single zipped file that contains a *copy* of your data source.

When sharing Tableau files in a network environment, check your access to that resource. If you use one of the resources below, check if you have basic access to the resource outside of Tableau.

- Drive Mappings
- Universal naming convention (UNC) path
- SharePoint access
- Database access
- Server access

2.5.4 Rename a Data Source

If you have successfully connected to a data source, the new data source is displayed at the top of the **Data Source** page. Click the data source name if you want to *rename* the data source.

2.5.5 Remove or Close a Data Source

Right-click the **Data Source** connection at the top of the **Data** pane, or use the **Data** menu to close the data source.

2.5.6 Save Data Sources – *.tds

Customizations you make to data sources can be saved in a Tableau TDS file. The TDS file includes the data source connection information. TDS files do not include visualizations or dashboards. Saved **Data Sources** are shown in the bottom left corner of the **Start** page. TDS files are located in "My Tableau Repository" in the folder "Datasources." In MacOS, you will find this folder in "Documents." The data sources in my MacOS hard drive are shown in Figure 2.21.

By default, Tableau includes the *Sample Superstore.tds* and *World Indicators.tds* saved data sources, which point to the **Sample-Superstore.xls** and **World Indicators. hyper** files, respectively. Many examples in Tableau Help or the Tableau Public website use these data sources. The data structure for Tableau's samples is already in the perfect format and is an excellent example of "tall data." Note that the option to create a saved data source is not available in packaged workbooks. Later in this chapter, we address tall data in "Combining Data." To create a TDS file, follow the steps below. You can also <u>export data sources to a Tableau Server</u> for others to use. In Alteryx, there is a tool with an option to include a *.tds file when outputting a *.hyper data file to a connected Tableau server.

1. On the **Data** menu, select the particular data source connection ("Orders," for example).

2. Once you have selected a connection, choose "Add to Saved Data Sources."

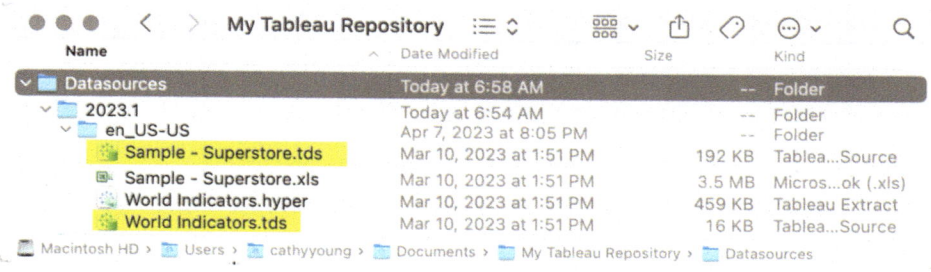

FIGURE 2.21
My Tableau Repository.

2.6 Replace a Data Source

When you select the "Replace Data Source" option in Tableau, Tableau's "Field Type Detection and Naming Improvements" algorithm reruns. The algorithm analyzes data types and column names again. It picks up new or removed fields and keeps *existing* custom fields, data types, renamed fields, groups, etc.

To avoid errors when you <u>replace a data source</u> file, *rename your flat file* to force Tableau's "Field Type Detection and Naming Improvements" algorithm to rerun. There is a great article on Tableau's website about how to replace an existing data source.

Let's say you add fields in an Excel file and do not change the Excel file name. When you next open the Tableau workbook, you might see a message stating, "An error occurred while communicating with the data source" and additional errors about an unbound field. To avoid errors during development, I add a date and time stamp to my flat data file names and use "Edit Connection" to change to the new file, as shown in Figure 2.22. Whenever possible, I use a data source (*.tds file) from a Tableau server to reduce these types of errors.

2.6.1 Change the Connection to a New File

In this example, my original file was *Data1.xlsx*. I have a new file named *Data2.xlsx* with the same fields and schema (field names and data types).

1. On the **Data Source** page, hover over the connection name in the top left corner of the screen until a drop-down arrow appears, as shown in Figure 2.22.
2. Click the drop-down arrow to open the *context menu* and choose "Edit Connection."
3. Finally, browse to select the new file *Data2.xlsx*.

2.6.2 Overview

Tableau copies some information, such as calculated fields, to the <u>new data source</u>. To save time, focus only

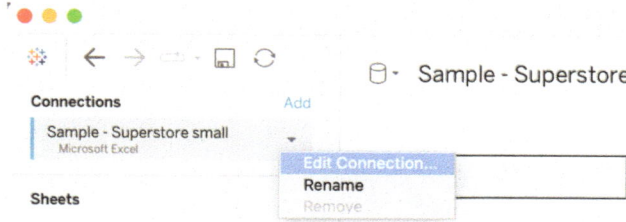

FIGURE 2.22
Edit connection.

on fields used in worksheets or parameters that apply to all worksheets. Make a note of these settings in case you have to update the objects in the new data source.

- Case-Sensitive Field Names
- Renamed Fields and Aggregation
- Field Data Types
- Field Roles
- Aliases
- Sets
- Parameters
- Combined Fields

2.6.3 What Is Not Copied?

It is worth noting that Tableau does not copy all information to the new data source. In my experience, even if it does copy sets, I have to recreate sets and update references manually. Combined fields may have the same issue depending on your version of Tableau. To check what is copied in your version of Tableau, go through the steps to replace the data source in a duplicate copy of the workbook and look at the **Data** pane fields and their *default properties*. In *"Section 4.3 Field Default Properties" on page 76*, we look at those settings. Certain items, such as the following, can be problematic. These items are **not** copied or may have issues:

- Custom fields that are <u>not used on any work sheet</u>. Tableau flags fields that are only used as parameter values or that are only used in other calculated fields as "not used."
- Field default properties (such as *Number Format* or *Color* settings)
- Assigned color and shapes or sort orders for **discrete** fields
- Combined fields
- Sets
- Data source filters

2.6.4 Field Names Are Case Sensitive

If you created a set from the "Region" field, and the field is capitalized in the new data source as "REGION," you'll have to recreate the set manually. Tableau field names are case-sensitive.

2.6.5 Renamed Fields and Aggregation

On the **Data Source** page, check if any fields in the original data source were renamed or if they use a different level of aggregation – for example, Sum(Sales) vs. Sales. You can identify renamed fields because the "Field Name" and "Remote Field Name" are different, as shown earlier in Figure 2.3.

2.6.6 Field Data Types

Sometimes, field types change with a new data source, causing problems. If a field is "red" after replacing a data source, check that field data types match the original. For example, "Order ID" is a string in the original data source and changes to a number in the new data source.

2.6.7 Check Fields in Parameter Lists Are Not Hidden

Edit parameters to check if data source fields are populating the list of parameter values. Unhide any fields used in parameters. Right-click the field in the **Data** pane and uncheck "Hide."

2.6.8 Unused Fields

Decide if you want to keep any *unused* fields you created, such as bins, groups, combined fields, totals, table calculations, and other calculated fields. These types of *unused* fields are not copied into the new data source when you choose "Update Data Source." Tableau identifies fields only used to populate

FIGURE 2.23

Tip: To make it easier to copy custom fields to the new data source, I copy them to a new folder in the **Data** pane, as outlined in the step-by-step instructions that follow. Do this step before you replace the original data source to avoid issues.

parameter list values or only used in other calculated fields as "not used."

The first step is gathering details to prepare to replace the fields. On a worksheet, click the drop-down arrow at the top of the **Data** pane on the right and check "Hide unused fields." When you next choose "Show Hidden Fields," the hidden fields are light gray, helping you focus on important fields. If you selected several fields to copy and any of the selected fields is "hidden (light gray)," the copy option is removed from the fields' *context menu*.

2.6.9 Roles: Measures, Dimensions, Discrete, and Continuous

In Tableau, a "Role" refers to whether a field is **continuous**, **discrete**, a measure, or a dimension. The "Describe" option, which we examined in *"Section 1.4.3 Describe" on page 32*, shows the field's details, such as a **continuous measure**. Make a note of whether fields are dimensions or measures. If the new data source field roles do not match, Tableau appends (1) to the new field name, and there is an invalid error.

2.6.10 Replace References

Once fields have the correct data types, roles, or new names, you can replace references to point to the new field name. I like this option because Tableau replaces all references on all worksheets at once. This step only applies when there is another field and you want to replace the original field. Right-click the original field in the **Data** pane and choose "Replace References" from the field's *context menu*. Tableau changes references in filters, calculated fields, sets, etc., to point to the new field. After the change, you may want to rename the new field if Tableau added the suffix (1).

2.6.10.1 *Unhide Worksheets*

To create a complete list of worksheets in the workbook, unhide worksheets used in dashboards or tooltips. On a dashboard, select the worksheet name in the **Dashboard** pane on the left. Worksheets in a dashboard have a blue check mark. You can also right-click the worksheet or dashboard tab along the bottom of the workspace and choose "Unhide All Sheets." To unhide worksheets used in a *Tooltip*, first select the worksheet with the tooltip in the bottom tabbed area. Only sheets with embedded tooltip sheets have the "Hide All Sheets" and "Unhide All Sheets" options.

2.6.10.2 Data Source Filters

<u>Data source filters</u> are not copied into a new **Data Source** and must be recreated manually.

2.7 Replace a Data Source, Step-by-Step Instructions

In this process, I create a new worksheet and a new data source. In Step 3, I add a field from the new data source to the new worksheet. The last step is to "Replace the Data Source." Tableau copies over custom objects when you replace a data source, but things often do not go as planned. For this reason, I copy my custom fields first to avoid some of the frustration and errors. You can skip the step to copy fields to a new folder, and if you encounter issues, go back and manually copy objects.

2.7.1 Sign In to a Tableau Server

If your new data source is on a Tableau server, follow these steps to log in. You will need your Tableau server and project name to log in to a Tableau server.

1. Open a browser and go to your Tableau server. The server name is the first part of the URL – like **Server1.TableauAtWork.net**. Do not include the site name at the end of the URL, for example, **/*/airw/MySite1/home**.

2. If you're not already logged into the Tableau server, open Tableau, and on the **Data Source** page, select "Tableau Server" at the top of the blue *Connect* pane on the left. Alternatively, on the **Server** menu, choose **Sign In**.

3. In the **Tableau Server Sign In** window, type the name of the server, as shown in Figure 2.24.

2.7.2 Connect to the New Data Source

1. Make a backup copy of the Tableau workbook before replacing the data source. If you also have a data file, as opposed to a live database or server connection, backup the data file as well.

2. Open Tableau, and at the top of the **Data Source** page, click the drop-down arrow next to the cylinder icon, as shown in Figure 2.25. Select "New Data Source" at the bottom of the pop-up window. Select a new connection for a data source like "Tableau Server" at the top of the blue **Connect** pane on the left. Alternatively, select a connection to an Excel file or some other type of data.

2.7.3 New Worksheet for New Data Source

Because "Replace Data Source" may be unavailable unless you have at least one worksheet that uses a field from the *new* data source shown in Figure 2.26, the first step is to create that worksheet.

1. Create a new worksheet with at least one field from the *new* data source. While on the worksheet page, select the new data source from the drop-down menu at the top of the **Data** pane.

2. Add any field from the *new* data source to the **Rows** shelf.

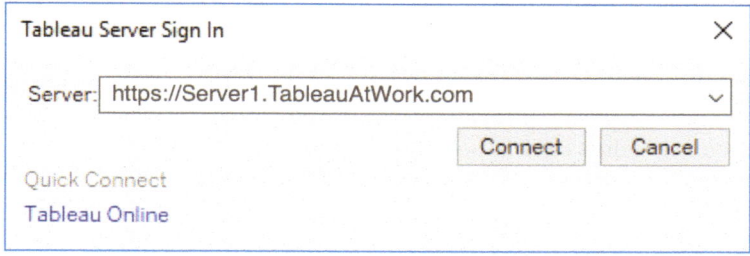

FIGURE 2.24
Tableau Server Sign In.

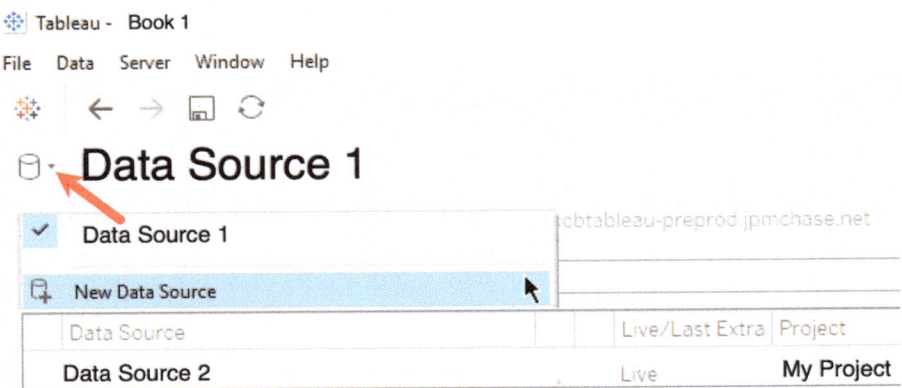

FIGURE 2.25
The drop-down arrow to open the Context menu.

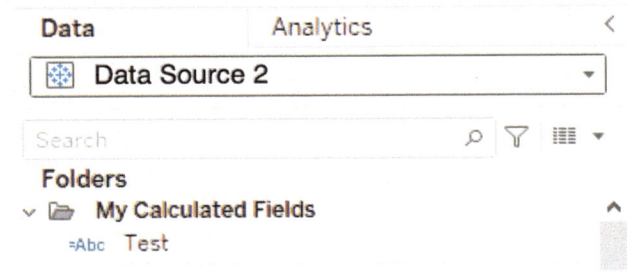

FIGURE 2.26
The new data source.

2.7.4 Create a Folder for Custom Fields

This step is optional, but I like to organize all my calculated fields, bins, and groups in a folder. In my experience, I've had to manually recreate *sets* and *combined fields* in the new data source so I don't copy those objects.

1. Create a new calculated field, "Test," in the *new* data source. At the top of the **Data** pane, click the drop-down arrow to open the *context menu* and choose "Create Calculated Field."

2. Select the "Test" field and click the drop-down arrow to open the field's *context menu*. Select "Group by Folder."

3. Repeat Step 2 to open the field's *context menu* and select "Folders -> Create Folder" with the name *My Calculated Fields*.

4. Repeat Step 3 and select "Folders -> Add to Folder" to select the new folder *My Calculated Field*s.

2.7.5 Copy Custom Fields

While Tableau copies custom fields (calculated fields, bins, and groups) that are used in the worksheets, some settings, like assigned colors and shapes or sort settings for **discrete** fields, are not copied to the new data source. I recreate *sets* and *combined fields* in the new data source rather than copying them over. To avoid these types of issues, I copy my custom fields into the new data source before I replace the data source.

1. After creating a folder, "My Calculated Fields," copy custom fields into the folder. Note that calculated fields begin with an equal sign. To see unused fields, select the drop-down arrow at the top of the **Data** pane and select "Show Unused Fields." Unused fields are grayed out. Before proceeding, right-click any field you want to keep to open the field's *context menu* and choose "Unhide."

2. At the top of the **Data** pane, select the *original* data source and select all objects in the *My Calculated Fields* folder. Right-click and choose "Copy." Because you can't copy hidden fields, make sure you don't accidentally select a hidden field (light gray).

3. Return to the new worksheet using the *new* data source, right-click anywhere in the white area of the **Data** pane, and choose "Paste." While the new fields are still selected, right-click to open the fields' *context menu* and move the fields into the "My Calculated Fields" folder in the new data source.

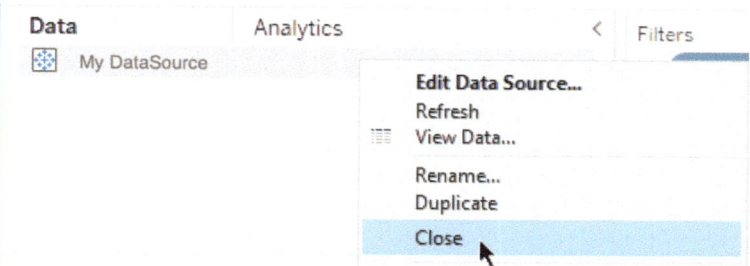

FIGURE 2.27
Close the original data source.

2.7.6 Custom Shapes and Colors and Sort Settings

Make a note of custom shapes and colors for **discrete** fields in the original data source so you can apply the changes in the new data source. Right-click a field in the **Data** pane to open the field's *context menu* and choose default properties. Note that when you update custom shapes and colors, you may have to remove the field from the *tile* on the **Marks** card and add it back to see the changes. Also, note fields used in views that have *sorting* applied.

2.7.7 Replace the Data Source

1. As a precaution, look for errors and warnings as outlined in the next section. Make sure there are no red fields, red exclamation marks, or other warnings before proceeding to step 2.

2. While still on the **new worksheet** with a field from the new data source, select "Replace Data Source" from the **Data** menu at the top of the workspace. When prompted, select the old and new data sources.

3. Before closing the original data source, check again that there are no errors or warnings and make corrections as needed. As a precaution, save the Tableau workbook before the next step.

4. Finally, in the **Data** menu, select the *old data source* and then select "Close," as shown in Figure 2.27. If you need to undo this action, click "Undo" (the back arrow in the toolbar).

2.7.8 Look for Trouble

Unhide all worksheets and dashboards and look for red fields or red exclamation marks in the view or **Data** pane. Along the bottom, right-click each worksheet or dashboard tab and select "Unhide all." Check worksheets because there may be a hidden

chart inside a worksheet tooltip. Also, look for new fields with the suffix (1).

- Compare the custom fields in the old data source to the new data source, looking for *missing or new* fields. When the field role is different, Tableau renames the new field with the suffix (1). See the next section to replace those field references.

- Check that the assigned *colors* and custom *shapes* and *sort* settings for **discrete** fields are correct.

- Check that *sets* are populated with the new data source's members (values).

- Check that *parameter* list values populated with field data are correct and use a field from the new data source.

- Check that the *sort settings* on worksheets are okay and that there are no warnings.

- Look for red fields in the **Data** pane or on the **Rows** or **Columns** shelf, the **Filters** shelf, the **Measure Values** shelf, or any *tiles* on the **Marks** card. If there are multiple mark types, check each layer on the **Marks** card. A red pill indicates that something changed so that the field no longer works properly. Replace the field with the "new" correct version, and the red pill disappears. After I verify a sheet, I change the sheet color to green.

2.7.8.1 Filter Selections

Since the underlying data may be different, I changed all the filter selections to "All" to avoid confusing my users.

2.7.9 Fixing Issues After Replacing a Data Source

Often, the simplest way to resolve an error is to drag the new field from the data source on top of the old red field. In cases like *sets* and *combined fields*, you may have to recreate the set and update all *references* to use the new object. Each Tableau release improves this process, so there may be differences from what I have outlined.

When replacing a data source, errors might include fields with a suffix (1) added to the name, red exclamation marks, warnings, or red pills. Fixing the warnings is easy enough by following the steps below, but it can be time-consuming.

- Are there warnings? Are fields missing? Can you replace a red field with a new calculated field?

- Are there warnings for calculated fields where a *field name* has a different case? Tableau field names are case-sensitive. Edit the calculated field and replace the existing field name with the new field name.

- Do *sets* have warnings? Right-click the original set and select "Edit, Set." Note the set configuration. Right-click the new source field in the **Data** pane for the new data source. Select "Create, Set" and recreate the original set configuration.

- Is the *aggregation* different for a field? Look for a red exclamation mark. If so, drag the new field on top of the old field. For example, a new field might already be aggregated as an average. Hence, you no longer need to aggregate the data with "AVG(field name)."

- Change the field's *role*. For example, open the field's *context menu* and choose "Convert to Measure" or "Convert to Discrete."

- Change the field *data type*. Open the field's *context menu* and choose "Change Data Type."

- Once the fields have the correct data types and roles, you can replace references to point to the new field, as outlined below.

2.7.9.1 Replace References

When there is a red exclamation mark next to a field, you may need to adjust the data type or role and then replace the old-field reference with a new field. Right-click the original field in the **Data** pane and choose "Replace References" from the *context menu*. Tableau changes references in filters, calculated fields, sets, etc., to point to the new field. After the change, you may want to delete the old field and rename the new field if Tableau added the suffix (1) to the new field name.

2.7.9.2 Update Parameter Lists

If the parameter list values look wrong, check the field that populates the parameter list is not hidden. Also, if you are using a Tableau server data source, make sure the data is refreshed.

2.7.9.3 Adjust Row-Level Security

If you are using a calculated field for *row-level security*, add the filter field to your **new worksheet**. If appropriate, apply the filter to "All using this data source."

2.7.9.4 Adjust Blend Relationships

If you are using two or more published data sources, check blend relationships on every worksheet are okay. On the **Data** menu, select "Blend Relationships" and choose fields from the new data sources. Also, add the "linking" field from the second data source to the *Detail* tile on the **Marks** card if the field is not already in the view.

2.8 Create an Extract

To create an <u>extract</u> file, move to any worksheet, right-click the connection at the top of the **Data** pane, like "Orders (Sample Superstore)," and select "Extract Data…" from the *context menu*. When you publish to Tableau Public, the first step is to create an extract *.<u>hyper</u> file.

1. You can also select "Extract" from the **Data** menu. Select the particular *data source connection* to see extract options. In Figure 2.28 I selected the "Orders (Sample - Superstore)" connection.

2. Once you select a connection, you can choose to "Extract Data." The **Extract Data** pop-up window opens with options for filtering and more, as shown in Figure 2.29. Filtering the extract data results in a smaller file.

2.8.1 Add an Extract Filter

Click the "Add" button in the middle of the pop-up **Extract Data** dialog window to see a list of fields, as shown in Figure 2.30.

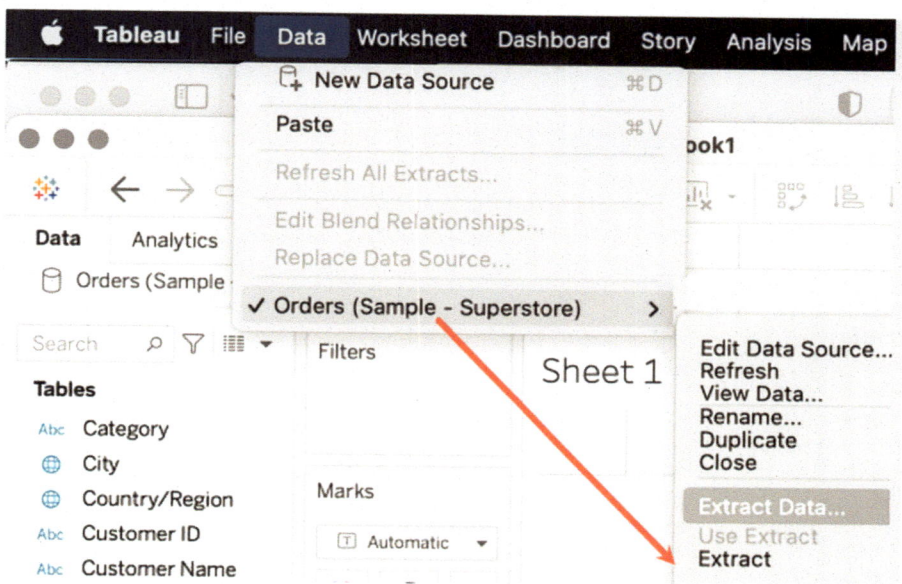

FIGURE 2.28
Select the Data Source and then Extract.

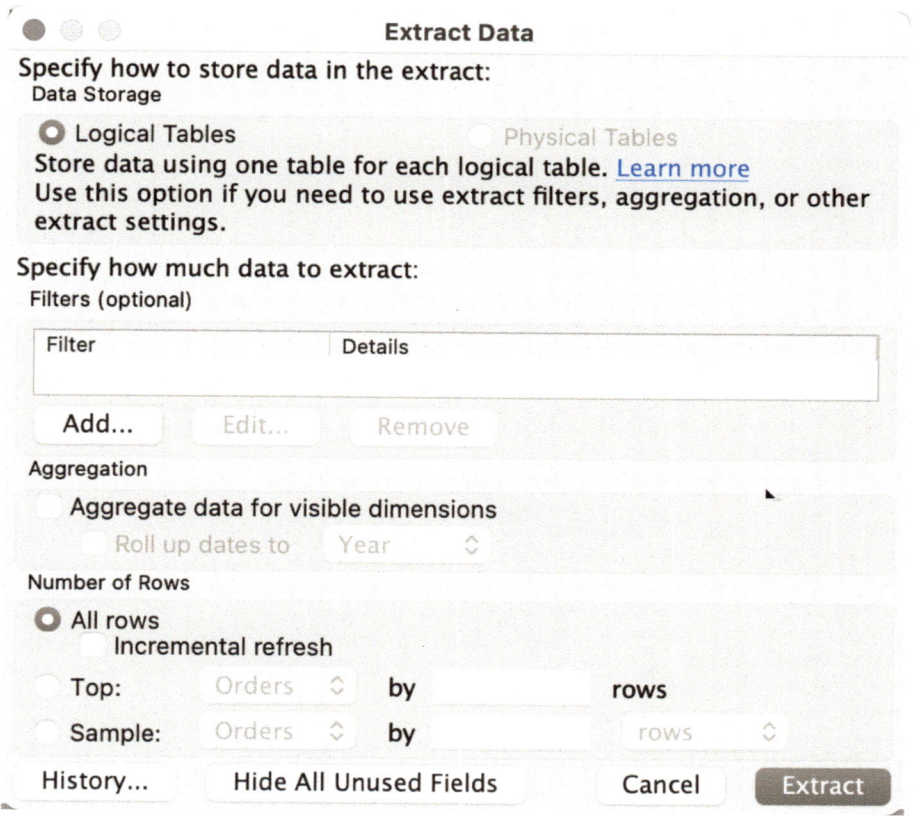

FIGURE 2.29
The Extract Data Dialog Window.

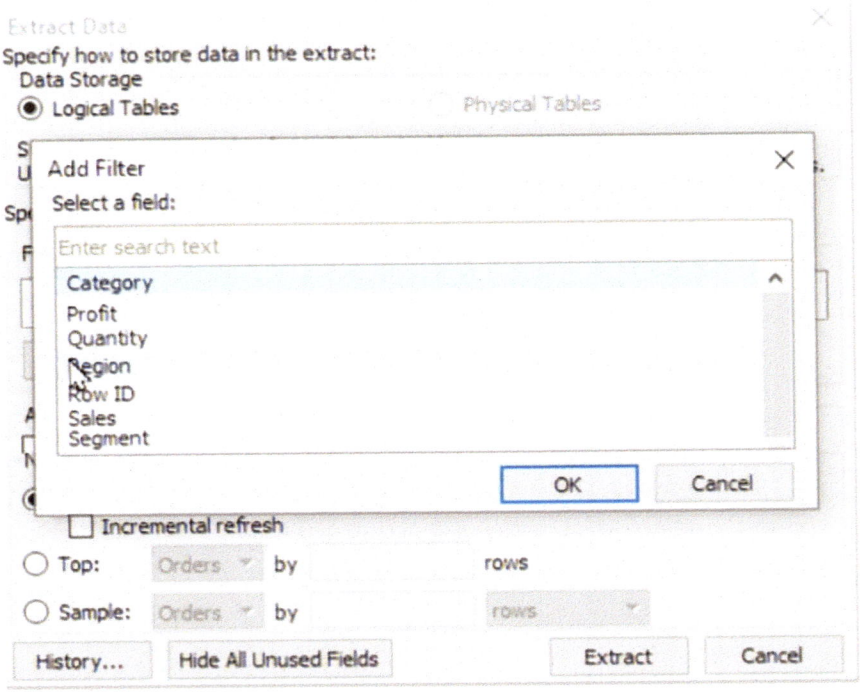

FIGURE 2.30
Add an Extract Filter.

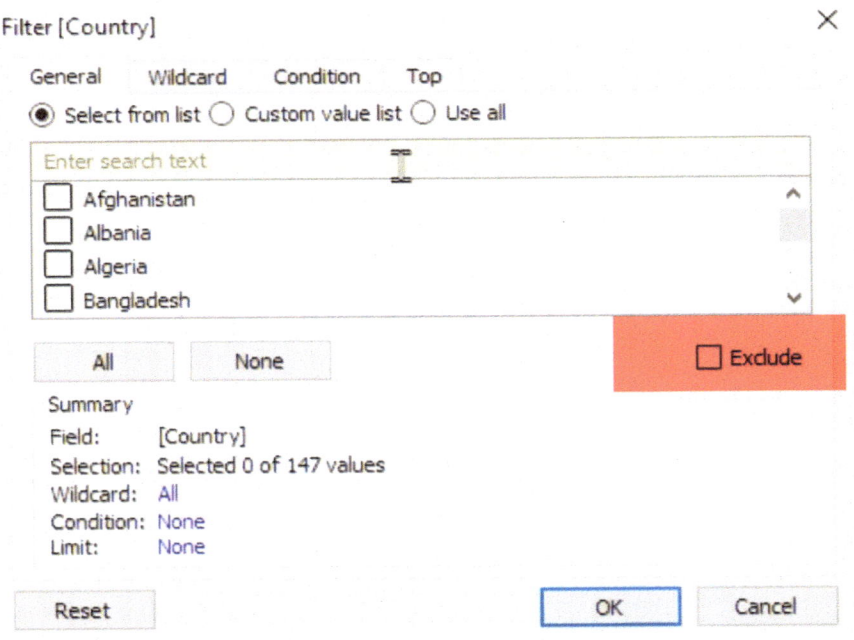

FIGURE 2.31
Filter Details.

After you select a field, the normal filter options are displayed. You can "Exclude" values, select some or all values, use wildcards in your filters or conditions, or set "Top N" filter details, as shown in Figure 2.31.

2.8.2 Aggregate Data

Under the filter section at the bottom of the **Extract Data** window, as shown in Figure 2.32, there are choices for aggregation, which may decrease the file size and improve performance.

Extract Data

Specify how to store data in the extract:

Data Storage

◉ Logical Tables   ○ Physical Tables

Store data using one table for each logical table. Learn more
Use this option if you need to use extract filters, aggregation, or

Specify how much data to extract:

Filters (optional)

Filter	Details
Country	keeps United States

[Add...] [Edit...] [Remove]

Aggregation

☑ Aggregate data for visible dimensions

☑ Roll up dates to [Year ▼]

| Year |
| Quarter |
| Month |
| Day |

Number of Rows

◉ All rows

FIGURE 2.32
Filter aggregation for dates.

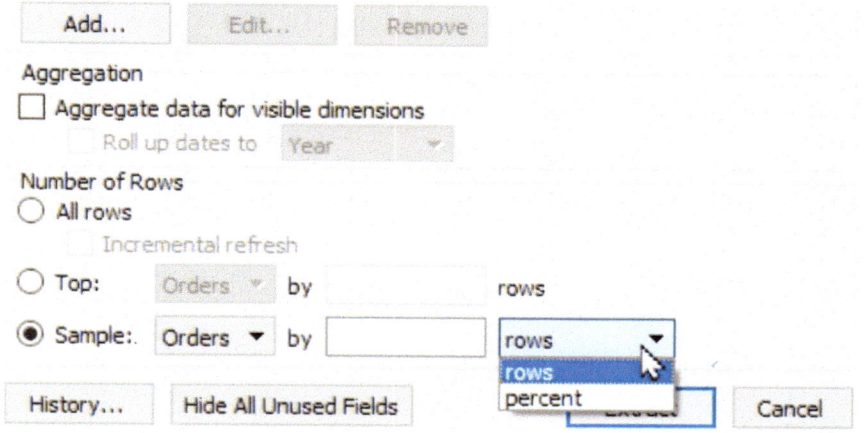

FIGURE 2.33
Number of rows for extract.

2.8.3 Number of Rows

In this dialog at the bottom of the **Extract Data** screen in Figure 2.33, you can choose how many records to include in the extract, with options for all, "top N" number of rows, or a sample size. Check "Incremental refresh" in the *Number of Rows* section to configure refresh options.

As mentioned earlier, there is a button at the bottom of the **Extract Data** dialog window to "Hide All Unused Fields."

3

Tableau Terminology

In this topic, we discuss

Dimension Fields

Measure Fields

Measure Names, Measure Values, Count Roles

Discrete vs. Continuous

Calculations, Groups, Sets, Bins, and Placeholders

Aggregation

To understand Tableau Desktop, you need to grasp Tableau's unique terminology. As you delve deeper into Tableau features, you might find yourself referring to the explanations in this chapter. Dates in Tableau are a topic that warrant a separate chapter and are covered in Chapter 9, as well as parameters, tooltips, actions, and hierarchies in Chapter 15.

3.1 Dimension Fields

Dimension fields are qualitative or categorical. They describe what, when, or who. For example, a *Regions* field might have Europe, Middle East & Africa (EMEA) and North America (NAM) values. Another example is a *Products* field, where the product members (or values) are laptops and desktops. Dimensions typically add row or column *headers* to a view and affect the level of detail in the view. We look at the level of detail in **Chapter 11**.

Tableau adds date fields to the "Dimensions" section of the **Data** pane. If you changed a date field to a "measure" and want it to be a dimension again, click the field to open its *context menu* to switch back to "dimension." To describe the *level of detail* for a sales view with [Country] and [State] fields, you might refer to the total sales in the state of Florida within the country of "USA," as compared to total sales for the state of New York within the country of "USA." In **Chapter 11**, we examine how the level of detail affects the aggregation.

3.1.1 Combined Dimension Fields

"Section 8.15 Sorting Segments Within a Stacked Bar" on page 187 illustrates the importance of a **dimension**

field when combining fields. To sort segments within a stacked bar, you create a new "Combined" field from two **dimension** fields. To check if a field is a dimension, right-click the field in the **Data** pane to open the field's *context menu* and select "Describe."

3.2 Measure Fields

Measure fields have numeric or quantitative values. For example, *Sales* field values are numbers reflecting amounts. The *sum of all sales* is an aggregation calculation that returns a numerical value. When you add a measure to a view, Tableau automatically aggregates the measure. By default, aggregation for measure fields in Tableau is a "Sum." Measures add an axis to a view. The color palette for a **continuous** measure field has diverging colors, while a **discrete** measure field uses categorical colors. I explain **continuous** and **discrete** after we look at "Roles."

In Figure 3.2, the [Sales] field on the **Columns** shelf is a *measure* aggregated with the sum function. The field name is shown as **SUM(Sales)**. In the **Data** pane, the [Sales] field has a green # pound sign to the left of the field name, indicating this measure is a number. The [Sales] field is below the line in the **Data** pane, indicating it is a *measure*. Mathematical calculations use *measure* fields. A **continuous** measure field adds a field with a **green** background or pill to the view, as shown in Figure 3.2.

In Figure 3.3, a # pound sign above the [Qty] and [Sales] field names indicates that the fields are of the number data type. When [Qty] is in the top area of the **Data** pane, it is a *dimension*. When [Sales] is below the line, it is a *measure*.

In the **Data** pane, you can drag a measure field to the *dimension* area to change the field to a dimension,

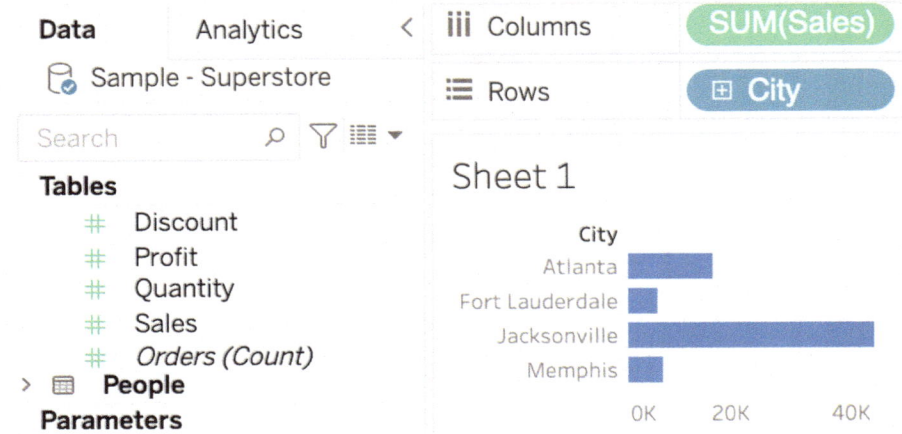

FIGURE 3.2
The measure field sales on the Columns shelf.

Abc Sheet1 **Fruit**	# Sheet1 **Qty**	📅 Sheet1 **Order Date**	# Sheet1 **Sales**
Cherry	1	8/30/2020	1.3500
Mango	2	9/4/2020	2.6000
Nectarine	4	10/8/2020	7.3200
Fig	11	11/16/2020	12.3200
Lime	9	12/4/2020	15.5700

FIGURE 3.3
Data Source Fields.

or vice versa, to change a dimension to a measure, as shown in Figure 3.4.

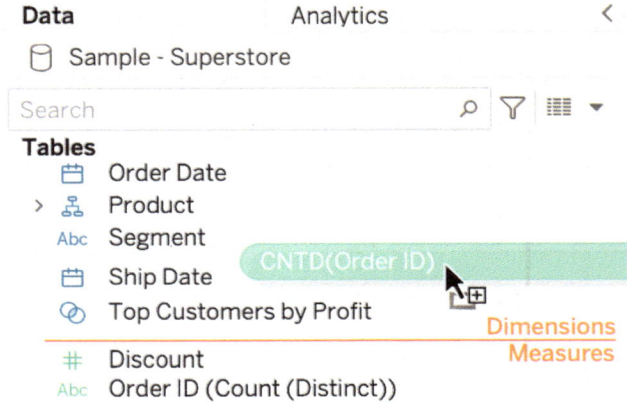

FIGURE 3.4
Drag a field to change to a dimension.

3.3 Measure Names, Measure Values, and Count

Measure Names and *Measure Values* fields are Tableau-generated fields containing all the measure names in your data source and the measure values. A **Measured Values** shelf is added below the **Marks** card when you use these special fields, as shown in Figure 3.6. Initially, fields on the **Measured Values** shelf use a field's default aggregation. Many examples use these special fields, such as:

- *"Section 8.14 Hover to Choose a Field for Sorting" on page 181* demonstrates adding or removing fields from the view using the **Measured Values** shelf.

- *"Section 13.6.3 Separate Color Legends" on page 298* formats [Measure Values] color legends.

Tableau automatically creates [Latitude] and [Longitude] fields when it recognizes geographic data. In Figure 3.5, Tableau created *Latitude* and *Longitude* fields because this data has a *State/Province* field. Tableau also automatically generates a field to count records in the data source table. When you hover over a generated field name in the **Data** pane, a tooltip describing the generated field appears, as shown in Figure 3.5.

3.3.1 Measure Values Shelf

To add multiple columns to the view, add [Measure Names] to the **Rows** shelf or the **Columns** shelf and [Measure Values] to the *Text* tile on the **Marks** card, as shown in Figure 3.6. Tableau adds a **Measure Values** shelf to the view with all available measure fields. To remove a field, drag it off the **Measure Values** shelf, thus adding [Measure Names] to the **Filter** shelf, reflecting the filtered field(s).

To change the order of columns, rearrange the fields on the **Measure Values** shelf, as shown in Figure 3.6.

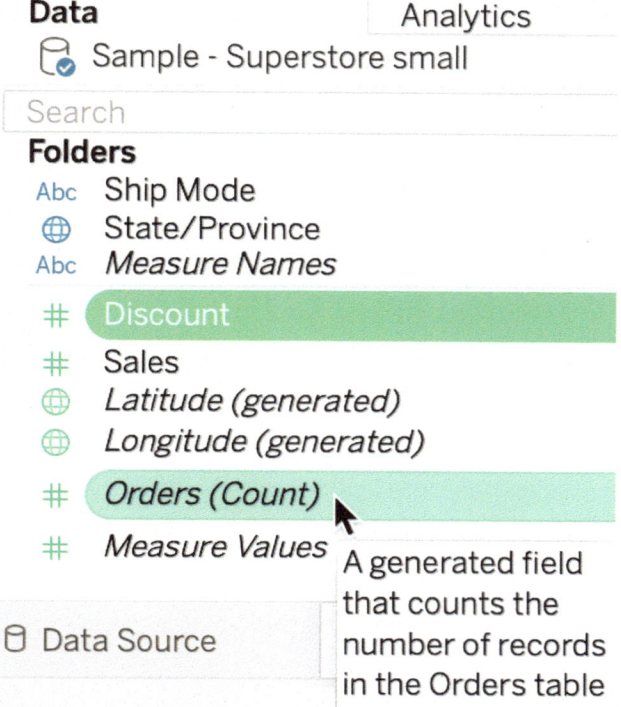

FIGURE 3.5
The count field.

Click and drag a field on the **Measured Values** shelf until an arrow line indicates the new location and then drop the field. A small sort icon appears on the right side of the [Measure Names] field because the fields are manually sorted.

When you add the [Measure Values] field to the *Color* tile on the **Marks** card, you can choose to use separate color legends for each field. For an example, check out *"Section 13.6 Legends and Controls"* on *page 298*.

3.3.2 Count

Each table has a Tableau generated field representing the total number of records or rows of data in a table. Look for a *table name* (Count) field in the **Data** pane. For instance, a table named "Returns" would contain a field called **Returns(Count)**. The bottom left corner of the screen also displays a count of the number of rows of data used in the view. In Figure 3.5, the [Orders(Count)] field at the bottom of the **Data** pane reflects how many orders are in the table. *"Section 14.23 KPIs and BANs (Big Numbers)"* on page *347* uses this count field for a Key Progress Indicator (KPI).

3.4 Roles

Tableau assigns a data type and **role** to every field. While I could easily grasp the idea of a measure (number) vs. a dimension (a category like types of

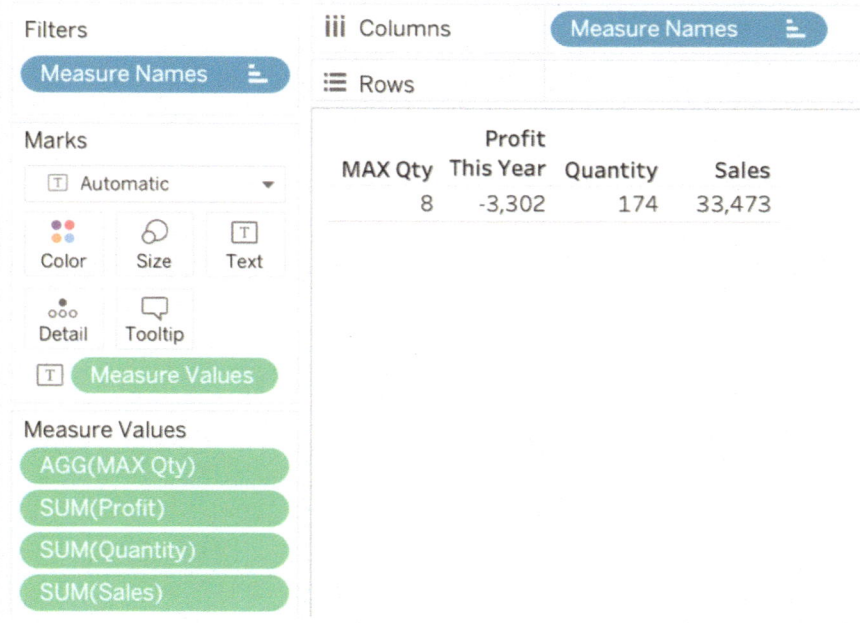

FIGURE 3.6
The Measure Values shelf.

furniture), I did not understand why it mattered if the data was **discrete** or **continuous**. Tableau uses the **discrete** vs. **continuous** setting to describe *what happens when you add a field to the view*. If the field adds headers, it is **discrete**. It is **continuous** if it creates an axis for a range of values. A **role** is a combination of:

- A **discrete** or **continuous** setting
- A measure or dimension

Let me expand on that idea a bit. Four possible combinations exist, although the first two are the most common.

- **Discrete** Dimension
- **Continuous** Measure
- **Continuous** Dimension
- **Discrete** Measure

If unsure what role a field has, right-click the field name in the **Data** pane and choose "Describe." In Figure 3.7, the field [Price(bin)] is a **continuous** dimension.

3.4.1 Geographic Role

Tableau automatically geocodes data it recognizes and assigns a geographic role. It also generates [Latitude] and [Longitude] fields, as shown in Figure 3.5. Right-click a field in the **Data** pane and select "Geographic Role" to add or change the role, as shown in Figure 3.8. If you drag [Latitude] to the **Rows** shelf

Describe Field	
Price (bin)	
Role:	Continuous Dimension
Type:	Numeric bin
Bin size:	0.400000
Remote column:	[Sales With Price].[Price]
Remote type:	Double-precision floating-point number
Status:	Valid
The domain for this field has not been loaded. Click "Load" to retrieve.	

FIGURE 3.7
Describe field.

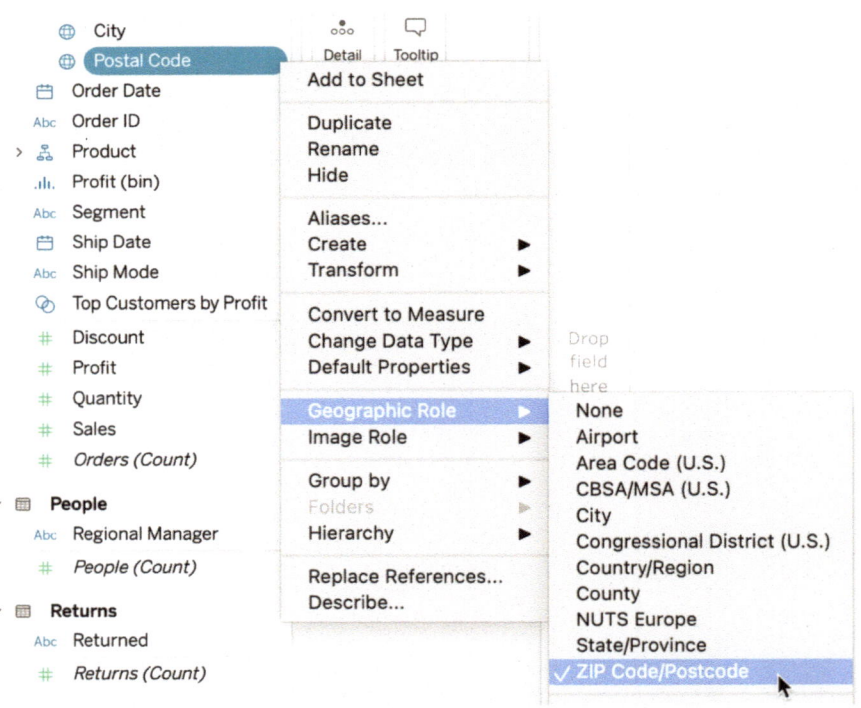

FIGURE 3.8
Geographic role.

and [Longitude] to the **Columns** shelf, Tableau creates a map visualization.

3.5 Discrete vs. Continuous

The color of a field name in a view has a **blue** or **green** background, depending on whether the field has a **discrete** or **continuous** setting. **Discrete** fields on a view create *headers*, while **continuous** fields create an *axis*.

Figure 3.9 has **discrete** dates with *headers* along the bottom of the visualization. The [MONTH(Order Date)] field has a blue background to indicate the **discrete** setting. The [SUM(Sales)] field is a **continuous** range of values along the *y-axis* (the vertical axis on the left). The shape of the colored field is often called a "pill."

In Figure 3.10, I changed the date field [MONTH(Order Date)] to a **continuous** range. Tableau automatically changes the mark type to a "line" and changes the background color for the [MONTH(Order Date)] field to green. Instead of headers along the bottom, there is a range of values along the bottom. A **continuous** field on the **Columns** shelf creates a **horizontal** or x-axis. I also added tick marks for each month to illustrate this is a range of values.

3.5.1 Blue vs. Green

When you move your mouse over the **Data** pane, a blue or green background highlights the field name. Depending on the role, the icon to the left of a field is also blue or green. You can add fields in many places on your view, such as the **Columns** shelf, **Rows** shelf,

Marks card, **Filters** shelf, or **Pages** shelf. In the previous example, the **continuous** field [Sales] had a green background, and the **discrete** field [City] had a blue background.

3.5.2 Discrete

Discrete values are single values that are individually distinct and separate. For example, a field with a **discrete** date part, "MONTH," is displayed with a **blue** background (sometimes called a blue pill) creating *headers* in the view.

- A **discrete** field on the **Columns** shelf creates horizontal *headers* from left to right.
- A **discrete** field on the **Rows** shelf creates vertical *headers* on the left.

In Figure 3.11, when I click the month "Apr" in the x-axis at the bottom of the view, the field's *context menu* has the options "Rotate Label" and "Show Header" because "Order Date" is **discrete**. If the field were **continuous**, the field's *context menu* would have options for an axis.

A field with a data type of string or Boolean is always **discrete**. Because Tableau assigns a **blue** background to a **discrete** field, a dimension with a string value is always **blue**.

Dates can be **discrete** or **continuous**. A **continuous** dimension date adds a field with a **green** background to the view.

The Figure 3.12 has two **continuous** fields: the [Sales] field is on the **Rows** shelf, and [Qty] is on the **Columns** shelf. The fields are **green** to indicate they are **continuous**. Earlier, I said **continuous** fields create axes. In Figure 3.12, the vertical y-axis reflects [Sales] amounts from $0.00 to $15.00, and the horizontal x-axis reflects [Qty] from 0 to 10.

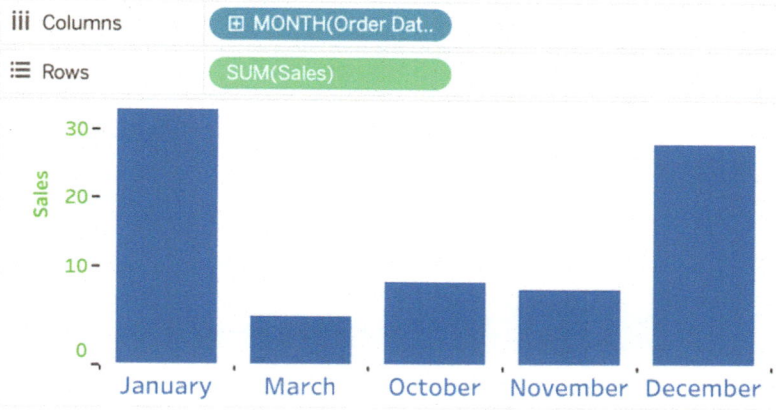

FIGURE 3.9
Discrete month headers.

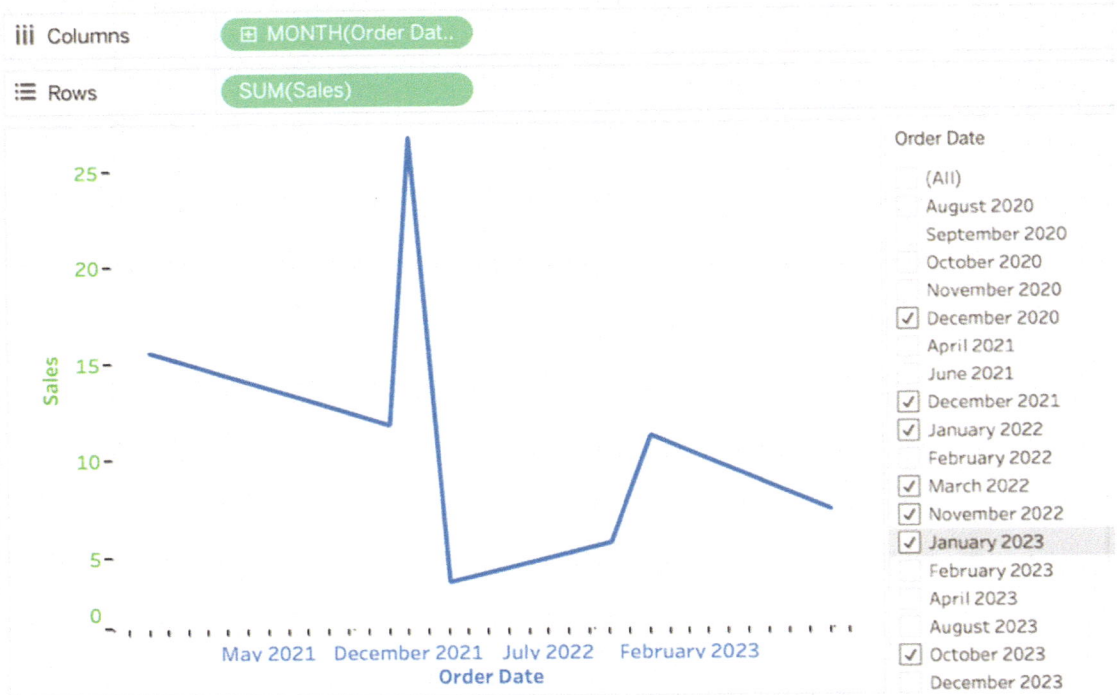

FIGURE 3.10
A continuous date axis.

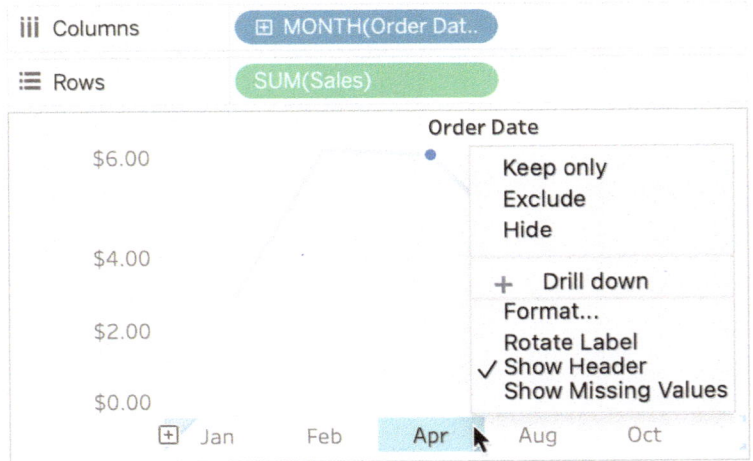

FIGURE 3.11
The discrete context menu.

3.5.2.1 Change Qty to Discrete

Suppose I want to change [Qty] in Figure 3.13 to a **discrete** field. In the **Columns** shelf, I click the drop-down arrow on the [Qty] field to open the field's *context menu*. I select **Discrete** to change the **continuous** setting to **discrete** values.

After you change [Qty] to **discrete**, the field on the **Columns** shelf changes color to blue. The x-axis now shows the numbers 1 to 11 as headers, as shown in Figure 3.14.

For this analysis, I want to know the quantity on hand, so I add [Fruit] to the *Color* tile or "property"

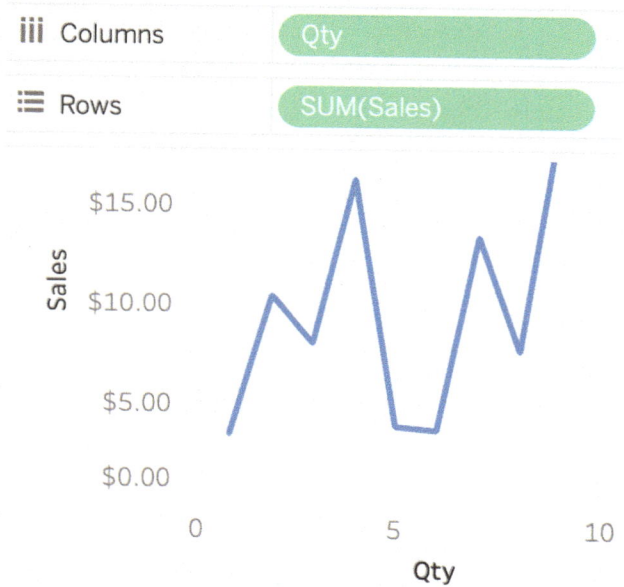

FIGURE 3.12
A y-Axis and an x-Axis chart.

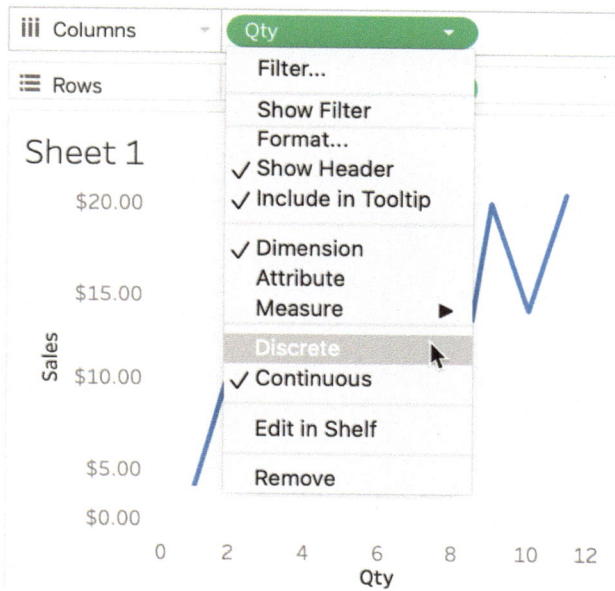

FIGURE 3.13
Discrete and Continuous in the Context Menu.

on the **Marks** card, as shown in Figure 3.15. Because nectarine sales are high and I am running low on quantity, I decided to reorder nectarines.

3.5.2.2 Categorical Color Palette

The color palette for a **discrete** field uses categorical colors.

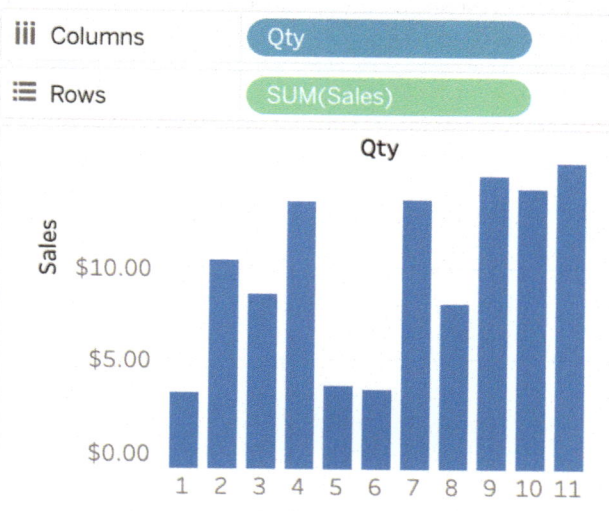

FIGURE 3.14
Qty headers.

3.5.2.3 Sorting Discrete Data

Let's go back to the first **discrete** example. If I click the [MONTH(Order Date)] field on the **Columns** shelf, the field's *context menu* has an option to "Sort" the values, as shown in Figure 3.16. Also, both sort tools are active in the toolbar at the top of the workspace. **Continuous** fields cannot be sorted, as shown in Figure 3.22.

3.5.3 Continuous

As we just saw, a **continuous** field creates an axis on the view, and the field name has a **green** background. For example, a **continuous** date field adds a timeline of date values from the beginning to the end of the month.

In the previous example, the **continuous** [Sales] field on the **Rows** shelf created a vertical y-axis. A **continuous** field on the **Columns** shelf creates a horizontal x-axis. In Figure 3.18, I use the "swap" tool in the toolbar so that [Sales] is on the **Columns** shelf, creating a **continuous** x-axis of $0.00 to $20.00.

Figure 3.19 shows a view with a **discrete** date field on the left and a **continuous** date field on the right.

[Order Date] is **continuous** in Figure 3.20. When I right-click the x-axis at the bottom of the view, there is an option, "Edit Axis," where you can configure the range, scale, title, or tick marks.

3.5.3.1 x- and y-Axis

Continuous fields on the view represent a range of values on an *x-axis* or a *y-axis*. Tableau creates axes for **continuous** fields on the **Rows** shelf or the **Columns**

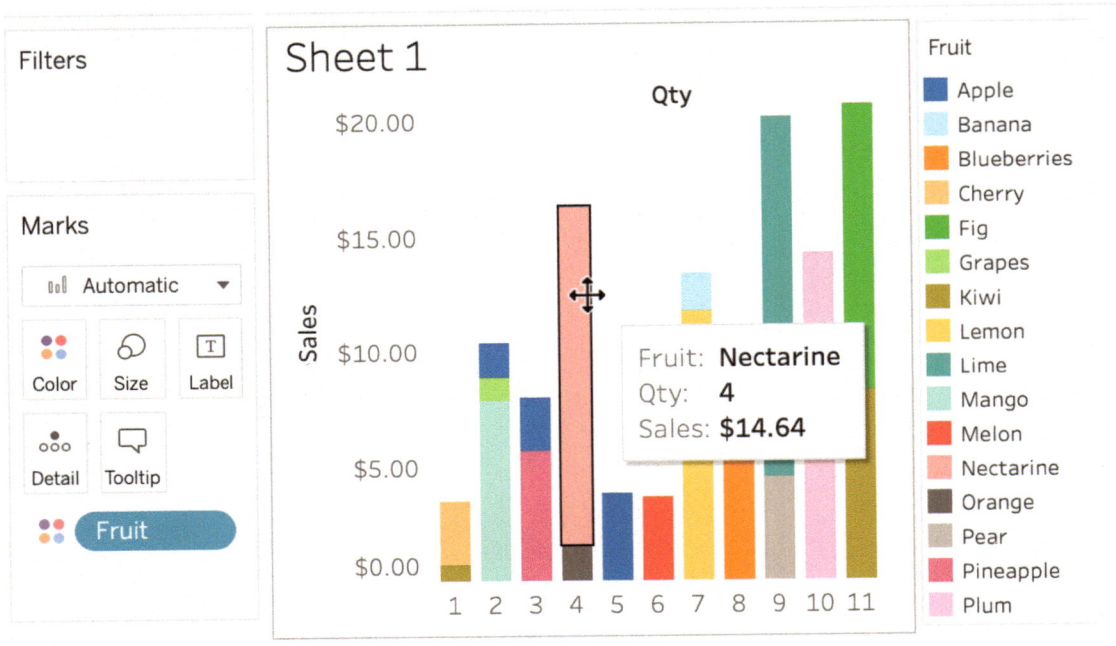

FIGURE 3.15
Sales vs. quantity.

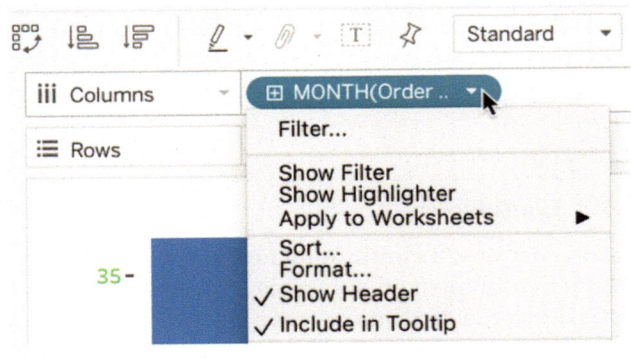

FIGURE 3.16
Sort in the context menu.

FIGURE 3.17

Tip: *Sorting is unavailable for continuous values, as you'll see in the next topic.*

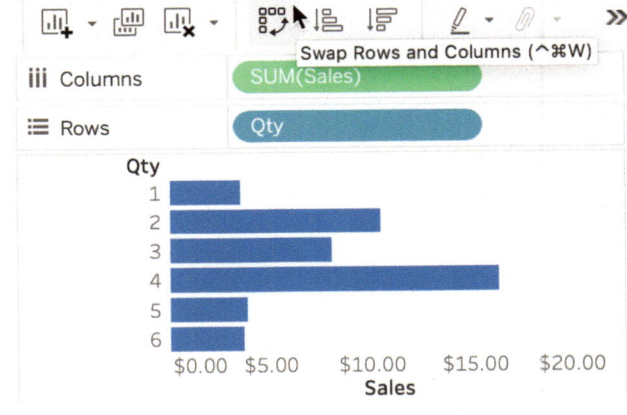

FIGURE 3.18
Swap.

- A **continuous** field on the **Rows** shelf creates a *y-axis*.
- A **continuous** field on the **Columns** shelf creates an *x-axis*.

The **visualization** on the left has the **continuous** field [Sum(Sales)] on the **Rows** shelf. A vertical y-axis for [Sales] on the **Columns** shelf is shown on the left side of the visualization.

shelf. The chart on the right in Figure 3.21 has a **continuous** [Sales] field on the **Columns** shelf. A horizontal **x-axis** ranging from 0 to 2000K is displayed. The **discrete** field [Country/Region] on the **Rows** shelf creates *headers* on the left side.

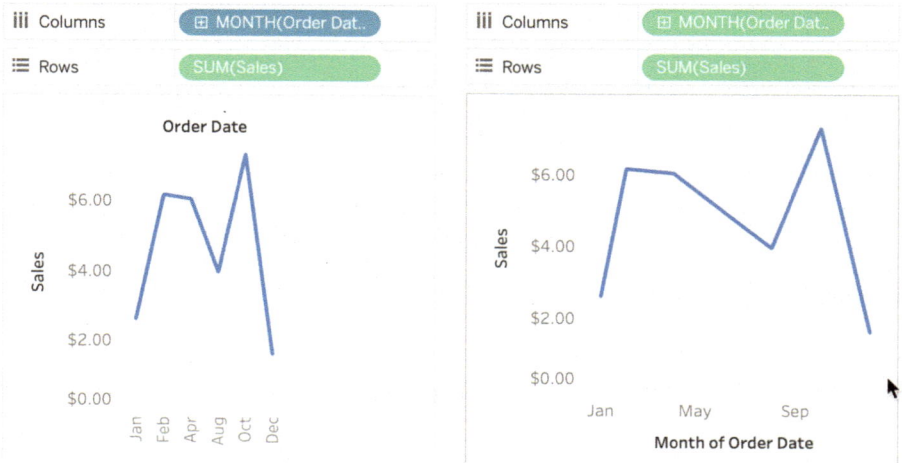

FIGURE 3.19
Discrete vs. continuous.

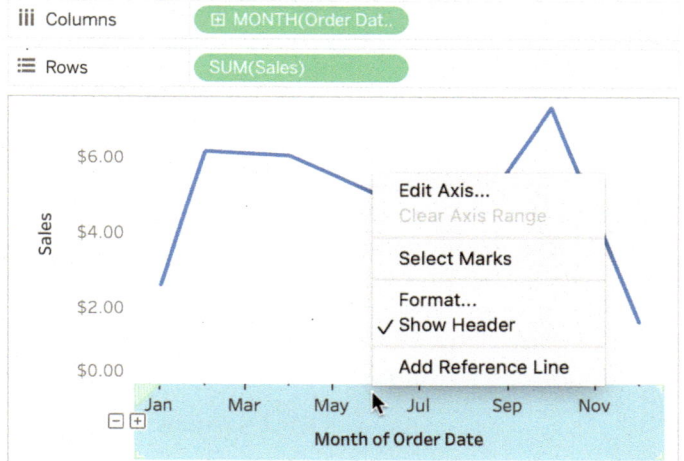

FIGURE 3.20
Date axis.

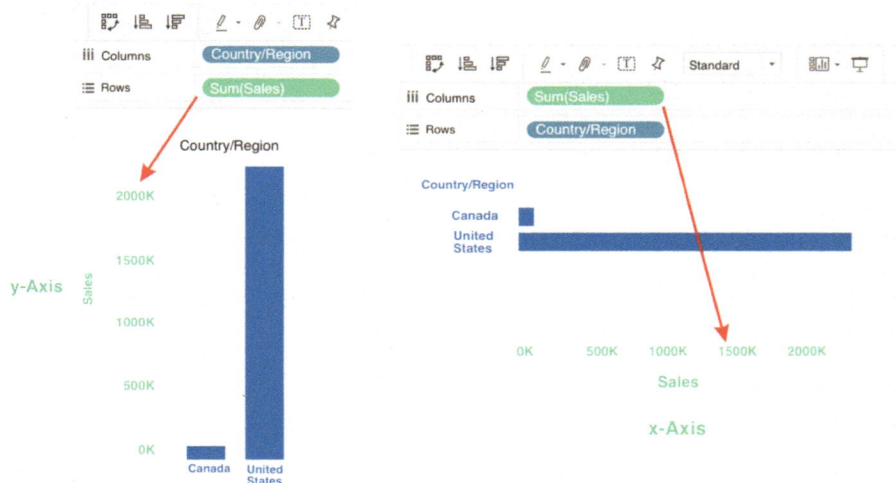

FIGURE 3.21
y-Axis and x-Axis.

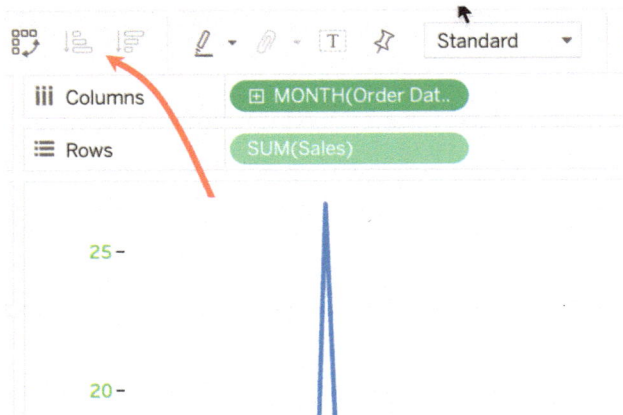

FIGURE 3.22
Grayed out Sort tools.

3.5.3.2 Continuous Color Palette

A **continuous** field uses a diverging color palette or "Stepped Colors" to group values into bins.

3.5.3.3 Unable to Sort Continuous Data

Let's go back to the first **continuous** example. Suppose I click the [Order Date] field on the **Columns** shelf after changing the field from **discrete** to **continuous**. In that case, the field's *context menu* no longer has an option to "Sort" the values. The sort tools at the top of the workspace are also grayed out, as shown in Figure 3.22 because the sort menu is not available for **continuous** fields.

3.6 Calculations, Groups, Sets, Bins, and Placeholders

In addition to the fields from your data source, you can create new fields such as combined fields, groups, sets, bins, hierarchies, table calculations, placeholder calculations, and other calculated fields.

Custom fields and totals add granularity and flexibility to your visualizations. "Totals" add row subtotals, column subtotals, and grand totals to a visualization, as discussed in *"Section 11.15 Totals" on page 253*. With these fields, you can add color, filter data, aggregate data, and interact with a visualization. In later chapters, we examine these elements in more detail.

- Totals
- Placeholder Fields
- Table Calculations
- Combined Fields

- Calculated Fields
- Groups
- Bins
- Sets
- Hierarchies

Discrete <u>bins</u> are created from measures, but you can convert the bin into a **continuous** field for a histogram chart, as shown in *"Section 7.2.2.2 Histogram Charts" on page 119*.

3.6.1 Table Calculations

Table calculations are an easy way to show rank or running totals and include these calculations.

- Difference From
- Percent Difference From
- Percent From
- Percent of Total
- Rank
- Percentile
- Running Total
- Moving Calculation

Table calculations are applied to a measure field, with a delta triangle to the right of the field name (Figure 3.23).

We examine table calculations in **Chapter 10**.

3.6.2 Groups

In the **Data** pane, a paperclip indicates a **Group**. Groups are a subset of *dimension* members. When your data is too granular, you can create a broader group or subset of data. I like that I can reuse a group in multiple views. *"Section 8.5.6 Filtering with Sets and Groups" on page 167* illustrates using a group to filter.

3.6.2.1 Create Groups

There are several ways to create groups.

1. Create a *visual grouping* by selecting *marks* on the canvas. Hold down the *Control* key and click with your mouse to select marks. Marks are dots, lines, bars, etc., on the canvas. In MacOS, use the *Command* key. Right-click selected marks to open the *context menu* with

FIGURE 3.23
A table calculation with the delta triangle.

additional choices, or hover the mouse over marks until a tooltip opens.

Select **Group** from the *context menu* or click the tooltip's group icon (a paperclip). After you create a group, Tableau adds the new group field to the **Data** pane. If this is the first group for that dimension field, Tableau adds the new group to *Color* on the **Marks** card.

2. After selecting headers in the view, hover your mouse over the headers and click the group icon in the tooltip. In Figures 3.24, I selected "Blueberries" and "Lemon" to create a new [Fruit (group)]. The new group [Fruit (group)] replaces the original field on the **Rows** shelf, and the group field is added to the **Data** pane, as shown below.

3. Another way to create a group is to click the field's drop-down arrow on the **Data Source** page to open the field's *context menu*.

4. Finally, in the **Data** pane, select a field, right-click to choose "Create" from the field's *context menu*, and then click "Group." The **Edit Group** dialog window opens, as shown below (Figures 3.25).

3.6.3 Sets

Sets are custom fields that aggregate data to add granularity and flexibility to your visualizations. Sets are a subset of data aggregated into In/Out categories. You cannot create sets on *measures*; you can only

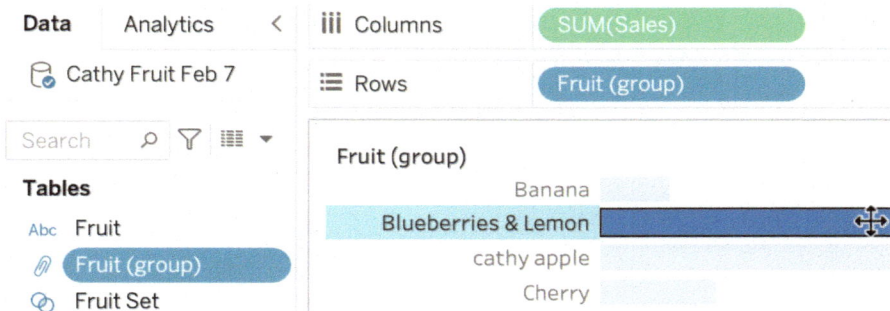

FIGURE 3.24
The New Fruit Group.

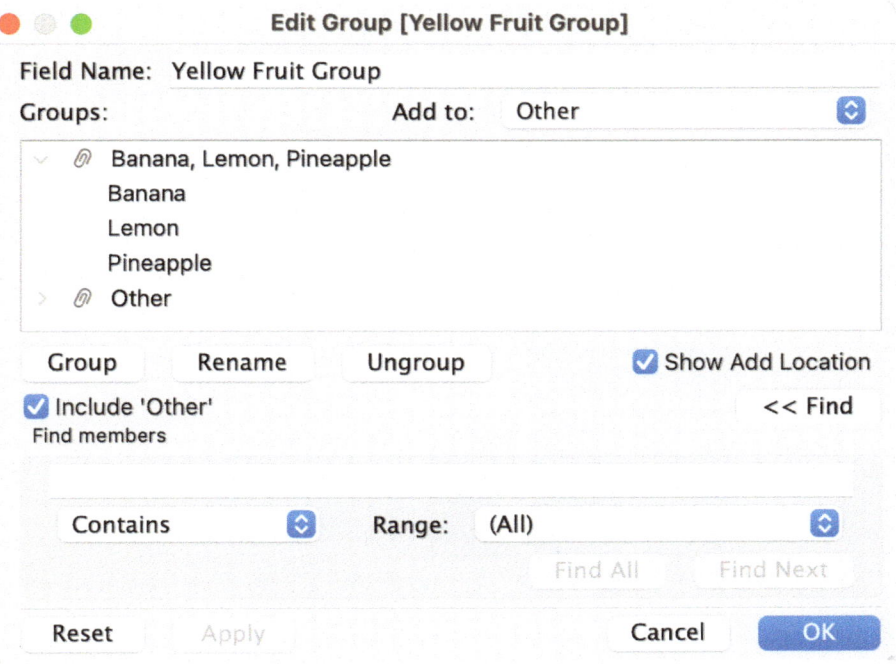

FIGURE 3.25
Edit the new group.

create sets on *dimensions*. A set has a Venn diagram icon in the **Data** pane to the left of the field name. Unlike groups, sets can have *fixed* or *dynamic* members. For the field [Produce], a set of "Red Produce" might contain only "red bell peppers" and "red apples." If you manually select the values "red bell peppers" and "red apples" to include in the set, those are *fixed* or static members. Using a conditional statement or calculation to select produce with "red" in the name is a dynamic set. A dynamic set changes as the data changes. You can combine sets by selecting one or more sets and ensuring both sets use the same dimension or field.

- The example *"Section 14.23 KPIs and BANs (Big Numbers)" on page 347* uses a set.
- The example *"Section 8.13 Click Data Points to Sort with a Set" on page 175* uses an In/Out set.

You can also use sets in filters, and when you display the **Set Control**, users can interactively choose set members or use the *In/Out* values. The default values in the **Set Control** are "In" and "Out." In the **Set Control**, click the value "In" and choose "alias" to change the value.

Right-click the set name on the **Filters** shelf to switch between "Show Members in Set" and "Show In/Out of Set." When filtering with sets, the filter condition is "True" or "False," meaning the marks are in the set or not in the set. I like sets for filters because Tableau's Order of Operations applies a set filter before measure,

dimension, or table calculation filters. *"Section 8.1 Filter Logic and the Order of Operations" on page 158* has more information on the Order of Operations. An expression should test for <u>Boolean</u> values (true or false) when you use sets in calculated fields. Finally, sets also support "Set Actions," which we see in action a bit later in *"Section 15.1.8 Drill Down with a Set Action" on page 359* that uses a set with a hierarchy.

3.6.3.1 *Create a Static Set*

Tableau Public file

> https://public.tableau.com/views/ CreateaSet001/Dashboard1?:language=en- US&:sid=&:redirect=auth&:display_ count=n&:origin=viz_share_link

> YouTube Video: https://youtu.be/IPkMehvRktE? si=cjh63D9gq1Hvql-3

1. Once you have added fields to the view, you can select data points or "marks" to create sets. Marks are dots, lines, bars, etc., on a chart. Hold down the Control key and click with your mouse to select marks. In MacOS, use the Command key. You can also select "headers" to select entire rows or columns for the set. In this example, three marks are selected (Figures 3.27).

2. After selecting marks, hover your mouse over the selected marks for a few seconds to open

FIGURE 3.26

Tip: *To create a static set quickly, right-click a dimension field in the* **Data** *pane and select "Create: Set." You can also select marks on a view, right-click, and choose "Create Set."*

FIGURE 3.28

Tip: *When you select marks, you can create sets, groups, or a filter to exclude or include selected marks.*

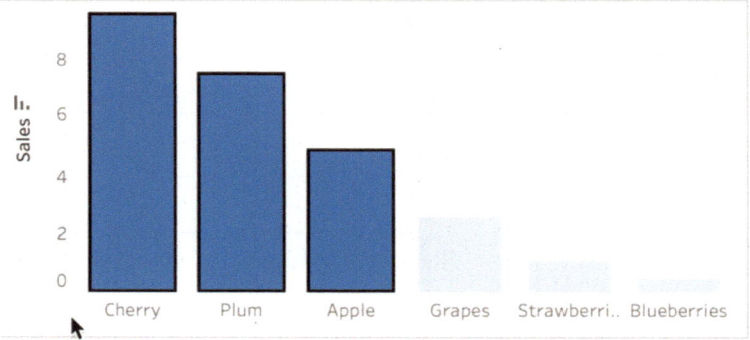

FIGURE 3.27

Three marks are selected in the view.

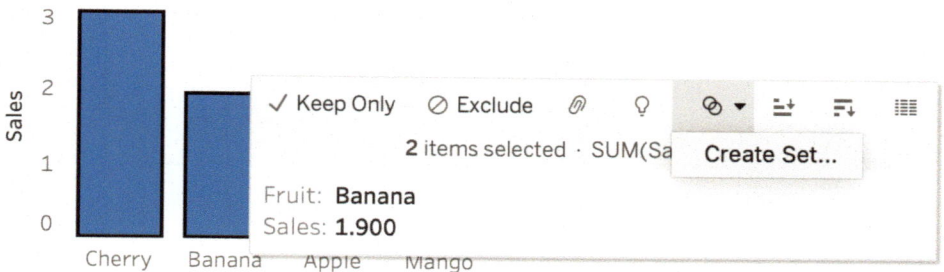

FIGURE 3.29
The Drop-Down Menu to Create a Set.

FIGURE 3.30
The Create Set Dialog.

the tooltip. Click the *Venn diagram icon* in the tooltip window to create a set (Figures 3.29).

3. The dialog window opens. Because you are creating a static set from *selected* marks, the only options are "Exclude" the members or "Add to Filters shelf." (Figures 3.30)

3.6.3.2 Conditional Sets

With a conditional or dynamic set, you use a condition, custom formula, or calculation to select members. Options include:

- Top 10
- Min
- Max
- >=
- <=

Conditional sets are ideal to answer questions. Let's say I want a set that shows the top three fruits by sales. In this example, I use a dynamic set that changes as the data changes. The set creates two panes in this

"small multiples" view. The panes represent members "in" or "out" of the set.

1. I create a set and use the "Top" option with the [Sales] field, as shown below (Figure 3.31).
2. Next, I added the [Sales] field and the [Fruit – Top 3 Sales] set to the **Rows** shelf. Tableau creates a small multiples chart, reflecting the members "In" the set (the top three Sales) at the top of the canvas and others not in the set below.
3. Right-click the word "In" on the axis and choose "Edit Alias." The pop-up menu shows the axis' *context menu* and the axis on the left below the menu has a blue highlight. I type the new alias, "Top 3." I repeated this step to add an "Out" alias with an empty string "" (Figure 3.32).
4. After I changed both set *aliases*, the finished chart clearly shows the top three sales because I added "Fruit" to the *Color* tile on the **Marks** card (Figure 3.33).
5. Another way to change aliases is to click the "In" word in the **Color Legend** in the bottom left corner of this example and choose "Edit Alias" (Figure 3.34).

3.6.3.3 Combined Sets

Select two sets in the **Data** pane on the left and right-click to open the *context menu*. Choose "Create Combined Set," as shown in Figure 3.35.

3.6.3.4 Filter with Sets

When you use a set as a filter, you have two options: *Show Members in Set* or *Show In/Out of Set*, as shown in Figure 3.36. After adding a field to the **Filters** shelf, right-click the drop-down arrow to see options or to edit the set. *"Section 14.23 KPIs and BANs (Big Numbers)" on page 347* demonstrates these options.

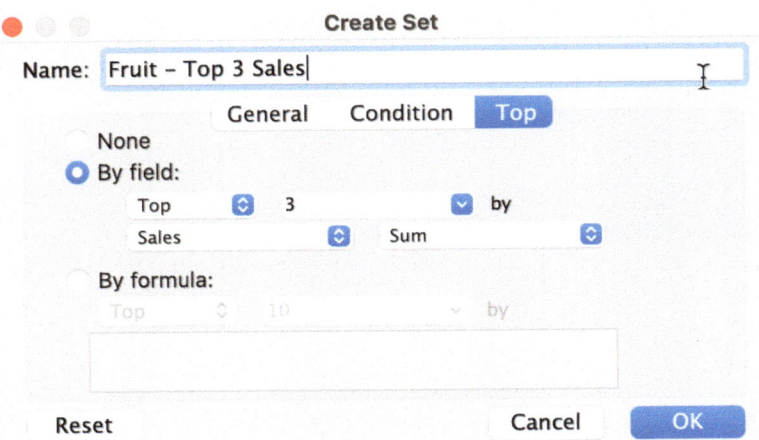

FIGURE 3.31
The Top Tab of the Create Set Dialog.

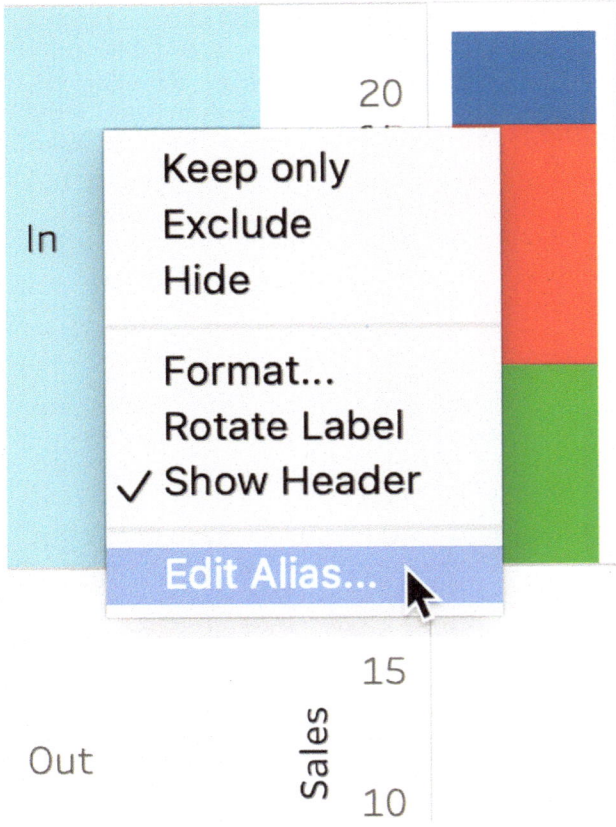

FIGURE 3.32
Edit Alias for Axis Field.

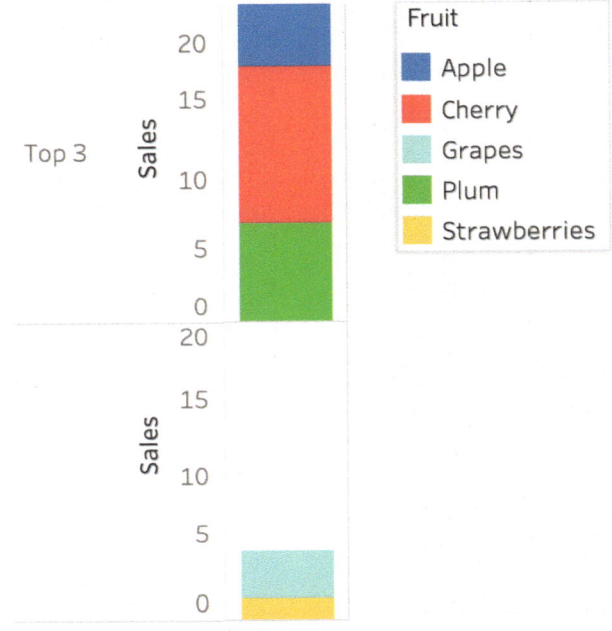

FIGURE 3.33
The Updated Chart with Aliases.

3.6.4 Placeholder Fields

Dual-axis charts with "Placeholder" fields can add different colors, shapes, marks, and more to a chart in a stacked or layered effect, as shown in several **Chapter 6** examples. These "Placeholder" or "Dummy" fields are usually an in-line expression like "MIN(1)." Placeholders are calculated fields where the value is unimportant. All that matters is a field in the view. I use placeholder fields in examples in later chapters.

"Section 6.5 Donut Chart" on page 112

"Section 8.13 Click Data Points to Sort with a Set" on page 175

3.6.3.5 *Set Control*

To display a **Set Control** for dynamic sets *used in a view*, right-click the set name in the **Data** pane and choose "Show Set." In Figure 3.37, the **Set Control** displays the members instead of the *In/Out* choices.

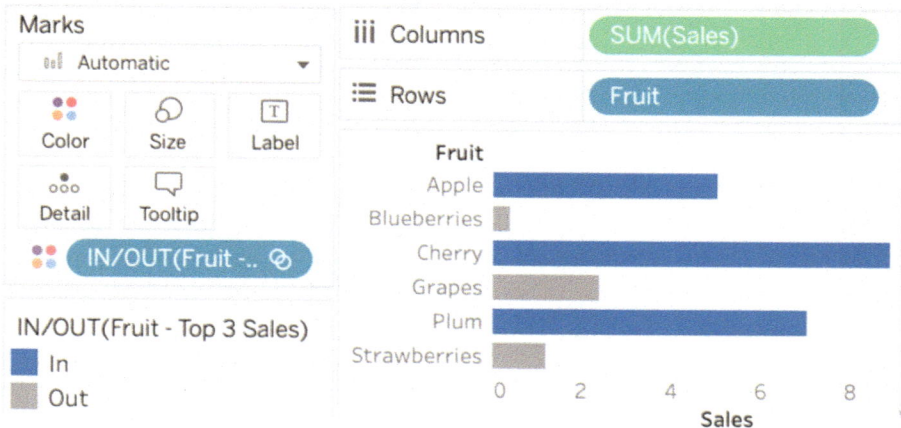

FIGURE 3.34
The Set Control in the Bottom Left.

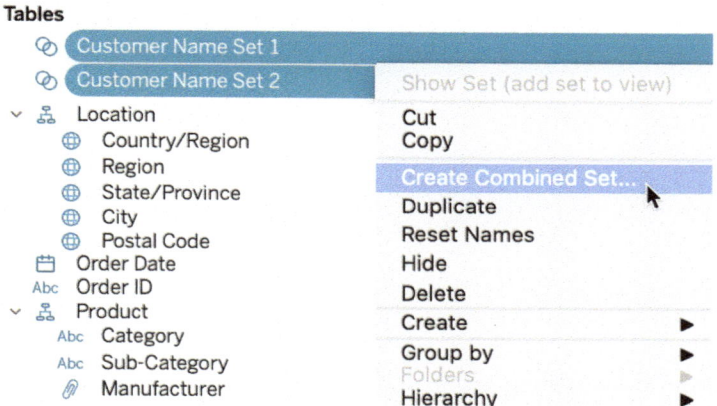

FIGURE 3.35
Create a Combined Set.

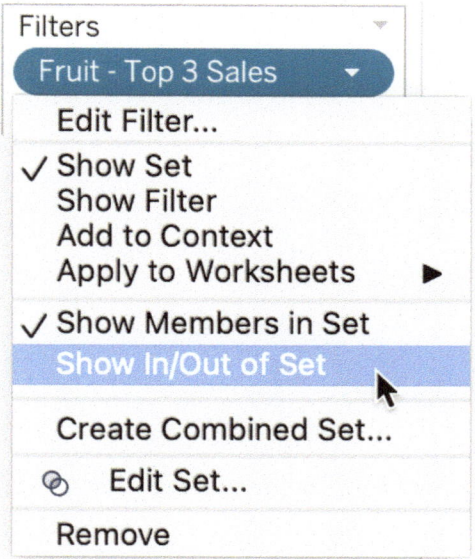

FIGURE 3.36
Filter Set Options.

Set Control (Fruit - Top 3 Sales)

- ☑ (All)
- ☑ Apple
- ☑ Blueberries
- ☑ Cherry
- ☑ Grapes
- ☑ Plum
- ☑ Strawberries

Limit

Top 3 by SUM([Sales])

FIGURE 3.37
The Set Control.

"Section 8.14 Hover to Choose a Field for Sorting" on page 181

"Section 12.21 Arrows Comparing Two Values" on page 287

"Section 13.6.4 Custom Color and Shape Legend (Diamond)" on page 298

"Section 13.8 Placeholder Fields" on page 302

"Section 14.23 KPIs and BANs (Big Numbers)" on page 347

Of all the examples, *"Section 13.6.4 Custom Color and Shape Legend (Diamond)" on page 298* best illustrates the power of placeholders. This example is my favorite method for moving a diamond shape to the perfect location. The example in *"Section 6.5 Donut Chart" on page 112* illustrates how to name a placeholder field.

3.7 Aggregation

Aggregation is a fundamental concept in Tableau. Tableau aggregates data using calculations like SUM() or AVG(). When I add the [Sales] field to a chart, Tableau aggregates the data for all sales, as shown in Figure 3.38. Tableau renders a scatter plot with two dots because I have two measures in this example. If I only had one measure field on the view, there would be one dot.

After I turn off aggregation, Figure 3.39 shows all sales. If you do not want aggregation, on the **Analysis** menu, uncheck "Aggregate Measures."

Earlier, we looked at an aggregated measure in the "Dimension Fields" and "Measure Fields" topics. In *"Section 11.4 Aggregation and Level of Detail" on page 227*, I explore aggregation and provide examples of level of detail expressions.

3.7.1 The Visualization Level of Detail

When you add dimension fields to a view, you create a deeper aggregation. The fields in a view represent the **Visualization Level of Detail** or Viz LOD. Tableau's

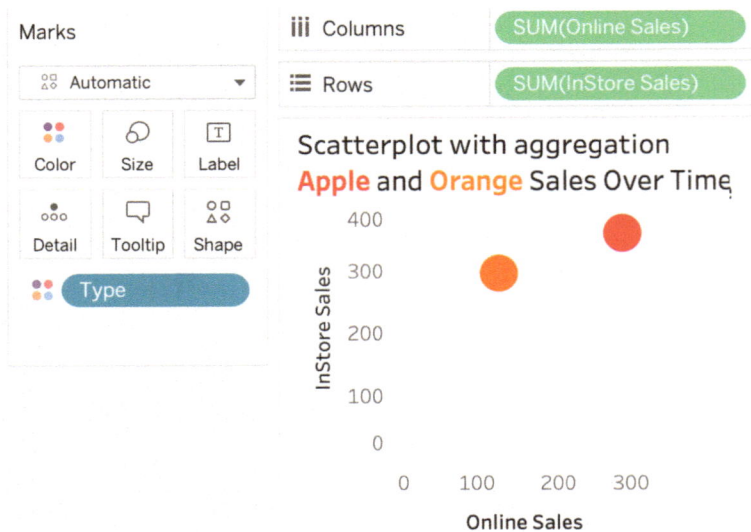

FIGURE 3.38
Aggregated sales.

Scatterplot with no aggregation
Apple and **Orange** Sales Over Time

FIGURE 3.39
No aggregations.

level of detail expressions are invaluable when controlling data in calculations or the view itself. What happens if a view shows a count of *Fans* per *Zip*, and you also want to see a count of *Fans* as an average of **all** *Fans* per *State*? A *level of detail* or *LOD calculation* is the solution to include fields in calculations where the fields *are not part of the view* or a different aggregation.

3.7.2 Aggregations, Addressing, and Partitioning

Tableau's addressing and partitioning affect how totals or other aggregations are calculated. For example, use "Table Down" to total columns and "Table Across" to total rows. Tableau automatically identifies some fields for *addressing* and others for *partitioning*. "*Section 10.4 Compute Using*" *on page 212* examines this topic more, including the "Compute Using" options for table calculations.

3.7.3 Aggregate Functions

Before we jump into ways to influence aggregation, let's look at the functions that aggregate field data. By default, Tableau aggregates measure data with **Sum()**, so when you drag a measure field like [Sales] onto the view, you will notice Tableau changes it to **Sum(Sales)**.

- Sum
- Count
- Average
- Min
- Max

To change the type of aggregation for a field, right-click the field to open the field's *context menu*. Select "Measure" and then choose an aggregation. When you drag a field on the view, you can also use the **Drop Field** *context menu* to choose a level of aggregation, as shown in the next topic.

3.7.4 Context Filters to Decrease Scope

Use **Context Filters** to decrease the scope of data used in a calculation. Let's say you have a filter where the [Sub-Category] field value is "Bookcases," and there are a million rows of [Sub-Category] data. If you set that filter as a **Context Filter**, you drastically reduce the data before any other filters or calculations are applied because Tableau processes **Context Filters** before "Top N" filters, Totals, Table Calculations, and other operations.

Chapter 8 examines Tableau's **Order of Operations**, which defines how Tableau processes filters, calculations, and other operations.

4

The Language of Data

In this topic, we discuss

Types of Data
Nulls, *, All, and None
Field Default Properties
Data Pane Icons Aggregation
The Tableau Data Model
Data Structure
Combining Data
Working with Data

In this chapter, we'll look at default properties for formatting data and explore how to work with and combine data.

4.1 Types of Data

Ideally, Tableau automatically identifies the correct data types when you connect a data source.

Common data types are shown below. Tableau icons also provide visual clues.

Strings
Dates
Numbers (Integers or Floats)
Boolean (True–False)
Geographic Role

Because dates are critical to many visualizations, I explore them in detail in **Chapter 9**. Earlier, we looked at the Geographic roles assigned by Tableau based on latitude and longitude values.

4.1.1 Field Type Detection and Naming Improvements

Tableau automatically detects the data type (date, string, and number) and renames fields based on "Field Type Detecting and Naming Improvement" rules. For example, field names that end with "Number" are treated as a dimension or string data types, and underscores in field names are replaced with a space. Tableau recognizes dates in the ISO format yyyy-MM-dd.

If you prefer the original field name, click the arrow next to it on the **Data Source** page and select "Reset name." When Tableau connects to a data source, it adds date fields to the "Dimensions" section at the top of the **Data** pane.

4.1.2 Change the Data Type of a Field

During data analysis, you may change a field's data type to match the purpose of the field. For example, suppose the field [Order Number] has only numbers, then Tableau may identify the field as a measure field when it needs to be a dimension. While working on a view, you can change a field data type in the **Data** pane. Select a field in the **Data** pane and click the drop-down arrow to open the field's *context menu*. On the **Data Source** page, click the small icon above the field name and select the new data type, as shown in Figure 4.1.

FIGURE 4.1
Data Types for Fields.

DOI: 10.1201/9781003566458-5

4.2 Nulls, *, All, and None

Let's briefly explore the unique data you might see in Tableau, such as "Nulls," "*," "All," and "None."

4.2.1 Nulls

Nulls are always a possibility when working with data. *Null* values impact your calculations or show up in your charts in other ways. When a line suddenly drops to zero, you may have nulls in your data. Nulls are not necessarily an issue. For instance, you may want to know when there were no errors during the month. If you are calculating a percent change compared to the previous month, you need to account for nulls in your data.

Nulls might occur naturally in your original data source or can be introduced when you combine data sources with joins. Relationships also preserve null values. If you have only one table for a data source, you need not be concerned about the nulls caused by using multiple tables. If you use multiple tables and data sources, pay close attention to how you configure blends, joins, and table relationships to avoid introducing null values.

Table calculations can also introduce null values. For instance, the first year would have a null value in a year-over-year calculation. The function ZN (fieldname) returns 0 if the field value is null. *"Section 11.8.4 ZN()" on page 232* has additional information on working with nulls.

4.2.1.1 Null Indicator

Tableau warns you when nulls are mixed with your data using a small "Null" indicator, usually in the bottom right corner of the data, such as "3 Nulls."

At the bottom of the **Format** pane are options for "**Special Values (e.g. NULL)**," as shown in Figure 4.2.

4.2.2 All

The "All" value is similar to an asterisk, except that "All" indicates multiple rows having the same value. Initially, you may not have duplicate values, but the "All" value may appear as data changes over time. Tableau has an online article on using parameters to work around this common issue. In *"Section 9.11 Avoid 'All' in a Date Title" on page 208*, the example uses a parameter and calculated field to add a date to the worksheet title.

4.2.3 None

When you filter a data, there is always a chance that no data is returned. Usually, this is not an issue unless

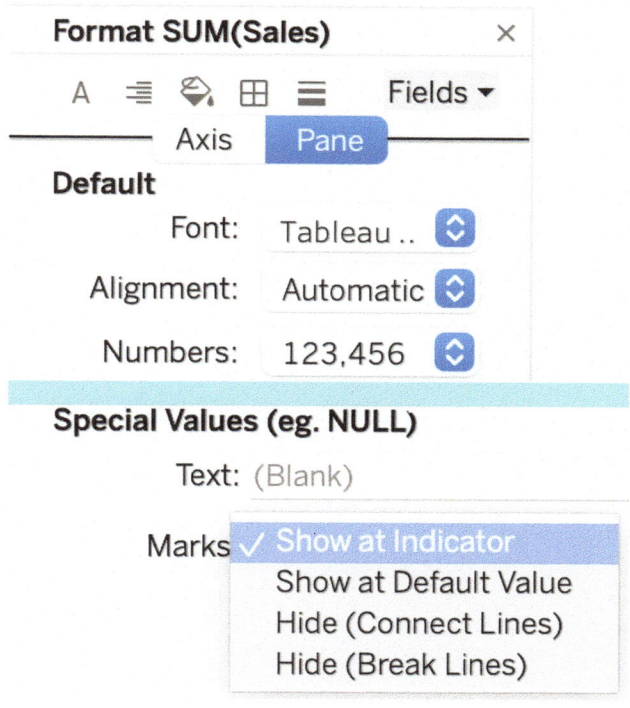

FIGURE 4.2
Special Values.

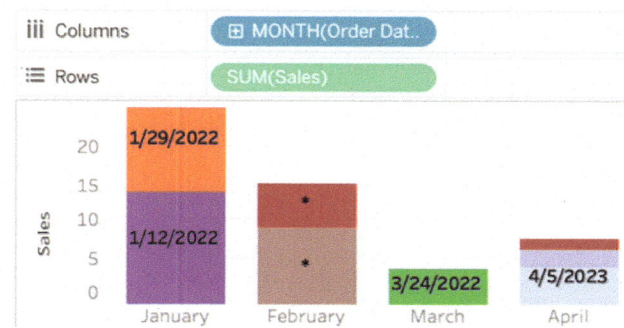

FIGURE 4.3
Asterisks Indicating Aggregated Data.

you use fields in your "title" and Tableau displays "None." *"Section 9.6.2 Worksheet for Date Title" on page 199* illustrates an alternative for "None" values.

4.2.4 * Asterisk

When Tableau aggregates data, you may see an * (asterisk). The asterisk indicates multiple values in a single mark. In Figure 4.3, February has asterisk values.

February has an asterisk symbol (*) instead of a date label. When I select the February marks and choose "View Data," the **Summary** tab has asterisks in the [Order Date] column as shown in Figure 4.4. Select the "Full Data" tab in the left pane to see all rows.

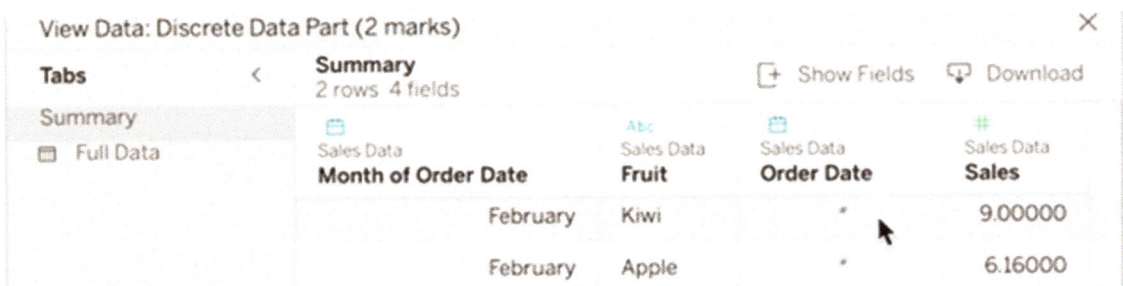

FIGURE 4.4
The Order Date Column.

4.2.5 No Data

The absence of data can be challenging in Tableau. Tableau displays a row count in the bottom left corner of a worksheet screen. If there are no rows of data, Tableau does not create a chart. For example, I have a key progress indicator (KPI) for the current month, and there is no data for the last two months. I cannot use current report date values for a report date heading because there is no data.

As a work-around, I can add a measure to the *Text* tile on the **Marks** card so Tableau has at least one row of data to create a chart. Since I only want to see data for the current month, I remove all text from the **Text Editor.** In this way, Tableau creates a blank chart with a title. I then add a calculated field to retrieve last month's date to the *Detail* tile on the **Marks** card. The only thing on the **visualization** is the date field in the title.

When you have a dashboard object like a KPI sheet with no rows of data, you can set the height in the worksheet's *context menu*, as explained in *"Section 14.6.3 Size: Edit Height or Width" on page 312.* This height option is useful when you have a row of KPI charts to align.

4.3 Field Default Properties

Each field instance on the view can have unique **default properties** for number format, aggregation, sort order, color, etc. The choices vary depending on the type of field. To apply the settings in any view, set **default properties** for that field in the **Data** pane. In *"Section 12.14 Default Properties" on page 280,* we also look at the options for formatting with **default properties**. When replacing a data source, **default properties** are not copied.

4.3.1 Describe Fields: Comments

When creating a visualization for others, I like to add comments about the original database or source of record, especially if several fields have similar names

and it is not obvious which field is relevant. When several databases are combined or manipulated in an external program like Alteryx, it is helpful to know if the data types changed along the way and where and how the field was added.

4.3.2 Dimension Fields

Default properties for "Dimension" fields include:

- Comment
- Color
- Shape
- Sort

A field's **default properties** apply to any view, but you can change the properties for a particular view. When you choose a field's default color, adding that field to the *Color* tile on the **Marks** card applies the color setting. For example, the "Segment" field has three values, including *Home Office.* When I change the color for the "Home Office" value to orange, the *Home Office* mark is orange whenever I add "Segment" to the *Color* tile. We look at color settings in *"Section 7.3 The Color Property" on page 139* and in *"Section 12.14.1 Color" on page 281.*

4.3.3 Measure Fields

Default Properties for "Measure" fields include:

- Comment
- Color
- Number format…
- Aggregation
- Total Using…

4.3.3.1 Number Fields

Default properties for "Number" fields include the settings below. *"Section 12.11 Format Field: Axis,*

Numbers" on page 276 has an example that sets the default "number format."

- Comment
- Color
- Shape
- Aggregation
- Sum
- Average
- Median
- Variance (Pop.)
- Count
- Count (Distinct)
- Minimum
- Maximum
- Percentile
- Std. Dev
- Std. Dev (Pop.)
- Variance

The default aggregation for measures in Tableau is "Sum," as shown in Figure 4.5.

4.3.4 Date Fields

Default properties for date fields include:

- Comment
- Color
- Shape
- Date Format
- Sort
- Default Year Start Day

4.4 Data Pane Icons

In the previous chapter, you may have noticed several icons representing data types, roles, and other custom fields when we looked at the **Data** pane. We examine these icons in detail in later chapters (Figures 4.6–4.14).

4.5 The Tableau Data Model

The Tableau Data Model organizes tables into *logical* and *physical layers*. When you drag two tables from the same data source onto the canvas, Tableau attempts to create a *relationship* between the tables. In addition to the logical and physical layers, Tableau creates *blends* when there are two distinct data sources. Next, we look at layers and blends in more depth.

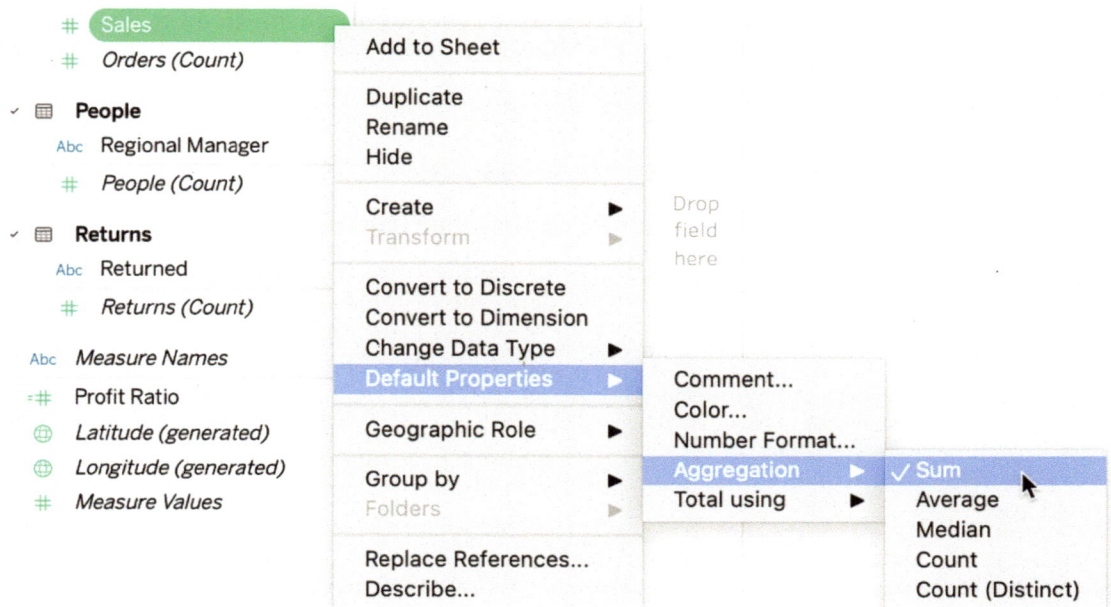

FIGURE 4.5
Default Aggregation.

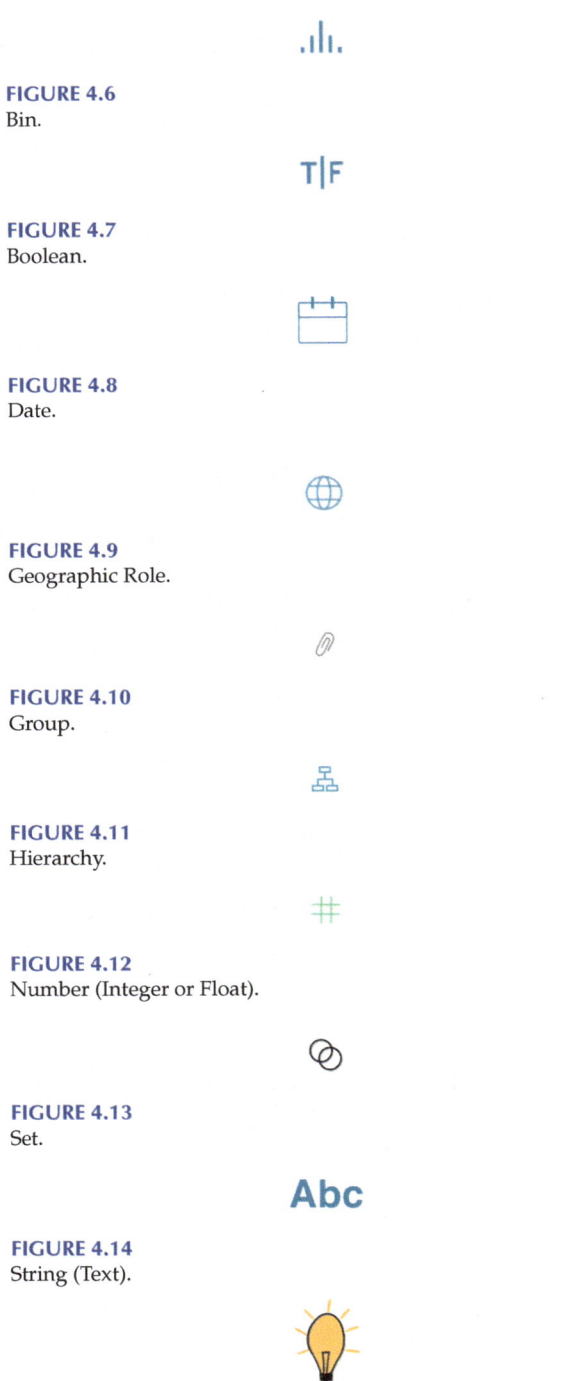

FIGURE 4.6
Bin.

FIGURE 4.7
Boolean.

FIGURE 4.8
Date.

FIGURE 4.9
Geographic Role.

FIGURE 4.10
Group.

FIGURE 4.11
Hierarchy.

FIGURE 4.12
Number (Integer or Float).

FIGURE 4.13
Set.

FIGURE 4.14
String (Text).

FIGURE 4.15
Tip: Because joins and unions do not account for different levels of granularity between tables, use relationships or blends for different levels of granularity.

4.5.1 Logical Layer

When we looked at the **data source** page earlier in Chapter 2, the first image was the *logical layer*. The **canvas** has lines indicating relationships between the

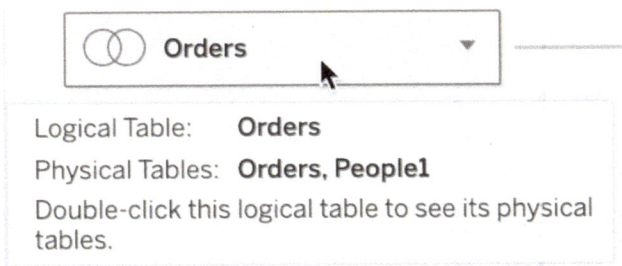

FIGURE 4.16
The Logical Layer.

Orders table and the *People* and *Returns* tables. The default **canvas** view is this *logical layer*. Relationships are created in the logical layer and are good when there are different levels of granularity or detail between the tables. We look at relationships in the next topic, "Combining Data." In Figure 4.16, when I hover my mouse over the logical table "Orders," a pop-up tooltip indicates there are physical tables below.

4.5.2 Physical Layer

Joins and **Unions** are configured at the *physical layer* in Tableau. Double-click the logical table name "Orders" to see the physical tables. The *physical layer* is underneath the logical layer. Relationships are created in the *logical layer*. Joins and unions are created in the *physical layer*. Figure 4.17 shows the *physical layer* of an *inner join* between two tables.

After you close the *physical layer* and return to the *logical layer*, a small join icon to the left of the table name indicates a join at the *physical layer*. Chapter 5, "Row Level Security with Two Connections in a Data Source," illustrates the logical and physical layers.

4.6 Data Structure

To demonstrate the importance of the structure of data, one of Tableau's first topics in its online help is "Structure Data for Analysis." The first time I prepared data for Tableau, I grouped my data and summarized totals. With my first chart, I learned this is the exact opposite of how data should be structured for Tableau! Instead, you want the simplest form of data or "tall data." Chances are you will have to clean up data before using a data source in Tableau.

- Remove header and footer rows
- Remove totals

FIGURE 4.17
The Physical Layer.

FIGURE 4.18
Tip: To set the default date format for all date fields in a data source, click the data source **name** at the top of the **Data** pane. Select "Date Properties" from the context menu.

- Try to have fewer columns and more rows or tall data
- Use valid dates. 2023-12-31 instead of "Jan." (Figure 4.18)

4.6.1 Partitioning

Partitioning refers to how you divide up the data. When there are two dimensions, [Country] and [State], you can partition the data into countries, states, or all the data. In *"Section 10.1 Table Calculation Scope" on page 209*, we look at scope partitioning and addressing in detail as they relate to table calculations.

4.6.2 Valid Dates

In the world of Tableau data, you should use real dates. Figure 4.19 shows a common format used in Excel. The data is broken into the months Jan, Feb, and Mar. Convert these text values to real dates like 2023-01-31. I tend to use the last day of the month, quarter, or year, but any date is okay if it makes sense for your data.

4.6.3 Remove Totals

The previous data includes sum totals in the last column on the right. However, including a sum total is unnecessary because Tableau aggregates data based on the fields in the view. Figure 4.20 shows the data after removing the total column and using real dates in the headers.

4.6.4 Tall Data

Finally, this data can be simplified by combining the date columns into one "Date" column, resulting in a

Quantity Sold				
Type	**Jan**	**Feb**	**Mar**	**Total**
Football	3	5	7	15
Baseball	1	7	25	33
Soccer	2	25	4	31

FIGURE 4.19
Month Headers.

Quantity Sold			
Type	**1/31/23**	**2/28/23**	**3/31/23**
Football	3	5	7
Baseball	1	7	25
Soccer	2	25	4

FIGURE 4.20
Date Headers.

"tall" table, as shown in Figure 4.21. Tall data is the best data structure for Tableau.

Figure 4.22 illustrates another data set with three columns of price data.

The three price columns can be combined into one field called "Price," as shown in Figure 4.23. The process is the same as the earlier example, where we combined three columns into the "Date" column.

4.7 Combining Data

Tableau combines data with relationships, joins, unions, and blends. If you plan to use a published data source on a Tableau server, relationships and joins are only available if you use Tableau Prep.

Type	Date	Qty
Football	1/31/23	3
Football	2/28/23	5
Football	3/31/23	7
Baseball	1/31/23	1
Baseball	2/28/23	7
Baseball	3/31/23	25
Soccer	1/31/23	2
Soccer	2/28/23	25
Soccer	3/31/23	4

FIGURE 4.21
Tall Date Data.

Type	Price	Qty
Football	<$10	3
Football	$10-$15	5
Football	$16-$20	7
Baseball	<$10	1
Baseball	$10-$15	7
Baseball	$16-$20	25
Soccer	<$10	2
Soccer	$10-$15	25
Soccer	$16-$20	4

FIGURE 4.23
Price Column with Tall Data.

Quantity Sold			
Type	Price <$10	Price $10-$15	Price $16-$20
Football	3	5	7
Baseball	1	7	25
Soccer	2	25	4

FIGURE 4.22
Price Columns.

FIGURE 4.24
Tip: You can combine several columns into one column with any new column name you like, such as "Combined Fields."

4.7.1 Relationships

The default method for combining data in Tableau is a relationship. To create a relationship, drag two tables from the left pane onto the canvas. Tableau draws a red line between the tables and prompts you to configure the relationship, as shown in Figure 4.25.

With relationships, the data is loosely combined so that tables are queried separately, similar to a deferred join. Relationships are "context-aware," in that data is brought together within the context of a visualization based on its dimensions. They are created in the logical layer and are good when there are different levels of granularity or detail between the tables. They do not merge data into a new table – like joins.

While relationships and data blending address the issue of different granularity in tables, relationships are more powerful than data blending. We look at

data blending in the following topic, "Data Blending." Relationships are one way to avoid the data duplication that can occur with joins.

4.7.2 Joins

Joins merge data based on common fields and create a new, fixed table with added columns. Joins are created at the *Physical Layer*. Tableau follows the general convention for join types and supports:

- Inner Join
- Left Join
- Full Outer Join
- Right Join

One data source can have multiple Excel worksheets from the same workbook, and you can join the tables if the joining fields are of the same data type. Depending on how you set up a join, you could unintentionally cause a Cartesian join, null values, or duplicate data. For example, Table 1 has 10 rows,

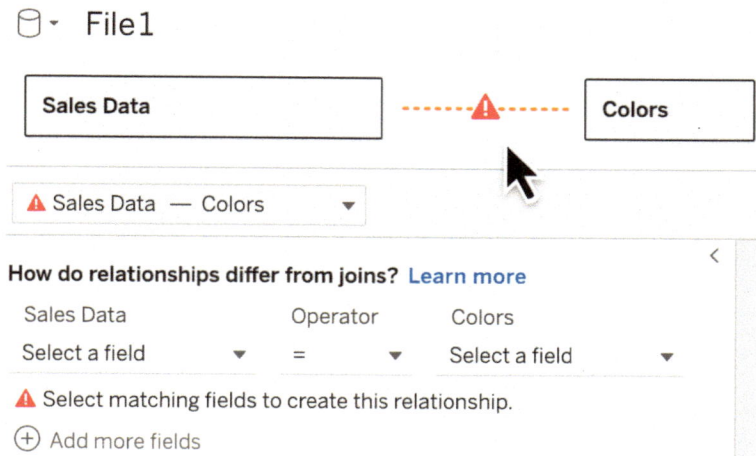

FIGURE 4.25
Click the Red Line to Configure the Relationship.

FIGURE 4.26
Tip: Relationships preserve null measures. You cannot use relationships with published data sources on a Tableau server.

and Table 2 has 20. A Cartesian join results in 10x20 or 200 rows, which is probably not what you intended. Check your row count to be sure the result is correct.

4.7.3 Inner Join

An *Inner Join* is the default join in Tableau. The resulting table includes values that match from both tables. In Figure 4.27, the tables "Price per dozen" and "Inventory" are combined with an inner join. The bottom of the figure illustrates the data after the join, where only the Baseball and Soccer records remain.

4.7.3.1 Create an Inner Join

In the next example of an *inner join*, my Excel workbook has two worksheets, "Sales Data" and "Colors." In this exercise, I will drill down into the *physical layer*. Once connected, the worksheets become *tables* in Tableau.

1. Drag the "Sales Data" sheet from the left pane onto the **canvas**.
2. Double-click "Sales Data" to move to the *physical layer*. Alternatively, you can hover over "Sales Data" and click the drop-down menu to open it. The canvas changes, and

Price per dozen

	Ball	Price
	Football	$25
	Baseball	$18
	Soccer	$10
	Golf	$15

Inventory

	Ball	Price
	Baseball	50
	Soccer	200
	Bowling	300
	Softball	140

Inner Join

	Ball	Price	Inventory
	Baseball	$18	50
	Soccer	$10	200

FIGURE 4.27
An Inner Join.

Tableau adds a header "Sales Data is made of 1 table" above the gray box "Sales Data." (Figure 4.28).

3. Drag "Colors" onto the white area of the **canvas**. Tableau creates an *inner join*, as shown below. If you drag "Colors" on top of the "Sales Data" table, Tableau prompts you to create a union (Figure 4.29).

To edit the join, click the join icon in the middle of the page.

4.7.4 Left Join

A *Left Join* includes all records from the left table and matched records from the right table. If a record in the

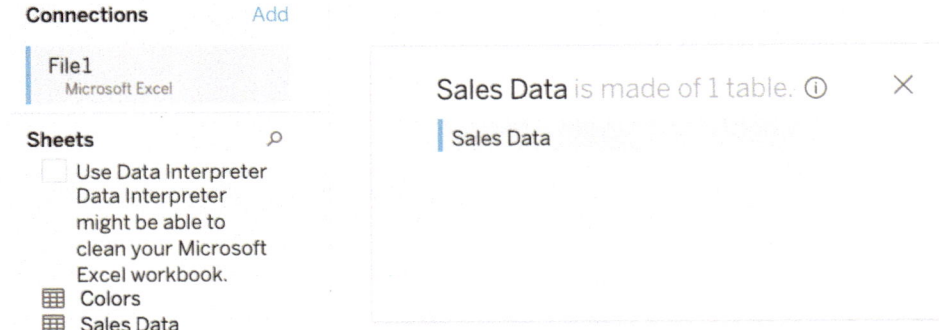

FIGURE 4.28
The Physical Layer for the Sales Data Table.

FIGURE 4.29
The Inner Join Between Sales Data and Colors.

left table does not match any records in the right table, a null value is created. In Figure 4.30, the Bowling and Softball records in the right table were dropped. *Inventory* for "Football" and "Golf" is null in the new table.

4.7.4.1 Create a Left Join

Continuing the previous example, I want to change the connection to a *left join*.

1. If you are not already on the *physical layer*, double-click "Sales Data" to move to the *physical layer*.
2. Click the join icon to open the **Join** dialog window.
3. Click the *Left* icon at the top of the pop-up window and select the field [Fruit] for both sides of the join clause, as shown below (Figure 4.31).

Price per dozen		Inventory	
Ball	**Price**	**Ball**	**Price**
🏈 Football	$25	⚾ Baseball	50
⚾ Baseball	$18	⚽ Soccer	200
⚽ Soccer	$10	🎳 Bowling	300
🏐 Golf	$15	🥎 Softball	140

Ball	**Price**	**Inventory**
🏈 Football	$25	
⚾ Baseball	$18	50
⚽ Soccer	$10	200
🏐 Golf	$15	

FIGURE 4.30
A Left Join.

FIGURE 4.31
The Join Edit Window.

Price per dozen	
Ball	**Price**
Football	$25
Baseball	$18
Soccer	$10
Golf	$15

Inventory	
Ball	**Price**
Baseball	50
Soccer	200
Bowling	300
Softball	140

Price per dozen	
Ball	**Price**
Football	$25
Baseball	$18
Soccer	$10
Golf	$15

Inventory	
Ball	**Price**
Baseball	50
Soccer	200
Bowling	300
Softball	140

Full Outer Join

Ball	Price	Inventory
Baseball	$18	50
Soccer	$10	200
Bowling		300
Softball		140
Football	$25	
Golf	$15	

FIGURE 4.32
Outer Join.

Right Join

Ball	Price	Inventory
Baseball	$18	50
Soccer	$10	200
Bowling		300
Softball		140

FIGURE 4.33
A Right Join.

4. Tableau keeps all records in the left "Sales Data" table and any matching records from the "Colors" table.

4.7.5 Full Outer Join

In my experience, you do not often use a *Full Outer Join*, which contains all records from both tables, as shown in Figure 4.32. Unmatched records on either side of the join create null values. The "Football" record is not in the inventory table, so the "Inventory" field is null in the new table.

4.7.6 Right Join

A *Right Join* includes all records from the right table and only matched records from the left table, as shown in Figure 4.33. When a value from the right table does not match with that of the left table, you will see a null value. In this example, the right table record "Bowling" does not exist in the left table, and the right join creates a null value in the "Price" field.

4.7.7 Unions

Unions are configured at the *physical layer* in Tableau, and rows are appended to combine multiple tables. Tables must have the same or similar column structure

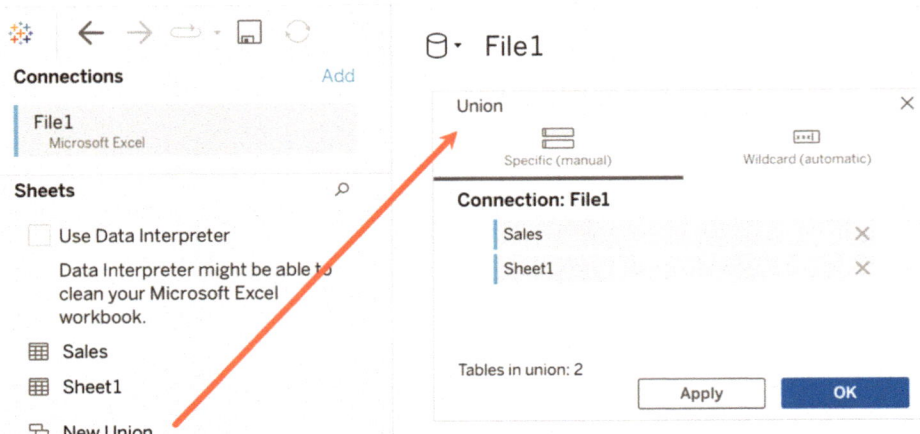

FIGURE 4.34
The Union Dialog Window.

and *come from the same connection*. For example, if Sheet1 from *Sales.xlsx* has eight records and Sheet2 has two records, a **union** creates a table with ten records. Both Sheet1 and Sheet2 must be from the same *Sales.xlsx connection*. **Union All** returns duplicate values if present.

1. Connect to a data source with two tables. In the bottom left corner, click "New Union" or drag the "Union" tool onto the canvas.

2. Drag both tables into the **Union** window and click OK (Figure 4.34).

4.7.8 Data Blends

Blends address different levels of detail and are less powerful than relationships. Blends work with published data sources. A blend queries each data source separately; the data is never combined. A blend simulates a left join and is specific to a particular **view**. If you have three views, there are three separate blends. Blends are context-aware based on the dimensions in the view. When you combine a *primary* and *secondary data source* directly in a *view*, Tableau attempts to create a "Blend."

Data sources need a common dimension for the blend. Tableau queries data sources independently and then visualizes data in the view like a left join. Blending is most appropriate when **comparing measures** that have a similar scale and unit. If the scales of the two measures are drastically different, trends may be distorted.

The first field you add to a **view** establishes the *primary* data source. You can only use Tableau's [Measure Names] and [Measure Values] fields from the primary data source for that view. Suppose *Table 1* is the *primary* data source. In that case, Tableau includes all fields from *Table 1* and only matched fields from the

secondary data source. From the **Data** menu, you can edit *Blend Relationships*.

A *blend* aggregates and then presents results. If *Table 1* has multiple values that match *Table 2*, when Tableau aggregates the data, you may see an asterisk symbol *. The asterisk indicates multiple values in a single mark.

- Blends work with published data sources. A published data source is located on a Tableau server.

- The **Data** menu only allows editing a data blend if two data sources are in the workbook.

- Blends query each data source independently and then aggregate the data.

4.8 Working with Data

Whether you want to check your calculations or resolve an error, sometimes you have to delve deeper into your data.

4.8.1 View and Export Data

My first experience with Tableau was editing an existing Tableau file. I wondered what the source data looked like, and I had no idea where to look. On the **Data Source** page, there are table structures such as fields, columns, and rows. There are other places throughout Tableau to view the underlying data as it relates to a particular context or within the view's level of detail, as shown below. There are also several places to export or download data.

- On the Analysis menu, select View Data
- View Data in the worksheet **Data** pane
- View Data on the **Data Source** page
- View Data from a selected mark
- Tooltips

The **Analysis** menu has a choice to **View Data**, which also opens the **View Data** detail window to see data used in a worksheet. Various menus and tools open the "**View Data**" dialog window, with options to "Download" or export data. On the **Analysis** menu at the top of the screen, select "View Data" to open the window.

4.8.1.1 Full Data Tab

When I select the **Full Data** tab on the left side of the **View Data** detail window, I can see multiple dates for Kiwi fruits in February, as shown in Figure 4.35.

It is easy to overlook the "Show Fields" button on the right side of the **Full Data** tab, but this is a great place to see and download all your data. At the top of the pane, "Show Fields" allows you to choose all the fields in the data source or a subset of fields, as shown in Figure 4.36.

4.8.1.2 The View Data Icon in a Tooltip

Hover over a mark until the "Tooltip" appears. Then, click the *data* icon on the far-right corner of the pop-up window, as shown in Figure 4.37.

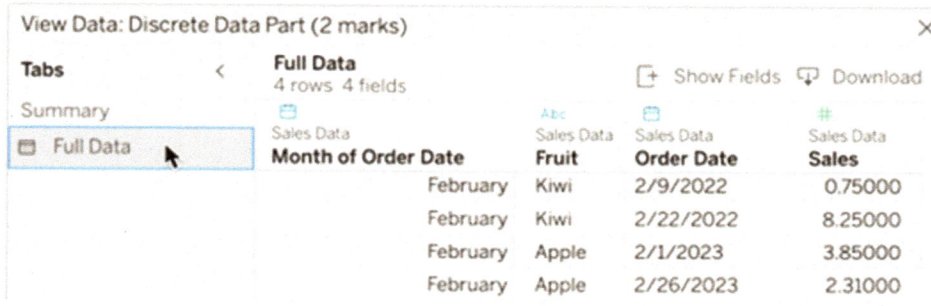

FIGURE 4.35
The Full Data Tab.

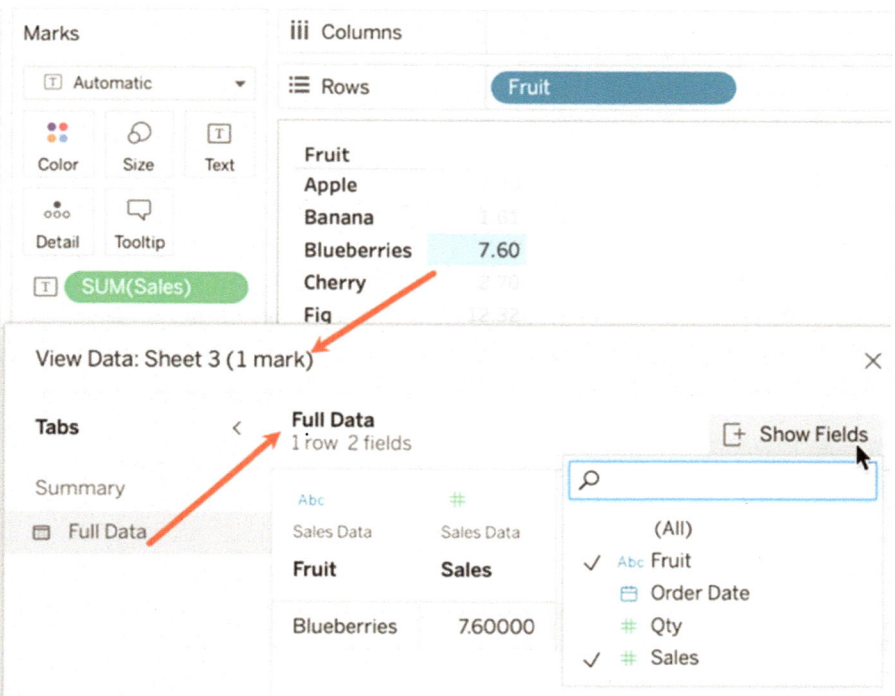

FIGURE 4.36
Show Fields Button.

4.8.1.3 Summary

The **summary** card shows aggregation based on the fields and filters in the view. Select "Show Summary" on the **Worksheet** menu to open the **Summary** card.

FIGURE 4.37
Show Data Icon.

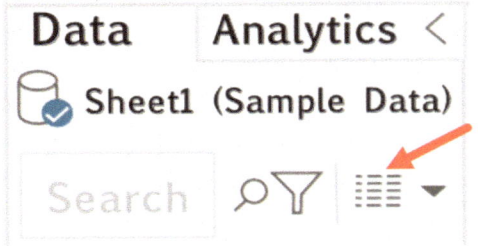

FIGURE 4.38
The View Data Tool.

4.8.1.4 View Data in a TWBX File

A packaged Tableau file (.twbx) is actually a compressed file. If you rename the file extension to "zip," you can click the file and choose "Extract" to see the original images and data source files. If you download a workbook from Tableau Public, the data source is a *.hyper file. Double-click the *.hyper file to open it in Tableau, and then on the **Data Source** page, select the **Data** menu and "Export Data to CSV."

4.8.1.5 View Data from the Data Pane

In the **Data** pane of a worksheet, click the View Data tool as shown in Figure 4.38. The **View Data** window opens with an option to *Show Fields* or *Download*.

The **View Data** pop-up window opens with details about the data, as shown in Figure 4.39. The slider bar at the bottom of the window shows fields with the data type and sample data.

- The Data Source is on the top left.
- Table names are on the left.
- Row and field counts are in the middle area.

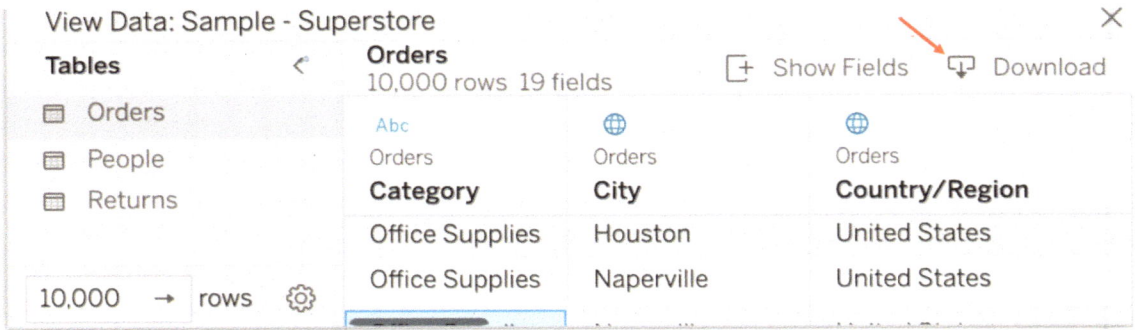

FIGURE 4.39
The **Download** Button in the **View Data** Screen.

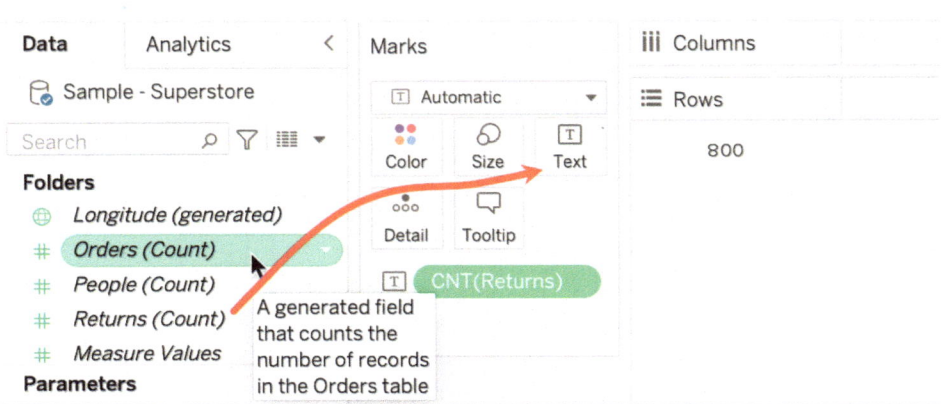

FIGURE 4.40
The Text Tile.

- The **Show Fields** button is in the top-right quadrant.
- The **Download** button is in the top right.

4.8.1.6 View Data for Selected Mark(s)

On the canvas, right-click a **mark** and select "View Data" from the *context menu*. The earlier example, "Create a Static Set," showed how to create a set from selected marks. *"Section 9.2.2 Select Marks on the View to View Data" on page 196* explores how to select marks on the view to view the data.

4.8.2 Check the Data

One way to validate chart data is to drag fields onto the *Text* tile in a new view, as shown in Figure 4.40. During development, consider using a smaller subset of data. For example, instead of 100,000 rows of data, use 1,000 rows of relevant data. I like to choose 2–3 data points that represent each category or filter in my visualization.

When replacing Excel charts with Tableau charts, I check my work by exporting Tableau data to Excel and creating the same chart view to confirm if the data matches, even if that is not the final visualization. Seeing the old and new charts side by side is a great validation test that business partners appreciate.

5

A Chart with a View

In this topic, we discuss

Preparation
Show Me
Create a Chart
Share Charts and Dashboards
From Data to Insights
Designing a Visualization
Publish to Tableau Server or Tableau Public

Once you have a data source, you are ready for the fun part of creating a visualization! By default, Tableau creates "Sheet 1" as your first worksheet. To add additional sheets, you can use the "New Worksheet" icon in the toolbar or the icons in the bottom right corner. There are three simple ways to create charts with different mark types.

- The **Marks** card
- Add fields to the **Rows** or **Columns** shelves.
- The **Show Me** Button

5.1 Preparation

While I enjoy the creative process of building charts and designing visualizations, I grow annoyed with myself if I have to interrupt my train of thought to clean up my data. To save you from that frustration, here are a few suggestions to prepare your data to use in Tableau.

1. Is your data laid out in a "Tall" format, as shown in *"Section 4.6.4 Tall Data" on page 79*?

2. After connecting Tableau to a **Data Source**, are the field names and data types what you expect, given that Tableau Field Type Detection and Naming Improvements can change data during the import process?

3. Are date values in a "Date" format, that is, 2025-01-31, instead of "January"?

4. If you have data on several worksheets in an Excel file, are column names consistent across worksheets?

5. Do you want to "rename" any fields so they make more sense for your audience?

6. Make a list of the key fields you need for your visualizations. Do you need to create new fields or split a field into new fields?

7. What questions are you trying to answer? For example, is the business asking why volumes have dropped and full time employees (FTEs) are unchanged?

8. Consider creating a data "Extract" or a smaller version of a large data set to use during development. I prefer to move my data to a Tableau server as a *.hyper file and connect my data source to the server. This saves aggravation later when moving from a flat file to a server data source.

9. Since Tableau will aggregate data, consider removing the "Total" fields to avoid confusion.

10. Ultimately, I must document field mappings as part of our corporate process. I like to add these "Comments" as default properties for each field. Field comments are helpful when someone asks, "Where did that data come from?" and save time when I am completing documentation later. More importantly, this helps me focus on the fields that matter.
    - Where did the field come from?
    - Which measure fields are important?
    - What does the data represent?
    - Which date field is critical?

11. Take a moment to familiarize yourself with the data.
    - Do you recognize a department name in a particular field?
    - Can you tell which fields are used to create a calculated result?
    - Is there an apparent relationship between the two fields?

DOI: 10.1201/9781003566458-6

- Do you have fields with no data or all Null values?
- Should some data be converted to friendly names?

  For example, Areas 1, 2, 3, and 4 represent North, South, East, and West, respectively.

- Are your geographic fields correct? Did Tableau create Latitude and Longitude fields?

12. Draw a mock-up for your design and possibly include field names or values to serve as a reference. This type of mock-up is also useful when validating calculations and values. I would not use such bright colors in an actual dashboard, but the example below illustrates this idea (Figure 5.1).

13. Save time by setting the default date format for all fields in a *Data Source*. In the **Data** pane, click the *Data Source* name and select "Date Properties" from the *context menu*.

5.2 Show Me

With **Show Me**, Tableau can suggest different views based on selected fields or fields already in the view.

These views use various combinations of *Mark Types* and other elements. Select fields in the **Data** pane on the left and then click the "Show Me" button in the toolbar in the top-right corner of your screen. Choose one of the views that is not grayed out, and Tableau will draw the visualization for you. As we saw in *"Section 3.5.3 Continuous" on page 63*, **continuous** fields create an *axis*. Discrete fields add column *headers* or row *headers*. A **continuous** example is a timeline of date values from the first of the month through the end of the month.

5.3 Create a Chart

This first example illustrates how to create a stacked bar chart by dragging fields onto the canvas, shelves, or cards. In this example, I am creating a stacked bar chart with several colors in each bar to indicate granularity further. I also illustrate how to drill down into the hierarchy of categories and sub-categories. If you have a question about this exercise, I will summarize the steps at the end of the example.

5.3.1 Which Chart (Mark Type) Should I Use?

The choice of charts, or "Mark Type," can be intimidating at first. But it won't be long before you are

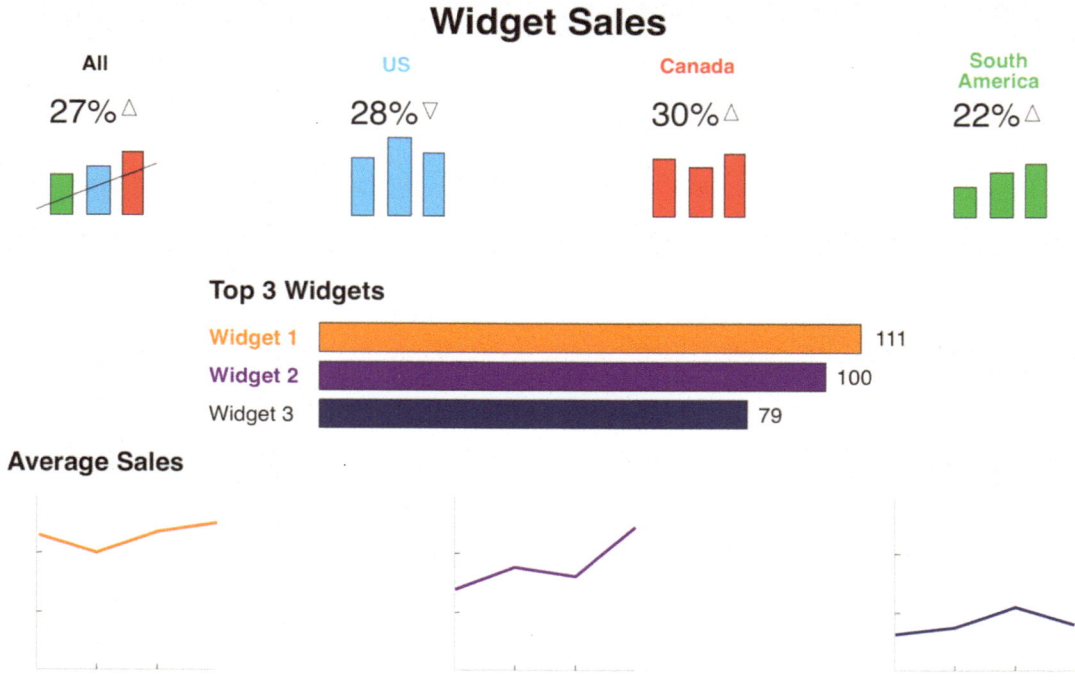

FIGURE 5.1
A Mock-up of a Dashboard Design.

cruising through the choices and discarding mark types that don't make sense. For example, if you do not have a continuous measure, you cannot use a histogram, and you probably should not use a line chart. There is no way to do a density chart unless you have massive amounts of congested data – think radar chart.

5.3.2 Drop Field

When we drag fields onto the canvas, a **Drop Field** window opens. Click a field in the **Data** pane and drag it onto the canvas, a shelf, or a card. In MacOS, use option-drag. For example, you can use the **Drop Field** behavior with the **Columns** shelf, **Rows** shelf, *Detail* tile, or *Text* tile. From the **Drop Field** dialog, you can choose the field's aggregation, as shown in Figure 5.2 where I am dragging the [Qty] field onto the canvas. Otherwise, the measure field default aggregation SUM() is used. The **Drop Field** dialog box varies depending on the type of field, as shown in *"Section 8.5.4 Date Filters" on page 165*.

5.3.3 Steps to Create the Visualization

1. Connect to the *Sample Superstore* data source and drag the [Sales] field from the **Data** pane on the left to the **Rows** shelf. The field is aggregated as a Sum, which is the default Tableau aggregation. Because this is a **continuous** field, the field has a green background.

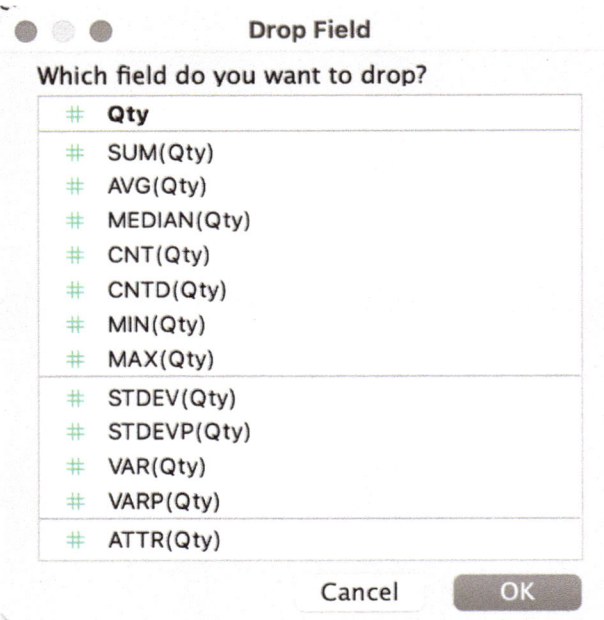

FIGURE 5.2
The **Drop Field** Dialog Window.

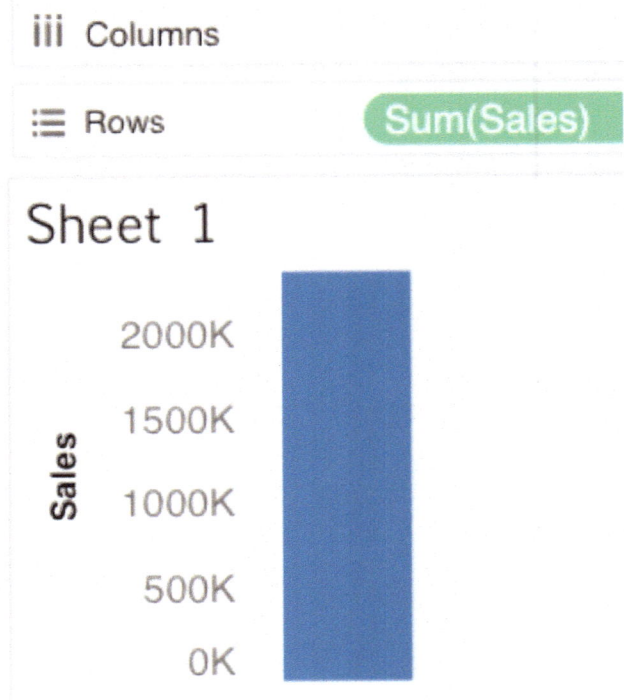

FIGURE 5.3
Sales from 0 to 2000.

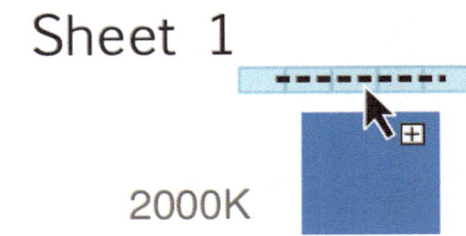

FIGURE 5.4
Drag the Field onto the Chart.

A blue bar is added to the view with a *y*-axis scale from 0K to 2000K (Figure 5.3).

2. Drag the [Category] field onto the view and hover over the top of the blue bar. A dashed black line appears with a blue highlight around the black line (Figure 5.4).

3. Drop the field onto the canvas, and Tableau will add it to the **Columns** shelf.

   Because the [Category] field is a **discrete** dimension, it has a blue background, or "pill," as shown below. Since there are three members for the **Category** field, Tableau updates the view to show three blue bars (Figure 5.5).

4. In Figure 5.5 a small plus (+) symbol on the left side of the **blue** [Category] field name on

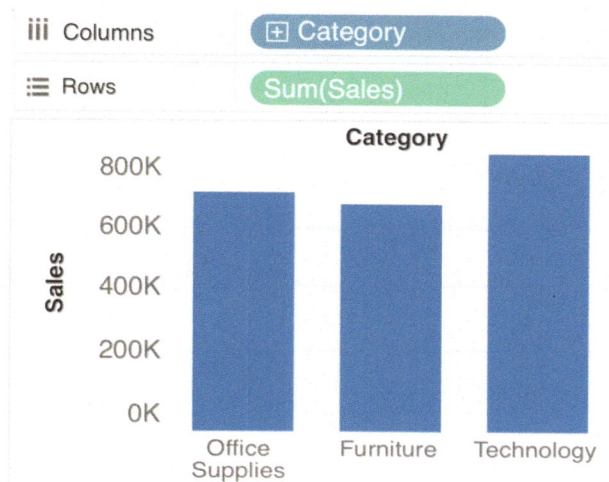

FIGURE 5.5
Bars for Each Category.

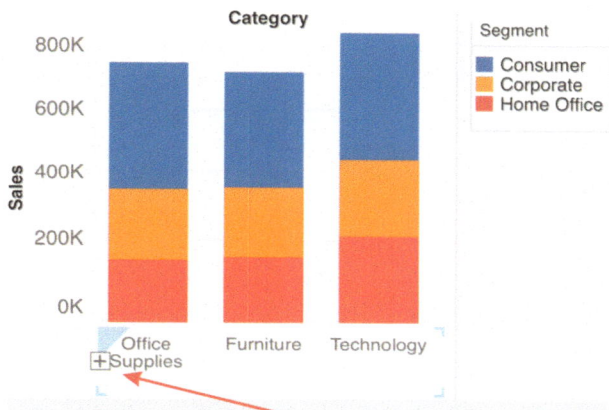

FIGURE 5.6
The Plus Symbol for a Hierarchy.

the **Columns** shelf indicates the field is part of a hierarchy. Click the plus symbol to drill down into the hierarchy. The *Field Label* at the top of the canvas also changes to "Category/Sub-Category." For now, click the minus symbol to drill back out.

5. Add the [Segment] field to *Color* on the **Marks** card to create a stacked bar chart. If you hover your mouse over the bottom of the view, the plus symbol is displayed, indicating you can drill down into the hierarchy from this location (Figure 5.6).

5.3.4 Validate and Test

To validate calculations or chart aggregations, I like to use a temporary worksheet and add fields to the *Text* tile of the **Marks** card, add a calculated field to a

tooltip, use the **Summary** card, or view the data. If using Excel workbooks, you can build pivots and compare Tableau to the Excel pivots.

1. Add the field to the *Tooltip* tile on the **Marks** card and hover over the mark to view the *Tooltip*.
2. Create a new sheet and drag the calculated field to the *Text* tile on the **Marks** card.
3. On the **Worksheet** menu, select "Show Summary."
4. Open the "View Data" window as outlined in *"Section 4.1.2 Change the Data Type of a Field" on page 74*.
5. Look at the number of marks, row count, and other calculations in the *Status Bar* along the bottom left edge of the screen.
6. If applicable, compare Tableau aggregations to Excel pivots.

5.3.5 Data and Fields

This chart is based on the *Sample Superstore* data source and utilizes these fields.

- Sales
- Category
- Segment
- Sub-category

The data type for the [Sales] field is a "Number (decimal)." In this view, [Sales] is a **continuous** field on the **Rows** shelf that creates an axis on the view. Because the field is on the **Rows** shelf, this is a vertical *y*-axis.

5.3.5.1 Category

The [Category] field is a **discrete** dimension with a "String" data type. Because [Category] is **discrete**, headings are added to the view – in this case, column headings are added because [Category] is on the **Columns** shelf. As expected, the **discrete** field has a blue background or "pill."

5.3.5.2 Sub-category

The [Sub-category] dimension field has a "String" data type and is part of a hierarchy. To illustrate drilling down into a hierarchy, I briefly use the [Sub-category] field, although it is not shown in the final visualization.

5.3.5.3 Segment

The [Segment] dimension field adds categorical color to my stacked bars and has a "String" data type.

5.3.6 Components or Elements

There are three elements to this view.

- Columns Shelf
- Rows Shelf
- The *Color* tile on the Marks card

5.3.7 Columns Shelf

The [Category] field is on the **Columns** shelf. [Category] is a **discrete** field and is blue in color. There is a plus symbol to the left of the field name, indicating the field is part of a hierarchy.

5.3.8 Rows Shelf

The [Sales] field is on the **Rows** shelf and uses the Sum() aggregation. It is green, indicating that it is **continuous**.

5.3.9 Color Tile and Color Legend

The [Segment] field is on the *Color* tile on the **Marks** card, which adds a **Color Legend** on the right side of the chart, as shown in Step 5. You can click and drag the **Color Legend** to a different area of the view.

5.4 Share Charts and Dashboards

There are several ways to share your Tableau visualizations with others, using either the **File** menu or the **Server** menu in Tableau Desktop. You can choose what to export and how to deliver the files. If your audience will print a PowerPoint in gray scale, check that the colors and shapes are appropriate. When a monthly report is filtered to six different supervisors and delivered as a PowerPoint, consider using a story with pre-filtered dashboards. If the audience uses Tableau Server or Tableau Desktop, you can include interactive features like filter drop-downs, parameters, actions, or tooltips.

- Export selected sheets or dashboards to a PowerPoint file.
- Save the file as a packaged workbook (*.twbx) file.

- Extract just the data as a *.hyper file.
- Publish the data source to a Tableau server.
- Publish your Tableau workbook directly to the server.

For users new to Tableau server, I include a story with instructions on how to use interactive features like filters, email, and highlighting. For complex dashboards, I include a button to a dashboard with "instructions" that my business partners share regarding the business process and how to interpret the data.

5.4.1 Export to PowerPoint

- On the **File** menu, select "Export as PowerPoint."

5.4.2 Package the Workbook

A packaged workbook embeds all information in the file, and users with Tableau Desktop can open the file. Because it includes the data, a packaged workbook avoids issues with drive letter mappings. You can also upload a packaged workbook to a **Tableau server**.

- On the **File** menu, select "Export Packaged Workbook."

A packaged Tableau file (.twbx) is actually a compressed file. If you rename the file extension to "zip," you can extract the data files. In MacOS, click the file and choose "Extract" to see the original images and data source files.

5.4.3 Extract Data

In Tableau Desktop, select the connection to your data source from the **Data** menu and choose "Extract Data."

5.4.4 Publish the Data Source to a Tableau Server

You can publish the data source in Tableau Desktop version 2023 and above. When you publish a data source to a Tableau server, you will need to upload a *.hyper file. Programs like Alteryx can also publish

FIGURE 5.7

Tip: If you hide unused fields before creating an extract, the extract is smaller, which improves performance. This step is beneficial as it reduces the size of the extract, making it more efficient to work with.

*.hyper files to Tableau servers. Depending on your environment, there can be a slight lag in refreshing data from a Tableau server. I believe the benefits of working with a data source on a Tableau server outweigh the aggravation of a potential slight delay.

1. In Tableau Desktop, from the **Server** menu, sign in to your Tableau server.
2. On the **Server** menu, select "Publish Data Source."

   Tableau has a series of articles on publishing data sources and workbooks.

   https://help.tableau.com/current/pro/desktop/en-us/publish_overview.htm

   Publish the Workbook to a Tableau Server or Tableau Public

   If your workbook has a connection to a data source on a Tableau server, skip to Step 2.

1. In Tableau Desktop, select the connection to your data source from the **Data** menu and select "Extract Data."
2. In Tableau Desktop, from the **Server** menu, sign in to your Tableau server.
3. On the **Server** menu, select "Publish Workbook."

5.5 Publish to Tableau Server or Tableau Public

To share your Tableau file on a Tableau server or Tableau Public, first create a data extract as outlined in *"Section 2.4 Connect to a Data Source" on page 43*. You can skip this step if your data source is already on the Tableau server. Then, in Tableau Desktop, select "Tableau Public" or "Tableau Server" from the **Server** menu. I usually review my dashboards and worksheets and "unselect" everything before saving the file.

After logging in to Tableau Public and publishing the visualization, select "My Profile" from the account icon to browse and open your visualization on Tableau Public.

1. Under *Settings*, enable "Allow Access."
2. Click the *Share* icon and copy your URL.

5.5.1 Optimize Performance

To optimize your workbook so that it opens and renders the page quickly, hide unused fields and run the optimizer on the **Server** menu. If you have "static" filters, consider changing them to context filters.

5.5.2 Row-Level Security

To restrict access to the data, use row-level security (RLS). The USERNAME() function returns the name of the user that is signed in to the Tableau server. A calculated field on the **Filters** shelf matches the user's name to each row of data.

USERNAME() = [Employee]

In Tableau Desktop, my username is lowercase, while on my Tableau server, it's in uppercase. I cast USERNAME to uppercase in my calculated field to ensure the calculation works in either environment.

UPPER(USERNAME()) = [Employee]

Tableau's online help has articles on row-level security and user functions.

https://help.tableau.com/current/server-linux/en-us/rls_options_overview.htm?_gl=1*1sct2i1*_ga*MTYzM

5.5.3 Row-Level Security with Two Connections in a Data Source

When you have connections to two different worksheets (or tables) in your data source, you can join the tables by a common field like [Employee] and then filter to a [Manager] field. I have two Excel worksheets in this example, and I create a join between the "Data" and "Managers." After you create the data source connection to an Excel workbook's worksheet, Tableau refers to the worksheets as "tables."

You cannot join two published data sources on a Tableau server. For more information, view the Tableau help or *"Section 4.7.8 Data Blends"* on page 84.

https://help.tableau.com/current/pro/desktop/en-us/joining_tables.htm

Both worksheets have an [Employee] column or field, as shown in Figures 5.8 and 5.9.

To begin, move to the **Data Source** page and add a new *Data Source* connection to the "Sales" workbook and the "Data" worksheet. The *logical layer* is shown in Figure 5.10.

Click the "Add" link in the **Connections** pane on the left to add a second connection to the "People.xlsx" workbook, as shown in Figure 5.11. Do not drag the "Managers" worksheet onto the canvas yet. First, double-click the "Data" table in Figure 5.11 to move to the *physical layer*. We looked at the *physical* and *logical layers* in Chapter 4's topic, "The Tableau Data Model."

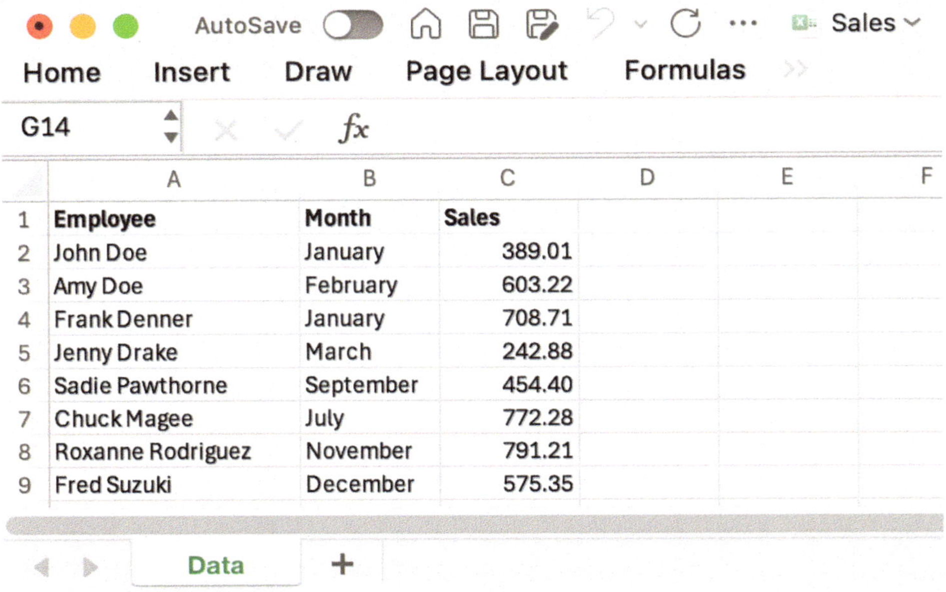

Employee	Month	Sales
John Doe	January	389.01
Amy Doe	February	603.22
Frank Denner	January	708.71
Jenny Drake	March	242.88
Sadie Pawthorne	September	454.40
Chuck Magee	July	772.28
Roxanne Rodriguez	November	791.21
Fred Suzuki	December	575.35

FIGURE 5.8
The Sales.xlsx "Data" Worksheet.

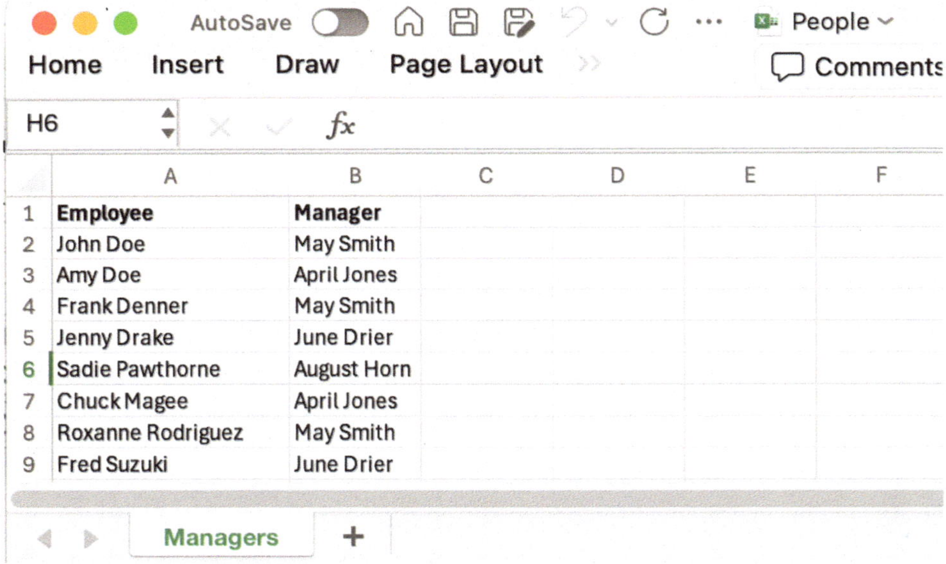

Employee	Manager
John Doe	May Smith
Amy Doe	April Jones
Frank Denner	May Smith
Jenny Drake	June Drier
Sadie Pawthorne	August Horn
Chuck Magee	April Jones
Roxanne Rodriguez	May Smith
Fred Suzuki	June Drier

FIGURE 5.9
The People.xlsx "Managers" Worksheet.

Figure 5.12 displays the *physical layer*. Drag "Managers" under the "Data" table on the canvas.

Tableau automatically creates a join between the two [Employee] fields, as shown in Figure 5.13.

Create a calculated field to compare the USERNAME() and [Manager] fields, as shown in Figure 5.14.

On a worksheet, add the new calculated field [Row-Level Security] to the **Filters** shelf and select "True." You could also check "Exclude" and choose "False," as shown in Figure 5.15.

Finally, add the calculated field to the **Filters** shelf. Because of the filter, in Figure 5.16, I see no data in the view. To save time with other views, apply the filter to "All Using This Data Source."

If you'd like to see the filtered view from the perspective of another user signed in to a Tableau server, use the "Filter as User" drop-down in the bottom right

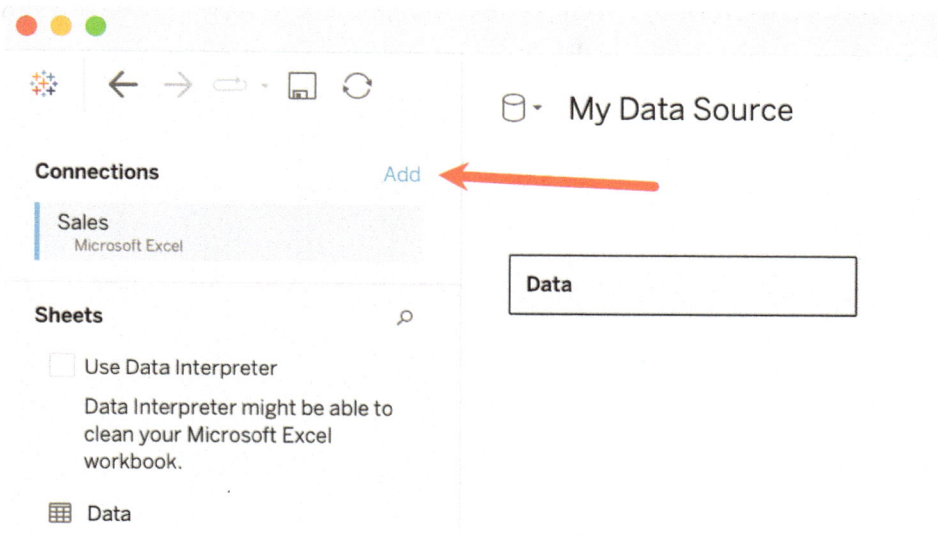

Add Another Connection to the Data Source.

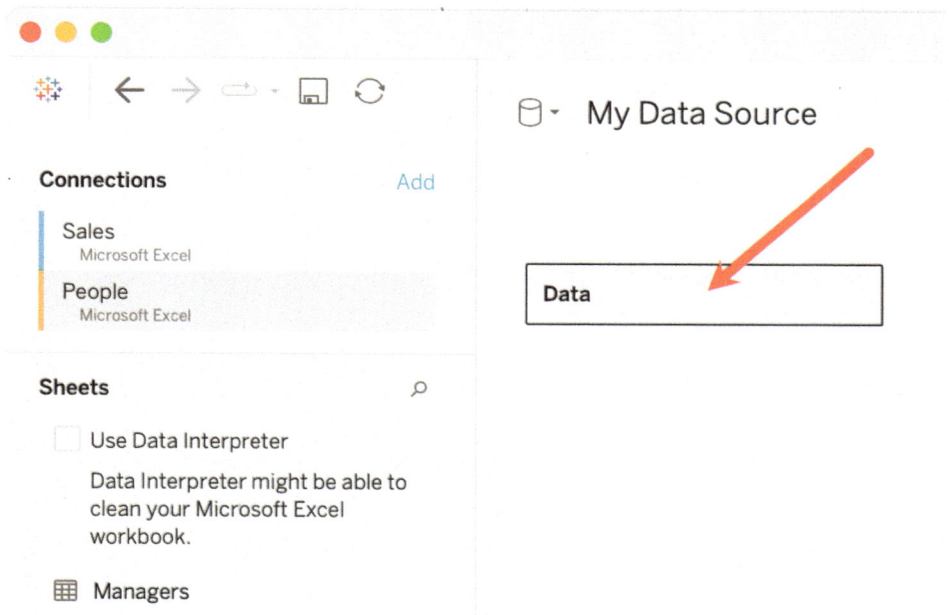

Double-click the "Data" Table.

area of the workspace to select the user's name, as shown in Figure 5.17. When you're done testing, choose "Reset Filter."

5.6 From Data to Insights

Visual analytics is both an art and a science. As a designer, you have the power to influence your audience and provide valuable insight into business

problems. Begin by gathering input from your intended audience. What questions do they want answered? What message should the visualizations show?

Develop a narrative to guide the reader from the initial questions through insights and end with decision points, opportunities, or solutions. Provide additional context where needed.

5.6.1 Start with a Question

While each situation is unique, one of these questions below may resonate with your audience.

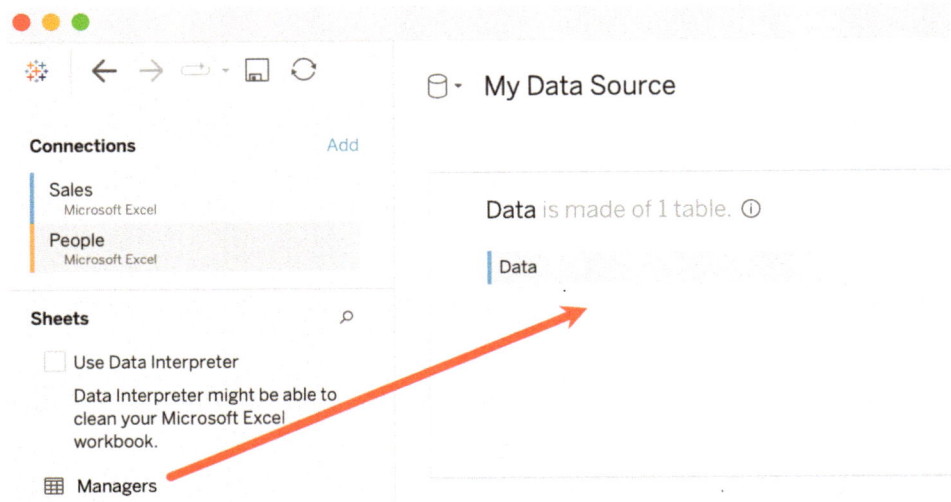

FIGURE 5.12
Drag the "Managers" Table Onto the Canvas.

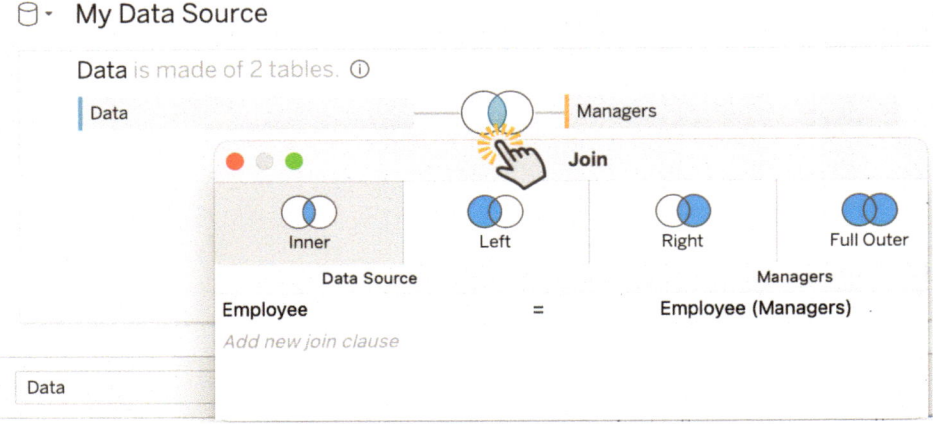

FIGURE 5.13
Click to Edit the Join.

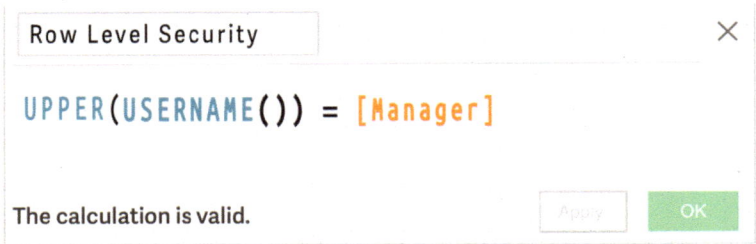

FIGURE 5.14
Row-Level Security Calculated Field.

Sometimes, data may come from a nontraditional source. For example, we're all used to spreadsheets and databases, but there is intrinsic data everywhere, although you may have to stop and look for it. For example, when discussing which Tableau topics and terms are important, I could create a word cloud chart of the top 20 words in this book.

- What are the **concerns**?
- What is the **problem**?

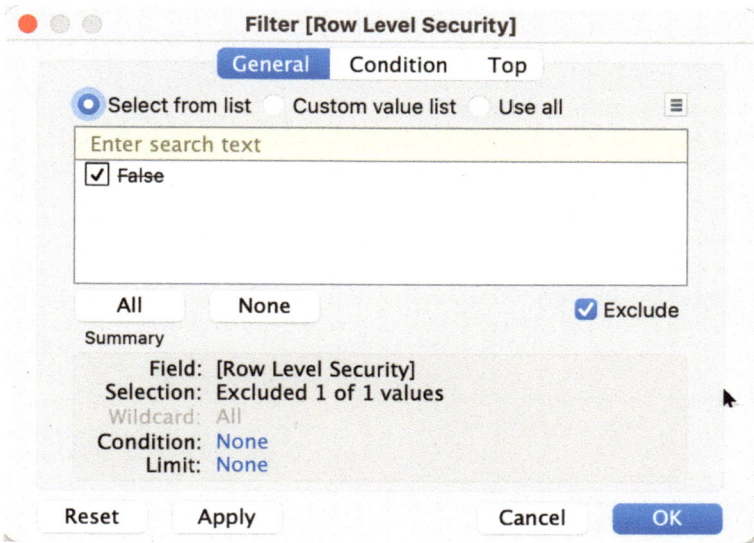

FIGURE 5.15
Filter.

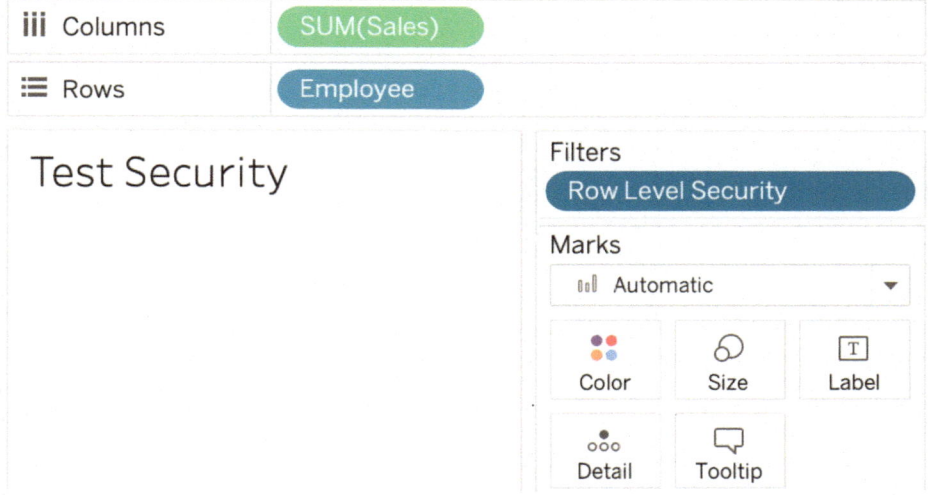

FIGURE 5.16
The Filtered View.

- How did the numbers **change over time**?
- What is the **percentage** of the total?
- What is the price **range** for most of our products?
- **What changed** (other than COVID-19) in the last five years?
- Unit costs are increasing, and we don't know why. Car repair appointments have dropped because customers are driving less. Mechanic FTEs are unchanged, causing unit costs to increase. New standards require mechanic training, decreasing productivity.

- Half of the company's expenses are **related** to real estate holdings.
- What makes one item **different** from another?
- Are there key contributing factors like economic instability or a pandemic?
- Who is affected? Does the problem affect store employees, delivery drivers, or particular corporate groups?
- Are there **trends**?
- Is there one person who consistently outranks others over three years? How do employee **rankings** compare to each other?

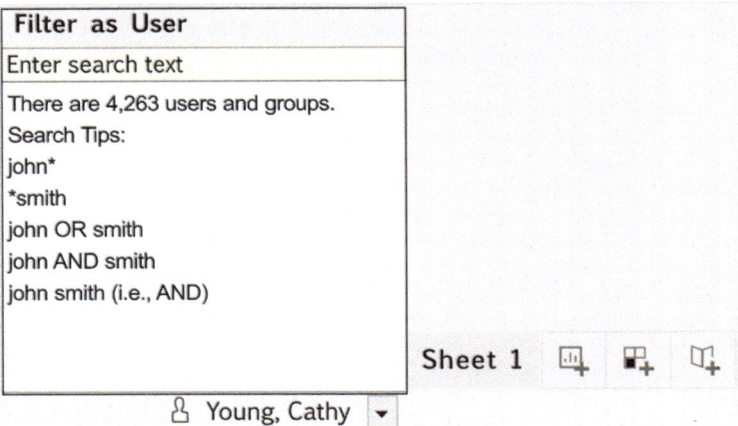

FIGURE 5.17
Filter as User.

- What are the top five accidents for older adults?
- What are the three **most profitable** and **least profitable** products?
- What are the **top five** causes of shipping delays per state?
- How have lost shipments changed over time? Which procedures reduced lost shipments? Which procedures had no impact? Which procedures cost the most to implement? How much time or money can we save by removing procedures that have no effect?
- Are we meeting **targets or goals**? What outside influences are preventing us from meeting our goals? Which sales people achieved their sales target?
- Where can we save money? What are the top expenses?
- How are the southern states performing **compared** to the other regions?
- Can you **compare** sales for two products or regions?
- What product has the most significant potential for growth or profit?
- What are the **bottom** three products? Which products cost the most to warehouse and have the smallest profit margin?
- Do the majority of delivery times fall within the accepted SLA or **range**? Has this metric improved over time?
- What is the price **range** for most of our products, and how does it compare to profitability?
- Is profitability for some products decreasing?

- Are the majority of staff meeting their goals? Which staff did not meet their goal?

5.6.2 Analyze the Data

Spend time analyzing the data. What are the key fields? What data formats are available? Is there a source of record for data you can use to clean the data? Did you gather insights from the data?

- Is there an apparent relationship between the two fields?
- Do you have fields with no data or all Null values?
- Add additional data if you need a longer timeline, more categories, or additional fields for calculations.

5.6.3 What Message Do You Want to Convey?

What solutions or answers have you uncovered? Were there insights you want to share with the audience?

- What needs to change?
- Why might there be objections to the solution?
- What are the key risks?

5.6.3.1 Example 1

To focus attention on targets, use these chart types:

- Bullet charts
- Reference lines, bands, and distributions

FIGURE 5.18
Two Charts Showing the Change in Price.

5.6.3.2 Example 2

How are the southern states performing compared to the other regions? A *group* or *set* is an excellent way to define classifications. Let's say I want a set that shows the top three states by sales. Use a dynamic set that changes as the data changes.

5.6.3.3 Example 3

What product has the greatest potential for growth or profit? When you filter to one area, does the "scale" change? For example, if you filter to technology, the profit scale (axis) changes from 1–50 to 1–350.

5.6.3.4 Example 4

This chart answers the question, "What happens if you increase the price by 10 cents?" (Figure 5.18)

5.6.3.5 Example 5

When you compare two values, like the *difference* between the current month and the previous month or the *change* in the first and last values, do you see an insight into performance? How does one value compare to all values? Can you relate parts to the whole? Use custom number formats with arrows to highlight the change. Labels at the beginning and end of the line call attention to changes.

5.6.3.6 Example 6

What are the bottom three products? A "Rank" table calculation or a calculated field can zero in on these numbers using the color property or *Shapes* on the **Marks** card.

5.6.4 Tell a Story

Develop a narrative that highlights insights. State the problem or question and then provide the solution or actionable outcome. The words used to frame the question influence the answer the audience chooses.

The pandemic is going to kill one million people. We must implement the vaccine program to save 10,000 people.

The pandemic is going to kill one million people. The health program will cost $400 million and save only 10,000 people.

Engage the audience and focus their attention with a narrative or storyboard about the problem and solution.

Past -> Present -> Future

Beginning -> Middle -> End

5.6.4.1 *Beginning*

- What is the central problem?
- Provide a high-level walkthrough of the story.
- Describe data and what it represents or means.
- Explain terminology.
- Who is involved with this work?
- Highlight your insights.

5.6.4.2 *Middle*

- What are the solutions or options?
- Give more background and details.
- What are the causes of this problem?

5.6.4.3 *End*

- Summarize your conclusions.
- What is the desired solution?
- List clear takeaways or next steps.

5.6.5 Target Your Audience

- What is a common thread on which to base your story?
- Is your audience familiar with the material?
- Should you use different terminology?
- What story beginning would get the audience's attention?
- Who will use your visualizations? Are they executives, managers, or regular employees?

5.7 Designing a Visualization

One principle of visual hierarchy is to position the most important information in the top left corner of the page. The Gestalt Principles of Design is a fascinating look at how humans perceive data, and it asserts that we notice preattentive attributes before we consciously focus on a chart. This principle means that before we "pay attention" to something, our brain does "preattentive processing" without conscious thought. Tableau has an interesting article on preattentive attributes like size, shape, and color.

5.7.1 Preattentive Attributes

- Color best draws attention, and you can tweak with saturation
- Size
- Bold is better than italic
- Shapes

5.7.2 Best Practices

- Refrain from using too many colors. Do not reuse colors or use similar colors.
- More than three visualizations on a dashboard are too many. Start with a high-level chart and then drill down into smaller charts. Mix detailed or expert charts with high-level charts.
- Avoid clutter.
- Reduce the number of fields in one visualization. If necessary, split the data into small charts.
- Start numerical axes at zero.
- Time data should flow from left to right and be **continuous**. There should be no gaps in months, days, etc.
- Turn a column (vertical) chart into a bar chart (horizontal).
- Emphasize important data and call attention to cells or values.

5.7.3 Review Your Visualizations

Don't look at the chart for a while and then look at it with fresh eyes.

- Does your title explain the question and your conclusion?
- Do you use consistent colors and formatting?
- Should I sort the bar chart?
- Can I use shape and color to highlight one or several values?

- Would the chart benefit from annotations or mark labels?
- Does the chart need a trend line or reference line?
- Are the tooltips relevant and formatted properly?
- Should you add highlighting, shading, row dividers, or column dividers?
- Would my audience like to drill down with a hierarchy from region to state to city?
- Would it make sense to add symbols or "% change" at the top of the bars?
- Do the chart or dashboard titles make sense and follow a logical path or timeline?
- Can you change axis labels from 1,000,000 to 1M or match axis colors to mark (field) colors?
- Should you add custom-colored shapes to create a color/shape legend or create a coordinated color legend from values?
- Is each chart relevant to the story?
- If printed, does it fit on the page?
- Can you remove or add anything?

5.7.4 Audience Feedback

Live presentations present the opportunity to garner audience feedback.

- What is the first thing you noticed when looking at this chart?
- Were there times you felt lost or confused?
- Did you hear something you thought was interesting or important?
- Did questions occur to you?
- Did you have objections during the presentation?
- Did you understand the visualization?
- Ask the reviewer if anything caught their eye as you were explaining the visualization.

How will the audience use the charts or dashboards? Can you add a story with instructions about goals or guidance interpreting the chart? If users are new to Tableau server, should you add dashboards with help on common tasks?

6

Storytelling with Charts

In this topic, we discuss

Blend Measures into a Single Axis
Dual-Axes Charts
A Small Multiples View
Donut Chart
Stacked Bar Chart

In this chapter, we focus on <u>multiple-measure charts</u>. We'll examine dual-axes charts with two separate axes and blended axes with only one axis. You can blend two measures to share the same axis in the same pane. Blending is best for measures with similar scales; for example, both scales fall between zero and one million. Blending measures add [Measured Names] to the **Filters** shelf and [Measured Values] to the **Rows** or **Columns** shelf, as shown in the example "Stacked Bar Chart" later in this chapter. That example also has [Measure Names] on the *Color* tile of the **Marks** card. In contrast, a "Small Multiples" view has multiple panes representing two or more measures or dimensions.

Dual-axes charts have two or more measures with individual axes in the same pane. When dual-axes charts have different mark types, such as a line and bar, they are called "combination charts." When you synchronize the axes on dual-axes charts, Tableau hides one axis. When there are two or more measure fields on the **Rows** shelf or **Columns** shelf, each measure field has its own layer on the **Marks** card, as shown in Figure 6.1. Often, charts use a "placeholder" or "dummy" field, where the field value does not matter. Instead, the additional layer on the **Marks** card is the important feature.

In Figure 6.1, I created two placeholder fields with the simple expression **MIN(1)**. I named the fields Layer 1 and Layer 2. To add a name for placeholder fields, begin the calculation with *//comment*, press Shift + Enter, and type Min(1). Now, I have two layers on the **Marks** card, each with separate properties for the type of marks (bar, line, etc.) or color, size, shape, label, detail, etc. Therefore, instead of six properties, I have 12. "*Section 7.1 Marks Card: Tiles*" *on page 116* examines the **Marks** card in more detail.

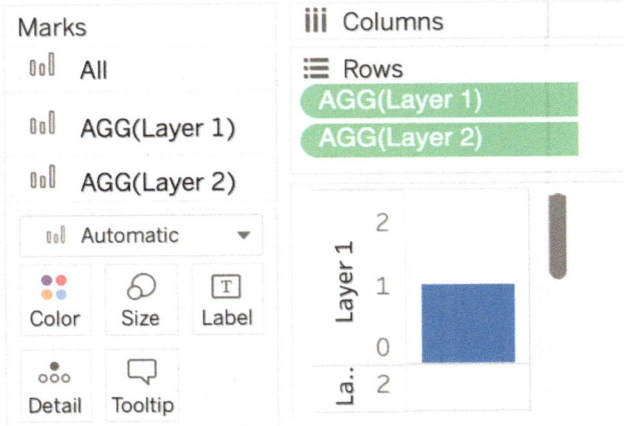

FIGURE 6.1
Layers on the Marks card.

6.1 Blend Measures into a Single Axis

To create a blended chart, <u>blend two measure fields</u> so that they share the same axis. With blended charts, all measure fields are on the **Measure Values** shelf, and the [Measure Values] field replaces the measure fields on the **Rows** or **Columns** shelf. A blended axis chart is ideal in these cases:

- You only want a single mark type.
- You want 2+ measure fields on the **Measure Values** shelf.
- The visualization has a single axis.

Add [Sales] to the **Rows** shelf to create a blended axis chart. Drag [Profit] onto the view and drop it at the vertical [Sales] axis. Tableau moves both [Profit] and [Sales] onto a new **Measure Values** shelf under the **Marks** card and also changes the two fields [Sales] and [Profit] on the **Rows** shelf to the [Measure Values] field. There is still one axis, and Tableau automatically added the generated field "Measure Names" to *Color* on the **Marks** card, as shown in Figure 6.2.

DOI: 10.1201/9781003566458-7

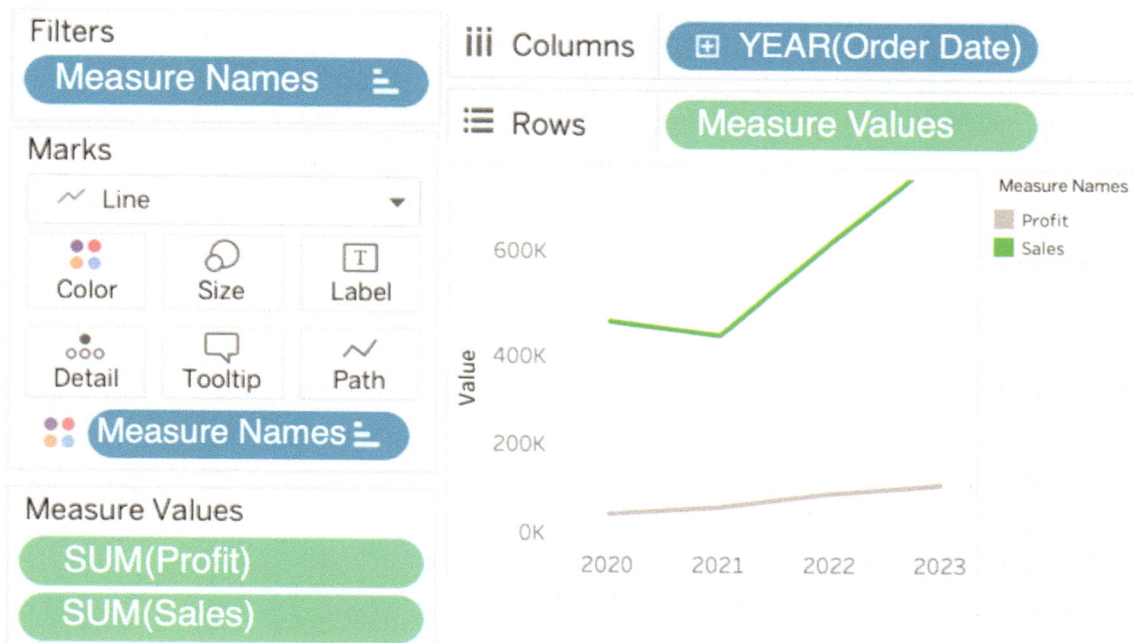

FIGURE 6.2
Blended chart.

Tableau Public file:

> https://public.tableau.com/views/blendedaxis_
> 17111206719300/Dashboard1?:language=
> en-US&publish=yes&:sid=&:display_count=
> n&:origin=viz_share_link

6.2 Dual-Axes Charts

Charts with two measures with separate ranges or independent axes layered on top of each other are "Dual-axes" charts. Dual-axes charts with multiple mark types, such as a bar and line, are called "Combination Charts." For example, chart one has sales from 0 to 500 in North America, and chart two's sales in South America range from 0 to 2,000. Two measure fields on the **Rows** or the **Columns** shelf create a dual-axes chart, where the two measure fields combine to create a "super bubble."

The next example is a **Dual-axes** chart with "Line" and "Area" marks from the [Sales] and [Profit] fields. The chart is also a combination chart because "Sales" is an "Area" chart, and "Profit" is a "Line" chart, corresponding to an "Area" mark and a "Line" mark on the **Marks** card.

1. Drag [Sales] to the **Rows** shelf. The view shows a blue bar.

2. Change the **Mark type** to "Area" using the drop-down arrow on the **Marks** card. The view now displays a vertical line instead of a vertical bar. The view looks as expected, although it does look odd (Figure 6.3).

If you do not want the default aggregation *SUM*, right-click the field in the **Data** pane and drag the field onto the view to see the **Drop Field Menu** with other aggregation choices. Alternatively, you could click the field on the **Rows** shelf to open the field's *context menu* and change the aggregation. We look at aggregation in detail in *"Section 11.4 Aggregation and Level of Detail" on page 227*.

3. Drag [Profit] to the right of the [Sales] field on the **Rows** shelf.

4. To create a dual-axes chart, click the drop-down arrow on the [Profit] field and select "Dual-axes." This option is only available on the second field on the right side of the **Rows** shelf. The green background for both fields changes to a "super bubble," as shown below, indicating that this is now a dual-axes chart (Figure 6.4).

The two fields on the **Rows** shelf correspond to two *mark layers* on the **Marks** card. Right now, both marks are "Area" marks. There are three shelves on the **Marks** card. The two

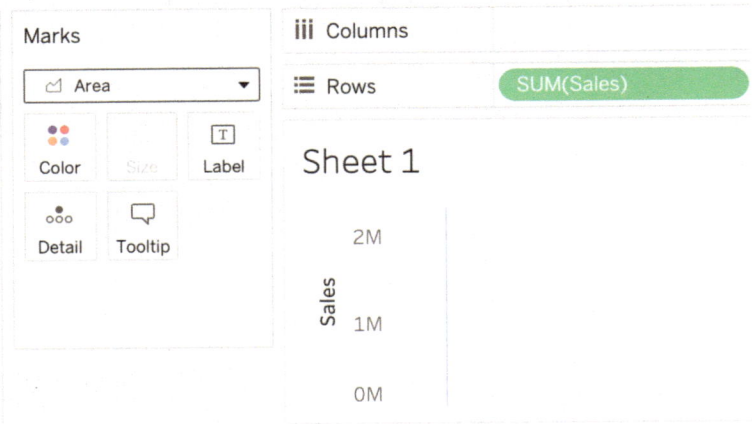

FIGURE 6.3
The mark type is the Area.

FIGURE 6.4
A super bubble of two measure fields.

fields each have a layer on the **Marks** card, and there is a third layer, "All."

- All
- Sum (Sales)
- Sum (Profit)

Under the heading "Marks" in the top-left corner of the **Marks** card, the "All" layer indicates you are editing all marks. When the "All" layer is selected, the drop-down **mark type** is "Multiple," as shown below. Changes to "All" properties (like color or tooltip) affect both layers (Figure 6.5).

Two field mark layers appear stacked at the bottom of the **Marks** card. When you click on either the **Sum(Sales)** or the **Sum(Profit)** layer, changes apply only to that mark layer.

5. Drag the generated field **Measure Names** from the **Data** pane to the *Color* tile on the **Marks** card to add a <u>Color Legend</u> to the view.

6. Drag [Order Date] to the **Columns** shelf and change the aggregation to "Month" for the *date value*. You can also use the plus symbol to drill down into the date values. The [Order Date] field is in the top area of the **Data** pane because it is a dimension. A line divides dimensions at the top from measures below

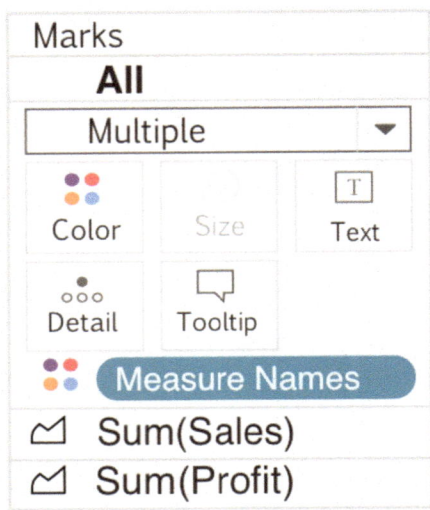

FIGURE 6.5
The "All" Layer in the Marks Card.

the line. The date field is **green**, indicating that the *date value* is a **continuous** dimension. For more information on date values, see *"Section 9.3 Date Values"* on page 196 (Figure 6.6).

7. I want the **SUM(Sales)** layer to be a "Line" mark, so I change the "Sales" mark type to "Line." Click to select the **Sum(Sales)** layer in the **Marks** card. The layer **Sum(Sales)** is bold, indicating the selected layer. From the drop-down menu, change the mark type to "Line," as shown in (Figure 6.7).

When you select the layer **Sum(Profit)**, the "Path" tool disappears because the **Sum(Profit)** layer is an "Area" mark.

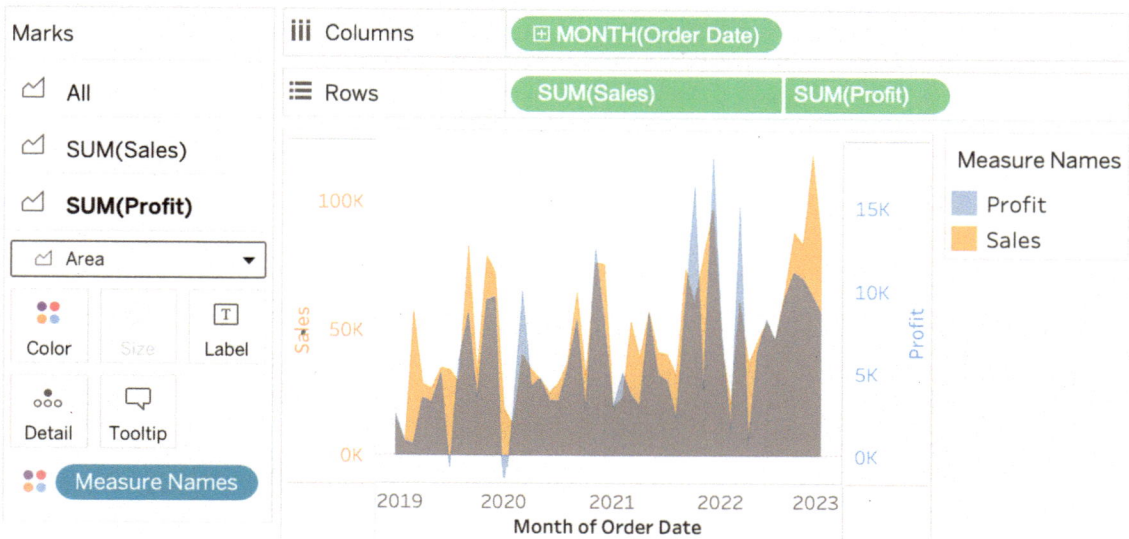

FIGURE 6.6
The worksheet with a continuous measure date.

FIGURE 6.7
The Path tool in the Marks card.

The **Marks** card now has a *Path* tool to the right of the *Tooltip* tile (Figure 6.7).

8. Right-click the **Profit** axis in the view and choose "Synchronize Axis" to create the new dual-combination chart in (Figures 6.8).

It synchronizes the axis, as shown in *"Section 10.2.1 Pareto Chart With a Running Total and Percent of Total Table Calculation" on page 210*.

6.3 Multiple Charts in One View

As shown in Figure 6.10, adding two measure fields to a chart creates two individual axes with independent scales and two panes from the "small multiples" view. In *"Section 3.6.3 Sets" on page 67*, I used a set based on the dimension [Fruit] to create two charts in the same view.

Tableau Public file:

> https://public.tableau.com/views/4_1_Dual_ Axes_Area_Line/MultipleChartsOnePane?: language=en-US&publish=yes&:sid=&: display_count=n&:origin=viz_share_link

6.4 A Small Multiples View

In this example, my view has nine values for [Fruit], and I want to break the chart into nine separate panes. This type of visualization is a "Small Multiples" view. A placeholder field adds a layer for headings. Because I set mark opacity to 0% in Step 7, the layer has no visible marks, only labels. I create two calculated fields for [Row Index] and [Column Index]. The INDEX() function is a table calculation, and both fields have the "Compute Using" set to the [Fruit] field. **Chapter 10** has more information on

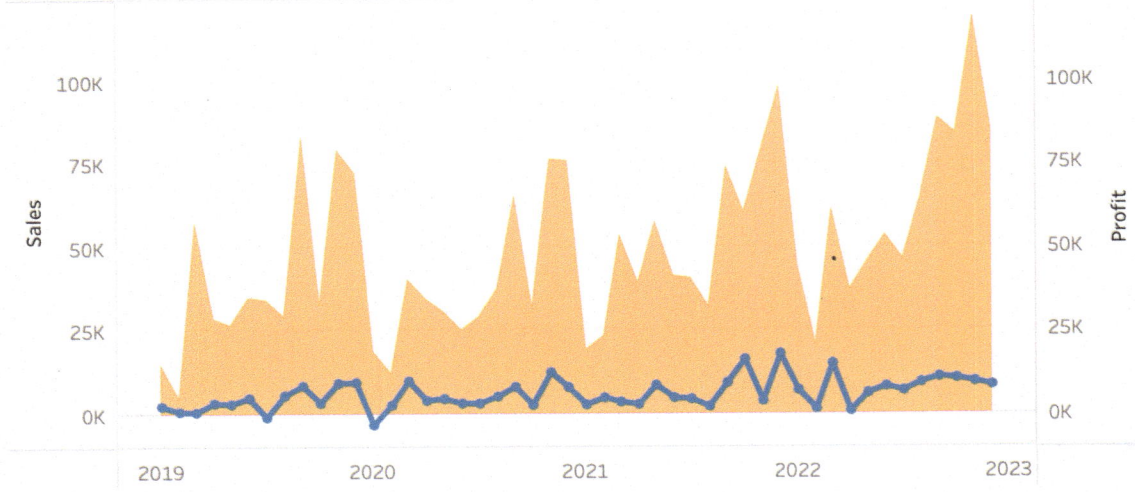

FIGURE 6.8
A dual-axis chart.

FIGURE 6.9
Tip: Another way to add the second field to the view is to drag it onto the canvas on the opposite side of the first axis until a black dashed line appears. When you drop the field, Tableau creates the super bubble.

table calculations in *"Section 10.1 Table Calculation Scope" on page 209*. *"Section 8.14 Hover to Choose a Field for Sorting" on page 181* has three panes in one view. The link to the Tableau Public file is at the end of the exercise, along with a checklist of the elements and settings in the example.

6.4.1 Preview – The Finished Chart

The [Sales Ranges] field adds headers along the bottom of the chart (Figure 6.11).

6.4.2 Create the Visualization

1. Add a dimension field to the **Columns** shelf and a measure field to the **Rows** shelf. In this example, I have a dimension field called [Sales Ranges] and a measure field called [Sales].

2. Create the two index fields as outlined at the end of the example. Create the [Sales Ranges] field with an expression similar to this syntax.

   If [**Sales**] >= 10 then "Very Profitable" elseif [**Sales**] <100 and [**Sales**] > 7 then

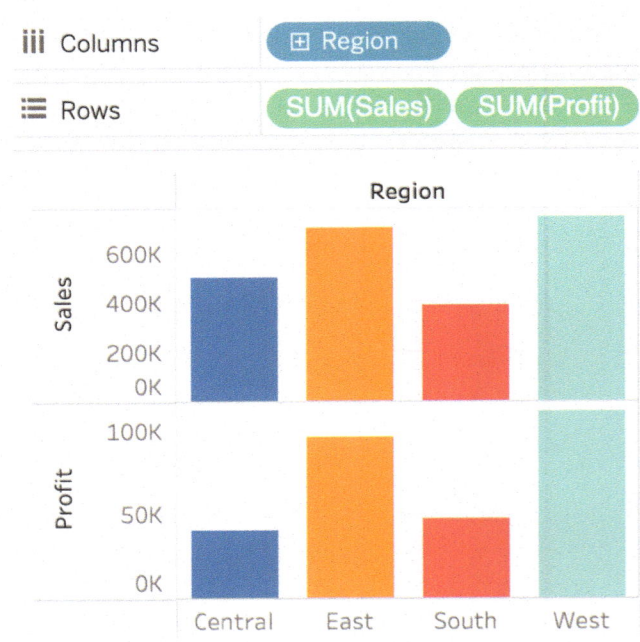

FIGURE 6.10
Multiple charts in one pane.

"Profitable" elseif [**Sales**] <100 and [**Sales**] > 4 then "Not bad" else "Why bother" end

If you wonder why [**Sales**] has an extra space, my original table was called "Sales"; Tableau does not allow two objects with the same name.

3. Add the [Column Index] field to the **Columns** shelf as the first field and the [Row Index] field

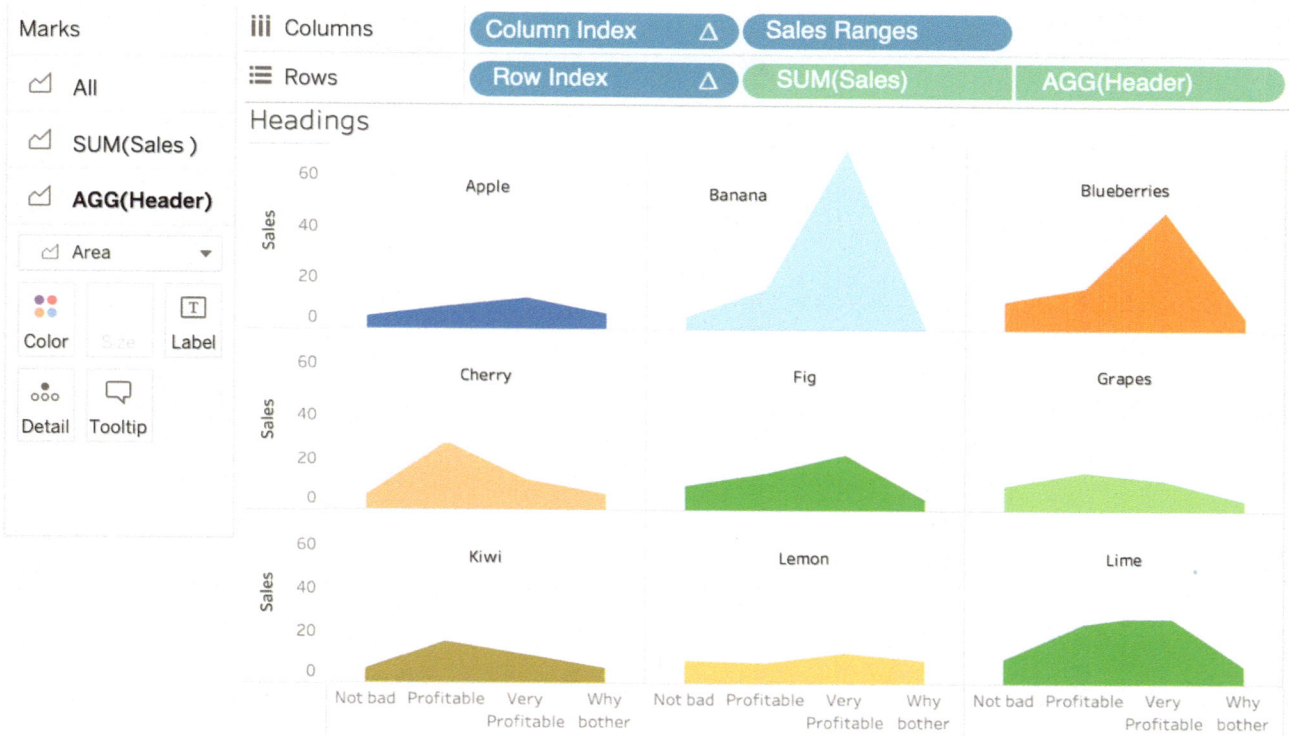

FIGURE 6.11
A small multiples view.

to the **Rows** shelf as the first field. The chart looks odd because we have not set the "Compute Using" option to the [Fruit] field (Figure 6.12).

4. Right-click the [Column Index] field on the **Columns** shelf to open the field's *context menu*. Select "Compute Using" and choose the [Fruit] field.

5. Repeat Step 4 for the [Row Index] field.

6. To add "headings" to the nine charts, I need a second layer or dual axis to add the [Fruit] field to the *Label* tile on the **Marks** card. Create a placeholder field on the **Rows** shelf with a MIN(1) value.

   In this example, I named the field [Header]. If you want to "name" the layer, begin the calculation with *//comment*, press Shift + Enter, and type *Min(1)*.

   Right-click the [Header] field on the **Rows** shelf to open the field's *context menu* and check "Dual-axes." (Figure 6.13)

7. The **Marks** card now has two layers – **SUM(Sales)** and **AGG(Header)**. Select the **AGG(Header)** layer and click the *Color* tile to change the *Opacity* to 0%, removing all visible marks from the view.

8. Remove any fields from the **Marks** card on this **AGG(Header)** layer. Add the [Fruit] field to

the *Label* tile on the **Marks** card. Now, there are labels on each of the nine charts (Figure 6.14).

9. Right-click the "Header" vertical y-axis on the right side of the view and select "Edit Axis," as shown in Step 8. The **Edit Axis** dialog window opens. In the "Range" section of the **Edit Axis** window shown below, select "Fixed" and change *Fixed start* and *Fixed end* to 0 to remove the scaling. After the change, the labels are near the top of the charts (Figure 6.15).

10. Right-click the "Header" y-axis again on the right side of the view and uncheck "Show Header." Right-click the [Row Index] vertical y-axis on the left side of the view and uncheck "Show Header."

    Alternatively, you could uncheck "Show Header" for both index fields. Right-click the field [Column Index] on the **Columns** shelf and uncheck "Show Header" in the field's *context menu*. Repeat for the [Rows Index] field on the **Rows** shelf.

11. Edit the "Column Index" horizontal x-axis at the top of the view and uncheck "Show Header."

12. The "Label" position is slightly over the area mark in the "Banana" chart. Click to select the "Banana" label and then drag the label slightly to the left.

FIGURE 6.12
The chart with bow index fields.

FIGURE 6.13
The Rows and Columns shelf.

13. Another way to position the headings closer to the top of each chart is to change the value on the [Header] field to *Min(10)* and then use "Edit Axis" to set the range to *Fixed start* 0 and *Fixed end* 1.

6.4.2.1 Validate and Test

As outlined in *"Section 5.3.4 Validate and Test" on page 91*, validate calculations or chart aggregations with a temporary chart. To check values, add fields to *Text* or *Tooltip* tiles on the **Marks** card, use the **Summary** card, or view the data.

Tableau Public file:

https://public.tableau.com/views/9chart son1views1069/9ChartsDashboard?:language= en-US&:sid=&:display_count=n&:origin= viz_share_link

6.4.3 Fields

6.4.3.1 Row Index

The calculated field [Row Index] expression uses the table calculation function INDEX() along with the DIV() function. [Row Index] is the first field on the **Rows** shelf (Figure 6.16).

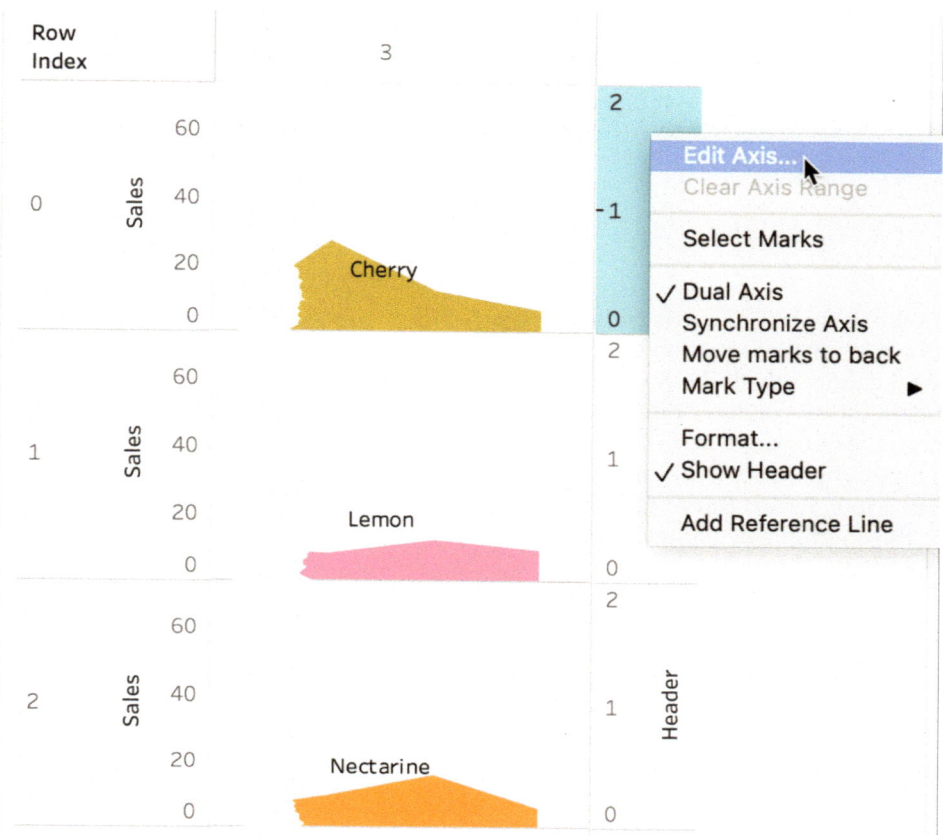

FIGURE 6.14
Edit the top-right axis.

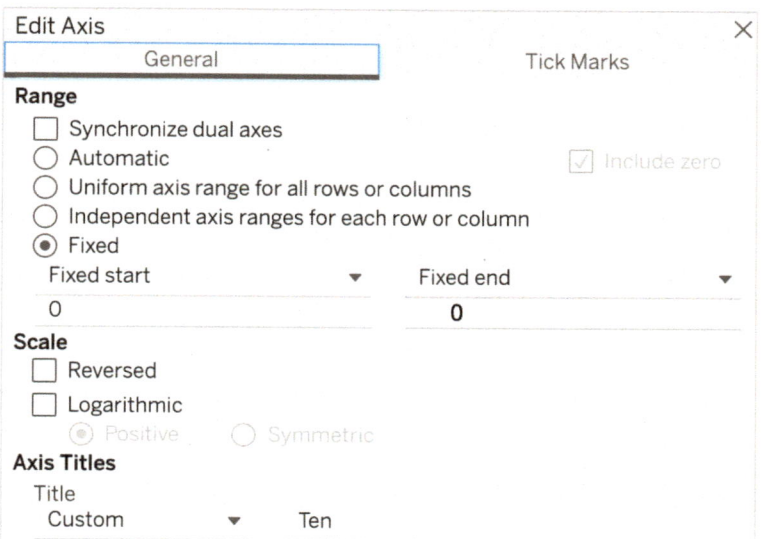

FIGURE 6.15
The **Edit Axis** dialog box.

FIGURE 6.16
Row Index calculated field.

Let's break down the [Row Index] equation to see what Tableau does. Looking at the equation's **INDEX() -1** part, the negative -1 changes the INDEX values to zero-based numbering. Let's say you have nine rows of data where the row index values are 1 to 9. The expression **INDEX() -1** changes these index numbers to zero-based values from 0 to 8. I want three columns of data for this chart, so the column calculation is divided by three. The following table shows the values.

	Row Index field		
Row	**Index()**	**After -1**	**Div() by 3**
1	1	0	0
2	2	1	0
3	3	2	0
4	4	3	1
5	5	4	1
6	6	5	1
7	7	6	2
8	8	7	2
9	9	8	2

[Row Index] is on the **Rows** shelf, and "Compute Using" is set to the [Fruit] field (Figure 6.17).

6.4.3.2 Column Index

The [Column Index] calculated field is similar to the [Row Index] field in that it also uses the INDEX() function. [Column Index] is the first field on the **Columns** shelf, and "Compute Using" is set to the [Fruit] field. This equation also uses the Modulo % operator to divide by three and return the remainder (Figure 6.18).

	Column Index field		
Row	**Index()**	**After -1**	**Modulo % 3 – Remainder**
1	1	0	0
2	2	1	1
3	3	2	2
4	4	3	0
5	5	4	1

6	6	5	2
7	7	6	0
8	8	7	1
9	9	8	2

I added the two new index fields to a new sheet to test whether the calculated fields work correctly. In the following example, the two index fields have the values I expect, so I am ready to use them in my view (Figure 6.19).

6.4.3.3 SUM(Sales)

The measure field [Sales] is the first measure field on the **Rows** shelf, creating a layer called **SUM(Sales)** on the **Marks** card.

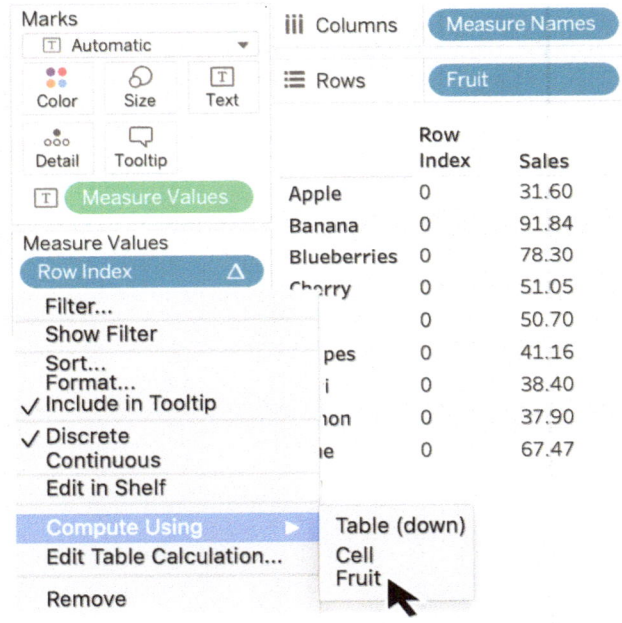

FIGURE 6.17
Compute using option.

FIGURE 6.18
Column index.

	Row Index along Table (Down)	Sales	Column Index along Table (Down)
Apple	0	31.60	0
Banana	0	91.84	1
Blueberries	0	78.30	2
Cherry	1	51.05	0
Fig	1	50.70	1
Grapes	1	41.16	2
Kiwi	2	38.40	0
Lemon	2	37.90	1
Lime	2	67.47	2

FIGURE 6.19
Row and Column indices.

6.4.3.4 The Placeholder Field [Header]

The [Header] placeholder field calculation is MIN(1), and I named the field "Header." Begin the calculation with *//Header*, press Shift + Enter, and type Min(1). [Header] is the second measure field on the **Rows** shelf. Right-click it to open its *context menu* and check "Dual-axes." This new field creates a second layer on the **Marks** card called **AGG(Header)**.

6.4.3.5 Sales Ranges

[Sales Ranges] is the second field on the **Columns** shelf.

6.4.3.6 Fruit

The [Fruit] field is on the *Color* tile on the **SUM(Sales)** layer of the **Marks** card (Figure 6.20).

[Fruit] is also on the *Label* tile on the **AGG(Header)** layer of the **Marks** card. Because marks are transparent on this layer, only the text "Labels" is shown in the view. In this case, the labels are the [Fruit] values or members (Figure 6.21).

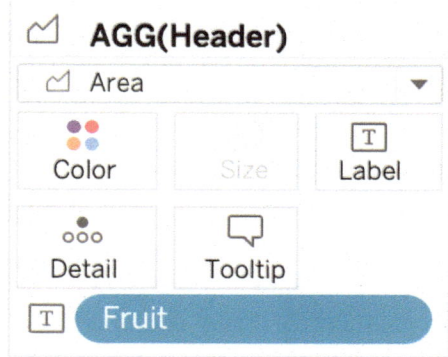

FIGURE 6.21
Label tile.

6.4.3.7 Marks Card

This dual-axis chart has the [Sales] field with a **SUM(Sales)** layer. The mark type is "Area." The placeholder field [Header] creates a second layer called **AGG(Header)** on the **Marks** card. I use the **AGG(Header)** layer for labels.

6.4.3.8 AGG(Header)

Because I added a placeholder field called [Header] to the **Rows** shelf, the **Marks** card has a layer called **AGG(Header)**. The mark type is "Area." The *Color* tile's *Opacity* is 0%; the area marks for this layer are transparent.

6.4.3.9 SUM(Sales)

The mark type on the **SUM(Sales)** layer is "Area."

6.4.3.10 Mark Type

Select "Area" from the drop-down on the **Marks** card for both layers.

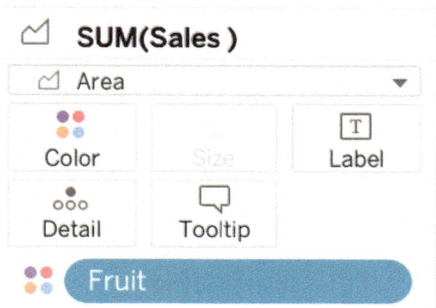

FIGURE 6.20
Color tile.

6.5 Donut Chart

A donut chart is created with two "Pie" charts and two **continuous** measure fields. The two fields create two layers, and both are a "Pie" mark. One pie chart mark is a small white circle that appears to be inside the colored pie chart. The colored pie chart shows the region sales and the white pie chart shows the total sales. In this example, I want to see the percentage of "Furniture" sales compared to "Overall" sales.

Tableau Public file:

> https://public.tableau.com/views/Donut
> Charts1042/DonutChart?:language=en-US&
> publish=yes&:display_count=n&:origin=
> viz_share_link

6.5.1 Preview – The Finished Chart

The two placeholder measure fields, [Outside Ring] and [Inside Circle], are on the **Rows** shelf, as shown in the following image (Figure 6.22).

6.5.2 Create the Visualization

1. Add two placeholder calculated fields to the view. I name the calculated fields to make identifying each layer easier.

   Double-click on the **Rows** shelf and type "//Outside Ring" followed by *Shift + Enter*. Then, type "Min(1)" and Enter.

   Tableau displays a new field on the **Rows** shelf, [AGG(Outside Ring)] (Figure 6.23).

FIGURE 6.23
The Outside Ring layer.

2. Repeat step one to create another placeholder "Min(1)" field named [Inside Circle]. There are two layers on the **Marks** card, as shown below. To make changes that affect both layers, select the "All" layer. To change a particular layer, click the layer name. **AGG(Inside Circle)** is bold in this example because I selected that layer (Figure 6.24).

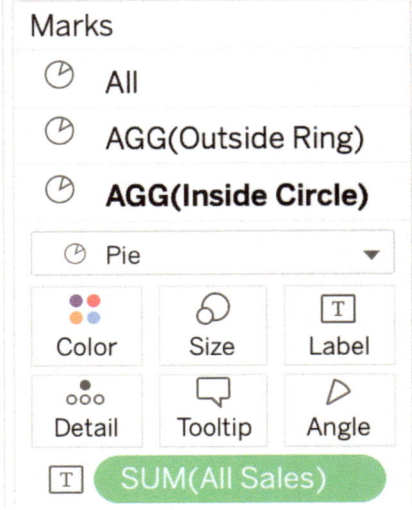

FIGURE 6.24
The Inside Circle layer.

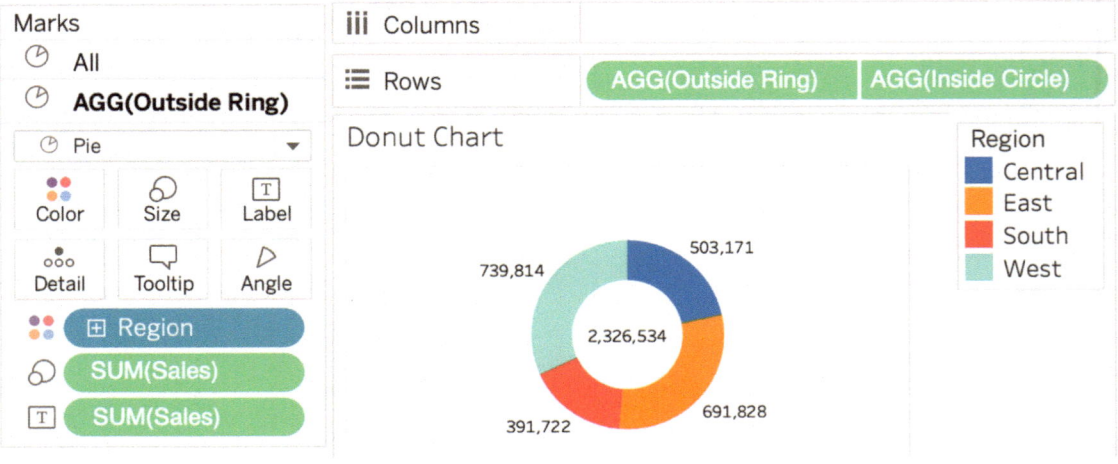

FIGURE 6.22
The Donut chart.

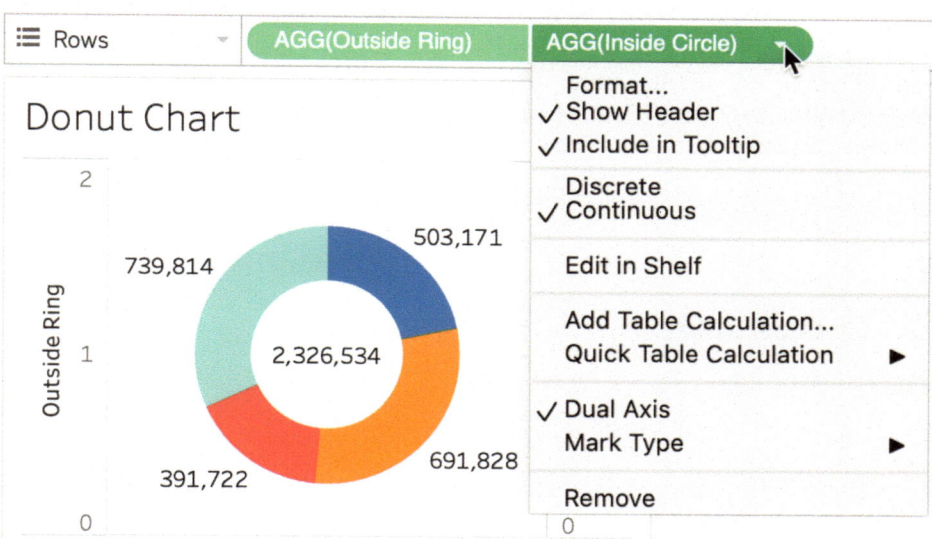

FIGURE 6.25
The dual-axis setting.

3. Select the second calculated field on the right side of the **Rows** shelf, [AGG(Inside Circle)]. Click the drop-down arrow to open the field's *context menu* and choose "Dual Axis." The "Dual Axis" option is only available on the *context menu* for the second field on the right side of the **Rows** shelf. The green background for both fields changes to a "super bubble," indicating that this is now a dual-axes chart (Figure 6.25).

4. From the toolbar at the top of the workspace, change "Fit" to "Entire View." (Figure 6.26)

5. In the **Marks** card, use the drop-down arrow on each layer to set the **Mark type** to "Pie."

6. Select the **AGG(Outside Ring)** layer on the **Marks** card. Add the **continuous** measure field [Sales] to the *Size* and *Text tiles* on the **Marks** card. Add the dimension field [Region] to the *Color* tile (Figure 6.27).

   To display the **Color Legend**, on the **Analysis** menu, choose "Legends" to toggle the **Color Legend Control** display. We look at LOD calculations in *"Section 11.12 Level of Detail Expressions" on page 238*.

7. Create a new calculated field called [All Sales] with a Fixed LOD for the sum of [Sales], as shown below (Figure 6.28).

FIGURE 6.27
The Size tile.

8. Select the **AGG(Inside Circle)** layer and add the new calculated field [All Sales] to *Text* on the **Marks** card.

FIGURE 6.26
Fit entire view.

FIGURE 6.28
The calculated field all sales.

9. In the **Marks** card, select the **AGG(Inside Circle)** layer and adjust the size so the inside pie (the white circle) is smaller than the outside pie (the colored ring). Click the *Color* tile on the **Marks** card and change the color to *white* (Figure 6.29).

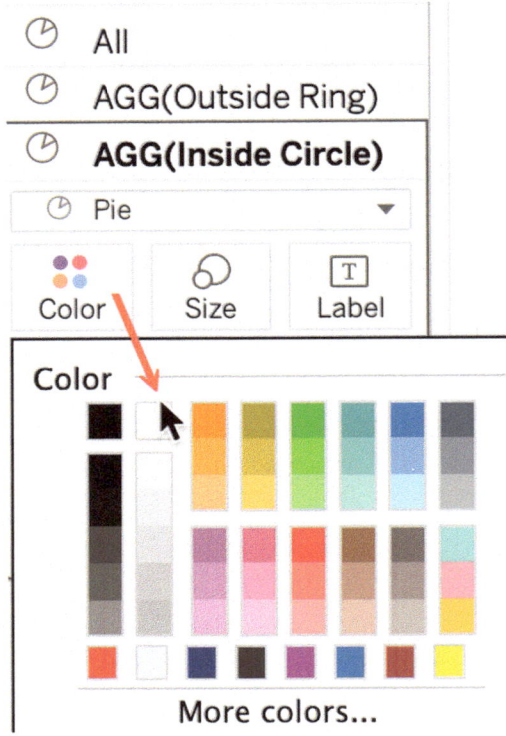

FIGURE 6.29
The color tile options.

6.6 Stacked Bar Chart

A Stacked Bar chart is an extension of a blended axis chart with two or more measures in the same pane. Continuing with the first chart at the beginning of this chapter:

[Order Date] is on the **Columns** shelf.

The [Measure Values] field is on the **Rows** shelf.

The [SUM(Sales)] and [SUM(Profit)] fields are on the **Measure Values** shelf.

1. Change the **Mark type** to "Bar." (Figure 6.30)

2. If you want [Profit] to be at the bottom of the bars, on the **Analysis** menu under "Stack Marks," select "Off." (Figures 6.31)

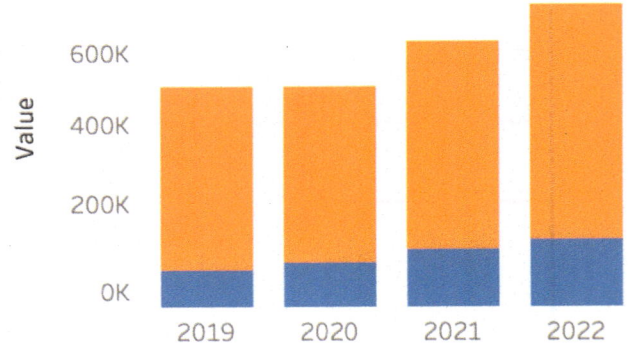

FIGURE 6.31
The stacked bar with stacked marks off.

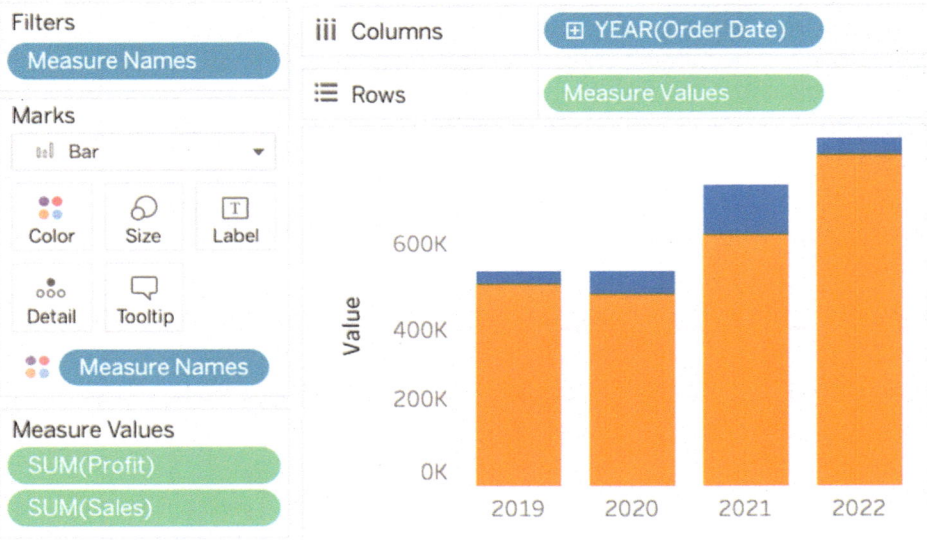

FIGURE 6.30
The stacked bar with two measure fields.

FIGURE 6.32

Tip: *I usually review my dashboards and worksheets and "unselect" objects before saving the file.*

After logging in to Tableau Public and publishing the visualization, select "My Profile" from the account icon to browse and open your visualization on Tableau Public.

1. Under *Settings*, enable "Allow Access."
2. Click the *Share* icon and copy your URL.

7

Visual Details

In addition to the shelves we looked at in **Chapter 1**, you can drag fields onto tiles on the **Marks** card to add colors, sizing, shapes, and more. The **Marks** card controls the *mark type* and *properties*. Depending on the kind of mark selected, different property tiles are displayed. Tableau adds the corresponding controls and legends to the view as you add fields to tiles on the **Marks** card, and it encodes chart marks with color, text, shapes, and other properties. You can use fields more than once. For example, the same field might be on the **Columns** shelf, the **Filters** shelf, and the *Color* tile and *Text* tile on the **Marks** card.

A *Tooltip* appears when users move their mouse over marks in the view. With the *Tooltip* tile, you can choose tooltip content and format text, add field data, URL links, other charts, and more. With Tableau Desktop or Tableau server, users can interact with a view and display a "tooltip" as they move their mouse over a data point.

7.1 Marks Card: Tiles

The property tiles include Angle, Color, Size, Text, Detail, Path, Shape, Tooltip, and more (Figure 7.1–7.9). Different tools are available (or grayed out) depending on the "type of mark" selected in the drop-down. For example, the **Pie** mark type includes the "Angle" tool. To configure the property *Color*, click on the *Color* tile. Click on any of the tiles to configure that property.

The properties apply to charts even when no field exists on that tile. For example, the *Color* tile and *Size* tile settings can change the default color or size of bars. *"Section 14.16 Horizontal Radial Buttons to Change Filters" on page 323* changes the default shape color to black on a shape chart. Later in this chapter, the topic, "Default Color," changes the default color to orange.

In Figure 7.10, I dragged three fields onto different tools or properties on the **Marks Card**. A small icon with four colored circles to the left of the field [Segment] indicates that this field is on the *Color* tile. The [Quantity] field is on the *Size* property, and the icon is two circles. The [Region] field is on the *Shape* tile. Notice the plus sign to the left of the [Region] field name, indicating that the field is part of a **Hierarchy** of related fields.

FIGURE 7.1
Angle.

FIGURE 7.2
Color.

FIGURE 7.3
Detail.

FIGURE 7.4
Label.

FIGURE 7.5
Path.

DOI: 10.1201/9781003566458-8

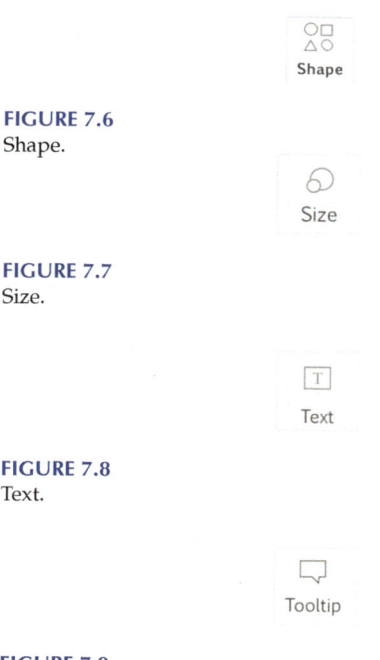

FIGURE 7.6
Shape.

FIGURE 7.7
Size.

FIGURE 7.8
Text.

FIGURE 7.9
Tooltip.

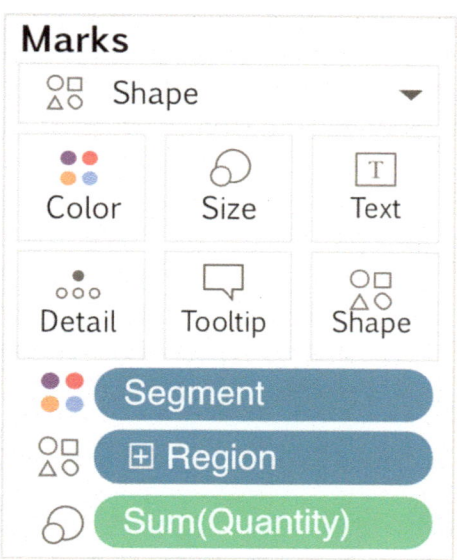

FIGURE 7.10
Color, shape, and size.

7.2 Types of Marks

The type of mark establishes the kind of chart, such as a text table, bar chart, line chart, or shape. Figure 7.10 shows a *Shape* tile because the **Mark** type is **Shape**. There is an *Angle* tile when the **Mark** type is a **Pie** chart. A *Path* tile is added to the **Marks** card for a line chart, as shown in Figure 7.11. To change the mark

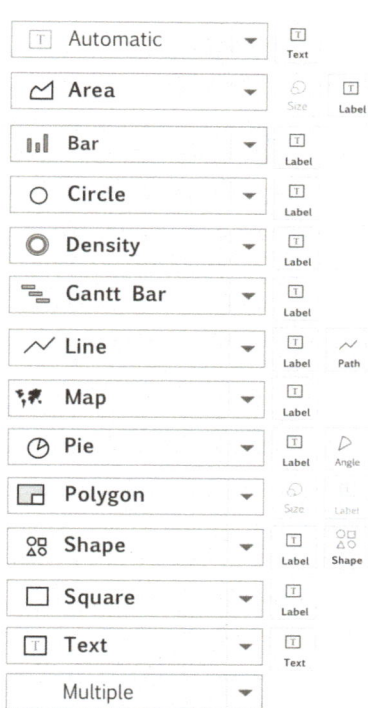

FIGURE 7.11
Mark properties.

type for a chart, use the drop-down menu, as shown in Figure 7.11.

Visualizations like *Bullet* charts start with a mark type and add new elements. For example, a *Bullet* chart is a **Bar** mark type with a reference line and can also include a reference line distribution band. A *Scatter plot* is a shape chart with two measure fields. Some charts do not have any fields on the **Columns** or **Rows** shelves. I add examples of specific charts as we look at various mark types.

Different tiles are available or grayed out, depending on the "type of mark" selected. For example, a **Pie** mark adds the "Angle" tool. The *Size* tile is grayed out for the **Area** and **Polygon** marks. The *Label* tile is also grayed out for a **Polygon** mark. "*Section 6.2 Dual-axes Charts*" *on page 103* demonstrates how the *Path* tool is only shown for a **Line** mark. In the previous example, the *Mark Type* is "Automatic" because Tableau selects the best mark type. Figure 7.11 highlights the different tiles available for the various **Mark Types**.

7.2.1 Multiple Marks

As shown in the previous chapter, adding another measure field, or a second instance of a measure field,

FIGURE 7.12

Tip: With dual-axis charts, you can right-click a mark on the canvas and change the mark type, which is a fun way to explore different combinations of mark types.

to the **Rows** shelf or **Columns** shelf creates a dual-axis chart. The **Marks** card has multiple layers when multiple measure fields are on the **Columns** or **Rows** shelf. We looked at several charts in **Chapter 6** that had multiple layers. You can have up to four layers – with two measures on the **Columns** shelf and two on the **Rows** shelf. Two different mark types are called a combination chart. In MacOS, click-drag the field from the **Data** pane onto the **Rows** shelf or **Columns** shelf to add a second instance of the same field.

In Figure 7.13, there are two fields, [Sales] and [Profit], on the **Columns** shelf, which creates two layers: SUM(Sales) and SUM(Profit). Multiple layers allow you to add color, text, and other visual effects to the worksheet layers. **Chapter 6** looked at a "Donut" chart and two pie charts based on two measure fields and a dual axis.

7.2.2 Bar Charts

Today, I see horizontal bar charts more often than vertical bar charts. Horizontal bar charts are more attractive and allow for longer headers, text labels, or comments. A line chart on top of a bar chart comparing values can show trends. Check out Robert Rouse's Tableau Public file "Bar Chart Menu" for some excellent examples of bar charts. A lollipop chart is a combination of a bar and a circle chart, as shown in Figure 7.14.

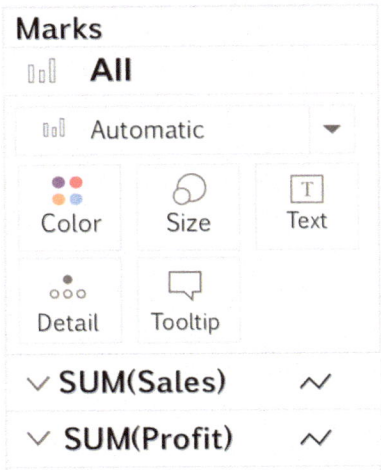

FIGURE 7.13
Two layers.

FIGURE 7.14
Lollipop chart.

7.2.2.1 Rounded End for Bar Charts

A bar chart with rounded ends combines bar and circle marks with a placeholder field.

Tableau Public file:

https://public.tableau.com/views/Rounded Barss1091/RoundedBars?:language=en-US&:sid=&:display_count=n&:origin= viz_share_link

1. Connect to the *Sample Superstore* data source and create a bar chart. Add [Sales] to the **Columns** shelf and [Sub-category] to the **Rows** shelf.

2. Click the drop-down arrow for [Sub-category] to open the field's *context menu*. Select "Sort" by the "Field" [Sales] in descending order.

3. Drag a second instance of [Sales] to the **Columns** shelf to create a second bar chart in the view (Figure 7.15).

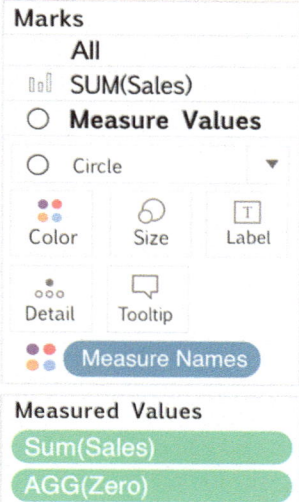

FIGURE 7.15
The mark type of Circle.

4. Create a placeholder field. Click the drop-down arrow at the top of the **Data** pane to open the *context menu*. Select "Create Calculated Field," as shown in Figure 7.16. Name the field [Zero] (Figure 7.17).

5. Drag the [Zero] field to the axis at the bottom of the second pane on the right.

6. Tableau adds the **Measure Values** shelf and adds [Measure Values] to the **Columns** shelf. Tableau also adds the [Measure Names] field to the **Rows** shelf and the **Filters** shelf (Figure 7.18).

7. Right-click the [Measured Values] field on the **Columns** shelf (Figure 7.19) and select "Dual-Axis."

   Tableau adds the [Measure Values] field to the *Color* tile on the **Marks** card.

8. Select the **Measure Values** layer in the **Marks** card (Figure 7.20) and change the type of mark to "Circle."

9. Right-click the axis and choose "Sychnronize" (Figure 7.21).

10. Remove [Measured Names] from the **Rows** shelf.

11. On the **Marks** card, click the *Circle* tile to change the marks to the same color (Figure 7.22).

12. Select the **Measured Values** layer and adjust the circle's shape and size, as shown in Figure 7.23.

7.2.2.2 Histogram Charts

Histogram charts are good for showing the distribution of **continuous** data and answering questions like, "Does the majority of production fall within the accepted SLAs (service level agreements)?" It is interesting to compare histogram charts to see whether a trend is changing over time. Histogram charts are great for answering other questions like these.

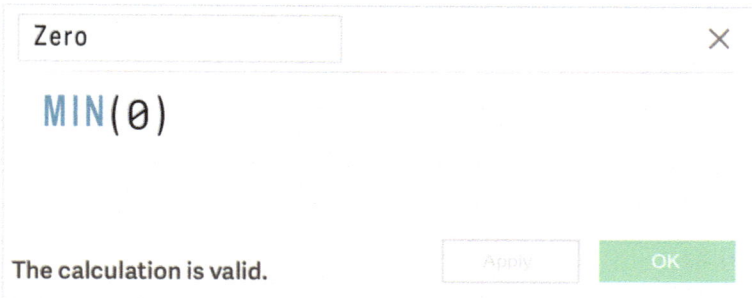

FIGURE 7.16
The Calculated Field Zero.

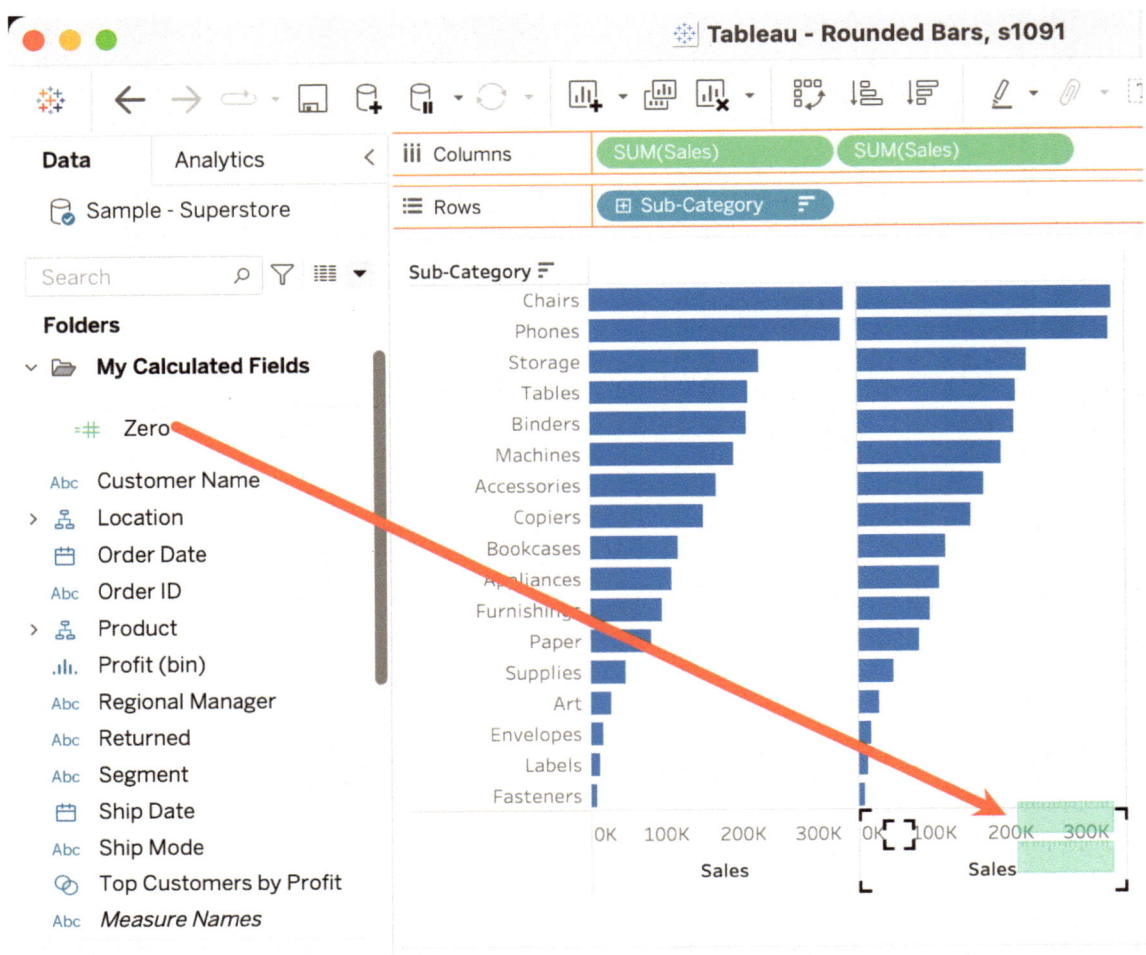

FIGURE 7.17
Drag the field to the x-axis.

- Are the majority of staff meeting their goals?
- What is the price for the majority of our products?
- Are most items profitable?
- Are delivery times within accepted SLAs?

Figure 7.24 groups the [Price] field to create three bins and then shows a *count* for each bin.

Tableau Public file:

    https://public.tableau.com/views/
        Histograms1041/Histogram?:language=en-
        US&publish=yes&:sid=&:display_count=n&:
        origin=viz_share_link

To quickly create a histogram chart, select the **continuous** measure [Price] in the **Data** pane and "Histogram" in the **Show Me** dialog in the top-right corner of the screen. The resulting histogram chart groups the [Price] field to create three bins and shows a count for each bin. In Figure 7.24, I can easily see the majority of my items are under $.80. **Show Me** changed the new [Price(bin)] field to **continuous** on

the **Columns** shelf and added CNT(Price) to the **Rows** shelf.

To add labels, control-click the [CNT(Price)] field and drag it to the *Label* tile on the **Marks** card. Most histogram charts do not have an outline or gap between the bars. Double-click the *Color* tile on the **Marks** card and select "Border" to change or remove the bar outline. If you have bins for a histogram chart and there are gaps in the data, right-click (control-click in MacOS) the headers or axis and choose "Show missing values." The next topic, "Bins," looks at the numeric dimensions of a histogram chart.

7.2.2.3 Bins

Bins are new numeric dimensions created from **continuous** measures and used in histogram charts. Bins are like buckets of values for a given range. You can edit a new [Bin] field in the **Data** pane if you want to adjust the size of the bins, as shown in Figure 7.25.

FIGURE 7.18
The Measure Values shelf in the bottom left.

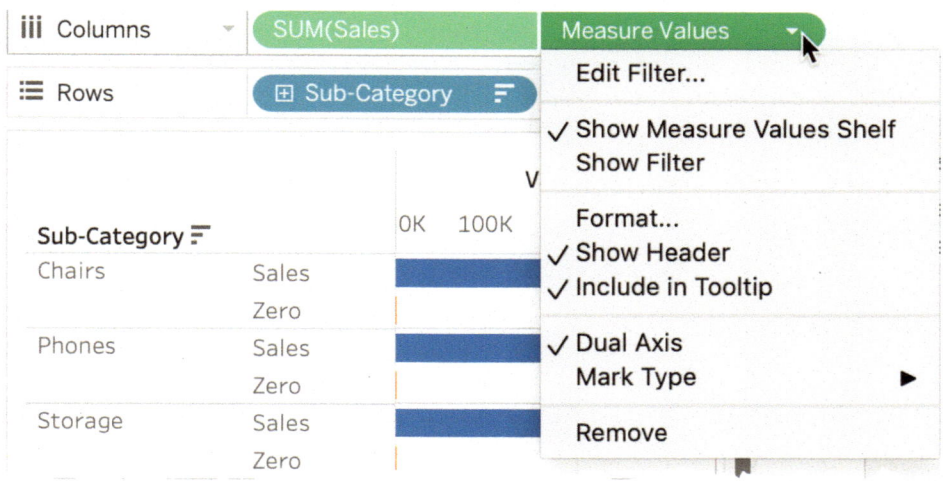

FIGURE 7.19
Select dual-axis.

7.2.3 Circle Marks

Box-and-Whisker plots, Word Clouds, Donut Charts, and Sparklines are all **Circle** marks. A **Circle** mark adds a *Shape* tile to the **Marks** card. You will often see *Color* and *Size* properties used with **Circle** charts, as shown in Figure 7.27. We created a donut chart in *"Section 6.5 Donut Chart" on page 112.*

7.2.3.1 Sparkline

A Sparkline is a combination chart with two mark types: **Line** and **Circle**. Circle shapes are at the end of the lines. In Figure 7.30, I create a calculated field [Dots] on *Color* on the **Marks** card for the "Circle" layer to indicate if the data is trending up or down.

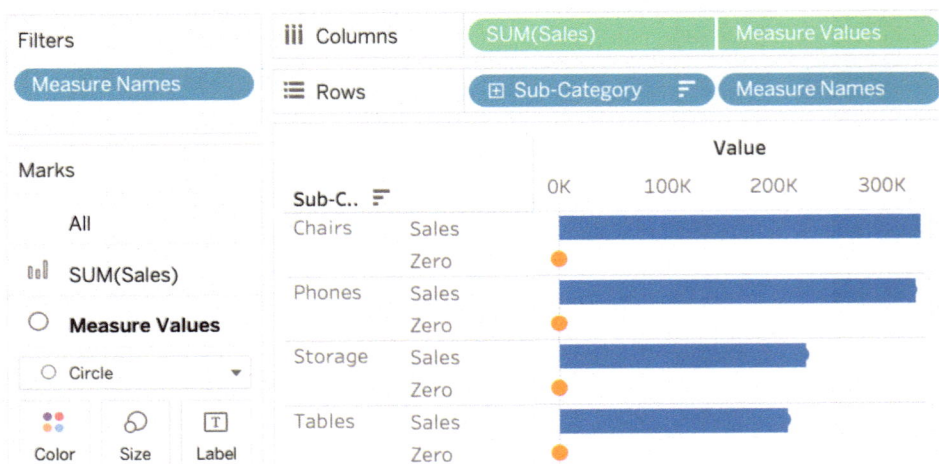

FIGURE 7.20
The **Measure Values** layer.

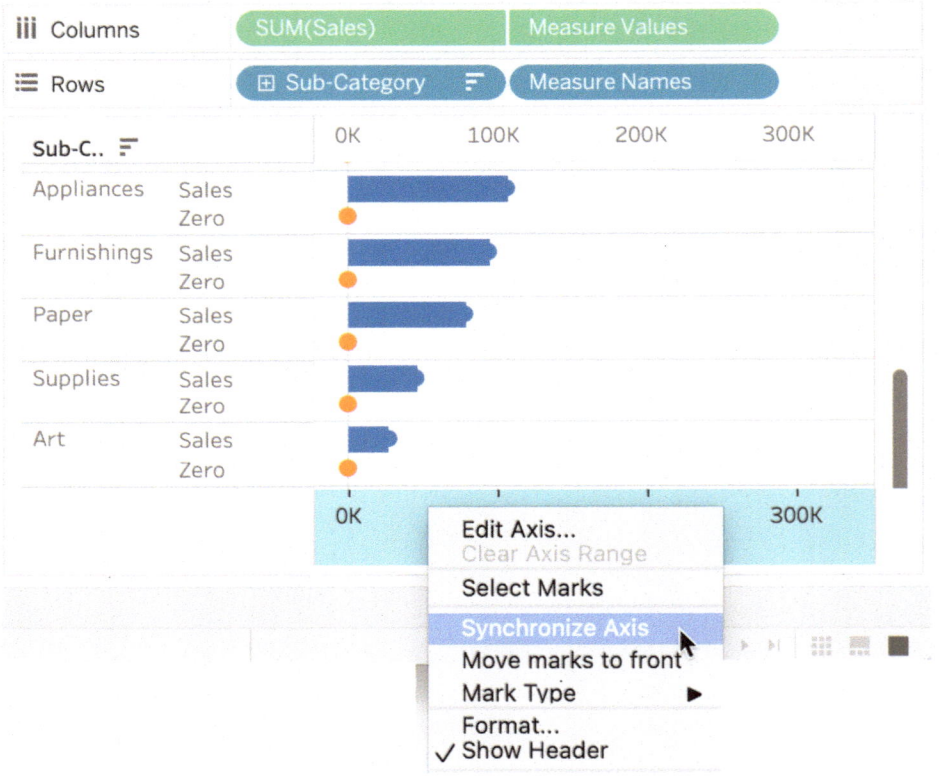

FIGURE 7.21
The **Axis Context** Menu With the **Synchronize Axis** option.

Tableau Public file:

https://public.tableau.com/views/Sparklines
1062/Sparkline?:language=en-US&:sid=&:
display_count=n&:origin=viz_share_link

1. Add the field [MONTH(Order Date)] to the **Columns** shelf. On the **Marks** card,

click the drop-down arrow and select the **Line** mark type.

2. Create a calculated field called [Dots] (Figure 7.28).

3. Add the [Sub-Category], [Sales], and [Dots] fields to the **Rows** shelf. [Sales] and

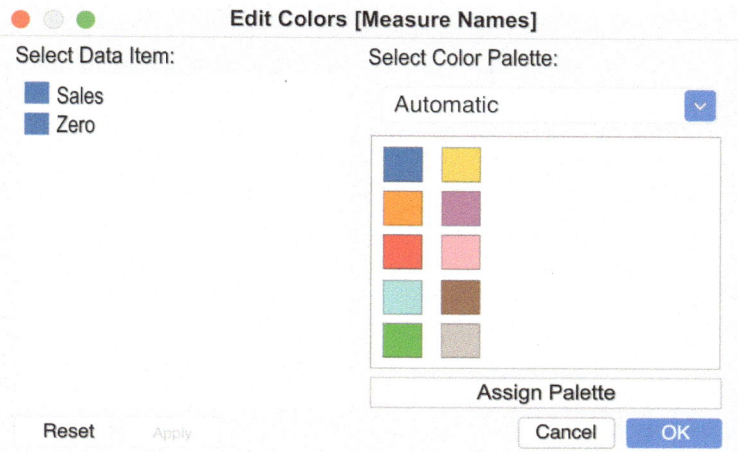

FIGURE 7.22
The **Edit Colors** dialog box.

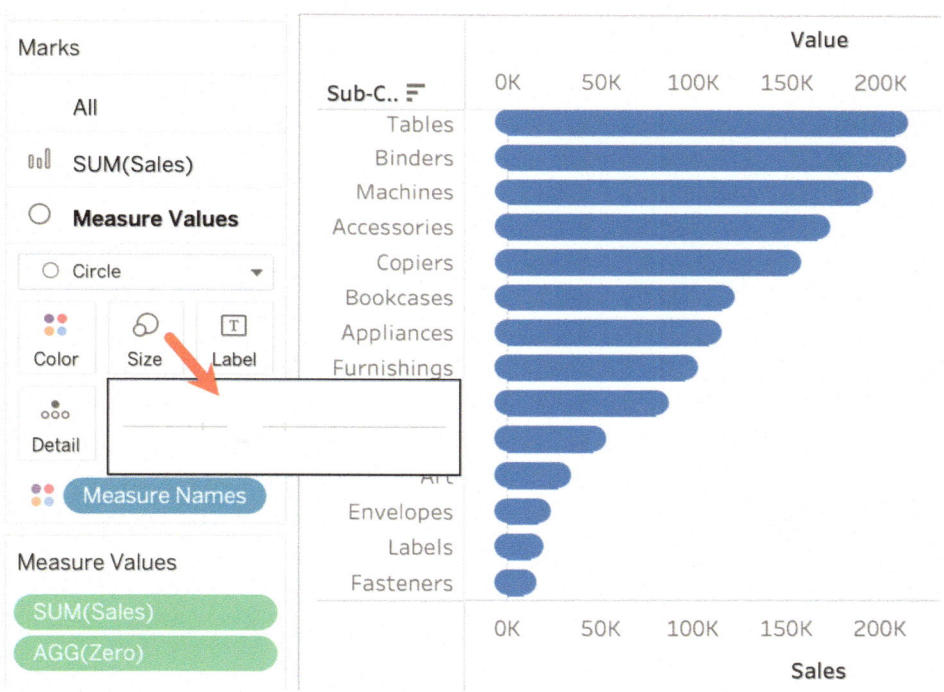

FIGURE 7.23
The **Measure Values** Layer in the **Marks** card.

[Dots] are measure fields, so the **Marks** card has two layers.

Select **Line** from the drop-down menu on the **SUM(Sales)** layer on the **Marks** card.

4. Right-click the [Dots] field on the **Rows** shelf and check "Dual-axis." Change the mark type to **Circle** on this **Dots** layer.

5. Create another calculated field called [MOM Performance]. This field is a True/False or Boolean data type and returns either True or False Figure 7.29. Comments in calculated fields begin with //.

6. Select the **Dots** layer and add the new [MOM Performance] field to the *Color* tile on the **Marks** card.

7.2.3.2 *Word Clouds*

Another **Circle** chart is the *Word Cloud*, as shown in Figure 7.31. At work, I have used live word clouds in

team meetings to rate how a sprint (software release) went, and they're a lot of fun.
    Tableau Public file:

> https://public.tableau.com/views/word
> clouds1083/WordCloud?:language=en-US&
> publish=yes&:sid=&:display_count=n&:
> origin=viz_share_link

7.2.3.3 Box-and-Whisker Plots

A *Box-and-Whisker* plot, or "Box Plot," is based on a **Circle** mark on the **Marks** card. This chart type is not a good choice if you only have a few data points. *Reference Lines* show the upper and lower range, which is 1.5 times the width of the adjoining box, as shown in Figure 7.32. First, we will examine the elements of a Box-and-Whisker plot, followed by an example to create the chart.

Box-and-Whisker plots utilize a *Reference Band* to show the middle 50% of data, as shown in Figure 7.33.

Box-and-Whisker plots show data distribution along a **continuous** axis. Box-and-Whisker plots show the outliers, the median, the mode, and where most data points lie in the "box," as shown in Figure 7.34.

The whiskers in Figure 7.35 are reference lines indicating the maximum and minimum values.

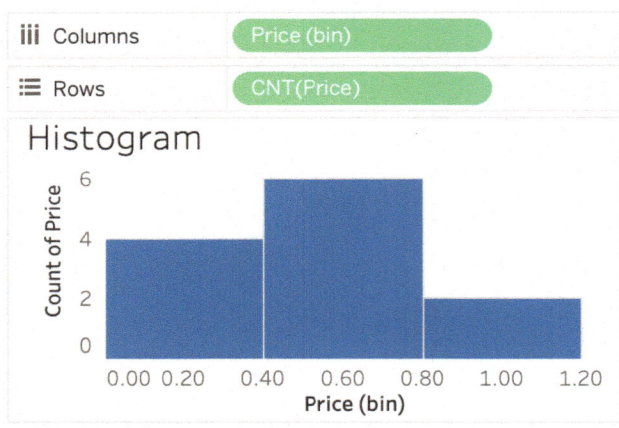

FIGURE 7.24
Histogram.

7.2.3.4 Create a Box-and-Whisker Plot

The steps to create a *Box-and-Whisker* plot follow. You can also select the fields and click the **Show Me** button in the top-right corner to select "Box-and-Whisker Plots."
    Tableau Public file:

> https://public.tableau.com/views/
> BoxandWhisker1074/Dashboard1?:
> language=en-US&publish=yes&:sid=&:
> display_count=n&:origin=viz_share_link

1. Add a **continuous** measure to the **Rows** shelf and a dimension field to the *Detail* tile on the **Marks** card.

2. Click the drop-down in the **Marks** card to change the *mark type* to **Circle** (Figure 7.36).

3. Right-click the axis and choose "Add Reference Line." In the "Add Reference Line, Band, or Box" pop-up window, select "Box Plot" in the top right corner. Set the properties for the box plot.

4. To change the box plot later, right-click on the axis and choose "Edit Reference Line (Figure 7.37)." If the axis is hidden, select the field on the **Rows** shelf, right-click to open the field's *context menu*, and select "Show Header."

7.2.4 Text Marks

A visualization with **Text** as the mark type is similar to a spreadsheet, pivot table, or crosstab. It is a good way

FIGURE 7.26
Tip: *Bins are not aggregated. You cannot create a bin from a calculated field with an aggregation like SUM([Sales]).*

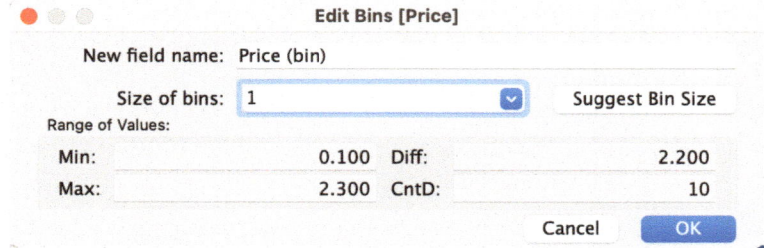

FIGURE 7.25
Edit Bins.

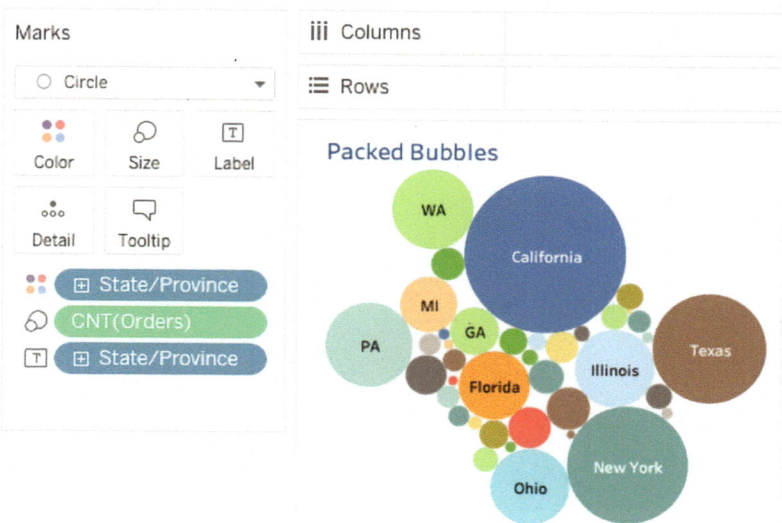

FIGURE 7.27
Circle Marks – packed bubbles.

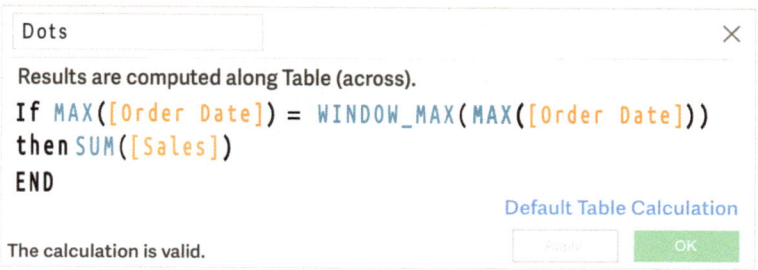

FIGURE 7.28
The calculated field dots.

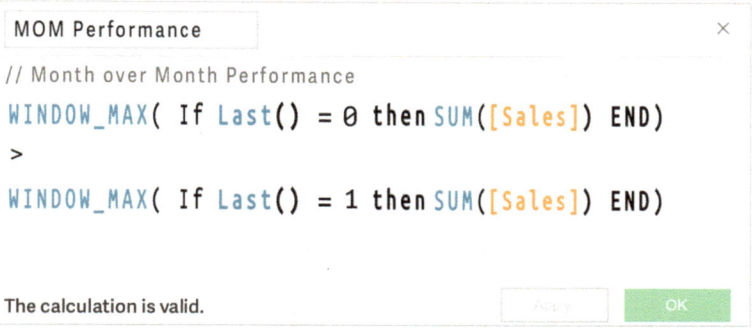

FIGURE 7.29
The calculated field MOM performance.

to compare multiple measures. In Figure 7.38, the red arrow points to the mark type; in this case, **Text**, which is not the same as the *Text* tile or text property.

7.2.5 Square Mark Type

A highlight table is a **Square** mark type with diverging colors. Waffle charts, Panel charts, Tile Grid Maps, and Tree Maps (Figure 7.68) all use the **Square** mark type. These topics have more information on highlight tables:

"Section 7.3.7 Highlight Table – Include Totals in Color" on page 143

"Section 7.3.3.2 Diverging Color Palette" on page 140

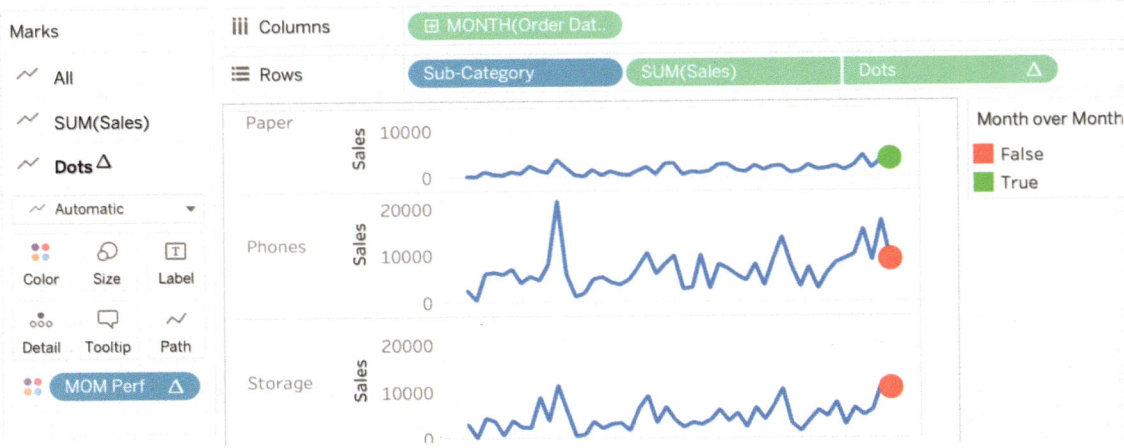

FIGURE 7.30
The Sparkline chart.

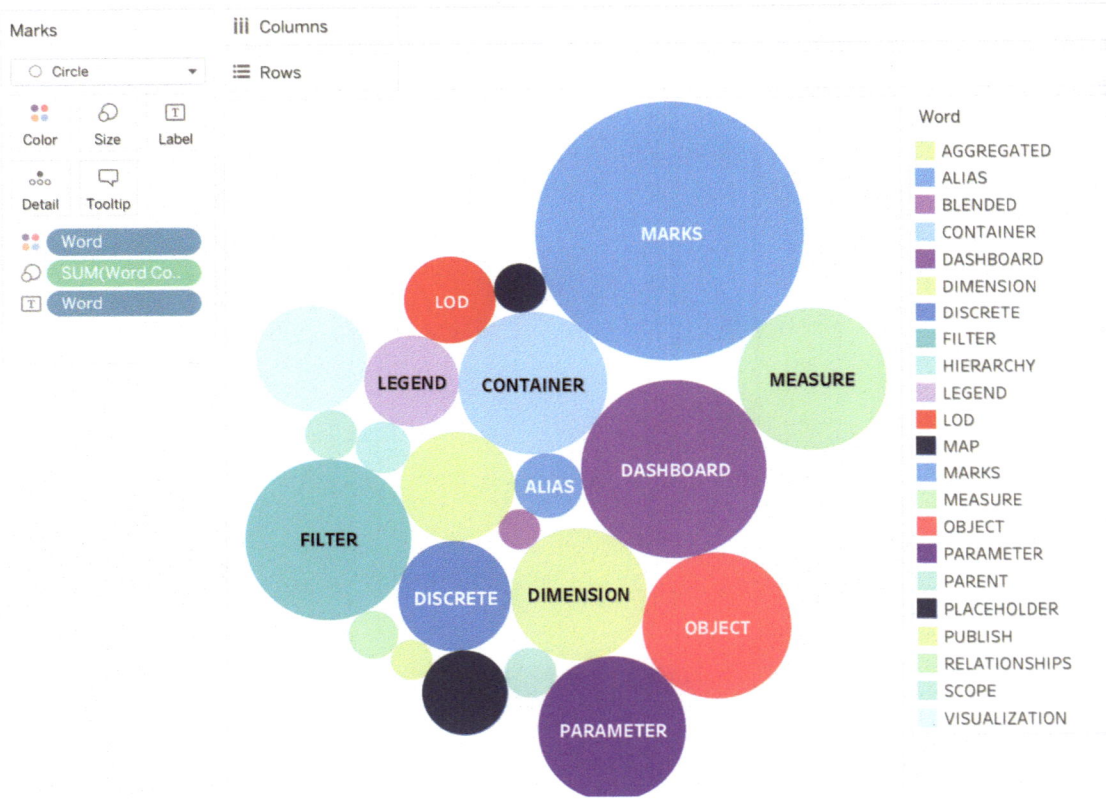

FIGURE 7.31
Word Clouds.

7.2.5.1 *Heat Maps*

<u>Heat Maps</u> are similar to **Highlight Tables**. For Heat Maps, I use color to indicate RAG (Red-Amber-Green) ratings so the viewer can quickly focus on problem areas. The mark type is a "Square." The *Highlight Table – Include Totals in Color* section *on page 143* demonstrates this type of chart.

7.2.6 **Gantt Bar Charts**

<u>Gantt Bar charts</u> are often combined with other marks to create beautiful multi-layer charts. Figure 7.39 is a dual-axis chart with a Gantt Bar chart with black lines. To create a Gantt Bar, select a date field, **continuous** measure field, and dimension field and open the **Show Me** button in the top-right corner of the

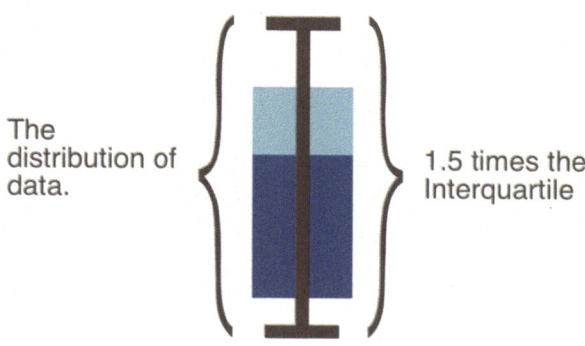

FIGURE 7.32
Box-and-Whisker distribution of data.

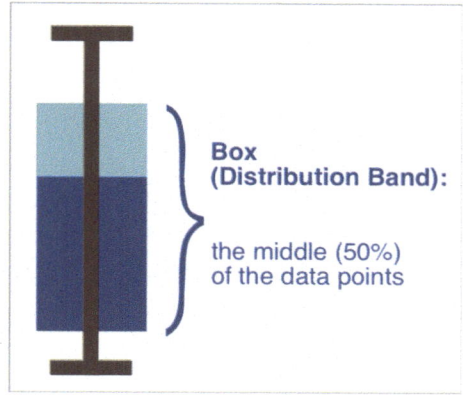

FIGURE 7.33
The middle 50% of the data points.

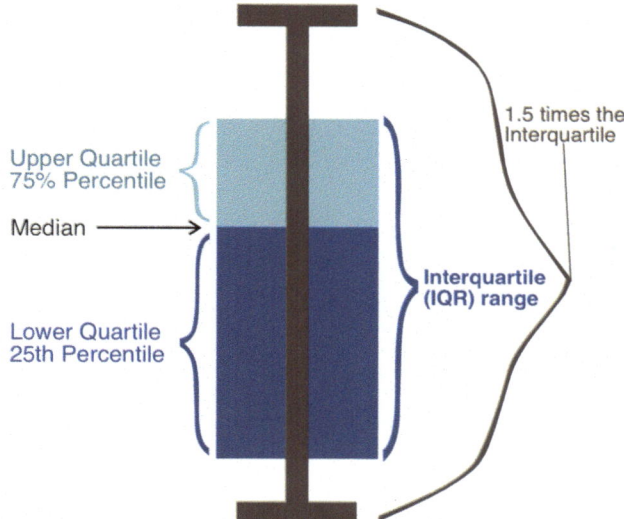

FIGURE 7.34
The median, upper quartile, and lower quartile.

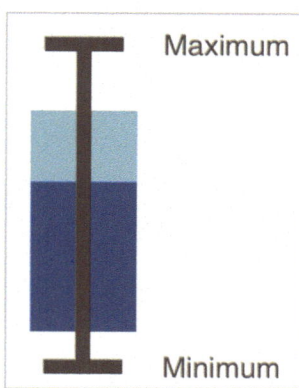

FIGURE 7.35
Minimum and Maximum Whiskers

1. Drag two measure fields to the **Rows** shelf. Change the mark type to Gantt Bar.

2. Drag a dimension field to the **Columns** shelf.

3. Right-click the second field on the right side of the **Rows** shelf and choose "Dual-Axis." This option is only available on the second field. The green background for both fields changes to a "super bubble," indicating that this is now a dual-axes chart.

4. Click within the right axis on the chart and choose "Synchronize Axis."

5. Right-click the second field on the **Rows** shelf and uncheck "Show Header" (Figure 7.40).

Tableau Public file:

> https://public.tableau.com/views/ Ganttcharts1078/GanttBar?:language=en- US&publish=yes&:sid=&:display_count=n&: origin=viz_share_link

7.2.6.1 *Bullet Graph*

After creating a Gantt Bar chart, you can use the "Show Me" option to create a Bullet Graph or follow these steps to build one from scratch by combining a bar chart and a Gantt chart. For another example, the topic "Section 7.8.3 Bullet Graph with a Reference Line and Distribution Band" on page 127 has a second distribution reference line.

Tableau Public file:

> https://public.tableau.com/views/Bullet Graphs1075/Dashboard?:language=en- US&:sid=&:display_count=n&:origin= viz_share_link

1. Drag two *dimension* fields to the **Rows** shelf; in this case, [Region] and [Country / Region].

desktop. *"Section 9.12 Time Duration for Gantt Bar, Waterfall and Resume" on page 208* also has a Gantt Bar chart.

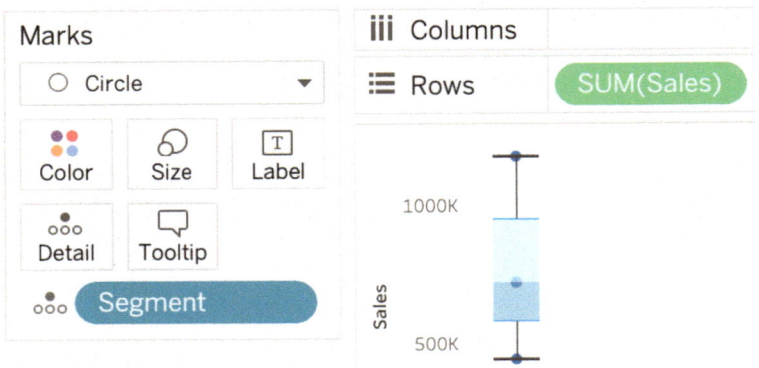

FIGURE 7.36
The Circle Mark type.

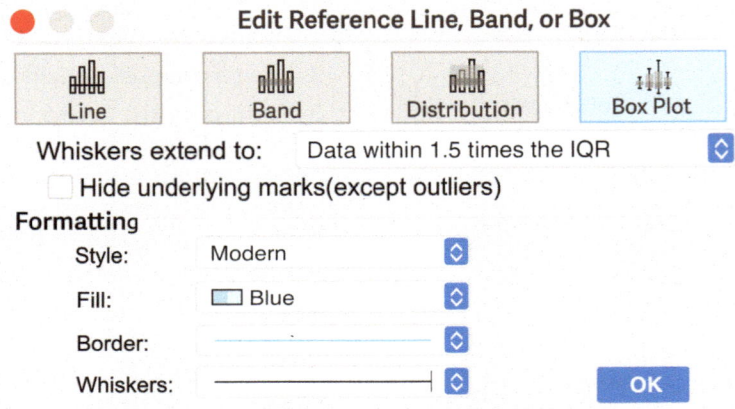

FIGURE 7.37
The **Edit Reference Line** dialog box.

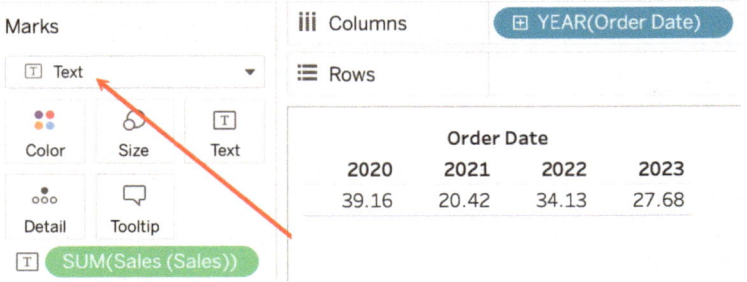

FIGURE 7.38
Text table.

2. Drag the first *measure* field, [Sales], to the **Columns** shelf.

3. Use the *Sort* tool in the "Sales" axis (Figure 7.41) to apply a descending sort. Hover the mouse over the axis until the sort tool appears.

4. Change the size of the bar line (Figure 7.42). Click the *Size* tile on the **Marks** card. We want the mark size to be narrower so the line stands out after we add the reference line.

5. Drag the second measure field [Returned sales] to *Detail* on the **Marks** card.

6. Select the **Analytics** pane on the left and drag a *Reference Line* onto the canvas (Figure 7.43). A pop-up appears where you can select *Table*, *Pane*, or *Cell*. Choose *Cell*.

7. In the **Edit Reference Line, Band, or Box** window (Figure 7.44), select the measure field [Returned Sales] from the **Value** drop-down list with an aggregation of "Sum." At the bottom of the window, choose the "Fill Above" and "Fill Below" colors.

   If you do not see the field [Returned Sales] in the drop-down list, right-click it on the *Detail* tile on the **Marks** card to open its *context menu* and ensure that the *measure* is checked instead of the *dimension*.

8. Right-click within the body of the chart and choose "Format." Change *Grid Lines* to "None (Figure 7.45)."

7.2.7 Shape Marks

Shapes are often used with combination charts to add additional detail to a view. Later, we will look at the role of <u>pre-attentive attributes</u> like shape and color. A **Shape** mark is also an excellent way to add RAG (red-amber-green) ratings to your view. Scatter plots are another chart type with a "Shape" mark type. These examples use shape marks:

"Section 7.2.7.4 Transparent Shapes to Call Attention to Some Marks" on page 129

"Section 14.23 KPIs and BANs (Big Numbers)" on page 347

"Section 12.21 Arrows Comparing Two Values" on page 287

"Section 13.6.4 Custom Color and Shape Legend (Diamond)" on page 298

"Section 14.16 Horizontal Radial Buttons to Change Filters" on page 328 also illustrates how to use custom shapes. In that example, I changed the default color to black to emphasize one shape. In the **Chapter 13** example, "Custom Color and Shape Legend," I created a yellow diamond shape so that the **Shape Control** would also show a yellow diamond.

Once you have set the mark type to "Shape," click the *Shape* tile on the **Marks** card to assign shapes to individual marks. In some situations, you might not see all values or marks. In that case, you can temporarily adjust the chart by changing filters or adding fields to the view. Hence, you see all possible values and can assign shapes to all values.

7.2.7.1 Custom Shapes and Colors

You can add custom shapes to the "Shapes" folder in the "My Tableau Repository" folder. Create a **new sub-folder** to add your shapes in the \My Tableau Repository\Shapes folder with the *.svg and *.png extension. In MacOS, this folder is in my "Documents" folder, as shown in Figure 7.47.

To add custom colors, edit the file *Preferences.tps*. In this example, I added a transparent palette with a transparent color. The *Preferences.tps* file is the only way to add a truly transparent color to Tableau, as shown in the example, "Call Attention to Marks with Transparent Shapes and Color," that follows.

- If custom shapes are black, you also need to add the same shape field to *Color* on the **Marks** card.
- If custom shapes do not appear correctly after a visualization is uploaded to a Tableau Server, ensure that they are in a separate sub-folder.

7.2.7.2 Charts with Only Shapes

To create a chart with only shapes, drag one field to the *Detail* tile on the **Marks** card and another to the *Shapes* tile, as shown in Figure 7.48. *"Section 14.23 KPIs and BANs (Big Numbers)"* on page 347 includes a shape chart.

7.2.7.3 Timeline Chart

The simplest form of a shape chart is a *Timeline* chart with a date field on the **Columns** shelf and a place-holder field on the **Rows** shelf, as shown in Figure 7.49. The [Fruit] field is on the *Detail* tile on the **Marks** card. In this example, I formatted the zero lines as a thick black line.

Tableau Public file:

```
https://public.tableau.com/views/
Timeline_17088770298420/Timeline?:
language=en-US&:sid=&:display_count=n&:
origin=viz_share_link
```

7.2.7.4 Transparent Shapes to Call Attention to Some Marks

Similar to the chart I created in *"Section 13.6.4 Custom Color and Shape Legend (Diamond)"* on page 298, Figure 7.50 is a dual-axis combination chart with **Area** and **Shape** marks and corresponding layers. I assigned blue circle shapes for the two *Min* and *Max* values. The other circle marks (between Min and Max) on the **Shape** layer use a transparent shape.

7.2.7.5 Examples of Colored Up and Down Arrows

Colored arrows call attention to changes and comparisons, as shown in these examples.

"Section 7.3.6 Color Positive and Negative Numbers" on page 142

"Section 12.11.6 Number Format: Custom Arrows" on page 276

"Section 12.21 Arrows Comparing Two Values" on page 287

"Section 14.23 KPIs and BANs (Big Numbers)" on page 347

7.2.7.6 RAG Ratings

RAG (red-amber-green) rating charts often use color and shapes. For example, a dual-axis chart has text and shapes, and red circles call attention to metrics that are performing poorly.

7.2.7.7 Use a Transparent Shape to Remove Blue Shading

The visualization in Figure 7.51 is a **Text** mark that displays a blue background when you select a mark. On a key progress indicator (KPI) dashboard, this blue shading might be annoying.

Change the mark type on the **Marks** card to **Shape** to remove the blue background. After you change to a transparent shape, only the text label is visible; in this case, "8." Double-click the *Shape* tile on the **Marks** card, click the shape in the "Select Data Item" pane on the left, and in the right pane, select the custom transparent shape (Figure 7.56 and 7.57) as shown in Figure 7.52. The shape is transparent when I move my mouse off the selected shape on the left. Tableau Public has some great examples that use transparent shapes.

7.2.7.8 Call Attention to Marks with Transparent Shapes and Color

This example of a combination chart has **Bar** and **Shape** marks (Figure 7.58). The red diamond shapes call attention to the top three sales. Also, see the "Custom Color and Shape Legend (Diamond)" in Chapter 13, which adds additional features to the chart.

Tableau Public file:

```
https://public.tableau.com/views/Top3
diamondshapelegends1073/Diamond
placement?:language=en-US&:sid=&:
display_count=n&:origin=viz_share_link
```

1. Connect to a data source like the *Sample Superstore* and drag a dimension field to the **Rows** shelf and a measure field like [Sales] to the **Columns** shelf.

2. Create a calculated field [Color and Shape Top 3] using **Rank()** to identify the top 3 sales (Figure 7.53).

3. Create a placeholder field on the **Columns** shelf (Figure 7.54). To create an in-line calculation for a placeholder field, right-click or double-click on the shelf and start typing on the **Rows** or the **Columns** shelf.

4. On the **Marks** card, the new **AGG(Min(1)) layer** is shown. Click the drop-down arrow to change the **Mark** type for the **AGG(Min(1)) layer** to **Shape** (Figure 7.55).

5. Next, I want to make this a dual-axis chart, similar to the examples in **Chapter 6**. To create a dual-axis chart, click the drop-down arrow on the [MIN(1)] field on the **Columns** shelf and select "Dual-Axis." This option is only available on the second field on the right side of the shelf. The green background for both fields changes to a "super bubble," indicating that this is now a dual-axis chart.

6. Drag the [Color and Shape Top 3] field to both the *Color* and *Shape* tiles on the **Marks** card.

7. Click the *Color* tile on the **Marks** card and click the "Edit Colors" button. A dialog window opens. Double-click the colored icon to the left of the "True" value. Type a hex code for a red color. In MacOS, when the *Digital Color Meter* application opens, select "RGB Sliders" from the drop-down menu. Click the ellipsis or three dots on the right and choose "Display." You should see a box where you can type in the "Hex Color #."

8. Next, assign a transparent color to the "False" value. The hexadecimal code for a transparent color has 00 at the end of "#FFFFFF00." Tableau only allows seven characters in the pop-up, so create a palette with the hexadecimal code in the *preferences.tps* file, as shown earlier. In the example below, I have added a palette called "Transparent," and the transparent color is displayed on the right as a black box.

9. I added a transparent *.png file to my "Custom" shapes folder as outlined in the next topic, "Shape Marks, Add Custom Shapes." You can make a transparent image file or download one from the internet.

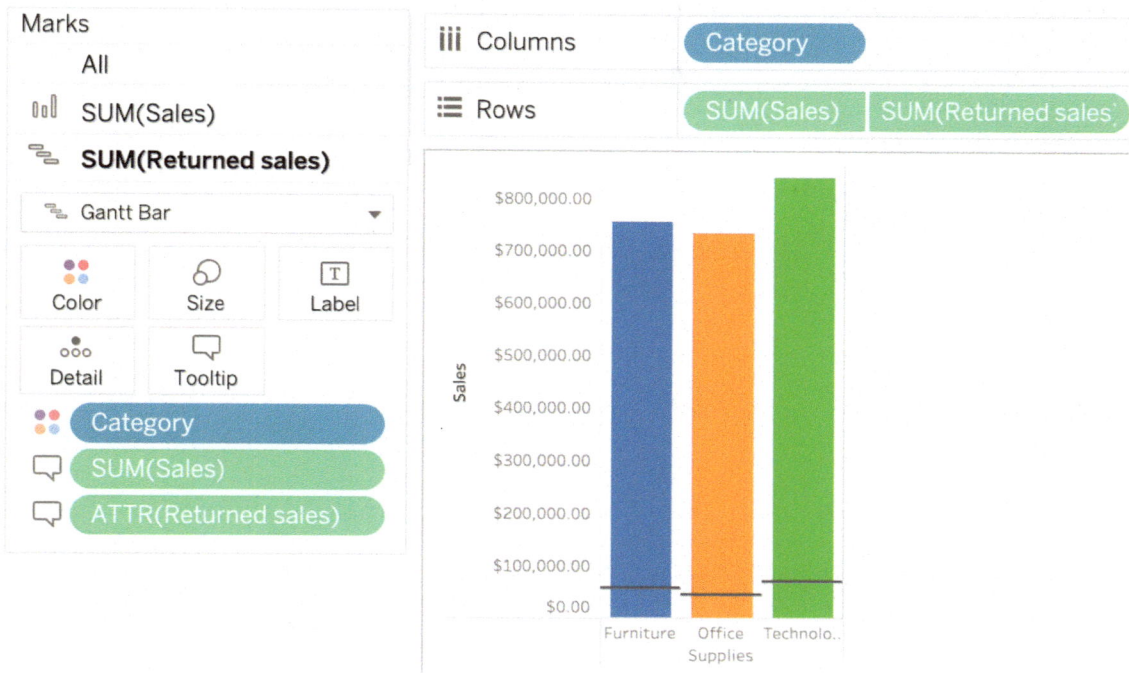

FIGURE 7.39
Gantt Bar Chart.

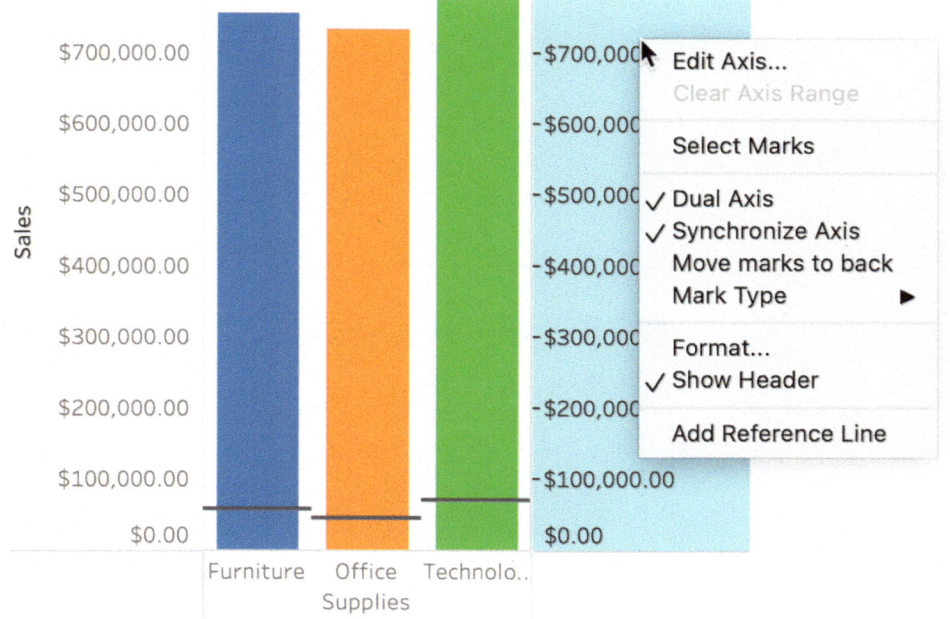

FIGURE 7.40
The axis context menu.

Click the *Shape* tile on the **Marks** card to open the dialog window. In the left pane, select "False" and browse in the right pane to select your transparent shape. When you move your mouse over the transparent shape in the right pane, a box indicates that it is selected. After assigning the transparent shape to "False," there is no visible shape on the left, indicating that the transparent shape is assigned.

FIGURE 7.41
The Sort icon in the x-axis.

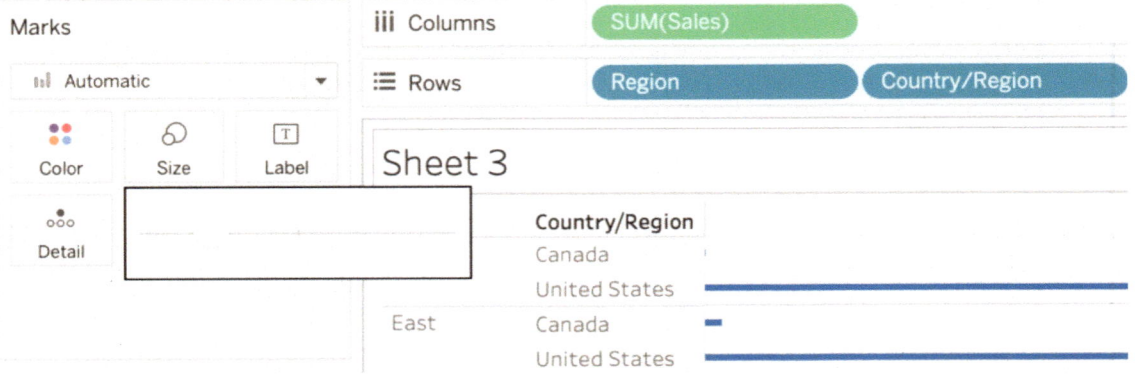

FIGURE 7.42
The Size slider on the Marks card.

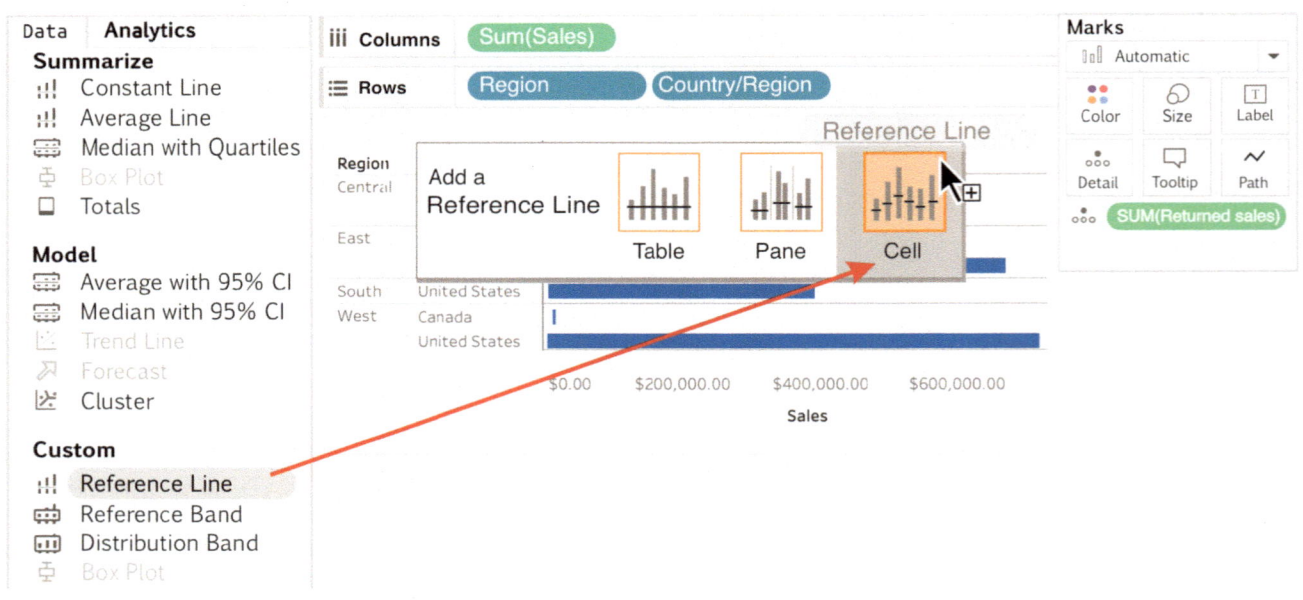

FIGURE 7.43
The Analytics pane.

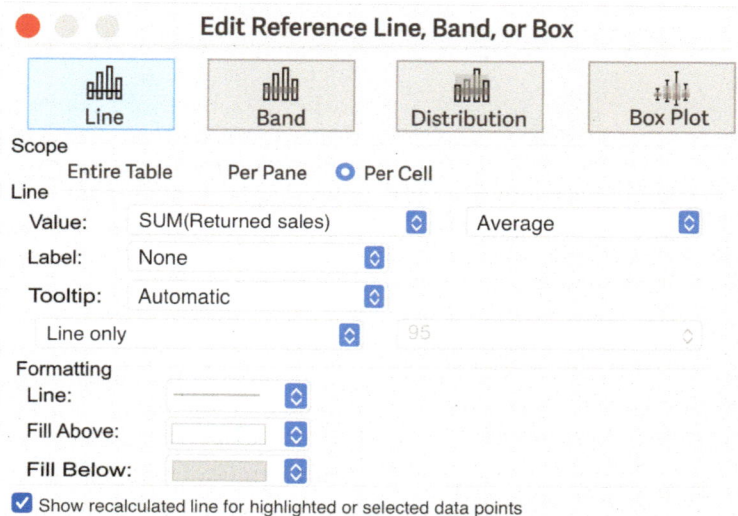

FIGURE 7.44
The **Edit Reference Line** dialog window.

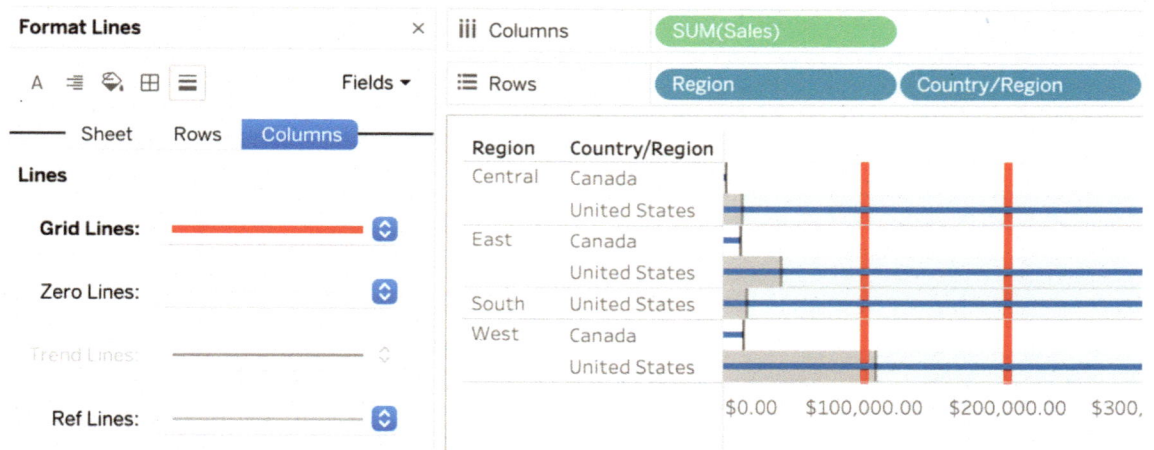

FIGURE 7.45
Grid Lines in the Format Lines pane.

10. Finally, I assign a diamond shape to the "True" value. The final chart is shown in Figure 7.58.

7.2.7.9 Scatter Plots

A scatter plot has at least two measures and adds the *Shape* tile to the **Marks** card, as shown in Figure 7.59. Scatter plots are good at showing the relationship between two items – in this case, [Profit] and [Sales].

Tableau Public file:

```
https://public.tableau.com/views/
Scatterplots1076/Scatterplot?:language=
en-US&:sid=&:display_count=n&:origin=
viz_share_link
```

7.2.7.10 Side-by-Side Circles

Tableau adds the *Shape* tile to the **Marks** card for Side-by-Side Circle charts because the mark type is a **Shape**, as shown in Figure 7.60.

7.2.8 Line Charts

Line charts are excellent for showing data changing over time or comparing data. If the **Mark** type is a **Line**, you can control the appearance of the lines (dashes, dots) with the *Path* property. In the previous chapter, the topic, "Dual-Axes Chart: Area and Line," used a *Path* tool. Tableau's blog site has a beautiful example of a shaded slope chart combining **Line** and **Area** marks. A **slope** chart is ideal for times when the

data changes gradually. *"Section 10.4.3 Slope Chart with a Rank Table Calculation" on page 215* illustrates rank calculations.

The data has null values if a line chart suddenly drops to zero. To prevent this behavior, exclude or remove null or zero values. To prevent a line from stopping and starting between panes, for example, a gap between years, change the date to a custom date part Month-Year.

7.2.8.1 Dumbbell Chart

A dumbbell chart combines *circle* and *line* mark types. A date field on the *Path* tile of the line mark type layer creates the bar, as shown in Figure 7.61.

Tableau Public file:

https://public.tableau.com/views/ Dumbbells1081/Sheet1?:language=en-US& publish=yes&:sid=&:display_count=n&: origin=viz_share_link

1. Add [Fruit] to the **Rows** shelf.
2. Add [Sales] to the **Columns** shelf.

⚙ **Preferences.tps**

```
~/Documents/My Tableau Repository/Preferences.tps ⌄        (functions) ⌄
1    <?xml version='1.0'?>
2 ▼  <workbook>
3 ▼      <preferences>
4 ▼      <color-palette name="Transparent" type="regular" >
5            <color>#FFFFFF00</color>
6 ┗      </color-palette>
7 ┗      </preferences>
8 ┗  </workbook>
```

FIGURE 7.47
The Preferences file.

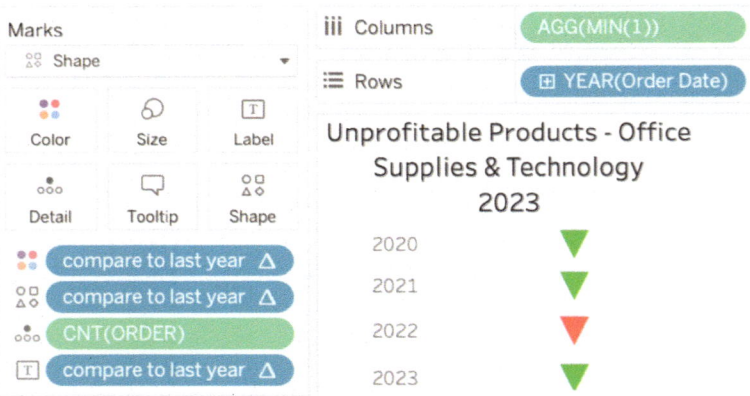

FIGURE 7.48
A Shape chart.

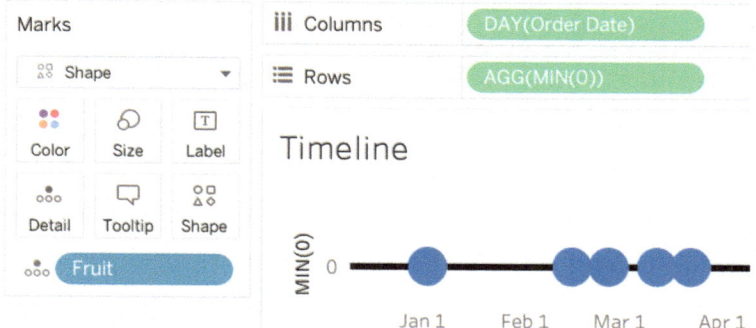

FIGURE 7.49
A Timeline chart.

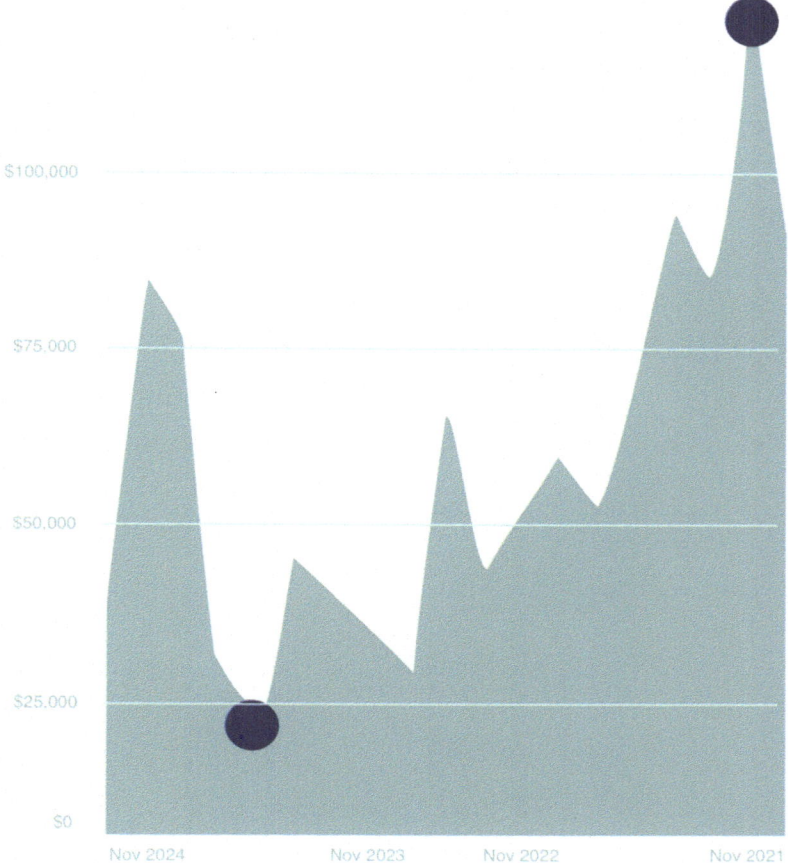

FIGURE 7.50
Minimum and maximum marks.

3. Change the *mark type* to "Line."

4. Add [Order Date] to the *Path* tile on the **Marks** card on the **SUM([Sales]) layer**.

5. Drag a second instance of [Sales] to the **Columns** shelf to create the **SUM(Sales) (2)** layer.

6. Change the second [Sales] field to dual-axes. Right-click [Sales] on the **Columns** shelf to open the field's *context menu*. Select "Dual-Axis."

7. Click the second axis at the top of the view and choose "Synchronize Axis."

8. Uncheck "Show Header" for the second [Sales] field. Right-click [Sales] on the **Columns** shelf to open the field's *context menu*. Uncheck "Show Header."

9. On the **SUM(Sales)(2)** layer on the **Marks** card, change the mark type to *Circle*.

10. Add the date part YEAR(Order Date) to the *Color* tile on the **Marks** card on the **SUM(Sales) (2)** layer. The field is **discrete** and has a blue background (Figure 7.61).

7.2.9 Area Mark

An area chart is a line chart in which the area between the line and the axis is shaded with a color. These charts typically represent accumulated totals and need a date and measure field. **Chapter 6** introduced

an area chart, and *"Section 8.13 Click Data Points to Sort with a Set" on page 175* uses an area chart.

7.2.10 Density Mark

Density Maps remind me of radar maps showing concentrations of rain or snow. A **Density** map uses the *Details* tile on the **Marks** card with latitude and longitude fields.

Tableau Public file:

https://public.tableau.com/views/ DensityHighSchool/Density?:language=en-US&publish=yes&:sid=&:display_count=n&: origin=viz_share_link

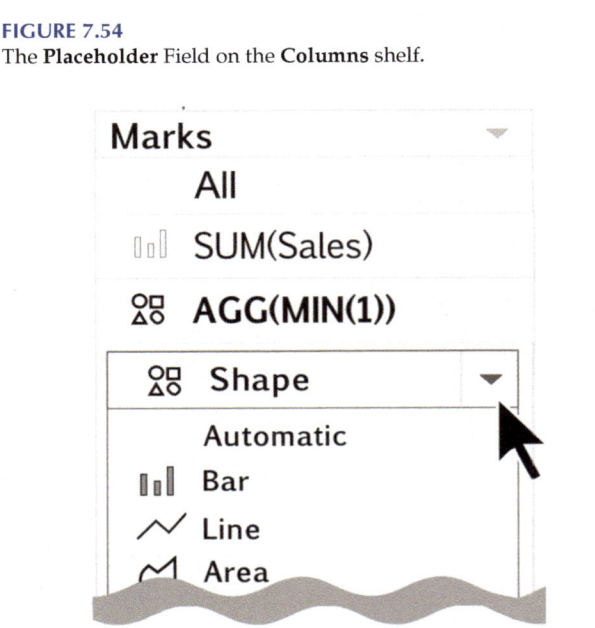

FIGURE 7.54
The **Placeholder** Field on the **Columns** shelf.

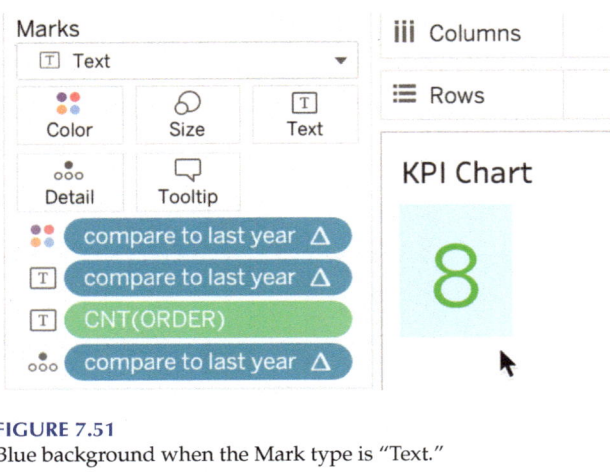

FIGURE 7.51
Blue background when the Mark type is "Text."

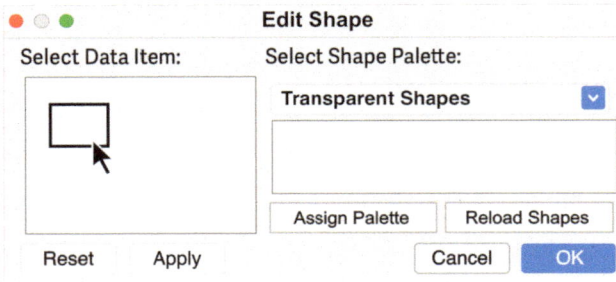

FIGURE 7.52
Transparent shapes.

FIGURE 7.55
The Shape Mark type.

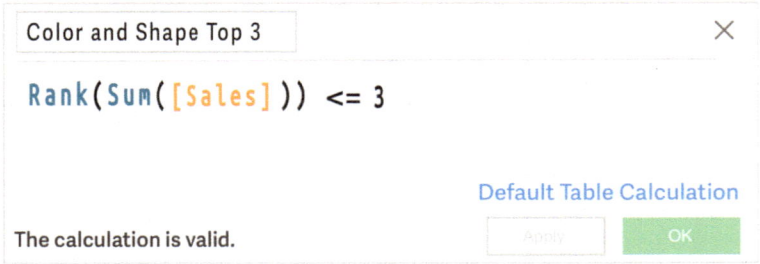

FIGURE 7.53
The Color and Shape Top 3 calculated field.

I downloaded school data from the New York City data hub at https://data.cityofnewyork.us to create this density chart. When I connected the data source, Tableau generated fields with geographic roles of latitude and longitude automatically because there is a postal code field in the data.

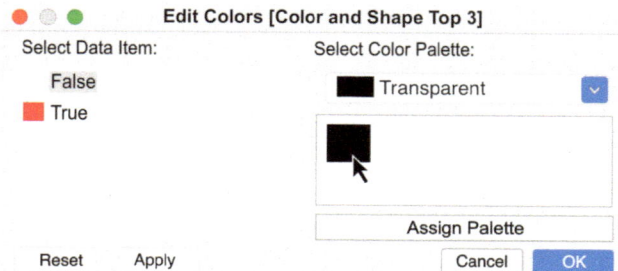

FIGURE 7.56
The **Edit Colors** dialog box.

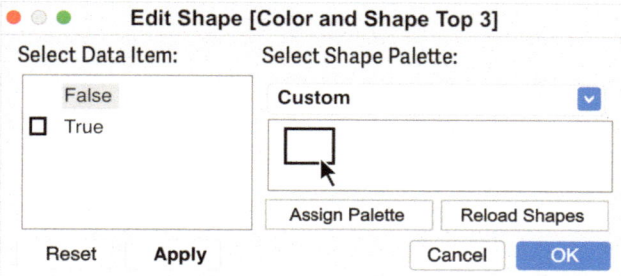

FIGURE 7.57
The **Edit Shape** dialog box.

1. Create a new worksheet and use the drop-down arrow on the **Marks** card to change the mark type to **Density**.

2. Select the [Longitude] and [Latitude] fields and drag them onto the canvas.

3. Drag the [Postal Code] field onto *Detail* on the **Marks** card.

4. Double-click the *Size* tile on the **Marks** card and move the slider to the right.

5. Double-click the *Color* tile on the **Marks** card and select one of the density color palettes. In Figure 7.62, I selected "Density Multi-color Light." If I increase the intensity setting on the *Color* tile, the red areas become darker.

7.2.11 Maps

Maps use latitude and longitude fields. Tableau auto-generates these fields when it recognizes location fields like zip codes or cities. Drag [Latitude] and [Longitude] fields onto the canvas and select the **Map** mark type from the drop-down on the **Marks** card, as shown in Figure 7.63.

You can use the **Map** menu to change the background map or other options. In Figure 7.64, I selected a satellite background.

Tableau Public file:

https://public.tableau.com/views/Ch5Maps/
Dashboard?:language=en-US&:sid=&:
display_count=n&:origin=viz_share_link

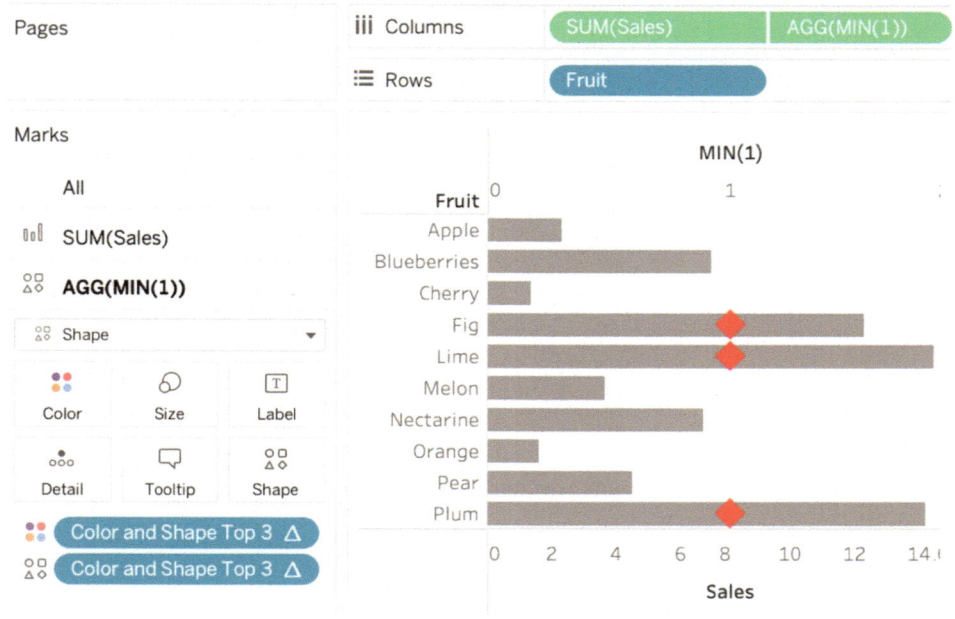

FIGURE 7.58
Horizontal bar chart with red diamonds.

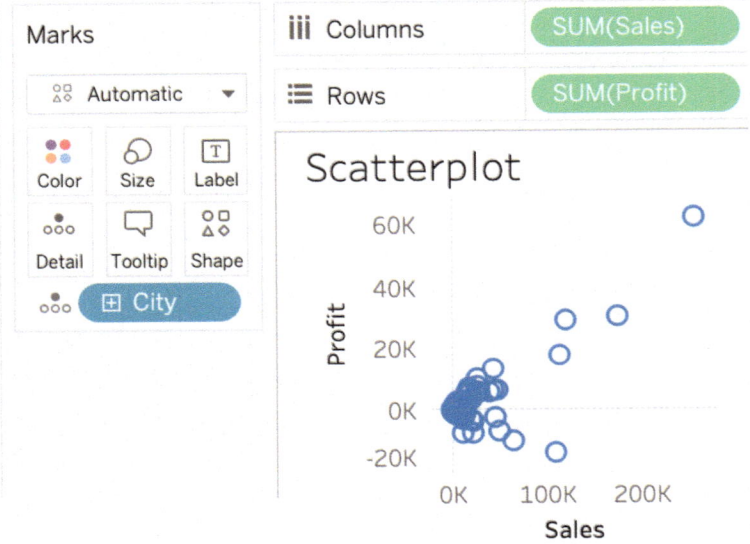

FIGURE 7.59
A Scatter Plot

FIGURE 7.60
Side-by-side circles.

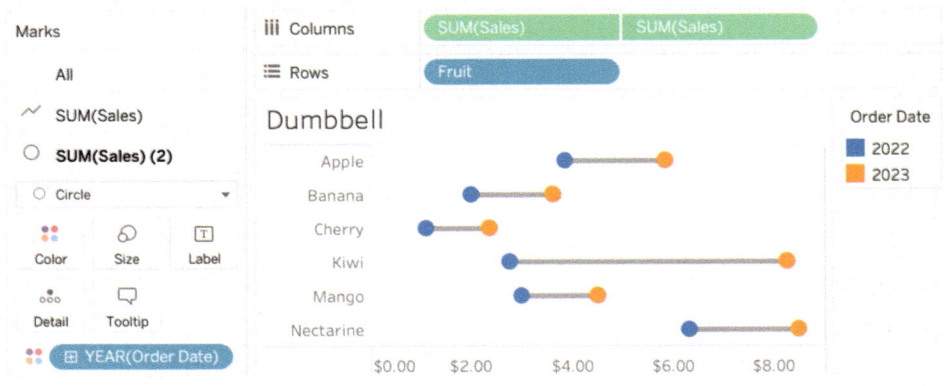

FIGURE 7.61
A Dumbbell chart.

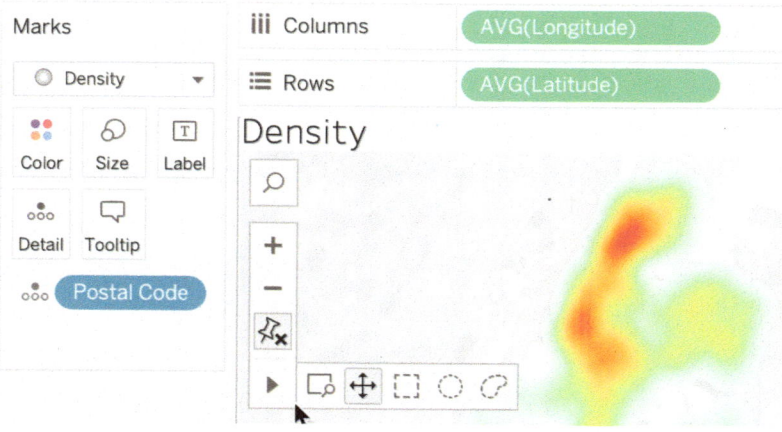

FIGURE 7.62
A density map.

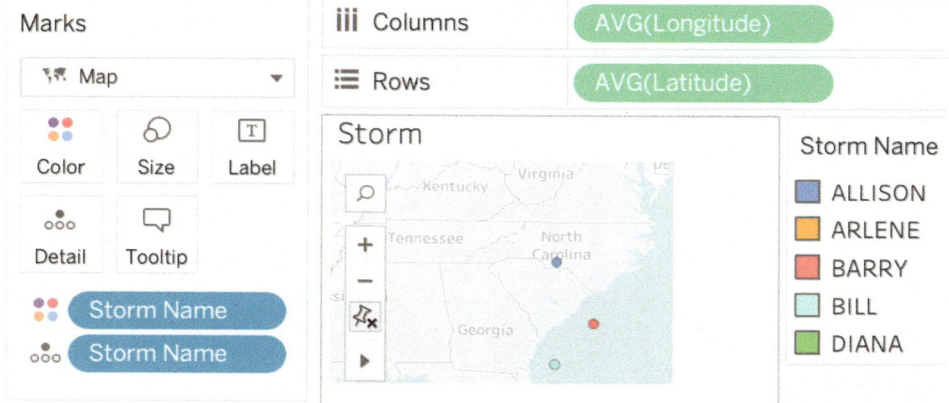

FIGURE 7.63
Map chart with a color legend.

7.3 The Color Property

The *Color* property controls the color of marks, or values, in the view in two ways:

- Default color for marks in the view.
- Fields on the *Color* tile of the **Marks** card.

The default color setting is handy for assigning a specific color to marks, values, or shapes. For example, you might want "Home Office" to always be blue and "Consumer" to be green.

"Section 14.23 KPIs and BANs (Big Numbers)" on page 347

"Section 12.21 Arrows Comparing Two Values" on page 287

7.3.1 Default Color

In Figure 7.65, neither chart has a field on the *Color* tile. The left chart has the default color blue, and I choose orange as the default color for the chart on the right. If you right-click the *Color* tile in the **Marks** card, you can select a default color that applies to all marks. If your company has an assigned color palette, change the default colors to match.

"Section 14.16 Horizontal Radial Buttons to Change Filters" on page 328 also illustrates how to change the default shape color to black to emphasize one shape.

7.3.2 Fields on the Color Tile

When I add the [State] field to the *Color* tile of the **Marks** card, Tableau adds a **Color Legend** on the right side of the view, as shown in Figure 7.66. Tableau uses

Storm

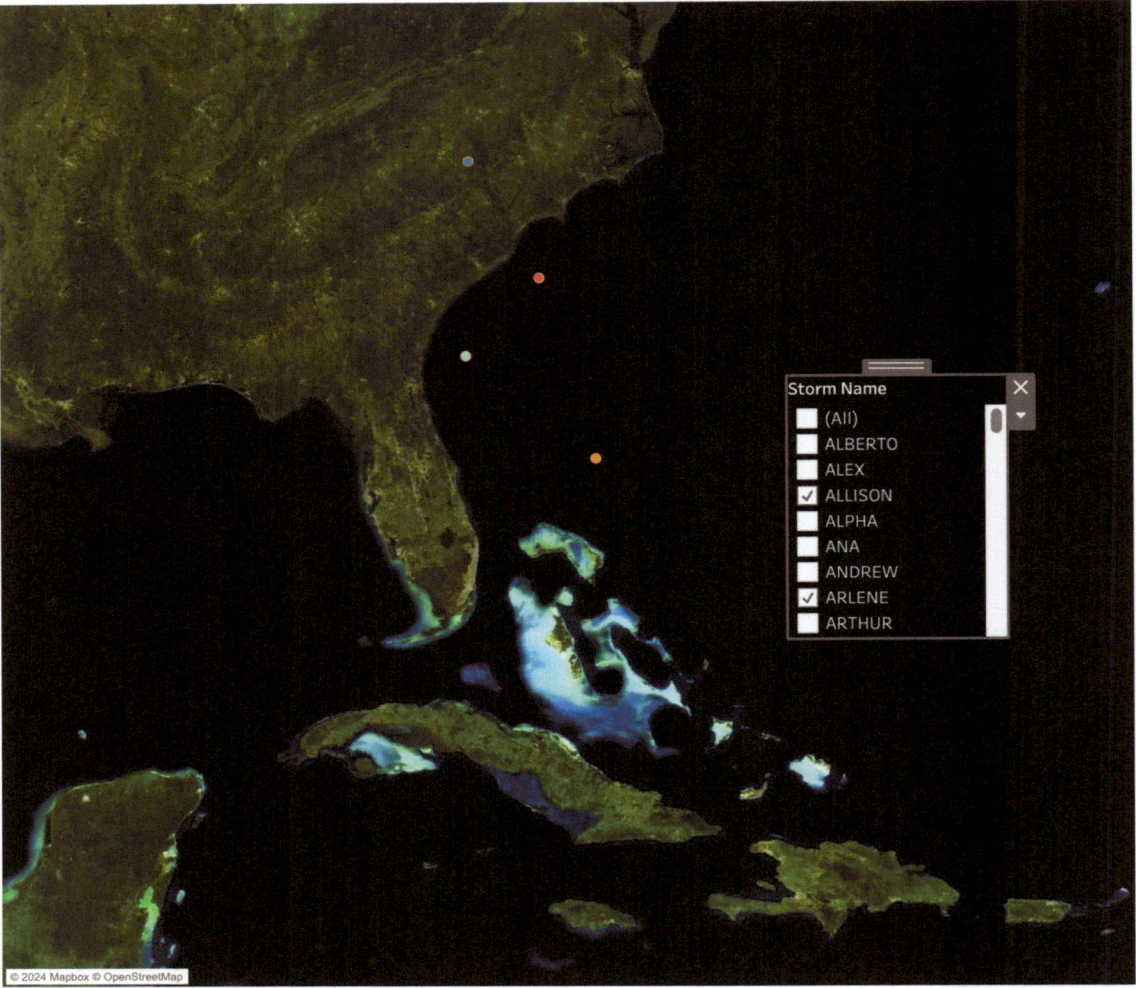

FIGURE 7.64
A Map chart.

a categorical color palette because [State] is a **discrete** dimension. I can assign different colors to individual marks.

You often will see dual-axis charts where the second measure field on the *Color* tile is a calculated field to show the regions that achieved their target or goal or some other comparison that relates parts to the whole. Groups and sets added to the *Color* tile are also a simple way to add color. *"Section 13.6.4 Custom Color and Shape Legend (Diamond)" on page 298* uses a calculated field to highlight the top three sales values. When you have a *continuous* field, the *Color* property uses a diverging palette or a stepped color that groups values into uniform bins. *"Section 13.6.3 Separate Color Legends" on page 298* formats [Measure Values] with a diverging palette.

7.3.3 Color Palettes

Tableau has two types of color palettes:

- Categorical
- Diverging

7.3.3.1 Categorical Color Palette

In the previous example with the [State] field on the *Color* tile, [State] is a **discrete** dimension. Tableau uses a categorical color palette for **discrete** values. Figure 3.15 has a categorical color palette for [Fruit].

7.3.3.2 Diverging Color Palette

A **continuous** field uses a diverging color palette, as shown in Figure 7.67, and can group values into bins

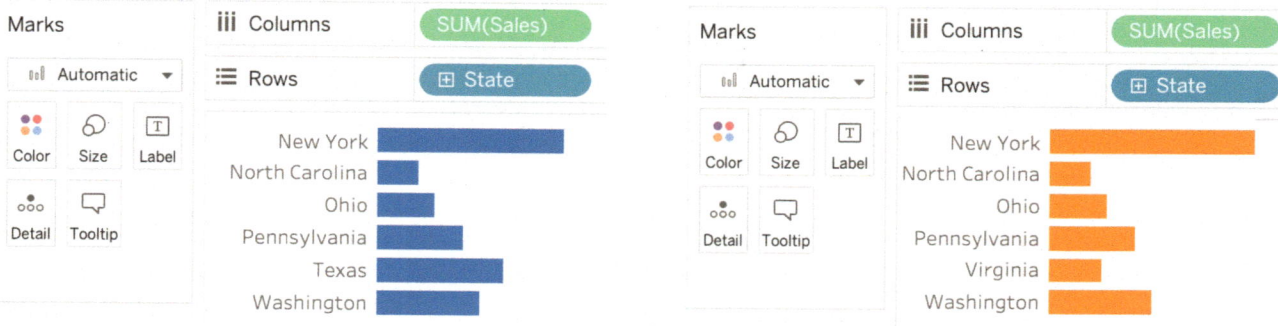

FIGURE 7.65
Default Color.

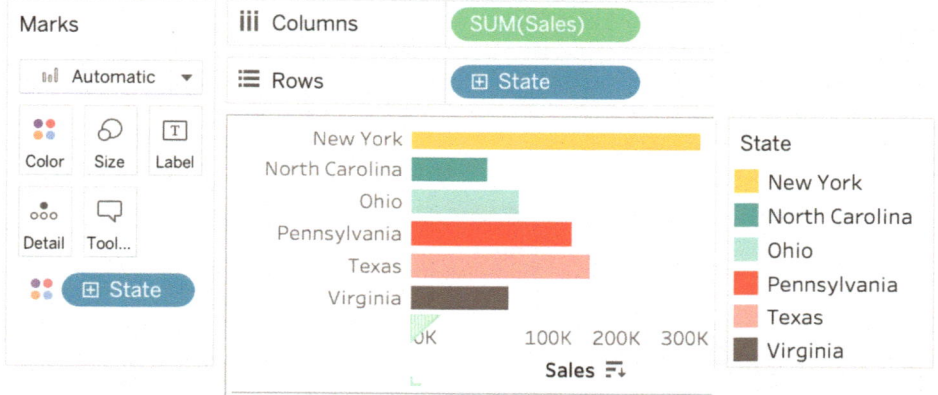

FIGURE 7.66
A Color legend.

with a "Stepped Color." We will look at stepped color in the topic "Color Positive and Negative Numbers" that follows.

Both treemaps (Figure 7.68) and highlight tables use a diverging color palette. Examples of highlight Figure 7.73 in *"Section 7.3.7 Highlight Table – Include Totals in Color" on page 143.* As shown in Figure 7.68, treemaps have no fields on the **Columns** or **Rows** shelves.

7.3.4 Assign Color to Marks

To assign colors to marks, click the *Color* tile. Because of filtering, you may not see all possible values. Temporarily adjust the chart by changing filters or adding fields to the view so you see all possible values. Sometimes, you will also have to remove a field from the *Color* tile and drag it back onto the *Color* tile to see the newly assigned colors.

7.3.4.1 Halo

In Figure 7.70, in the *Symbol Map Chart*, I changed the "Halo" option on the *Color* tile to surround marks

with a black outline border. To make marks stand out against a background image or map, surround each mark with a solid contrasting color or "halo."

To create a symbol map chart, download the New York City taxi zones file from https://data.cityofnewyork.us and follow these steps.

1. Select [Postal Code] and [Total Student 10/26] in the **Data** pane and click **Show Me** in the top-right corner of the screen. Select **symbol maps** in the second row. Tableau creates latitude and longitude fields from the [Postal Code] field and adds the new fields to the **Data** pane.

2. Use the drop-down arrow on the **Marks** card to change the mark type to "Density."

3. Add [Total Student 10/25] to the *Color* tile on the **Marks** card. Double-click the *Color* tile to increase the intensity to 70%. Also, add a dark halo color to the marks.

4. Use the *Size* tile on the **Marks** card to increase the size of the marks.

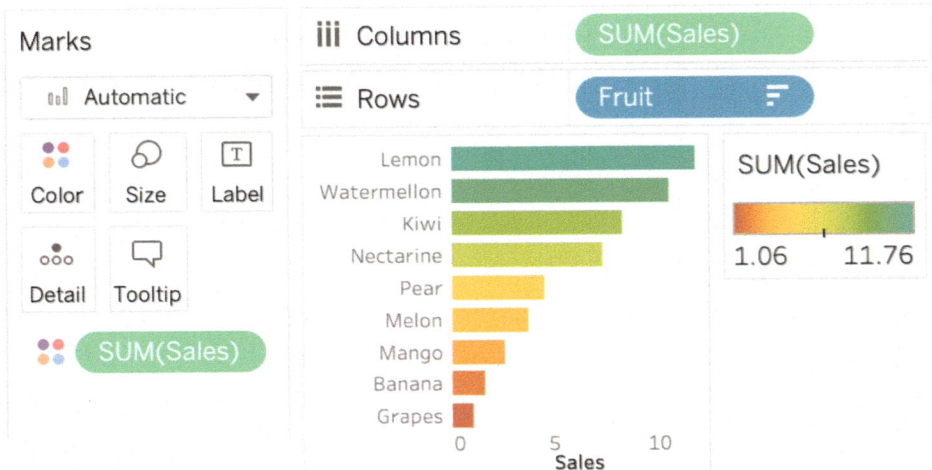

FIGURE 7.67
A diverging color palette.

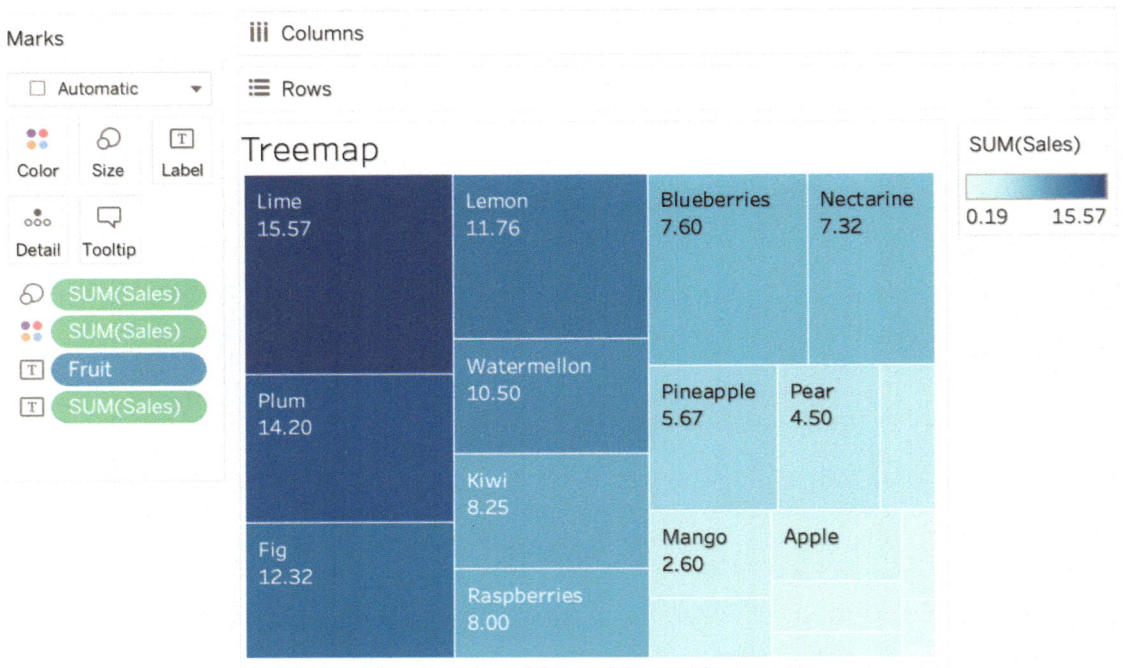

FIGURE 7.68
A Treemap chart.

7.3.5 Border or Outline Color of Bars

Double-click the *Color* tile on the **Marks** card to change or remove the outline around bars and select "Border."

7.3.6 Color Positive and Negative Numbers

With the option "Use Full-Color Range," <u>Tableau uses full intensity</u> for both positive and negative numbers. If you only have a few negative numbers,

uncheck "Use Full-Color Range." Add a **continuous** field to the *Color* tile on the **Marks** card to focus on positive vs. negative values. Edit the color palette to use "Stepped Color" with two "steps," as shown in Figure 7.71.

In Figure 7.72, the negative marks are red. *"Section 15.5 Switch Between Measures with Parameters" on page 369* uses a stepped color setting. Figure 12.4 also shows positive and negative marks.

7.3.7 Highlight Table – Include Totals in Color

In Figure 7.73, the *Grand Total* column on the right does not have the same colors as the body of the highlight table. A highlight table is a **Square** mark type with a diverging color palette because it has a **continuous** field. *"Section 13.1.7.1 Highlight Table – Mark Labels" on page 292* illustrates creating a highlight table.

Tableau Public file:

> https://public.tableau.com/app/profile/cathy.y7960/viz/HighlightTables1070/Dashboard1

Click the *Color* tile on the **Marks** card and then click the "Edit Colors" button. In the **Edit Colors** dialog window shown in Figure 7.74, check "Include Totals" in the bottom left corner.

After the change, the total column also has colors, as shown in Figure 7.75.

7.3.8 Match Label Colors to Bar Color

Matching mark labels to bar colors is a nice touch for your visualization. Select the *Label* tile and the **Font**

FIGURE 7.69

Tip: To choose new custom colors when assigning colors to values, double-click the assigned color in the left pane to open a "Color Picker" dialog.

drop-down arrow to open the *context menu* for fonts. Click the "Match Mark Color" button to match colors, as shown in Figure 7.76.

7.3.9 Show Color Legend(s)

You can show the **Color Legend** when there is a field on the *Color* tile in your view. When you add the [Measured Values] field to the *Color* tile on the **Marks** card, you can choose to use separate color legends for each field. For an example, check out *"Section 13.6 Legends and Controls" on page 298*. On the **Analysis** menu, select "Legends" to display a color legend.

7.3.10 Color Legend from Field Values

Create a worksheet to use as a "Color Legend" with a field on the *Text* and *Color* tiles of the **Marks** card. Create unique color legends by incorporating color in titles and using field values as part of the 'worksheet' that will be a color legend.

7.3.11 Opacity

Even when there is no field on the *Color* tile, you can double-click it and choose "More Colors" to change the default mark color, opacity, or border. When opacity is set to 0%, marks are invisible. Two measures with different opacity levels can make one mark stand out, as shown in Figure 7.77.

One way to add color to the visualization is to use a calculated field similar to the one in Figure 7.79 to

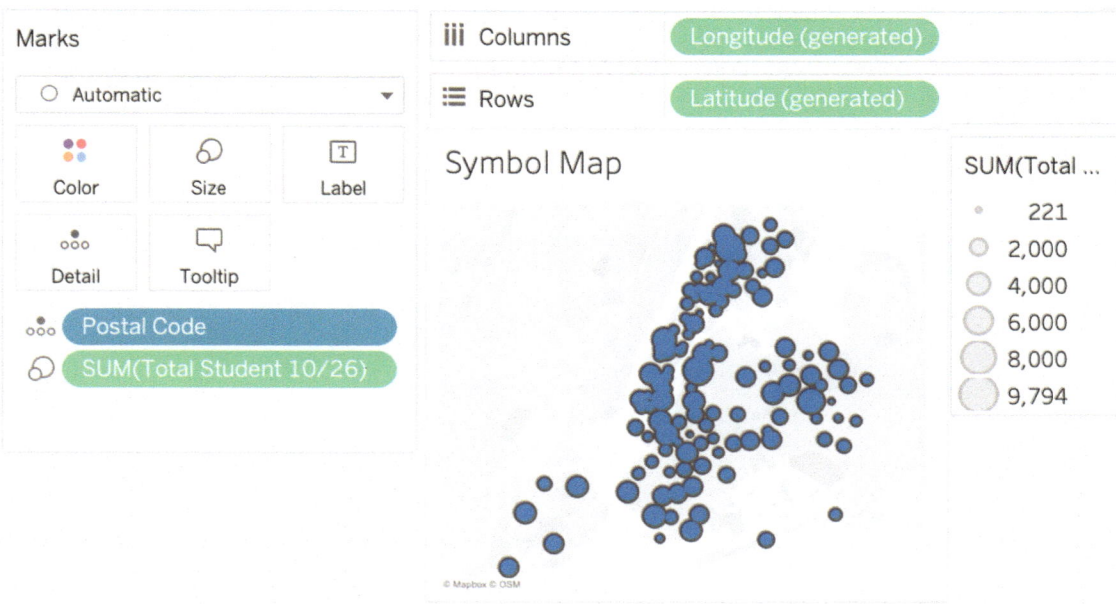

FIGURE 7.70

The Halo setting on a Map chart.

identify one value and assign that value to a different color. In the *Color* tile properties shown in Figure 7.78, I assign that value to a different color. I have two values on the left side of this example: "last" and "other."

The calculated field shown in Figure 7.79 uses the LAST() table calculation to select 2023 data. When added to the *Color* tile on the **Marks** card, I can assign a different color to the 2023 bar, as shown in Figure 7.77.

7.3.12 Transparency

To call attention or focus to a particular mark, assign a color like blue to one mark and assign a transparent color (hex code: #00FFFFFF) to the other marks, as shown in these examples:

"*Section 7.2.7.4 Transparent Shapes to Call Attention to Some Marks*" on page 129

"*Section 13.6.4 Custom Color and Shape Legend (Diamond)*" on page 298

FIGURE 7.71
Stepped color.

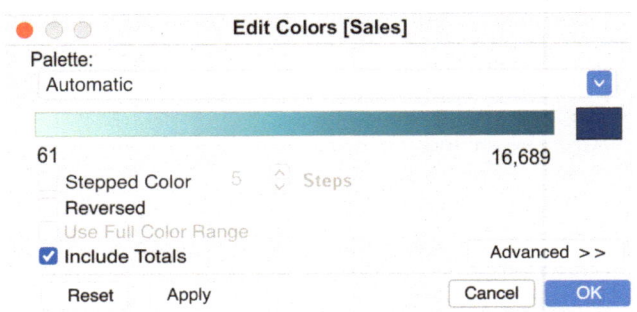

FIGURE 7.74
Include totals option.

FIGURE 7.72
Positive and negative marks.

Segment	2019	2020	2021	2022	Grand Total
Consumer	14,427	368		1,894	16,689
Corporate	3,150	61	1,483	3,572	8,267
Home Office		302	4,164	3,731	8,197

FIGURE 7.75
The grand total column with Colors.

FIGURE 7.73
A highlight table.

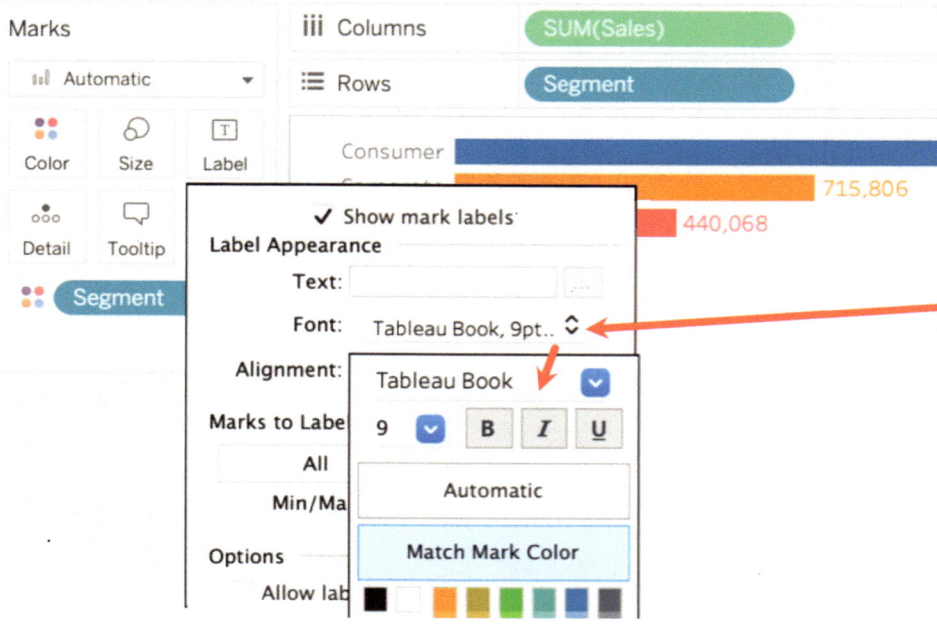

FIGURE 7.76
Match Mark Color.

FIGURE 7.77
Opacity.

7.3.13 Color Not Applied

When you have a field on the *Color* tile and color is not applied, check to see if the **Mark** type is "Shape." On the **Marks** card, select "Text" from the drop-down to change the **Mark** type to **Text** to see the assigned colors.

7.3.14 White or Special Colors

When you have a field on the *Color* tile on the **Marks** card, double-click the *Color* tile and choose "Edit Colors." On the left, double-click the item you want to change to white to open the "Color Picker" dialog. Select a white area on your screen using the dropper tool. You can select any color with the "Color Picker" dialog.

7.3.15 Color Tile Affects Lines in the View

In the formatting chapter, we examine *Lines* on the **Format Control Panel**. The **Marks** card *Color* tile can also add vertical lines to the view. Change the *opacity* to 0% with the *Color* tile to remove lines.

7.3.16 Call Attention to the Difference with Color

This example uses color to highlight whether sales are above or below the year-over-year goal of 1.1 times sales (Figure 7.81). This dashboard has two charts with the *same axis range*. Chart titles, axes, and field labels are hidden in both charts. The dashboard title is a dashboard text object. The *Floating* chart is on top of the *Background* chart and has blue lines representing sales **up to the goal line**. The *Background* chart bars are

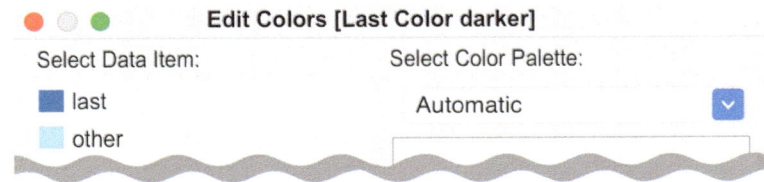

FIGURE 7.78
Edit Colors.

FIGURE 7.79
Calculated Field.

FIGURE 7.80

Tip: Suppose you use a calculated field to assign colors and change the calculation field's logic. In that case, you might have to remove a field from the *Color* tile and drag the field back onto the *Color* tile to see the newly assigned colors.

color-encoded red or green to reflect the difference between yearly sales and the goal.

While I like the visual aspect that calls out the difference from the goal, I would not recommend this type of chart if the underlying data might change because the axis ranges must match between the two charts.

Tableau Public file:

https://public.tableau.com/views/
AccentuatetheDifferencewithColors1089/
Dashboard1?:language=en-US&:sid=&:
display_count=n&:origin=viz_share_link

7.3.16.1 Preview the Finished Dashboard

The finished dashboard, as shown in Figure 7.81, has blue bars indicating sales up to the goal and red or green bars indicating the difference between sales and the goal. The reference line is the goal.

7.3.16.2 Create the Visualization

1. Connect a new workbook to the *Sample Superstore* data source. Create a [Goal] field with a calculation that the previous year's sales increased by ten percent (Figure 7.82).

2. Create a new field [Background Bar to display] (Figure 7.83). If sales are under the goal, I display the [Goal] value, which I ultimately encode in red. When sales are under the [Goal], the *Floating* chart shows a blue bar for [Sales], and the gap between sales and the goal is red.

3. Create a new worksheet *Background* and add the [Background Bar to display] field to the **Rows** shelf (Figure 7.84). Because the [Goal] is a year-over-year calculation, there is no bar for the first year. I also added an annotation to show the best year was 2022.

   Note that the axis range is 0 to 799.75. When I create the *Floating* worksheet in Step 6, I want it to have a similar axis range.

4. Next, I want a text label showing the year-over-year difference in sales. I created a new field [Difference] and added it to the *Text* tile on the **Marks** card of the *Background* worksheet (Figure 7.85).

5. I create a new field [Bar color to display] and add it to the *Color* tile on the **Marks** card of the *Background* worksheet.

6. Click the worksheet title and uncheck "Show Title." Click field labels on the view and choose "Hide Field Labels." Uncheck "Show Header" for the [Floating Bar to Display] field (Figure 7.86).

7. Now, we will create the *Floating* worksheet. On the final dashboard, the blue bars on the *Floating* worksheet are on top of the *Background* worksheet. Create a new field [Floating Bar to display] (Figure 7.87).

   When [Sales] are **over** the [Goal], the green bars in the *Background* worksheet represent the amount **over** the [Goal]. In this case, the blue bars are not the total [Sales]; instead, they are the [Goal]. The green bar in the *Background* worksheet fills the gap between the [Goal] and [Sales], highlighting sales that are **over** the goal.

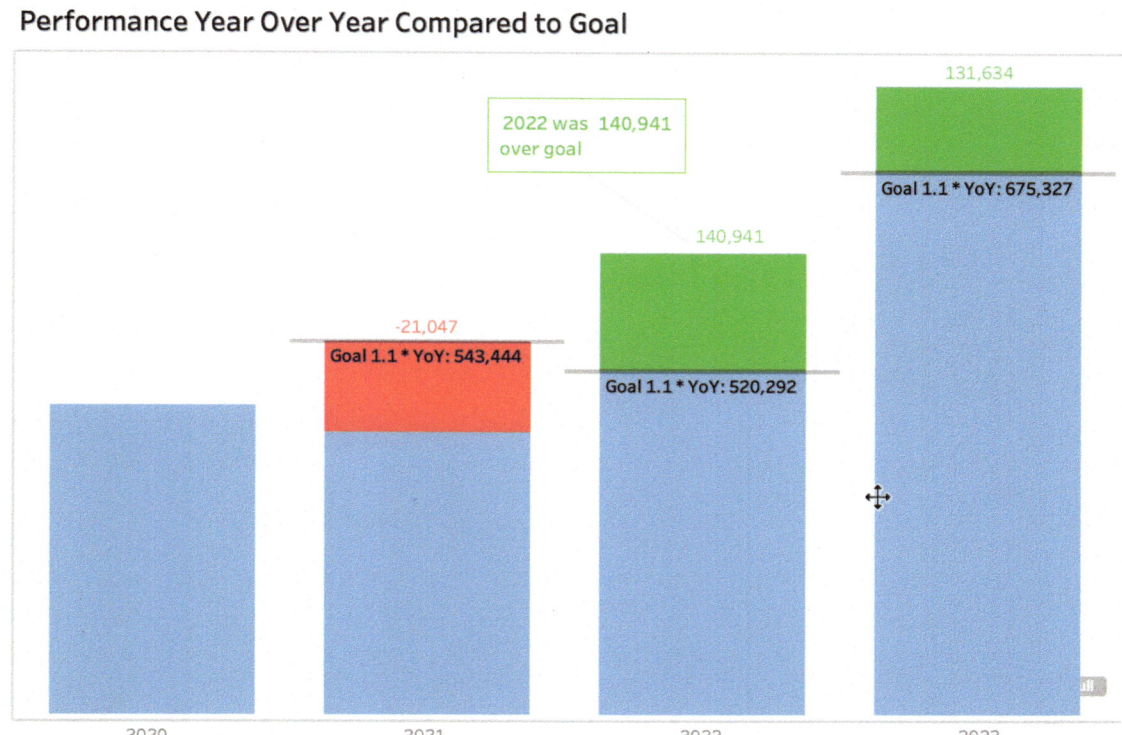

FIGURE 7.81
Dashboard Showing the Difference between Sales and Goals.

FIGURE 7.82
The Calculated field goal.

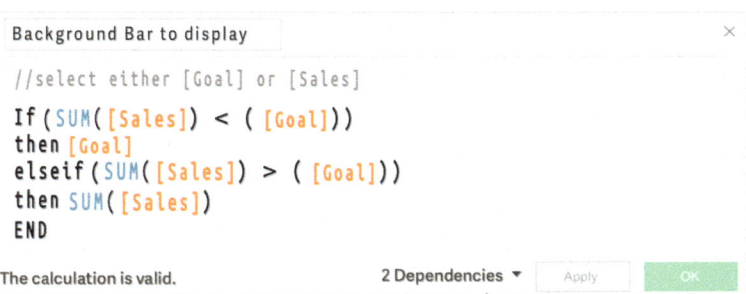

FIGURE 7.83
The calculated field Background bar to display.

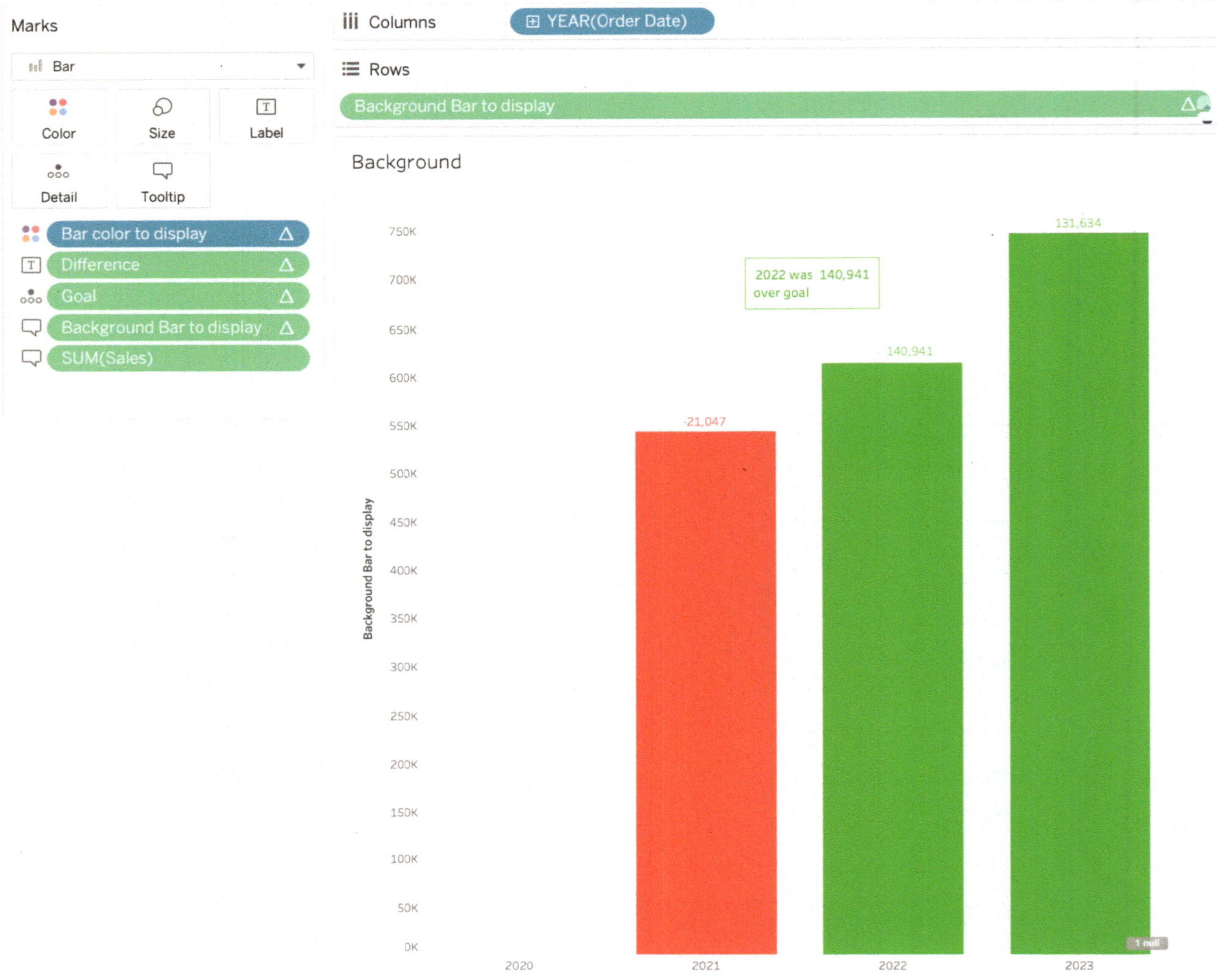

Marks

Bar

Color	Size	Label

Detail	Tooltip

Bar color to display △
Difference △
Goal △
Background Bar to display △
SUM(Sales)

Columns YEAR(Order Date)

Rows Background Bar to display △

Background

[Bar chart showing years 2020–2023 with a vertical axis "Background Bar to display" from 0K to 750K. The 2021 bar is red labeled -21,047, the 2022 bar is green labeled 140,941 with a callout "2022 was 140,941 over goal", the 2023 bar is green labeled 131,634. A "1 null" marker appears at bottom right.]

FIGURE 7.84
The Bar Chart.

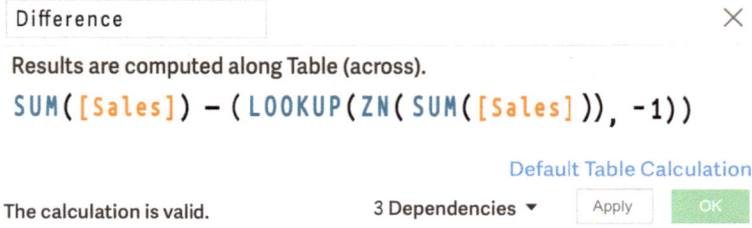

Difference   ×

Results are computed along Table (across).

SUM([Sales]) − (LOOKUP(ZN(SUM([Sales])), -1))

Default Table Calculation

The calculation is valid.   3 Dependencies ▼   Apply   OK

FIGURE 7.85
The Calculated field difference.

8. Add the [Floating Bar to display] field to the **Rows** shelf on the *Floating* worksheet to reflect sales up to the goal reference line. Right-click the axis and set the axis range to match the [Background] worksheet axis.

9. Click the worksheet title on the *Floating* worksheet and uncheck "Show Title." Click field labels on the view and choose "Hide Field Labels." Uncheck "Show Header" for the [Floating Bar to Display] field (Figure 7.88).

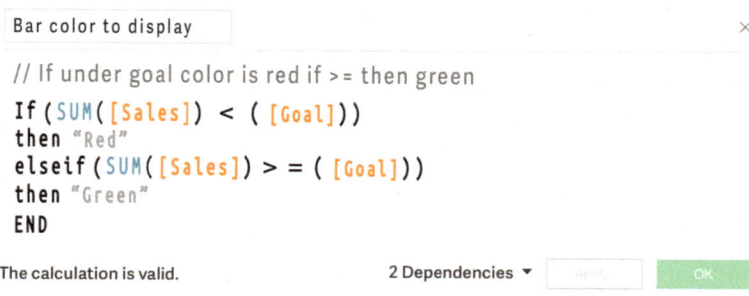

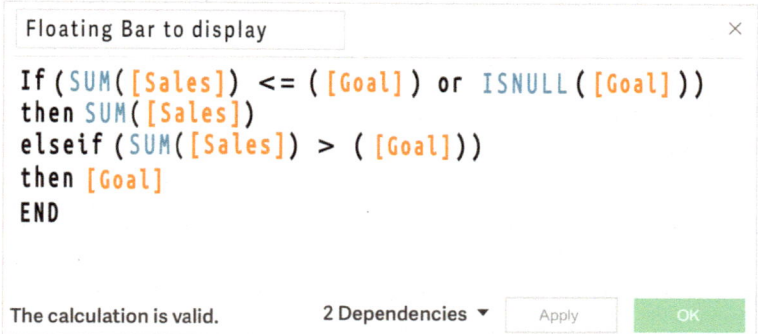

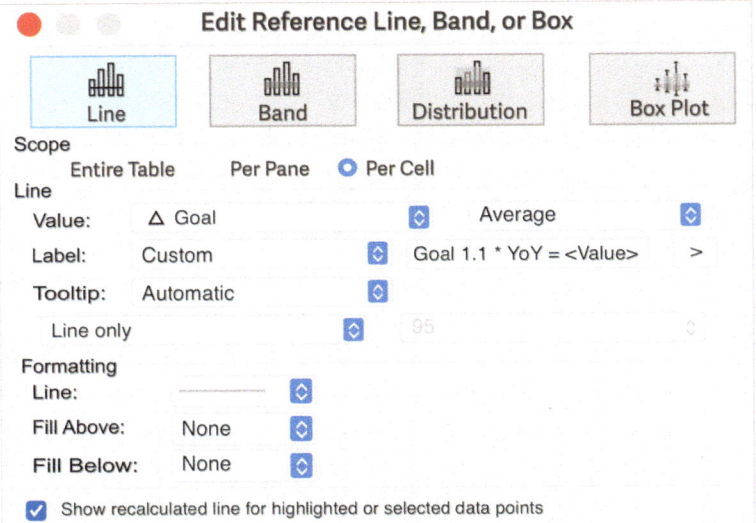

FIGURE 7.89
The **Edit Reference Line** dialog box.

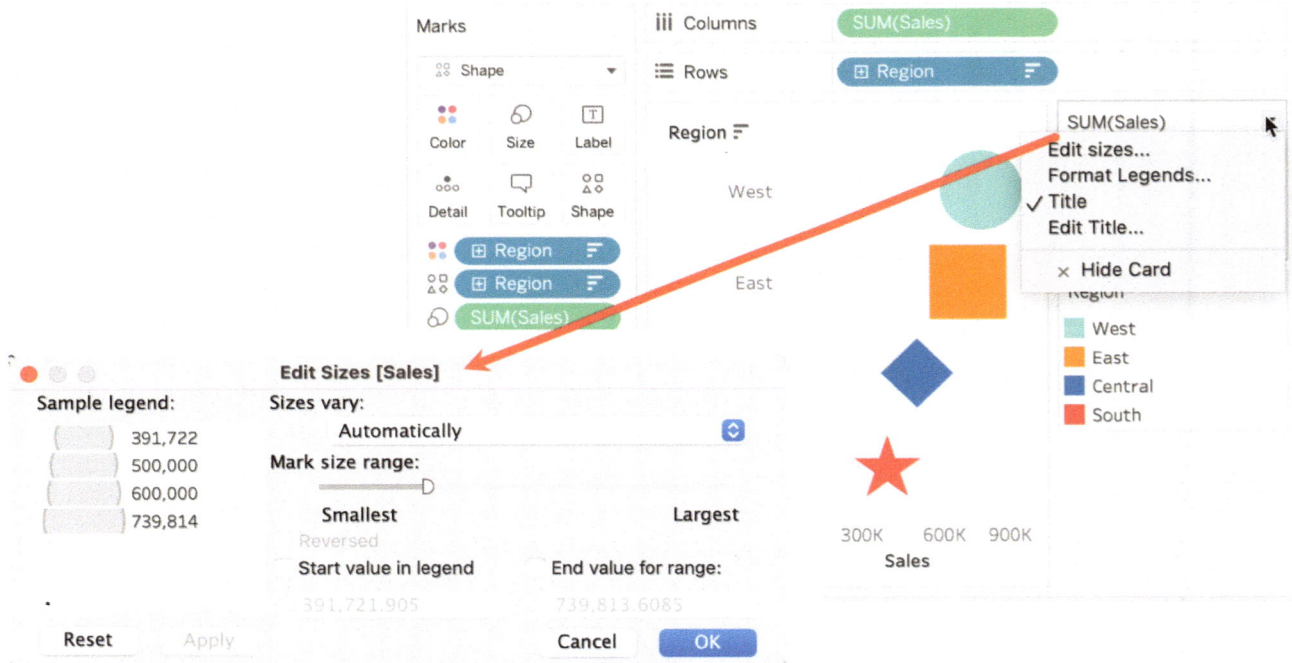

FIGURE 7.90
The Size legend.

10. To add a reference line to the *Floating* worksheet, I must add the [Goal] field to the *Detail* tile on the **Marks** card. On the left side of the view, move to the **Analytics** pane and drag the "Reference Line" onto the canvas. Select the options in Figure 7.89, adding a custom "Label" with the [Goal] value.

11. Create a dashboard and add a text object for the dashboard title. Drag the *Background* worksheet below the text object.

12. Drag the *Floating* dashboard over the *Background* worksheet as a floating object.

7.4 The Size Property

Generally, I use the *Size* property with **Shape** marks, but sometimes, you want to adjust bar sizes in a bar chart. Earlier, we looked at the topic "Bullet Chart," which uses the *Size* property. Because the [Sales] field is on the *Size* tile in Figure 7.90, there is a **Size Legend** on the right side of the screen. When you click the drop-down arrow on the **Size Legend**, the "Edit Sizes" dialog box opens, and you can adjust the various mark sizes. The **Edit Sizes** dialog box gives you more control over the size of marks compared to the slider bar in the *Size* tile.

The *Size* property behaves differently depending on whether a field is **continuous** or **discrete**. In the following example, the [Sales] field is on the **Rows** shelf, and there is no field specifically on the *Size* tile. The **continuous** [Sales] field is a green pill, and when I click on the *Size* tile, the pop-up has radial buttons for "Manual" or "Fixed," as shown in Figure 7.91.

7.5 The Text or Label Property

The "Text" or "Label" property formats the text values of fields added to the *Text* tile on the **Marks** card. If you do not see the mark "labels" on the view, choose "Show Mark Labels" from the **Analysis** menu. The *Text* property also sets text alignment. Figure 7.92 has two fields on the *Text* tile.

In this case, I want both text values on the same line. To edit the *Text* property, click the *Text* tile on the **Marks** card to open the pop-up dialog with choices for "Text" and "Alignment." Click the *ellipsis* to the right of the **Text** box, as shown in Figure 7.94.

The **Edit Label** window opens with the fields on separate lines, as shown in Figure 7.95. By default, Tableau arranges them on separate lines when you have two or more fields on the *Text* tile. Click the *Text* tile to edit the text so values are on the same line.

After editing the text, click **OK** to save the changes. The **Insert** button on the right side of the **Edit Label** window allows you to add fields to the label, as shown in Figure 7.96. Select the button and click the drop-down to open the *context menu*.

After resizing the columns, the visualization in Figure 7.97 displays the text on one line.

"Section 11.13.2 The Visualization without LoD Calculations" on page 241 demonstrates how to add fields to the *Text* or *Label* property on the **Marks** card. In *"Section 6.3 Multiple Charts in One View" on page 105*, a placeholder field on the *Label* tile on the **Marks** card adds a second layer for headings.

7.5.1 A Heading for a Field on the "Text" Tile

To add a heading to a field on the *Text* tile of the **Marks** card, create a calculated field with the heading text. See *"Section 13.4.2 A Heading for a Field on the Text Tile" on page 295* for an example.

7.5.2 Text Values Not Shown

When adding a field to the *Text* tile on the **Marks** card, if you do not see any values in the view, adjust the formatting so the text is visible.

1. As a test, add the field to the *Tooltip* tile and hover over the mark to view the *Tooltip*.

2. You may need to adjust the formatting or column width if you see the data in the *Tooltip* but not in the view. For example, change these format settings:

- Round a number with six precision points to one decimal point.

- Adjust the font size on the *Text* tile.

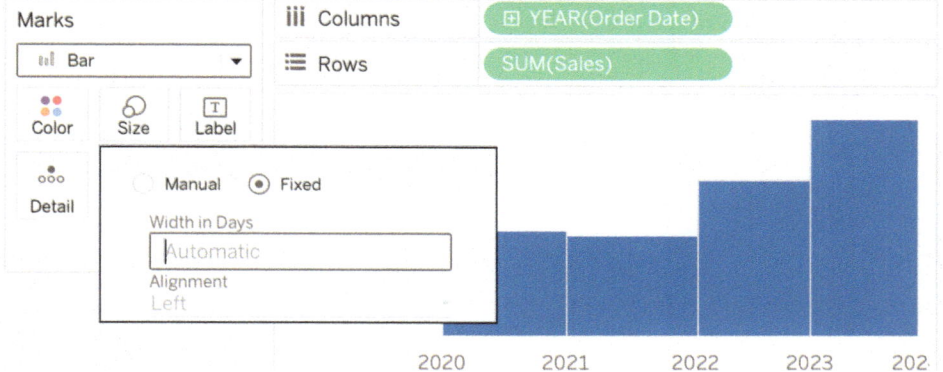

FIGURE 7.91
Fixed size.

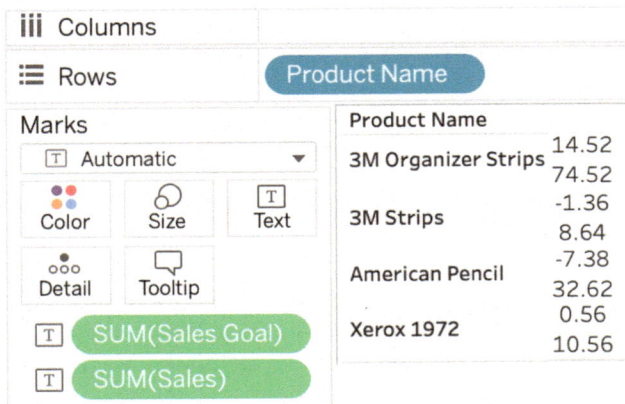

FIGURE 7.92
The Text tile.

FIGURE 7.93
Tip: If you have already formatted a text field and want to replace it, drag the new field on top of the old field to keep the text formatting.

FIGURE 7.94
Edit Text.

7.6 The Detail Tile

When you want to use fields in calculations and aggregations but do not want the field data visible in the view, add the field to the *Detail* tile on the **Marks** card. The example, "Only Shapes," which we looked at earlier, uses the *Detail* tile. These examples also use the *Detail* tile:

7.6.1 Field Not Available

If you are trying to use a field in a tooltip or as a visualization object in general and it is unavailable, add it to the *Detail* tile on the **Marks** card.

7.7 Tooltips

A *tooltip* is displayed when you hover your mouse over one or more marks in the visualization, as shown in Figure 7.98. You can choose tooltip content with the *Tooltip* property on the **Marks** card, including formatting text and adding field data, URL links, or even other charts. Using Tableau Desktop or Tableau server, viewers can interact with a view and display a *tooltip* as you move your mouse over a data point. We look at tooltips in more detail in **Chapter 15** on *page 360*.

Tooltip fields do not have to be part of the main body of the chart, but they must be on the *Tooltip* or *Details* property on the **Marks** card. I like to use *tooltips* to show different aggregation levels compared to the view. For example, the visualization shows sales by region and I also want to see all sales. In that case, I suggest adding a calculated field in the *tooltip* that shows the sum of all sales in all regions. In the example in Figure 7.98, the tooltip displays the sum of 1,755 in the gray area at the top of the tooltip. The sum of the two *selected* marks, 1,120 and 635, is 1,755.

7.8 Reference Lines

We looked at many chart examples that used reference lines in this chapter. Reference lines delineate a chart. For example, marks that meet a sales goal value versus marks that did not meet the sales goal. In this chapter, we created several reference line examples.

- Gantt Bar Marks
- Bullet Graph

To create a reference line, select the **Analytics** pane on the left and drag *Reference Line* onto the canvas, as

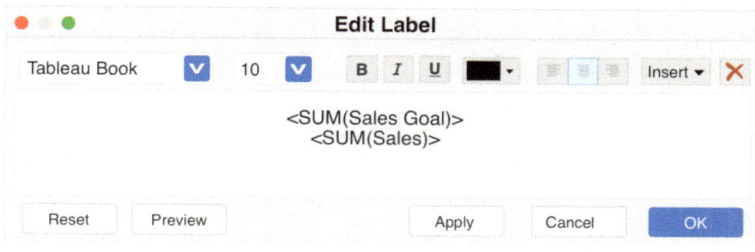

FIGURE 7.95
Edit Label.

FIGURE 7.96
Edit Label Insert button.

Product Name	
3M Organizer Strips	Goal: 14.52. Actual: 74.52
3M Strips	Goal: -1.36. Actual: 8.64
American Pencil	Goal: -7.38. Actual: 32.62
Xerox 1972	Goal: 0.56. Actual: 10.56

FIGURE 7.97
Edited Text.

shown in Figure 7.99. The **Edit Reference Line, Band, or Box** screen opens with scope choices at the top: *Table*, *Pane*, or *Cell*. Choose *Cell*. To manually type a specific value, use the "Constant" setting. For example, if you want a goal of 120% or a "Constant" value of 1.2, on the right side of the **Edit Reference Line, Band, or Box** screen, select "Constant" from the drop-down menu as shown in Figure 7.99. Instead of a constant, you can also use any measure field.

Chapter 11's "INCLUDE" topic on *page 239* uses two reference lines with a custom label that includes a field value. A field must be part of the view to be used in a reference line; in this case, it was on the *Detail* tile of the **Marks** card.

If you cannot grab the reference line to edit or delete the line, try clicking the axis to open the context menu. You can also use this context menu to add a reference line.

7.8.1 Reference Line with Shading

When reference lines are combined with a parameter, viewers can set the reference line limits – in this case,

the profit goal, as shown in Figure 7.100. We look at parameters in **Chapter 15**.

For this reference line, the fill above it is light green, and the fill below it is gray, as shown in *Figure 7.101*. The Reference Line Itself Is Green.

7.8.2 Format Reference Line

The default formatting for a reference line is on the right in Figure 7.102. I find the light shading hard to read, so I click on the reference line and choose "Format." After formatting the opacity and color, the left chart is easier to read.

7.8.3 Bullet Graph with a Reference Line and Distribution Band

This bullet graph example in Figure 7.104 has a reference line and a distribution band for comparing this year's data to last year's.

7.8.3.1 Create the Visualization

1. Connect a new workbook to the *Sample Superstore* data source. Create a field [Last Year] for last year's sales and add the field to the *Detail* tile on the **Marks** card.

If **YEAR([Order Date])** = 2020 then **[Sales]** end

2. Create a field [This Year] for this year's sales and add it to the **Columns** shelf.

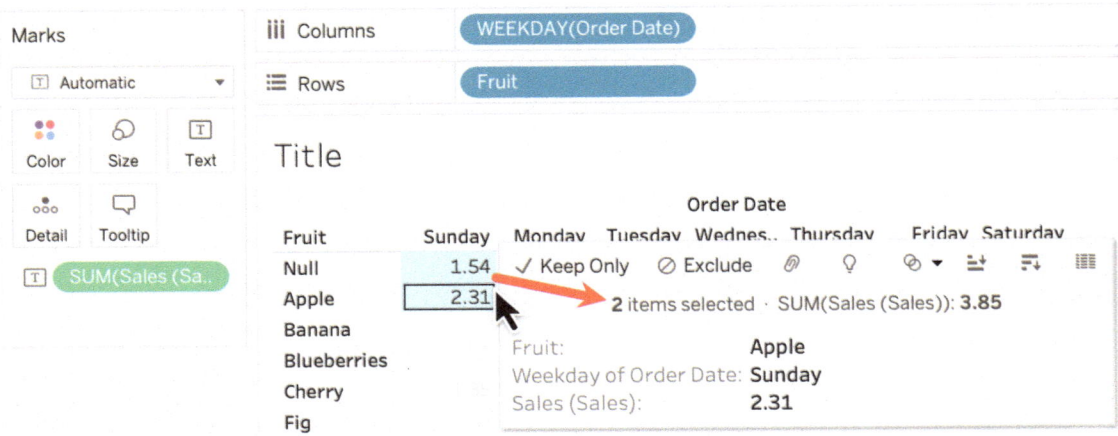

FIGURE 7.98
Tooltips

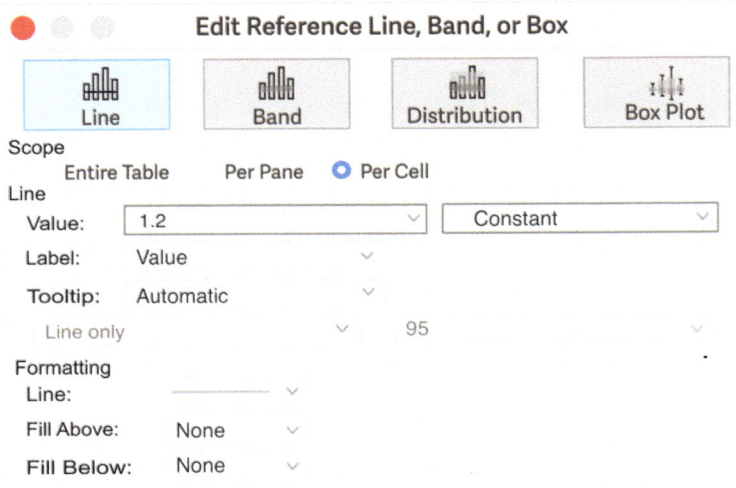

FIGURE 7.99
Reference Line dialog box.

If **YEAR**(**[Order Date]**) = 2021 then **[Sales]** end

3. Drag the [Category] field under the [Segment] field in the **Data** pane to create a hierarchy.

4. Use the *Size* tile on the **Marks** card to narrow the bar width.

5. Right-click the **Axis** and select "Add Reference Line."

- At the top of the **Edit Reference Line, Band, or Box** screen, choose "Line."

- The **Scope** is "Per Cell."

- In the **Line** section, select [SUM(Last Year)] for **Value**, and the aggregation is "Sum."

- For **Label**, use the drop-down arrows to select "None."

- In the **Formatting** section, use the drop-down arrows to select a red color for "Line."

- At the bottom, uncheck "Show recalculated line for highlighted or selected data points." When a viewer selects marks on the view, a second recalculated line appears when this check box is enabled.

6. Add a second reference line (Figure 7.103). Right-click the **Axis** again and select "Add Reference Line."

- At the top of the **Edit Reference Line, Band, or Box** screen, choose "Distribution."

- The **Scope** is "Per Cell."

- In the "Computation" section, click the drop-down arrows for **Value** to see the choices for value. The default "Percentages" is 60, 80, and that is OK (Figure 7.101). Below "Percentages" for "Percent of," use the drop-down arrows to select the field "Sum(Last Year)." Also, change the aggregation to "Sum."

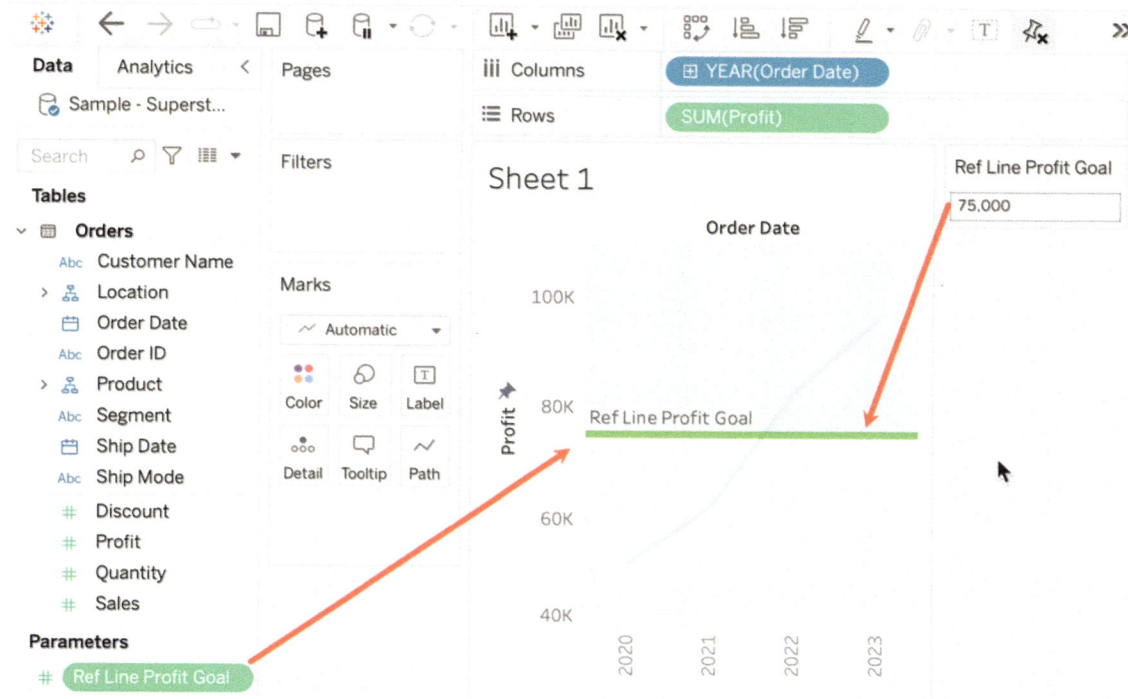

FIGURE 7.100
Shaded reference line.

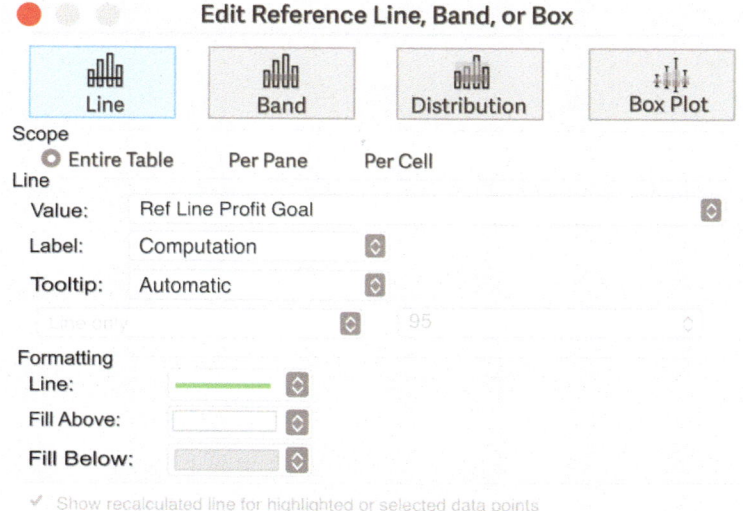

FIGURE 7.101
Reference line formatting.

- For the **Label**, use the drop-down arrows to select "None."
- In the **Formatting** section, check "Fill Below" on the right side. The "Fill" drop-down changes to a two-tone color. Use the drop-down arrows to select teal for "Line."

- At the bottom of the screen, uncheck "Show recalculated line for highlighted or selected data points."
7. Right-click the view and select "Format." Select the *Lines* tool at the top of the **Format** pane on the left. On the *Columns* tab, change **Grid Lines** to "None."

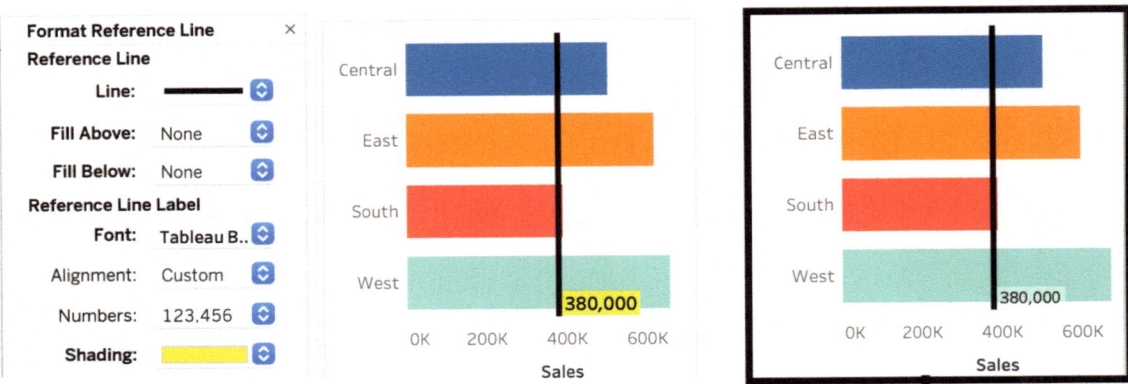

FIGURE 7.102
Format reference line.

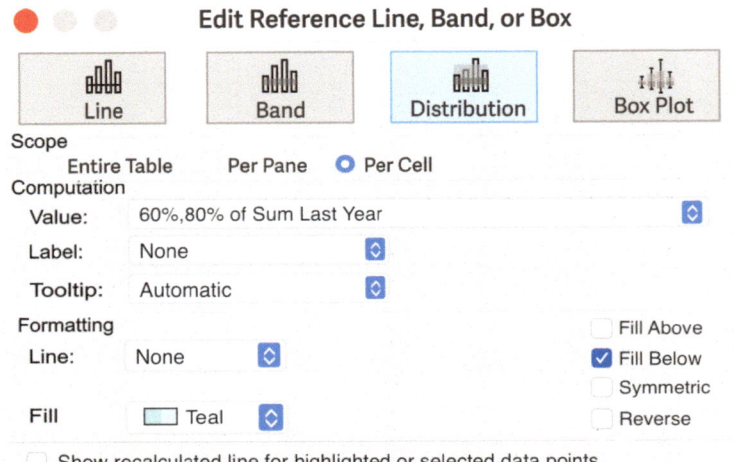

FIGURE 7.103
Uncheck show recalculated line.

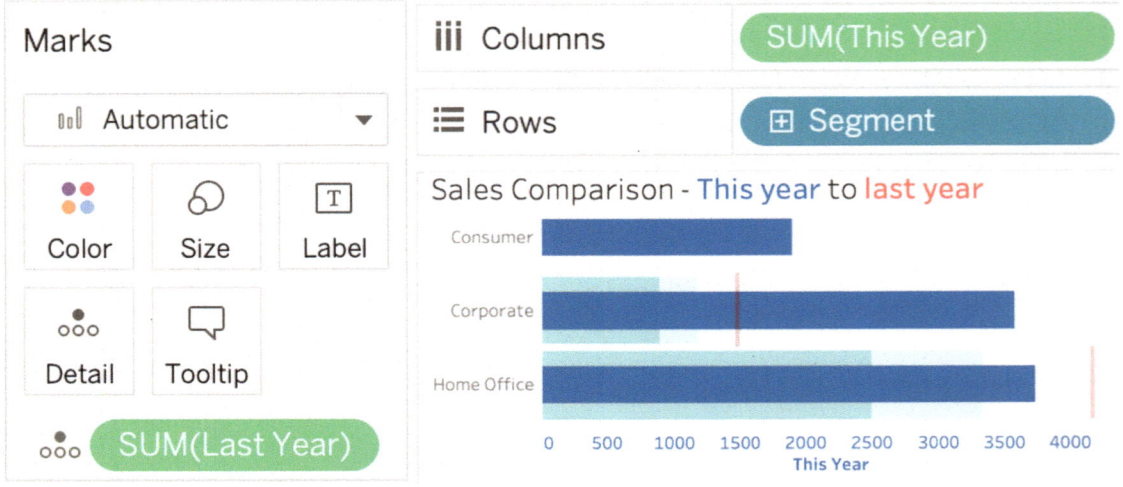

FIGURE 7.104
The Title with matching colors.

Change the **Grid Lines** to a thick white line on the *Rows* tab. If you do not want a gap between the bars, select "None."

8. Adjust the axis and title to indicate the mark and reference line colors (Figure 7.104).

7.9 Trend Lines

To create a trend line, add a date field to the **Rows** or **Columns** shelf and add a **continuous** measure field like [Sales] to the other shelf. From the **Analytics** pane on the left side of the screen, drag a *Trend Line* onto the view.

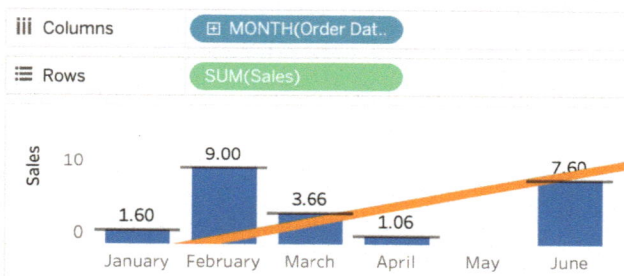

FIGURE 7.105
Trend line over mark labels.

7.9.1 Trend Line Overlaps Mark Label

Sometimes, you need to move a mark label, as in Figure 7.105, where a trend line intersects some of my mark labels. Click the *mark label* and then you can click-drag it to a new location.

7.9.2 Trend Line Grayed Out

There are several causes for a gray **Trend Line** in the **Analytics** pane. In this example, I have a custom date of MDY, which is a "Date Part," as shown in Figure 7.106. If I change the date field to something other than "custom," I can add a trend line. I do have a **continuous** field, which is required to create a trend line. If I added a dimension field to the **Color** tile on the **Marks** card, a **Trend Line** is unavailable. Experiment with the fields in the view to add a **Trend Line**.

7.9.3 Trend Line Color

When you right-click a trend line, you can choose to format color, thickness, and more. If the formatting is not applied correctly, right-click the trend line and choose "Edit All Trend Lines." Uncheck "Allow a trend line per color" under "Options" to ensure that trend line formatting colors are correctly applied.

7.9.4 Remove Trend Line

Select a trend line and click-drag it to remove it from the visualization.

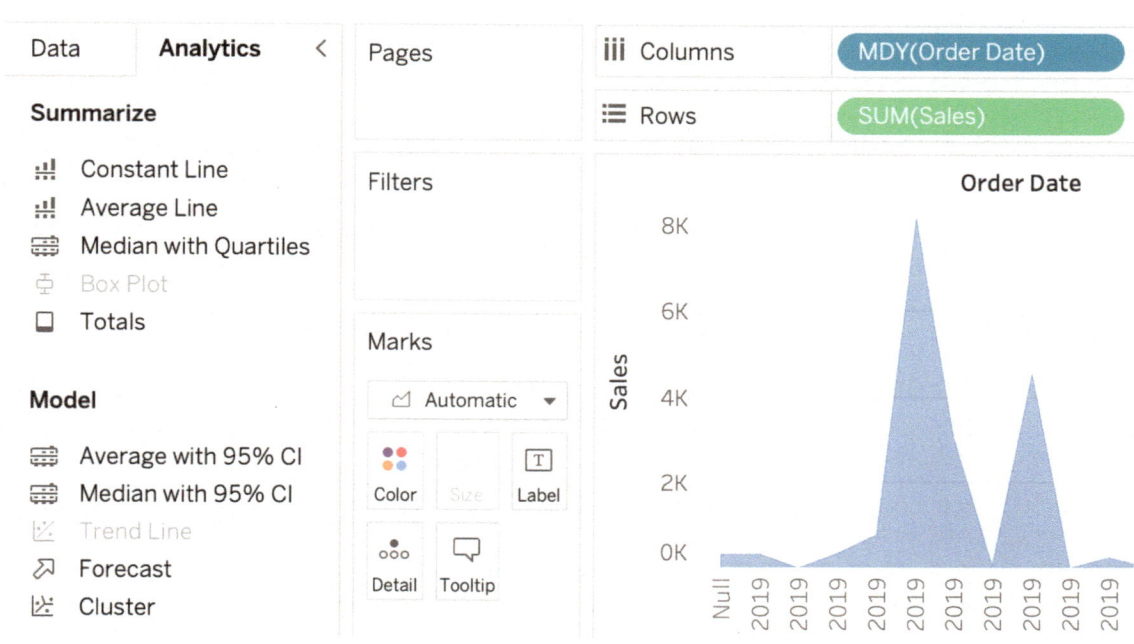

FIGURE 7.106
MDY date field.

8

Filter and Sort

In this topic, we discuss

<u>Filters</u> are integral to Tableau. They include extract filters, data source filters, and filters using data fields, as well as special fields you create, like groups, sets, or parameters. You can also use "filter actions" so that when a user clicks or hovers over a data point in one sheet, it filters other sheets. Finally, you can apply the same filter to one or more worksheets, even across data sources.

8.1 Filter Logic and the Order of Operations

There are two key considerations when understanding how filters work in Tableau.

- The Filter Order of Operations
- Filters Are Computed Independently by Default

8.1.1 Order of Operations

Earlier, we briefly touched on Tableau's **Order of Operations**, which outlines how Tableau processes filters, calculations, and other operations, as shown in Figure 8.1. **Fixed** *Level of Detail* calculation field filters compute independently of the view and any *dimension* filters because **Fixed** LOD calculations are above *Dimension* filters in Tableau's **Order of Operations**.

8.1.2 How Tableau Applies Filters

Tableau applies filters *individually* in a preset order. By default, <u>filters</u> in Tableau are computed independently and work on the entire data set. In Figure 8.2, Tableau displays one row after all three filters are applied.

The type of filter and Tableau's **Order of Operations** determine the order in which filters are applied. In Figure 8.3, the *Top N* filter is applied before a *Dimension* filter, and a *Dimension* filter is applied before a Measure filter.

Let's say I only want purple fruit in my results; for that, I must apply the **Color** filter first. A Tableau *context filter* is applied before *Top N, Dimension,* or *Measure* filters, ensuring the **Color** filter is applied first. An example of independent filters in the topic **Context Filters** follows.

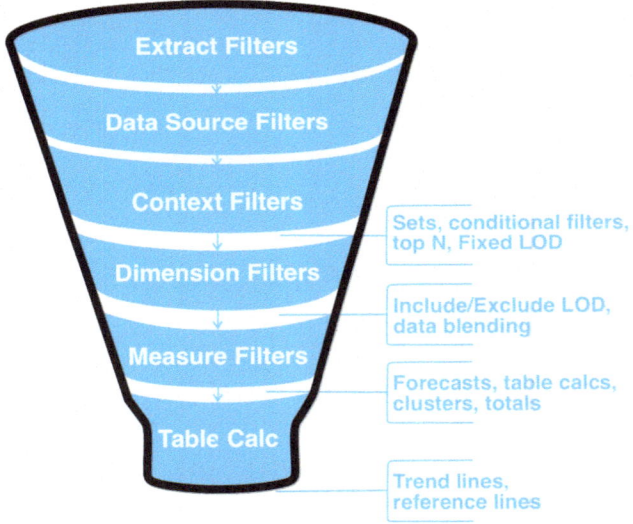

FIGURE 8.1
Order of Operations.

Filters		Fruit	2022
Fruit		Plum	$14.20
Color:Purple			
MIN(Qty)			

FIGURE 8.2
Three Fields on the Filters Shelf.

DOI: 10.1201/9781003566458-9

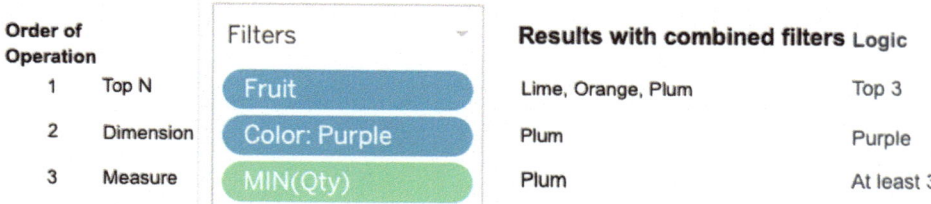

FIGURE 8.3
Comparing filters.

When you see unexpected results when filtering, go back to the <u>Order of Operations</u> to review what Tableau is doing behind the scenes. **Chapter 11** explores *Level of Detail* calculations. In the case of <u>discrete dimension filters with the four tabs General,</u> <u>Wildcard, Condition, and Top</u>, the settings on each of these tabs are *additive*. Tableau has a great YouTube video on filters at: https://www.youtube.com/watch?v=fyDY0_Ivy54

8.1.3 The "Apply to Worksheets" Setting

When you right-click a field on the **Filter** shelf and click the drop-down arrow to open the filter's *context menu*, choose "Apply to Worksheets" to customize how the filter is applied. There are four ways to apply filters to worksheets:

- All Using Related Data Sources
- All Using This Data Source
- Selected Worksheets…
- Only This Worksheet

Select "Apply to Worksheets" and then "Selected Worksheets…" from the **Filter Control** drop-down *Object Menu* to open the dialog window, as shown in Figure 8.4. If you are using row-level security, apply the filter to "All Using This Data Source."

In the bottom-left corner of the dialog window, the button "Select all on the dashboard" is a quick way to apply the filter to all dashboard worksheets.

Tableau allows you to <u>filter across data sources</u> if there is a related field. However, you cannot filter across published data sources on a Tableau server.

8.2 Create a Filter

When creating a field filter, the options vary depending on whether the field is a dimension, measure, or date. **Chapter 3** explored dimensions and measures. **Chapter 9** has more information on dates. Filters

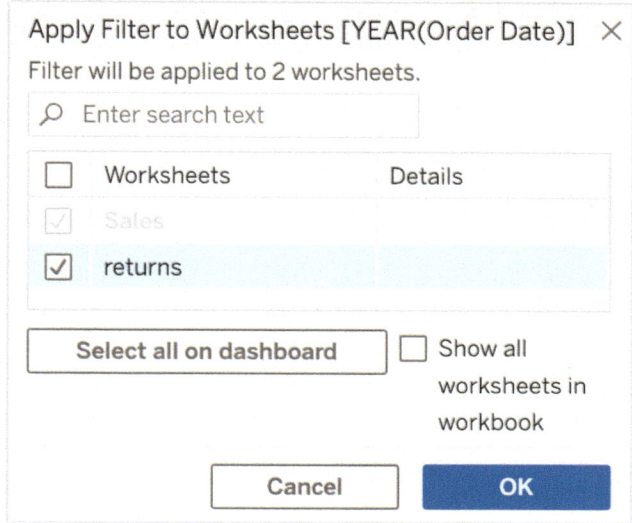

FIGURE 8.4
Apply Filter to Worksheets.

FIGURE 8.5
Tip: *To quickly see which worksheets are using a filter, hover over the field on the **Filters** shelf.*

either *include* or *exclude* members. In the example below, when I select an item from the list, like *Consumer*, the view is filtered to display only *Consumer*. There are four tabs for filters: *General, Wildcard, Condition,* and *Top*, as shown in Figure 8.6. Under the tabs are three radial buttons: *Select from list, Custom value list,* and *Use all*. "*Section 14.14 Dashboard Sheet Selection Menu*" *on page 317* lists the steps to create a *Custom value list* filter (Figure 8.6).

8.2.1 Select Marks to Create a Filter

Select marks on the canvas to quickly create a filter. When you hover over the selected marks, a tooltip

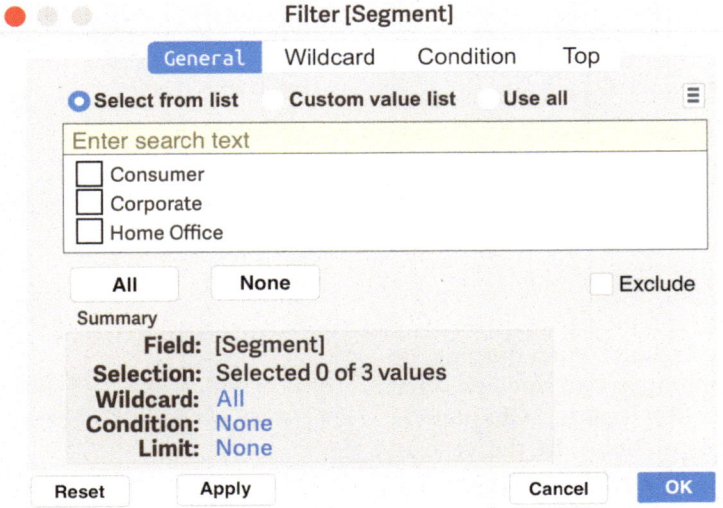

FIGURE 8.6
The Filter Window.

FIGURE 8.7
Warning: *When you have multiple filters on a dashboard, sometimes, you run into issues if some of the filters use "Only Relevant Values." If the filters do not work as expected, check the radial button "Use All," or change the filter to "All Values in Database."*

opens with choices to **Keep Only** or **Exclude**, as shown in Figure 8.8. For example, after you select **Keep Only**, Tableau adds the field to the **Filters** shelf with those marks selected. You can also right-click the marks to open the *context menu* with filter choices.

8.2.2 Select Headers to Filter Data

To filter entire rows or columns of data, right-click a header in the view. On the tooltip that appears, select "Exclude" or "Keep Only."

8.2.3 Filter from Fields on the Rows Shelf or Columns Shelf

To create a filter, right-click a field on the **Rows** or **Columns** shelf to open the field's *context menu* and select "Filter."

8.2.4 Exclude Nulls

The **Filter** pop-up window has four tabs and a check box on the right to "Exclude" values. In Figure 8.9, "Exclude" is checked, which means Null values are excluded.

In Figure 8.10, my year-over-year table calculation is null in the last year column. Suppose I click the small *Null indicator* in the bottom-right corner of the canvas. In that case, the dialog window choices are *filter* or *show data at default position*.

After I choose *Filter data*, Tableau creates the filter and adds the field to the **Filters** shelf with the settings, as shown in Figure 8.11.

8.3 Filter Controls

After adding fields to the **Filter** shelf, show the **Filter Control** to use interactive filters. You can also format

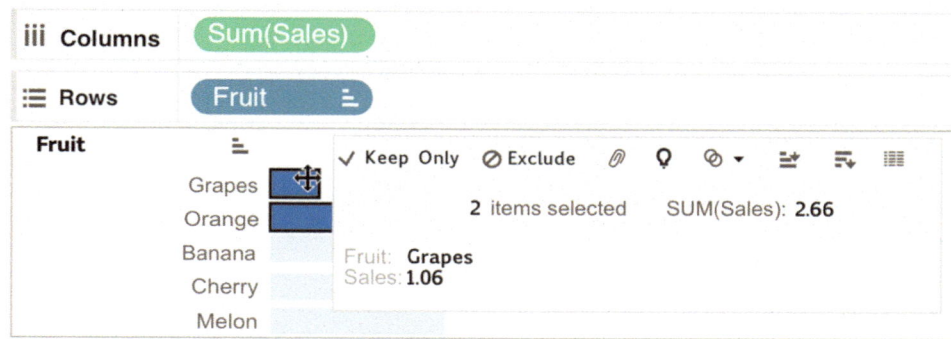

FIGURE 8.8
Tooltip.

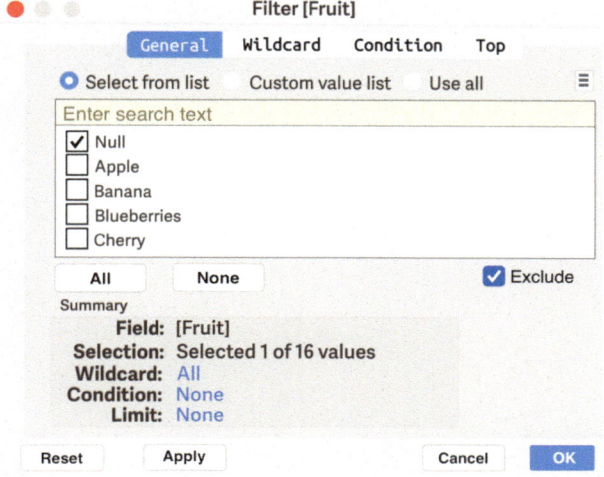

FIGURE 8.9
Exclude option.

the **Filter Control** and edit the title. To display a **Filter Control** on a worksheet, right-click the filter on the **Filter** shelf and select "Show Filter." On a dashboard, select a worksheet object; a dark-gray bounding box indicates that the worksheet is selected. Click the drop-down arrow in the top-right corner of the bounding box to open the *object menu*. Select "Filters" and then select one of the available fields from the list.

8.3.1 Formatting a Filter Control

In *"Section 1.7.2 Show, Hide, and Format Legends" on page 35*, we looked at a map with transparent controls and legends. By default, the background of a **Filter Control** is transparent, and the text is opaque, as shown on the dashboard in Figure 8.13. Select *Format Filter and Set Controls* from the **Filter Control's** drop-down arrow to change basic formatting when editing the map worksheet (Figure 8.12).

8.3.2 Only Relevant Values

With more than one filter, Tableau includes an option to filter "Only Relevant Values," which is a great way to limit the members of a filter list. When you have several filters on a worksheet, it may cause *Null* values. Try setting the filter to "Only Relevant Values" to remove *Null* values. Select the **Filter Control** and click the drop-down arrow to open the filter's *context menu* to adjust the setting.

8.3.3 Show Apply Button

If there is a lot of data to filter, you can show the "Apply" button in the **Filter Control**, so that Tableau waits to apply the filters. Right-click the filter to open the filter's *context menu*, select "Customize," and then "Show Apply Button."

8.3.4 Show "All" Value

To hide the "All" filter choice, select "Customize" in the Filter Control drop-down menu and then uncheck **Show "All" Value**.

8.4 Filter Actions

Filter actions are available for individual worksheets or dashboards. Filter actions are particularly useful when you want one sheet on a dashboard to control filtering on other sheets on the dashboard. For example, when a user selects data points in one chart on the dashboard, a dashboard "filter action" can filter other views on the same dashboard. At the end of the chapter, we will look at several examples that use parameter actions and set actions to filter the view.

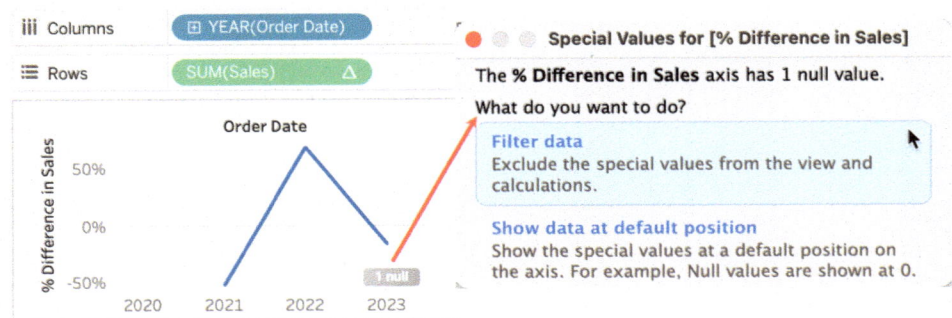

FIGURE 8.10
Year Over Year.

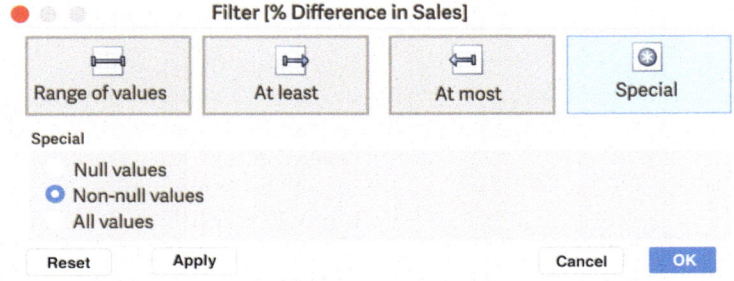

FIGURE 8.11
Filter Non-null Values.

FIGURE 8.12
Tip: *Note, if you change the color of the text title for a Filter or Parameter Control while working on a worksheet, you will not see that change until you view the Filter or Parameter Control on a dashboard.*

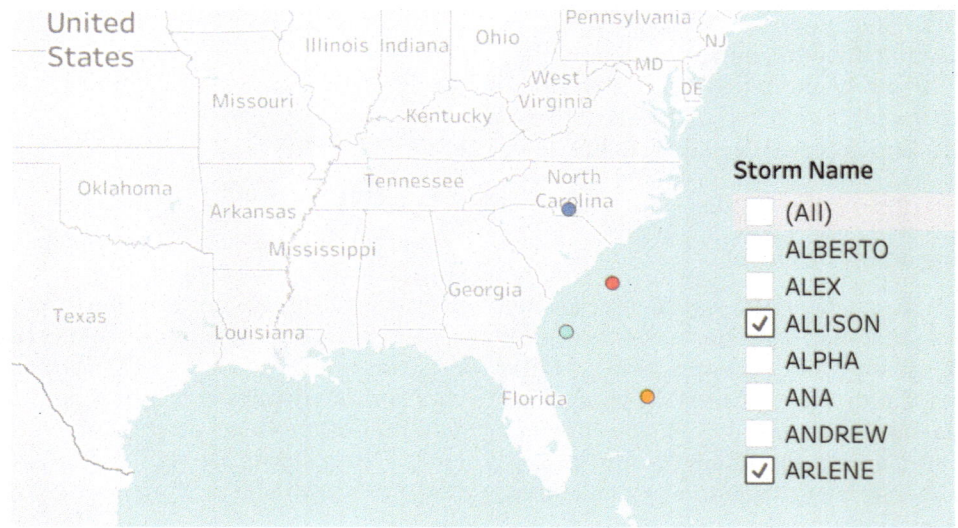

FIGURE 8.13
A Transparent Filter Control.

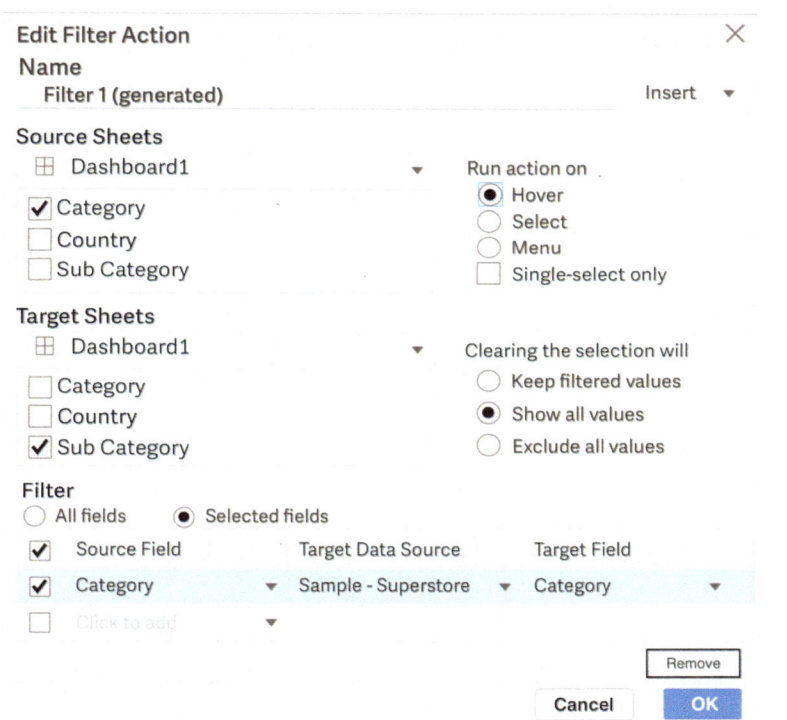

FIGURE 8.14
Filter Action.

FIGURE 8.15
Edit Filter Action.

Select a sheet on the dashboard to quickly create a dashboard filter action. In the top-right corner of the bounding box, click the drop-down arrow to select the **Filter** icon. When the filter is active, the **Filter** icon is filled in. You can also click the drop-down arrow to open the *context menu* and then select "Use as Filter." Tableau automatically generates a filter action, as shown in Figure 8.14.

To view and edit the new action, on the **Dashboard** menu, select "Actions." The **Actions** dialog window opens. The default setting for "Run On" is *Select*, and the "Fields" setting is "*All*." Click "Filter 1 (generated)"

and choose "Edit" to adjust the settings. In the following example, the three worksheets have different dimensions. The "Category" and "Sub Category" worksheets both have the [Category] field, so it makes sense to use [Category] as a filter for those two worksheets.

At the bottom of the **Edit Filter Action** window in Figure 8.15, the radial button "Selected fields" is active, and the *Category* field is selected. I also adjusted the **Source Sheets** and **Target Sheets** choices.

Suppose the source worksheet has more dimensions than the other sheets. In that case, Tableau displays a warning message "Missing fields on Clear All Filters" in the bottom left corner of the **Edit Filter Action** window.

Chapter 14 has numerous examples of filter actions.

- *"Section 14.19 A Reset All Filters Button" on page 339*
- *"Section 14.21 A Pop-Out Chart (Filter Action)" on page 343*
- *"Section 14.7.4 Filter Dashboard Sheets When Data Points Are Selected" on page 314*

8.5 Types of Filters

Let's briefly look at the types of filters you may encounter. We will look at the options and examples for these types of filters later in this chapter.

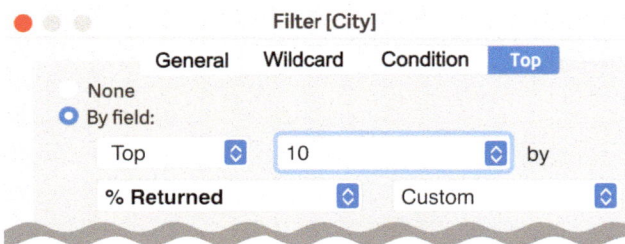

FIGURE 8.16
The Top Tab.

8.5.1 Table Calculation Filters

Create a calculated field with a table calculation, and add the new field to the **Filters** shelf.

8.5.2 Dimension Filters

When you add a dimension to the **Filter** shelf, the tabs are specific to the type of dimension, for example, a date field. For **discrete** dimensions, Tableau offers four tabs for filtering. Tableau combines the tab filters for that specific dimension. As we saw earlier, Tableau applies *Top N* filters before other dimensional filters. There are several examples of filters at the end of this chapter. It is worth noting that **Top N** filters do not show multiple values in the event of a tie. Use Rank() for that type of calculation.

8.5.2.1 Top N Filter

The [City] field is on the **Filters** shelf in Figure 8.16, and the **Top** tab is selected. I entered "10" in the **Top** value field, but you can also use the drop-down arrow to select a parameter or create a new parameter.

In the text table in Figure 8.17, the filtered view has ten rows. If the **Top N** filter is not returning the correct number of rows, make sure the radial button "Use All" on the **General** tab is selected.

Use parameters if you want to filter within a dynamic range of values. I have two parameters in Figure 8.18 so users can select the bottom and top sales. I switch to the *Condition* tab to add a condition to

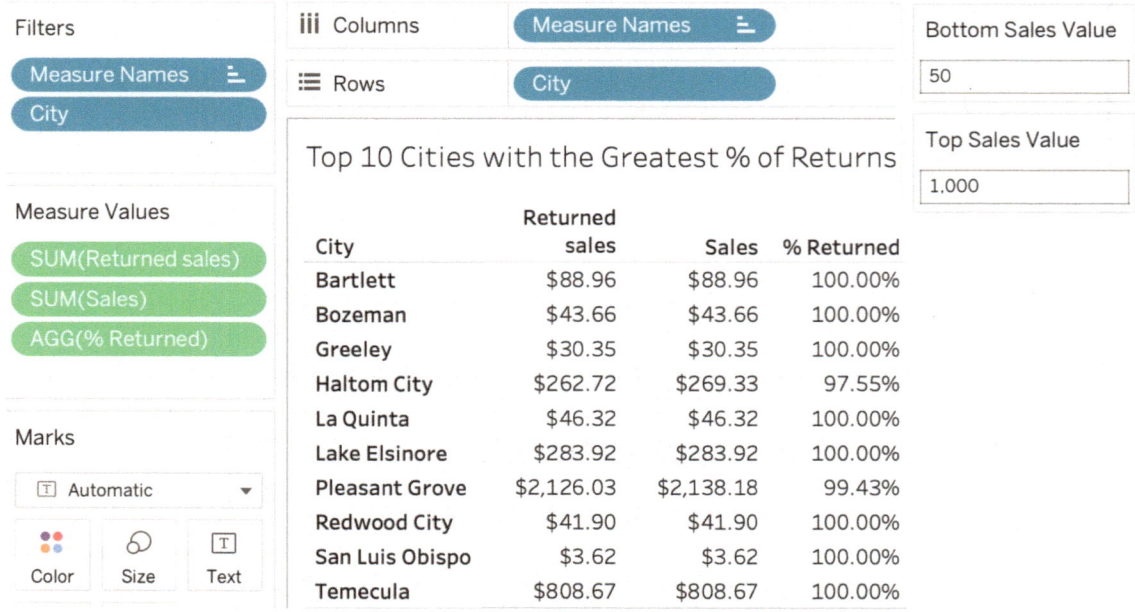

City	Returned sales	Sales	% Returned
Bartlett	$88.96	$88.96	100.00%
Bozeman	$43.66	$43.66	100.00%
Greeley	$30.35	$30.35	100.00%
Haltom City	$262.72	$269.33	97.55%
La Quinta	$46.32	$46.32	100.00%
Lake Elsinore	$283.92	$283.92	100.00%
Pleasant Grove	$2,126.03	$2,138.18	99.43%
Redwood City	$41.90	$41.90	100.00%
San Luis Obispo	$3.62	$3.62	100.00%
Temecula	$808.67	$808.67	100.00%

FIGURE 8.17
A Text Table.

this filter for the [City] dimension field. The purple fields in the formula are parameters.

Now, the chart filters to different rows, as shown in Figure 8.19.

There is another example of a parameter filter in *"Section 15.6.1 Switch Between Dimensions" on page 372.*

> When I used this logic in other views, I noticed that filtering did not work if my condition formula had ATTR() for aggregation. In that case, I changed my formula to use AVG([Goal]) so that filtering worked as expected.

8.5.3 Measure Filters

For measure fields, the button "At least" sets the floor value for the sort. The button "At most" sets the ceiling, as shown in Figure 8.20.

8.5.4 Date Filters

Date field filters are a great way to zero in on a particular range of data. When you drag a date field from the **Data** pane and drop it on the **Filter** shelf, you can choose the type of date filter. In Figure 8.21, I chose relative dates from the **Drop Field** dialog window and then the previous month in the **Filter** dialog window. The date field on the **Filters** shelf is green, indicating that it is a **continuous** field.

When I choose "Month" from the **Drop Menu**, I select a **discrete** date part value. Tableau opens a different **Filter** dialog window for **discrete** dates. In the bottom-left corner of the **Filter** dialog window in Figure 8.22, I check the box "Filter to the latest date value when the workbook is opened."

8.5.5 Context Filters

Tableau *Context filters* and *Level of Detail Expressions* are invaluable for controlling data in calculations or the view. By default, filters in Tableau are computed independently and work on the entire data set. A

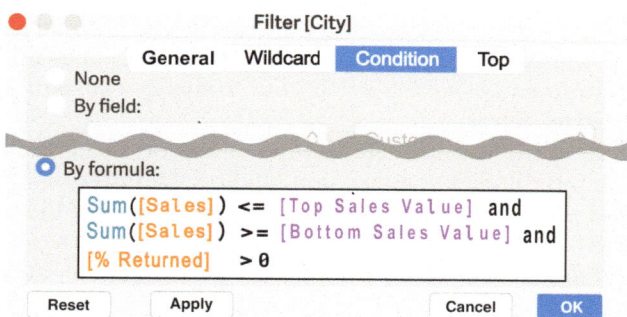

FIGURE 8.18
The Condition Tab.

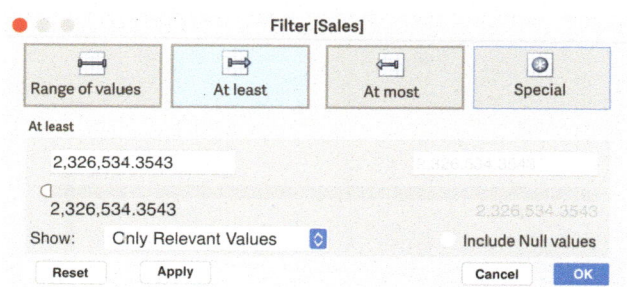

FIGURE 8.20
A Floor Filter That Uses At Least.

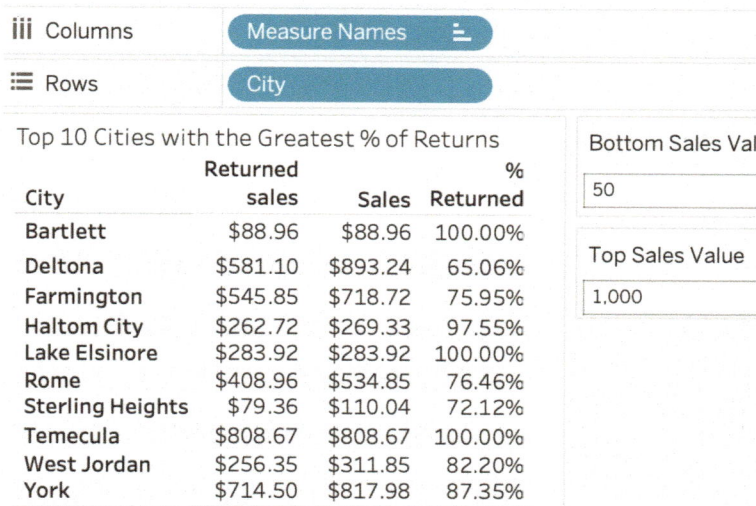

| Columns | Measure Names | |
| Rows | City | |

Top 10 Cities with the Greatest % of Returns

City	Returned sales	Sales	% Returned
Bartlett	$88.96	$88.96	100.00%
Deltona	$581.10	$893.24	65.06%
Farmington	$545.85	$718.72	75.95%
Haltom City	$262.72	$269.33	97.55%
Lake Elsinore	$283.92	$283.92	100.00%
Rome	$408.96	$534.85	76.46%
Sterling Heights	$79.36	$110.04	72.12%
Temecula	$808.67	$808.67	100.00%
West Jordan	$256.35	$311.85	82.20%
York	$714.50	$817.98	87.35%

Bottom Sales Val
50

Top Sales Value
1,000

FIGURE 8.19
Filtering with Parameters.

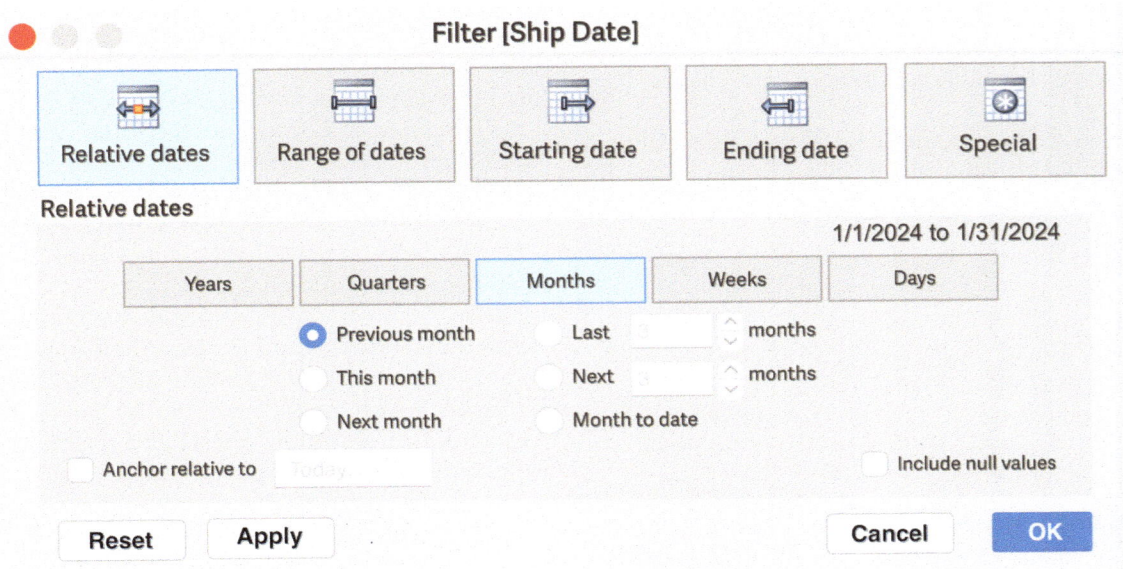

FIGURE 8.21
Continuous Date Filter Options.

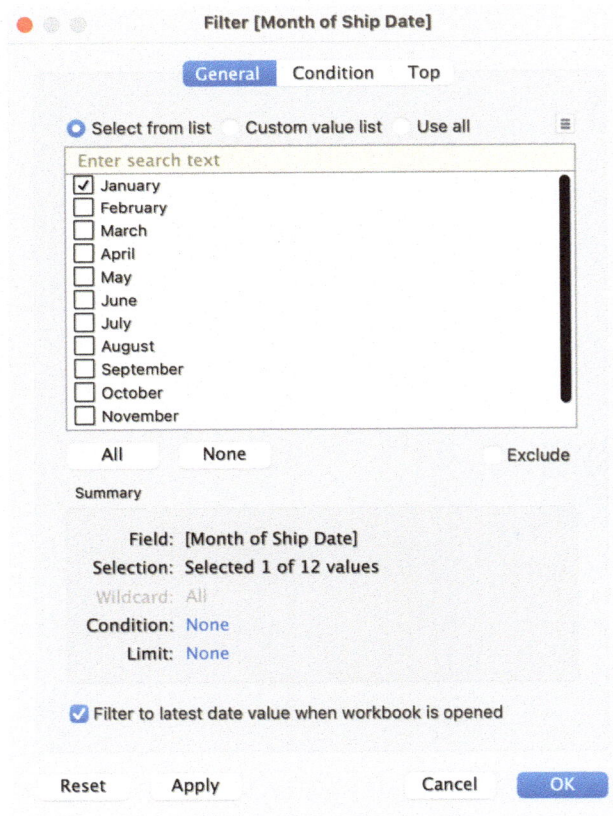

FIGURE 8.22
Discrete Date Filter Options.

context filter runs before most other filters, creating a temporary table, which all other filters use. *Context filters* apply to categorical (dimension) fields. While *context filters* limit scope and improve performance, Tableau recommends a single *context filter*. It does not recommend *context filters* if your audience constantly changes filters.

To apply a filter before other filters on the **Filters** shelf, right-click a dimension field on the **Filters** shelf and choose "Add to Context." The field on the **Filters** shelf changes to dark gray to indicate that this is a *context filter*. The next example adds a *context filter*.

8.5.5.1 Why Use a Context Filter?

When there are several filters, and you do not see the expected results, try changing one of the dimension filters to a *context filter*. In this example, I want to see the top three fruit sales for yellow fruit. There are four rows in the data that have yellow fruit.

1. First, let's see what happens if you add a [Fruit] filter to select the top three fruits based on [Sales], as shown below. Drag the [Fruit] field from the **Data** pane onto the **Filters** shelf (Figure 8.23).

2. Create another filter with the formula [Color] = "Yellow." You might expect Tableau to return the top three rows. However, Tableau returns only one row, as shown below (Figure 8.24).

3. To fix this issue, select the [Color] field in the **Filters** shelf and choose "Add to Context." The field background changes to a dark gray color, and I see three rows of data for "Yellow" fruit (Figure 8.25).

With a *context filter*, the order of operations changes how filters are applied. The chart in Figure 8.26 has only two rows of data after these filters are applied.

8.5.6 Filtering with Sets and Groups

The **Filter** dialog window has *General, Condition,* and *Top* options when filtering with sets and groups. We explored sets and groups in **Chapter 3**. The example *"Section 14.23 KPIs and BANs (Big Numbers)" on page 347* uses a set.

8.5.7 Extract Filters

To reduce the size of a data extract and improve performance, use extract filters. You can apply filters to the logical or physical tables when you create or edit an extract. We looked at extract filters in **Chapter 2**.

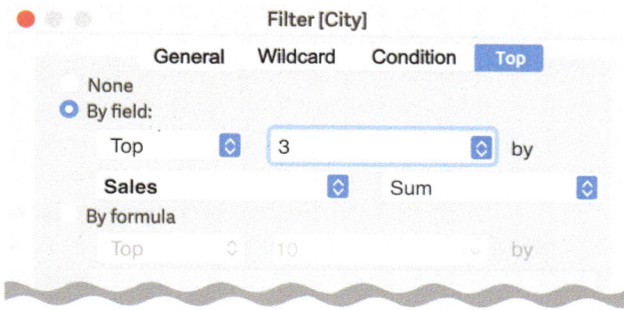

FIGURE 8.23
The **Filter Dialog** Window.

8.5.8 Data Source Filters

You can apply a filter globally to all worksheets from the same data source, as shown in this link: https://help.tableau.com/current/pro/desktop/en-us/filtering_global.htm

8.5.9 Filtering with Parameters

Earlier, I used two parameters in a filter formula on the *condition* tab. It is common to combine parameters and calculated fields to filter a view. Both worksheets and dashboards have an action called "Change Parameter." Generally, I create my parameters from the drop-down menu of the **Data** pane. Still, you can create a parameter when adding a filter, as shown in Figure 8.27.

The examples below illustrate filters and parameters, and in some cases, the **Parameter Control** acts as the filter.

- *"Section 9.13 Date Parameter in Axis Label" on page 208*
- *"Section 14.14 Dashboard Sheet Selection Menu" on page 317*
- *"Section 14.17 Horizontal Radial Buttons to Switch Sheets" on page 328*
- *"Section 14.16 Horizontal Radial Buttons to Change Filters" on page 323*
- *"Section 14.18 A Floating Container for Filters" on page 333*

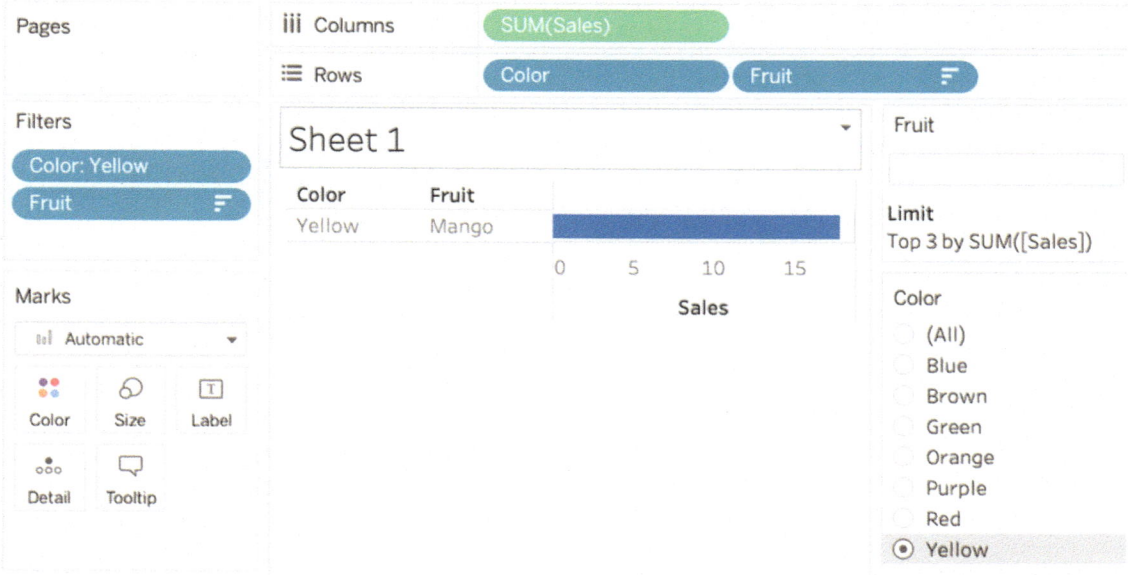

FIGURE 8.24
The **Color** Filter.

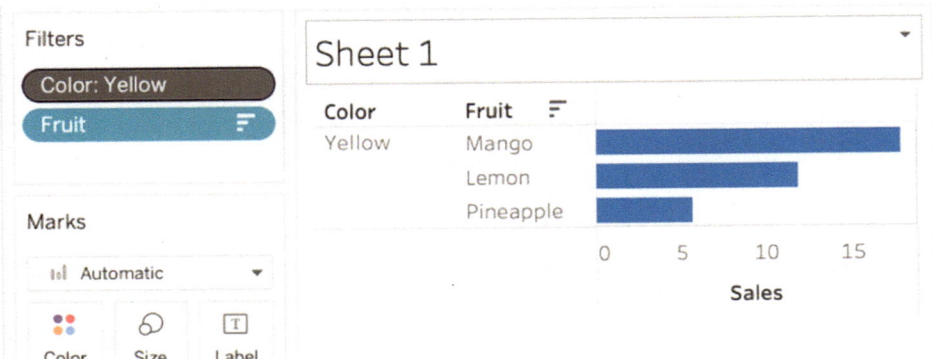

FIGURE 8.25
The Color Field with a Gray Background Color.

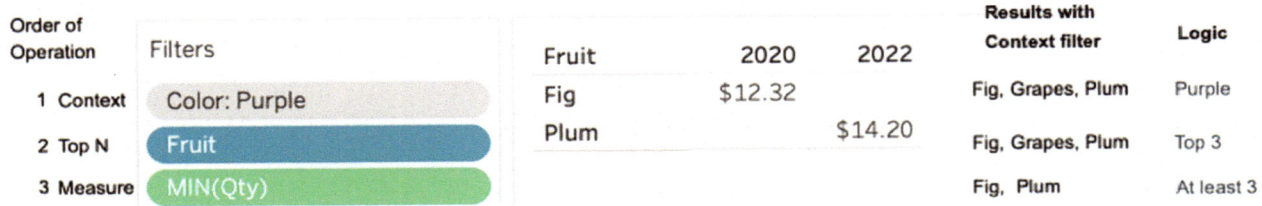

FIGURE 8.26
Filtered Chart.

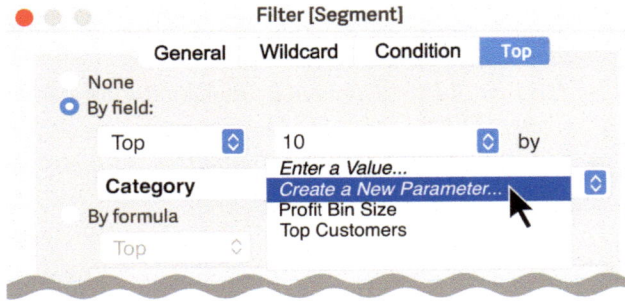

FIGURE 8.27
The Segment Filter with a Parameter.

- *"Section 15.5 Switch between Measures with Parameters" on page 369*
- *"Section 15.6.1 Switch between Dimensions" on page 372*

8.6 Testing Filters

When you use several filters on one visualization, I recommend testing every possible filter combination to ensure that the filter is what you intended. In Chapter 5, "Row-Level Security with Two Connections in a Data Source," I used the "Filter as User" option to see the view from the perspective of a user signed in to a Tableau server.

8.7 Filter Examples

Let's look at two examples of filtering: a condition filter and a table calculation filter.

8.7.1 Filter to Dynamic Range and Top N

In Figure 8.17, my users want to see the *top 10 returns* for sales within a dynamic range of sales; in this case, 50–1,000. First, I add the [City] dimension field to the **Filters** shelf. I use the "Condition" and "Top" filter settings. Two parameters allow users to choose a range of values. In the previous example, the parameters have these values.

- Bottom Sales Value = 50
- Top Sales Value = 1,000

In the **Data** pane, I right-click each parameter and check "Show Parameter." The two **Parameter Controls** are on the right side of Figure 8.17. On the *Condition* tab shown in Figure 8.28, I filter the range using the parameters.

After applying the "Condition" filter, I have a range of sales between the bottom and top values, and now, I want to find the *Top 10* of the "% Returned" within that range. The "Top" filter settings retrieve the *top 10 returns*, as shown in the *Top* tab in Figure 8.16.

8.7.2 Filter the View, Not the Underlying Data

Sometimes, you want to hide data from the view but still use the data in calculations. Tableau's "Table Calculations" can filter the view without filtering the underlying data. The Tableau Public and YouTube

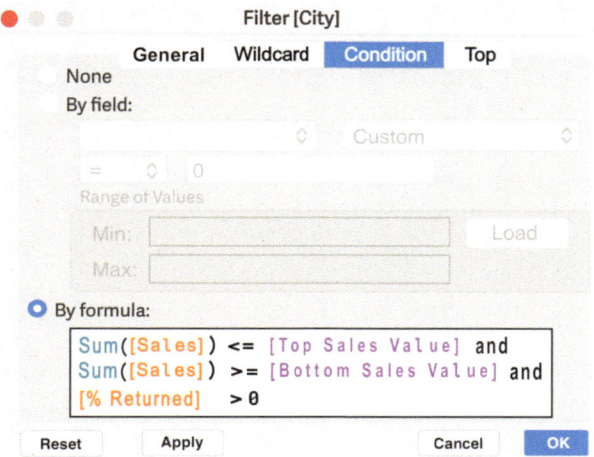

FIGURE 8.28
Filter Condition Tab.

links are at the end of the exercise, along with a check-list of the elements and settings in the example.

8.7.2.1 Introduction

In this example, I create a calculated field that uses a LOOKUP() table calculation. I filter the view with the new calculated field on the **Filters** shelf. To illustrate this filter, I created a second table calculation for a moving average calculation that uses data from the previous year, which is not showing on the view.

My sample Tableau file already has the "Average" view with [Order Date] on the **Rows** shelf and [Sales] on the *Text* tile on the **Marks** card, as shown in Figure 8.29.

In Figure 8.30, I create three charts for the dashboard.

8.7.2.2 Create the Visualization

Download the sample file from Tableau Public or rec-reate the "Average" view with the *Sample Superstore* data source. The field [Order Date] is on the **Rows** shelf, and the field [Sales] is on the *Text* tile of the **Marks** card, with an AVG() aggregation.

1. To create a copy of the "Average" view, right-click the sheet name along the bottom of the screen in the tabbed area and select "Duplicate."

2. Change the title for the new sheet to "Moving Average." Right-click the sheet tab along the bottom of the screen and select "Rename."

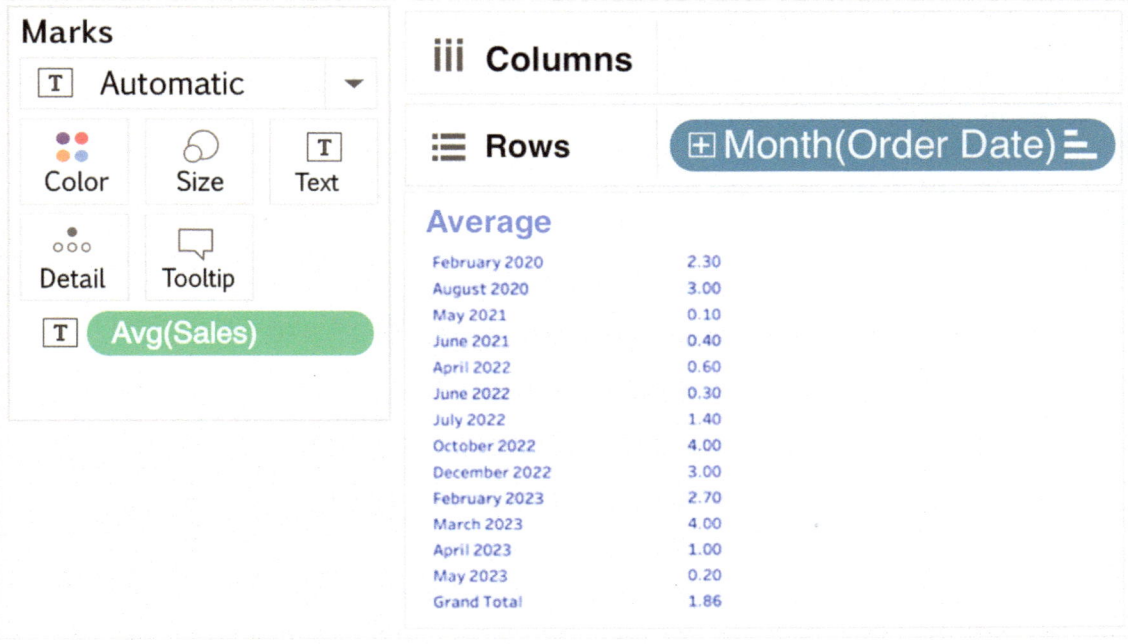

FIGURE 8.29
Preview – The Finished Chart Average View.

Filter a View, Not the Underlying Data

Average		Moving Average		Filtered Moving Average	
February 2020	2.30	February 2020	2.30	February 2023	3.23
August 2020	3.00	August 2020	2.65	March 2023	3.23
May 2021	0.10	May 2021	1.80	April 2023	2.57
June 2021	0.40	June 2021	1.17	May 2023	1.73
April 2022	0.60	April 2022	0.37	Grand Total	1.86
June 2022	0.30	June 2022	0.43		
July 2022	1.40	July 2022	0.77		
October 2022	4.00	October 2022	1.90		
December 2022	3.00	December 2022	2.80		
February 2023	2.70	February 2023	3.23		
March 2023	4.00	March 2023	3.23		
April 2023	1.00	April 2023	2.57		
May 2023	0.20	May 2023	1.73		
Grand Total	1.86	Grand Total	1.86		

FIGURE 8.30
Three Charts.

3. The [Sales] field should already be on the *Text* tile of the **Marks** card. Change the aggregation from the "Avg" calculation to a table calculation, "Moving Average." Right-click the field name [Sales] on the *Text* tile and select "Quick Table Calculation" from the drop-down *context menu*. Next, select "Moving Average."

4. Create a copy of the new "Moving Average" sheet.

5. Update the title for the new sheet to "Filtered Moving Average."

6. Create a new calculated field, [Date Lookup Filter]. At the top of the **Data** pane on the left, click the drop-down arrow to open the *context menu* and select "Create Calculated Field." In the calculation editor, enter the formula shown in the Chapter 12 example, "KPIs and BANs."

7. Right-click the new [Date Lookup Filter] field in the **Data** pane and select "Convert to Continuous."

8. Drag the new field [Date Lookup Filter] to the **Filters** shelf.

9. In the pop-up **Filter** dialog box, select only 2023 dates in the slider. Click OK. Because this is a **continuous** field, the filter has a slider for the date range. I only want 2023 dates for this chart (Figure 8.31).

10. Create a new dashboard and add the sheets to the dashboard. In the bottom-right corner of the workspace, click the dashboard icon to create a dashboard. A tooltip appears with the icon name if you hover your mouse over the icons.

In the new dashboard, drag the sheets from the **Dashboard** pane on the left and drop the sheets onto the dashboard view. As you drag the sheet, a gray box indicates where the view will be added.

8.7.2.3 *Validate and Test*

As outlined in **Chapter 5** *page 91*, validate calculations or chart aggregations with a temporary chart. To validate the visualization, add fields to *Text* or *Tooltip* tiles on the **Marks** card, use the **Summary** card, or view the data.

8.7.2.4 *Project Files*

Tableau Public file: https://public.tableau.com/views/FilterViewNotUnderlyingData002/FiltertheViewNottheUnderlyingData?:language=en-US&:display_count=n&:origin=viz_share_link
YouTube file:

https://youtu.be/f6hF-Eb-few

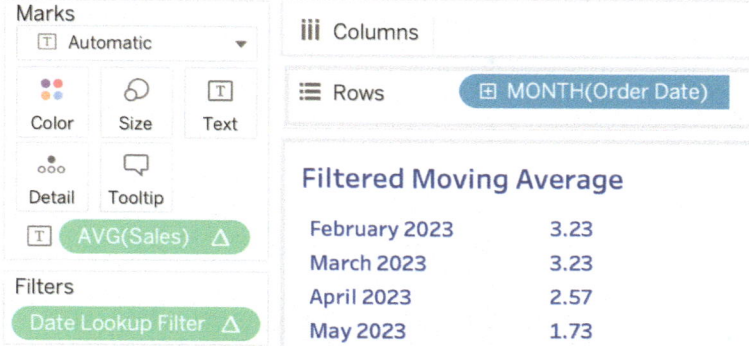

FIGURE 8.31
The Chart with 2023 Dates.

8.7.2.5 Data and Fields

This chart is based on the *Sample Superstore* data source and utilizes these fields.

8.7.2.5.1 Sales

The data type for [Sales] is a "Number (decimal)." In this view, [Sales] is a **continuous** field on the *Text* tile of the **Marks** card. Initially, the aggregation is "Avg" on the first visualization. I change it to a "Moving Average" table calculation on the other two visualizations. Because the field is on the *Text* tile, Tableau creates a traditional "Text" chart that looks like a spreadsheet.

8.7.2.5.2 Order Date

The data type for [Order Date] is a date. For the [Order Date] field, I choose the *Date Level* "Date Part" of "Month." A "Date Part" is **discrete**, and the field is blue on the **Rows** shelf.

8.8 Improve Filter Performance

When you add an interactive filter to a view, each filter requires a query. If you add a lot of interactive filters to your dashboard, it can cause the dashboard to take a long time to render.

> https://help.tableau.com/current/pro/desktop/en-us/perf_visualization.htm

8.9 Sorting

When laying out my table of contents for this book, I knew I wanted to include details on sorting simply because I initially found Tableau's sorting confusing. Once I started gathering notes on sorting, I realized how many ways there are to sort in Tableau. In this section, we will explore different ways to sort, some pitfalls to avoid, and some examples that utilize sorting to format the visualization or provide interactivity.

It is worth noting that Tableau sort options vary based on the type of field selected. For example, sorting is not available for a field with a **continuous** setting. When sorting within a stacked bar, use a *combined field*, as shown later in this chapter.

8.9.1 Default Sort Behavior

Tableau uses the innermost or deepest dimension field to sort when no field is selected for sorting. Since Tableau does not allow sorting with table calculation fields like "Rank," you can use this default sort behavior to apply sorting with a table calculation field. **Chapter 11** illustrates these steps in *"Section 11.10.5.1 Sort by Ranking Alternative"* on page 236.

8.9.2 What Can't You Sort?

Let me start by saying Tableau cannot sort some data. When I started with Tableau, I found it odd that there are some instances where there is no sort option for a field's *context menu*, such as:

- Table calculation fields
- Continuous fields
- Scatter plots with only continuous fields

8.9.2.1 Continuous Fields

In **Chapter 3**, when there were only **continuous** fields in *"Section 3.5.3.3 Unable to Sort Continuous Data"* on

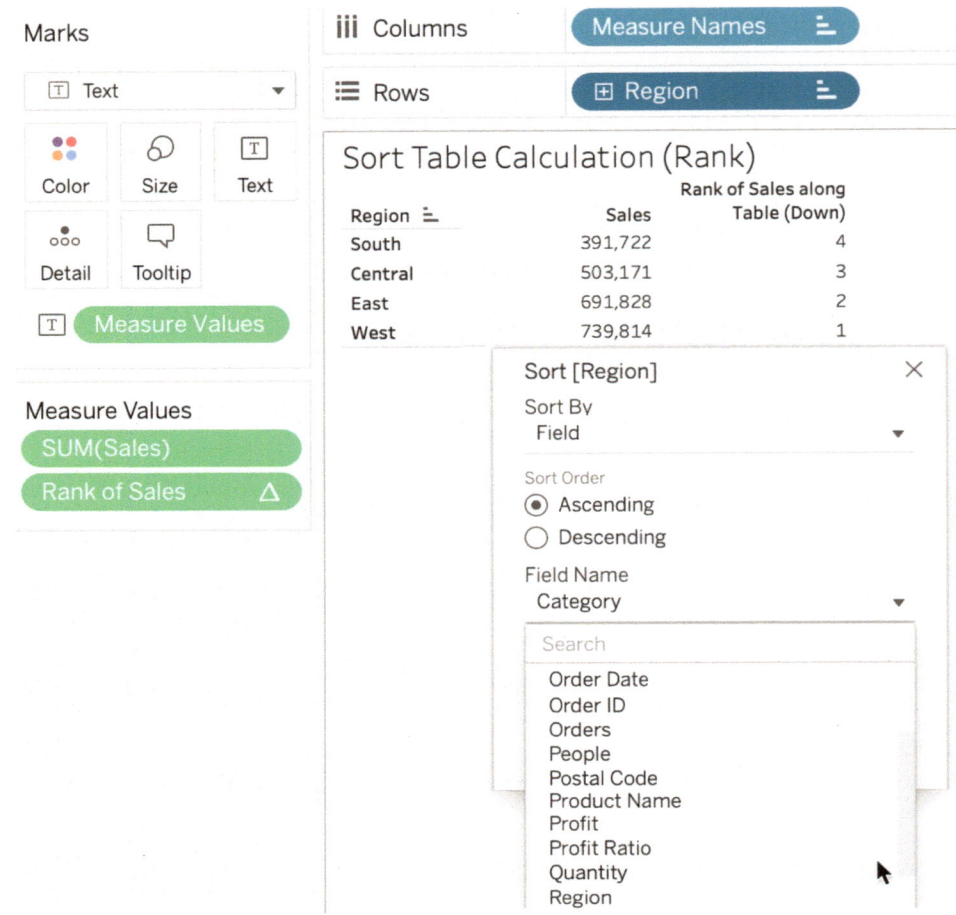

FIGURE 8.32
Sort by Choices.

page 66, the *Sort* buttons in the **Toolbar** at the top of the screen are grayed out. If you right-click the [Order Date] field on the **Columns** shelf, there is no option to "Sort" on the field's *context menu*.

8.9.2.2 Table Calculations Can't be Sorted

Along the same lines as **continuous** data, Tableau does not have the option to sort by a table calculation field. In the example, "Sort by Rank," that follows, I changed a table calculation field to **discrete** and added it to the **Rows** shelf to use the field for sorting.

8.9.2.3 Change a Continuous Field to Discrete for Sorting with Rank()

After adding a table calculation like "rank" to my visualization, there is no option to sort by the new table calculation field, "Rank of Sales," because Tableau does not let you sort by a table calculation, as shown in Figure 8.32.

8.10 Types of Sorting

8.10.1 Computed Sorts

The sorting I am most familiar with is a simple, computed sort. For these types of sorts, Tableau uses rules to determine the sort order, such as:

- Alphabetical Sorts
- Ascending or Descending Sorts
- Dynamic Sorts (Tableau updates sort order automatically)

8.10.2 Manual Sorts

You decide the sort order with a manual sort, which is then static. You apply a manual sort when you drag and drop field labels or names or drag the values on the view or in a legend. A dark bar indicates the new field location when you drop the field in a control or shelf, as shown in Figure 8.40. You can also reorder values with the arrows in the pop-up **Sort** menu.

8.10.3 Nested Sort

A **nested sort** sorts a column within another sorted column, as shown in Figure 8.33. *"Section 11.13 Fixed LoD Example" on page 241* has an example of a nested sort. *"Section 8.16.3 Sort by Date and SUM(Sales)" on page 189* also uses a nested sort.

8.11 How to Sort in Tableau

When sorting from an axis, header, or field label, you can click through the various options where one click

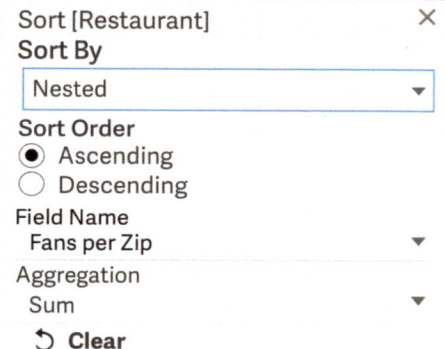

FIGURE 8.33
Nested Sort.

sorts descending, two clicks ascending, and three clicks clears the sort. In the example, at the end of this chapter, I use set and parameter actions to update sorting. There are many ways to sort in Tableau, as shown below.

- The **Sort** Dialog Box for a Field's *Context Menu*
- The **Toolbar** Sort Buttons
- Hover Over a Header
- Right-click a Header
- Drag Field Labels to Sort
- Hover Over Field Labels
- Use a Legend to Sort
- Click Axis to Sort
- Sort by Set
- Sort, Parameter Actions, and Set Actions

Let's look at the bar chart example in Figure 8.34 to explore how Tableau handles sorting. Looking at this sales chart, I'd like to sort [Sales] in descending order.

My first instinct is to click the [Sales] field on the **Columns** shelf. When I right-click the [Sales] measure field to open the field's *context menu*, there is no sort option, as shown in Figure 8.35.

The *Sort Descending* tool in the **Toolbar** at the top of the screen displays a tooltip when I hover my mouse over the icon, as shown in Figure 8.36. The tooltip describes how Tableau sorts, indicating that I must sort the [State/Province] field on the **Columns** shelf. To begin sorting in Tableau, I need to start with the

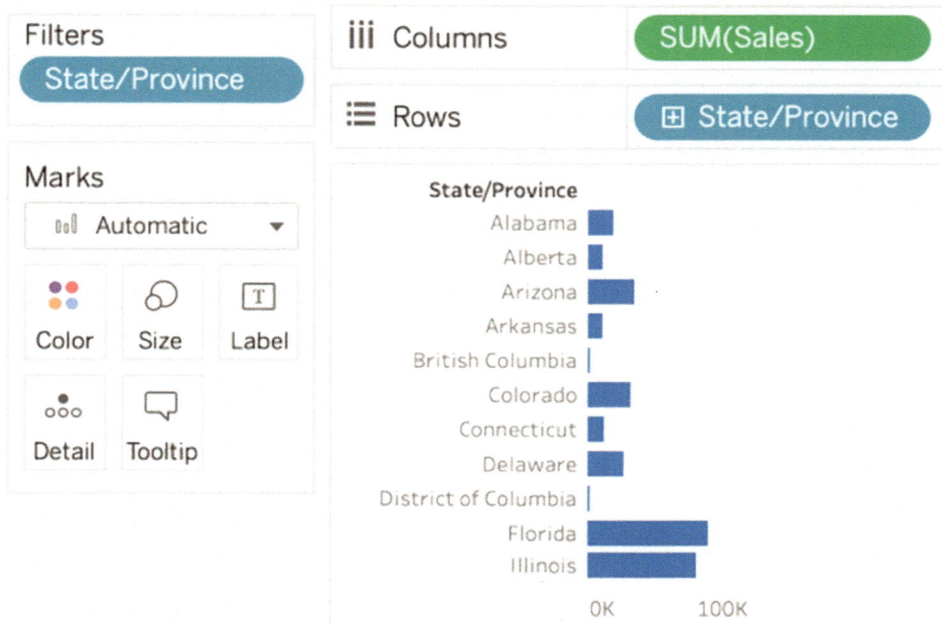

FIGURE 8.34
The Sales Chart.

discrete dimension field, not the **continuous** *measure* field [SUM(Sales)].

When I click the drop-down arrow for the [State/Province] field, there is a *Sort* option in the field's *context menu*, as shown in Figure 8.37.

The **Sort Dialog Box** opens when I select *Sort* from the *context menu*, as shown in Figure 8.37.

8.11.1 Sort Dialog Box

When you right-click a field in your view, choose "Sort" to open the **Sort Dialog Box**, as shown in Figure 8.38 Select the type of sort from the "Sort By" drop-down menu.

- Data Source Order
- Alphabetic
- Field
- Manual
- Nested

The dimension field [State/Province] was on the **Rows** shelf in Figure 8.37. When I select *Sort By* "Field"

and select the [Sales] field, the dialog box has a choice to sort by SUM of [Sales]. You can sort data based on any field, even if the field is not displayed in the view. Use the drop-down arrow shown in Figure 8.38 to change "Sort by" to "Field" and then use the drop-down arrow to select a field.

As shown above, you can select a particular field to use for sorting. The options in the **Sort** dialog box vary based on the field type.

8.11.2 The Toolbar Sort Buttons

When you use the **toolbar** sort buttons at the top of the screen, Tableau's default behavior is to sort the deepest dimension.

8.11.3 Hover Over Field Labels

Hover over a *Field Label* to display the sort dialog, as shown in Figure 8.39, and click the drop-down arrow to open the *context menu* with the sort options.

You can click through the various options when sorting from a field label.

- One click sorts descending.
- Two clicks sort ascending.
- Three clicks clear the sort.

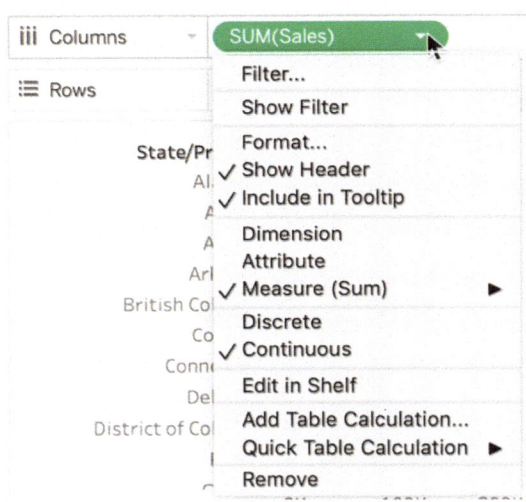

FIGURE 8.35
A measure field does not have a Sort option.

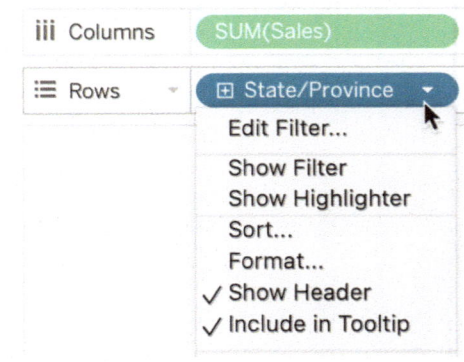

FIGURE 8.37
The field context Menu.

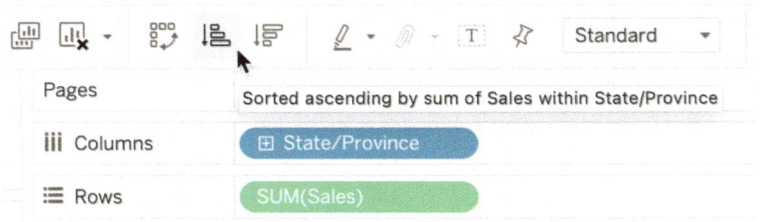

FIGURE 8.36
Sort icons in the Toolbar.

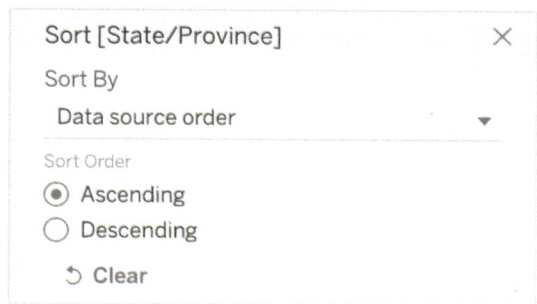

FIGURE 8.38
Sort by the sales Field.

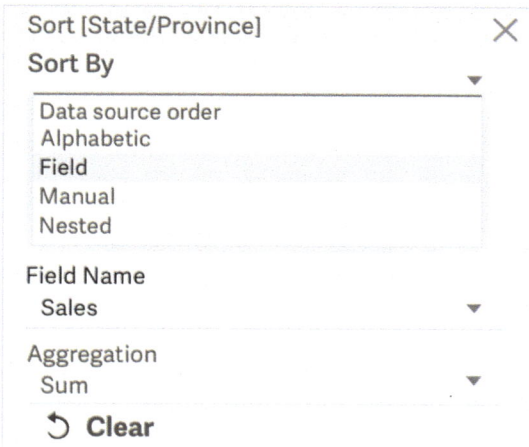

FIGURE 8.39
Sort dialog box.

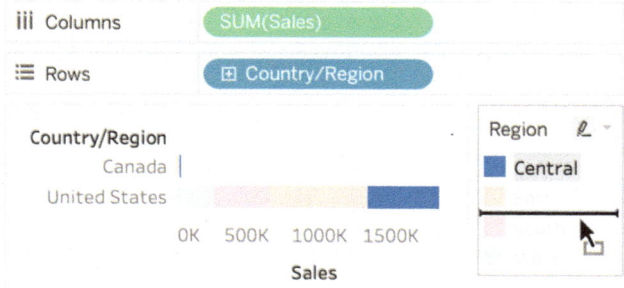

FIGURE 8.40
Legend sorting.

8.11.4 Use a Legend to Sort

There are several ways to sort using a **Legend**. Select a value in the legend and click and drag to sort manually. As you drag the field, a black line indicates the new field placement, as shown in Figure 8.40.

Click within the whitespace in a **Legend** and select *Sort* from the *context menu*, as shown in Figure 8.41.

Finally, the **Legend** drop-down arrow opens the **Legend's** *context menu*, which also has a *Sort* option to open the **Sort Dialog Box**.

8.11.5 Axis Sort Tool

Hover the mouse over the axis or click to sort instantly, as shown in Figure 8.42. An example of the axis sort tool is in *"Section 7.2.6.1 Bullet Graph" on page 127*. To avoid users accidentally "breaking" a view with incorrect sorting, uncheck "Show Sort Controls" in the **Worksheet** menu.

A *table calculation* axis and charts with only measures do not have sort icons on the axis.

8.12 Sort Examples

While sorting seems like a simple task, sorting in Tableau comes with some challenges. Hopefully, these examples will eliminate sorting roadblocks.

- Click Data Points to Sort with a Set
- Hover to Choose a Field for Sorting
- Sorting Segments within a Stacked Bar
- Sort by Rank Alternative
- Sort by Date and SUM(Sales)

8.13 Click Data Points to Sort with a Set

For this area chart, when a user clicks within the body of the area chart, the chart is re-sorted based on their selection. The link to the Tableau Public file is at the end of the exercise, along with a checklist of the elements and settings in the example.

When you click to select a mark in the view, a "Set Action" updates the set. The [Category] field on the Color tile is sorted by the [Category Sorter] field that uses the [Category Sort (Set)].

8.13.1 Preview – The Finished Chart

The finished area chart has a **Color Legend** on the right, as shown in Figure 8.43.

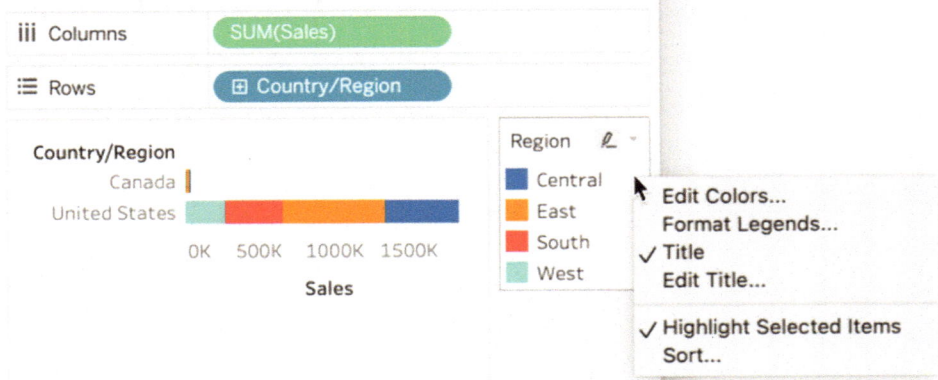

FIGURE 8.41
Context menu.

FIGURE 8.42
The Sort Tool in the Axis.

8.13.2 Create the Visualization

1. Create a calculated field called [% of Total Sales] after connecting to a data source like *Sample Superstore*. This expression uses the FIXED scoping keyword in the level of detail syntax (Figure 8.44).

   [Sales] / {**FIXED** [Sales]: **SUM**([Sales])}

2. Create the worksheet. Add [Order Date] to the **Columns** shelf. We want a **Continuous** field that creates a horizontal x-axis of dates along the bottom.

   Click the drop-down arrow of the [Order Date] field on the **Columns** shelf to open the field's *date context menu*. The items in the middle section of the *date context menu* are divided by a line. The choices above the line are *Date Part* levels. Below the line are *Date Value* levels.

   In the following image, I selected the "Year" *Date Value* and **Continuous** (Figure 8.45).

3. Add the new calculated field [% of Total Sales] to the **Rows** shelf (Figure 8.46).

4. Create another calculated field called [Category Sorter], as shown in Figure 8.48.

5. Create the last calculated field called [Calc to turn off highlighting]. This field is another example of a placeholder field (Figure 8.48).

6. Create a "Set" based on the [Category] field. Name the set [Category Sort (Set)].

In the **Data** pane, right-click the [Category] field, choose "Create," and then click "Set…" Select *Technology* and click OK (Figure 8.49).

7. Drag the [Category] field to *Color* on the **Marks** card. Sort this field by the calculated field [Category Sorter]. Right-click the [Category] field and choose "Sort" to open the **Sort Dialog Window**, as shown below. Select [Category Sorter] for the Field Name.

   On the **Worksheet** menu, choose "Actions" and click the "Add Action" button to open the drop-down *context menu*. Select "Change Set Values." The **Edit Set Action** dialog window opens, as shown in Figure 8.51. Now, when a user selects a mark in the view, Tableau updates the [Category Sort (Set)] (Figure 8.50).

   Name: *Update Category Set*

   Source Sheets: *Click to Sort by Category*

   Run action on: *Select*

   Target Set: *Category Sort (Set)*

   Running the action will: *Assign values to set*

   Clearing the selection will *Keep set values*

8. Add the calculated field [Calc to turn off highlighting] to the **Marks** card on the *Detail* tile (Figure 8.52).

9. On the **Toolbar** at the top of the screen, select the *highlight* tool and open the *context menu*. Select the field you created in step 5, [Calc to turn off highlighting].

FIGURE 8.43
A Chart with a Color Legend.

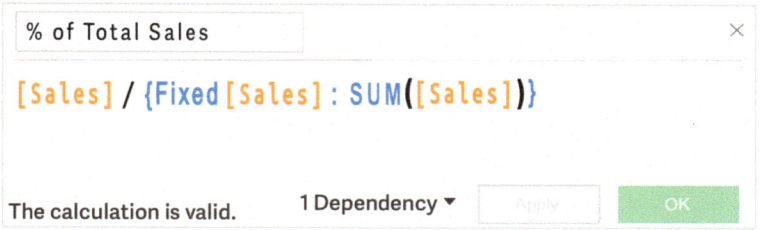

FIGURE 8.44
The Calculated Field % of Total Sales.

Tableau Public file:

> https://public.tableau.com/views/Click
> toSortUsingaSets1050/ClicktoSort
> byCategory?:language=en-US&:sid=&:
> display_count=n&:origin=viz_share_link

8.13.3 Worksheets

There is one area chart in this example.

8.13.4 Data and Fields

This dashboard utilizes these fields.

- Order Date
- Sales
- Price
- Qty
- Category

- Category Sorter
- % of Total Sales
- Calculation to Turn Off highlighting

8.13.4.1 Order Date

The [Order Date] data type on the **Columns** shelf is "Date." For the [Order Date] field, I chose a "Date Value" with a *Date Level* of "Year." I also select a **continuous** setting so the chart has an x-axis of date ranges along the bottom of the view.

8.13.4.2 Sales

The data type for [Sales] is a "Number (decimal)." In Figure 8.41, [Sales] is a **continuous** field on the **Rows** shelf. The field has a **continuous** setting, creating an axis on the view, and because the field is on the **Rows** shelf, this is a vertical y-axis.

8.13.4.3 Category

The [Category] field is a **discrete** dimension with a "String" data type. As expected, the field has a blue background or "pill" on the *Color* tile of the **Marks** card because it has a **discrete** setting. The sort configuration for [Category] is set to the field [Category Sorter].

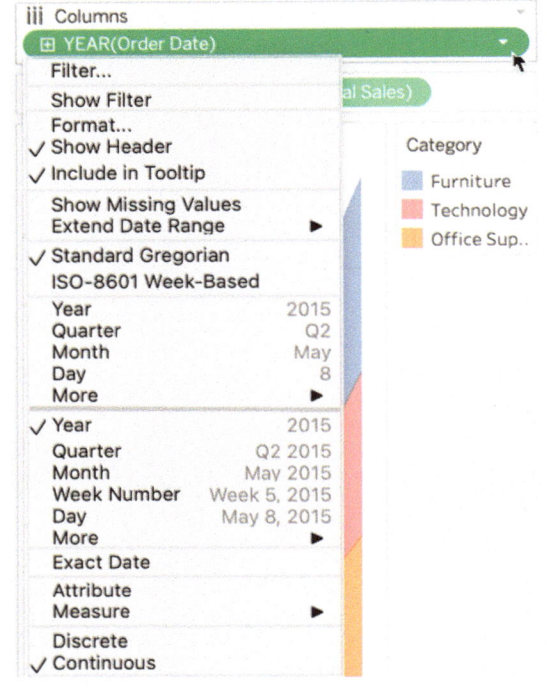

FIGURE 8.45
The Context Menu for Dates

FIGURE 8.46
The New Field on the Rows Shelf.

8.13.4.4 Calculated Fields

There are three calculated fields.

- Category Sorter
- % of Total Sales
- Calculation to Turn Off Highlighting

8.13.4.4.1 Category Sorter

The [Category Sorter] field changes the sorting of the [Category] field on the *Color* tile on the **Marks** card. When a user clicks on the view to select a mark, the "Change Set" action updates the [Category Sort (Set)]. So, for example, if "Furniture" is selected in the **Set Control**, the "Change Set" action updates the set to "Furniture." The [Category] field on the *Color* tile on the **Marks** card is sorted by the [Category Sorter] field. The expression returns [Sales] for the category in the set; in this case, "Furniture" sales.

8.13.4.4.2 % of Total Sales

Create a new calculated field called [% of Total Sales] with the **FIXED** level of detail expression shown below. **Chapter 11** has more information on level of detail expressions on *page 238*.

[Sales] / {**FIXED** [Sales]: **SUM**([Sales])}

8.13.4.4.3 Calculation to Turn Off Highlighting

This calculation field [Calc to turn off highlighting] is a placeholder field, so I can adjust highlighting in the last step. The value of a placeholder field can be anything. In the last step of this example, I set the highlighting tool to highlight with this placeholder field, in effect turning off highlighting.

8.13.5 Category Sort (Set)

A worksheet *action* that uses the [Category Sort (Set)] field updates the set when users click a mark on the visualization.

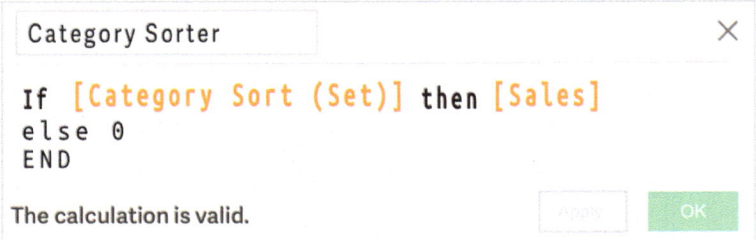

FIGURE 8.47
The Calculated Field Category Sorter.

FIGURE 8.48
The Calculated Field Calc to Turn Off Highlighting.

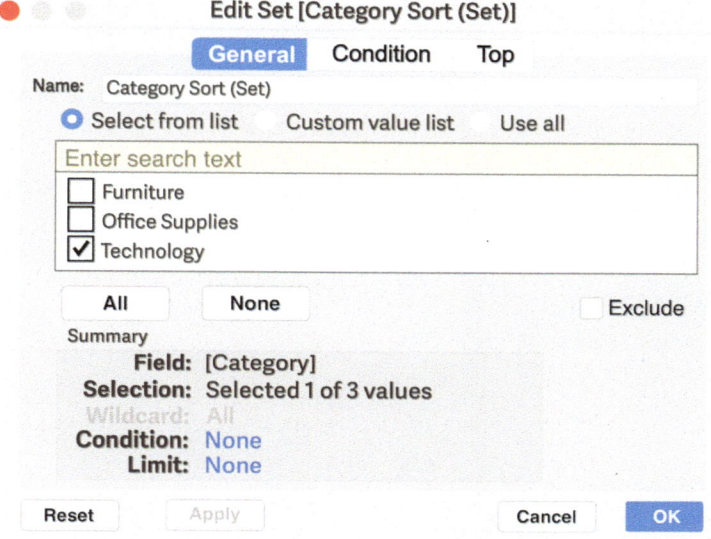

FIGURE 8.49
The **Edit Set** Dialog Window.

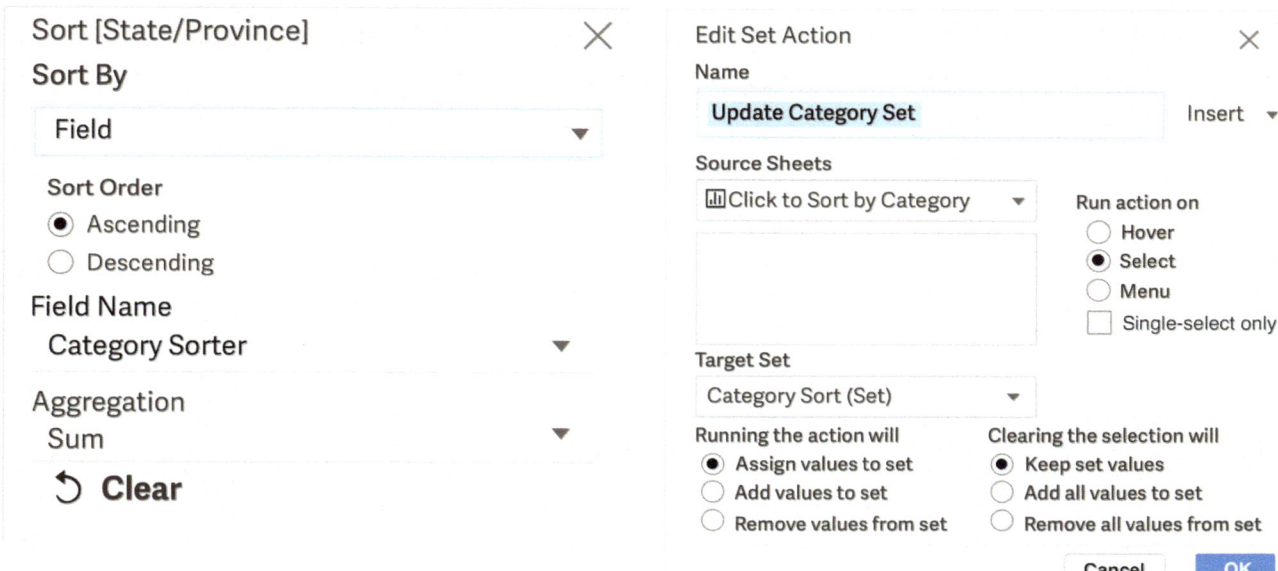

FIGURE 8.50
The Sort Dialog With Category Sorter.

FIGURE 8.51
The Edit Set Action Dialog Window.

8.13.6 Components or Elements

There are several elements to this view.

- Columns Shelf
- Rows Shelf

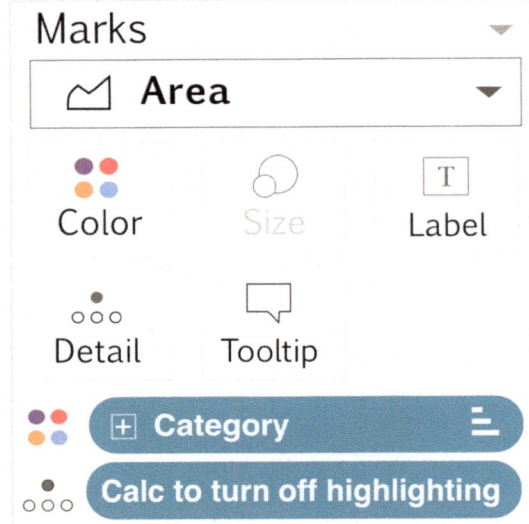

FIGURE 8.52
The Detail Tile of the Marks Card.

- Set Action
- Marks: Color (sorted by the calculation field)
- Toolbar: Highlight

8.13.7 Columns Shelf

On the **Columns** shelf, the data type for the [Order Date] field is a "Date" type. For the [Order Date] field, I choose the *Date Level* "Date Value" of "Year." With the **continuous** setting, the field creates a horizontal x-axis.

   Click the drop-down arrow of a date field to open the field's *date context menu*. The items in the middle section of the *date context menu* are divided by a line. The top part above the line has *Date Part* levels. The bottom part of the **Date** *context menu* is actual *Date Values*.

8.13.8 Rows Shelf

The LOD calculated field [% of Total Sales] is on the **Rows** shelf.

8.13.9 "Change Set Values" Action

A "Change Set Values" action links the [Category Sort (Set)] with the calculated field [Category Sorter] so

FIGURE 8.53
A Dashboard with Sort Choices.

that when a user clicks a category data point on the chart, the action updates the members of the set.

8.13.10 Marks: Details

Add the [Calc to turn off highlighting] field to the *Detail* tile on the **Marks** card to make the field available for visualization.

8.13.11 Marks: Color

Add the [Category] field to *Color* on the **Marks** card. This [Category] field is then sorted by the calculated field [Category Sorter].

8.13.12 Toolbar: Highlight

When you click to select a mark on the visualization, Tableau's default behavior highlights the mark, and all other marks are changed to gray. To turn this behavior off, select the *highlight* tool in the **Toolbar** and open the *context menu*. Select the field you created in step 5, [Calc to turn off highlighting].

8.14 Hover to Choose a Field for Sorting

When I first saw this bar chart example, I was intrigued. After trying the sorting, I was surprised at

how insightful it was to see the price of the most expensive fruit and then compare the values to the sales and quantity sold for that same fruit.

8.14.1 Introduction

In this example of a "small multiples" view, there are three panes of bar charts in one worksheet. I added the worksheet to a dashboard and created a parameter action. When someone hovers over the field name above that chart, Tableau sorts that chart, and the [Fruit] headers on the left are also reordered. The link to the Tableau Public file is at the end of the exercise, along with a checklist of the elements and settings in the example.

8.14.2 Preview – The Finished Dashboard

In Figure 8.53, the finished dashboard is sorted by [Qty] because I hovered the mouse over [Qty] at the top of the dashboard.

8.14.3 Create the Visualization

1. Connect to the data source like the *Sample Superstore*. Create a "Bar Chart" worksheet with three measures on the **Columns** shelf: [Sales], [Price], and [Qty]. Add [Fruit] to the **Rows** shelf (Figure 8.54).

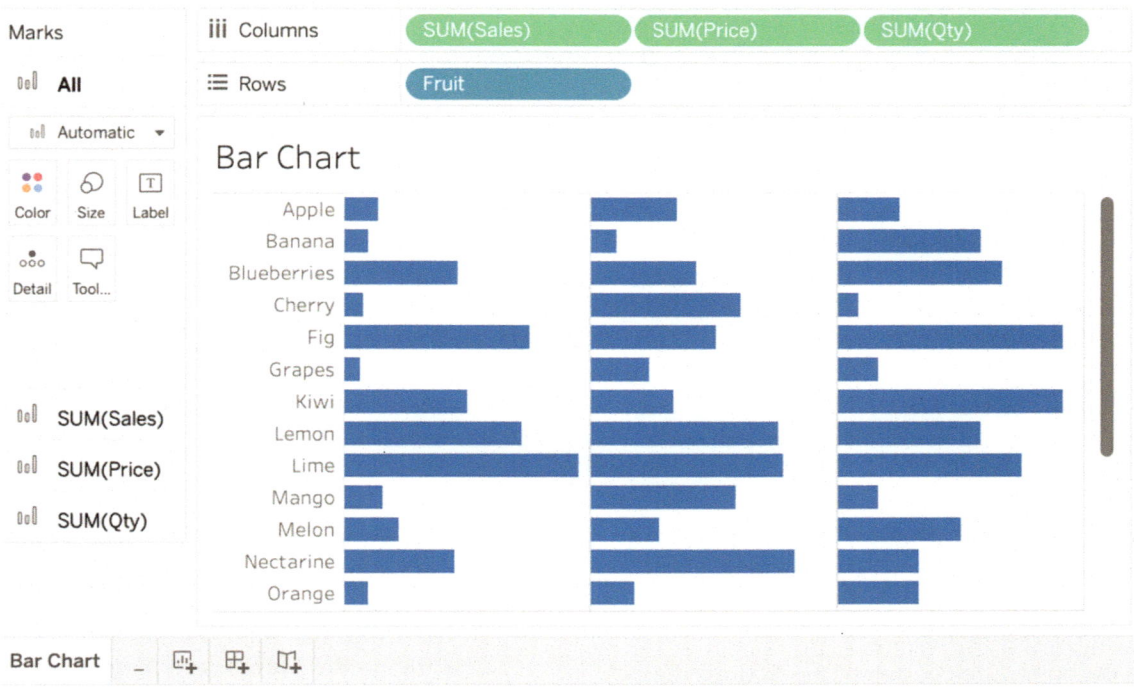

FIGURE 8.54
The Basic Chart with Three Panes.

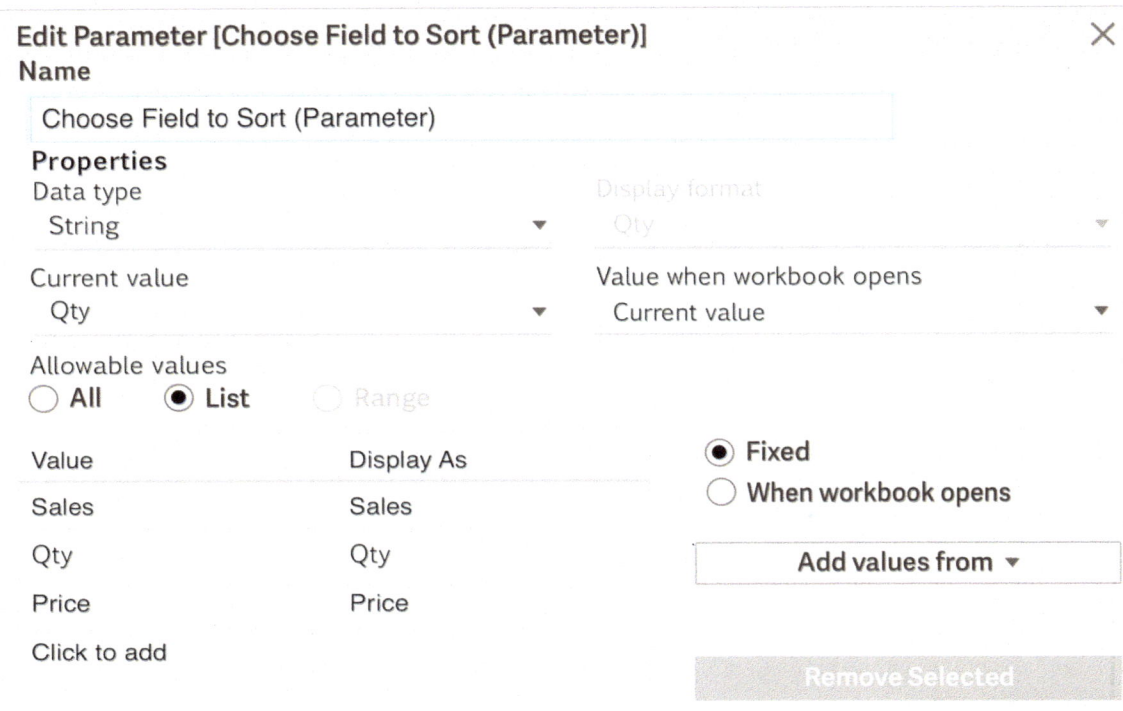

FIGURE 8.55
The **Edit Parameter** Dialog Window.

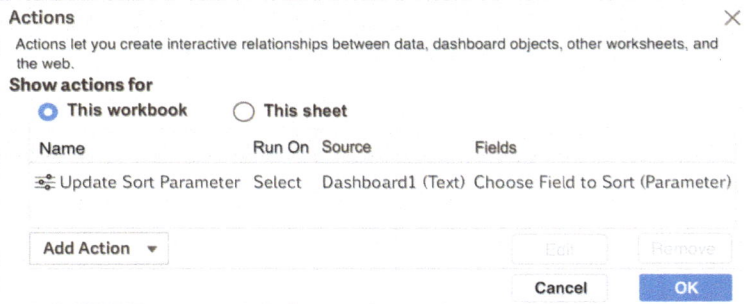

FIGURE 8.56
The **Edit Parameter Action**.

2. Create a parameter called [Choose Field to Sort (Parameter)] (Figure 8.55).

3. Display the **parameter control**. In the bottom-left corner of the **Data** pane, click the parameter's drop-down *context menu* and choose "Show parameter." This step is optional but does show how the parameter changes when you hover over a mark at the top of the dashboard.

4. On the **Dashboard** menu, select "Actions" to open the **Actions** dialog window.

In the bottom-left corner of the **Actions** dialog window shown above, click the "Add Action" button and select "Change Parameter" (Figure 8.56).

5. Create a calculated field called [Calc field for sorting].

6. Click the [Fruit] field's drop-down arrow on the **Rows** shelf and choose "Sort" from the *context menu*. For "Sort by," select "Field" and the new calculated field [Calc field for sorting], as shown below (Figure 8.58).

7. Create another worksheet called "Text" for the three text values based on the [Measure Names] field. Add the [Measure Names] field to the **Columns** shelf, **Filters** shelf, and the *Text* tile on the **Marks** card. Filter the field as shown below (Figure 8.59).

8. Add [Measure Values] to *Detail* on the **Marks** card to add the three field names to the view.

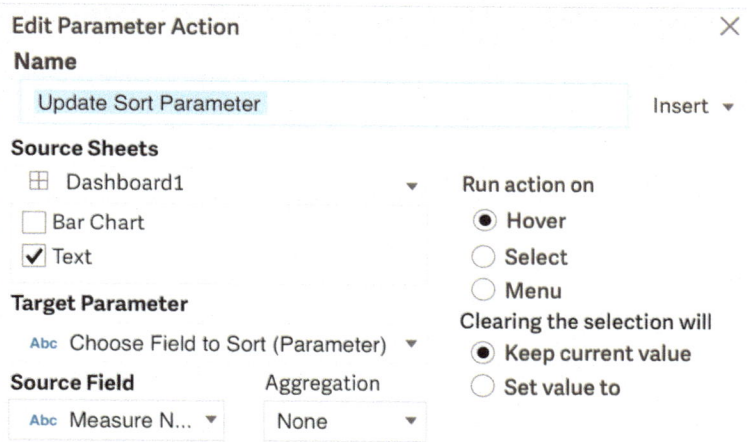

FIGURE 8.57
The Calculated Field "Calc Field" for Sorting.

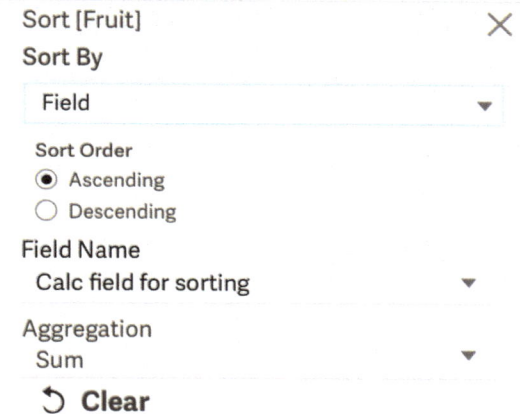

FIGURE 8.58
The Sort[Fruit] Dialog Window.

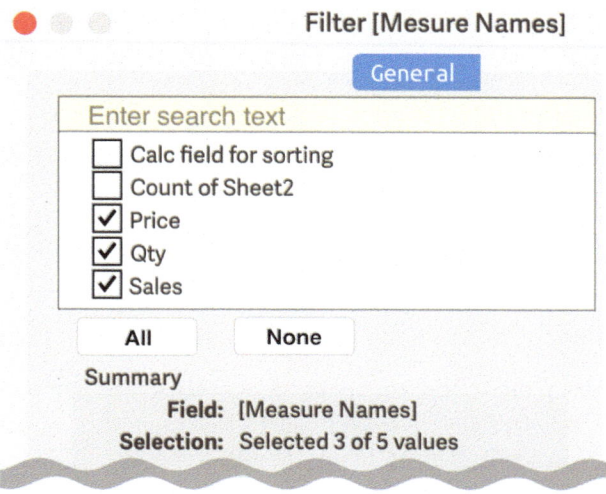

FIGURE 8.59
The **Filter** Dialog Window.

You only want three fields on the **Measured Values** shelf, as shown along the top right of the canvas below. The placeholder field on the **Rows** shelf adds a bit of space on the left side of the canvas (Figure 8.60).

9. Create a dashboard and add the two worksheets. The "Text" worksheet with the *Sales, Price*, and *Qty* values is at the top of the dashboard, and the "Bar Chart" worksheet is below (Figure 8.61).

10. Create a dashboard parameter action called "Update Sort Parameter" with the settings shown below (Figure 8.62).

Setting	Value
Name	Update Sort Parameter
Source Sheets	Text
Run action on	Hover
Target Parameter	Choose Field to Sort (Parameter)
Clearing the selection will	Keep current value
Source Field	Measured Names
Aggregation	None

8.14.4 Testing

Hover over "Sales" at the top of the canvas and then hover over another mark – the chart sorts based on where you move your mouse.

8.14.5 Project Files

Tableau Public file:

> https://public.tableau.com/views/Hovertochoosefieldforsorting51052/Dashboard?:language=en-US&publish=yes&:sid=&:display_count=n&:origin=viz_share_link

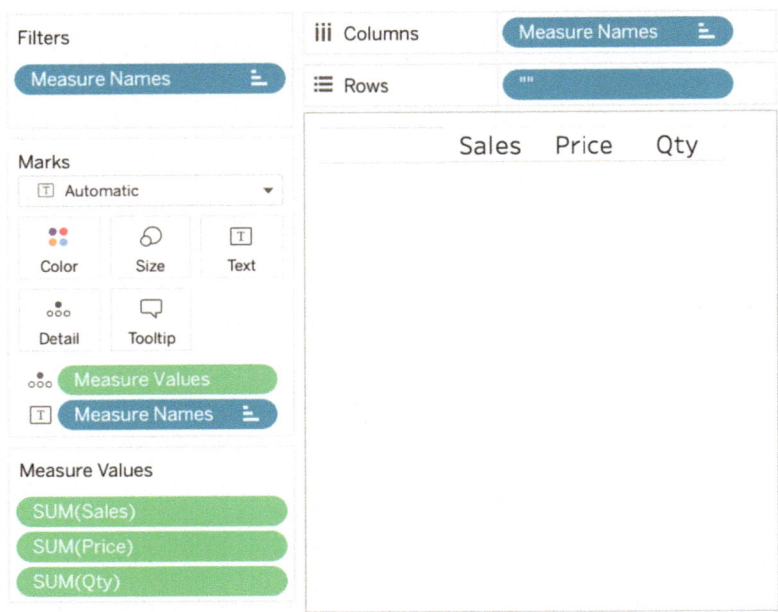

FIGURE 8.60
The Measure Values Field on the Detail Tile.

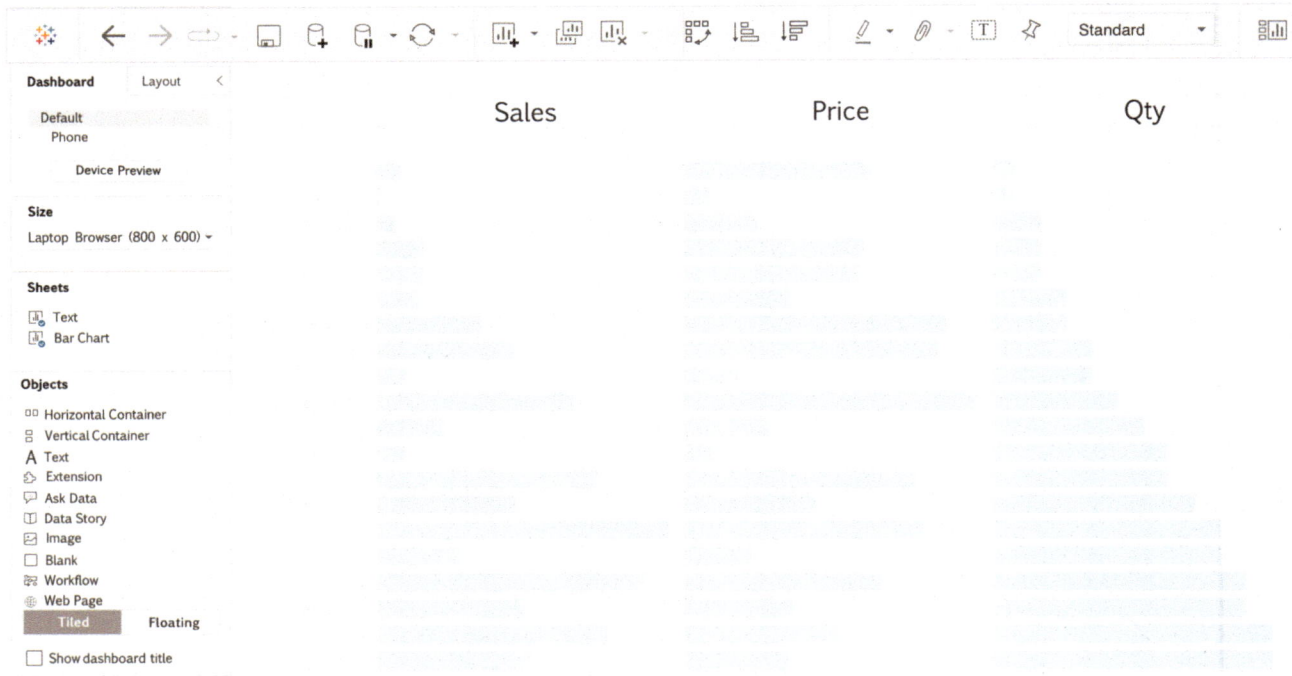

FIGURE 8.61
The Dashboard.

8.14.6 Worksheets and Dashboard

In this example, there are two worksheets on one dashboard.

8.14.7 Bar Chart Worksheet

The "Bar Chart" worksheet has three fields on the **Columns** shelf, as shown in Step 1, which creates three panes. The aggregation for all three fields is SUM(), as shown in Figure 8.64.

SUM(Sales), SUM(Price), SUM(Qty)

The [Fruit] dimension field is on the "Bar Chart" worksheet's **Rows** shelf. With a **discrete** setting, the field creates header rows on the left side of the view. This dimension field is also sorted by the field [Calculation field for sorting].

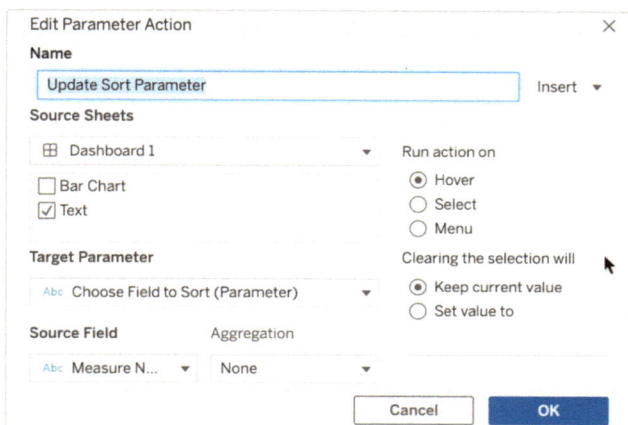

FIGURE 8.62
The **Edit Parameter Action** Window.

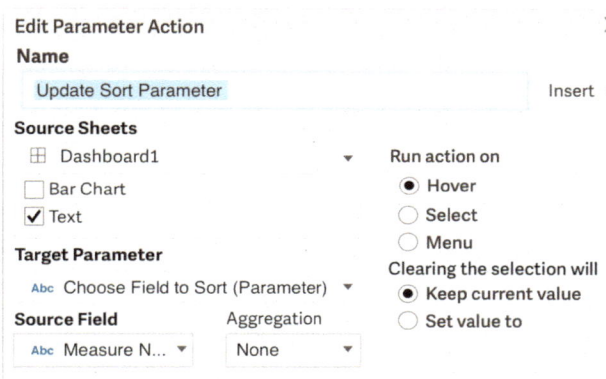

FIGURE 8.63
The **Columns** Shelf.

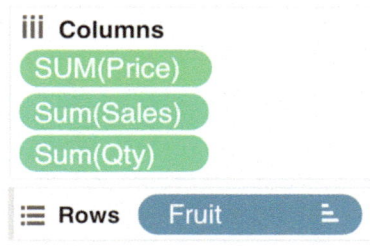

FIGURE 8.64
Measure Names on the Columns Shelf.

8.14.8 Text Worksheet

The "Text" worksheet only has the field [Measure Names] on the **Columns** shelf. [Measure Values] is on the *Detail* tile on the **Marks** card, as shown in Figure 8.65. Tableau adds the **Measured Values** card to the view. When I add the [Measure Names] field to the **Columns** shelf, Tableau also adds [Measured Names]

to the **Filters** shelf. I sorted [Measured Names] in ascending order in this example, or Sales, Price, Qty, as shown Figure 8.65.

As shown in Step 8, the "Text" worksheet has a "Placeholder" dimension field with the expression for a blank string on the **Rows** shelf. The placeholder field expression is "".

8.14.9 Data and Fields

This dashboard utilizes these fields.

- Sales
- Price
- Qty
- Fruit
- Measured Names
- Measured Values
- Calculation Field for Sorting
- A Placeholder Field for Sorting

The data type for **[Sales]** is a "Number (decimal)." In the "Bar Chart" worksheet, [Sales] is a **continuous** field on the **Columns** shelf. This **continuous** field creates an axis on the view, and because the field is on the **Columns** shelf, this is a horizontal x-axis.

In the "Bar Chart" worksheet, **[Price]** is on the **Columns** shelf. **[Price]** is a **continuous** field, so it creates a second chart in the view with an x-axis. In the "Bar Chart" worksheet, **[Qty]** is also on the **Columns** shelf. **[Qty]** is a **continuous** field, so it creates a third chart in the view with an x-axis.

The **[Fruit]** field is a **discrete** dimension with a "String" data type. As expected, the field has a blue background or "pill" because it is **discrete**. Since [Fruit] is on the **Rows** shelf, header rows are created on the left side of the view.

8.14.10 Measured Names

The three field names are **discrete** values in the [Measured Names] field. Tableau automatically generates this field. In this "Text" worksheet, I am using [Measured Names] in three places.

- Columns Shelf
- Filters Shelf
- Marks Card: Text Tile

8.14.11 Calculated Fields

There are two calculated fields.

- Calculation Field for Sorting
- A Placeholder Field

8.14.11.1 *"Calc Field for Sorting"*

This calculated field uses a case statement to choose which field is sorted. The [Fruit] field is sorted using the [Calc Field for Sorting] on the "Bar Chart" worksheet.

8.14.11.2 *Placeholder*

There is an empty string field on the "Text" worksheet. This "Placeholder" field is simply used to align the "Text" worksheet on the dashboard. A placeholder field is a simple calculation; in this case, a blank string. " "

8.14.12 Components or Elements

There are several elements in this workbook on the two worksheets.

- Columns Shelf
- Rows Shelf
- Measure Values Shelf
- Filters Shelf
- Parameter
- Parameter Control
- Change Parameter Action

8.14.13 Filters Shelf

The **Filters** shelf has the [Measure Names] field on the "Text" worksheet. The **Filters** shelf is not used on the "Bar Chart" worksheet. This filter lets you choose which fields are on the **Measure Values** card.

8.14.14 Marks Cart: Text

For the "Text" worksheet, the field [Measure Names] is on the "Text" tile of the **Marks** card.

8.14.15 Measure Values Card

Because [Measure Names] is on the **Columns** shelf of the "Text" worksheet, and I also added [Measure Values] to *Detail* on the **Marks** card, the corresponding **Measure Values** card is added with the three fields, as shown in Figure 8.65. In this case, the aggregation is SUM().

- SUM(Sales)
- SUM(Price)
- SUM(Qty)

8.14.15.1 *Parameter*

The parameter called [Choose Field to Sort (Parameter)] uses a "Change Parameter" dashboard action with a calculated field called [Calc field for sorting].

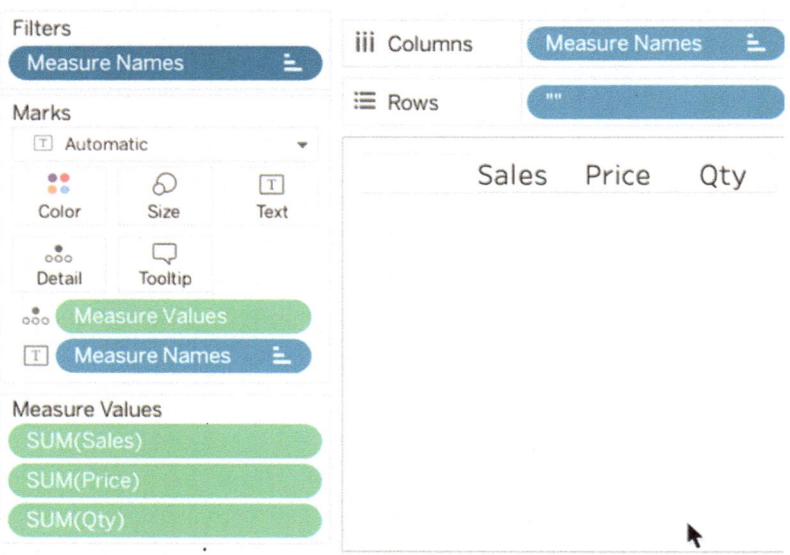

FIGURE 8.65
The Measure Values Card.

8.14.15.2 Change Parameter – Dashboard Action

The "Change Parameter Action" links the calculated field [Calc field for sorting] with the parameter [Choose Field to Sort (Parameter)].

8.14.15.3 Parameter Control

By showing the **Parameter Control** for the parameter [Choose Field to Sort (Parameter)], you allow users to choose a different parameter value and interactively change filtering. I used a very descriptive name here, but you could use anything that makes sense (Figure 8.66).

8.15 Sorting Segments within a Stacked Bar

This exercise uses a "combined field" to sort segments within a stacked bar chart. You can only create a "combined field" from dimension fields.

> Choose Field to Sort (Parameter)
> ○ Sales
> ⦿ Qty
> ○ Price

FIGURE 8.66
Field to Sort.

Tableau Public file:

> https://public.tableau.com/views/Sort
> SegmentsinStackedBar/Dashboard1?:
> language=en-US&publish=yes&:sid=&:
> display_count=n&:origin=viz_share_link

8.15.1 Preview – The Finished Worksheet

In Figure 8.67, the segments in each bar use the dimensions [Fruit] and [Month] to sort by [Sales].

8.15.2 Create the Visualization

1. Create a new calculated field called [Month for Sorting]. In this example, I use the MONTH() function.

   MONTH([Order Date])

2. Select the two dimension fields [Fruit] and [Month for Sorting] in the left **Data** pane and right-click to open the *context menu*. Select *Create Combined Field* (Figures 8.68).

3. Add the [Fruit] field to *Color* on the **Marks** card. Right-click the field and choose "Attribute" from the *context menu*. Changing the field aggregation is a **critical** step to sort the segments within an individual bar (Figure 8.70).

4. Add the new combined field [Month for Sorting & Fruit (Combined)] from Step 2 to *Detail* on the **Marks** card.

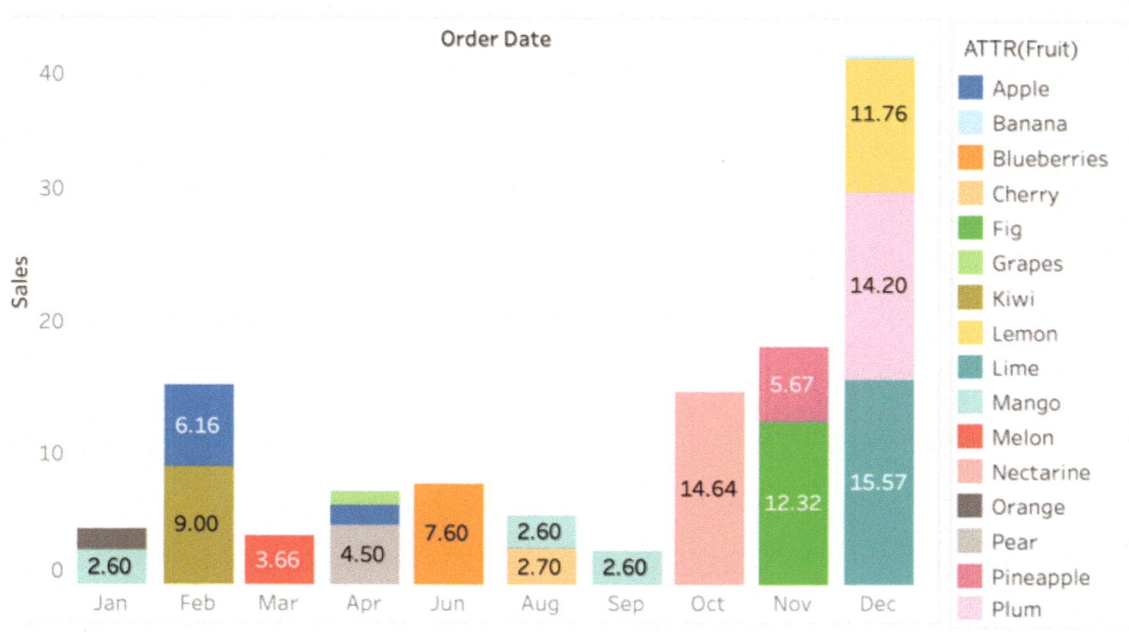

FIGURE 8.67
Bar Chart with Segments.

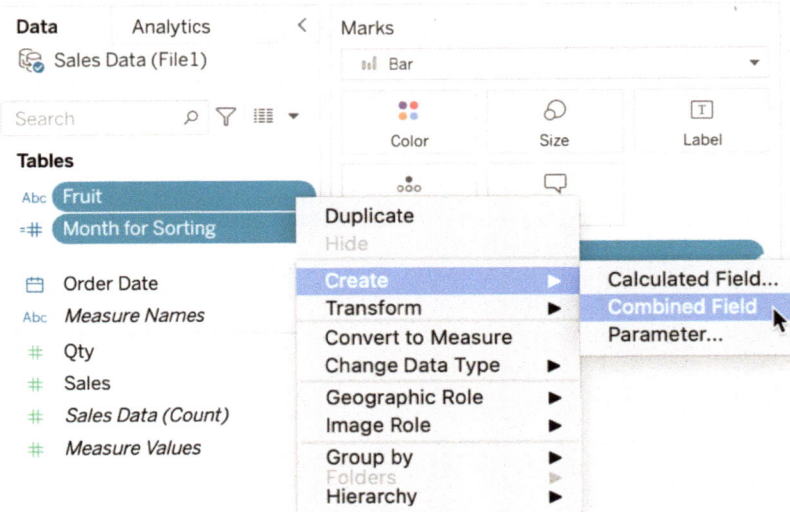

Figure 8.68 The Choice to Create a Combined Field.

FIGURE 8.69
Tip: *To check if a field is a dimension, right-click the field in the **Data** pane to open the field's context menu and select "Describe."*

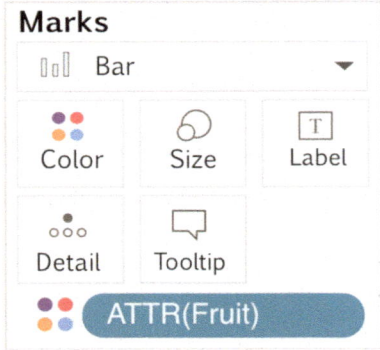

FIGURE 8.70
The Marks Card.

5. On the **Marks** card, click the drop-down arrow for the [Month for Sorting & Fruit (Combined)] field and choose "Sort." Configure the options shown below.

Month for Sorting & Fruit (Combined)

Setting	Value
Sort By	Field
Sort Order	Ascending
Field Name	Sales
Aggregation	Sum

6. Add [Sales] to *Label* on the **Marks** card so mark labels are shown as numbers within the bars, as shown in Figure 8.71.

7. The finished chart is shown in Figure 8.67. The segments in each bar are sorted, and the largest sales are at the bottom.

8.16 Sort by Rank Alternative

In **Chapter 11**, I use a quick table calculation for rank in *"Section 11.10.5.1 Sort by Ranking Alternative" on page 236*. While you cannot select a table calculation field in the **Sort Dialog Box**, you can add the table calculation field to the **Rows** or **Columns** shelves. Then, Tableau uses the field for sorting.

1. Add [Measured Names] to the **Columns** shelf. Tableau adds the **Measured Values** shelf to the view. Add [Region] to the **Rows** shelf.

2. Create a field [Rank of Sales] with a table calculation of "RANK()."

3. Add the field [Rank of Sales] to the **Rows** shelf. Right-click the field to change it to **Discrete**, as shown below. After the change, the field background changes from green to **blue** (Figure 8.72).

4. On the **Rows** shelf, drag the [Rank of Sales] field to the left so that it is the first field on the **Rows** shelf. The chart shows both fields and is sorted by the first field on the shelf (Figure 8.73).

5. Right-click the field [Rank of Sales] on the **Rows** shelf and uncheck "Show Header" (Figure 8.74).

6. The view now only shows one instance of the [Rank of Sales] field (Figure 8.75).

8.16.1 Project Files

Tableau Public file:

> https://public.tableau.com/views/Sort
> SegmentsinStackedBar/Sales?:language=
> en-US&:display_count=n&:origin=
> viz_share_link

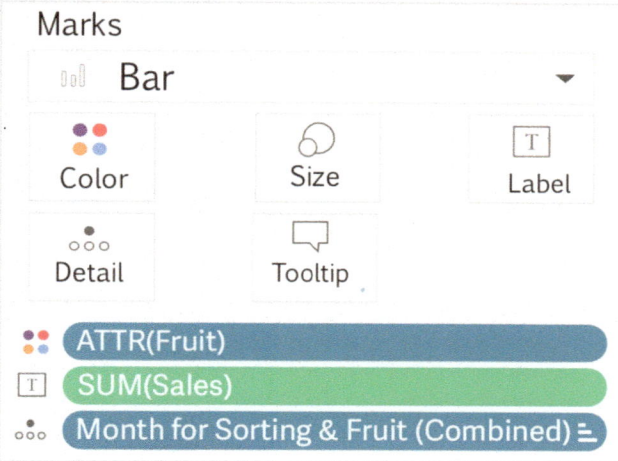

FIGURE 8.71
The Marks card with the sales field on the Label tile.

8.16.2 Fields

The worksheet has five fields, as shown in Figure 8.76. I created the [Month for Sorting] as a dimension field from [Order Date]. I also created a new combined field called [Month for Sorting and Fruit (Combined)].

- Order Date
- Month for Sorting
- Sales
- Fruit
- Month for Sorting and Fruit (Combined)

8.16.3 Sort by Date and SUM(Sales)

In this example, I want to sort by dates and then sales. The month separates the view into panes, and I want to sort within each pane.

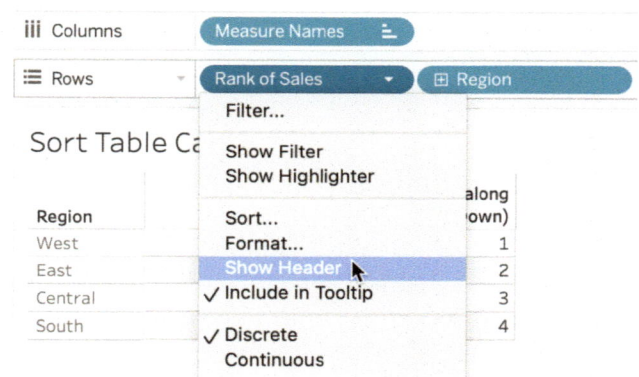

FIGURE 8.73
The **Rank of Sales** Field on the **Rows** Shelf.

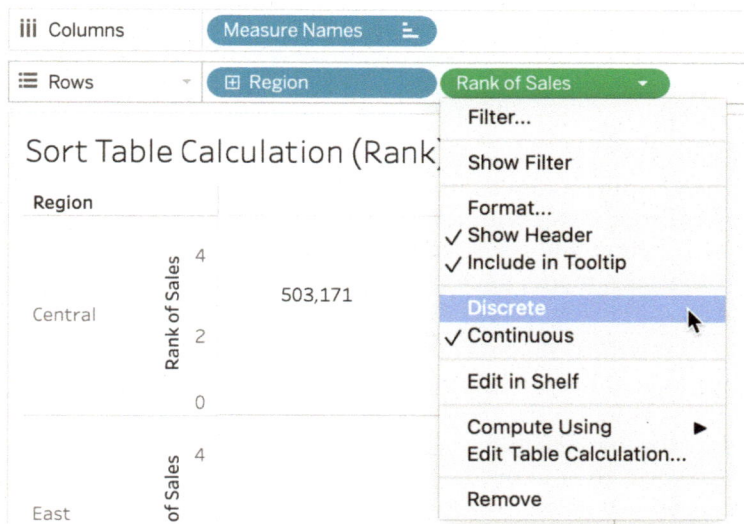

FIGURE 8.72
Change the Field to Discrete.

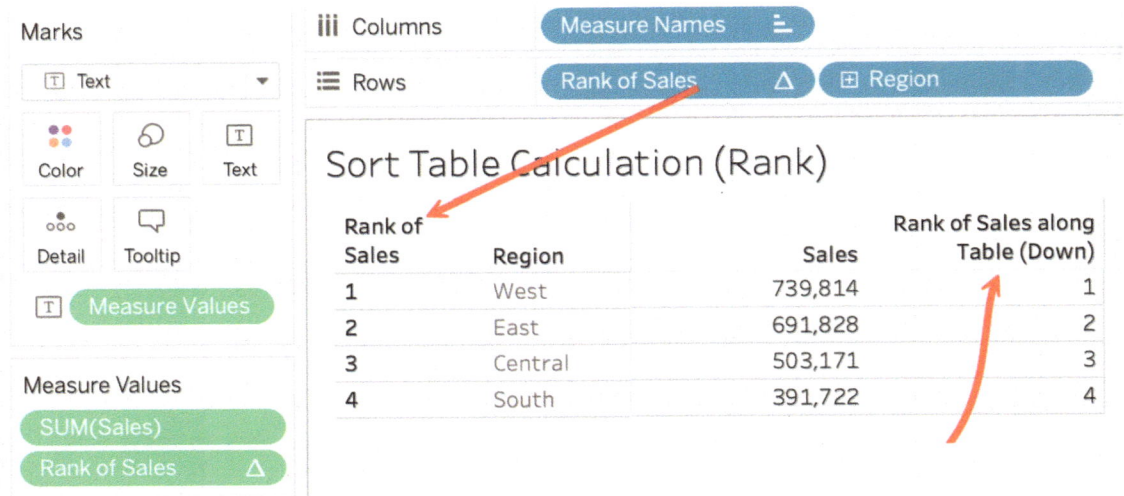

FIGURE 8.74
The **Show Header** Option.

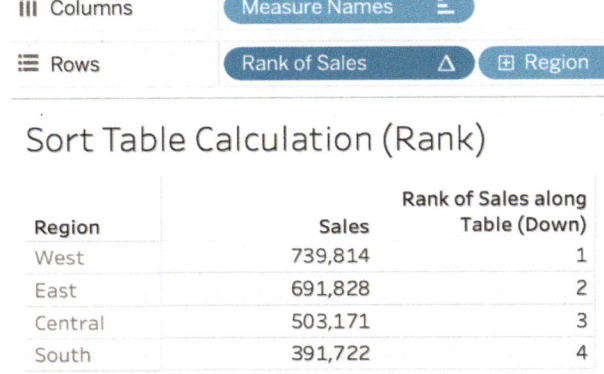

FIGURE 8.75
The **Rank** Field on the Right.

1. Create a simple unsorted chart using the sample superstore data source, as shown below (Figure 8.77).

2. Look at the view when I apply a descending sort for the date field [Order Date] with *data source order*. As shown below, the dates are sorted correctly, but the sales marks have no sorting (Figure 8.78).

3. Let's take a moment to see the different sorting options before we look at the final sort in step 4. If I change the sorting on the [Order Date] field to *Nested*, the bars within each pane will not be sorted correctly, and the dates will be out of order, as shown below (Figures 8.79 and 8.80).

> When I sort the [Category] field with the *Nested* option, the bars are sorted properly, but the dates are no longer descending.

4. Using the descending [Order Date] sort option from step 2, I add a second sort on the [Category] field, as shown below. Now, my dates are sorted in descending order, and my sales are also in descending order for each month (Figure 8.81).

8.17 Sort Columns or Marks

These two topics are not about sorting field data but rather how to sort the order of columns or marks.

8.17.1 Sort the Order of Columns on the Canvas

Click and drag a field name on a shelf to change the order of columns. If you are using [Measure Values], as discussed in *"Section 3.3 Measure Names, Measure Values, and Count" on page 58*, rearrange the fields on the **Measure Values** shelf. Click and drag a field until a red line indicates the new location and then drop the field. A sort icon is displayed to the right of the [Measure Names] field on the **Rows** or **Columns** shelf, indicating the fields are sorted manually. However, you can change the sort order.

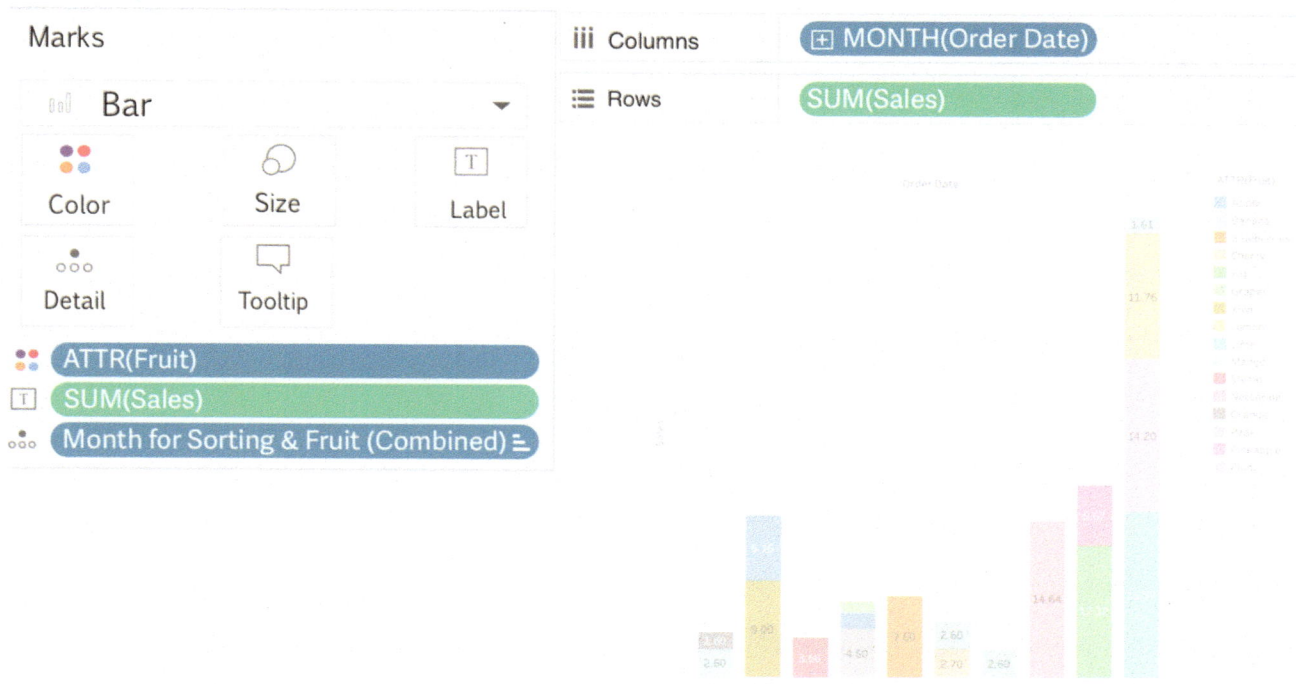

FIGURE 8.76
The **Marks** Card.

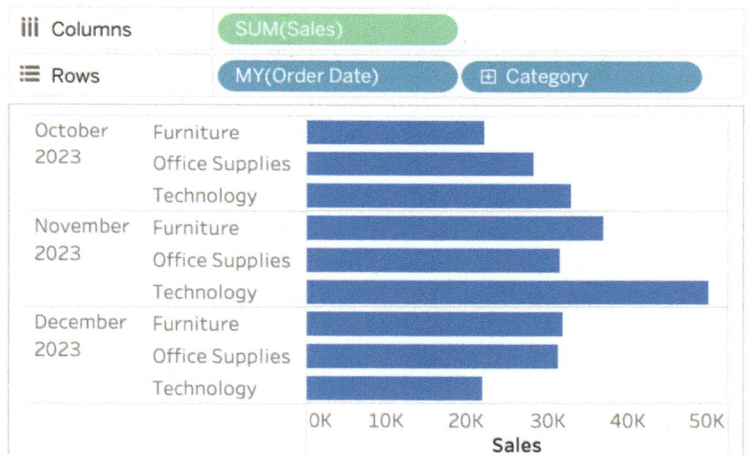

FIGURE 8.77
The Unsorted Bars.

8.17.2 Sort to Bring a Mark to the Front

You can use sorting for a categorical "dimension" field to bring one line (mark) to the front of the visualization so that it is on top of other lines. For example, if you are looking at country data and want the USA line to be at the forefront of the chart, sort the country values so that the USA is first. In the case of multiple fields on the **Measure Values** shelf, drag the field to change the stacking order of the marks. Change the categorical sort order to bring the "Accessories" line to the top of the page so it is not hidden under other lines, as shown in Figure 8.82.

You can also click an **Axis** and choose "Move marks to front," as shown in *"Section 12.12 Bring a Mark to the Forefront" on page 278.*

FIGURE 8.78
Sort by the Date Field.

FIGURE 8.79
A Nested Sort by the Order Date.

FIGURE 8.80
Sort by Category.

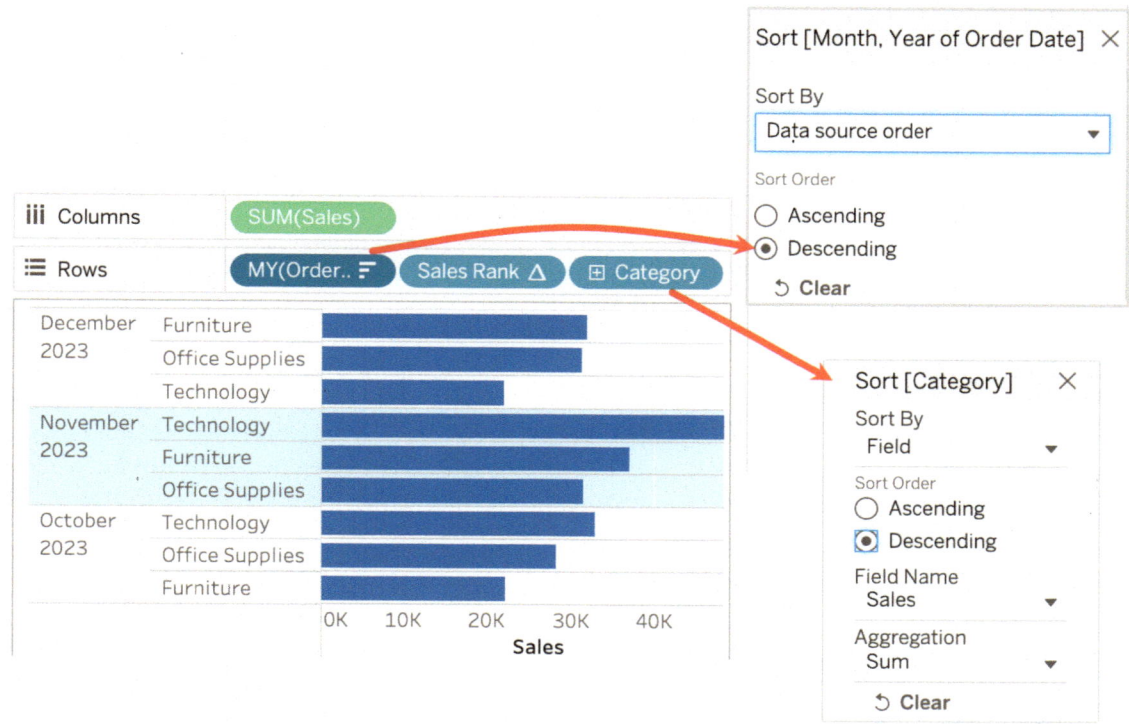

FIGURE 8.81
The Sort Option by Order Date and Category.

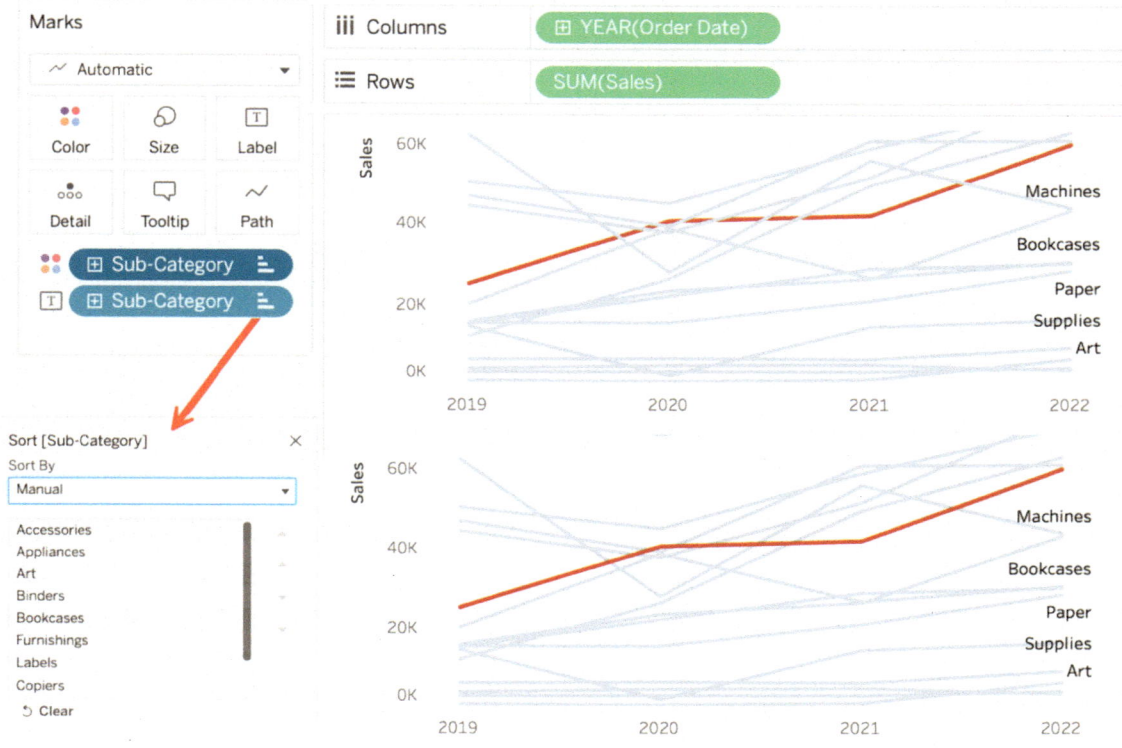

FIGURE 8.82
Bring Line to the Front.

9

Dates

In this topic, we discuss

In this chapter, I wanted to discuss how to use date data in Tableau and explore the differences between **date values** and **date parts**, a fundamental concept in Tableau. I only briefly touch on common date expressions since excellent examples are available online. Tableau is very flexible when working with date fields. That is to say, fields with a "date" type. When Tableau connects to a data source, Tableau adds date fields to the "Dimensions" section of the **Data** pane. If you have changed a date field to a "measure," click the field to open the field's *context menu* to switch back to "dimension."

For Tableau data, try to use dates like "2023-01-31" whenever possible instead of a title like "January." Figure 4.19 is a common format used in Excel. The data is broken into the months *Jan, Feb,* and *Mar,* as shown in *"Section 4.6.2 Valid Dates" on page 79.* In Chapter 4, we also looked at the importance of the data type "date" and tall data in the topic "Data Structure," where we converted the months *Jan, Feb,* and *Mar* into dates in the format "2024-01-31."

In both cases, you choose whether to include the year, quarter, month, weekday, or the entire date. Tableau displays a small plus sign to the left of the field name to indicate you can drill down from year to quarter to month, etc. If the date includes time, there are hours, minutes, and seconds. Date parts aggregate all dates in the data set, so two dates that are the same date and time (7:00 AM) **aggregate** the values $1.55 and $1.90 to $3.45, as shown in Figure 9.15. For example, date parts reflect four instances of the month "May" when the data spans from 2021 to 2024.

Date values reflect a particular date, on the other hand. The additional choice of discrete or continuous determines whether to add headers or an axis with a range of dates to a view. For filtering, the discrete date field would have the individual years 2021, 2022, 2023, and 2024, while the continuous date field would have a slider to indicate a range of dates.

- Date Parts (usually discrete but can be continuous)
- Date Values (usually continuous but can be discrete). To change the *date level*, click the date field's drop-down arrow to open the *date context menu*, as shown in Figure 9.1. The items in the middle section of the *date context menu* are divided by a line. The top part has **date part** levels. The bottom part is the actual **date values**.

The bottom section of the *date context menu* allows you to choose **discrete** or **continuous**. A **discrete** field creates headers like January, February, and March. A **continuous date value** adds an axis to the view. In the previous example, **discrete** and the **date part** *Month* are checked. Let's look at these items in detail, focusing on the differences and how the data is affected.

9.1 Date-Level Settings

When you drag a field onto the view, Tableau prompts you to choose a date level. Tableau uses the date levels in the two categories when working with date fields.

9.2 Date Parts

Date parts are aggregated to reflect **ALL** instances of that **date part**, such as the month of July for any year. A **discrete** date part of "year" displays individual years in a **Filter Control**. Some date parts are shown below. When you add fields to columns or shelves, the selected

DOI: 10.1201/9781003566458-10

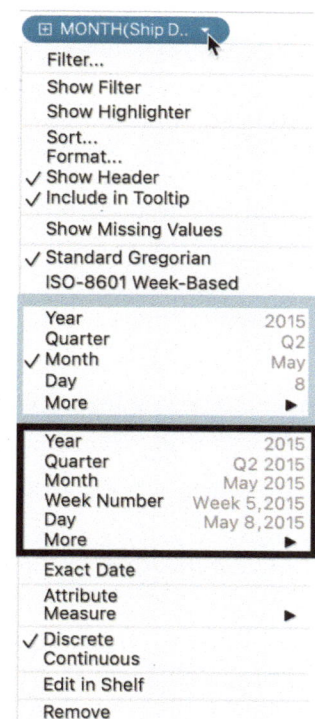

FIGURE 9.1
The Date Context menu.

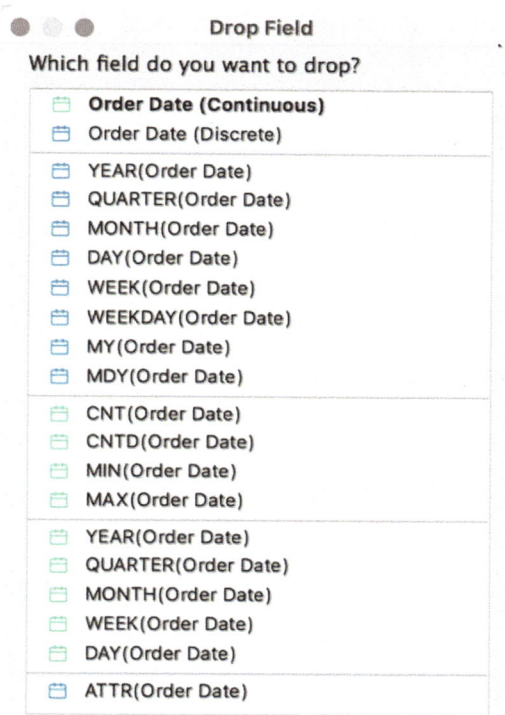

FIGURE 9.2
The **Drop Field** context menu.

date part YEAR is displayed in uppercase, as shown in Figure 9.3. When you use date parts in functions, they are displayed in lowercase, as shown in Figure 9.28.

- year
- quarter
- month
- day
- weekday (day of the week, like Tuesday)
- week
- hour
- minute
- second

When **date parts** are **discrete** and the data source includes data across four years, there are four instances of the month "May." In the same example, the **date part** "Day" reflects every instance of the 8th day of the month across four years or 48 instances of the day "8." In the **Data** pane, select a date field and drag it to the **Columns** shelf. In MacOS, use the *Option* key and drag the field to the **Columns** shelf. The **Drop Field** *context menu* is displayed with date-level options, as shown in Figure 9.2.

I use the **date part** "YEAR" with a **discrete** "Date Level" to create the year headings, as shown in Figure 9.3.

To see the difference between **date parts** and **date values**, select the **date part** "Month" from the top half

FIGURE 9.3
Discrete date headings.

of the date field's *context menu*, as shown in Figure 9.4. In the **Columns** shelf, right-click the field [Order Date] on the **Columns** shelf to open the date field's *context menu*. In the following example, when you select "Month" from the top half of the *context menu*, Tableau automatically checks **discrete**, and the field is blue on the **Columns** shelf.

You cannot format a custom **date part** like MY([Order Date]) in the **Format** pane. Instead, to format a date, use any **date part** or **date value** except "Custom." The advantage of a custom date part is that it prevents a line from stopping and starting because of panes, for example, a gap between years.

To see the difference between **discrete** and **continuous** dates, right-click the field *Order Date* in the **Columns** shelf to open the *date context menu*. Select

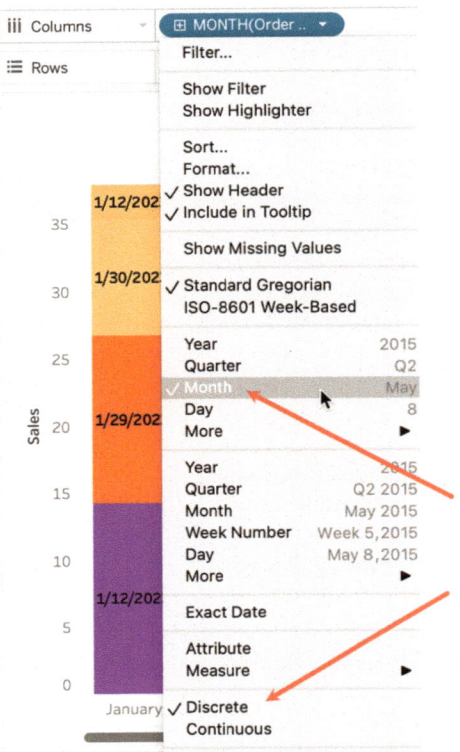

FIGURE 9.4
A discrete month in the Date Field's context menu.

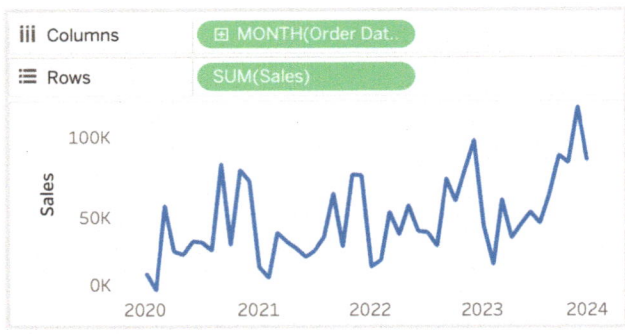

FIGURE 9.5
x-Axis.

"Month" from the top half of the *context menu* and **continuous** near the bottom of the menu. Tableau redraws the chart with an x-axis along the bottom, as shown in Figure 9.5.

Select the **Date Value** "Week Number" from the bottom half of the *context menu* and check **discrete** as a comparison. Finally, change to **continuous** to see the change in the view.

9.2.1 Year and Month

When displaying several **date parts**, add the date field to the shelf and use the field's plus symbol to expand the **date parts**. In Figure 9.6, I expanded the field from year to quarter, then to month, and then removed the "quarter" **date part** blue pill from the shelf.

9.2.2 Select Marks on the View to View Data

In *"Section 4.2.4 * Asterisk" on page 75*, I had a chart with sales data by month. With the marks selected, right-click the January bar and select "View Data" from the pop-up *context menu*, as shown in Figure 9.7. Tableau displays the "View Data" window, as shown in Figure 9.10.

To see the data behind the "January" bar, click the view and drag the mouse to select all the segments in the bar. The mouse pointer changes to a square, as shown in the top-left corner of Figure 9.8. As you drag the mouse, a gray highlight box is displayed.

With the marks selected, right-click the January bar and select "View Data" from the pop-up *context menu*, as shown in Figure 9.9.

Tableau displays the "View Data" window, as shown in Figure 9.10.

The data has four rows and includes the month "January" from 2022 and 2023.

9.3 Date Values

Date values reflect a particular date and are truncated to a specific level. For example, when the date is *2023-08-31*, and I select the "Year" **date value**, the axis

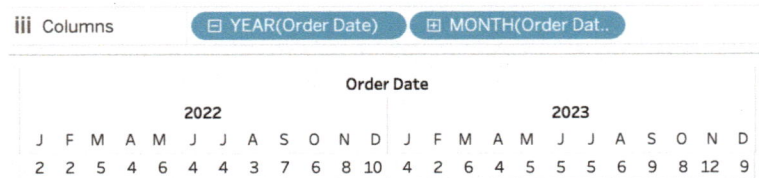

FIGURE 9.6
Expand date parts.

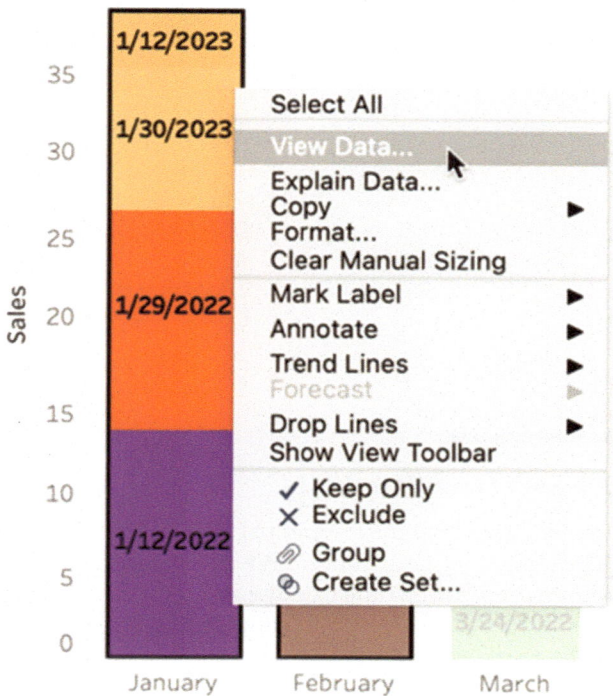

FIGURE 9.7
View Data from Context menu.

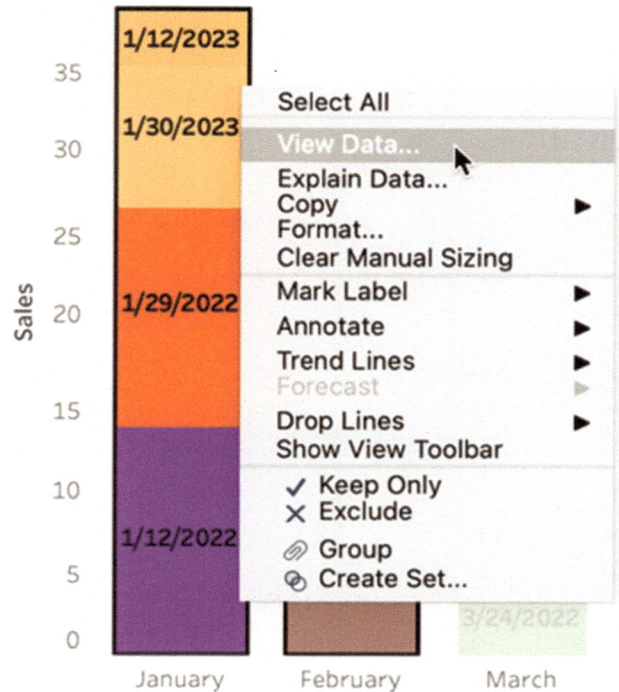

FIGURE 9.9
View Data from Context menu.

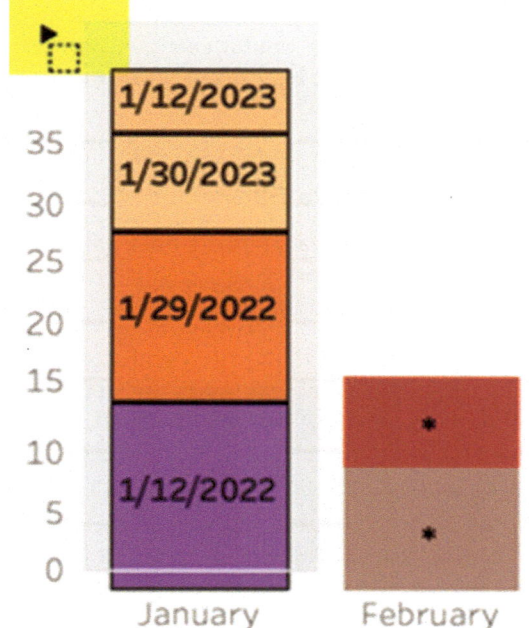

FIGURE 9.8
Highlight box in top-left corner.

displays *2023*. Drag [Order Date] to the **Columns** shelf and change the aggregation to "Month" at the bottom of the date field's *context menu*. This is a **date value**. In this example, I checked the **continuous** setting in the date field's *context menu*, and the field is green. If you click the small plus symbol to the left of the field name, Tableau drills down to the lower **date value**; in this case, *Month* (Figure 9.10).

We look at date functions in *"Section 11.8.2 MAX() and MIN()" on page 232*. Chapter 11 also has details on aggregation.

9.3.1 Change to a Date Value

Next, I use the date field's *context menu* to change the "Order Date" field from a **discrete** blue **date part** to a **continuous** green **date value** in Figure 9.12. When I select "Month" from the bottom half of the date field's *context menu*, Tableau checks **continuous**, and the field color is green.

The bar chart also changes to reflect the **date values**, as shown in Figure 9.13.

9.4 Comparing Date Parts and Date Values

To illustrate the difference between **date parts** and **date values**, let's look at two charts showing "hours" over several days. The data source has four rows, and two of the rows are 7:00:00AM, as shown in Figure 9.14.

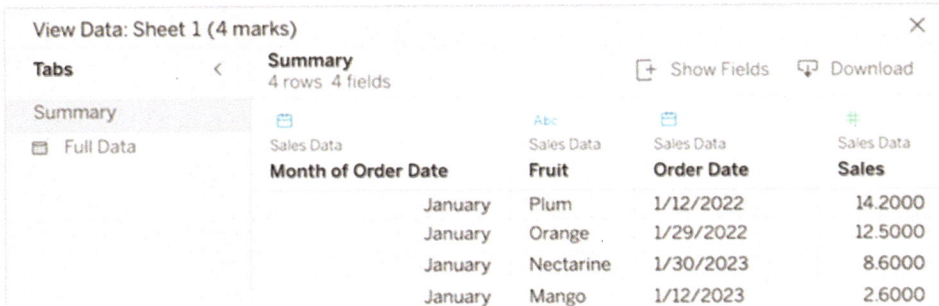

FIGURE 9.10
View Data window.

FIGURE 9.11
Month date value.

FIGURE 9.12
Continuous in date Context menu.

In Figure 9.15, the chart on the left uses a **date part** to show an x-axis with hours over a 24-hour range, with each "hour" containing an aggregate value over a series of *days*. There are three data points because the two 7:00 AM values ($1.55 and $1.90) are aggregated to $3.45.

The second chart shows the individual **date values** with four data points.

9.5 ISO Date Standards

Tableau uses ISO date standards. ISO is the Industry Standards Organization. When importing data sources or creating date calculations, ISO dates use the format 2023-02-25. The ISO standard sets the first day of the week as "Monday."

9.6 Discrete vs. Continuous Dates

"Section 3.5 Discrete vs. Continuous" on page 61 also examines the difference between **continuous** and **discrete** dates.

9.6.1 Add Date Parts to Titles

In this example, I illustrate adding **date parts** for your title as month, day, and year. In this instance, the "Exact Date" option would also work.

1. Create a new field [Date Title] with the expression: TODAY(). Tableau adds the field to the **Data**pane, and if you hover over the field, a blue background indicates the field is **discrete**.

2. Drag the [Date Title] field from the **Data** pane to the *Detail* tile on the **Marks** card. The field name is [YEAR(Date Title)], and the field has a blue background because it is the **discrete date part** "Year."

3. Click the plus symbol to the left of the [YEAR(Date Title)] field name on the *Detail* tile to drill down into the **date parts**. A new field [QUARTER(Date Title)] is added to the *Detail* tile.

I do not want the quarter **date part**, so I click the drop-down arrow on the [QUARTER(Date Title)] field

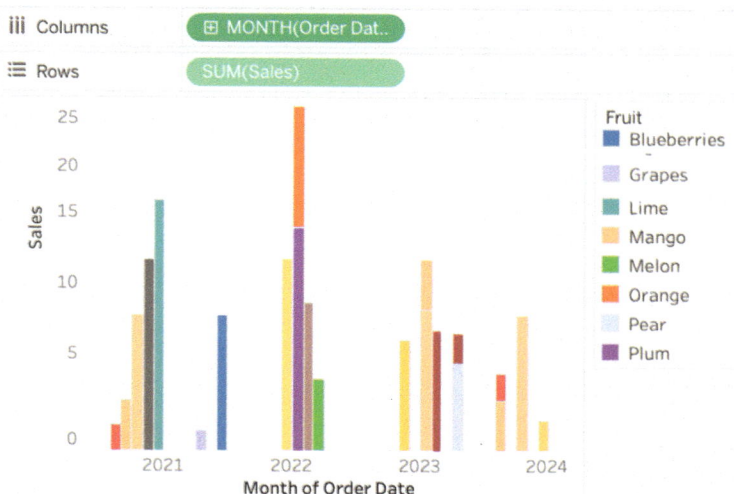

FIGURE 9.13
New Date values in x-axis.

Abc	#	📅	#
Sales Data 2023	Sales Data 2023	Sales Data 2023	Sales Data 2023
Fruit	**Qty**	**Order Date**	**Sales**
Apple	5	2/1/2023 7:00:00 AM	1.55
Mango	2	2/5/2023 10:00:00 AM	1.00
Cherry	3	2/3/2023 12:00:00 PM	3.00
Banana	1	2/4/2023 7:00:00 AM	1.90

FIGURE 9.14
Original data.

and select the **date part** "Month" from the *date context menu*. I select the first instance of "Month" on the *context menu* above the line. The field is still blue.

4. Now, the field is [MONTH(Date Title)]. I click the plus symbol on the left side of the [MONTH(Date Time)] field and select the **date part** "Day."

5. Finally, I double-click the title to open the **Edit Title** window. If the title is not showing, on the **Worksheet** menu, select "Show Title." Then, I click the drop-down arrow on the **Insert** menu and choose the date fields, as shown in Figure 9.16.

9.6.2 Worksheet for Date Title

In Figure 9.19, I create a separate sheet for the title to avoid "None" or "All" values in my title.

1. Drag the [Order Date] field from the **Data** pane to the *Text* tile on the **Marks** card.

2. Right-click the field on the *Text* tile to open the field's *date context menu*. Select "Measure" and then "Minimum." Also, select "**Continuous**."

3. Repeat Step 2 and select "Maximum."

4. Click the *Text* tile and remove all fields from the "Edit Label" box, as shown in Figure 9.17.

5. Double-click the title to open the **Edit Title** window. If the title is not showing, on the **Worksheet** menu, select "Show Title." Then, click the drop-down arrow on the **Insert** menu and select the two fields (Figure 9.18).

6. The finished worksheet is shown in Figure 9.19.

9.7 Formatting and Default Properties

9.7.1 Formatting All Dates in a Data Source

Save time by setting the default date format for all fields in a *Data Source*. Click the *Data Source* name at the top of the **Data** pane and select "Date Properties" from the *context menu*, as shown in Figure 9.20. Tableau online help has a section for supported date format symbols. I often pick one of the suggested formats so that Tableau fills in the expression; then, when I switch to custom formatting, I have a starting point.

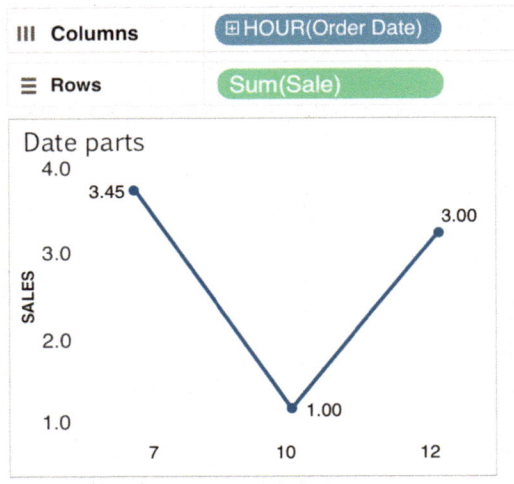
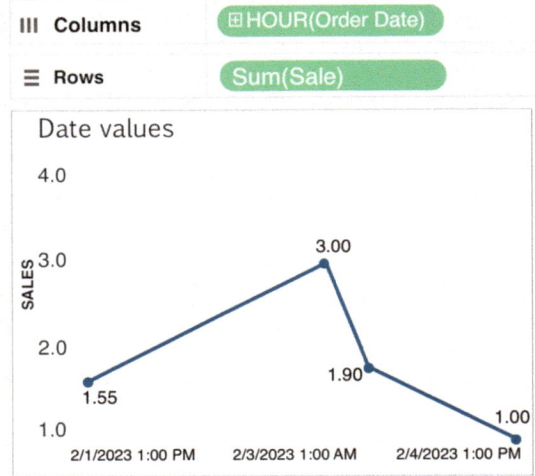

FIGURE 9.15
Date parts vs. date values.

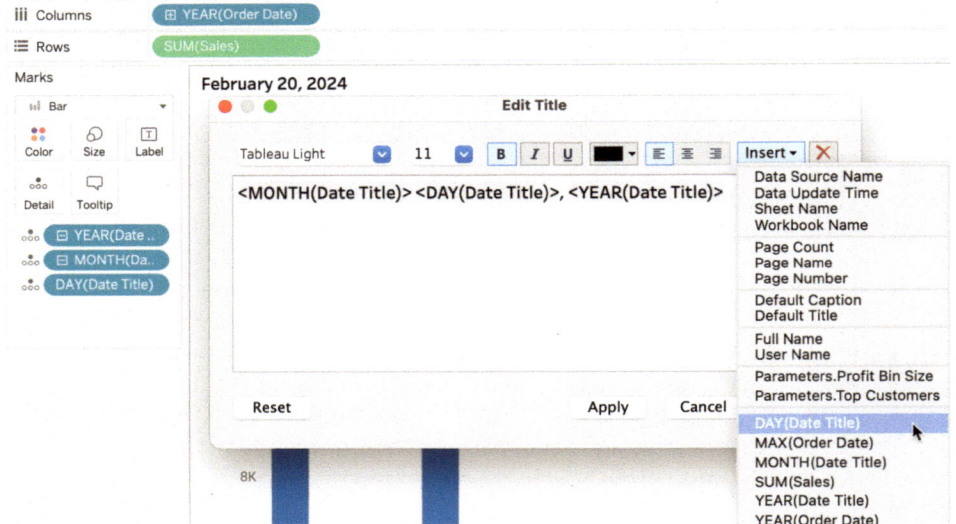

FIGURE 9.16
The **Edit Title** dialog box with the **Insert** fields drop-down list.

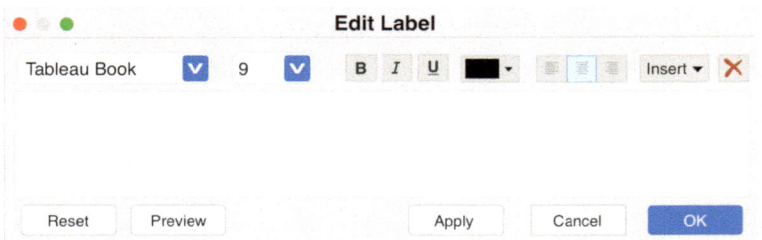

FIGURE 9.17
The **Edit Label** dialog box.

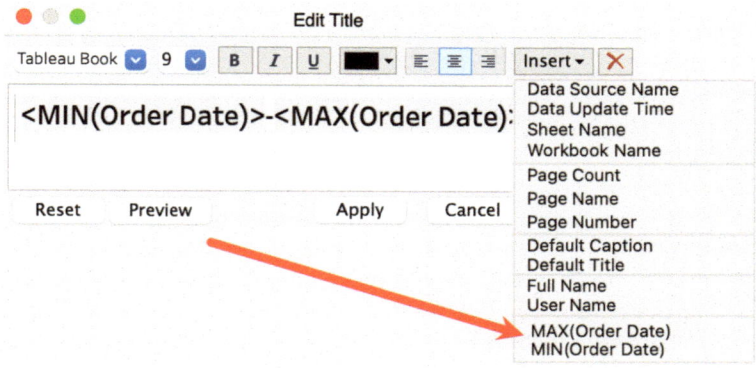

FIGURE 9.18
The **Edit Title** dialog box.

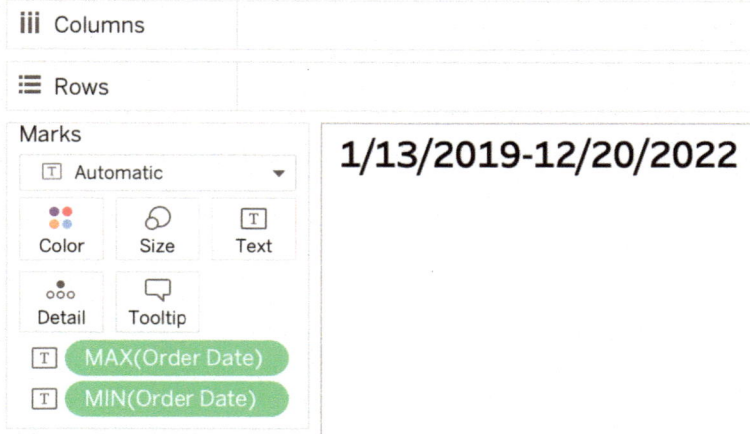

FIGURE 9.19
The completed worksheet with the Title.

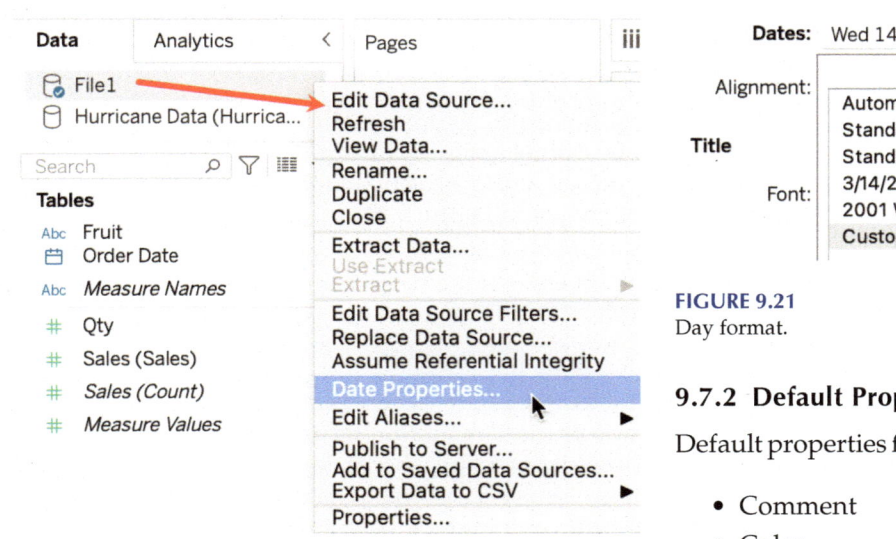

FIGURE 9.20
Date properties.

FIGURE 9.21
Day format.

9.7.2 Default Properties for Dates

Default properties for date fields include these settings:

- Comment
- Color
- Shape
- Date Format
- Sort
- Default Year Start Day

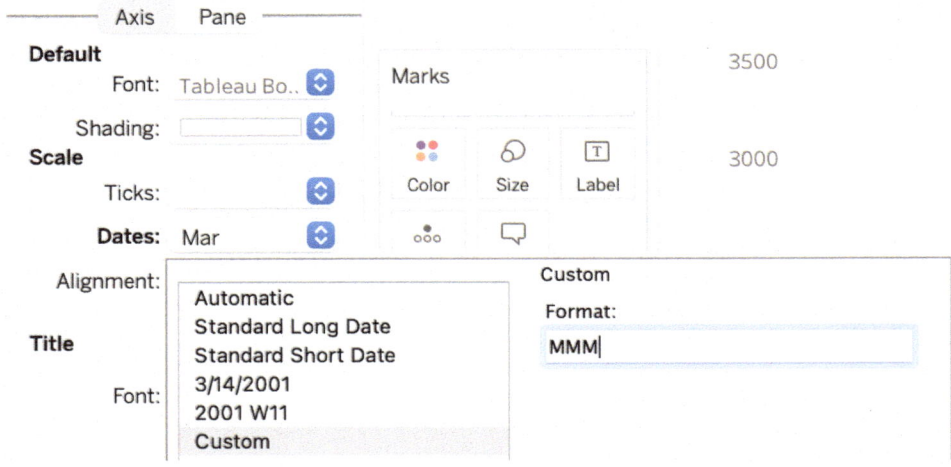

FIGURE 9.22
Month format.

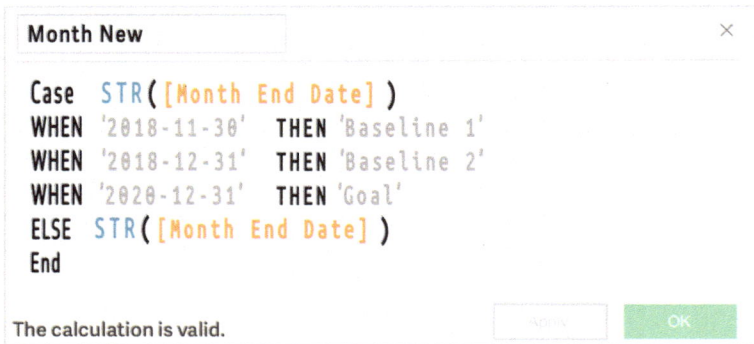

FIGURE 9.23
Calculated field for Date Aliases.

9.7.3 Date Symbols

Tableau uses specific symbols when formatting dates. Follow this link and scroll down to the section "Supported date format symbols" for more information.

> https://help.tableau.com/current/pro/desktop/
> en-us/dates_custom_date_formats.htm

When I type the symbol "dddd" shown in Figure 9.21, Tableau displays the day of the week or "Wednesday."

9.7.4 Abbreviate Month in the Axis

To display months with abbreviations on the axis, in the **Format** pane, select the *Axis* tab and scroll down to the "Scale" section. Click the drop-down arrows for **Dates**, choose "Custom," and type MMM. Instead of "March," Tableau shows "Mar," as shown in Figure 9.22. *"Section 12.11 Format Field: Axis, Numbers" on page 276* also looks at formatting the axis.

9.8 "Alias" for a Date Field

In *"Section 2.2.4 Create an Alias" on page 42*, I mentioned you cannot assign an alias to a date field. Alternatively, you can create a calculated field to do the same thing, as shown in Figure 9.23.

9.9 Date Functions

Tableau supports several date functions. On the right side of the **Calculation Editor**, select "Date" from the drop-down to see a list of date functions. The explanations also specify what data type the function returns: a string, integer, or date. Date functions use arguments such as the **date part** of "month" or the "start_of_week" argument. While there are too many examples to count on the internet, I like this cheat sheet with a Tableau workbook you can download.

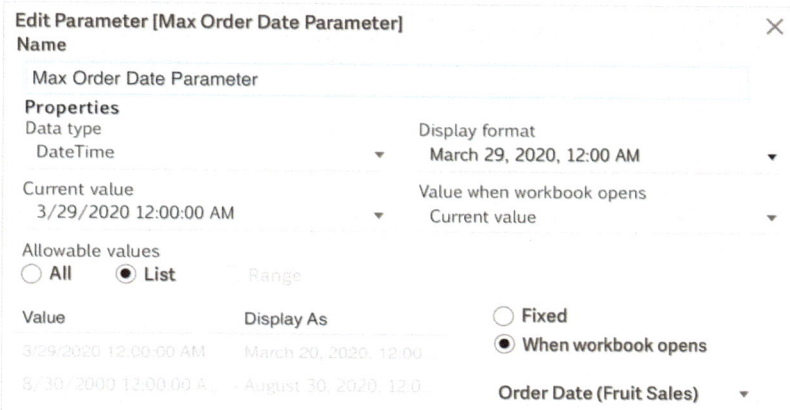

FIGURE 9.24
The **Edit Parameter** dialog window.

FIGURE 9.25
The calculated field Max Date parameter.

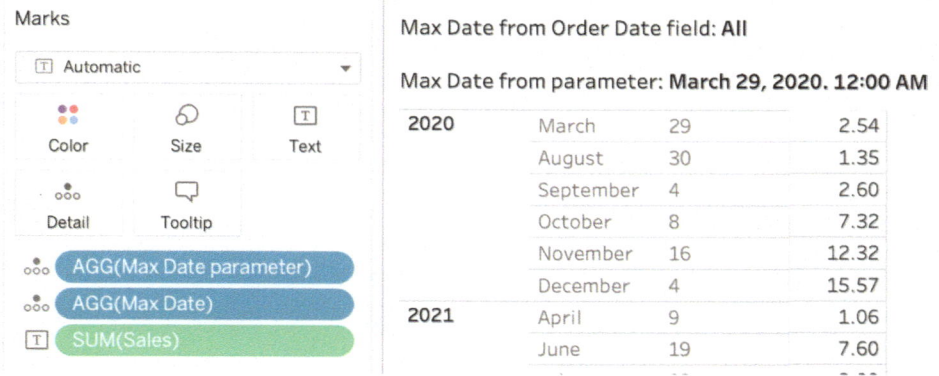

FIGURE 9.26
The finished chart.

https://www.flerlagetwins.com/2021/02/dates.html *"Section 11.5 The Calculation Editor" on page 228* has additional details on the calculation editor.

9.9.1 Date Literal

The format for using a date in an expression is shown below. To use a date literal in an expression, enclose the date with the #pound signs.

#9/24/2023#

9.9.2 Expressions for Filtering vs. Returning a Date

There is a slight difference in how to write an expression to return a date, as opposed to using the expression to filter dates. This expression returns a date or 9/1/2023 12:00:00 AM. DATETRUNC returns the date to the first day of the month when I use the **date part** "month."

DATETRUNC('month', #9/24/2023#)

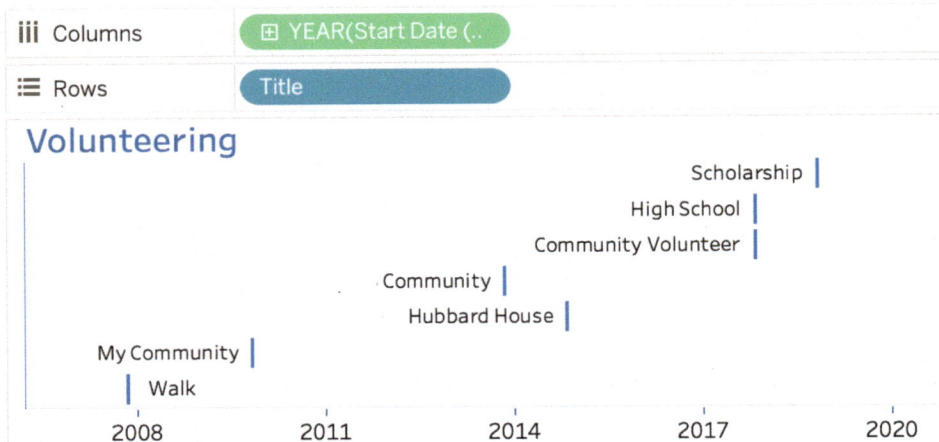

FIGURE 9.27
Gantt Bar Chart.

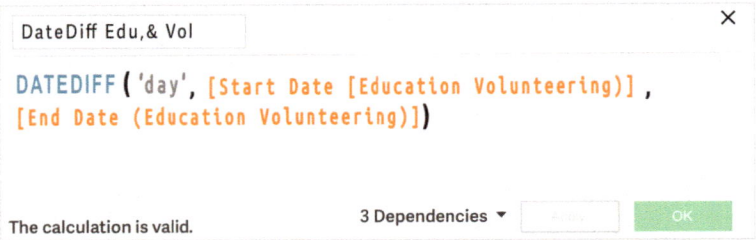

FIGURE 9.28
DATEDIFF calculation.

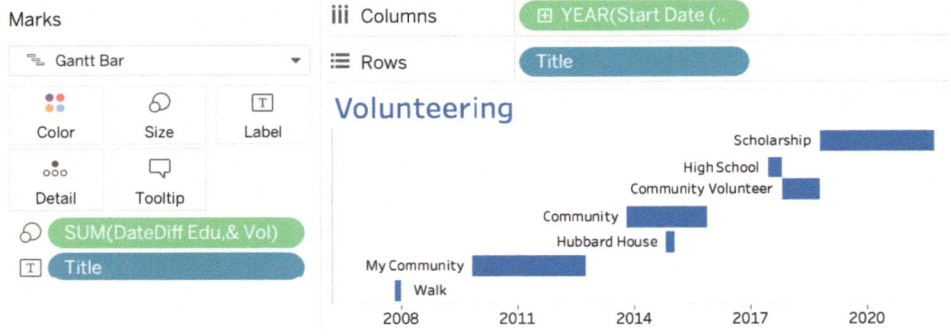

FIGURE 9.29
Gantt Bars with duration.

The next expression on the **Filter** shelf returns records between the dates. When I opened this chart on January 26, 2024, Tableau filtered data to December 2023, the last month. The first line in the expression uses the DATEDIFF() function to retrieve "whole" months, and the last line limits dates to the most recent whole month.

```
DATEDIFF ('month', [Order Date], Today())>=1
AND
DATEDIFF ('month', [Order Date], Today()) <2.
```

9.9.3 DATEPART() and DATENAME()

The DATENAME() function returns the **date part** as a string, for example, "Monday." The next example uses the **date part** "weekday" and returns the first two characters.

```
LEFT(DATENAME('weekday', [MyDateField]), 2)
```

The DATEPART() function returns the name of the specified **date part** as an integer. The next example

FIGURE 9.30
Waterfall chart.

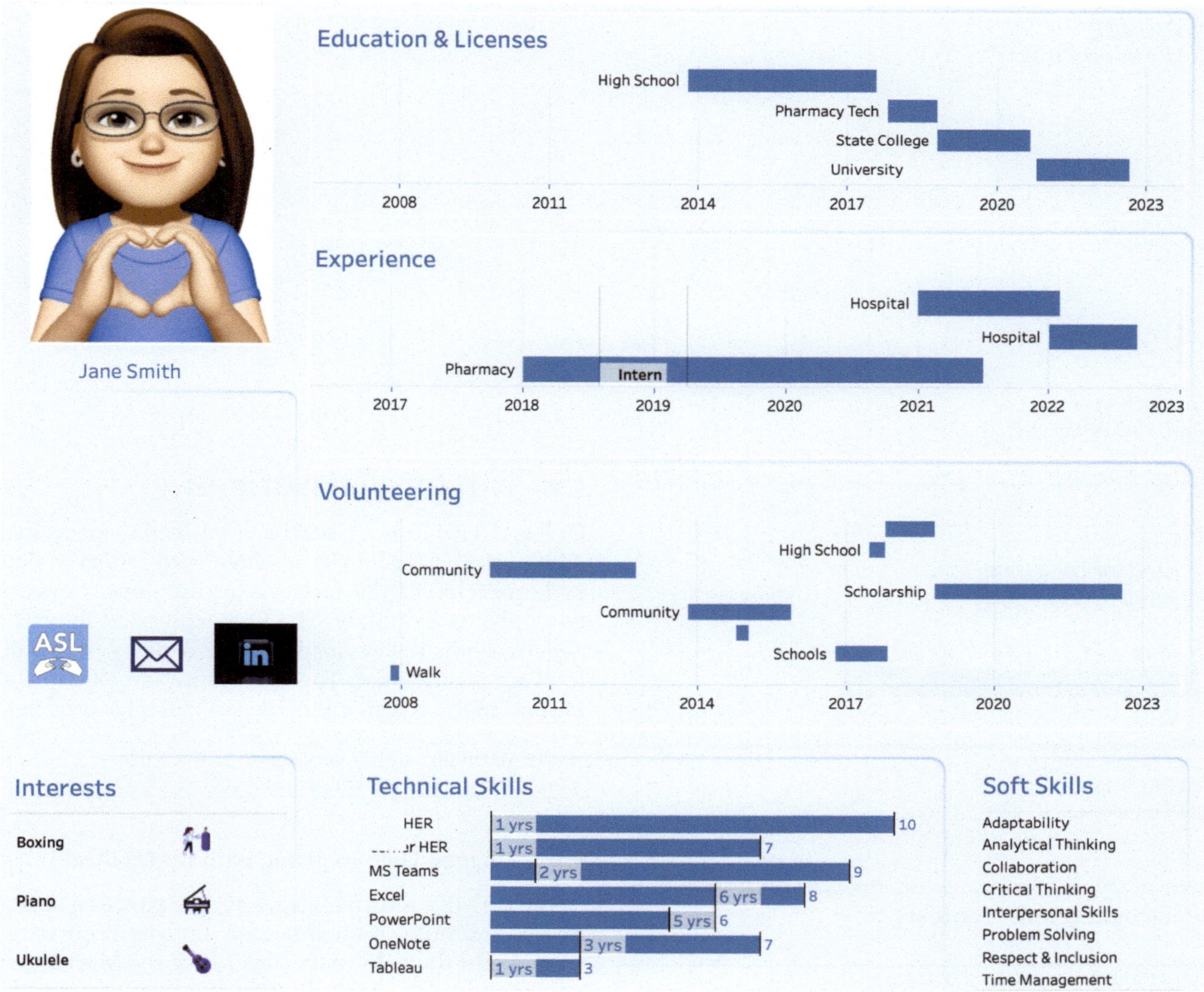

Education & Licenses

High School
Pharmacy Tech
State College
University

2008   2011   2014   2017   2020   2023

Experience

Hospital
Hospital
Pharmacy   Intern

2017   2018   2019   2020   2021   2022   2023

Volunteering

Community
High School
Community   Scholarship
Schools
Walk

2008   2011   2014   2017   2020   2023

Jane Smith

ASL   ✉   in

Interests

Boxing

Piano

Ukulele

Technical Skills

HER	1 yrs	10
...or HER	1 yrs	7
MS Teams	2 yrs	9
Excel	6 yrs	8
PowerPoint	5 yrs	6
OneNote	3 yrs	7
Tableau	1 yrs	3

Soft Skills

Adaptability
Analytical Thinking
Collaboration
Critical Thinking
Interpersonal Skills
Problem Solving
Respect & Inclusion
Time Management

FIGURE 9.31
A resume combining a Waterfall chart, Time Duration, and Gantt Bar.

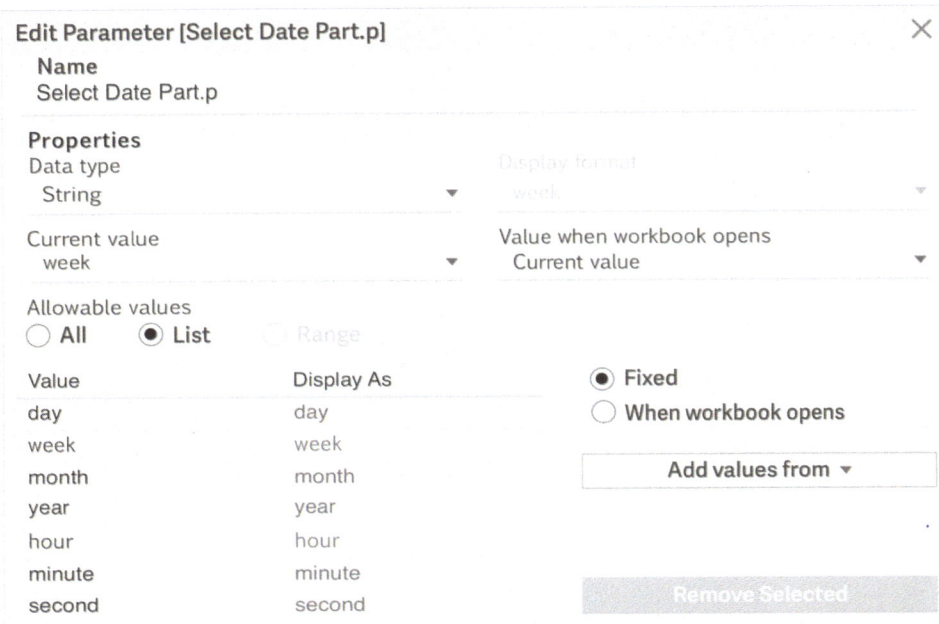

FIGURE 9.32
The Parameter Control.

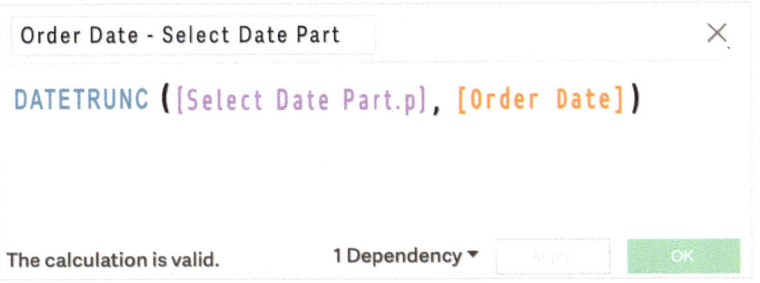

FIGURE 9.33
The Calculated field.

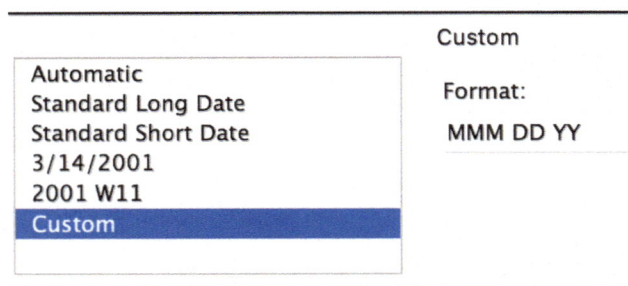

FIGURE 9.34
The Format pane.

returns 2 for February, while the DATENAME() function would return "February."

> DATEPART('month', #2023-02-25#)

9.9.4 DATEADD() and DATEDIFF()

DATEADD() adds or subtracts an increment from a **date part**, such as "day" or "year" and returns a date and time. DATEDIFF() returns the difference between two dates as a number. The first expression returns a negative ten. If I reversed the two dates, it would return a positive ten. The Time Duration example at the end of the chapter uses the DATEDIFF() function.

> **DATEADD**('day', -10, [**Order Date**])
> **DATEDIFF**('year', [**Order Date**], today())

9.9.5 Change Date to String with DATENAME()

DATENAME() returns the given **date part** as a string. In this example, the expression returns "February" when I add the field to the *Text* tile of the **Marks** card on February 20, 2024. If you want to try out the various expressions, add a test field to the *Text* tile of a new worksheet.

DATENAME('month', TODAY())

9.9.6 DATE()

This expression uses three date functions to find the last day of the last month. The right side of the expression returns the first date of today's month. The left side of the expression has a negative one to change to the last month.

Expression: DATE(DATEADD ('day', -1, DATE(DATETRUNC('month', today()))))

Returns: 9/1/2024 12:00:00 AM

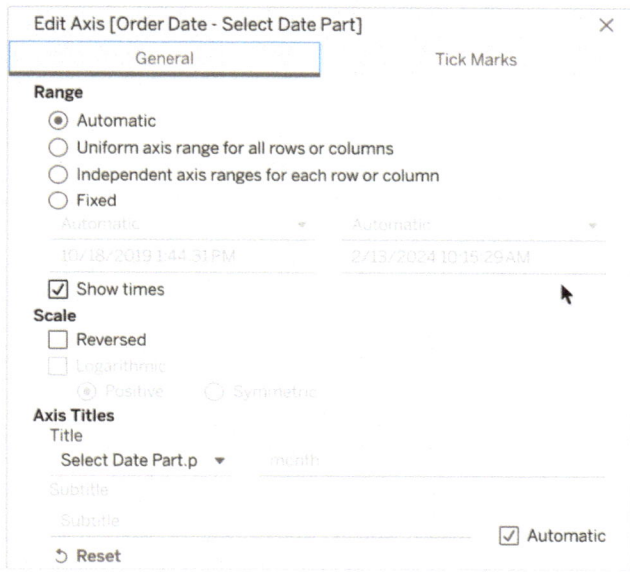

FIGURE 9.35
Edit the Axis Label.

9.9.7 DATETRUNC()

The DATETRUNC() function is like rounding, returning a date at the level indicated by the first argument in parentheses. This function returns a date and time. Because the argument is "month," this expression returns the first day of the month.

Expression: DATETRUNC('month',#9/24/2024#)
Returns: 9/1/2024 12:00:00 AM

The next example returns the first day of the *month*, or **9/1/2023**, because the argument is the **date part** "week." "Monday" is the start day for the week.

Expression: DATE(DATETRUNC('week', #9/24/2024#, 'Monday'))
Returns: 9/23/2024

9.9.8 MIN() and MAX() with Dates

MIN(*fieldname*) returns the earliest date in *fieldname*. MIN(*fieldname1, fieldname2*) compares the two dates and returns the first date. MAX() is similar to MIN(), except it is the latest date. MAX() is also useful for finding the largest amount or most recent date. The next topic, "Avoid 'All' in a Date Title," combines MAX() with a parameter.

9.10 Data Refresh Date in Title

When my data source is on a Tableau server, I cannot use the Tableau-generated field "Data Update Time." This field is in the drop-down **Insert** menu when editing a title. Tableau displays the last data source refresh time, which may not be the last time data was updated.

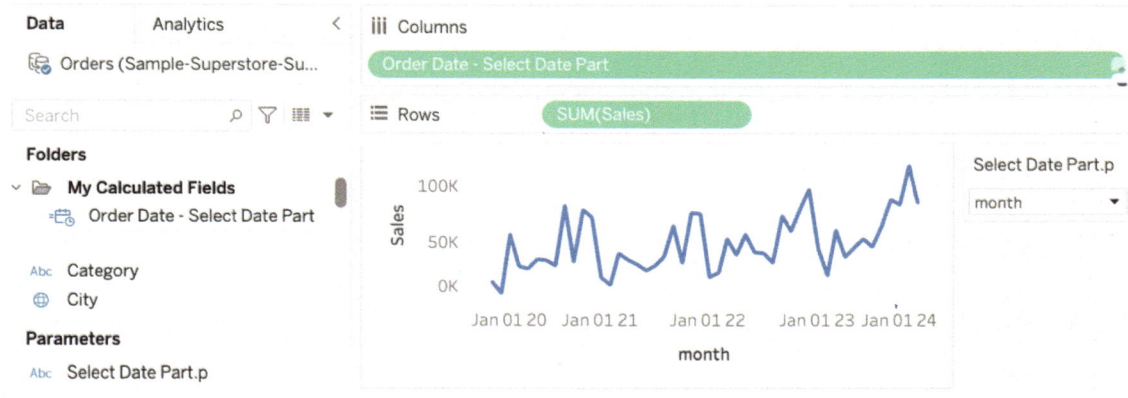

FIGURE 9.36
The parameter control on the right.

A workaround to provide a data date is to add the date when you create the original data source. For example, if you are using the Alteryx connector, "Publish to Tableau Server," you can add an update field using an Alteryx function like *DateTimeNow*() before output.

9.11 Avoid "All" in a Date Title

Even with valid dates for a title, you may have "All" in your title instead of a date because of identical values. You may not see these values initially, but the "All" value may appear as the data changes. Tableau suggests handling "All" values by creating a parameter and using that in a calculated field. A word of caution: if you use a field to populate the parameter, and it is only used in the parameter, do not "hide" the field, or the parameter will return the current date. This example looks at the difference between two calculated date fields.

Tableau Public file:

> https://public.tableau.com/views/Work aroundforAllinDatetitles1084/Title?: language=en-US&:sid=&:display_count=n&: origin=viz_share_link

1. Connect to the Sample Superstore data source and create a new worksheet.

2. Create a parameter "Max Order Date Parameter" with *list* values from the [**Order Date**] field (Figure 9.24). In the bottom-right area, select the field to be used "When workbook opens."

3. Create a calculated field [Max Date] with this expression:

MAX([Order Date])

4. Create another calculated field [Max Date parameter] as shown in Figure 9.25:

5. Set the default date format for the field [Max Date parameter] using the custom format below. Right-click the field in the **Data** pane to open the field's *context menu*, choose "Default Properties," and then "Date Format." Select **Custom** and enter this expression in the format box:

mmmm dd, yyyy. HH:mm AMPM

6. Add both fields to the *Detail* tile of the **Marks** card so you can use the fields in the title.

7. Double-click the title and click the drop-down arrow for **Insert** in the top-right corner of the

pop-up window. Add both fields to the title. In this example, the [Max Date] has a value of "All," and the [Max Date Parameter] field has the correct date (Figure 9.26).

9.12 Time Duration for Gantt Bar, Waterfall, and Resume

In the Gantt Bar chart in Figure 9.27, I want the bar length to reflect the time between the start and end dates instead of just a vertical line.

Tableau Public file:

> https://public.tableau.com/views/Gantt-Time DurationWaterfalls1077/Waterfall?: language=en-US&publish=yes&:sid=&: display_count=n&:origin=viz_share_link

Using the **DATEDIFF()** function in Figure 9.28, I created a calculated field [**DATEDIFF Edu. & Vol**] to find the duration of the event. I add the field to the *Size* tile on the **Marks** card.

Now, Figure 9.29 shows that the bars reflect the duration of each activity.

I create a Waterfall chart when I swap the fields on the **Columns** and **Rows** shelves (Figure 9.30). A resume is another practical application for this type of chart.

The completed dashboard combines several worksheets, as shown in Figure 9.31.

9.13 Date Parameter in Axis Label

To switch between date parts like year or month, create a date parameter and use a calculated field with the DATETRUNC() function and a date part. This example is similar to *"Section 15.5 Switch Between Measures with Parameters" on page 369.*

1. Create the parameter as shown below. Right-click the parameter name to display the **Parameter Control** (Figure 9.32).

2. Create the calculated field and add it to the **Columns** shelf (Figure 9.33).

3. Right-click the axis and choose "Format." In the **Format** pane, change the date format (Figure 9.34).

4. Right-click the axis and choose "Edit Axis." Near the bottom of the **Edit Axis** window, in the Title section, click "Custom" to select the parameter from the drop-down list (Figure 9.35).

The finished chart with the parameter control on the right is shown in Figure 9.36.

10

Table Calculations

In this topic, we discuss

Table Calculation Scope
Add a Table Calculation
Quick Table Calculations
Compute Using

Table calculation fields compute data based on fields in the current view (the view level of detail) and require an aggregate expression like SUM(Sales). Calculations are applied to a **measure** field, and a delta triangle appears to the right of the field name (Figure 10.1).

When *right-clicking* a field in the view, two options to create a table calculation appear on the field's *context me*nu. The "Quick Table Calculations" option is a simple way to add common table calculations like year-over-year or rank to the visualization. With the other option, Add Table Calculation, you have more control. Tableau gives guidance while setting up the table calculation. You can also create calculated fields that use table calculation functions like "Lookup()," as shown in *"Section 12.21 Arrows Comparing Two Values" on page 287.*

Regardless of how you create a table calculation, you can choose how to apply the calculation with the *"Compute Using"* options. Tableau uses "table" and "pane" to decide how to apply table calculations. Tableau further segments the calculations using "across" for rows or "down" for columns. You only see pane options when multiple dimensions are in a view, like the fields [Category] and [Sub-category].

A table calculation filter affects the view but does not affect the underlying data. **Chapter 8** shows this behavior in *"Section 8.7.2 Filter the View, Not the Underlying Data" on page 169.* Another example is *"Section 14.23 KPIs and BANs (Big Numbers)" on page 347.*

Tableau does not have an option to sort by a table calculation field. In *"Section 11.10.5.1 Sort by Ranking Alternative" on page 236,* I changed a table calculation field to **"Discrete"** and added it to the **Rows** shelf so I could use Tableau's default sort behavior as a substitute for field sorting.

Chapter 11 examines table calculation functions, such as the "INDEX()" topic on page 234, which illustrates the scope. **Chapter 12** also uses the table calculation function LOOKUP() in *"Section 12.21 Arrows Comparing Two Values" on page 287.* **Chapters 6, 7, and 9** provide examples of using "Rank" to emulate a sort, filter, and perform other table calculations.

10.1 Table Calculation Scope

The first consideration when creating a table calculation is the **scope** of the table calculation. Scope defines how to group the calculation based on the dimension fields in the view. These dimension fields are called *partitioning* or *addressing* fields. **Chapter 11's** topic, "FIRST() on page 232," includes an example of table calculation scope. *Partitioning* fields are used to group the data, and then the calculation is performed on the remaining dimension fields. When creating table calculations, the first question is, what is the scope? Tableau uses these three terms to define scope:

- Table
- Cell
- Pane

"Table" indicates that Tableau uses the entire table for the calculation. Cell calculates at the individual cell level. A pane refers to a group of data determined by dimension fields. For example, if you have 30 rows of inventory data for three states, the state field can group the data into three panes. The next question is about what **direction** or *addressing* Tableau should use for the calculation. Tableau uses four directions for table calculations:

- Across
- Down
- Across, then Down
- Down, then Across

FIGURE 10.1
A Green measure field.

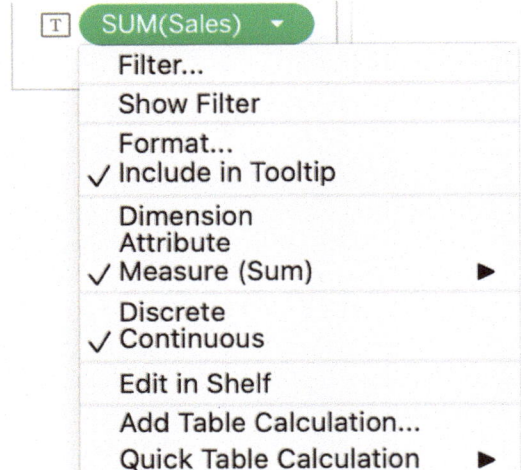

FIGURE 10.2
Adding a Table Calculation.

<u>Addressing and partitioning</u> affect how Tableau calculates totals or other aggregations. We looked at aggregations in several examples already, and **Chapter 11** specifically looks at different types of aggregation on page 227, like SUM(). The default behavior in Tableau for table calculations is "Table (Across)." We examine many examples of "Compute Using" in this chapter. Rather than having one or two visualizations with many fields, <u>improve performance</u> by spreading the data across five or six visualizations.

10.2 Add a Table Calculation

To add a new table calculation, right-click a field on the **Rows** or **Columns** shelves and select "Add Table Calculation" or "Quick Table Calculation," as shown in Figure 10.2. *"Section 11.10.5.1 Sort by Ranking Alternative" on page 236* uses a "Quick Table Calculation" to create a new field and edit it in the **Data** pane. You can also add a table calculation by creating a calculated field that uses table calculation functions. Another way to create a table calculation is to add a table calculation function to a calculated field, as shown in **Chapter 11** on *page 232*.

The **Table Calculation** window is divided into three areas.

- Calculation Type
- Compute Using
- Relative To

When you select a "Calculation Type," Tableau highlights the new calculated values in yellow on the view. To see the new calculations immediately on the canvas, choose different "Calculation Types" or "Compute Using" options in the **Tableau Calculation** window. Based on the "Calculation Type" you choose, the view is updated with the new table calculation, as shown in Figure 10.3.

When choosing the calculation type, "Running Total," a choice for aggregation is added to the dialog window, as shown in Figure 10.4, and includes:

- Sum
- Average
- Minimum
- Maximum

10.2.1 Pareto Chart with a Running Total and Percent of Total Table Calculation

Because Figure 10.4 is a running total calculation, the bottom of the dialog window has a new option to "Add secondary calculation" in the bottom left corner. When I check "Add secondary calculation," the right side of the window has options for the "Secondary Calculation Type." On the left side, the **Primary Calculation Type** is *Running Total*, and the aggregation under that is "Sum." This secondary calculation is the *Percent of Total* (Figure 10.4).

Next, I will use this table calculation to create a <u>Pareto chart</u> with two measure fields. The Pareto Principal is named after Vilfredo Pareto, who observed that 80% of the land was owned by 20% of the people. Eventually, this principle came to mean that 80% of the consequences come from 20% of the causes. And yes, there is a chart for that!
Tableau Public file:

```
https://public.tableau.com/views/Pareto
    Charts1086/Pareto?:language=en-US&:
    sid=&:display_count=n&:origin=viz_
    share_link
```

1. Connect to the *Sample Superstore* data source and add [Sales] to the **Rows** shelf and [Sub-category] to the **Columns** shelf.

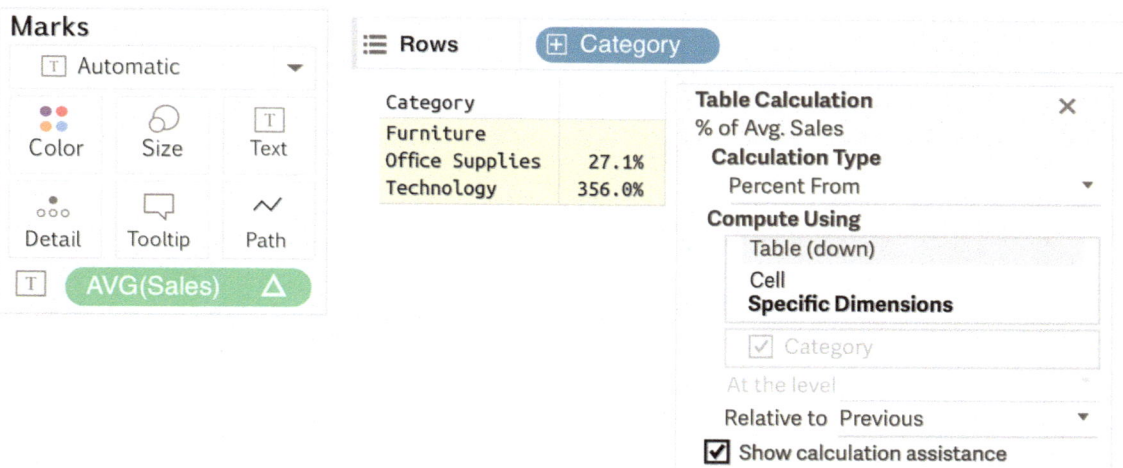

FIGURE 10.3
Table Calculation window.

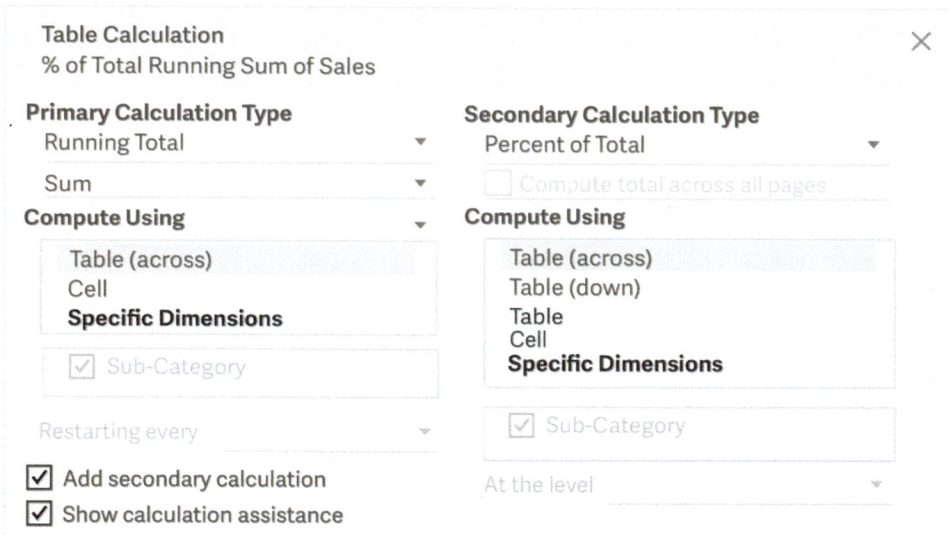

FIGURE 10.4
Running total.

[Sales] creates a vertical y-axis on the left side of the chart.

2. On the **Marks** card, use the drop-down arrow to select "Bar" as the mark type.

3. Select the [Sub-Category] field on the **Columns** shelf and click the drop-down arrow to open the field's *context menu*. Choose "Sort" and then add a descending sort using the field [Sales], as shown in Figure 10.5.

4. To create a dual-axis chart, drag [Sales] to the right side of the view until a green rectangle and dashed black line appear, as shown in Figure 10.6. Drop the field.

Tableau creates another layer on the **Marks** card, and the two measure fields become a super bubble on the **Rows** shelf (Figure 10.7).

5. Select the [SUM(Sales)] field on the right side of the **Rows** shelf and click the drop-down arrow to open the field's *context menu*. Select "Add Table Calculation…" and configure the table calculation with the running total and percent of the total, as shown in Figure 10.4.

6. Select the table calculation layer SUM(Sales) on the **Marks** card and change the **Mark** type to "Line," as shown in Figure 10.8. Click the *Color* tile and change the line color to orange.

The new Pareto chart is shown in Figure 10.9.

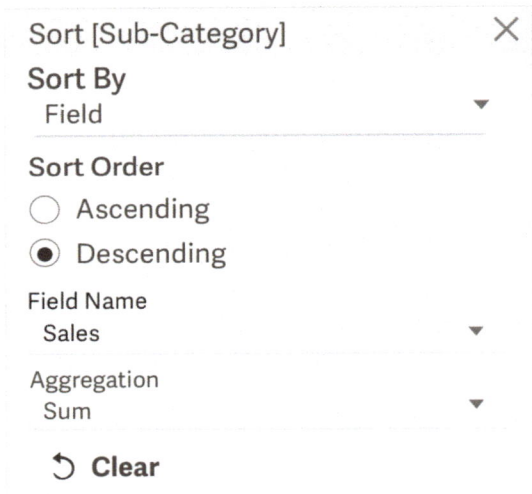

FIGURE 10.5
Sort descending.

FIGURE 10.8
The Line Mark type in the **Marks** card.

you have in your view. *"Section 11.10.5.1 Sort by Ranking Alternative" on page 236* creates a new quick table calculation field. If you want to save the calculation, drag the new field from the view into the **Data** pane. Right-click a field *on the view* and select "Quick Table Calculation" to add a new calculation.

- Running Total
- Difference From
- Percent Difference From
- Percent From
- Percent of Total
- Rank
- Percentile
- Moving Average
- YTD Total
- Compound Growth Rate
- Year-over-Year Growth
- YTD Growth

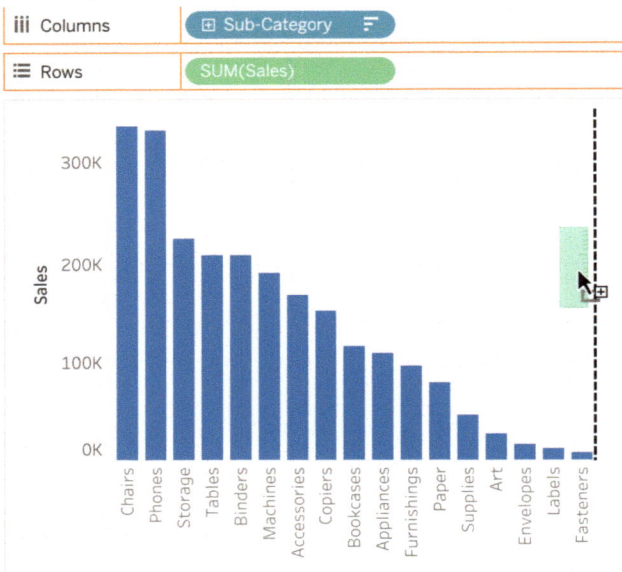

FIGURE 10.6
Drag the Field and Drop on the right side.

When using a year-over-year calculation, the first year is null. Rank is a quick table calculation and also a function used in calculated fields. When creating a table calculation for rank, you can choose how to handle duplicate values or ties, as shown in Figure 10.10.

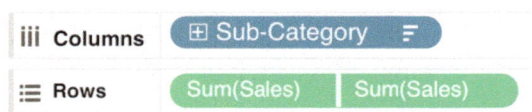

FIGURE 10.7
Two measure fields on the Rows shelf.

10.3 Quick Table Calculations

Quick Table Calculations are an easy way to show rank or running totals and include the calculations shown below, which vary depending on what fields

10.4 Compute Using

When creating a table calculation, below the *Calculation Type* are choices for *Compute Using*, as shown in Figure 10.11. These choices vary based on the view's number of columns or rows based on the fields on the **Rows** or **Columns** shelves.

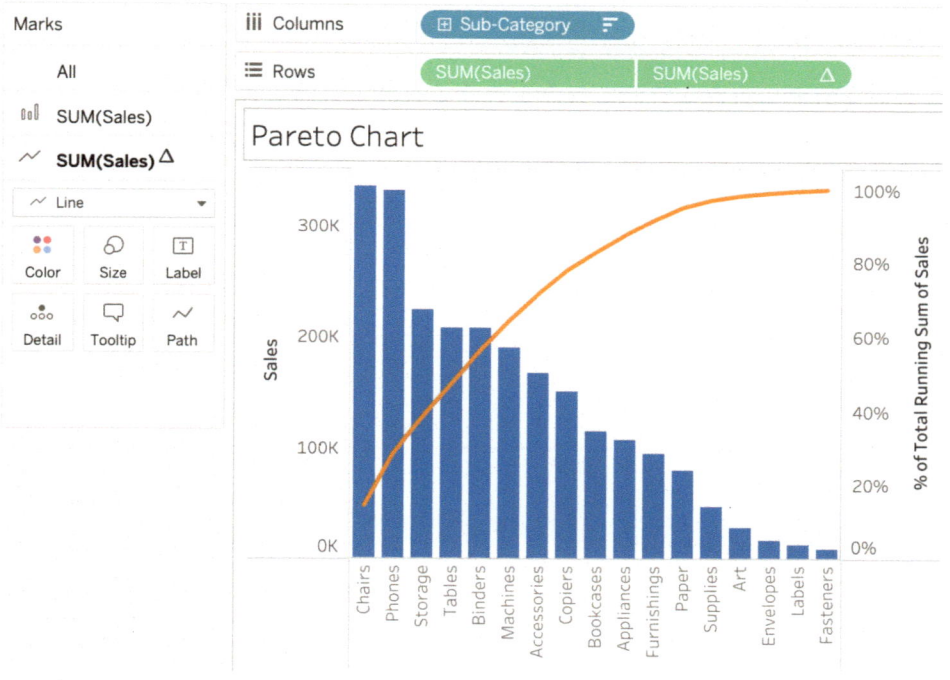

FIGURE 10.9
The Pareto chart.

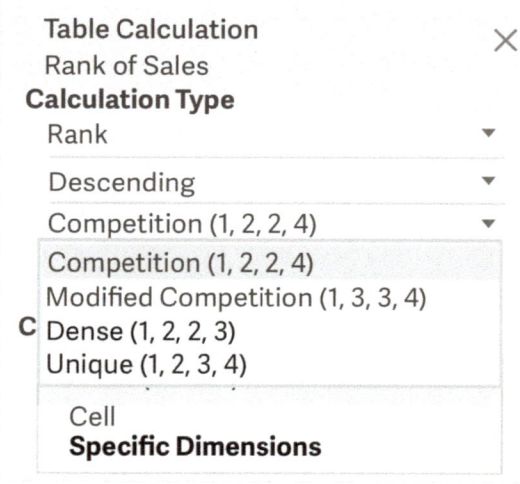

FIGURE 10.10
Rank.

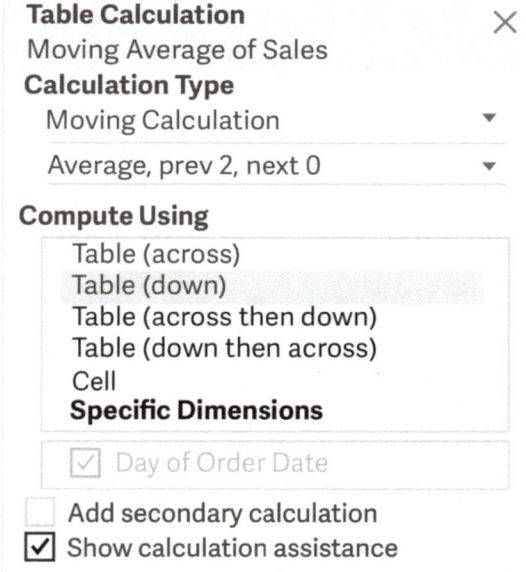

FIGURE 10.11
Compute using choices.

10.4.1 How "Compute Using" Groups Data in Table Calculations

When dragging a new table calculation field onto the *Text* tile of the **Marks** card, Tableau assigns the **scope** and **direction**, for example, "Table (scope), Down (direction)." In Figure 10.12, the "Row Index" value changes when the [Color] value changes, as expected. The [Color] value defines the pane. *"Section 6.3 Multiple Charts in One View" on page 105* uses a table

calculation with the INDEX() function and sets "Compute Using" to the "Fruit" field.

10.4.2 Compute Using: Specific Dimensions

When you select **Specific Dimensions**, you can also choose fields from the view. In Figure 10.13, I added the

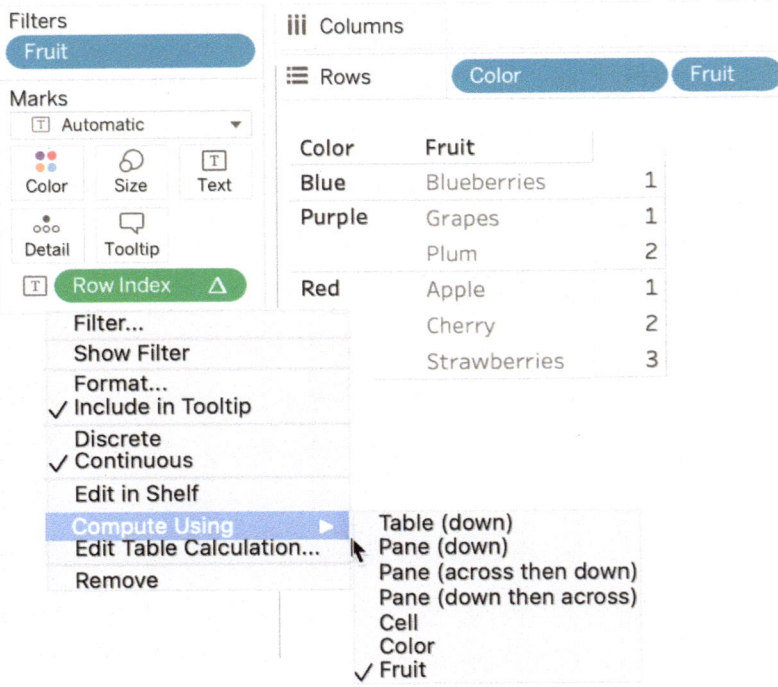

FIGURE 10.12
Compute using menu.

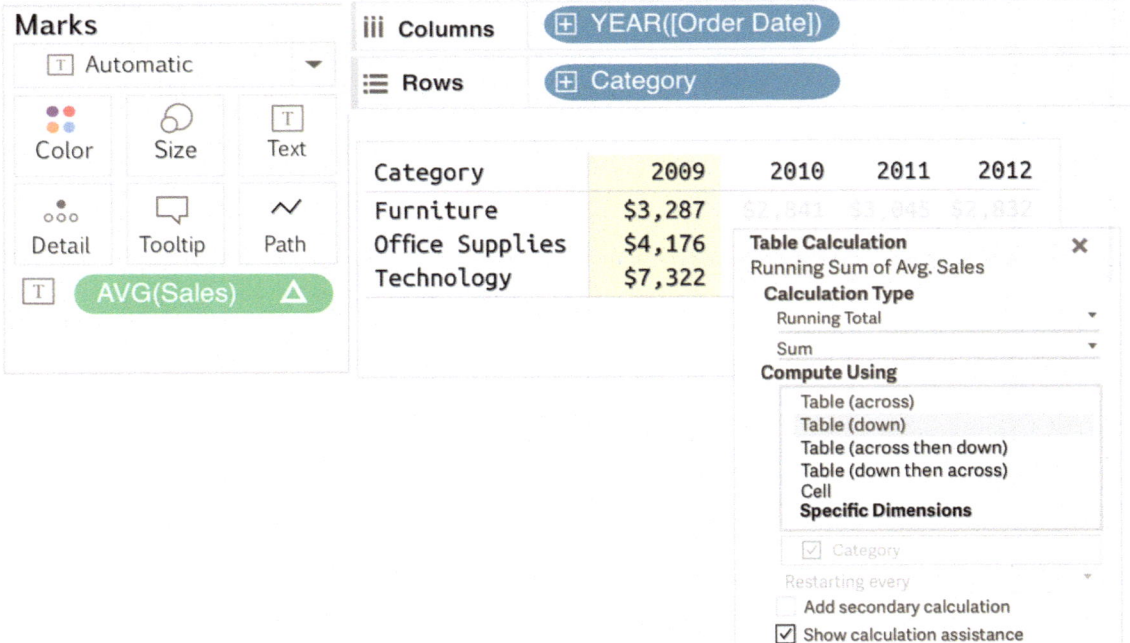

FIGURE 10.13
Compute using: specific dimensions.

[Order Date] and [Category] fields to the view. I use the "YEAR" **date part** for [Order Date]. If I right-click the "AVG(Sales)" field on the *Text* tile of the **Marks** card, I can edit the table calculation. Tableau shows "Table(down)" for "Compute Using" and applies yellow to the first column in the view (Figure 10.13).

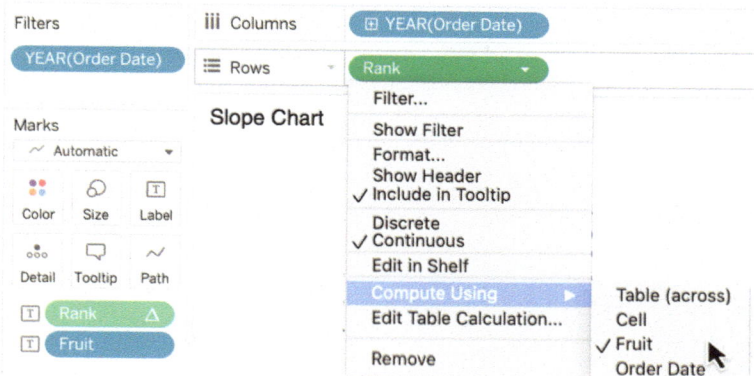

FIGURE 10.14
Compute using the fruit field.

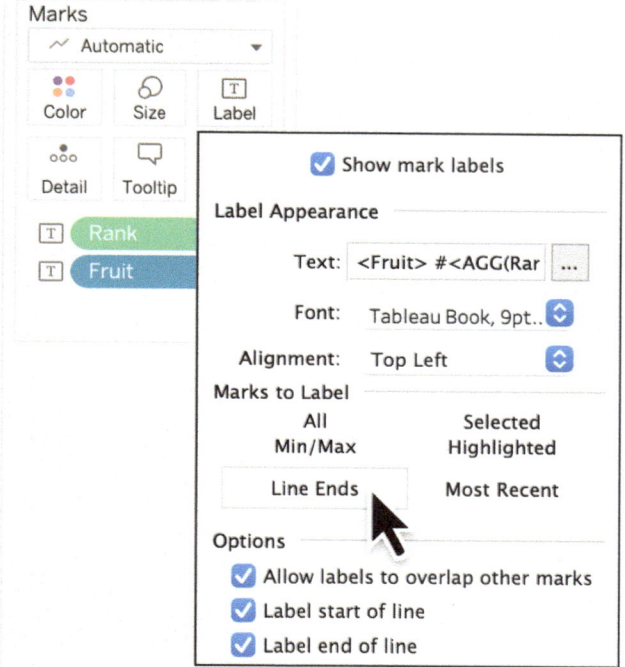

FIGURE 10.15
Show Mark Labels at Line Ends.

10.4.3 Slope Chart with a Rank Table Calculation

This slope chart includes the "Rank" table calculation, and the "Compute Using" value is set to the field [Fruit]. The link to the Tableau Public file is at the end of the exercise, along with a checklist of the elements and settings in the example.

1. Add [Order Date] to the **Columns** shelf using the **discrete** "YEAR."
2. Add [Fruit] to the *Text* tile of the **Marks** card.
3. Add [Sales] to the **Rows** shelf. Change the aggregation from Sum(Sales) to the table

calculation "Rank." Set **Compute Using** to [Fruit] so the [Fruit] sales ranking is computed within the partition YEAR(Order Date).

4. Drag the new table calculation field from the **Rows** shelf to the *Text* tile on the **Marks** card. Also, drag the new field to the **Data** pane and rename the field [Rank] (Figure 10.14). Both instances of [Rank] on the view should have the **Compute Using** setting as [Fruit].

Click the *Label* tile, change the **Marks to Label** to "Line Ends," and adjust the alignment to *Top Left*, as shown in Figure 10.15.

5. In the "Label Appearance" section, click the ellipsis on the right to edit the text label and open the **Edit Label** window. In Figure 10.16, the expression uses the [Fruit] and [Rank] fields.
6. Edit the [Rank] **axis** and select "Reversed" so the rankings start with one at the top. Right-click the [Rank] **axis** on the left side of the view (Figure 10.17) and select "Edit Axis."
7. Right-click the [Rank] field on the **Rows** shelf and uncheck "Show Header."
8. To move the [Order Date] "Year" headers to the *top* of the view, select "Table Layout" on the **Analysis** menu. Under "Advanced," uncheck "Show innermost level at bottom of view when there is a vertical axis" (Figure 10.18).
9. Right-click [Fruit] and check "Show Highlighter" (Figure 10.19). Also, add [Fruit] to the **Color** tile on the **Marks** card.
10. Add [Order Date] to the **Filters** shelf and select two years.
11. Right-click the canvas and select **Format**. Select the **Lines** icon at the top of the **Format**

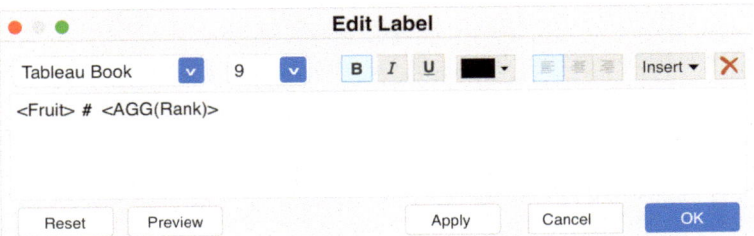

FIGURE 10.16
The **Edit Label** dialog box.

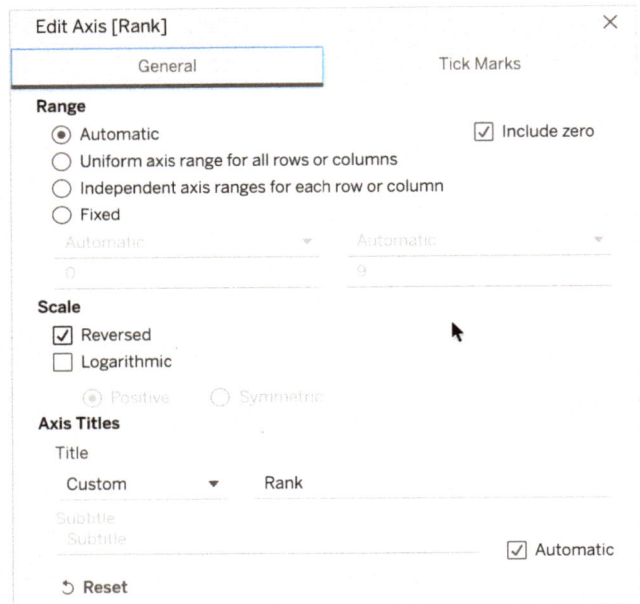

FIGURE 10.17
The **Edit Axis** dialog box.

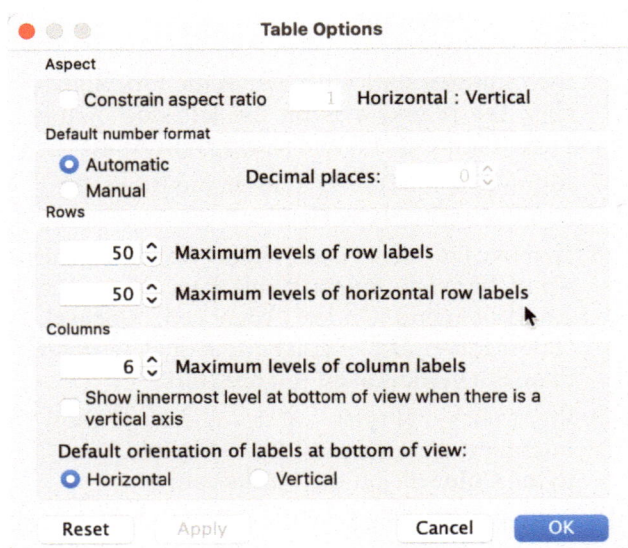

FIGURE 10.18
Table options.

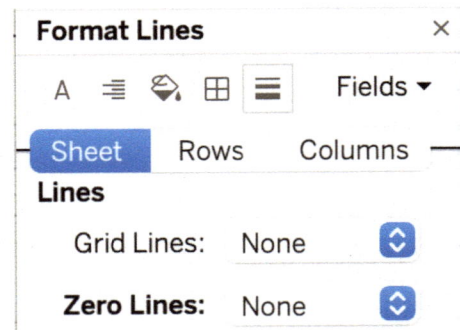

FIGURE 10.19
The Show Highlighter option.

FIGURE 10.20
Zero Lines.

pane on the left and click the *Sheet* tab. Change *Grid Lines* and *Zero Lines* to "None," as shown in Figure 10.20.

The finished *slope* chart is shown in Figure 10.21.

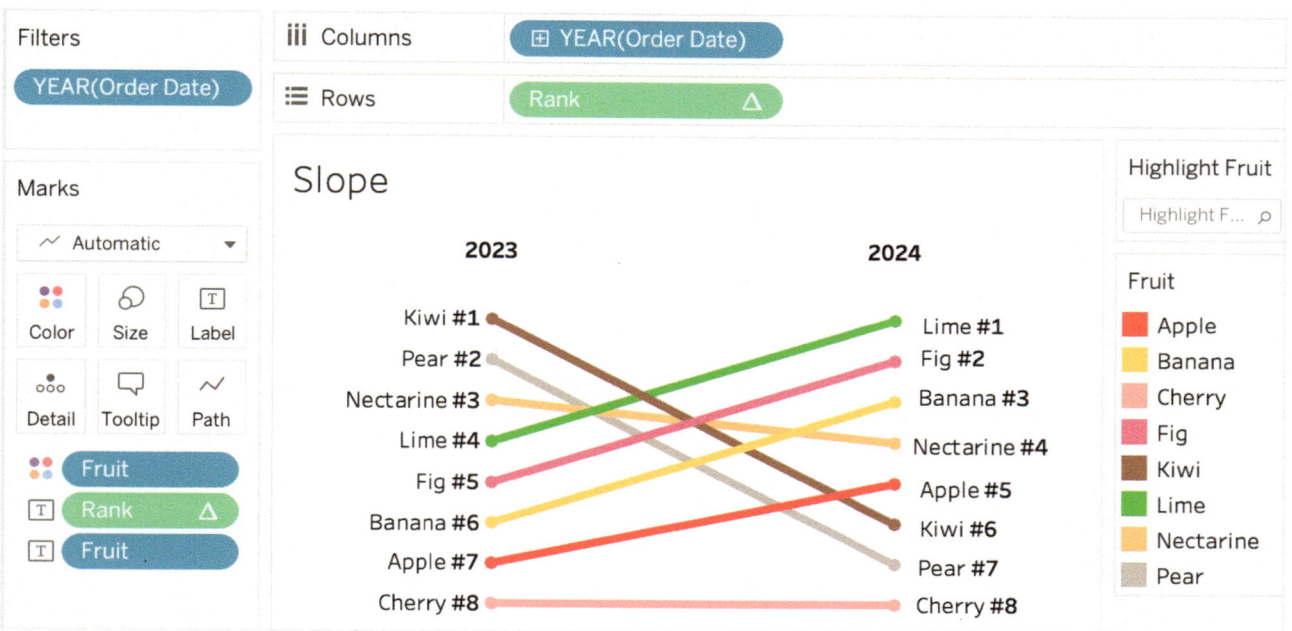

FIGURE 10.21
A Slope chart.

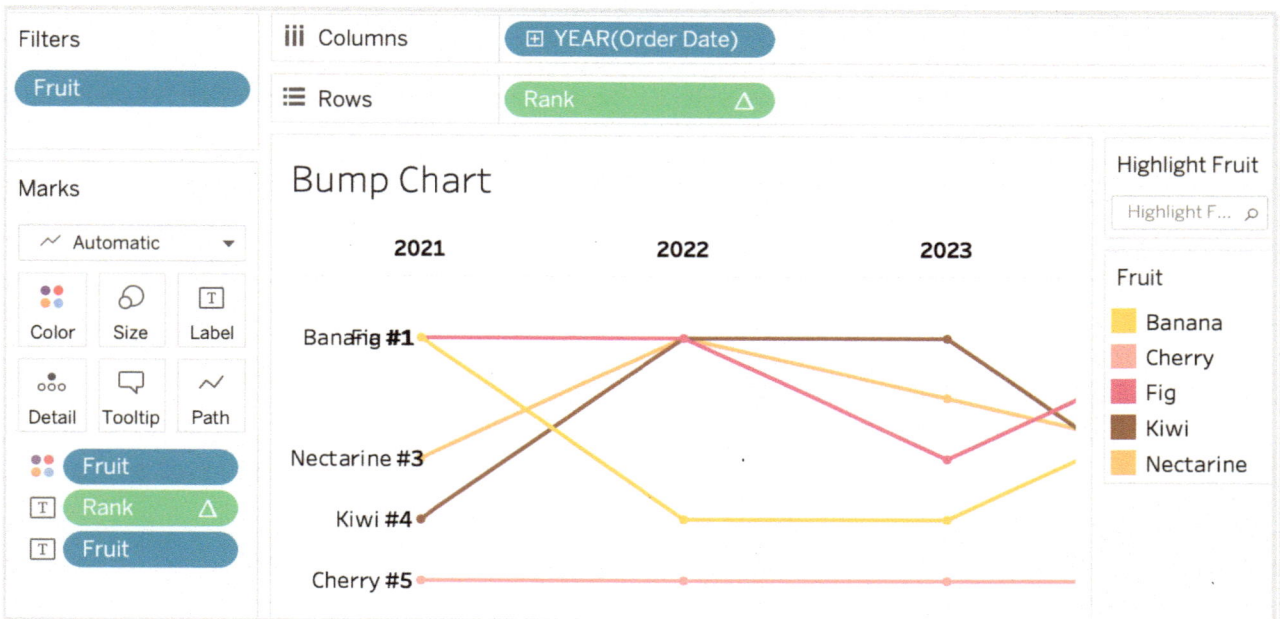

FIGURE 10.22
A Bump chart.

If I take the date filters off the slope chart, it is a *bump* chart, as shown in Figure 10.22.

Tableau Public file:

https://public.tableau.com/views/Slopeand
BumpChartss1085/Slope?:language=en-
US&:sid=&:display_count=n&:origin=
viz_share_link

10.4.4 Compute Using: Table Across

Tableau computes **Table Across** from left to right and restarts the *running total* table calculation after every partition. The "First()" example in *"Section 11.10.3.1 Filter to Top 5 using INDEX()" on page 235* uses **Table Across**. In Figure 10.23, Tableau restarts the running total every time the [fruit] field value changes.

Compute Using: Table Across

			2020	2021	2022	2023
Q1	Jan	Mango				2.60
		Orange			1.60	1.60
	Feb	Apple				6.16
		Kiwi			9.00	9.00
	Mar	Melon			3.66	3.66
Q2	Apr	Apple				1.54
		Grapes		1.06	1.06	1.06
		Pear				4.50
	Jun	Blueberries		7.60	7.60	7.60
Q3	Aug	Cherry	1.35	1.35	1.35	2.70
		Mango				2.60
	Sep	Mango	2.60	2.60	2.60	2.60
Q4	Oct	Nectarine	7.32	7.32	7.32	14.64
	Nov	Fig	12.32	12.32	12.32	12.32
		Pineapple			5.67	5.67
	Dec	Banana				1.61
		Lemon			11.76	11.76
		Lime	15.57	15.57	15.57	15.57
		Plum			14.20	14.20

Sales

			2020	2021	2022	2023
Q1	Jan	Mango				2.60
		Orange			1.60	
	Feb	Apple				6.16
		Kiwi			9.00	
	Mar	Melon			3.66	
Q2	Apr	Apple				1.54
		Grapes		1.06		
		Pear				4.50
	Jun	Blueberries		7.60		
Q3	Aug	Cherry	1.35			1.35
		Mango				2.60
	Sep	Mango	2.60			
Q4	Oct	Nectarine	7.32			7.32
	Nov	Fig	12.32			
		Pineapple			5.67	
	Dec	Banana				1.61
		Lemon		11.76		
		Lime	15.57			
		Plum			14.20	

FIGURE 10.23
Compute using: table across.

In Figure 10.23, the original sales data has a dark outline on the *right side*. The new values for the "table across" total are applied for each row, as shown on the *left side* of the diagram. In "**Q2** Apr for *Grapes*," the 2021 total of $1.06 is carried across unchanged, moving left to right to 2022 and 2023 as a running total. Tableau restarts counting for each row, and the last column of each row is the row total.

10.4.5 Compute Using: Table Down

Table Down computes vertically from the top row to the bottom row of the table. It restarts at the top after every partition; in this case, each column. In this example, the partition is "Year." The original sales data has a dark outline on the *right side* in Figure 10.24. The value for each year (partition) is a *running total* moving from the top of the column to the bottom of that column. A running total adds each value to the last and displays the *total* to that point. For 2020, if you were to add up all the values in the original table on the *right side*, the total for 2020 would be $39.16, as shown on the *left side* of the diagram.

The "**Q3** Sept Mango" total is $3.95, which is the sum of $1.35 + $2.60 for "Aug" and "Sep" values in 2020, which you can see in the box on the *right side*. Next, Tableau adds $7.32 for a running total of $11.27 in "Q4 Oct." At the bottom of each column, or year,

Tableau displays the total for that year. Then, the table calculation restarts counting in the first row for the next column, which, in this case, is the year 2021.

10.4.6 Compute Using: Table Across, Then Down

For **Table Across, Then Down**, Tableau computes left to right, continues to the next row computing left to right, and so on until the end of the table. The panes reflect the innermost field; in this case, the date quarters on the left.

The first row in the box on the *right side* of Figure 10.25 is $2.60 in 2023, and the second row in Q1 is $1.60 in 2022. At that point in the calculation, the sum is $4.20, as shown in the table on the left side, where numbers are rounded to one precision point. For this calculation, the final running total is $121.4 for "Plum" in 2022.

10.4.7 Compute Using: Table Down, Then Across

Tableau computes a running total for each column for "Compute using" **Table Down Then Across**; in this example, the column is "Year."

For consistency in this table, I used the **Format** menu to change the [Sales] field's default "Number Format" to two precision points (decimals). The new table calculation values are on the *left side* in Figure 10.26, and

Compute Using: Table Down

			2020	2021	2022	2023
Q1	Jan	Mango				2.60
		Orange			1.60	2.60
	Feb	Apple			1.60	8.76
		Kiwi			10.60	8.76
	Mar	Melon			14.26	8.76
Q2	Apr	Apple			14.26	10.30
		Grapes		1.06	14.26	10.30
		Pear		1.06	14.26	14.80
	Jun	Blueberries		8.66	14.26	14.80
Q3	Aug	Cherry	**1.35**	8.66	14.26	16.15
		Mango	1.35	8.66	14.26	18.75
	Sep	Mango	**3.95**	8.66	14.26	18.75
Q4	Oct	Nectarine	11.27	8.66	14.26	26.07
	Nov	Fig	23.59	8.66	14.26	26.07
		Pineapple	23.59	8.66	19.93	26.07
	Dec	Banana	23.59	8.66	19.93	27.68
		Lemon	23.59	20.42	19.93	27.68
		Lime	39.16	20.42	19.93	27.68
		Plum	39.16	20.42	34.13	27.68

Sales

			2020	2021	2022	2023
Q1	Jan	Mango				2.60
		Orange			1.60	
	Feb	Apple				6.16
		Kiwi			9.00	
	Mar	Melon			3.66	
Q2	Apr	Apple				1.54
		Grapes		1.06		
		Pear				4.50
	Jun	Blueberries		7.60		
Q3	Aug	Cherry	**1.35**			1.35
		Mango				2.60
	Sep	Mango	**2.60**			
Q4	Oct	Nectarine	7.32			7.32
	Nov	Fig	12.32			
		Pineapple			5.67	
	Dec	Banana				1.61
		Lemon		11.76		
		Lime	15.57			
		Plum			14.20	

FIGURE 10.24
Compute using: table down.

Compute Using: Table Across Then Down

			2020	2021	2022	2023
Q1	Jan	Mango				2.6
		Orange			4.2	
	Feb	Apple				10.4
		Kiwi			19.4	
	Mar	Melon			23.0	
Q2	Apr	Apple				24.6
		Grapes		25.6		
		Pear				30.1
	Jun	Blueberries		37.7		
Q3	Aug	Cherry	39.1			40.4
		Mango				43.0
	Sep	Mango	45.6			
Q4	Oct	Nectarine	52.9			60.3
	Nov	Fig	72.6			
		Pineapple			78.3	
	Dec	Banana				79.9
		Lemon		91.6		
		Lime	107.2			
		Plum			**121.4**	

Sales

			2020	2021	2022	2023
Q1	Jan	Mango				2.60
		Orange			1.60	
	Feb	Apple				6.16
		Kiwi			9.00	
	Mar	Melon			3.66	
Q2	Apr	Apple				1.54
		Grapes		1.06		
		Pear				4.50
	Jun	Blueberries		7.60		
Q3	Aug	Cherry	1.35			1.35
		Mango				2.60
	Sep	Mango	2.60			
Q4	Oct	Nectarine	7.32			7.32
	Nov	Fig	12.32			
		Pineapple			5.67	
	Dec	Banana				1.61
		Lemon		11.76		
		Lime	15.57			
		Plum			14.20	

FIGURE 10.25
Compute using: table across, then down.

Compute Using: Table Down Then Across

			2020	2021	2022	2023
Q1	Jan	Mango				96.31
		Orange			61.18	
	Feb	Apple				102.47
		Kiwi			70.18	
	Mar	Melon			73.84	
Q2	Apr	Apple				104.01
		Grapes		40.22		
		Pear				108.51
	Jun	Blueberries		47.82		
Q3	Aug	Cherry	1.35			109.86
		Mango				112.46
	Sep	Mango	3.95			
Q4	Oct	Nectarine	11.27			119.78
	Nov	Fig	23.59			
		Pineapple			79.51	
	Dec	Banana				121.39
		Lemon		59.58		
		Lime	39.16			
		Plum			93.71	

			2020	2021	2022	2023
Q1	Jan	Mango				2.60
		Orange			1.60	
	Feb	Apple				6.16
		Kiwi			9.00	
	Mar	Melon			3.66	
Q2	Apr	Apple				1.54
		Grapes		1.06		
		Pear				4.50
	Jun	Blueberries		7.60		
Q3	Aug	Cherry	1.35			1.35
		Mango				2.60
	Sep	Mango	2.60			
Q4	Oct	Nectarine	7.32			7.32
	Nov	Fig	12.32			
		Pineapple			5.67	
	Dec	Banana				1.61
		Lemon		11.76		
		Lime	15.57			
		Plum			14.20	

FIGURE 10.26
Compute using: table down, then across.

the original values are in the box on the *right side*. In the table on the *left side*, the final total of all values is $121.39 in the "Dec *Banana* row."

10.4.8 Compute Using: Pane Down

In the example in Figure 10.27, "Month" is used for partitioning the **Pane Down** aggregation, and "running total" is the type of calculation. The new table calculation values are on the *left side* of the diagram, and the original values are in the box on the *right side*.

With **Pane Down**, the table calculation runs top to bottom for the month "**Q2** Apr." Each year column has a total for "**Q2** Apr." In "**Q2** April 2021," sales for *Grapes* were $1.06. The table calculation ends with the *Pear* row in the 2021 column for $1.06 in 2021.

In "**Q2** April 2023," sales for *Apples* were $1.54. The table calculation continues and adds *Pear* sales of $4.50 in 2023, and the final running total for April 2023 is $6.04.

10.4.9 Compute Using: Pane Down, Then Across

Before discussing Figure 10.28, take a short break because this explanation will take a while. It would help if you read the entire topic without pausing because when you read the diagrams in the second half, it will start to make more sense.

For **Pane Down then Across**, within the pane, Tableau starts computing from the top down to the bottom in the first column, moves up to the first row in the pane and the second column, and continues to the bottom of the pane or the last row for the quarter [**Q3** Aug]. The dimension fields in the view determine the pane; in this case, quarter and month. In this example, I focus on August sales in any year because I use the **discrete date parts**.

The Chapter 11 "FIRST()" example uses **Pane Down Then Across**.

This table calculation initially seems odd because Tableau takes all values for the [Fruit] field and adds them to each pane, expanding the number of rows. Figure 10.28 is all sixteen possible sales on the

FIGURE 10.27
Compute using: pane down.

FIGURE 10.28
All sales.

Table Calc

			Order Date			
			2020	2021	2022	2023
Q2	June	Pineapple			7.60	
		Plum			7.60	
Q3	August	Apple				1.35
		Banana				1.35
		Blueberries		1.35		
		Cherry	1.35			2.70
		Fig	1.35			
		Grapes		1.35		
		Kiwi			1.35	
		Lemon		1.35		
		Lime	1.35			
		Mango	1.35			5.30
		Melon			1.35	
		Nectarine	1.35			5.30
		Orange			1.35	
		Pear				5.30
		Pineapple			1.35	
		Plum			1.35	
	September	Apple				2.60
		Banana				2.60
		Blueberries		2.60		
		Cherry				2.60
		Fig				
		Grapes		2.60		
		Kiwi			2.60	
		Lemon		2.60		
		Lime				
		Mango	2.60			2.60
		Melon			2.60	
		Nectarine	2.60			2.60
		Orange			2.60	
		Pear				2.60
		Pineapple			2.60	
		Plum			2.60	
Q4	October	Apple				7.32
		Banana				7.32
		Blueberries		7.32		
		Cherry				7.32
		Fig				
		Grapes		7.32		
		Kiwi			7.32	
		Lemon		7.32		
		Lime				
		Mango				7.32
		Melon			7.32	
		Nectarine	7.32			14.64
		Orange			7.32	
		Pear				14.64

FIGURE 10.29
Compute using: Pane Down, Then Across.

left and no table calculations on the right. The 16 rows in Figure 10.28 become the 16 rows in "Q3Aug" in Figure 10.29.

I am interested in the *Cherry* sales of $1.35 in 2020 and 2023 and the *mango* sales of $5.20 in 2023.

The *Mango* sales of $2.60 in 2020 were not in August, so those sales are not included in the [**Q3 August**] table calculation. Of the *Mango* $5.20 total in 2023, only $2.60 was in August, so I ignore the Mango $2.60 in Q1 January.

On the *right side* of Figure 10.28, I have added quarter and month **date parts** to the visualization. The table shows that in [**Q3 August 2020**], Cherry sales were $1.35. In 2023, there were two sales: Cherry and Mango for $1.35 and $2.60, respectively.

2020	Cherry $1.35
2023	Cherry $1.35
2023	Mango $2.60

Figure 10.29 shows part of the text table after I add the table calculation with Compute Using: *Pane Down, Then Across*. The table layout has 16 rows each month or 224 total rows. There is a scroll bar on the *right side*. The three August sales are highlighted. The first sale in 2020 of $1.35 for *Cherry* is carried through to 2023,

with another sale for $1.35, making the running total $2.70. The calculation continues down the 2023 column to *Mango* and adds $2.60, so the final running total is $5.30 for "Q3 August."

As shown in Figure 10.30, for [**Q3 Aug**], #1 is $1.35 for *Cherry* in 2020. Tableau carries the total through 2021 and 2022, where there were no sales until *Cherry* in 2023 had sales of $1.35, bringing the running total to $2.70, as shown in the left side of Figure 10.30.

The next sale in 2023 is for $2.60 for Mango, bringing the new running total to $5.30 for [Q3 Aug]. The "Q3 Aug" calculation continues to the end of the pane, the last row with data in [Q3 Aug 2023]. At this point, Tableau is using all sales in 2023 in alphabetical order to decide the last row with data in 2023: Apple, Banana, Cherry, Mango, Nectarine, and Pear. In this case, the Pear row is the last in 2023. The new table calculation values are on the left side of Figure 10.30, and the original values are in the box on the right side.

Looking at the left side of Figure 10.30, you can see that Tableau now has a value in any row that originally had sales. In 2020, these categories had sales: Cherry, Fig, Lime, Mango, and Nectarine. In 2023, there were sales for Apple, Banana, Cherry, Mango, Nectarine, and Pear.

Compute Using: Pane Down Then Across

			2020	2021	2022	2023
Q3	Aug	Apple				1.35
		Banana				1.35
		Blueberries		1.35		
		Cherry	① 1.35			2.70 ②
		Fig	1.35			
		Grapes		1.35		
		Kiwi			1.35	
		Lemon		1.35		
		Lime	1.35			
		Mango	1.35			5.30 ③
		Melon			1.35	
		Nectarine	1.35			5.30
		Orange			1.35	
		Pear				5.30
		Pineapple			1.35	
		Plum			1.35	
	Sep	Apple				2.60

FIGURE 10.30
Compute using: Pane Down Then Across.

Compute Using: Pane Across Then Down

			2020	2021	2022	2023
Q3	Aug	Apple				
		Banana				
		Blueberries	①			②
		Cherry	1.35			2.70
		Fig	2.70			
		Grapes		2.70		
		Kiwi			2.70	
		Lemon		2.70		
		Lime	2.70			
		Mango	2.70			③ 5.30
		Melon			5.30	
		Nectarine	5.30			5.30
		Orange			5.30	
		Pear				5.30
		Pineapple			5.30	
		Plum			**5.30**	
	Sep	Apple				

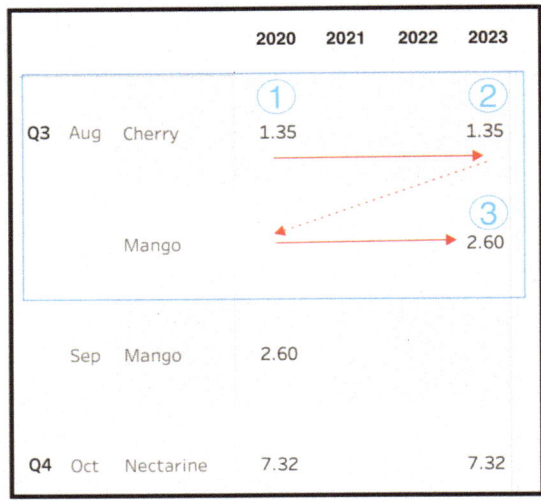

FIGURE 10.31
Compute using: Pane Across, Then Down.

10.4.10 Compute Using: Pane Across, Then Down

In Figure 10.31, "Month" is used for partitioning the **Pane Across, Then Down** aggregation, and "Running Total" is the type of calculation. The new table calculation values are on the *left side* of Figure 10.31, and the original values are in the box on the *right side*. Similar to the last calculation, Tableau expands the three "**Q3** Aug" rows on the right to 16 rows on the left.

The *Pane Across, Then Down* table calculation moves left to right, moves down to the next row, moves left and right, and so on until the end of the partition. The original values are in the box on the *right side*. For [**Q3** Aug], the box on the *right side* shows the three values used in the table calculation.

As Tableau does the table calculation on the *left side* of Figure 10.31, in the Cherry row, the #1 value of $1.35 is added to the #2 value of $1.35 for a running total of $2.70. The left side shows the running calculation for #2 as $2.70.

There are no new values until *Mango* in 2023, so all the numbers in between carry forward the running total of $2.70. Tableau adds $2.60 to the running total of $2.70, as shown in #3 on the *left side*, for a new running total of $5.30. Tableau carries $5.30 to the last row *Plum* in 2022 for [**Q3** Aug].

11

Calculations

Rather than call this chapter "Calculated Fields," I chose "Calculations" because you see calculated expressions and syntax throughout Tableau. Filters and sets also use calculation logic.

> Tableau's online help has an article on <u>best practices</u> for calculated fields, such as using case statements instead of nested If-Then-Else expressions to improve performance.

11.1 Types of Calculated Fields

In this chapter, we will create in-line calculations and calculated fields, including placeholder fields. We will also explore Level of Detail (LoD) syntax to work with different levels of aggregation. Finally, we review some practical examples that use calculated fields.

11.1.1 In-Line Calculations

To create an in-line calculation, click on the **Rows** or **Columns** shelf and start typing. This is also how you create placeholder fields. In the following example, I round the sum of [Sales].

```
AGG(ROUND(SUM([SALES]), 1))
```

11.1.2 Placeholders

"Section 3.6.4 Placeholder Fields" on page 70 introduced simple calculations like the three examples below, known as placeholder, throwaway, or dummy fields. "Placeholder" fields add different colors, shapes, marks, and more to a chart in a stacked or layered effect.

```
Min(1)  " "  Avg(0)
```

To create an in-line calculation for a placeholder field, right-click or double-click and start typing on the **Rows** or the **Columns** shelf. The example *"Section 6.5 Donut Chart" on page 112* illustrates this task. In Figure 11.1, after adding a placeholder field to the **Rows** shelf, I hid *Field Labels* to add "blank space" on the left side of the canvas.

If you drag the new placeholder field from the **Rows** shelf into the **Data** pane, you can rename and reuse it in other worksheets.

> If you want to "name" your layer, begin the calculation with //*layername*, press Shift + Enter, and type Min(1).

"Section 8.14 Hover to Choose a Field for Sorting" on page 181 is an interesting example that uses a *placeholder* field to format worksheet placement on a dashboard. *"Section 8.13 Click Data Points to Sort with a Set" on page 175* also has a placeholder field. In *"Section 12.21 Arrows Comparing Two Values" on page 287*, I create a *placeholder* field for the example, "Arrows Comparing Two Values."

11.2 Syntax

Tableau calculations include these components:

- Functions
- Fields

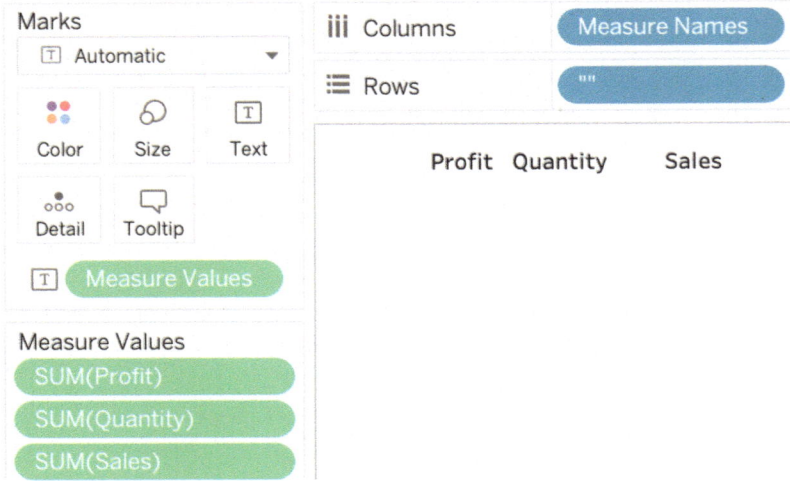

FIGURE 11.1
Placeholder on the Rows Shelf.

- Parameters
- Operators (symbols like = > < / +)
- Literal Expressions (constant values)

11.2.1 Calculated Field Data Types

In the **Data** pane, calculated fields have a small equal sign to the left of the field name and data type icon. Tableau combines the equal symbol with the data type symbol. In *"Section 4.1 Types of Data" on page 74*, we looked at Tableau's different data types, each requiring specific syntax.

Calculated Field – Number
Calculated Field – Boolean
Calculated Field – String

11.2.2 Comments

Comments in calculations begin with two forward slashes //. You can also use comments with in-line calculations. If you want to "name" a placeholder field, begin the calculation with //*name*, press Shift + Enter, and type Min(1).

11.2.3 Boolean

A <u>Boolean</u> field has the values *True* or *False*. For example, this syntax tests the value of the Boolean field **"Profit."** *"Section 14.16 Horizontal Radial Buttons to*

Change Filters" on page 323 looks deeper into Boolean values.

```
If [Profit] = True then "Profitable" else "Not Profitable" End
```

11.2.4 Functions

Functions are **blue** in the calculation editor.

11.2.5 Fields

Fields are **orange** in the calculation editor.

11.2.6 Parameters

Parameters are placeholder variables and are **purple** in the calculation editor.

11.2.7 Literal Expressions

Strings, Boolean values, numbers, and "Null" are all examples of literal expressions, such as:

"abc"
True or False
Null
1, 23.4, 300 (Numbers)
#2024-04-01#

This calculation returns a Boolean value of TRUE or FALSE.

```
If SUM( [Sales] ) > 10000 then TRUE else FALSE END
```

11.3 Mathematical Order of Operations

Tableau follows the standard mathematical order of operations. If there is more than one element in the same calculation, Tableau solves each calculation from *left to right*.

1. Elements in parentheses
2. Exponents
3. Division and multiplication
4. Addition and subtraction

As we see in *"Section 11.14 Weighted Average with Fixed LoD" on page 250*, Tableau solves each calculation from *left to right*. Tableau calculates the aggregation SUM(Sales) and then SUM(Profit) for the expression below. Finally, it divides those values to determine a percentage.

SUM(Sales) / **SUM**(Profit)

11.3.1 Elements in Parentheses

In this example, if I want the "addition" part of the expression (2 + 10) computed before the division part, I must use parentheses around the "addition" block of code. I often add parentheses as an extra visual clue in my calculations, even when they are not always required.

(2+10) / 6

In the following example, the addition calculation (90+3) and Sum(*fieldname2*) are performed before the division. Because the addition is within parentheses that calculation is first.

(90 + 3) / **Sum**(*fieldname2*)

11.3.2 Division and Multiplication

Division is expressed using a forward slash "/" character; in this case, the calculation is six divided by two.

6/2

Multiplication uses the asterisk. In this example, the calculation is five times three.

5 * 3

Tableau calculates left to right with division and multiplication in the same equation.

4 * 6 / 3 * 5

1st.	4 * 6 = 24
2nd.	24 / 3 = 8
3rd.	8 * 5 = 40

11.3.3 Addition and Subtraction

Tableau uses the plus symbol for addition and the dash for subtraction, as shown below.

56 + 1 - 7

11.4 Aggregation and Level of Detail

"Section 3.7 Aggregation" on page 72 introduced the concept of **Aggregation** and **LoD Expressions**. A regular aggregated calculation is at the *visualization* LoD. I think of the LoD as a grouping or pivot. The **dimension** fields used in the visualization change the *Viz Level of Detail*. *Level of Detail* expressions use aggregations that are different from the aggregation of the fields in the view. We look at *"Section 11.12 Level of Detail Expressions" on page 238*. In this example, I am aggregating the "SUM" of each measure field using the visualization partition.

SUM(*field1*)/**SUM**(*field2*)

"Section 10.1 Table Calculation Scope" on page 209 examined panes and scope (partitioning and addressing). As we examine aggregations and errors, this Tableau Public file has examples you may find helpful.

```
https://public.tableau.com/views/
    AggregationErrors/Sheet2?:language=
    en-US&publish=yes&:display_count=n&:
    origin=viz_share_link
```

Dimension fields use these types of aggregations: ATTR, COUNT, COUNTD, MIN, and MAX, while measures use aggregations like SUM or AVG, as shown in Figure 11.2. Some functions like ATTR, COUNT, MIN, and MAX apply equally to both dimensions or measures.

Tableau's default aggregation for measure fields is "SUM." When you drag a field into a view, the new calculation is SUM(*fieldname*). You can change the aggregation from the field's *context menu* to one of the aggregations for measure fields, as shown in Figure 11.2.

"Section 11.13 Fixed LoD Example" on page 241 includes COUNT(), SUM(), and AVG() aggregations.

11.4.1 Count(), CountD()

To count the number of records (rows), use the Count() or CountD() functions. CountD returns distinct

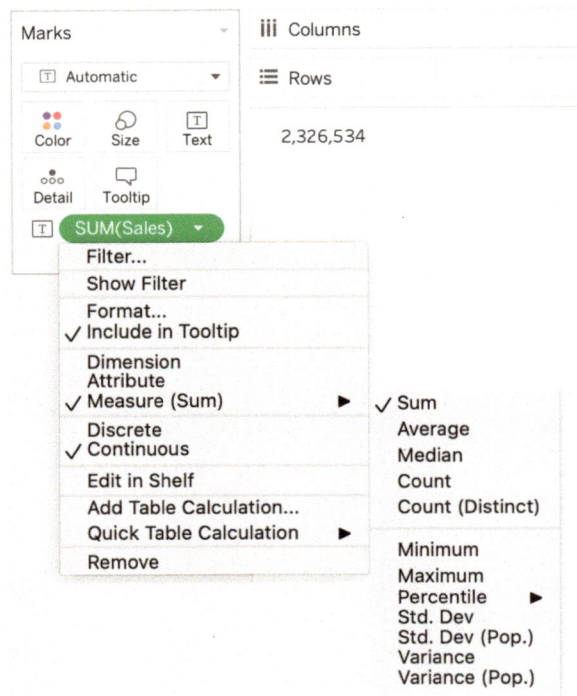

FIGURE 11.2
Aggregations for measures.

FIGURE 11.3
Warning: *Changing aggregation or the result type for a calculated field can cause a* **red** *exclamation mark when Tableau recognizes a change in the calculated field. If a red exclamation mark appears, drag the changed field on top of the old one, and the red exclamation mark should go away.*

values. Because CountD() is already an aggregation, you cannot combine it with another aggregated function like AVG(), as shown in Figure 11.4.

11.4.2 AVG()

Tableau only allows the AVG() function to be used with measure fields that are not aggregated. Instead of the AVG() function, I can calculate the average count of unique [Orders] over three months using an LoD, as shown in Figure 11.5.

11.4.3 Aggregation Errors

When you try to mix aggregate and non-aggregate fields or aggregate already aggregated fields, Tableau displays an error like "The calculation contains errors." In Figure 11.6, I had to remove the SUM() function because the field "Total State Sales" is already aggregated.

Using the ATTR(*fieldname*) function sometimes eliminates the aggregation error, as shown in Figure 11.7. In the **Calculation Editor**, search for "Aggregate" functions that might apply in your situation.

11.4.4 ATTR() – Dimension vs. Measure

While you can use ATTR() with dimensions or measures, there are some times when ATTR() causes an error. These two calculations in Figure 11.8 produce identical results when placed on the *Text* Tile of the **Marks** card (Figure 11.9).

However, when I try to use the first "Percent of Goal" calculated field that has the ATTR() function in a *filter condition*, it causes the error, "The field … is invalid," as shown in Figure 11.10. Because the expression has a measure field, in this case, Tableau expects the aggregation to be something like SUM or AVG, *not ATTR*.

11.5 The Calculation Editor

In the next topic, we explore several ways to create a new calculation in the **Calculation Editor**. On the right side of the **Calculation Editor,** the "Functions Reference" pane lists all Tableau functions grouped by category, as shown in Figure 11.11. For example, select the "String" category to see functions related to text or string values.

The white pane on the left side of the **Calculation Editor** is where you add code to your formula. Tableau's calculation interpreter ignores uppercase, lowercase, and whitespace – like spaces or tabs. Single or double quotes are OK, but you cannot mix them. Comments begin with two forward slashes //.

Operators !=, ==, =, (), <>

Logical AND OR NOT IN

Comparisons

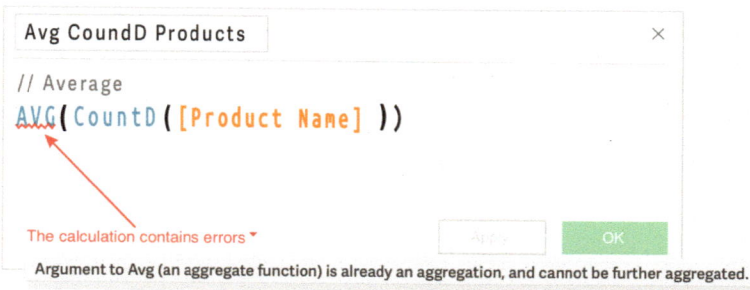

FIGURE 11.4
Aggregation error.

FIGURE 11.5
An AVG() calculation.

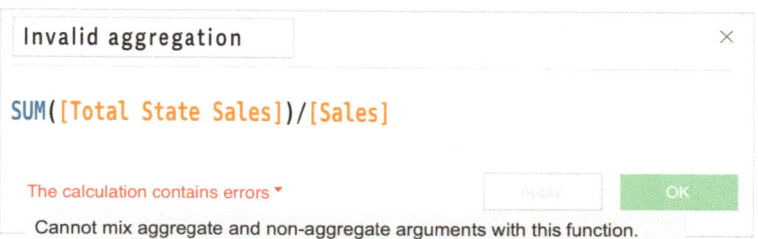

FIGURE 11.6
Cannot mix aggregate and non-aggregate arguments.

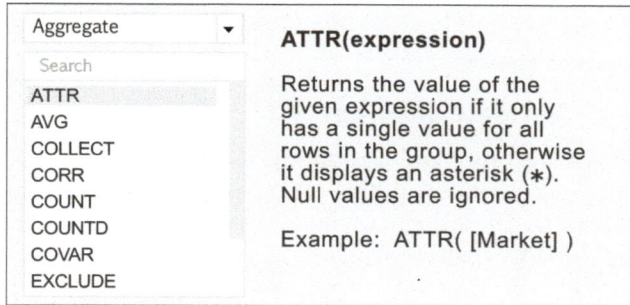

FIGURE 11.7
ATTR() function.

11.5.1 Add Fields to the Calculation

There are several ways to add fields to a calculation.

- Drag a field from the **Data** pane into the **Calculation Editor**.
- Start typing the field name, and Tableau auto-completes the name.

- Drag a field from the *view* into the **Calculation Editor**.

11.5.2 Preview Calculation

Use the "Apply" button in the **Calculation Editor** to see the result of an edited calculation before saving the new calculation.

11.5.3 Zoom or Font Size

In the **Calculation Editor**, press the CTRL and + keys on your keyboard (Command + in MacOS) to zoom in.

11.6 Create and Edit Calculated Fields

Open the **Calculation Editor** to begin creating calculated fields. While there are several locations where you can launch the **Calculation Editor**, I like to use the

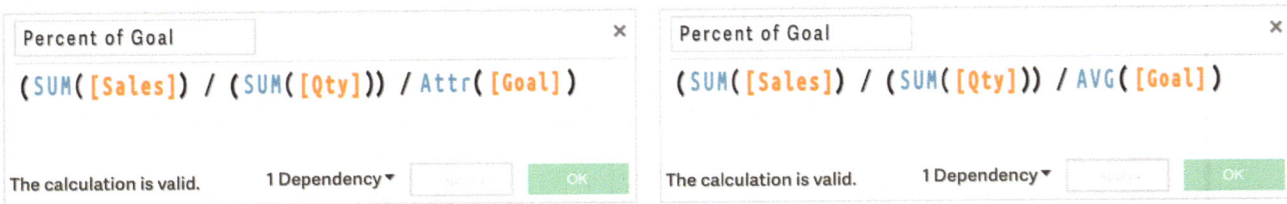

FIGURE 11.8
ATTR() and (AVG() calculations.

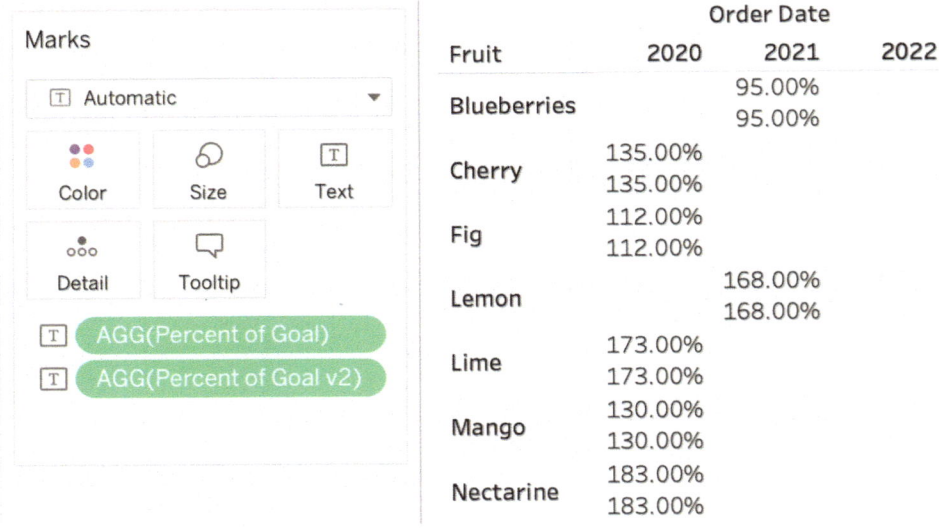

FIGURE 11.9
Same values for both calculations.

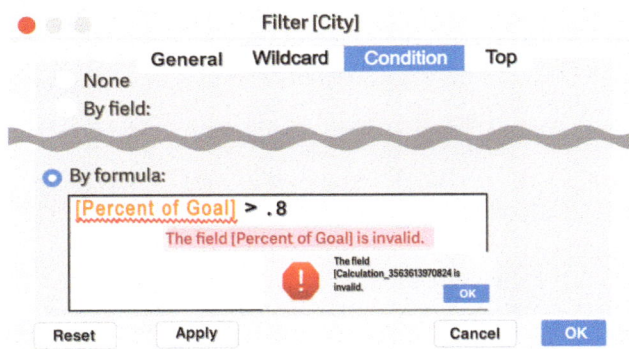

FIGURE 11.10
Error in filter formula.

Data pane menu. To edit a calculated field, right-click the field name in the **Data** pane and choose "Edit."

- In the **Data** pane, click the drop-down menu at the top to create a calculated field.
- Select a field in the **Data** pane and choose "Create, Calculated Field."
- From the **Analysis Menu**, choose "Create Calculated Field."

- On the **Data Source** page, click the drop-down menu for any field. The online <u>Tableau help</u> has additional information on calculation types.

11.7 Validate and Test

When testing and validating your visualizations, check calculations, filters, table calculations, aggregations, etc. There are many ways to validate your work, but I follow these steps.

1. Create a new sheet and drag the calculated field to the "Text" tile on the **Marks** card.
2. Add relevant fields to the *Tooltip* or *Text* tile. Earlier, in *"Section 11.4 Aggregation and Level of Detail" on page 227*, I added three fields to the *Tooltip* to check the "% of Total Sales" calculation.
3. The **Summary** card shows information for selected marks. If the **Summary** card is not

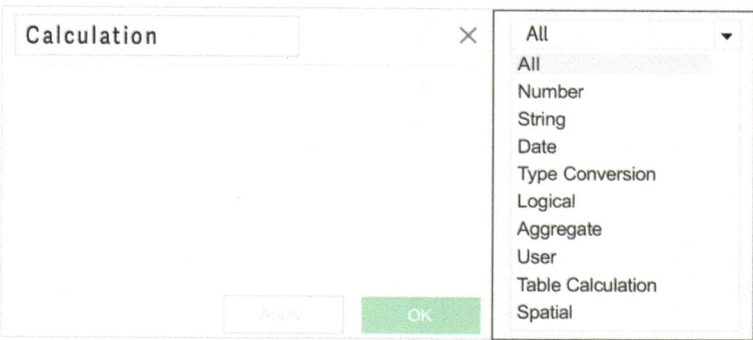

FIGURE 11.11
The Calculation Editor.

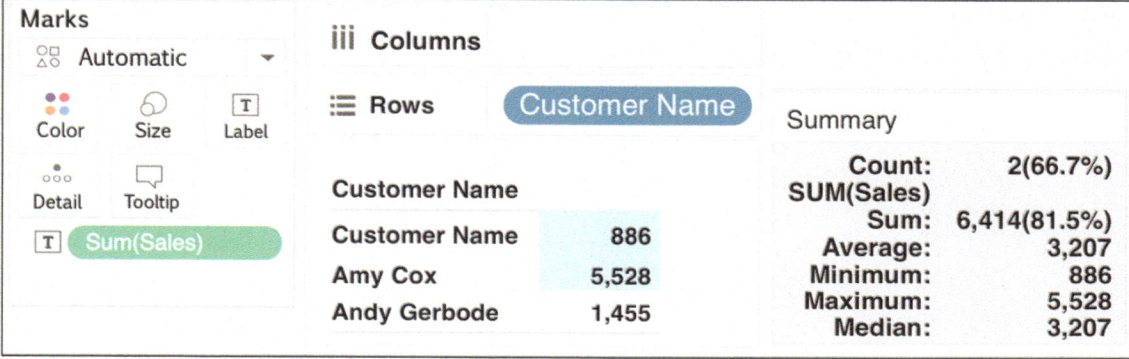

FIGURE 11.12
The Summary Card on the right.

open, on the **Worksheet** menu, select "Show Summary." I selected two out of three marks in this example; the "Count" is two on the **Summary** card. The "Sum" of the selected marks is 6,414, and the "Average" is 3,207 (Figure 11.12).

4. In *"Section 4.1.2 Change the Data Type of a Field" on page 74*, we looked at how to "View Data," using the **Analysis** menu -> "View Data" option to see data for the active worksheet view. Viewing the data is an excellent way to see the underlying data and the aggregation used in the visualization. You can also export data and create a pivot chart to cross-check your data.

5. Test using a smaller subset of data. I like creating a small data set representing each field's values. For example, I might use one year instead of all years from an [Order Date] field.

6. When you have multiple filters, check the different filter selections to be sure the data is what you expect. For example, if you are summarizing total counts, you may use a set filter.

Still, when you change to individual row counts, a more granular measure filter might give you the results you are looking for.

Suppose you want to see which worksheets are using a calculated field. In that case, Tableau displays a link to those worksheets in the bottom-right corner of the **Calculation Editor**.

11.8 Useful Functions

Tableau functions support the typical programming tasks. You can combine strings, convert one data type into another, perform mathematical functions or logical comparisons like if-then-else, and work with dates and numbers.

11.8.1 Case

A "Case" statement is a logical test where you want to test whether a field is a particular value. Case statements may be faster than nested If-Then-Else-End statements. The Tableau white paper, "Designing

FIGURE 11.13
Warning: When you change the result type of a calculation, the field background might change to red. To remove the red background, drag the new calculated field onto the original one.

Efficient Workbooks," looks at these performance issues in more detail. *"Section 8.14 Hover to Choose a Field for Sorting"* on page 181 has a case statement in a calculated field.

11.8.2 MAX() and MIN()

The MAX() function works with strings and dates to compare two values and aggregate data. *"Section 9.11 Avoid 'All' in a Date Title"* on page 208 looks at MAX() and uses a parameter and calculated field to add a date to the worksheet title.

11.8.3 ROUND()

The ROUND() function rounds a number to the given precision point. In this example, ROUND() returns two decimals. Earlier, the AVG example in the "Inline Calculations" topic also used ROUND().

```
Round([Sales], 2)
```

11.8.4 ZN()

You can replace missing values using the ZN() function in calculated fields. ZN(*expression*) returns the expression, and if its value is Null, it returns 0.

11.9 User Functions

In *"Section 5.5.2 Row-Level Security"* on page 93, we looked at the USERNAME() function for row-level security. Tableau's online help covers other user functions. I have a calculated field in the title of a "Welcome" worksheet on my main dashboard that uses the FULLNAME() function

    SPLIT (FULLNAME(), " ", 2)
    https://help.tableau.com/current/pro/desktop/
en-us/functions_functions_user.htm?_gl=1*1*
910qo*_ga*MTYzMjEzMDcxMS4xNzE5NzUyOTMz*
_ga_8YLN0SNXVS*MTcxOTc1MTcwNS4xLjEuMTcx
OTc1MjkzMi4wLjAuMA

11.10 Table Calculation Functions

In *"Section 10.1 Table Calculation Scope"* on page 209, we saw you can create a "Quick Table Calculation" from a field's *context menu*. Tableau also has functions you can use in expressions to create table calculations. In the **Calculation Editor**, if the expression is a table calculation, Tableau displays a message about the table calculation in the bottom-right corner just above the OK button. Now, let's look at the more common table calculation functions.

- First
- Last
- Index
- Lookup
- Rank
- Window Average
- Window Sum

> Tableau does not allow table functions inside a FIXED LoD expression.

11.10.1 FIRST()

A field that uses the FIRST() function returns the row number for the partition starting at 0. Both FIRST() and LAST() are also used with table calculation functions like LOOKUP() and WINDOW_ SUM() to specify the FIRST() row for the calculation. FIRST() starts with the current row "0" and counts backward to the first row in the partition. For this data, FIRST() returns 0 for the 2023 row, and the 2020 row is −3.

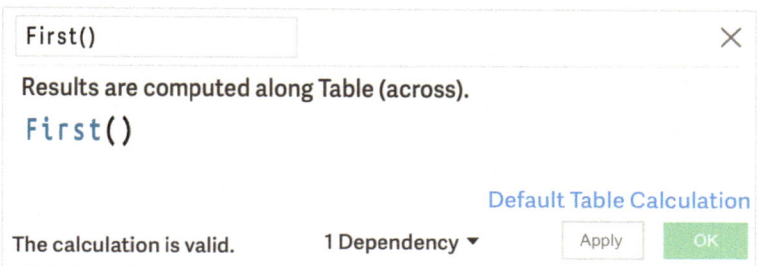

FIGURE 11.14
FIRST() function.

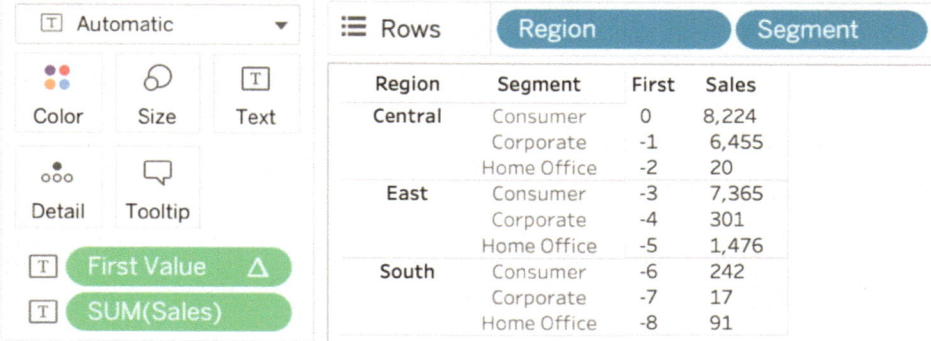

FIGURE 11.15
Default scope.

Order Date	Value returned by First([Order Date])
2023	0
2022	−1
2021	−2
2020	−3

If I save a new [First Value] field and then edit the field, I can see Tableau adds a yellow bar with the default scope, as shown in Figure 11.14. In *"Section 10.2 Add a Table Calculation" on page 210*, we looked at the scope (partitioning and addressing) in the topic, "Table Calculation Scope."

11.10.1.1 FIRST() Example

In Figure 11.14, Tableau explains the addressing and partitioning for the calculation as "Results are computed along Table (across)." Table is Tableau's default scope, and the direction is across. In Figure 11.15, the [First Value] field is the first column with marks. In this case, the marks are numbers.

Because I want to see the top sales within each region, I need to find the first (or top) value for each region. My table calculation uses "Pane (down then across)" for the "Compute Using" setting, as shown in Figure 11.16. In this example, the scope is "Pane," and the direction is "(down then across)."

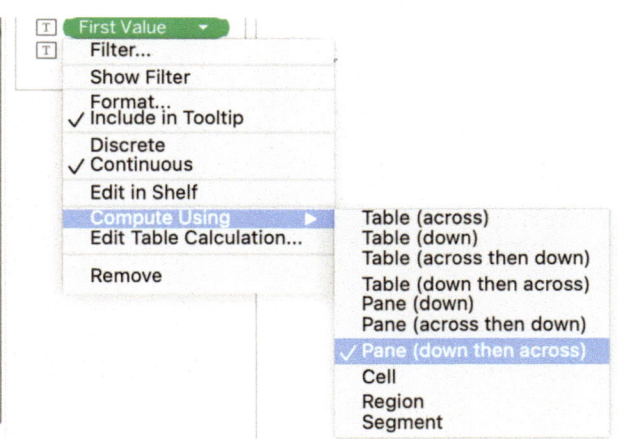

FIGURE 11.16
Compute using options.

After making the "Compute Using" change above, the first row in each pane is "0," as shown in Figure 11.17. The panes are grouped by the [Region] field, which is the leftmost field on the **Rows** shelf.

Finally, my manager wants to see only the top value in the chart, so I added the [First Value] field to the **Filter** shelf. The chart in Figure 11.18 shows only the top sales for each region.

11.10.2 LAST()

Both FIRST() and LAST() are used with table calculation functions like LOOKUP() and WINDOW_SUM() to determine the LAST() row for the calculation. In this example, the "2020" row is offset from the LAST() row by "3."

Order Date	Value returned by LAST([Order Date])
2020	3
2021	2
2022	1
2023	0

FIGURE 11.17
FIRST() function.

In *"Section 7.3.11 Opacity" on page 143*, the last bar is darker than the other bars. A calculated field identifies the mark to highlight, and I apply color differently for those marks.

IF **LAST()** = 0 THEN **SUM([HOURS])**

11.10.3 INDEX()

To find the current row in the partition, use the <u>INDEX()</u> table calculation function. INDEX() returns 1

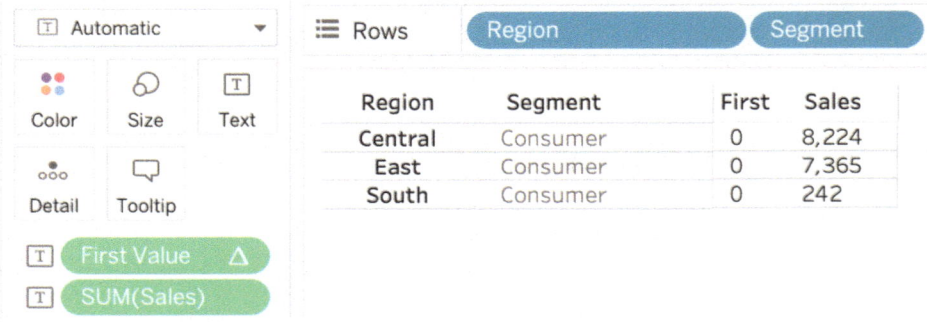

FIGURE 11.18
Updated chart.

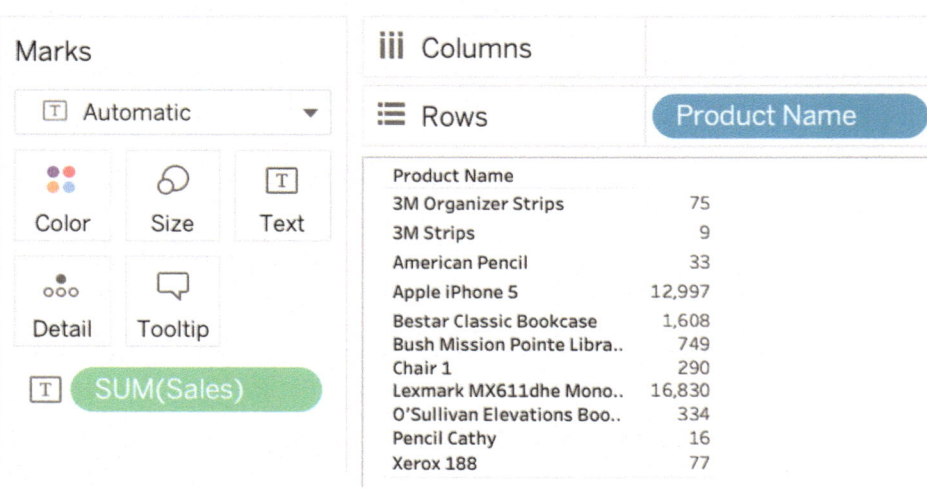

FIGURE 11.19
Sales chart.

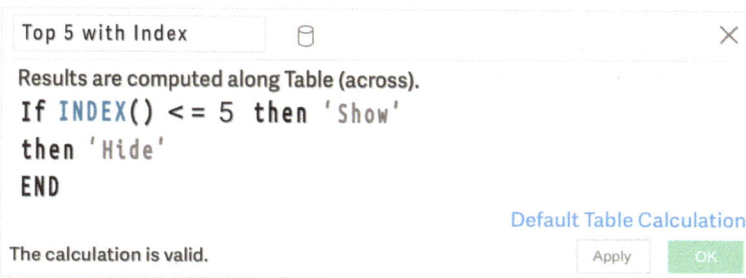

FIGURE 11.20
Top 5 with Index function.

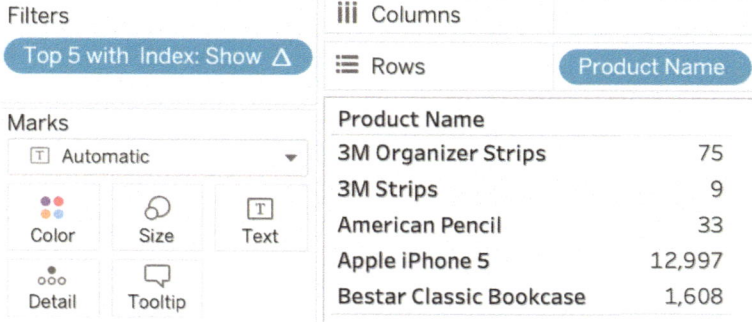

FIGURE 11.21
Filtering with Top 5 Index.

for the first row, as shown below. The next row, 2021, has an index value of 2.

Order Date	Value returned by First([Order Date])
2020	1
2021	2
2022	3
2023	4

In *"Section 6.3 Multiple Charts in One View" on page 105*, the example uses INDEX().

After adding a new calculated field with the INDEX() function to the view, when you right-click the field on the view, the field's *context menu* opens with an option to choose "Compute Using." Because this is a table calculation function, there are options for partitioning, like Table (Across). The view's **dimension** fields are listed at the bottom of the *context menu*, as shown in Figure 11.24.

11.10.3.1 Filter to Top 5 using INDEX()

To illustrate the INDEX() function, let's look at the simple sales chart in Figure 11.19.

The [Top 5 with index] calculated field in Figure 11.20 uses the INDEX() function to find the top 5.

After adding the new [Top 5 with Index] field to the **Filters** shelf in Figure 11.21, the view shows only the

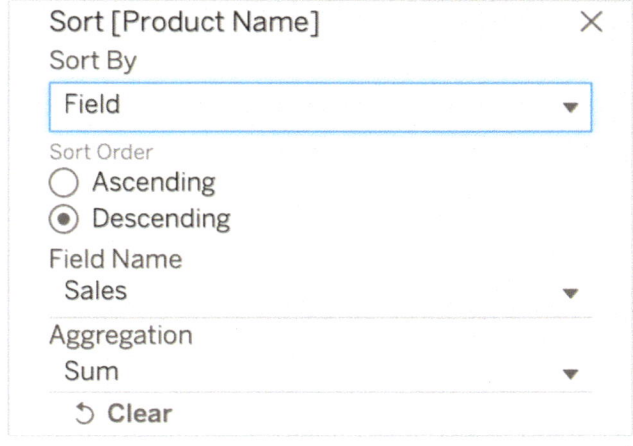

FIGURE 11.22
Sort by field.

first five rows of data, which are not the Top 5 values, because there is no sort.

In Figure 11.22, I apply a descending sort to the [Product Name] field using the [Sales] field.

After sorting the product names, the top 5 sales are correct, as shown in Figure 11.23.

In Figure 11.24, the filter sets the "Compute Using" option to Table(down). Depending on your scenario, you may need to adjust the "Compute Using" setting.

11.10.4 LOOKUP()

LOOKUP() is a table calculation function that is great for comparing two values, like the *difference* between the current month and the previous month or the *change* between the first and last values. LOOKUP() differs from PREVIOUS_VALUE, which returns the *calculation's value* when applied to the previous row. These examples use the LOOKUP() function.

- *"Section 7.3 The Color Property" on page 139*
- *"Section 8.7.2 Filter the View, Not the Underlying Data" on page 169*
- *"Section 12.21 Arrows Comparing Two Values" on page 287*

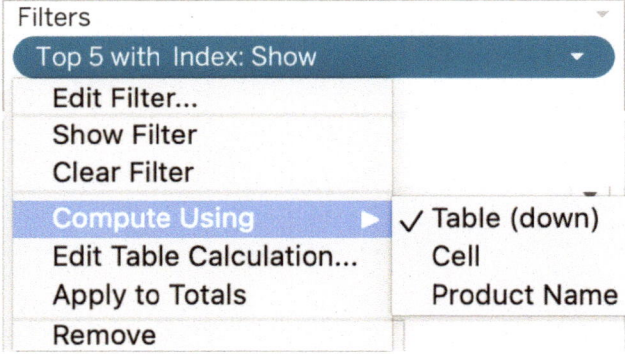

FIGURE 11.23
Top 5 sales.

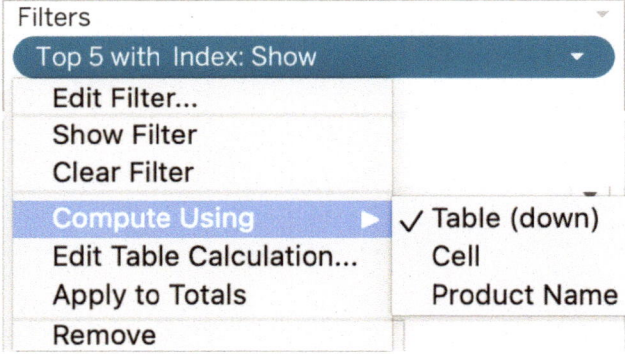

FIGURE 11.24
Compute Using: Table Down.

- *"Section 14.23 KPIs and BANs (Big Numbers)" on page 347*

In Figure 11.25, the -1 indicates the previous *column* because the *direction* is **Table (across)**. If I used **Table (down)**, the table calculation would return the previous *row*.

11.10.5 RANK()

The RANK() function creates a table calculation. Unlike the INDEX() function, identical values have the same rank in the event of a tie. I am using a descending rank in Figure 11.26 in a calculated field. *"Section 13.6.4 Custom Color and Shape Legend (Diamond)" on page 298* uses a RANK() calculation to add a shape and color to the top three sales values on a dashboard. *"Section 7.2.7.4 Transparent Shapes to Call Attention to Some Marks" on page 129* also utilizes the RANK() function.

11.10.5.1 Sort by Ranking Alternative

"Section 8.16 Sort by Rank Alternative" on page 188 used the **RANK()** function. The Tableau **Sort Dialog Box** does not include table calculation fields; however, as shown in that example, you can use Tableau's default sort behavior to apply sorting by adding a table calculation field to the **Rows** or **Columns** shelves.

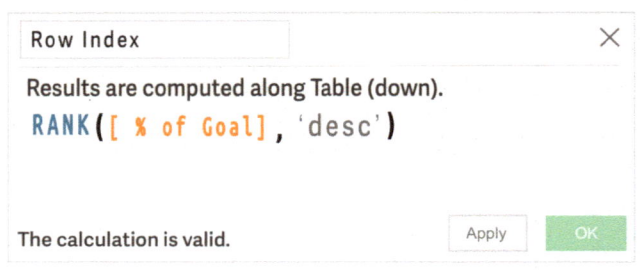

FIGURE 11.26
The Rank function.

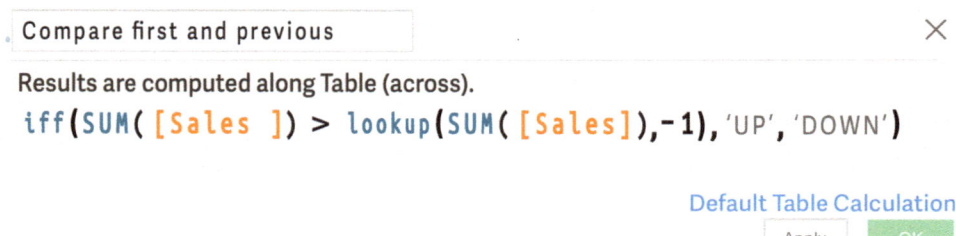

FIGURE 11.25
Lookup function.

1. Create a new field [Ranking] with the RANK() function. To do so, drag the [Sales] field to the **Rows** shelf, right-click it, choose *Quick Table Calculation*, and then "Rank." In the

   Table Calculation dialog window for "Compute Using," select "Table (down)," as shown below (Figure 11.27).

   Another option is to create a new calculated field [Ranking] with the RANK() function.

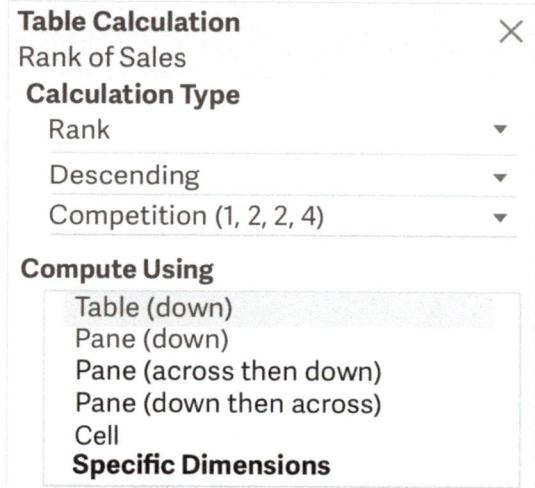

FIGURE 11.27
The Table Calculation Dialog Box.

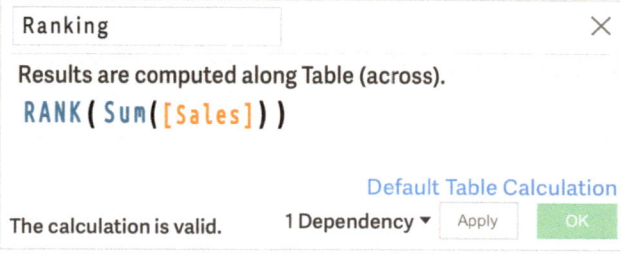

FIGURE 11.28
The calculated Field Ranking.

Because a table calculation must be aggregated, I use SUM() to aggregate [Sales] in this example (Figure 11.28).

If you omit the aggregation "SUM," Tableau displays a red warning at the bottom of the calculation editor window (Figure 11.29).

2. The [Ranking] field on the **Rows** shelf has a small delta triangle on the right side, indicating this is a table calculation. Right-click the field on the **Rows** shelf and use the drop-down arrow to open the field's *context menu*. Change the [Ranking] field to **discrete**. The field background (or pill) changes from green to blue, as shown below. Because Tableau sorts the table by the innermost field by default, in this case [Region], the ranking is out of order, or 1-3-4-2 (Figure 11.30).

3. Drag the [Ranking] field to the left so it is the first field on the **Rows** shelf or the innermost field. Immediately, Tableau re-sorts the table (Figure 11.31).

4. If you do not want to see the ranking in the view, right-click the field [Ranking] to open its *context menu* and uncheck "Show Header."

11.10.6 WINDOW_AVG

When you want an average of the values in your view, and you have a lot of filters making LoD calculations a challenge, use the WINDOW_AVG() table calculation function. The expression below returns a three-month average.

WINDOW_AVG([Sales], -2, 0)

To have Tableau create the field for you, add the [Sales] field to the *Text* tile of the **Marks** card and right-click the field to open the field's *context menu*. Select "Quick Table Calculation" and choose "Moving Avg." Drag this field from the **Marks** card to the **Data** pane and rename the field [Average Sales]. Now, you

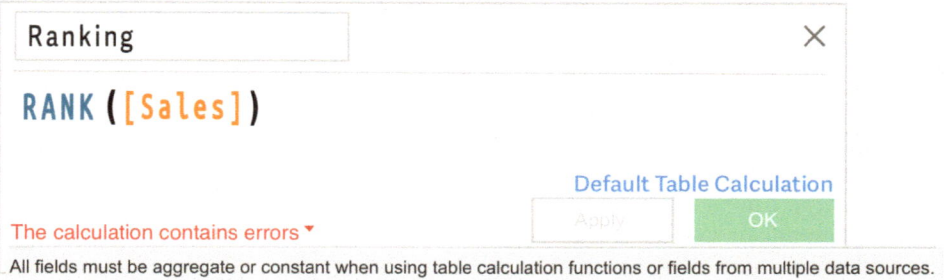

FIGURE 11.29
The Error Message for the Ranking Field.

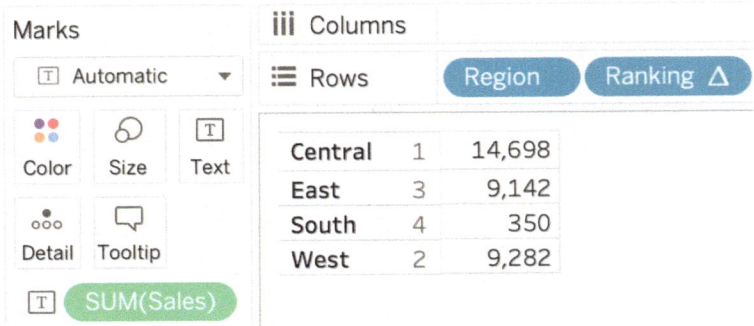

FIGURE 11.30
The Ranking Field on the **Rows** Shelf.

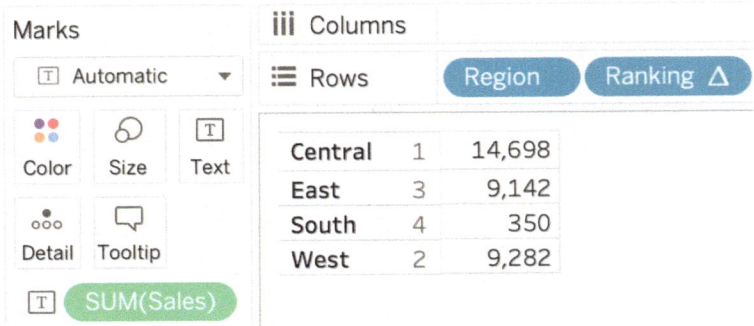

FIGURE 11.31
The Ranking Field on the **Rows** Shelf.

can edit the new field, as shown in Figure 11.32. Right-click the field in the **Data** pane to edit the new field.

11.10.7 WINDOW_SUM

The WINDOW_SUM table calculation sums the values within the window. The window starts at the current row, and you specify the FIRST() and LAST() rows as optional offsets. Figure 11.34 has no offset values and uses the entire partition. The example *"Section 6.5 Donut Chart" on page 112*, uses the WINDOW_SUM() calculation.

11.11 Level of Detail (LoD)

When you want to use a LoD different from the visualization, use "level of detail expressions." When you add dimensions to the view, the LoD changes from the entire file or row level and becomes more granular. For example, the next visualization has [Sales] by [State/Province] and [City]. I use LoD expressions to show city sales as a percentage of state sales. In Figure 11.35, the orange circles represent sales by city. I have an LoD expression, [% of State Sales], to calculate total sales for the [State/Province] represented by blue circles. Adding dimensions to the view increases the LoD.

- [City] is the most granular level of detail.
- SUM(Sales) for Calgary is 10,972.
- The total [Sales] for Alberta is 11,460.
- Calgary has 95.74% of sales for Alberta, or 10,972/11,460.

11.12 Level of Detail Expressions

LoD expressions allow you to control the level of aggregation and *dimensions* used in a calculation. An LoD calculation is the solution if a view shows a count of [Fans] per [Restaurant], and you also want to see the percentage of *Fans* compared to **all** *Fans*.

A fixed LoD expression computes independent of the view and *dimension* filters. "Fixed" LoD calculations are above *dimension* filters in Tableau's **Order of Operations**. They are applied before *dimension* filters, as shown in *"Section 8.13 Click Data Points to Sort with a Set" on page 175*.

> An LoD expression cannot use ATTR() or table calculation functions.

An LoD calculation can use any field regardless of whether it is part of the visualization. For example, an LoD calculation can include the *State* field, which does not have to be part of the visualization or viz LoD.

11.12.1 Scoping Keywords

LoDs use three scoping keywords:

EXCLUDE

FIXED

INCLUDE

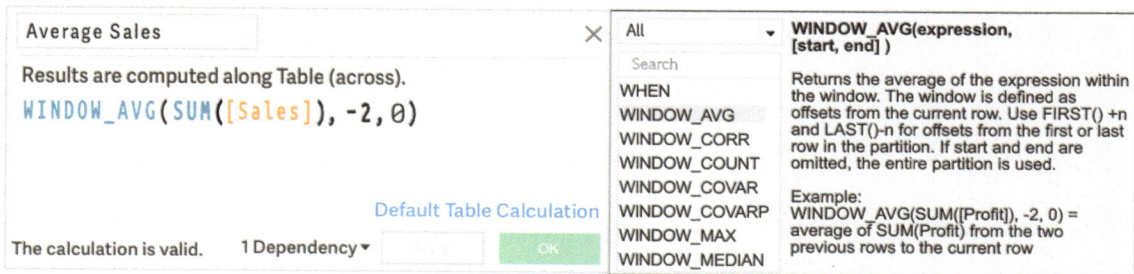

FIGURE 11.32
Quick Table Calculation.

FIGURE 11.33
Warning: *If you are using WINDOW_AVG or WINDOW_SUM and the calculation is wrong, turn on the row or column "Totals" on the **Analysis** menu to see if those totals look okay. If not, check filters and ensure you do not have a table calculation filter that filters the view but not the underlying data.*

11.12.1.1 EXCLUDE

EXCLUDE is less granular than the view because it *removes* the specified view dimensions. An EXCLUDE LoD expression always returns a measure.

11.12.1.2 FIXED

FIXED only uses fields in the LoD declaration and ignores any fields in the view other than *Context* filters. In line with *"Section 8.1 Filter Logic and the Order of Operations" on page 158*, FIXED also uses *Data Source* and *Extract* filters. A FIXED LoD expression can return a dimension or a measure. *"Section 8.13 Click Data Points to Sort with a Set" on page 175* utilizes a FIXED LoD expression.

11.12.1.3 INCLUDE

The INCLUDE keyword changes the view LoD to a more granular level by adding the specified dimensions to the dimensions already in the view. An INCLUDE LoD expression always returns a measure.

{ INCLUDE [Zip] : AVG([Fans]) }

I use a reference line to show the average restaurant fans per state. In Figure 11.36, I created the first reference line and included the value in the custom label. You can add field values to the label when you click the arrow on the right side of the custom label field in the middle of the **Edit Reference Line, Band, or Box** dialog window.

Using the earlier INCLUDE expression, I also want to show each state's average fans per zip. For the reference line to use the new field [Include Zip LoD], I add the field to the *Detail* tile on the **Marks** card, as shown in Figure 11.37.

11.12.2 LoD Declaration

An LoD expression is enclosed in curly braces and follows this format. The **Dimension Declaration** is optional.

{ **Scoping Keyword Dimension Declaration : Aggregate Expression** }

A sample LoD expression is shown below. The dimension field is [State]. This LoD expression tells Tableau to aggregate at the *State* level, regardless of the fields in the visualization. Here, the **Aggregate Expression** is **SUM**([Sales]).

{ FIXED [State] : SUM([Sales]) }

- This LoD expression uses a **FIXED** scope.
- The **dimension declaration** is the [State] field.
- The **aggregate expression** is **SUM**([Sales]).

FIGURE 11.34
WINDOW_SUM Calculation.

FIGURE 11.35
Aggregation example.

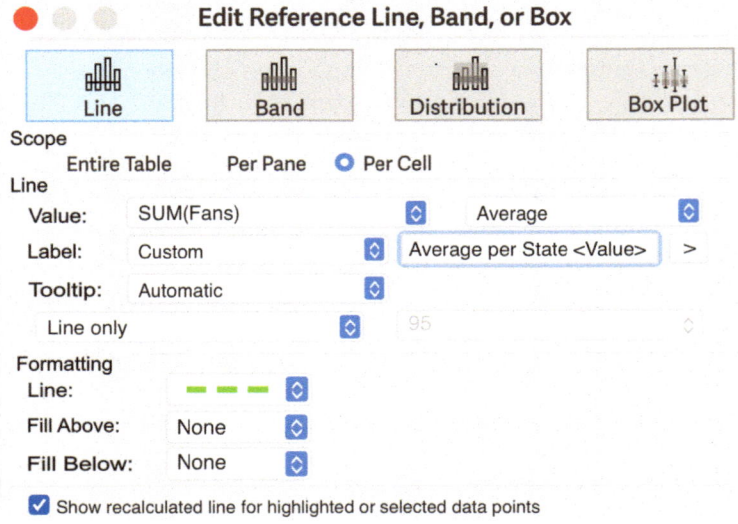

FIGURE 11.36
Reference Line with Custom Label.

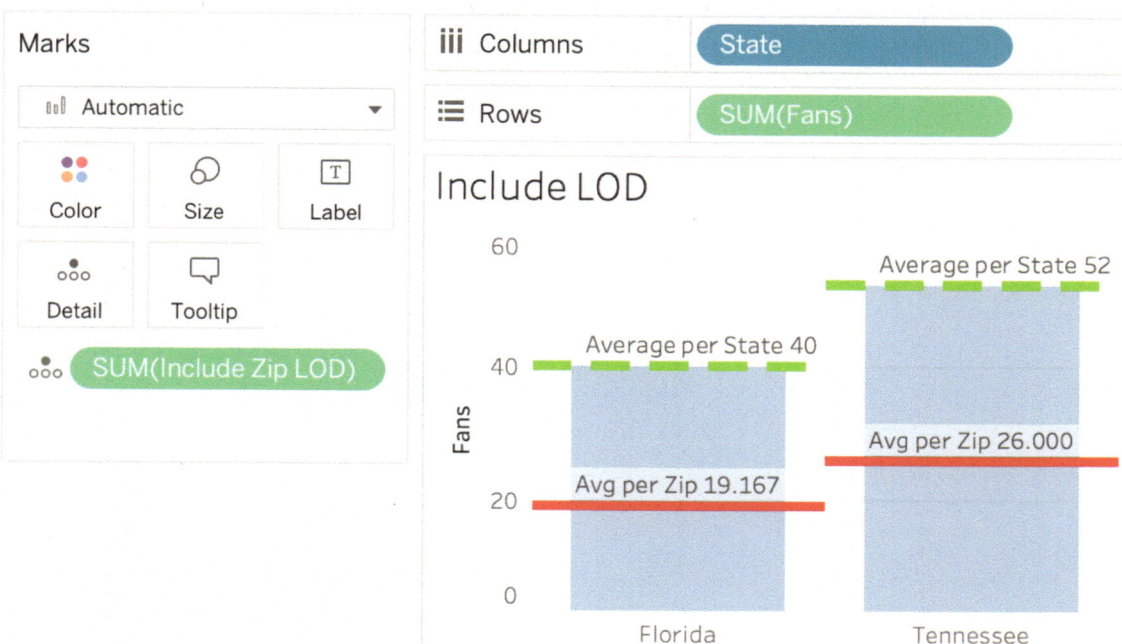

FIGURE 11.37
Two Reference Lines.

Multiple dimensions are separated by commas in the **dimension declaration**. In this LOD, there is a comma between [State] and [Restaurant].

{ FIXED [State], [Restaurant] : SUM([Sales]) }

- This LoD expression uses a **FIXED** scope.
- The **dimension declaration** uses the [State] and [Restaurant] fields.
- The **aggregate expression** is **SUM**([Sales]).

11.13 Fixed LoD Example

In this workbook with bar charts, we compare the Viz LoD to the LoD in two fixed LoD calculations. The data source is small, with only a few rows of data, to make the calculations easier to follow.

First, we look at the "No LoDs" worksheet and the "Count" and "Average" aggregations. Then, we look at percentage calculations on the "LoD Zip" and "LoD All Fans" worksheets. The links to the Tableau Public file and YouTube video are at the end of the exercise, along with a checklist of the elements and settings in the example. There is a copy of the data table if you

want to have that reference in front of you as we work through the exercise.

11.13.1 Comparing Visualizations

Before we create this workbook, let's examine the difference between a visualization with no LoDs and a visualization with an LoD calculation based on all records, as shown in Figures 11.38 and 11.39.

11.13.2 The Visualization without LoD Calculations

For this bar chart, "No LoDs," I want to see a count of [Fans] for various restaurants by [Zip]. The [Fans] and [Zip] fields define the Visualization level of detail or Viz LoD.

1. [Fans] is on the **Columns** shelf, and [Zip] and [Restaurant] are on the **Rows** shelf. [Restaurant] is configured with a *Nested* Sort by [Fans per Zip] and then by [Restaurant]. A nested sort is demonstrated in *"Section 8.10.3 Nested Sort" on page 173*.
2. Drag [Fans] onto the *Label* tile of the **Marks** card. The default aggregation in Tableau is SUM(Fans), which is what I want.

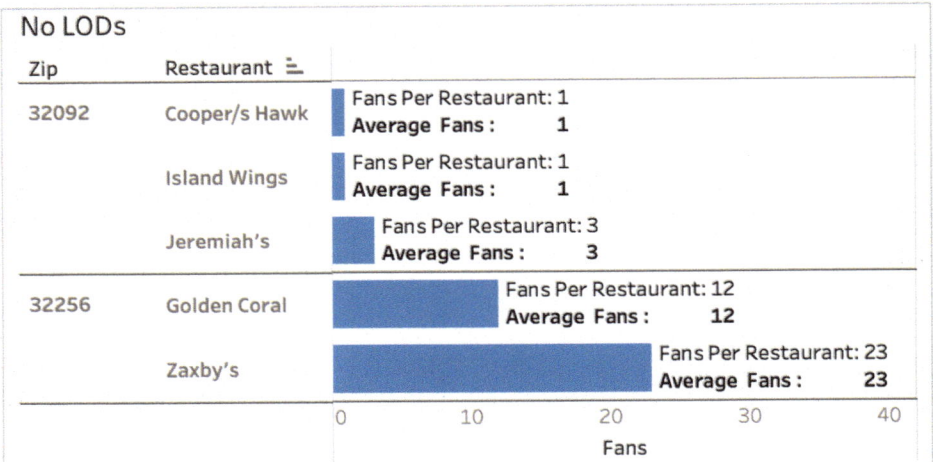

FIGURE 11.38
Chart with No LoDs.

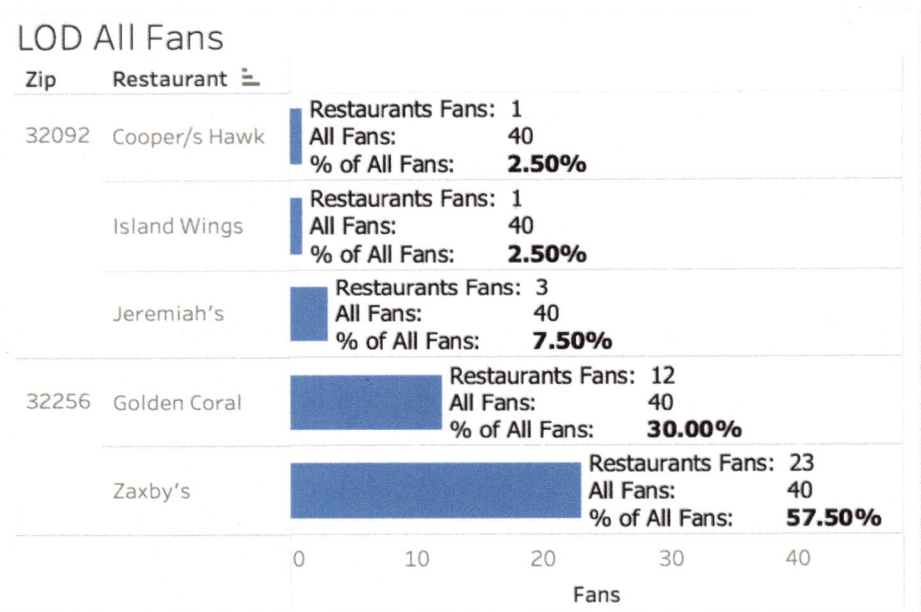

FIGURE 11.39
Chart with LoDs for All Fans.

3. Add a second instance of [Fans] to the *Label* tile on the **Marks** card and change the aggregation to "Average." In MacOS, click-drag the [Fans] field from the **Data** pane and drop it on the *Text* tile of the **Marks** card.

4. Click the drop-down arrow of the [Fans] field on the *Text* tile to open the field's *context menu*. Select "Measure(Sum)" and change the aggregation to "Average."

5. Click the *Label* tile on the **Marks** card and check "Show mark labels." Click the ellipsis tool on the

right to edit the text in the "Label Appearance" section in the "Text" line (Figure 11.40).

To add fields within the text:

- Click in the white box in the **Edit Label** window.

- Position the cursor where you want to place the field.

- In the top-right corner of the "Edit Label" dialog window, click the drop-down arrow for "Insert" and select the field.

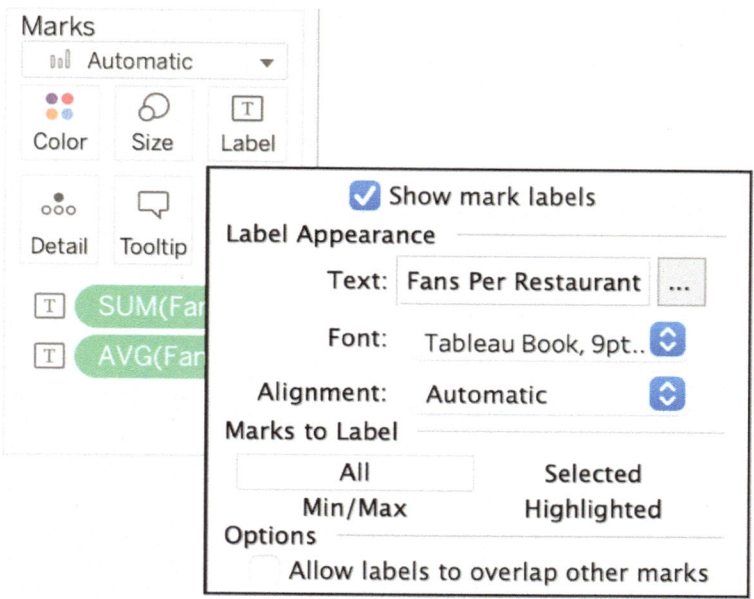

FIGURE 11.40
The Label Dialog window.

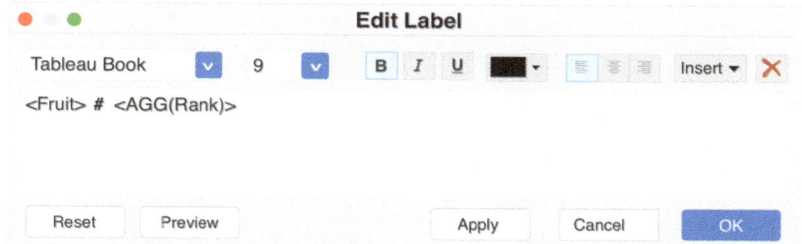

FIGURE 11.41
The **Edit Label** box.

Note only fields used in your view are shown in the **Insert** menu (Figure 11.41).

Now that you see the mark labels on the view, notice the average calculation is the same as the count because Tableau uses the Viz LoD. I want to see calculations based on ALL fans, so I need an LoD calculation (Figure 11.42).

11.13.3 The Visualization with an LoD Zip Calculation

This view, "LoD Zip," shows a count of *Fans* per *Zip* and *Restaurant*, but I also want to see the percentage of **all** *Fans* in the Zip.

1. Right-click on the sheet in the bottom tabbed area and choose "Duplicate." Rename the new worksheet "LoD Zip."

2. Change the aggregation of [Fans] on the **Rows** shelf to "AVG(Fans)." Right-click the field's drop-down arrow to open its *context menu*, select "Measure(Sum)," and change it to "Average" (Figure 11.43).

3. For this "LoD Zip" view, I do not use the field [AVG(Fans)] on the **Marks** card, and I remove that field.

4. Create the two calculated fields [Fans per Zip] and [% Fans per Zip].

   The [Fans per Zip] is an LoD expression and shows the sum of fans in each zip.

   • This LoD expression uses a **FIXED** scope.
   • The **dimension declaration** is the "Zip" field.
   • The **aggregate expression** is **SUM**([Fans]) (Figure 11.44).

5. I want to create a calculated field [% Fans per Zip], as shown below. The expression uses the LoD field [Fans per Zip] I created in step four (Figure 11.45).

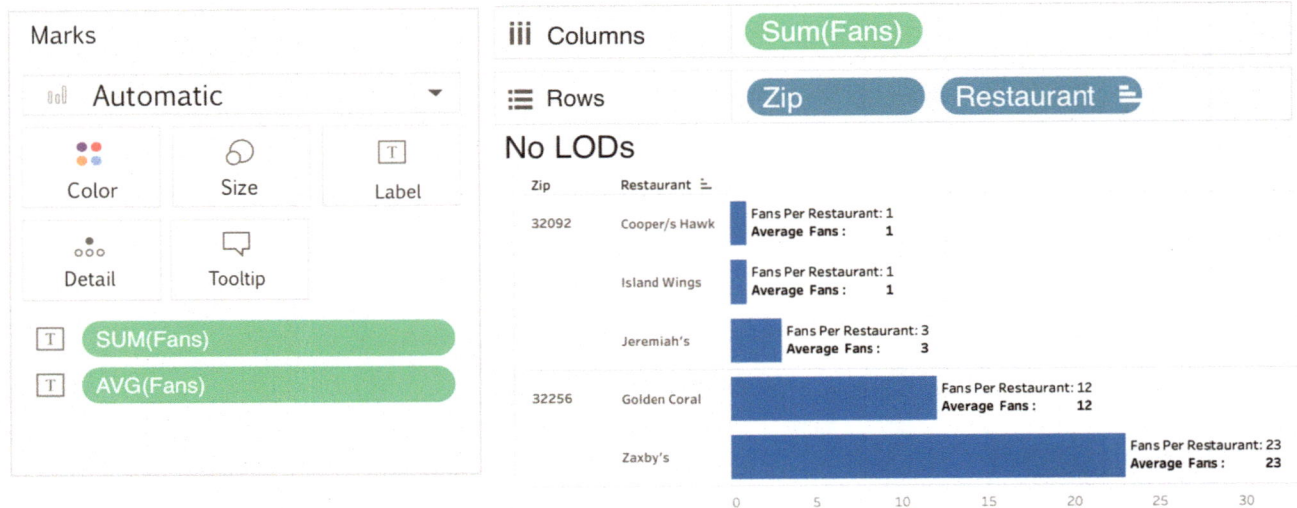

FIGURE 11.42
The No LODs worksheet.

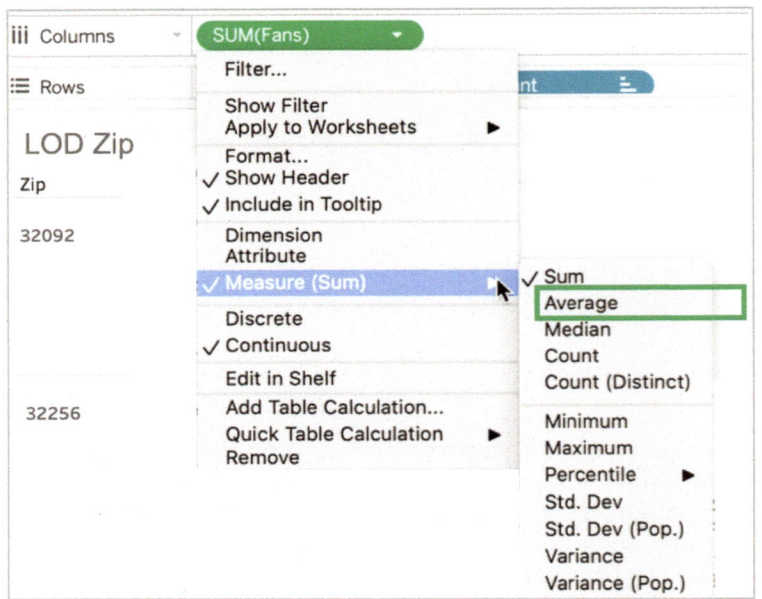

FIGURE 11.43
Change the Aggregation to Average.

6. Add both fields to the *Label* tile on the **Marks** card. Click the *Label* tile and check "Show mark labels." In the "Label Appearance" section of the "Text" section, click the ellipsis tool to edit the text to match this diagram (Figure 11.46).

Looking at the previous view, the [Fans Per Zip] total in the 32256 zip is 35, and the [Fans Per Zip] total in the 32092 zip is 5.

11.13.4 LOD All Fans Sheet

Figure 11.52 shows the "LOD All Fans" worksheet. While I could have created one calculated field for this percentage, I created several calculated fields so you can see how I arrived at the final expression.

1. Create the [All Fans] field. I am using the field [State] this time for the **dimension declaration** in the [All Fans] shown below. Add this new field to *Label* on the **Marks** card. I do not

FIGURE 11.44
The Calculated Field Fans Per Zip.

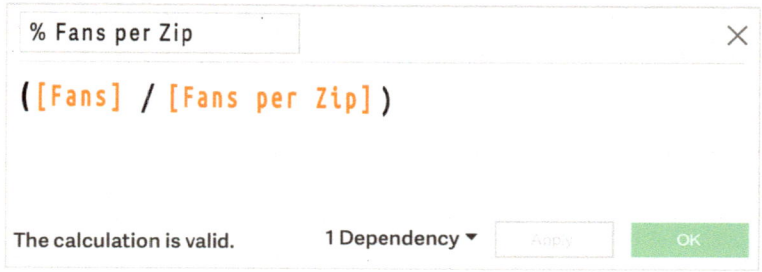

FIGURE 11.45
The Calculated Field % Fans Per Zip.

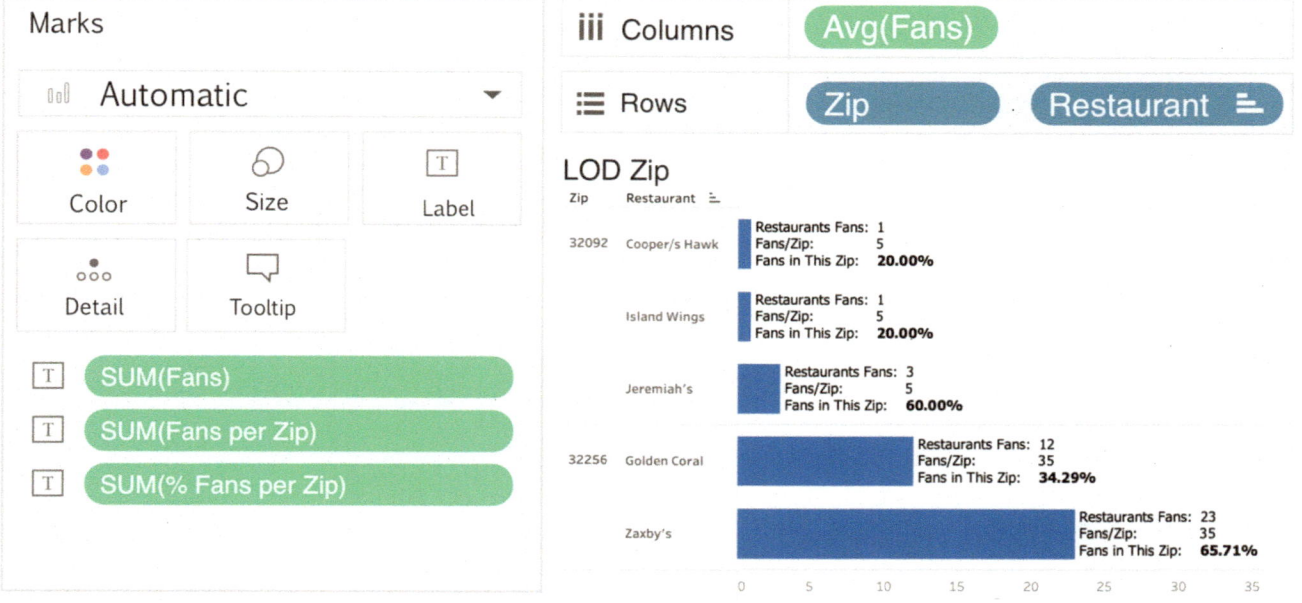

FIGURE 11.46
The LOD Zip Worksheet.

FIGURE 11.47
The calculated field % of all fans.

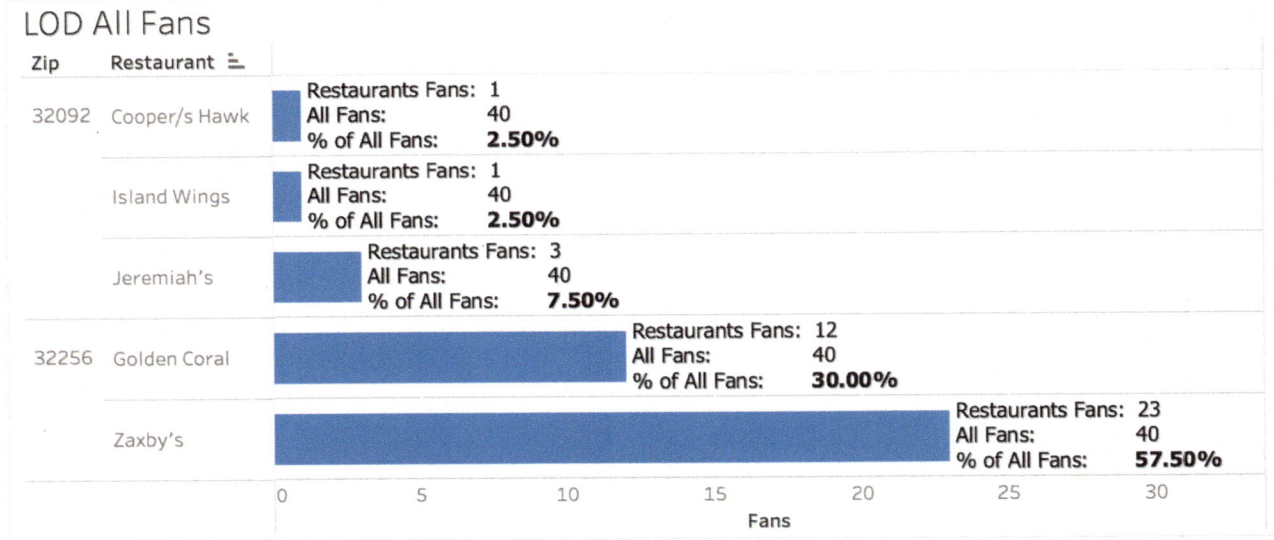

FIGURE 11.48
The LOD all fans worksheet.

use this field anywhere else. I only want it to illustrate the calculations on the view.

> { **FIXED** [State] : **SUM**([Fans]) }

2. Create the [% of All Fans] field. Add the field to *Label* on the **Marks** card (Figure 11.47).

> ([Fans] / { **FIXED** [State] : **SUM**([Fans]) })

- This LoD expression uses a **FIXED** scope.
- The **dimension declaration** is the "State" field.
- The **aggregate expression** is **SUM**([Fans]) (Figure 11.47).

    While [State] is not part of the view, I can still use it in an LoD expression. When we looked at the data earlier, you probably noticed that all my restaurants are in the same state, so, in essence, this calculation returns all data.

3. Edit the text as shown in Step 6 earlier, inserting the new fields. The text should match the example below (Figure 11.48).

11.13.4.1 Fixed LoD without a Dimension Declaration

Figure 11.49 illustrates another way to write the same expression for all records. This expression does not have a **dimension declaration**.

- This LoD expression uses a **FIXED** scope.
- There is no **dimension declaration** after the **FIXED** keyword.
- The **aggregate expression** in the LoD is **SUM**([Fans]).

11.13.5 Project Files

If you want to follow along with this example, download the Tableau Public file:

https://public.tableau.com/views/Fixed LoDofTotal/Dashboard1?:language=en-US& publish=yes&:sid=&:display_count=n&: origin=viz_share_link

FIGURE 11.49
Fixed LoD without a Dimension.

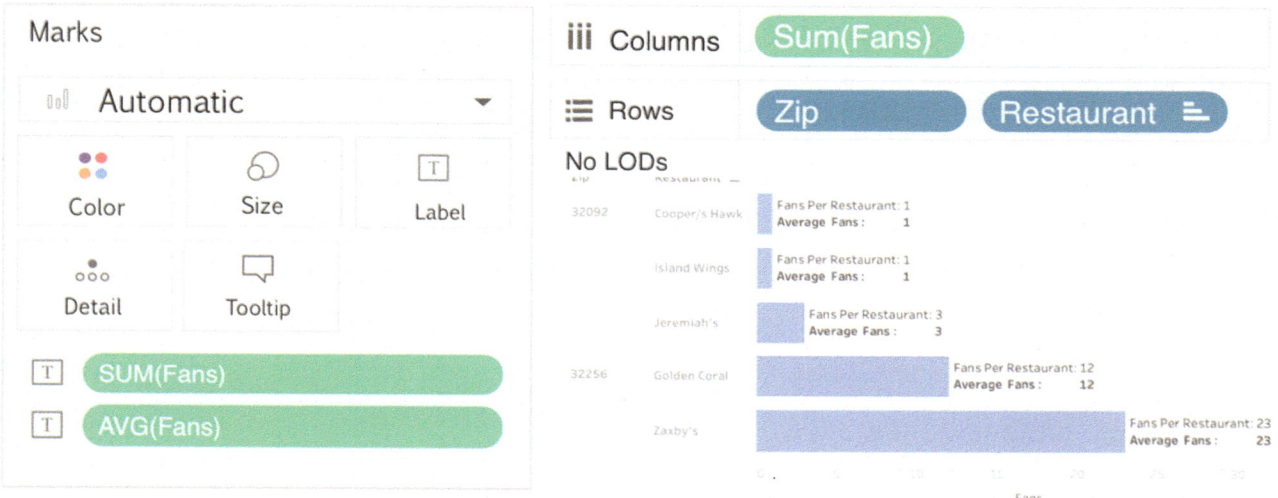

FIGURE 11.50
The No LODs worksheet.

11.13.6 Worksheets

There are three worksheets in this workbook.

- No LoDs
- LoD Zip
- LoD All Fans

11.13.6.1 No LoDs

The first worksheet, "No LoDs," is a basic bar chart, as shown in Figure 11.50.

11.13.6.2 LoD Zip

This "LoD Zip" worksheet in Figure 11.51 adds two LoD calculations to the *Text* tile of the **Marks** card.

11.13.6.3 LoD All Fans

The final worksheet in Figure 11.52, "LoD All Fans," uses two new fields.

11.13.7 Data and Fields

This workbook is based on a simple Excel file with four fields. I also create several calculated fields.

The data for this visualization is shown below (Figure 11.53).

[Fans] is a number field representing the number of fans of a particular restaurant and is a **continuous** field. [Fans] is on the **Columns** shelf of all worksheets, and the *Text* tile is on the **Marks** Card. I also use [Fans] in several calculated fields.

The [State] field is a **discrete** dimension with a "String" data type. As expected, the field has a blue background in the **Data** pane because it is **discrete**. I also use the [State] field in calculated fields.

The [Zip] field is a **discrete** dimension with a "String" data type on the **Rows** shelf. I use the [Zip] field in several calculated fields.

The [Restaurant] field is also a "String" field on the **Rows** shelf. I also added a "nested" sort.

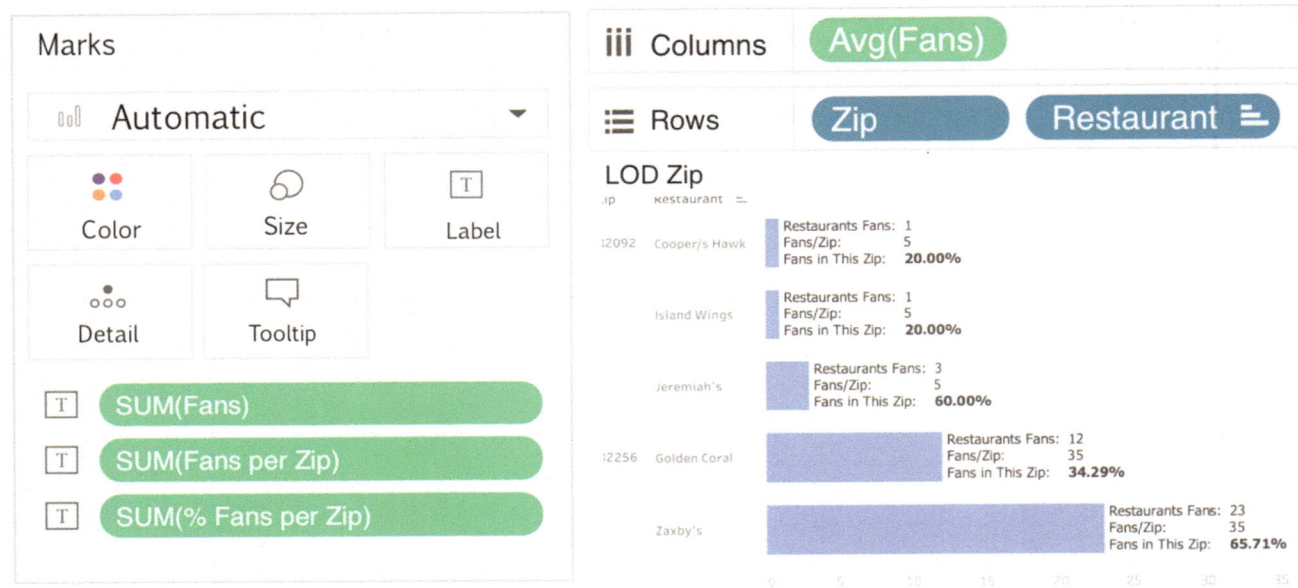

FIGURE 11.51
The LOD Zip worksheet.

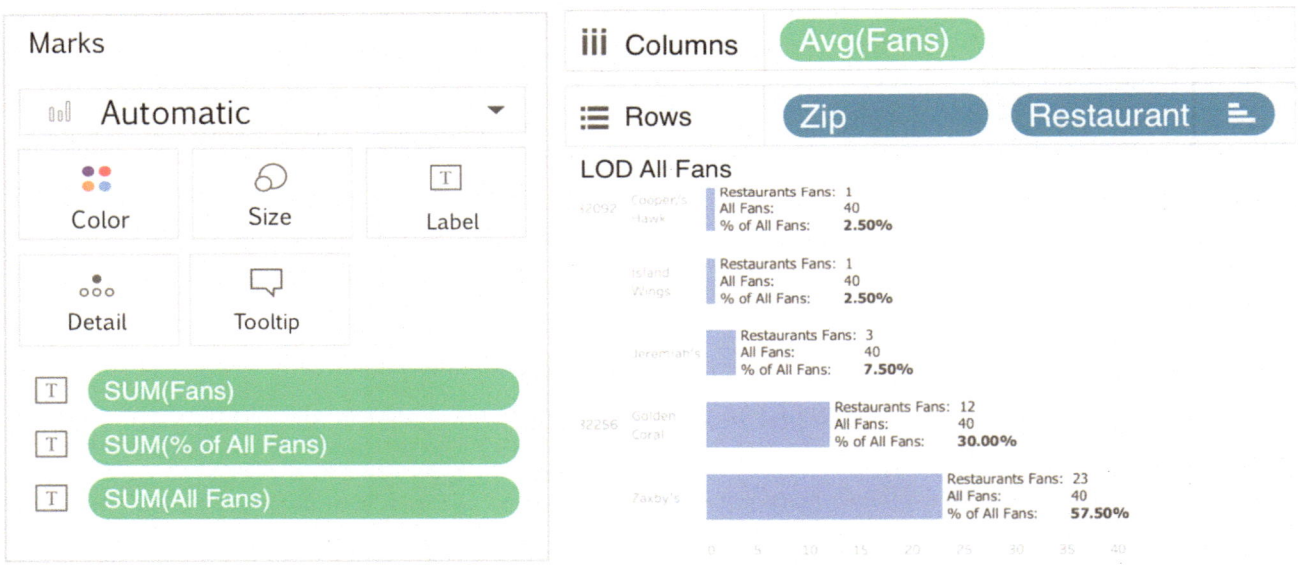

FIGURE 11.52
The LoD all fans worksheet.

11.13.8 Calculated Fields

The **[Fans per Zip]** field is used in the "LoD Zip" worksheet. This calculated field is only an LoD expression, as indicated by the enclosing curly braces. The scope is **FIXED**, and the **dimension declaration** is [Fans].

```
{ FIXED [Fans] : SUM( [Fans] ) }
```

The **[% Fans per Zip]** field is used on the "LoD Zip" worksheet. This calculated field computes a percentage using the previous [Fans Per Zip] LoD field. The outside enclosing parentheses are optional.

```
( [Fans] / [Fans per Zip] )
```

The **[All Fans]** field is used on the "LoD All Fans" worksheet and is an LoD expression. The scope is **FIXED**, and the **dimension declaration** is [State].

```
{ FIXED [State] : SUM( [Fans] ) }
```

The **[% of All Fans]** field is used on the "LoD All Fans" worksheet. This calculated field uses an LoD expression inside another calculation.

```
( [Fans] / { FIXED [State] : SUM( [Fans] ) } )
```

11.13.8.1 % of All Fans v2

This calculated field includes an LoD expression and is another way to write the [% of All Fans] calculation. The scope is **FIXED**, and there is no **dimension declaration**.

```
Sum( [Fans] ) / SUM( { FIXED : Sum( [Fans] ) } )
```

11.13.9 Components or Elements

There are several elements to this view.

- Columns Shelf
- Rows Shelf
- Marks Card: Label

11.13.10 Marks Card: Label

The fields on the *Label* tile on the **Marks** card vary depending on the worksheet.

Fans	Fans	Fans	Fans
State	**Zip**	**Restaurant**	**Fans**
Florida	32092	Cooper's Hawk	1
Florida	32092	Island Wings	1
Florida	32092	Jeremiah's	3
Florida	32256	Golden Coral	12
Florida	32256	Zaxby's	23

FIGURE 11.53
Data source.

FIGURE 11.54
The finished dashboard.

Weighted Average

Category	2020	2021	2022	2023	Weighted Avg
Furniture	96.37%	98.10%	96.41%	98.47%	97.34%
Office Supplies	84.75%	81.71%	80.89%	83.56%	82.73%
Technology	87.46%	79.41%	82.42%	81.34%	82.66%

Profit

Category	2020	2021	2022	2023	Total
Furniture	5,885	3,280	7,216	3,349	19,730
Office Supplies	23,489	25,178	35,613	41,743	126,023
Technology	22,310	33,563	39,836	50,834	146,543

Sales

Category	2020	2021	2022	2023	Total
Furniture	162,125	172,330	200,980	219,313	754,748
Office Supplies	154,014	137,670	186,374	253,835	731,893
Technology	177,901	162,993	226,580	272,419	839,893

Expense

Category	2020	2021	2022	2023	Total
Furniture	156,240	169,050	193,764	215,964	735,018
Office Supplies	130,525	112,492	150,760	212,092	605,870
Technology	155,591	129,429	186,744	221,585	693,350

FIGURE 11.55
Profit, sales, and expense data.

11.13.10.1 No LoDs

The [Fans] field is on the *Label* tile twice on the "No LoDs" worksheet. One instance uses a SUM aggregation, and the other uses an AVG aggregation.

Sum(**Fans**)

Avg(**Fans**)

11.13.10.2 LoD Zip

There are three fields on the *Label* tile for the "LoD Zip" worksheet, and all three use a SUM aggregation, as shown in Step 6.

Sum(**Fans**)

Sum(**Fans Per Zip**)

Sum(**% Fans Per Zip**)

11.13.10.3 LoD All Fans

There are three fields on the *Label* tile for the "LoD All Fans" worksheet, and all three use a SUM aggregation.

Sum(**Fans**)

Sum(**% of All Fans**)

Sum(**All Fans**)

11.14 Weighted Average with Fixed LoD

This example also uses a FIXED LoD expression with two fields, [Category] and [Order Date], in the **dimension declaration**. The LoD's **aggregate expression** is simply the calculated field [Avg Expense], which is already an aggregation.

avg({FIXED [Category], Year([Order Date]) : ([Avg Expense]) })

After the "Create the Visualization" exercise, there is a link to the Tableau Public file and a checklist of the elements and settings in the example.

11.14.1 Introduction

This text table shows expenses as a percentage of sales for each year. My audience wants the average calculation (the column on the right) as a weighted average, as shown in Figure 11.54. Think of this calculation as an average of averages.

Avg (96.37 + 98.10 + 96.41 + 98.47) = 97.34

11.14.2 Preview – The Finished Dashboard

I created several views with the data and the calculations to illustrate the difference between averages and weighted averages.

11.14.3 Create the Visualization

After connecting to my data source, I created three views: Profit, Sales, and Expense. This step is optional; I wanted the data available for you while I make the average views. Next, I add the three views to the dashboard, as shown below (Figure 11.55).

11.14.4 The Avg Expense View

For this view, I want to replace "SUM(Expense)" with "Avg Expense." I duplicated the "Expense" worksheet and dragged the new [Avg Expense] field on top of [Expense] on the *Text* tile on the **Marks** card. The default "average" aggregation in Tableau computes the average of all values across the row from left to right (Figure 11.56).

(**SUM**(Sales) / **SUM**(Profit)) * 100

Tableau adds a new column to the right of the [Category] values. In this example, I renamed the column [Average all Years]. Tableau first calculates the SUM(Sales) total of 754,748 and the SUM(Expense) total of 735,018 for this average calculation. Then, the average for [Furniture] across all years is calculated. Unfortunately, **97.39** is not what I was expecting. I want **97.34**.

(735,018 / 754,748) = **97.39%**

11.14.5 The Weighted Average Calculation

My audience does not like this default average calculation and wants to see a [Weighted Average] calculation like this.

(96.37 + 98.10 + 96.41 + 98.47) / 4 = **97.34**

Now, I am going to use the [Avg Expense] field in a new [Weighted Average] calculation with a FIXED

What is the Average Expense?

Category	2020	2021	2022	2023	Average all Years
Furniture	96.37%	98.10%	96.41%	98.47%	97.39%
Office Supplies	84.75%	81.71%	80.89%	83.56%	82.78%
Technology	87.46%	79.41%	82.42%	81.34%	82.55%

FIGURE 11.56
The average for all years.

FIGURE 11.57
Weighted Average Calculated Field.

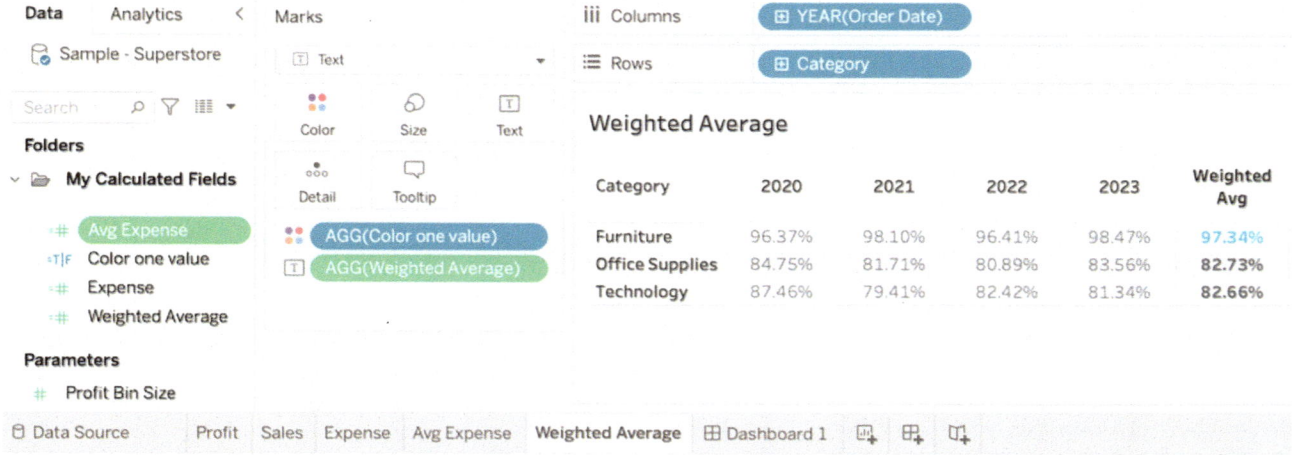

FIGURE 11.58
The Weighted Average View.

scope and two dimensions: [Category] and [Order Date].

- This LoD expression uses a **FIXED** scope.
- The **dimension declaration** uses the [Category] and YEAR([Order Date]) fields.
- The **aggregate expression** is [Avg Expense] (Figure 11.57).

11.14.6 The Weighted Average View

For this view, I duplicated the "Average" worksheet and dragged the new [Weighted Average] field on top of [AGG(Avg Expense)] on the *Text* tile on the **Marks** card. Tableau adds a new column to the right of the [Category] values. The calculation is **97.34** for furniture, which is the correct calculation: average of averages (Figure 11.58).

        https://public.tableau.com/views/
            WeightedAverages1047/Dashboard1?:
            language=en-US&:display_count=n&:
            origin=viz_share_link
        https://youtu.be/l8ysFcHBMKg?si=
            uIyd9JvVAUq4iZ1

11.14.7 Worksheets and the Dashboard

In addition to the dashboard, there are five worksheets in this workbook.

- Profit
- Sales
- Expense
- Avg Expense
- Weighted Average

11.14.8 Data and Fields

This chart is based on the *Sample Superstore* data source and utilizes these fields.

Order

Date

Category

Sales

Profit

Expense

Avg Expense

Weighted Average

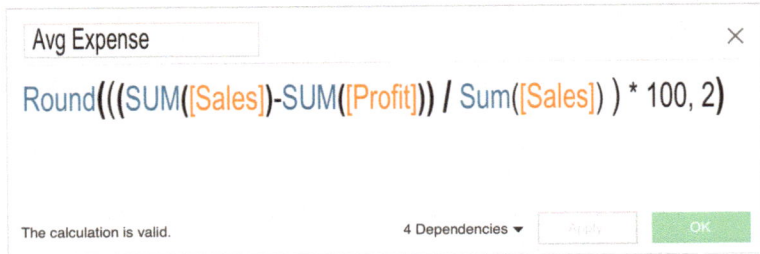

FIGURE 11.59
The Avg expense calculation.

11.14.8.1 *Order Date*

On the **Columns** shelf, the data type for [Order Date] is "Date." For the [Order Date] field, I am using a "Date Part" with the *Date Level* "Year."

> **Year(Order Date)**

11.14.8.2 *Category*

The [Category] field is a **discrete** dimension with a "String" data type. Because [Category] is a **discrete** dimension, headers are added to the view. In this case, row headings are added because [Category] is on the **Rows** shelf. As expected, the field has a blue background or "pill" because it has a **discrete** setting.

11.14.8.3 *Sales*

The data type for [Sales] is a "Number (decimal)." In this workbook, [Sales] is a **continuous** field in my calculated fields.

11.14.8.4 *Profit*

[Profit] is a number field and is also used in calculations.

11.14.8.5 *Expense*

[Expense] is a new calculated field with a data type of "Number." I am not using this field in the average calculation itself. Still, I did want to show how I calculated expenses using the [Sales] and [Profit] fields.

In the **Data** pane, the two green symbols to the left of the field name indicate that this new field is **continuous**. The equal symbol indicates that this is a calculated field, while the pound symbol indicates that it is a number field.

11.14.8.6 *Weighted Average*

[Weighted Average] is a new calculated field with a data type of "Number." The [Weighted Average]

calculated field uses the "avg" aggregation in a "FIXED" LoD expression. We explore this expression a bit later in this example.

> avg({FIXED [Category], Year([Order Date]) : ([Avg Expense]) })

11.14.8.7 *Avg Expense*

[Avg Expense] is a new calculated field with a data type of "Number." The new field uses the "Sum" aggregation with the [Sales] and [Profit] fields, wrapped in the **ROUND()** function (Figure 11.59).

11.14.9 Components or Elements

There are four elements to these views.

- **Rows** Shelf
- **Columns** Shelf
- Text Tile on the **Marks** Card
- Row Grand Totals

11.14.9.1 *Columns Shelf*

The [Order Date] data type on the **Columns** shelf is "Date." For the [Order Date] field, I chose the *Date Level* "Year." Because I checked **discrete**, the field is blue on the **Rows** shelf.

11.14.9.2 *Rows Shelf*

The [Category] field is a **discrete** dimension with a "String" data type. Because [Category] is a **discrete** dimension, *headings* are added to the view; in this case, row headings because [Category] is on the **Rows** shelf. The heading values are:

- Furniture
- Office Supplies
- Technology

FIGURE 11.60
The **Expense** field on the **Marks** card.

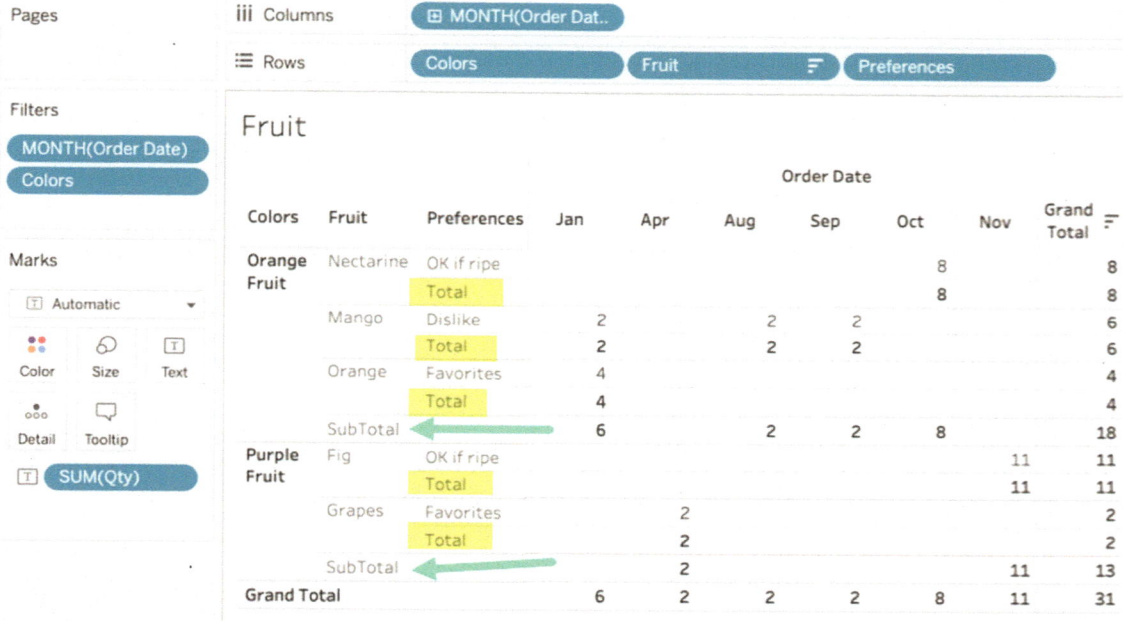

FIGURE 11.61
Subtotals in the View.

11.14.9.3 Text Tile on the Marks Card

The [Weighted Average] field on the *Text* tile on the **Marks** card reflects four years of data.

11.14.9.4 Row Grand Totals

Select "Totals" and "Show Rows Grand Totals" from the **Analysis** menu to add a grand total column on the right side of the chart.

11.14.10 Marks Card: Text

I use a different field on the *Text* tile on each view's **Marks** card to create three views to show Profit, Sales, and Expenses. In Figure 11.60 you can see the **continuous** field [Expense] is on *Text*.

To create the other views, I duplicated the worksheet and replaced the field on the **Marks** card (Figure 11.60).

11.15 Totals

Use the **Analysis** menu or **Analytics** pane to add totals to the view. From the **Analytics** pane, drag "Totals" onto the view. A pop-up window, "Add Totals Dialog," opens. Drop "Totals" onto one of these options.

- Subtotals
- Column Grand Totals
- Row Grand Totals

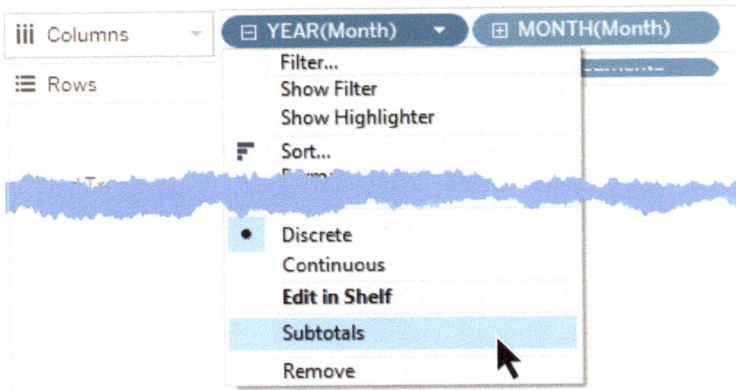

FIGURE 11.62
Subtotals on the Field's Context Menu.

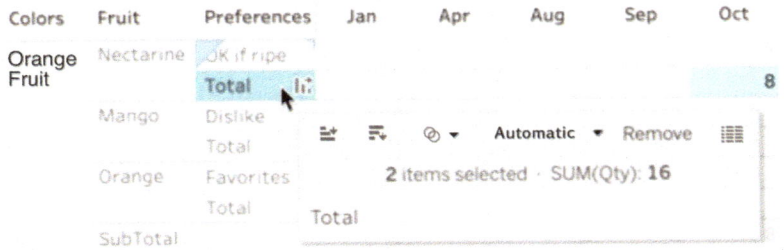

FIGURE 11.63
The Remove Option in the Tooltip.

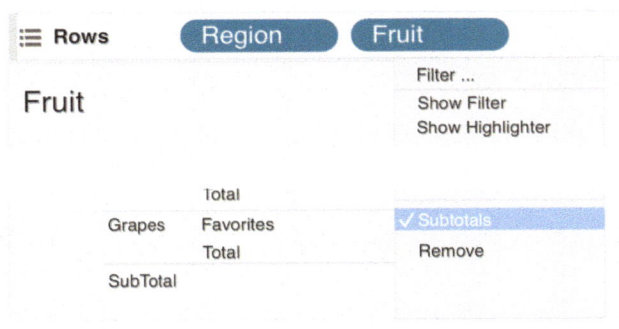

FIGURE 11.64
The **Subtotals** Option in the Field's Context menu.

To add totals, as shown in Figure 11.61, on the **Analysis** menu, select "Totals" and then "Add all subtotals."

Tableau adds "Subtotals" to the field's *context menu*, as shown in Figure 11.62. Depending on the granularity of the view, the *Subtotals* option may not be applicable.

11.15.1 Format Totals

In the **Format Field** pane on the left, on the *Header* tab, format the font in the "Totals" or "Grand Totals"

section. You can also right-click within the "total" area of the chart and choose "Format" from the *context menu*.

In the previous example, all totals are enabled, but in this example, I only want the row "Subtotals." There are two ways to remove the row "Totals."

1. Select any **Total** on the view, and select "Remove" in the pop-up *tooltip* in the upper right corner (Figure 11.63).
2. Right-click the field [Fruit] on the **Rows** shelf and uncheck "Subtotals" (Figure 11.64).

In the following example, I want to turn grand totals off for one column. Figure 11.65 has column grand totals, but I do not want a total for the [Quantity] column.

Because I need to turn off totals for a specific field, I right-click the field name on the **Measure Values** shelf to open its *context menu*. I select "Total using Automatic" and then I choose "Hide."

11.15.2 Include Totals in the Color Property

In the case of a highlight table, you can configure the "Color" property on the **Marks** card to include totals,

FIGURE 11.65
Grand Totals – Columns.

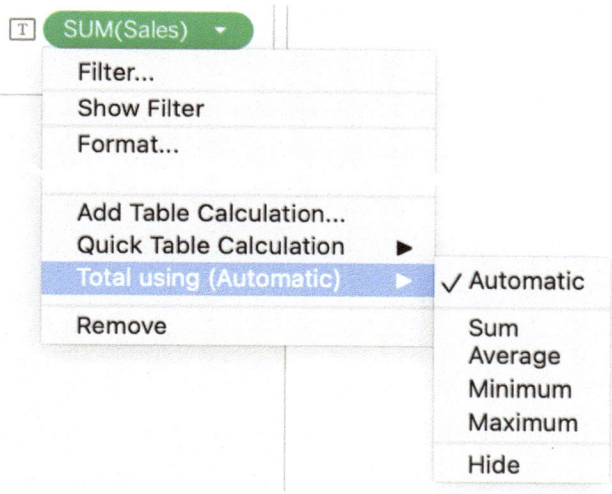

FIGURE 11.66
Total using option in the Field's Context menu.

as shown in *"Section 7.3.7 Highlight Table – Include Totals in Color" on page 143.*

11.15.3 Total Using Sum, Average, Minimum, or Maximum

I like to add average totals using the "Total using" setting on the field's *context menu*, as shown in Figure 11.66. Because I've added totals to the view, there is a choice to "Hide" totals at the bottom of the *context menu*.

12

Formatting

My largest collection of notes covers formatting a visualization because Tableau has dozens of ways to format chart elements. This chapter highlights my favorite formatting choices while illustrating how to utilize nuanced formatting. For example, when we look at lines, I highlight how the options vary depending on the mark or chart type. We also examine how a slight change in "Row Divider" settings impacts lines. To explore additional topics related to formatting, check out the chapters below.

- Dates (**Chapter 9**)
- Labeling (**Chapter 13**)
- Dashboard headings (**Chapter 14**, page 316)

12.1 Elements of the View

Before we look at formatting details, I have labeled the common view elements related to formatting. This example from *"Section 7.3.7 Highlight Table – Include Totals in Color" on page 143* is a basic text or crosstab chart. It has headers from two dimension fields and a column for grand totals. Figure 12.1 does not have the *field label* for the [Order Date], but the *field label* for the [Segment] field on the **Rows** shelf is visible. To see the [Order Date] field label, go to the **Analysis** menu, select "Table Layout," and check "Show Field Labels for Columns."

Let's look at axis charts that show positive and negative values and see the difference when we "swap" the fields on the **Rows** and **Columns** shelves. The **continuous** field [Profit] is on the **Columns** shelf. It creates a horizontal x-axis ranging from negative 5 to 20. The field label "State/Province" is visible in Figure 12.2, and the values from the [State/Province] field create headers underneath the field label.

After swapping fields, the [Profit] field is on the **Rows** shelf and creates a vertical y-axis. Figure 12.4 illustrates the "Field Label" for the [State/Province] field at the top of the canvas. If you have two **continuous** fields on the **Rows** shelf, there are two vertical y-axes on the left and right sides of the chart.

Figure 12.3 shows the headers [Discount] and [Profit] derived from the special Tableau [Measure Names] field. You can format all columns at once by applying format settings to the [Measure Names] field or select individual fields like [Profit] and apply formatting to only that field.

12.1.1 Format an Object

The easiest way to format an object is to right-click it in the view and open the **Format** pane; this also applies to formatting a text object on a dashboard. The **Format** menu is another way to open the **Format** pane (Figure 1.35).

DOI: 10.1201/9781003566458-13

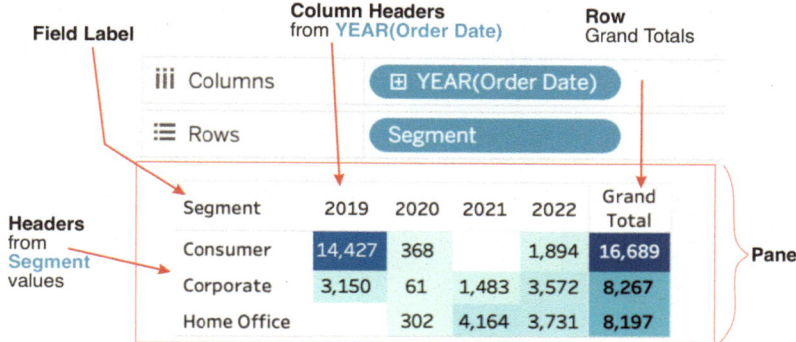

FIGURE 12.1
View objects.

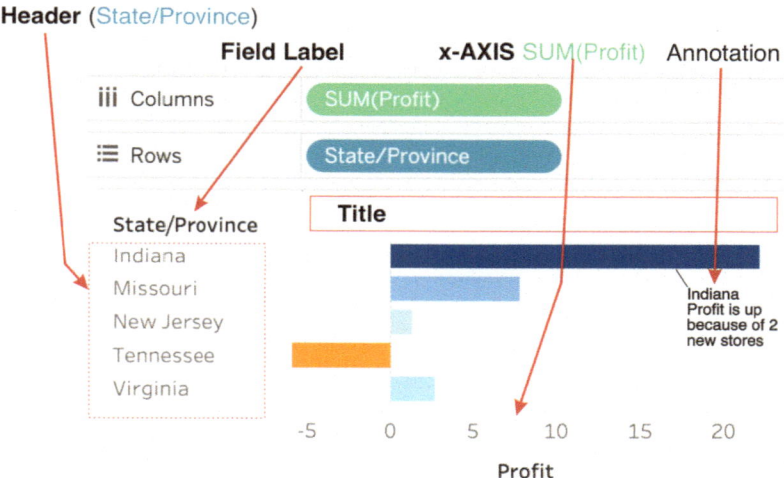

FIGURE 12.2
Field label and headers.

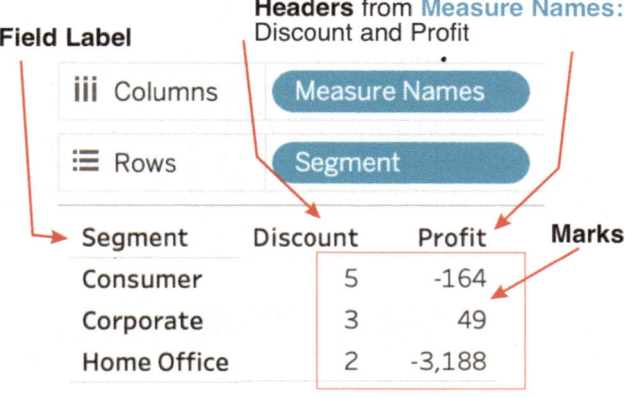

FIGURE 12.3
Headers.

12.2 Format Control Panes

The **Format Control** pane is the central location for formatting. When you right-click an object on your worksheet, the object's *context menu* has a "Format" choice that opens a **Format Control** pane specific to that object. The contents of a **Format Control** pane vary depending on the type of object selected. A bold heading in the top-left corner of the **Format Control** pane indicates the object type. Another way to open a **Format Control** pane is to use the **Format** menu at the top of the Tableau screen. In Figure 12.6, the **Format Control** pane heading in the top-left corner is **Format Font**.

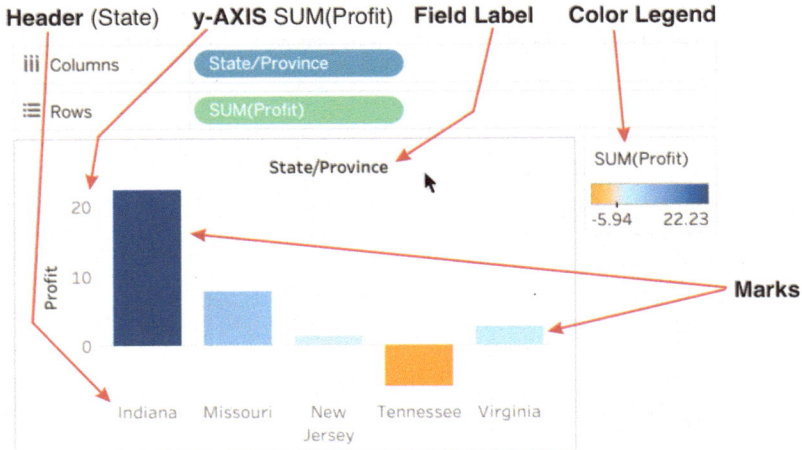

FIGURE 12.4
y-axis and color legend.

FIGURE 12.5
Tip: Tableau applies format changes to the view immediately, so you will see the view change as you adjust the Format pane settings.

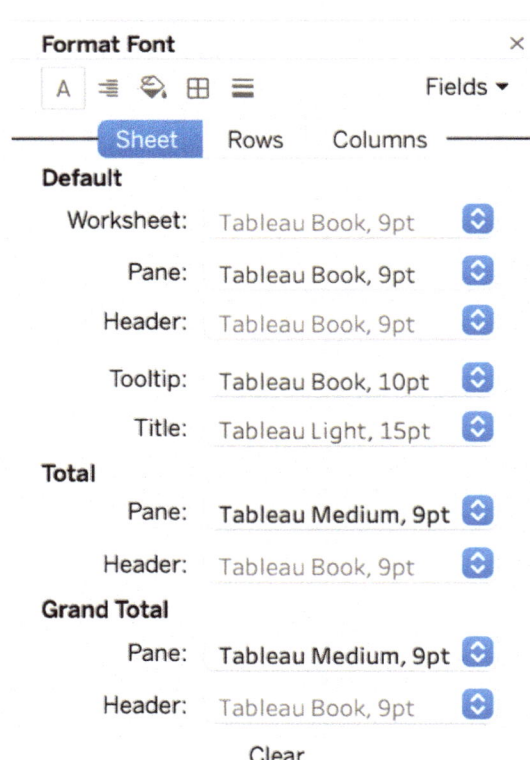

FIGURE 12.6
Format Font.

Each **Format Control** pane has tool icons at the top, a row of various tab groups below, and sections with different options.

- Tools
- Tab Groups
- Options

> When you update an item in the **Format** pane, the title is bold. If you right-click the bold item title, you can "clear" the changes. If you kept the default setting, the clear button at the bottom of the pane is unavailable.

12.3 Fonts

You can set the font style for the entire workbook and change the font for every element on the worksheet. Right-click within the body of the chart and choose **Format** from the *context menu*. On the Sheet tab, select the default font.

12.4 Alignment

In addition to aligning text within a column or row, you can control the direction of header text so that text

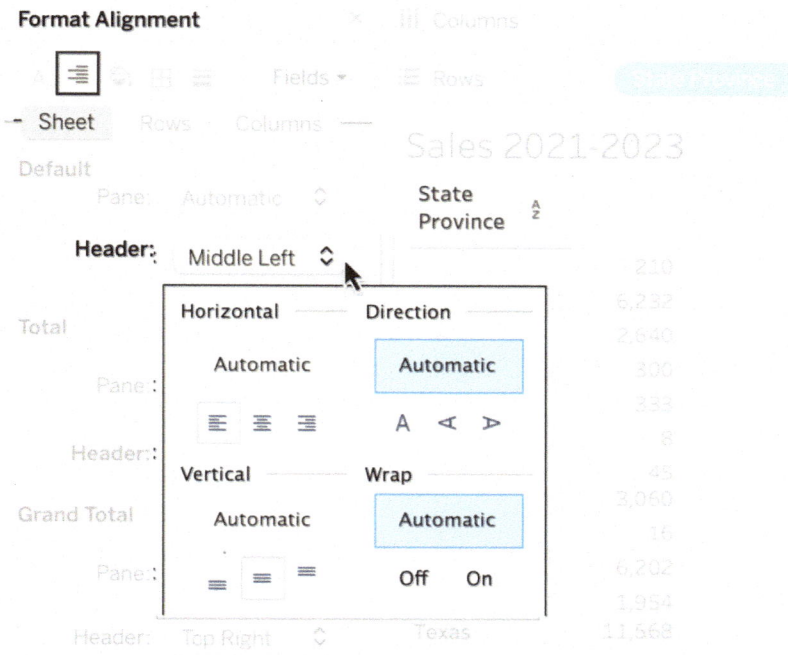

FIGURE 12.7
The **Format Alignment** pane.

is horizontal or vertical. To rotate header text, see the topic, "Format Menu, Rotate Labels." *"Section 12.18 Analysis: Table Layout" on page 286* looks at handling empty rows that throw off alignment. Alignment settings include:

- Horizontal – left, right, or center.
- Vertical – top, middle, or bottom.
- Wrap Headers.
- Vertical Text: top-to-bottom or bottom-to-top.

12.4.1 Vertical Alignment

This example is something you use sparingly. Still, I sometimes have headers that span 2-3 rows, and I want to control the vertical alignment. My header below is "State Province." To illustrate alignment options, I center the heading.

1. From the **Format** menu at the top of the screen, select the "Alignment" tool. The **Format** control pane opens on the left.
2. Select the Sheet tab.
3. Click the drop-down arrow for "Alignment" to select settings for *Header* (Figure 12.7).
4. Select the "Columns" tab, as shown below. In the bottom-right corner of the **Format**

Alignment drop-down menu, there are options for control wrapping (Figure 12.8).

12.4.2 Center Column Values

There are several ways to change alignment to center data within a column, such as using the "Alignment" tool in the **Format** pane. The examples that follow set alignment at these levels:

- A field or all fields with the special [Measure Names] field.
- The Sheet.
- Within the *Text* tile on the **Marks** card with the "Alignment" setting in the **Edit Label** box.

12.4.2.1 Format Pane

Follow these steps to align the [Customer Name] column using the **Format** pane. In this example, the [Customer Name] field is on the *Text* tile of the **Marks** card.

1. Right-click within the column on the canvas and choose "Format." The **Format** control pane opens on the left. You could also select a field from the "Fields" drop-down at the top-right corner of the **Format** control pane.

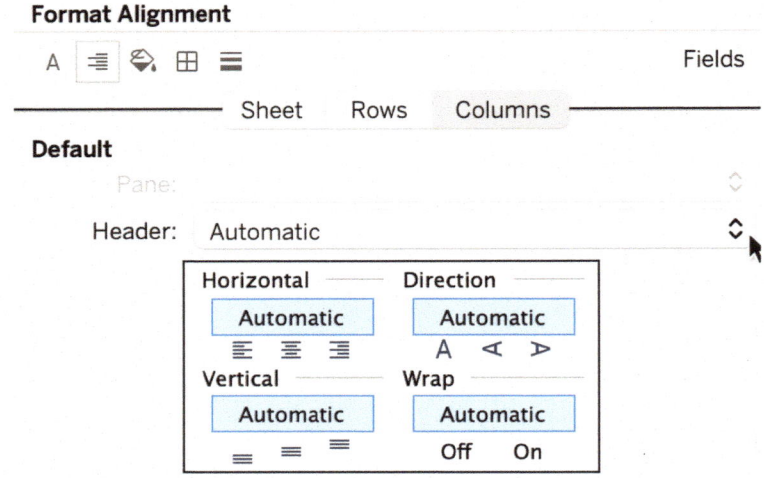

FIGURE 12.8
The Header Options for alignment.

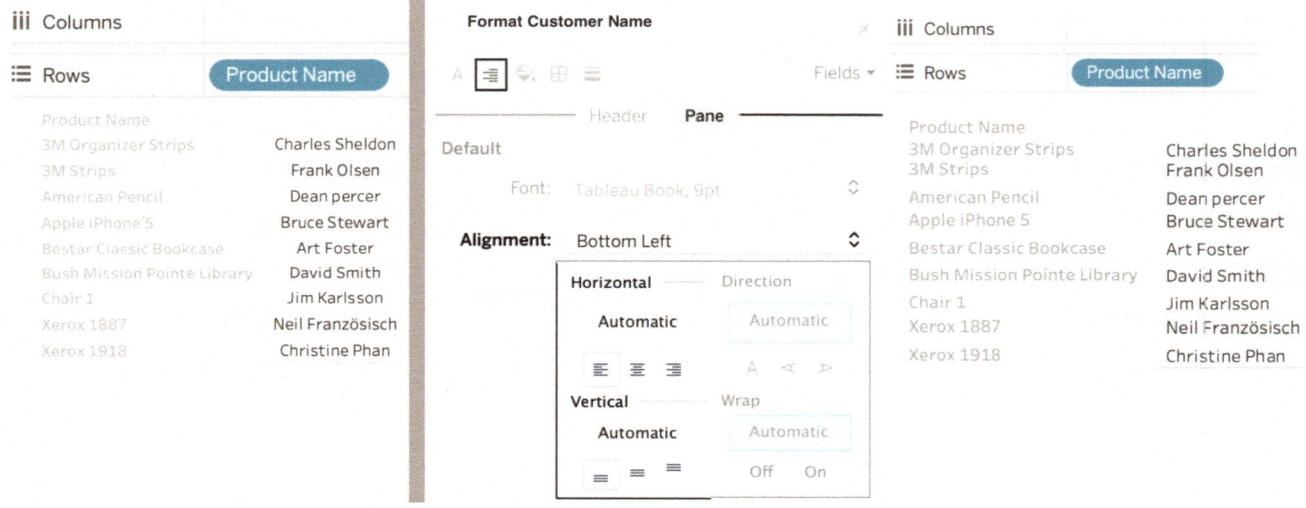

FIGURE 12.9
Formatting the Customer Name Field's alignment.

2. In the top-left corner of the **Format** control pane, click the "Alignment" tool and select the *Pane* tab.

3. In the "Default" section of the **Format** control pane on the left, click the drop-down arrow for "Alignment" and select the appropriate alignment buttons. The customer name is center-aligned on the left side of the following image. After the change, you can see the left alignment in the example on the right side (Figure 12.9).

When you drag a number field like [Sales] onto the *Text* tile, Tableau adds a column to the visualization, as shown in Figure 12.10. To change the appearance of the numbers, right-click anywhere in the column and choose "Format."

In Figure 12.11, I have [Measure Values] on the *Text* tile of the **Marks** card. I can use [Measure Values] to format several fields at once.

12.4.2.2 Text Tile Alignment

To center the [Measure Values] column numbers vertically, click the *Text* tile on the **Marks** Card and change alignment to "Middle Center," as shown in Figure 12.12.

After the change, the numbers are centered in the columns, as shown in Figure 12.13.

12.4.3 Text Tile – Edit Label

To align row data horizontally, use the "Alignment" tool in the **Format** pane. While my **Format Alignment** control pane is set to "Middle Center" in Figure 12.14, the numbers are slightly below the "Product Name" headers.

When I check the *Text* tile on the **Marks** card, I can see in Figure 12.15 that the first rows are blank.

I caused empty rows while experimenting and moving fields around in my visualization.

After I remove the blank rows, the numbers line up horizontally as expected, as shown in Figure 12.16.

12.4.4 Format Pane – Measure Values

Follow these steps to the center columns for the chart in Figure 12.17. In this example, [Measure Values] is on the *Text* tile of the **Marks** card.

1. Right-click within the column and choose "Format." The **Format** pane opens on the left.

2. In the **Format** pane, click the "Alignment" tool in the top-left corner and select the Sheet tab.

3. In the "Default" section, click the drop-down arrow for *Pane* and click the center alignment buttons, as shown below (Figure 12.18).

12.5 Shading

When we look at axis rulers in the following "Lines" topic, I use worksheet shading to make the background for a floating chart invisible. This setting is handy with layered or floating worksheets on a dashboard.

Shading is also handy if you are trying to identify a particular setting, such as a vertical line. Changing the

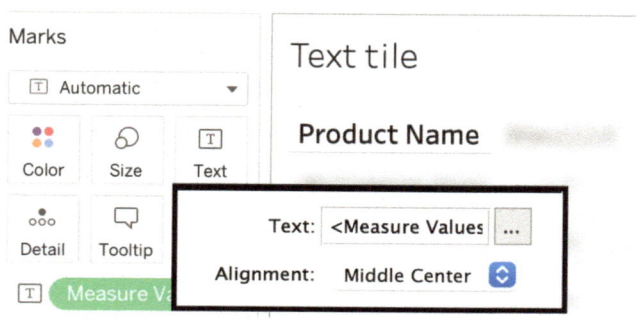

FIGURE 12.12
Text alignment.

Product Name	Discount	Quantity
3M Organizer Strips	2.50	24.00
3M Strips	0.20	2.00
American Pencil	0.00	14.00
Xerox 1963	0.20	2.00

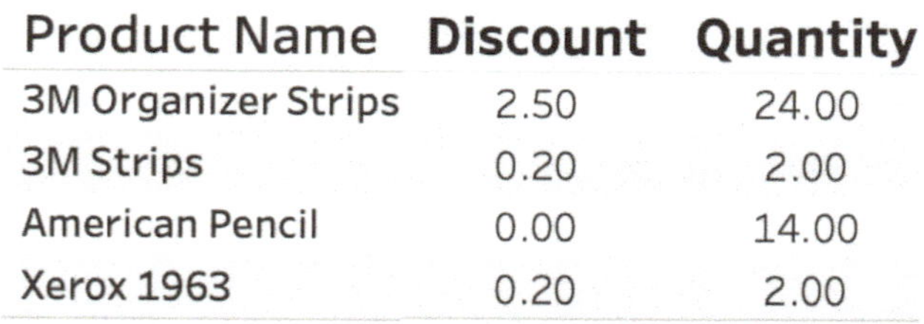

FIGURE 12.13
Centered numbers.

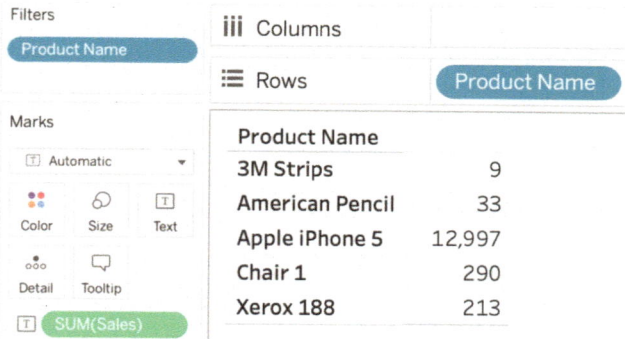

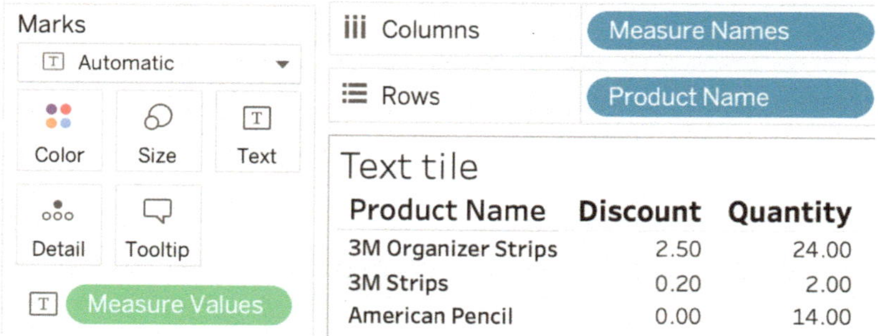

FIGURE 12.10
Text Column.

FIGURE 12.11
Measured values.

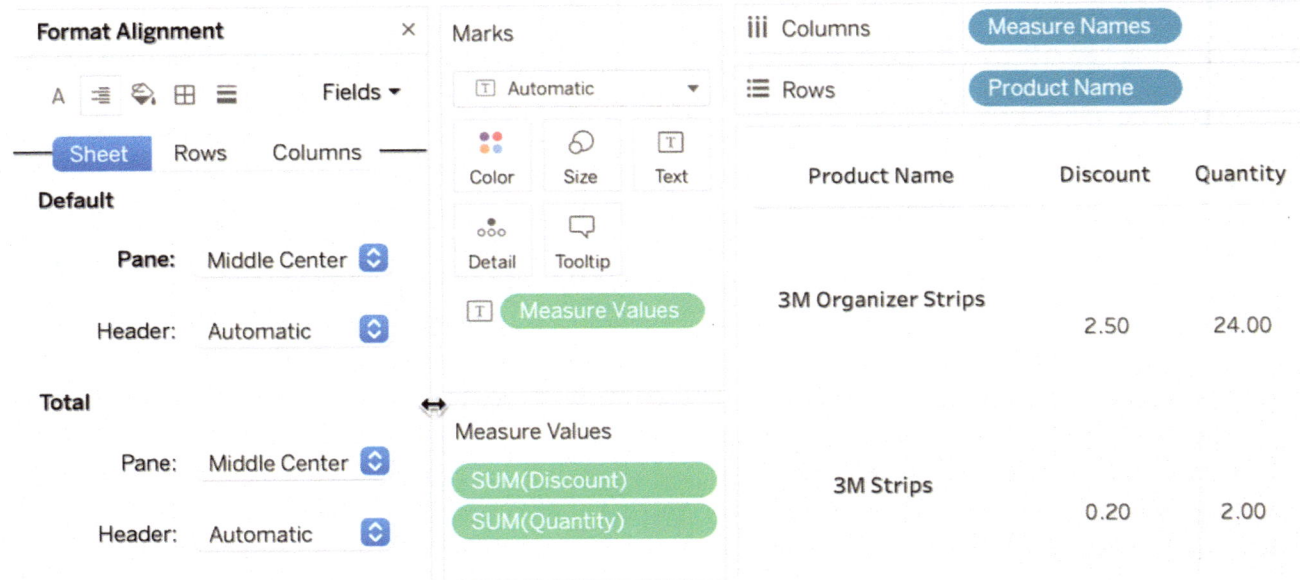

FIGURE 12.14
Numbers below headers.

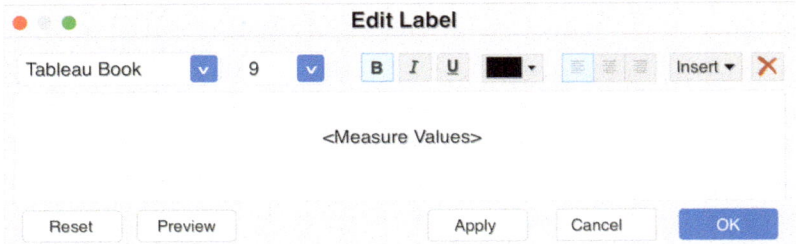

FIGURE 12.15
Edit Label dialog box.

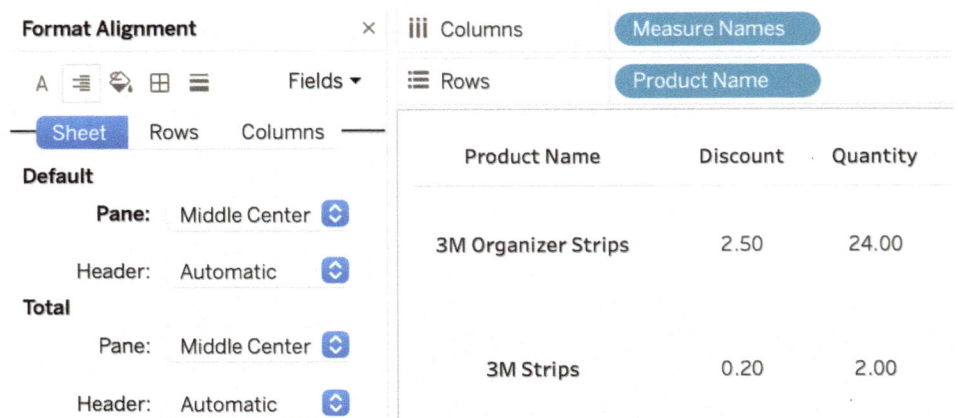

FIGURE 12.16
Numbers aligned to headers.

worksheet background to a dark color can make lines stand out, allowing you to find the correct line setting in the **Format** pane.

1. To open a **Format Shading** control pane from any worksheet, on the **Format** menu at the top of the screen, select "Shading…"

2. The **Format Shading** control pane opens on the left, and a box around the "Shading" tool indicates that this is the selected tool.

3. On the Sheet tab, set the "Worksheet" shading to "None."

In Figure 12.19, I'd like to change the light gray line at the bottom of the chart to dark gray. I use a contrasting color for shading to make lines and borders stand out.

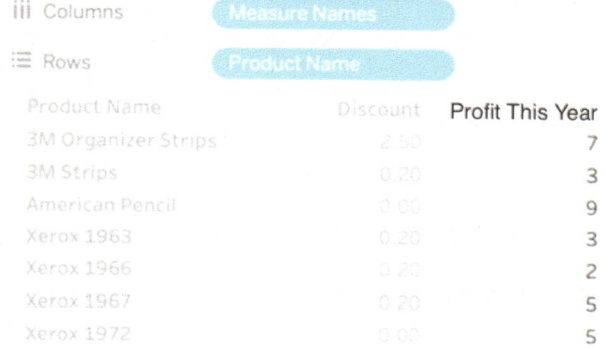

FIGURE 12.17
Numbers aligned to the right side of the Column.

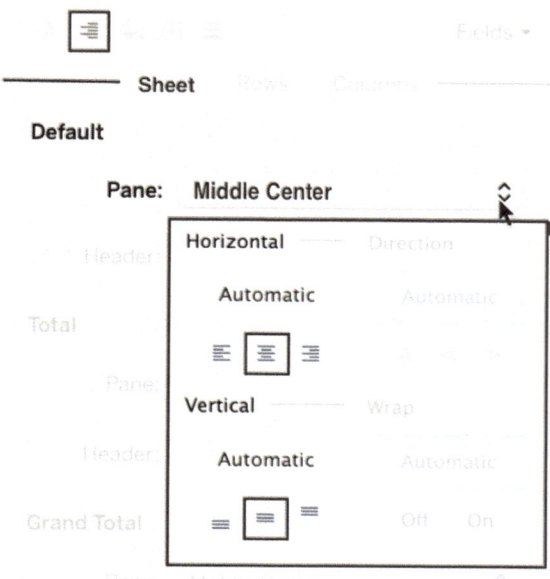

FIGURE 12.18
The **Format Alignment** pane.

I select the "Shading" tool and the Sheet tab in the **Format** pane. At the top of the **Format** pane, in the "Default" section, I click the drop-down arrow by **Worksheet** to change the background to dark gray, as shown in Figure 12.19.

In Figure 12.20, I selected the "Border" tool and the Rows tab. In the **Row Divider** section, I changed **Pane** to a thick red dashed line as an example.

12.5.1 Row Banding

To shade every other row, use the Shading tool and "Row Banding." Right-click within the body of the chart and select "Format." In the **Format** pane on the left, select the shading tool that looks like a paint pot at the top of the pane. On the Sheet tab, scroll down to change **Row Banding** for the *Pane* and *Header*. By default, row banding is active, so the headings *Pane* and *Header* are not bold in the left **Format Shading** pane in Figure 12.21. Bold headings in the **Format** pane indicate a change from the default setting.

Level also affects the shaded lines, as demonstrated in Figure 12.22, where I have dark shading for the "Apr" and "Dec" rows. In the **Format Shading** pane on the left, the **Level** indicator is on the right side of this example.

To apply the shading to the "City" and "Year" columns, I move the **Level** to the left, as shown in Figure 12.23. Be sure to *click* to select a level instead of trying to slide the toggle. Depending on the headers in the view, you may have to adjust the **Level** to extend

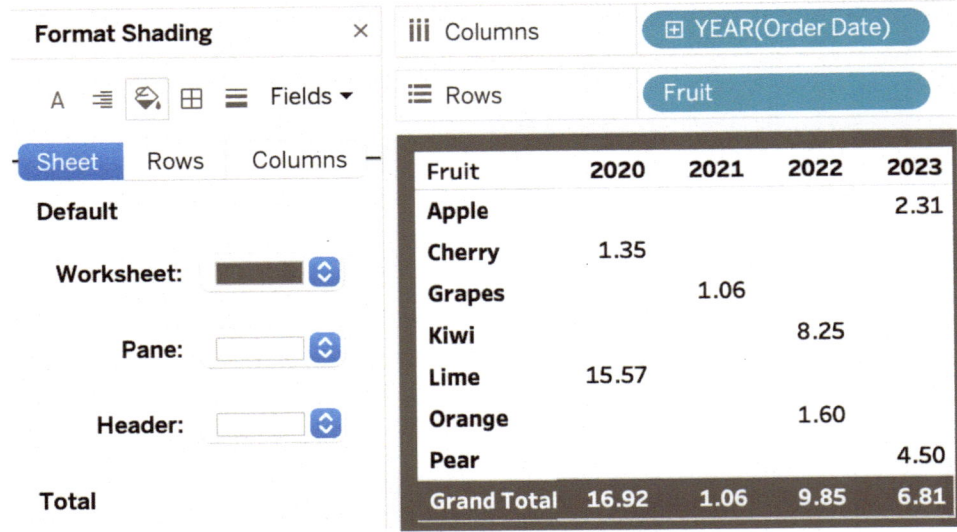

FIGURE 12.19
Worksheet shading.

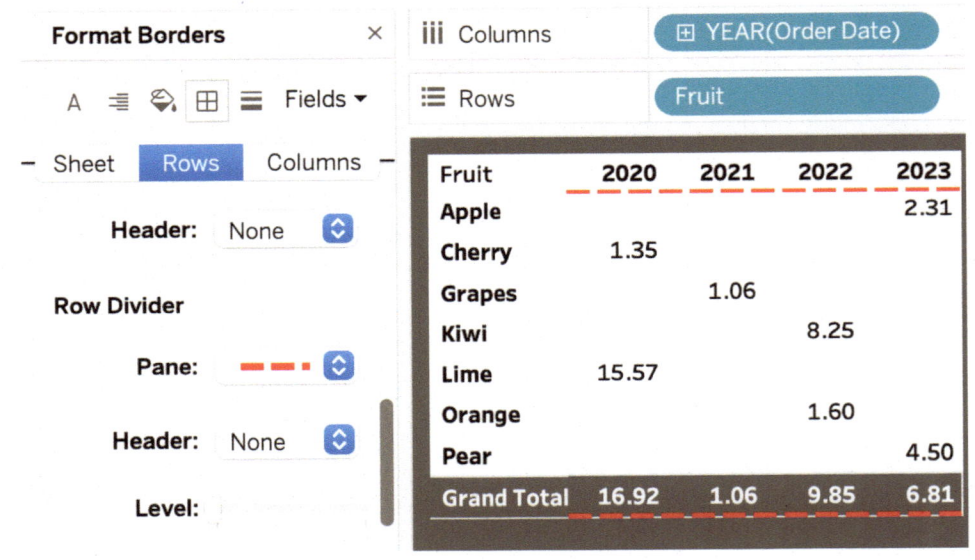

FIGURE 12.20
Row Divider: Pane.

the shading to include all headers, and it may not necessarily be to the left as in the previous example.

12.5.2 Column Banding

Select the shading tool in the **Format** pane on the left to adjust column banding. On the Sheet tab, scroll down to change **Column Banding**. In Figure 12.24, I shaded columns 2020 and 2022 and turned off **Row Banding**. You may need to turn off **Row Banding** so the entire column is shaded.

12.5.3 Worksheet Shading (Background)

Use the shading tool to set the background shading for the worksheet. At the top of the **Format** pane in the "Default" section, change the "Worksheet" color. *"Section 14.16 Horizontal Radial Buttons to Change Filters" on page 323* illustrates how to change shading. When a view has a dark background, it may help to use the "Halo" setting on the **Marks** card to make the mark more visible, as explained in *"Section 7.3 The Color Property" on page 139.*

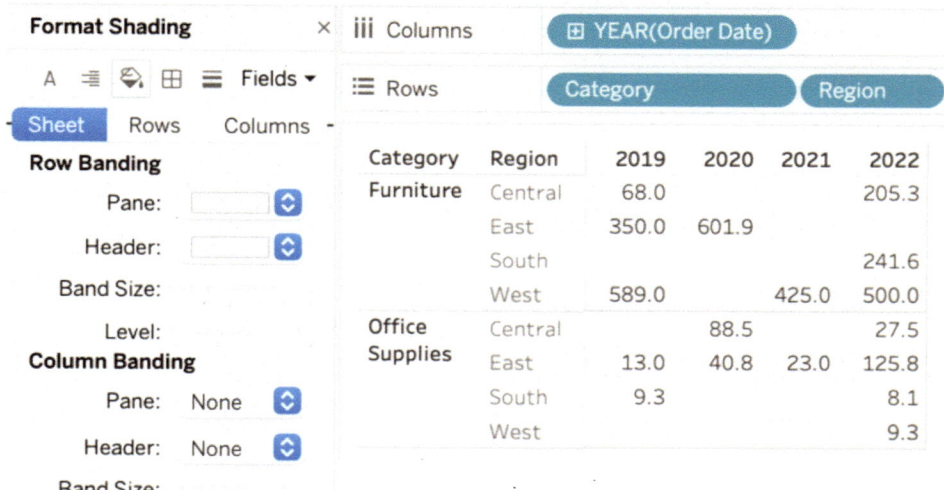

FIGURE 12.21
Row Banding on the Sheet tab.

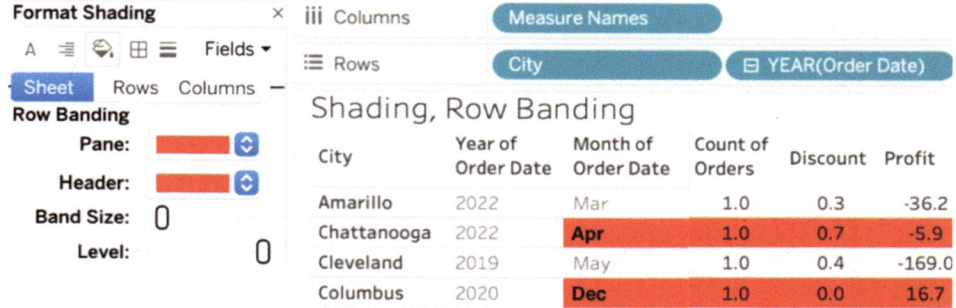

FIGURE 12.22
Row Banding: level.

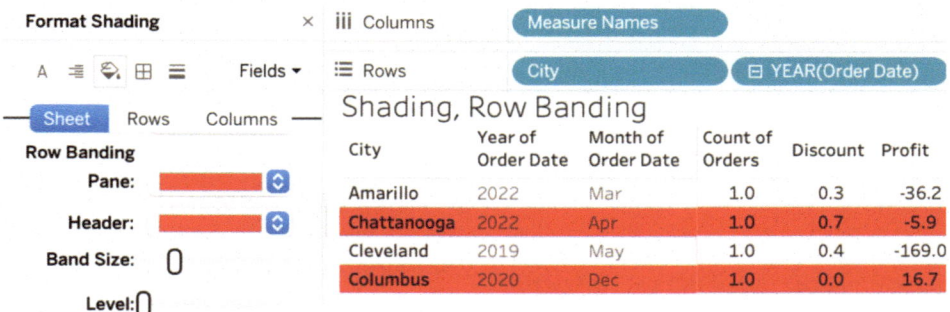

FIGURE 12.23
Level on the far left.

12.6 Borders

When working with shaded backgrounds, the borders tool creates a clean edge around the view, especially on a dashboard. In these examples, we explore several "mark types" to see how Tableau applies the same setting to different types of marks. I also included an example of the *Level* setting.

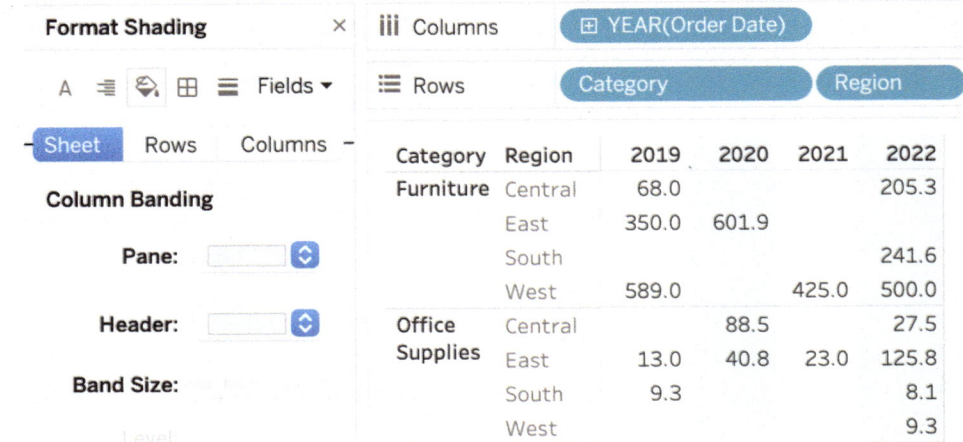

FIGURE 12.24
Column Banding.

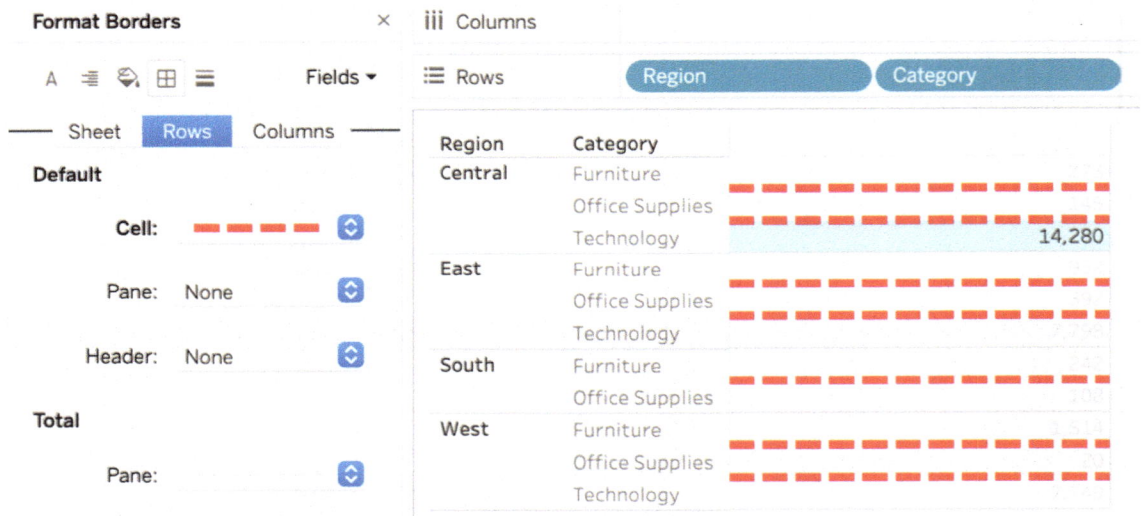

FIGURE 12.25
Cell borders.

12.6.1 Default: Cell

In Figure 12.25, the horizontal row of the dark red "Cell" *borders* between each row of data is distracting. To illustrate cell borders, I changed the lines in this example to thick, dashed red.

1. Right-click anywhere within the view and select "Format."

2. Click the *Borders* tool at the top of the left pane and select the Rows tab.

3. Click the drop-down arrows for *Cell* and adjust the formatting.

Figure 12.26 is another example of the same formatting setting with a shaded background. If you want a border around the entire cell, combine other formatting with the "Cell" borders.

12.6.2 Row Divider

In Figure 12.27, I change the horizontal line formatting. I selected the *Borders* tool in the **Format** control pane on the left. I am editing the **Row Divider** option on the Rows tab; use the "Columns" tab and the **Column Divider** section for vertical lines. *"Section 14.16 Horizontal Radial Buttons to Change Filters" on page 328* illustrates how to set the **Row Divider** to

Region	Category	Profit	Sales
Central	Furniture	-49	273
	Office Supplies	60	145
	Technology	-1,190	14,280
East	Furniture	-100	952
	Office Supplies	165	392
	Technology	1,157	7,798
South	Furniture	0	242
	Office Supplies	29	108

FIGURE 12.26
Cell Borders with shaded background.

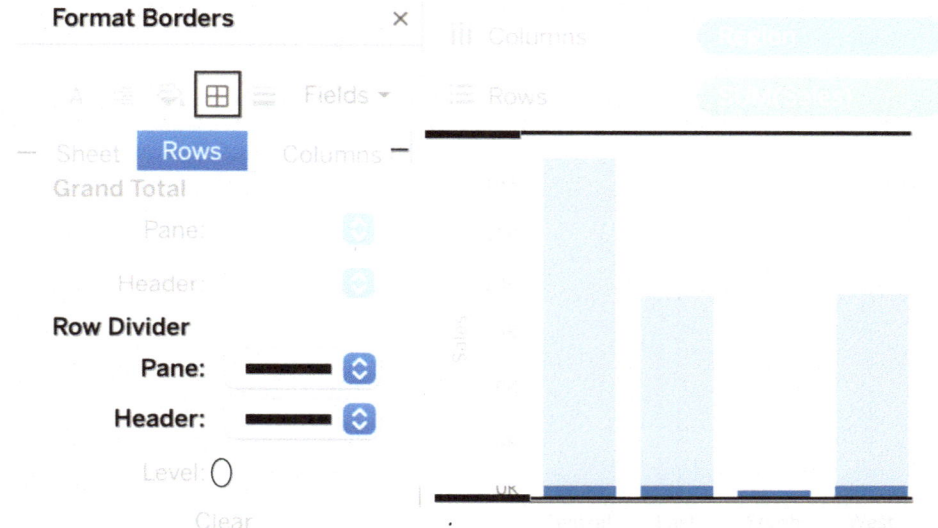

FIGURE 12.27
Row Divider.

"None." The earlier example, "Shading," also illustrated changing this setting.

1. Right-click anywhere within the view and select "Format."
2. Select the *Border* tool at the top of the **Format Borders** pane on the left, and then select the Rows tab for horizontal lines. Scroll down in the left pane to see the **Row Divider** section.
3. Click the drop-down arrows for *Pane* and *Header* and choose "None."

When looking at **Row Dividers** for a "Text" chart, you can customize the appearance of the lines in several ways. In the Figure 12.30, I scroll down to the **Row Divider** options in the **Format Borders** pane on the Sheet tab. I select the *Borders* tool at the top of the pane on the left. The "Row Divider, Pane" has dashed red lines, and the *Level* is 0.

4. When I click on the right side of the **Level** bar, Tableau adds lines between the rows. Note I did not click in the middle of the bar or try to "slide" the bar to the right (Figure 12.28).

12.6.3 Column Divider

The *Column Divider* border tool has the same options as a *Row Divider*, as shown in Figure 12.29. I selected the *Borders* tool for the **Column Divider** in the **Format** pane and adjusted the *Pane* setting to add dashed lines.

After I change the "Level," there are lines between the columns, as shown in Figure 12.29. I added dotted

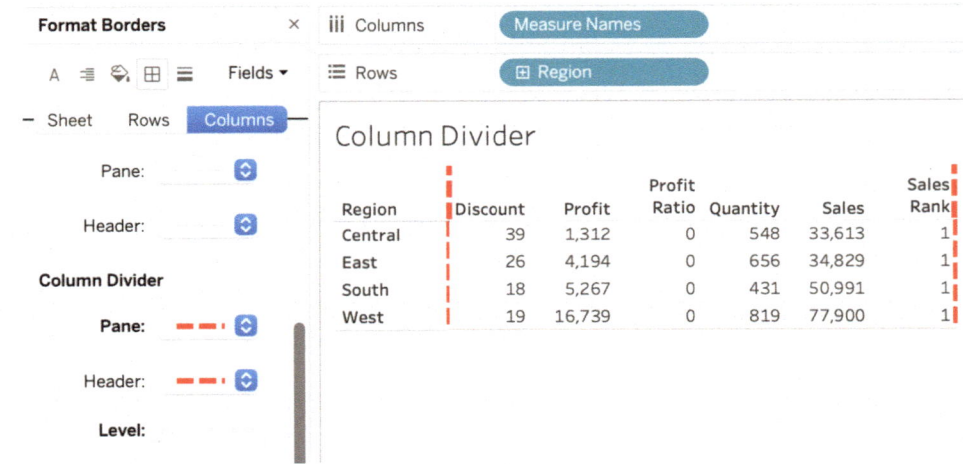

FIGURE 12.28
The Level Slider in the **Format Borders** pane.

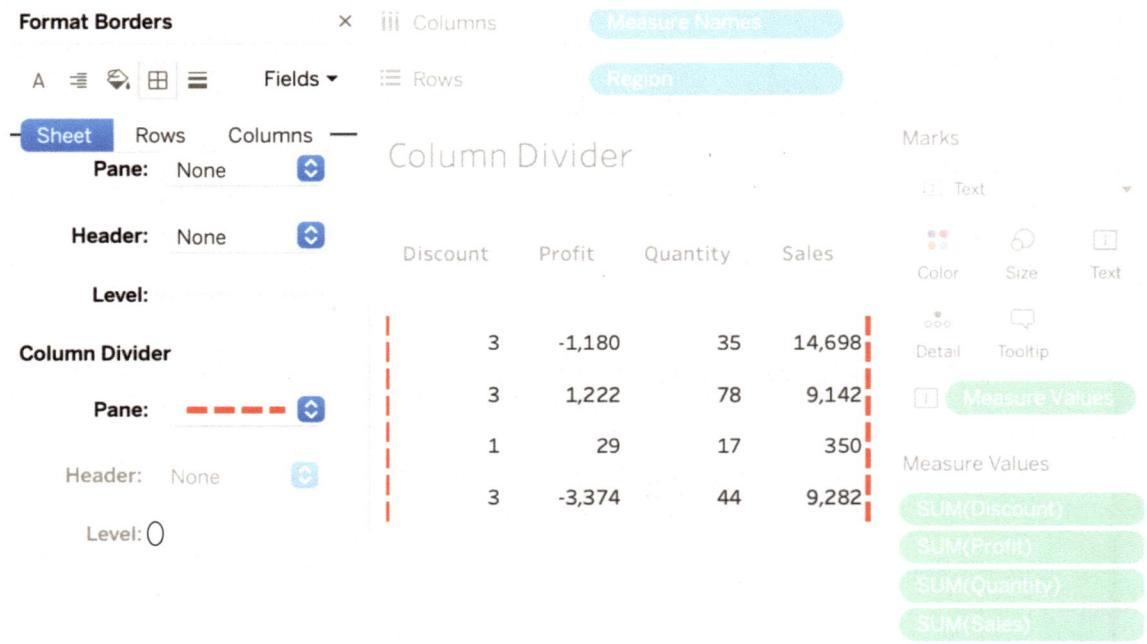

FIGURE 12.29
Column Divider.

"Header" lines using the *Borders* tool and the **Column Divider** *Header* setting.

Figure 12.31 is another example of borders. I want to turn the lines off between the data and the grand total column. I change the **Pane** setting in the **Total** area to "None" to remove the lines.

As with many formatting options, there is more than one way to change the formatting. In Figure 12.32, I selected the *Borders* tool and the Sheet tab in the **Format** pane. In the **Default** section, I changed the setting for the **Cell** to red dashed lines.

12.6.3.1 Divider between Columns

The *Column Divider* border tool option *Level* controls the dividers between columns. In Figure 12.33, the column divider for the **Pane** is orange between the [Region] column and the three-year columns from [Order Date]. Notice the **Level** slider is on the left side.

When I click the right side of the "Level" slider in Figure 12.34, Tableau adds dividers between the year columns. Depending on your background and line colors, a column divider can also add a bit of space between the columns.

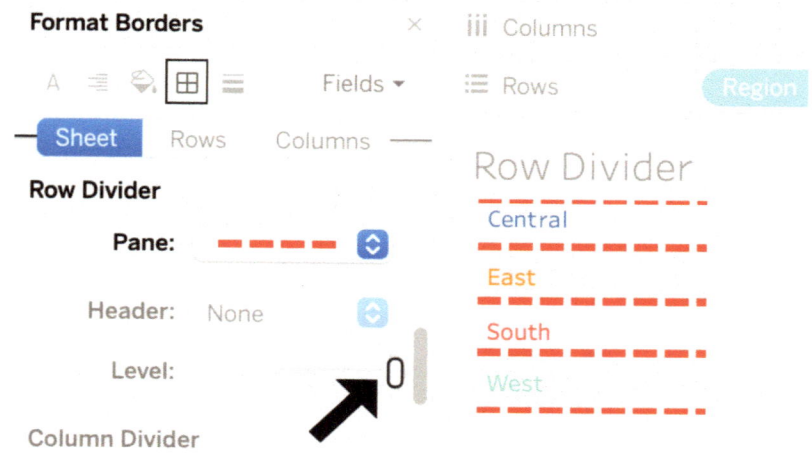

FIGURE 12.30
Column Divider vertical lines.

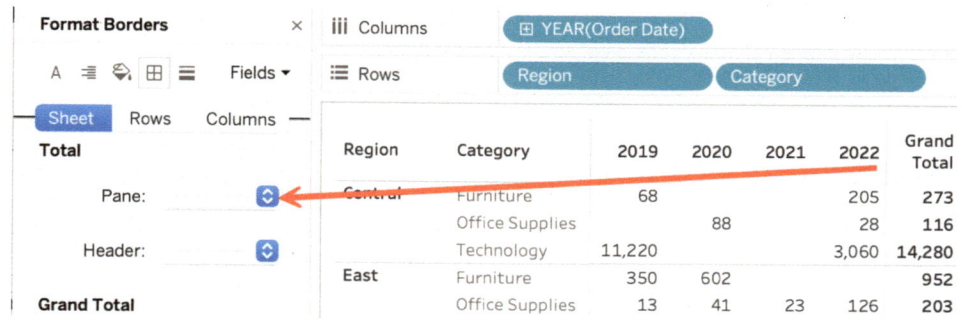

FIGURE 12.31
Pane borders.

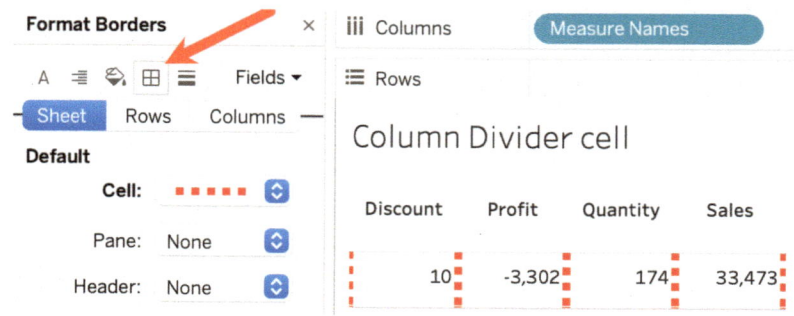

FIGURE 12.32
Sheet Tab, Cell.

12.7 Lines

When formatting lines, use the drop-down arrows to change the line *thickness*, *style*, *color*, and *opacity*, as shown in Figure 12.35. If I layer floating charts on a dashboard, I like to change the horizontal **Grid Lines** and **Axis Rulers** to "None." *"Section 10.4.3 Slope Chart with a Rank Table Calculation" on page 215* also changes the grid and zero lines (Figure 12.37).

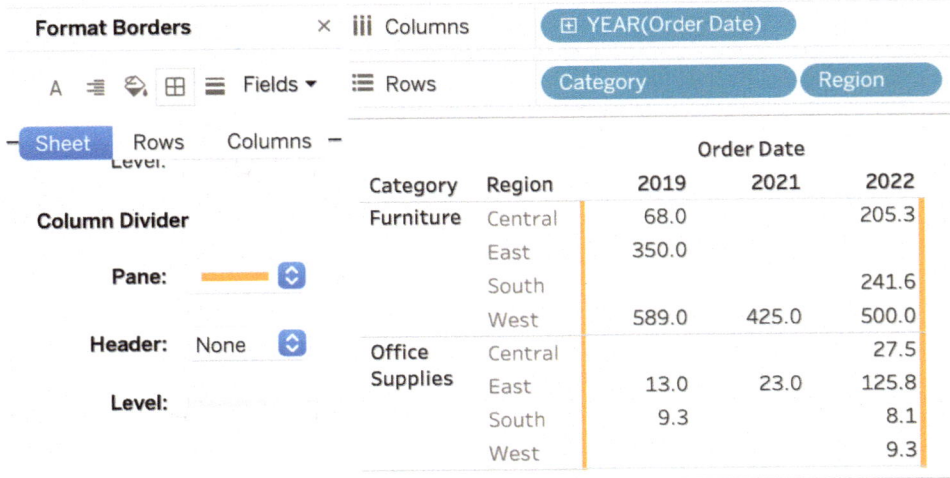

FIGURE 12.33
Column Divider: pane.

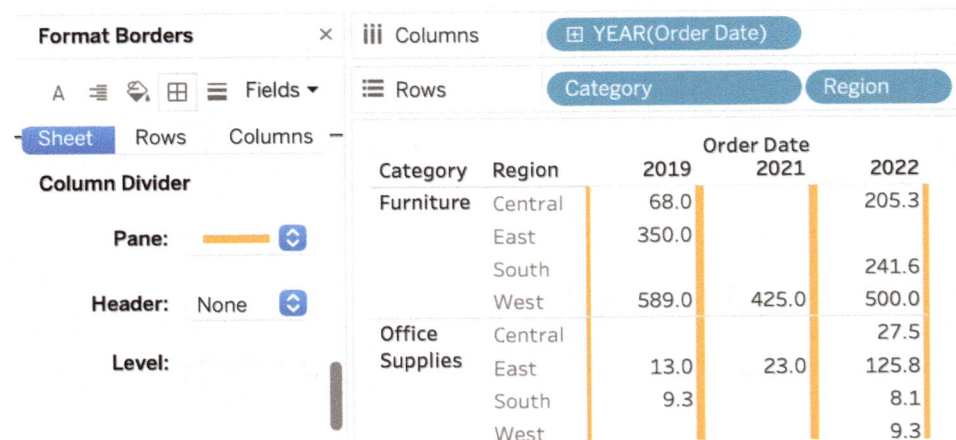

FIGURE 12.34
Column Divider: level.

12.7.1 Grid Lines

In Figure 12.37, I selected the "Lines" tool at the top of the **Format Lines** pane. The Columns tab is selected, and the **Grid Lines** are dark red dashed lines.

12.7.2 Format the Workbook Grid Lines

Another way to hide grid lines is to set the *opacity* to 0%. In Figure 12.38, in the **Format** menu, I selected "Workbook." In the *Lines* section, I used the drop-down arrow to open the color picker, and at the bottom, I set the opacity to 0%.

12.7.3 Horizontal Grid Lines

The *Grid Lines* setting for a text chart adds lines between the text rows, as shown in Figure 12.39.

In the bullet chart in Figure 12.40, the *Grid Lines* setting is a thick black line.

If you do not want a gap between the bullet bars, change *Grid Lines* to "None," as shown in Figure 12.41.

1. Right-click anywhere within the view and select "Format" to change horizontal lines.

2. Click the "Lines" tool at the top of the **Format** pane on the left and select the Rows tab for horizontal lines. Note, use the "Columns" tab to change vertical lines.

3. In this example, the grid lines are thick red. You could click the drop-down arrows for *Grid Lines* and choose "None" to remove the lines (Figure 12.42).

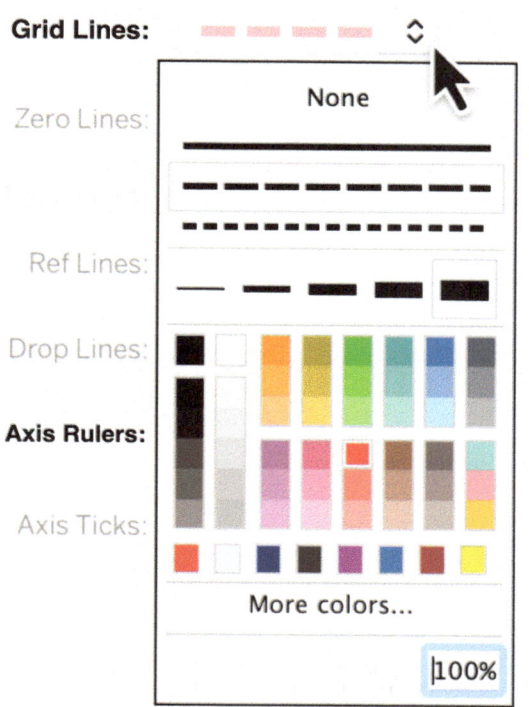

FIGURE 12.35
Grid Line drop-down options.

FIGURE 12.36
Tip: If you run across vertical lines between columns not controlled by the Borders or Lines settings in the Format control pane, check the Color tile on the **Marks** card and adjust the opacity to 0%.

12.7.4 Axis Rulers

By default, Tableau adds thin, light gray "Axis Ruler" lines to a chart. To illustrate the vertical "Axis Ruler" in Figure 12.43, I use a thick pink dashed line on the left side of the chart.

In Figure 12.44, I added the "Sales 2022" chart to a new dashboard as the chart on the bottom; I set the default background color to light blue. "Sales 2022" is the bottom chart. Next, I dragged the "Sales 2019"

FIGURE 12.38
Opacity.

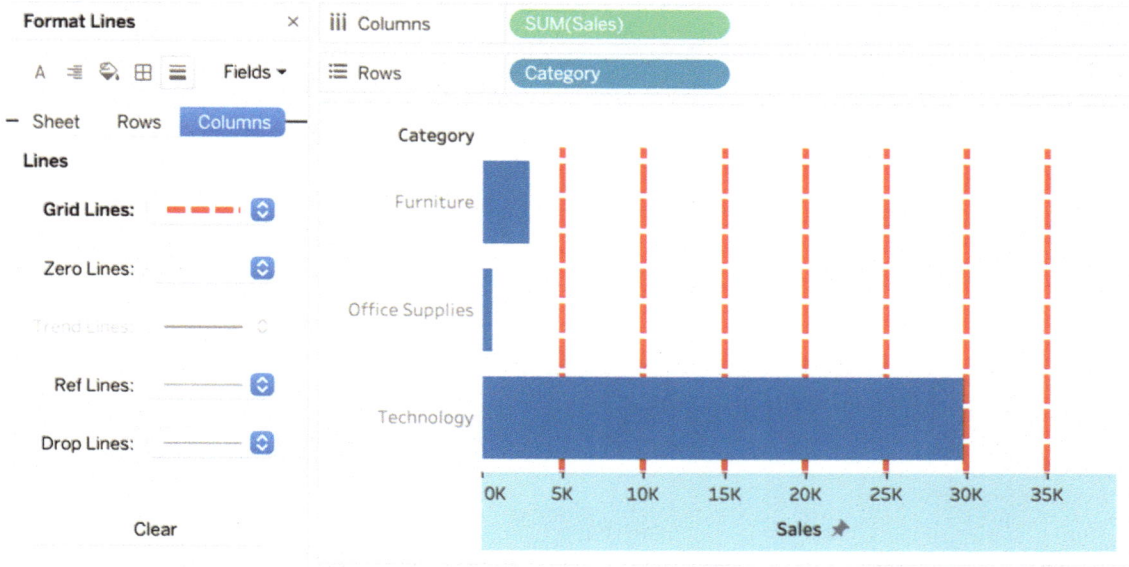

FIGURE 12.37
Columns: Grid lines.

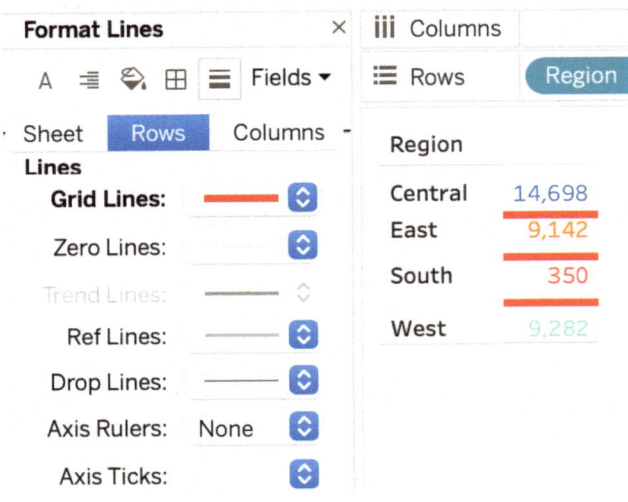

FIGURE 12.39
Rows: Grid lines.

chart onto the first chart as a floating object on top of the "Sales 2022" chart. **Chapter 14** has examples of floating objects and backgrounds. A dark-gray bounding box indicates that "Sales 2019" is still selected.

When I view the dashboard in "Presentation" mode in Figure 12.45, the vertical "Axis Ruler" stands out.

1. To remove the "Axis Ruler," right-click anywhere within the body of the "Sales 2019" chart and choose "Format."
2. At the top of the **Format** control panel on the left, select the "Lines" tool and then select the Rows tab.
3. Use the drop-down arrows for **Axis Ruler** to change the formatting to "None." The annoying dashed line is no longer visible, as shown below (Figure 12.46).

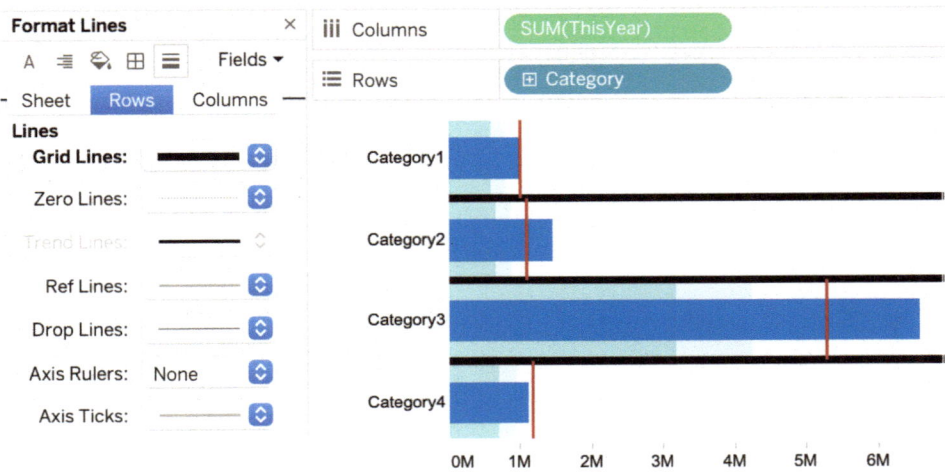

FIGURE 12.40
Thick Black Grid Line.

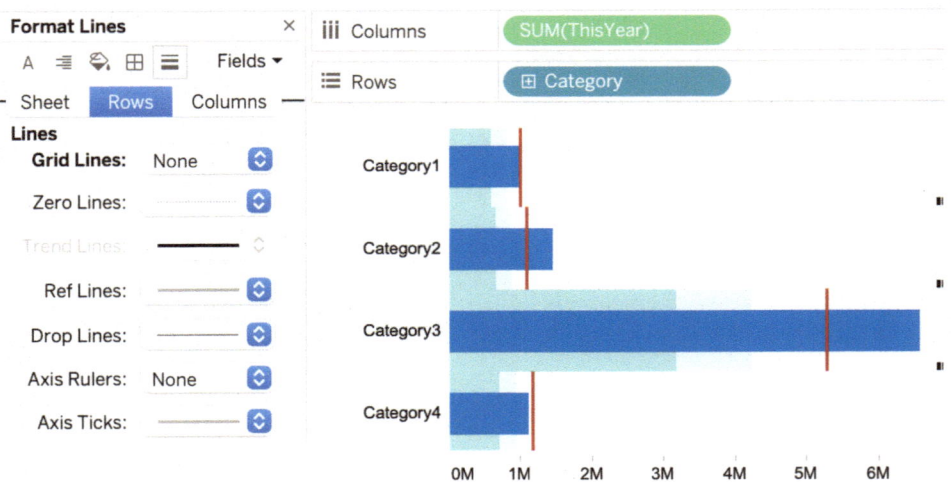

FIGURE 12.41
Grid Lines Set to "None."

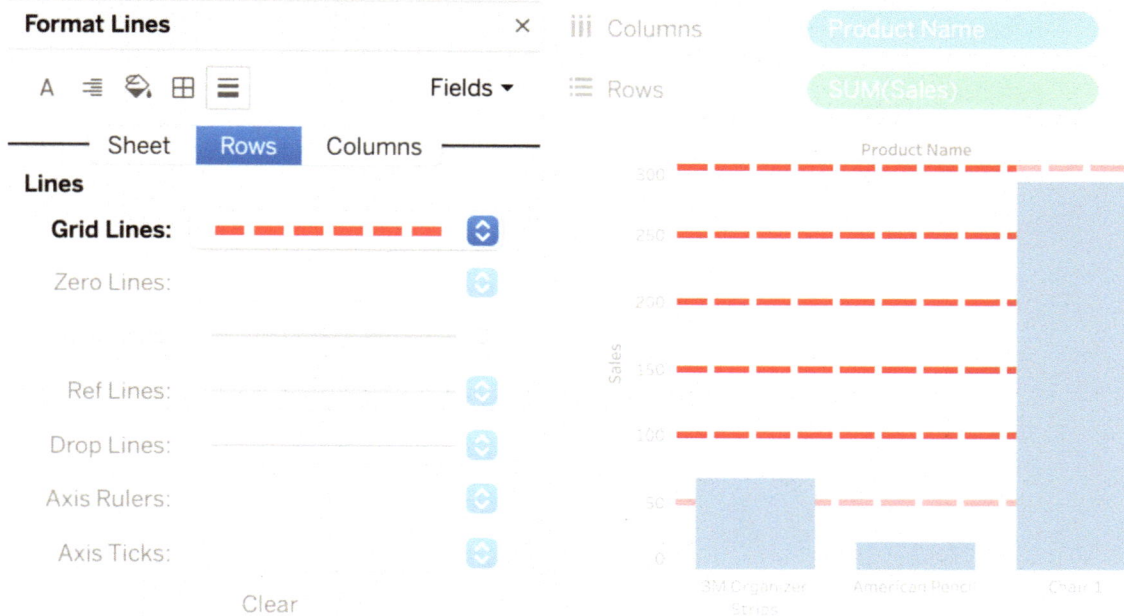

FIGURE 12.42
Format Grid Lines panel.

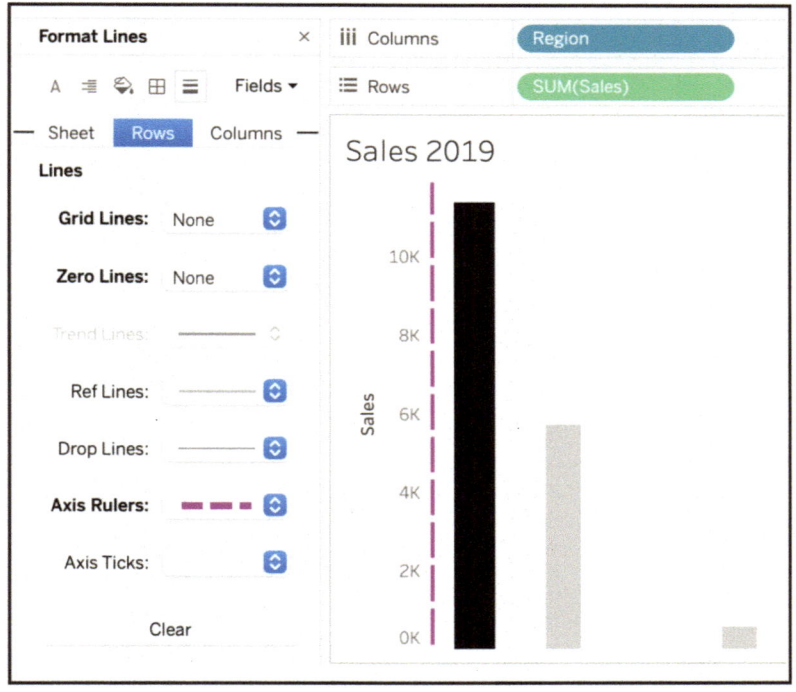

FIGURE 12.43
Vertical Axis Ruler.

12.8 Fields

When formatting a specific "Field," the [Measure Values] field, or the [Measure Names] field, the options vary based on whether the field is a dimension or a measure.

Measures have **Axis** and *Pane* tabs

Dimensions have **Header** and *Pane* tabs

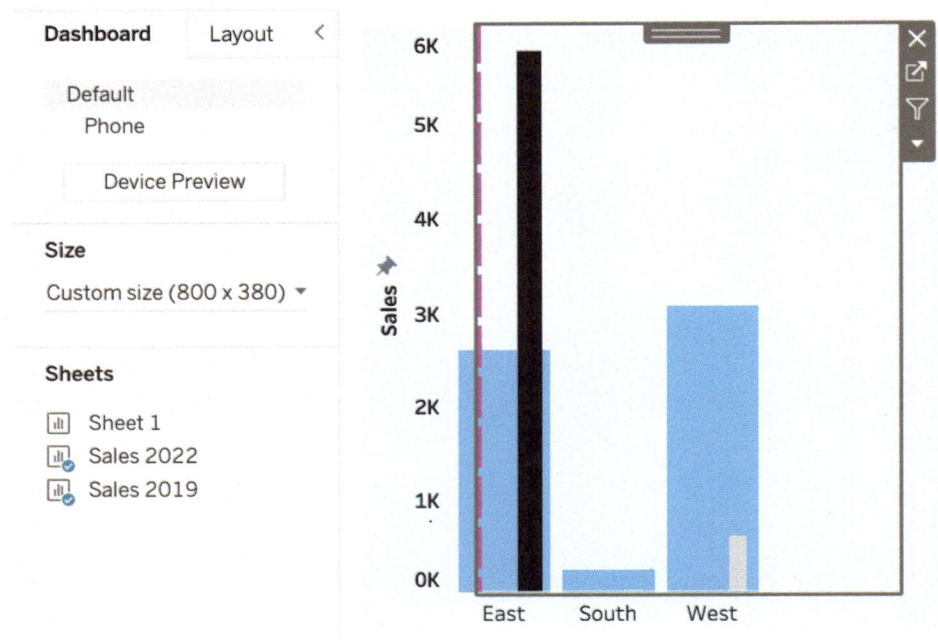

FIGURE 12.44
Sales 2019 Chart.

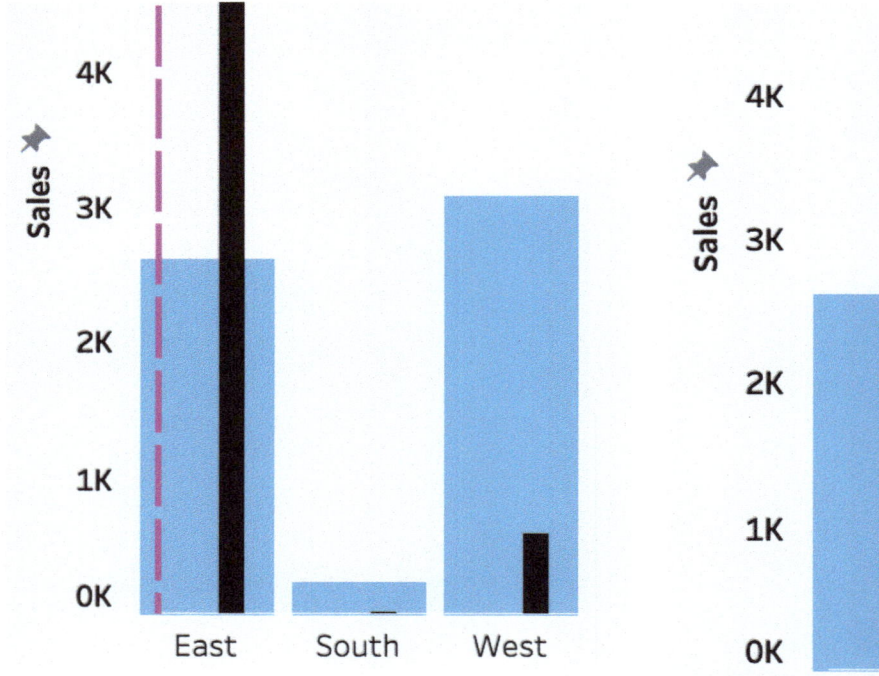

FIGURE 12.45
Pink Axis Ruler on the dashboard.

12.8.1 Header Tab

The **Format** pane for a "field" has several options. For example, the Header tab of the **Format** pane for the [Segment] field has the options shown in Figure 12.47.

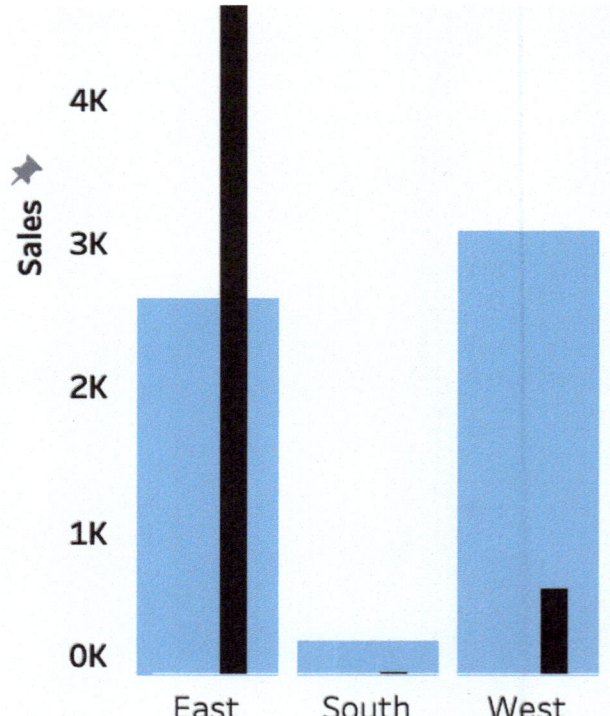

FIGURE 12.46
The Chart without the vertical Axis Ruler.

This setting applies to row headers or column headers. The pane title is **Format Segment** because I'm formatting the [Segment] field.

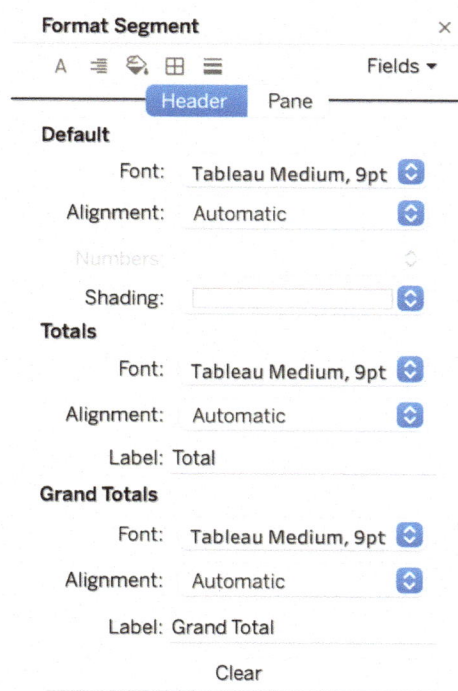

FIGURE 12.47
Formatting the Segment field.

12.8.1.1 *Format Totals*

In the **Format Field** *"fieldname"* pane on the **Header** tab, move to the **Totals** or **Grand Totals** section near the bottom to set the font for totals. You can also right-click within the "total" area of the view and choose "Format" from the *context menu*.

12.8.2 Cannot Format Date Field

When you select "More" and a "Custom" date part in the date field's *context menu*, you cannot format the date in the **Format** pane. Instead, use any date part or date value except "Custom."

12.9 Show Header/Hide Header

When you turn off "Show Header" for a discrete field, it hides the entire column for text charts. However, the data is still available for calculations. For other mark types like bars or lines, if the *axis* or *headers* are not displayed, select the field to open the field's *context menu* and choose "Show Header." *"Section 6.4 A Small Multiples View" on page 105* demonstrates how to show or hide a header.

Hiding the header of a "Rank" field is an interesting way to add sorting, as shown in *"Section 8.16 Sort by*

Rank Alternative" on page 188 where I add a "Rank" field and then "Hide" the header. For additional information, see the Tableau help article "How to hide a row or column."

12.9.1 Resize Column Header

To resize the column width, turn on "Show Header" and move your mouse between the headers or over the chart edge until a double arrow appears, and then *click-drag* the arrow. The "Cell Size" setting on the **Format** menu also adjusts the column width. However, if you place a worksheet with the "Cell Size" setting on a dashboard, you must use the "Standard" fit to see the new column width.

12.10 Axis

In Figure 3.12, we saw that Tableau creates axes for **continuous** fields on the **Rows** or **Columns** shelf.

12.10.1 Show or Hide Axis

You can hide or show an axis with the "Show Header" setting for a field on the **Rows** or **Columns** shelves. *"Section 6.5 Donut Chart" on page 112* example illustrates how to hide an axis.

12.10.2 Axis Labels

Because an axis is **continuous**, you may see sequential numbers at the axis ticks like 1, 2, 3. If you want to center labels under bars, you must change the field to **discrete**, thus adding headers you can center. *"Section 9.13 Date Parameter in Axis Label" on page 208* has a dynamic axis label from a field. *"Section 13.2 Axis Labels" on page 294* also examines axis labels.

For readability, consider replacing numbers like 12,000,000 with 12M.

12.10.3 Resize Axis Height

You might want to resize the axis height if you remove the title. To resize the height of an axis:

1. Position the cursor between the axis and the body of the chart until a double arrow appears, as shown in Figure 12.48.
2. *Click-drag* to resize the axis. Do not use the double arrow at the bottom of the axis, which changes the size of the entire chart.

12.11 Format Field: Axis, Numbers

In this section, we look at Tableau formatting for individual fields. There are several ways to format numbers in Tableau, and if none of the defaults are quite right, you can create a custom format. For this example, I use the *Currency (Standard)* option. These same choices are available on the *Pane* tab, and we will look at *Custom* and *Percentage* formats in those examples. The "Custom" setting is one way to add symbols.

- Automatic
- Number (Standard)
- Number (Custom)
- Currency (Standard)
- Currency (Custom)
- Scientific
- Percentage
- Custom

In Figure 12.49, the measure field [Sales] creates a vertical axis. Right-click on the axis and choose "Format." The **Format** *fieldname* pane opens on the left. On the

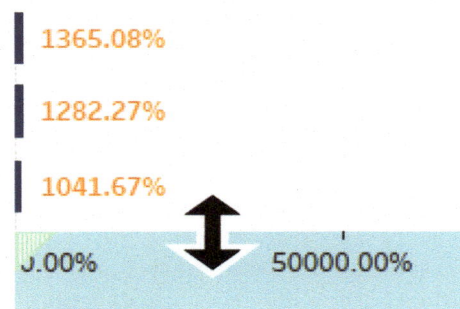

1365.08%

1282.27%

1041.67%

0.00%   50000.00%

FIGURE 12.48
Resizing the Axis Height.

Axis tab, scroll down to the **Scale**, *Numbers* section. In this section, you also change the number format from decimals to whole numbers.

12.11.1 Currency (Standard)

The formatting for a vertical or horizontal "axis" is found in the **Format** control pane for that measure *field*. When the *Axis Scale* is in whole numbers, and the marks on the view use decimals, I change the formatting to match. In Figure 12.50, the [Sales] field is on the **Columns** shelf, creating a horizontal x-axis at the bottom of the view, ranging from 0 to 15. I want the scale to be a currency, so I edit the number format.

When I right-click on the *Sales* axis at the bottom of the view and choose "Format," the **Format** control pane changes to "**Format SUM(Sales)**." On the *Axis* tab, the **Scale** section has a drop-down for *Numbers*. After I changed the *Numbers* format to **Currency (Standard)**, the axis numbers at the bottom of the chart reflect dollars, as shown in Figure 12.51.

12.11.2 Pane, Null Format

Tableau has options for handling special values like *Nulls*, as shown at the bottom of Figure 12.52, where the field [SUM(Sales)] is selected. Tableau adds the special values option when fields have null values.

12.11.3 Format Field: Pane

On the *Pane* tab, you can also format "Font," "Alignment," "Numbers," and "Totals" for the selected field.

12.11.4 Number Formats: Positive, Negative, and Zero

When formatting a field, Tableau provides several default formats for *Numbers*, such as the "Currency

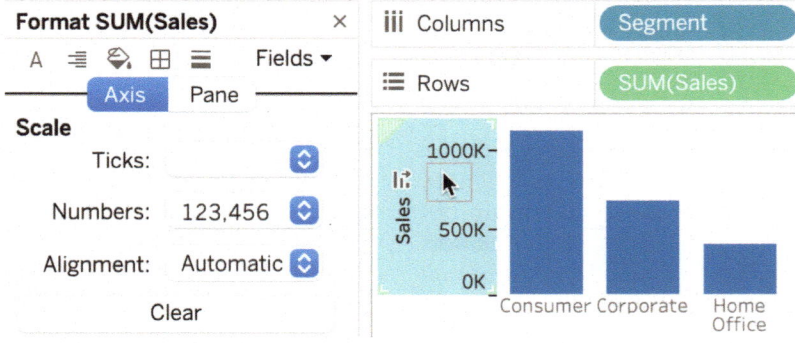

FIGURE 12.49
The Axis Tab: Scale, Numbers.

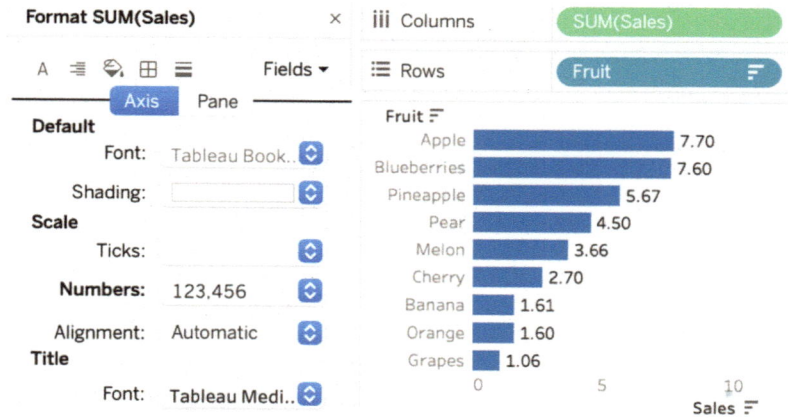

FIGURE 12.50
Formatting numbers.

FIGURE 12.51
Dollars in the bottom axis.

To focus on positive vs. negative values, add a **continuous** field to the *Color* tile on the **Marks** card, as shown in *"Section 7.3.3.2 Diverging Color Palette" on page 142.* Edit the color palette to "Stepped Color" with two "steps." *"Section 15.5 Switch Between Measures with Parameters" on page 369* uses a stepped color setting with positive and negative values. The "x- and y-axis" example at the beginning of this chapter in Figure 12.4 also shows positive and negative marks.

(Standard)" I used earlier. Before we walk through the following example, I will briefly examine Tableau's syntax for formatting numbers. When you select "Currency (Custom)," Tableau adds the dollar sign symbol **$** and formats the field with two decimals. To edit the syntax used by Tableau for "Currency (Custom)," first select a number value for **Numbers** in the *Default* section of the **Format** pane. This step is optional but gives you a starting expression to edit. Next, click "Custom" to edit the default expression, as shown in Figure 12.54. Tableau adds quotes around the dollar sign symbol "$." A semi-colon separates positive and negative formats in the expression. Tableau adds a minus symbol as part of the negative format, as shown in Figure 12.53. You can add any ASCII symbol, such as an arrow, triangle, or + plus symbol (Figure 12.54).

Mark Reid has a great guide for number formats at:

https://datavis.blog/2022/07/31/tableau-custom-number-formatting/

In addition to positive and negative formats, the third group applies to *zero* values. If you combine shapes with numbers, you should fill in the third group with a different symbol or leave the symbol blank. As shown in Figure 12.55, you could use "N/A" for zero values. To hide positive, negative, or zero values, just add the semicolon without a 0 or #.

In Figure 12.56, Tableau replaced the zero values for *3M Strips* with "N/A."

Tableau syntax uses "Microsoft Number Format Codes."

12.11.5 Number Format: Percentage

In the next example, Tableau added the **Measure Values** shelf to the visualization because the [Measure Values] field is on the *Text* tile of the **Marks** card. I want to change the "Number" format for the [% of Total SUM(Discount)] without affecting the [Profit], [Sales], or [Quantity] fields on the **Measure Values** shelf.

Follow these steps to change the number format for the [% of Total SUM(Discount)] table calculation field.

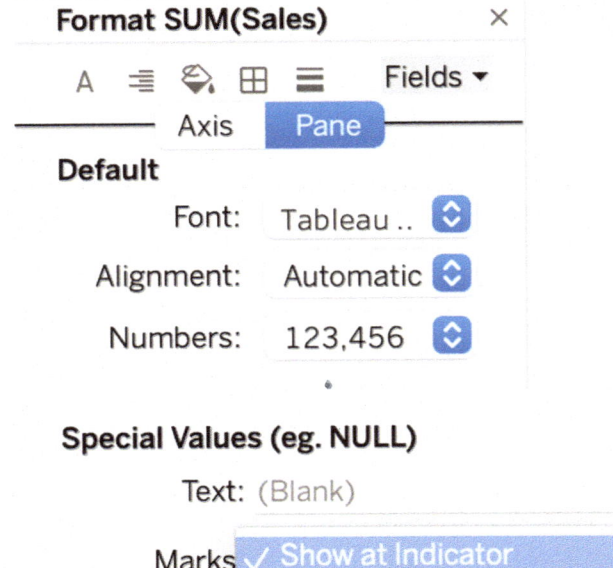

FIGURE 12.52
Special values.

FIGURE 12.53
Positive and negative formatting.

1. Right-click within the first column [Discount (% of Total)] and choose "Format." The **Format** pane opens on the left.

The small triangle to the right of the field name [% of Total SUM(Discount)] indicates this is a table calculation.

2. In the **Format** pane on the left, in the top-right area, click the **Fields** drop-down arrow to open the *context menu*. Select the field "% of Total SUM(Discount)." (Figure 12.57)

3. The **Format** pane changes the *Pane* tab to blue. The "Default" section has formatting choices for **Numbers**. Click the drop-down arrow to change the format to "Percentage" with 0 decimal places (Figure 12.58).

12.11.6 Number Format: Custom Arrows

A calculated field that shows the *difference* between the current month and the previous month or the *change* in first and last values adds value to visualizations. This example resembles *"Section 14.23 KPIs and BANs (Big Numbers)" on page 347*. *"Section 15.1.8 Drill Down with a Set Action" on page 359* also uses arrows.

To quickly show positive and negative numbers, edit the field's default format for *Numbers*, as shown in Figure 12.59. Hold down the **Alt** key and type 30 on the number keypad on a Windows computer for the up arrow. Alt31 is the ASCII code for a down arrow. In MacOS, open the *Notes* application and then open the *Symbol* window. Paste the symbols into *Notes* and copy and paste them into the Tableau format box. In MacOS, type Control + Command + Spacebar to open the *Symbol* window.

As mentioned in the previous example on positive and negative numbers, if you combine ASCII shapes with numbers, add a semi-colon to add another group at the end of the expression to format zero values. I'd recommend using a different symbol or leaving the format expression blank after the semicolon.

In Figure 12.60, the **Numbers** format for the [SUM(Arrows)] field displays only up and down arrows for this KPI.

If you want to call out a particular number, you can use two fields formatted with different sizes. In Figure 12.61, I duplicated my [Sales Goal] field and renamed it [Arrows] and then added it to the *Text* tile on the **Marks** card.

Finally, the *Text* property on the **Marks** card formats the "Arrows" field in a size nine font, and the [Sales] field is bold with a size of 14 font, as shown in Figure 12.62.

The arrow indicators are shown in Figure 12.63. I also added the [Compare to last month] field to the *Color* tile on the **Marks** card. The example "Arrows Comparing Two Values" that follows walks through the steps to create the chart.

12.12 Bring a Mark to the Forefront

Use sorting to bring one line (mark) to the front of the visualization so that it is on top of other lines. For example, if you are looking at country data and want the USA line to be at the forefront of the chart, sort the country values so that the USA is first.

If there are multiple fields on the **Measure Values** shelf, drag each field to a new location on the [Measure Values] shelf to change the stacking order of the marks. You can also click an axis and choose "Move marks to front," as shown in Figure 12.64.

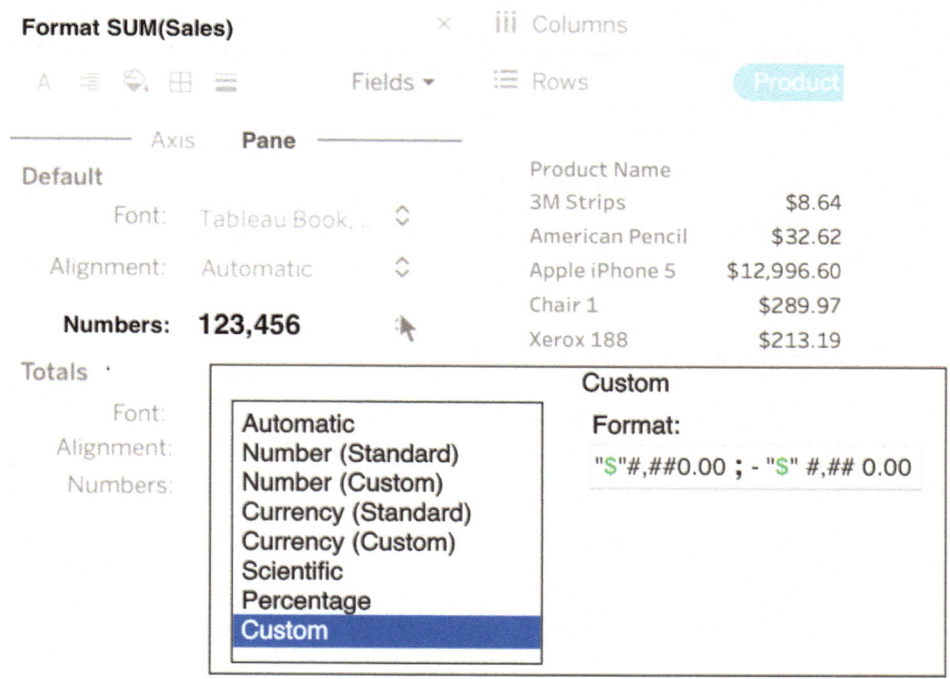

FIGURE 12.54
Custom number formats.

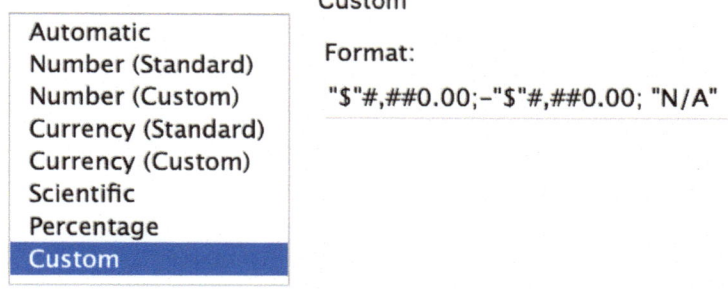

FIGURE 12.55
Zero formatting.

Product Name	
3M Strips	N/A
Chair 1	$289.97
O'Sullivan Elevations Bookcase, Cherry Finish	$334.00

FIGURE 12.56
Zero formatted as N/A.

12.13 Resize

Generally, to resize columns, rows, or the overall chart, you hover over a line or chart edge and *click-drag* to resize. Depending on what you are changing,

you may have to grab the line next to a heading, axis, or edge of the chart rather than a line by the mark. In the case of bars, use the *Size* tile on the **Marks** card to adjust the bar width. Hover at the outside edge of the chart until a *double arrow* appears and then *click-drag* to resize the entire chart, as shown in Figure 12.65.

> If the axis or header area is not shown, select the field on the **Rows** or **Columns** shelf to open the field's *context menu* and choose "Show Header."

Figure 12.66 shows the double arrows to resize the column width. If the chart is set to "Fit Width" or "Entire View," there are no double arrows.

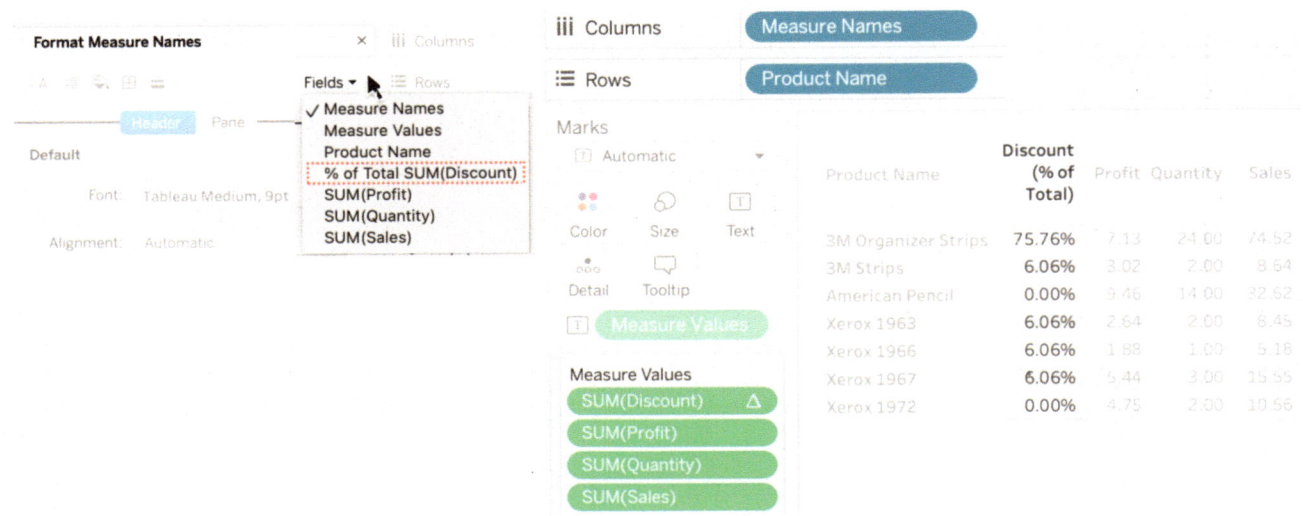

FIGURE 12.57
The drop-down for Fields.

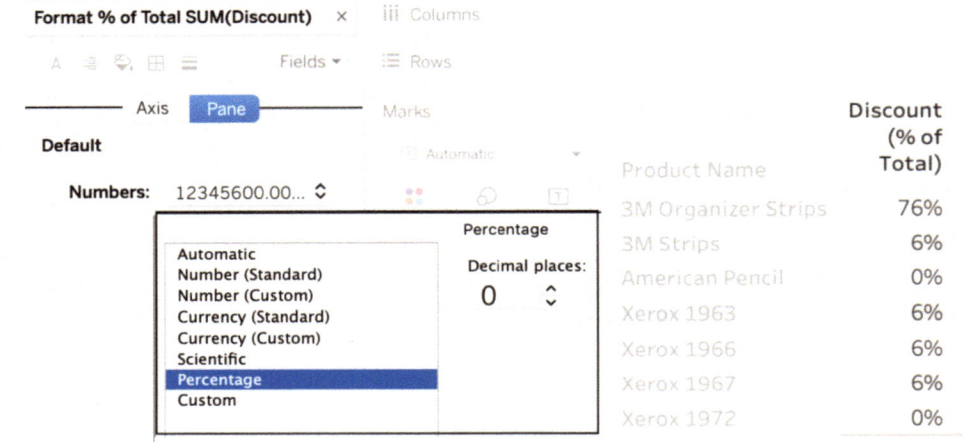

FIGURE 12.58
The Format Numbers drop-down box.

12.13.1 Resize Bar Width

To change the width of a bar, you can use "Size" in the **Marks** card or position the mouse between headers in the axis until a *double arrow* appears, as shown in Figure 12.67, and then drag to resize.

12.14 Default Properties

In *"Section 4.3 Field Default Properties" on page 76*, we looked at default properties for different types of data. Both dimension and measure fields have *Comment* and *Color* default properties. A dimension field also has *Shape* and *Sort*. A measure field might have *Number Format*, *Aggregation*, and *Total Using*, although choices vary more based on the field type. Earlier in this chapter, the topic "Format Field: Axis, Numbers" formats a measure field to set the **Numbers** format. In the case of measure fields, I like to set a field's "Default Properties" to change the **Numbers** format so the format applies anywhere I use the field.

As shown in Figure 12.68, the "Default Properties" settings vary based on whether the field is a dimension (on the left) or a measure (on the right.)

Please note that *default field properties*, such as **Number Format** or **Color**, are not copied when you replace a data source.

If the "Default Properties" are not working as expected, ensure you format the correct field. For example, when I use a *calculated field* to set a "Region," I have to set the default properties on the *calculated field*, not the original "Region" field.

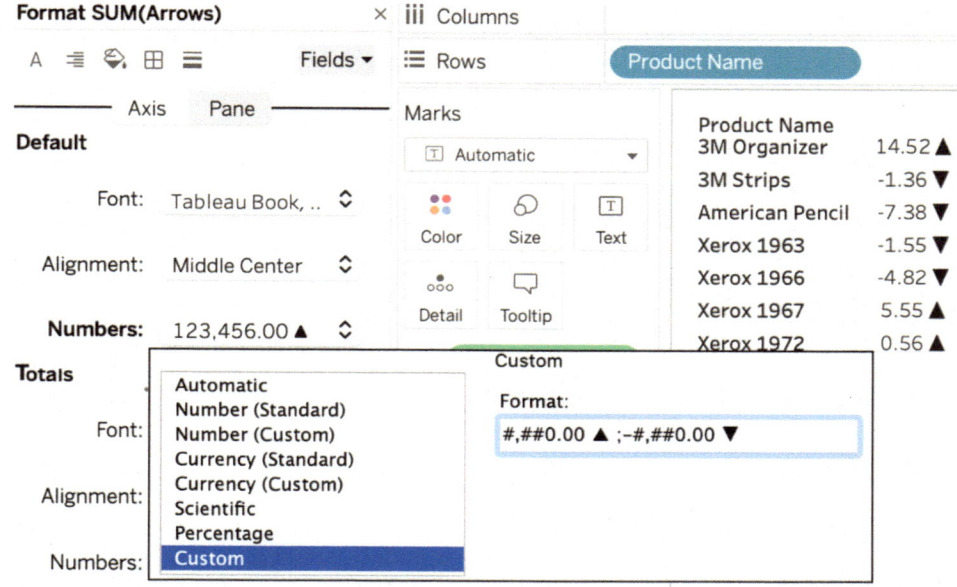

FIGURE 12.59
Add Symbols to the numbers format expression.

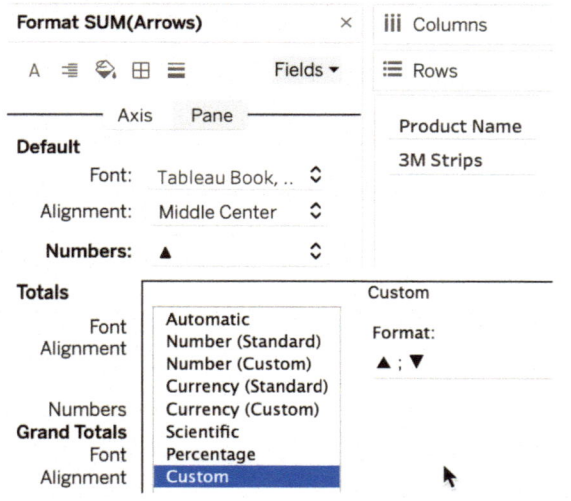

FIGURE 12.60
Custom Format with Arrows.

12.14.1 Color

A field's default properties setting for color is handy in case you want to assign specific colors to individual values. For example, the [Segment] field has three values, including *Home Office*. When I change the color for the "Home Office" value to orange, the *Home Office* mark is orange whenever I add [Segment] to the *Color* tile. We looked at the *Color* tile in *"Section 7.3 The Color Property" on page 139* and will look at color specifically at the end of this chapter.

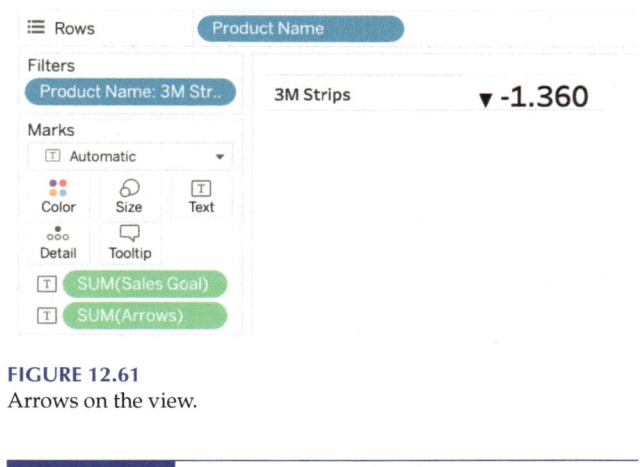

FIGURE 12.61
Arrows on the view.

12.15 Format Menu

The **Format Menu** is a fast way to jump to specific formatting options in the **Format** control pane. For example, earlier in the topic "Format Control Pane Tools," we looked at *Font, Alignment, Shading, Borders,* and *Lines.* The **Format Menu** also has additional options. **Chapter 13** has additional information for some of these formatting topics.

- Workbook
- Animations
- Reference Lines
- Drop Lines
- Annotations

FIGURE 12.62
Edit Label.

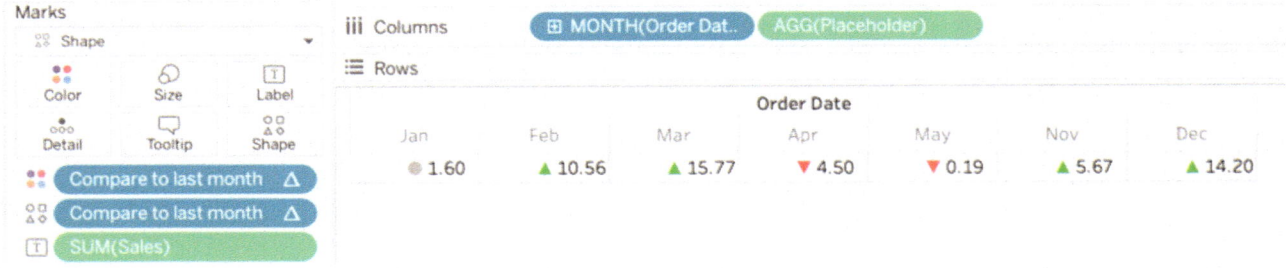

FIGURE 12.63
Arrow indicators.

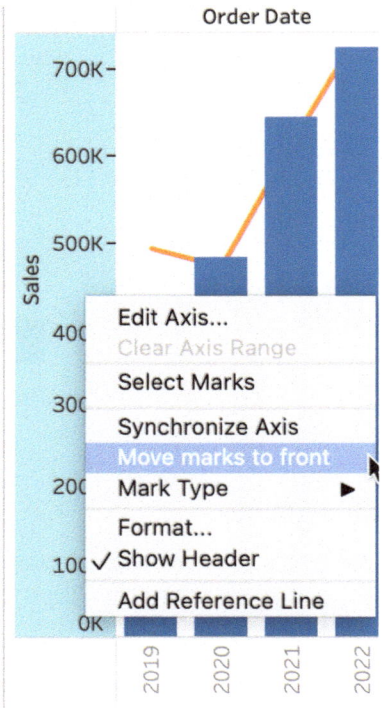

FIGURE 12.64
Move marks to the front.

- Title and Caption
- Field Labels
- Legends
- Filters

FIGURE 12.65
Resize column widths.

- Highlighters
- Parameters
- Cell Size
- Copy and Paste Formatting

12.15.1 Workbook

Setting format options at the Workbook level saves time. On the **Format** menu, select "Workbook" to change workbook settings, which control the default font and line settings for the entire workbook, as well as these settings.

- Highlighting (**Chapter 15** on *page 364*)
- Date formats for all fields in a *Data Source* (**Chapter 9,** *page 199*)

FIGURE 12.66
Resize the column width.

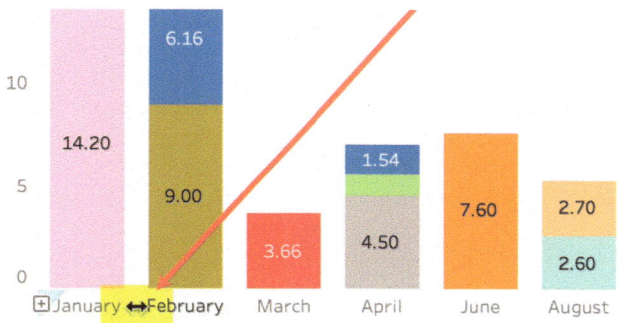

FIGURE 12.67
Double arrow in axis.

While not specific to the workbook, you can copy and paste formatting between worksheets as shown in the topic "Copy and Paste Formatting" that follows.

12.15.2 Animations

Select "Animations…" on the **Format** menu to change the animations' speed. In the **Animations** pane on the left, toggle animations on or off and adjust the duration.

12.15.3 Worksheet Title and Caption

When formatting a "Title and Caption," the **Format Title and Caption** pane controls "Shading" and "Borders." I use captions to describe a view or explain calculations. Select "Show Caption" on the **Worksheet** menu and double-click to edit captions.

Check "Show Title" on the **Dashboard**, **Worksheet**, or **Story** menu if you do not see the title. You can also toggle the "Show Title" option in the **Story** pane on the left when editing a story. On the *toolbar* at the top of the screen, click the drop-down arrow on the "Show/Hide Cards" button and select "Title" from the *context menu*. Toggle the check mark on or off to show or hide the worksheet title. Right-click the title and choose "Format" to open the **Format Title and Caption** pane, as shown in Figure 12.69.

For chart titles, check out *"Section 14.12.1 Include Field Data in the Dashboard Title" on page 316*, which combines the *Text* tile on the **Marks** card and the worksheet title to create a dashboard title. *"Section 9.11 Avoid 'All' in a Date Title" on page 208* uses a parameter and calculated field to add a date to a worksheet title, and "Worksheet for Date Title" illustrates an alternative for "None" values.

12.15.4 Filter and Set Controls

On the **Format** menu, select "Filters" to open the **Format Filter and Set Controls** pane. https://help.tableau.com/current/pro/desktop/en-us/formatting_worksheet.htm

12.15.5 Field Labels

Right-click the label on the view to format field labels, and select "Format."

"Section 13.3 Field Labels" on page 295 looks at field labels.

12.15.6 Legends

In *"Section 1.7.2 Show, Hide, and Format Legends" on page 35*, we looked at a map with transparent controls and legends. *"Section 7.3.10 Color Legend From Field*

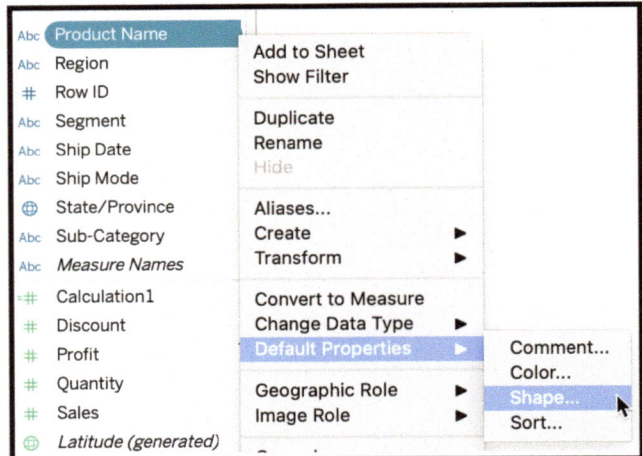
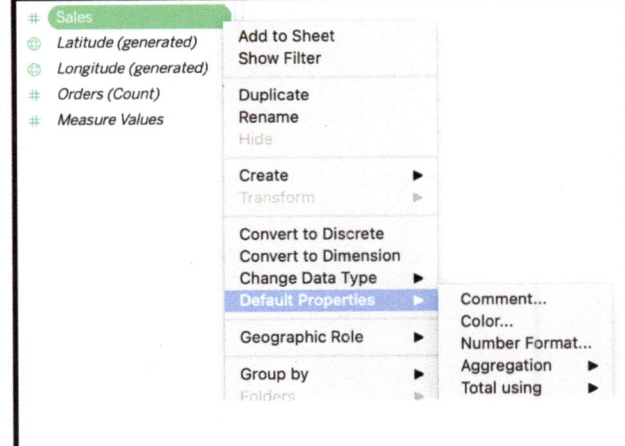

FIGURE 12.68
Comparing default properties on dimension or measure fields.

FIGURE 12.69
Worksheet title.

FIGURE 12.70
A text table with overlapping marks.

Values" on page 143 uses field data to create a color legend. Create unique color legends by incorporating color in titles and using field values as part of the color legend.

12.15.7 Cell Size

The text overlaps in the example shown in Figure 12.70. On the worksheet **Format** menu, select *Cell Size* and an option like *Text Cell* to fine-tune text spacing. A text cell has an aspect ratio of 3:1, and a *Square Cell* has an aspect ratio of 1:1. When text values overlap on a chart, make the cell size wider to allow for more room. Tableau will add a horizontal scroll bar if needed.

When you adjust the *Cell Size* for a worksheet used on a dashboard, use the *Standard* fit on the dashboard to see the new column widths.

12.15.8 Copy and Paste Formatting

After I adjust the formatting for one workbook, I usually copy and paste the formatting to other sheets in the workbook.

1. From the source worksheet, on the **Format** menu, select "Copy Formatting."
2. In the tab area at the bottom, right-click the name of the destination worksheet and select "Paste Formatting."

12.16 Worksheet Settings

The **Worksheet** menu has choices to show elements like *Title, Caption, Summary, Cards,* the *Toolbar,* or *Sort Controls,* as shown in Figure 12.71.

To avoid users accidentally "breaking" a view, uncheck **Show Sort Controls** in the **Worksheet** menu.

12.17 Headers

Column or row headings are automatically added for **discrete** fields on the **Rows** shelf or **Columns** shelf, as

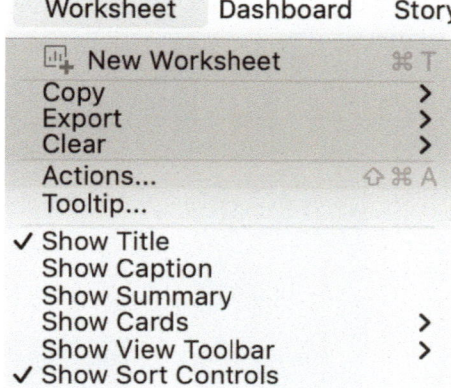

FIGURE 12.71
Show Sort Controls.

discussed in *"Section 3.5 Discrete vs. Continuous" on page 61*. Additional information on headers is available in *"Section 10.4.3 Slope Chart with a Rank Table Calculation" on page 215* that illustrates how to move headers.

There is no heading for a field on the *Text* tile of the **Marks** card, but you can create a calculated field to add a heading, as shown in *"Section 13.4.2 A Heading for a Field on the Text Tile" on page 295*.

Because KPIs sometimes involve the absence of data, *"Section 14.23 KPIs and BANs (Big Numbers)" on page 347* explores headings for charts without data.

12.17.1 Change Whitespace between Title and Column Headings

Drag the line just below the column headings to add additional room. If [Measure Names] is on the **Columns** shelf, right-click the field [Measure Names], and the **Format Measure Names** pane opens on the left. On the Header tab, change the alignment as shown in Figure 12.72.

When "Show Headers" is turned off and there is still a lot of space between the title and the data, check if "Show Empty Columns" or "Show Empty Rows" is checked on the **Analysis** menu under "Table Layout." The following topic, "Analysis: Table Layout,"

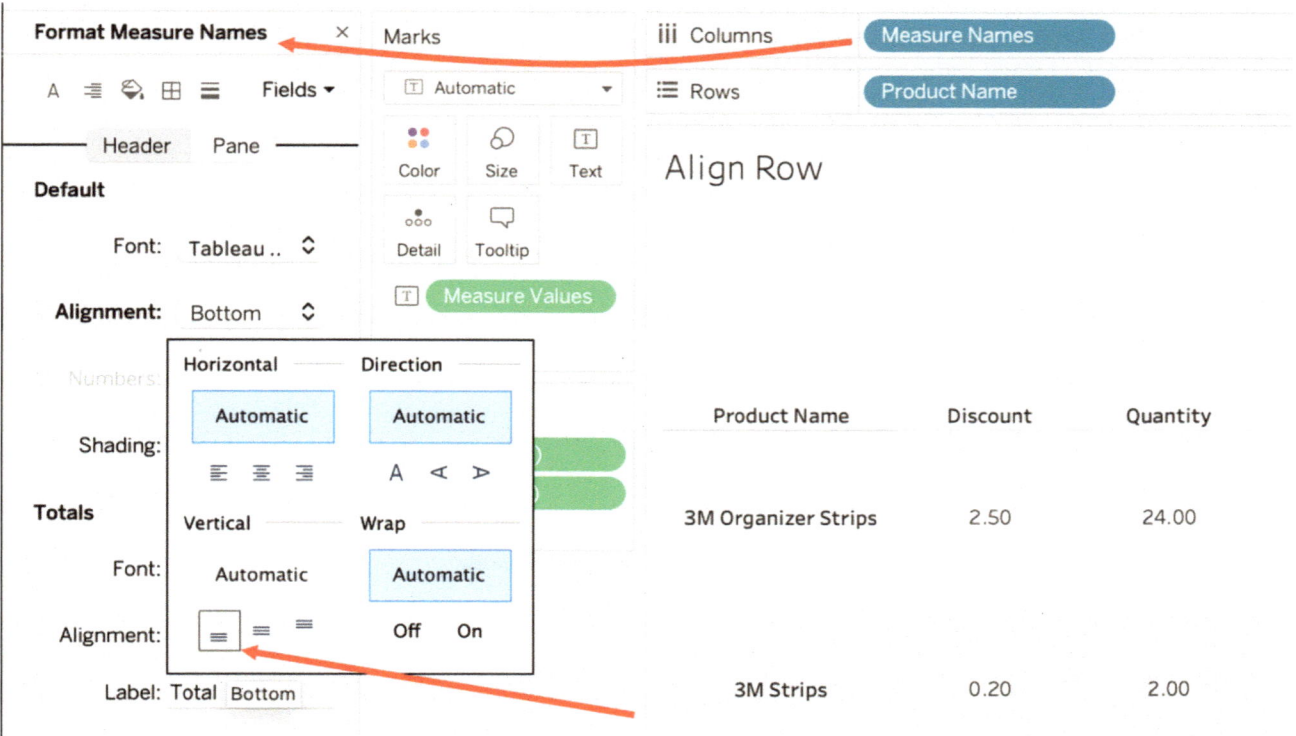

FIGURE 12.72
Format Measure Names pane.

explains how to show empty columns or rows to resolve this issue.

12.17.2 Dashboard Container for Headings

When I want to rename my column headings or reuse aliases more than once, I create a container on my dashboard with a text object for each heading. *"Section 14.12.2 Dashboard Container for Headings" on page 316* walks through how to make this type of container.

12.17.3 Rotate Header

In Figure 3.11 when I clicked on the month "Apr" in the bottom header area, the *context menu* has the options "Rotate Label" and "Show Header" because the [Order Date] field is **discrete**. If the field were **continuous**, options for an axis would be displayed.

12.17.4 Format Header for Totals

To format headings for totals, right-click on the header area and choose "Format." The **Format** pane opens on the left of the Header tab. Scroll down to the **Totals** area and change the "Label."

12.17.5 Headings Do not Line Up on a Dashboard

When you combine several charts on a dashboard, the heading's alignment can be off. The next topic, *"Section 12.18 Analysis: Table Layout" on page 286*, explains how to show empty columns or rows to resolve this issue.

12.18 Analysis: Table Layout

When tables have empty rows or columns, it can be useful to show the empty rows or columns, especially when comparing two charts on a dashboard, as shown in Figure 12.73. On the **Analysis** menu, select *Table Layout* and then check "Show Empty Rows" or "Show Empty Columns."

12.18.1 Show Empty Columns

If data does not line up correctly on a dashboard or there are large areas of blank space, check that "Show Empty Columns" is not checked. In Figure 12.74, there is a gap of two years.

If you have bins for a histogram chart and there are gaps in the data, right-click (control-click in MacOS) the headers or axis and choose "Show missing values."

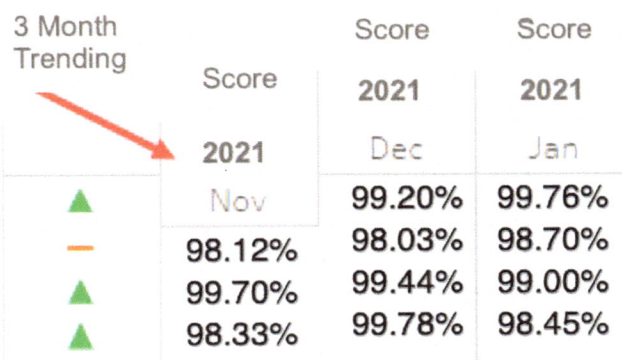

FIGURE 12.73
Headings not aligned.

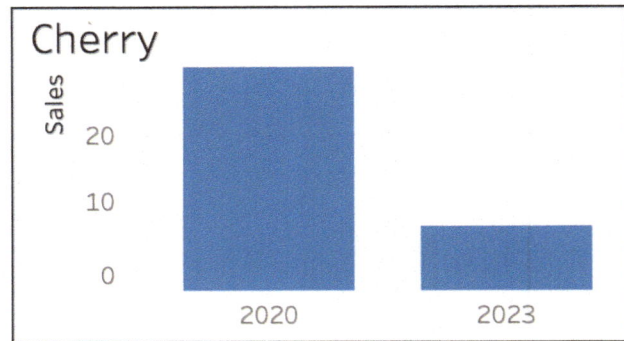

FIGURE 12.74
Marks.

12.19 Properties on the Marks Card

Chapter 7 examined the **Marks** card properties like *Color*, *Size*, and *Labels*. It is worth noting that these properties apply to charts even when there is no specific field on the *tile* itself. For example, the *Color* tile and *Size* tile settings can change the default color or size of bars. The *Label* tile on the **Marks** card affects the appearance of mark labels on the chart even when there is no field on the *Label* tile. We look at mark labels in more detail in *"Section 13.1 Mark Labels" on page 291*.

12.20 Reference Line Labels

When configuring the labels for reference lines, you can customize the text and add values and other settings in the **Edit Reference Line, Band, or Box** screen, as shown in *"Section 7.8.1 Reference Line with Shading" on page 153*.

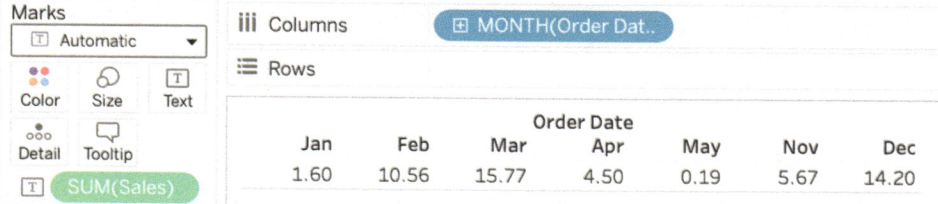

FIGURE 12.75
Order date and sales fields.

FIGURE 12.76
A Calculated field named Placeholder.

12.21 Arrows Comparing Two Values

Now that we have explored formatting, I want to look at an example with arrows. Another everyday use of arrows is to compare two fields or values; for example, current [Sales] are down compared to [Sales last month]. Colored arrows are also helpful in showing RAG ratings visually. Follow along as I combine *Shape* and *Color* tiles to create arrows. I have included many screenshots because the visualization changes dramatically with each step.

1. Add [Order Date] to the **Columns** shelf and [Sales] to *Text* on the **Marks** card (Figure 12.75).

2. Create a [Placeholder] field and add the field to the **Columns** shelf. The [Placeholder] calculation is unimportant, but having the field in the view adds additional formatting options (Figures 12.76 and 12.77).

3. On the **Columns** shelf, click the drop-down arrow for the [Placeholder] field and uncheck "Show Header" (Figures 12.78).

4. Create a calculated field [Compare to last month] to indicate "Up" or "Down" values. I use the table calculation LOOKUP() to find the previous month's value, as shown below (Figure 12.80).

5. Change the **Marks** card type to "Shape." Tableau adds a new *Shape* tile to the **Marks** card. Drag the new field [Compare to last month] to the *Shape* tile.

6. Click the *Shape* tile to open the "Edit Shape" dialog window. Select the "Down" value under **Select Data Item** in the left pane. In the right pane, use the drop-down arrow to select the "Filled" shape palette. Select the down arrow shape in the box under the palette name, as shown below (Figure 12.81).

7. Repeat step 6 for the other values, "Null" and "Up," selecting the appropriate *shapes*.

8. Add the [Compare to Last Month] field to *Color* on the **Marks** card. Click the *Color* tile to open the **Edit Colors** dialog window.

9. In the left pane, under "Select Data Item," select "Down." In the right pane, use the drop-down arrow to choose a "Color" palette. Select red for the "Down" value (Figure 12.82).

10. Repeat Step 9 for the other values, "Null" and "Up," selecting the appropriate *colors*. If you do not see a choice for "Up," remove the field [Compare to Last Year] from the *Color* tile, adjust filters so you see all possible values in the view, and then add the field back to the *Color* tile. Assign colors to all marks and then adjust filters to the original setting. The finished chart is shown in Figure 12.63.

12.22 Color

In **Chapter 7**, we looked at the role of the *Color* tile on the **Marks** card in "*Section 7.3 The Color Property*" on *page 139*. The previous topics that touched on color are shown below. Blue is the default color for marks, and black is the default color for text.

- Default Properties
- Default Color
- Categorical Palettes
- Range of Colors (for continuous)

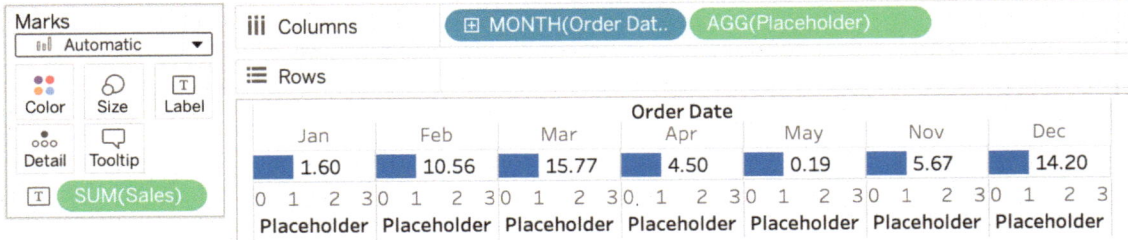

FIGURE 12.77

Add the Placeholder field to the Columns shelf.

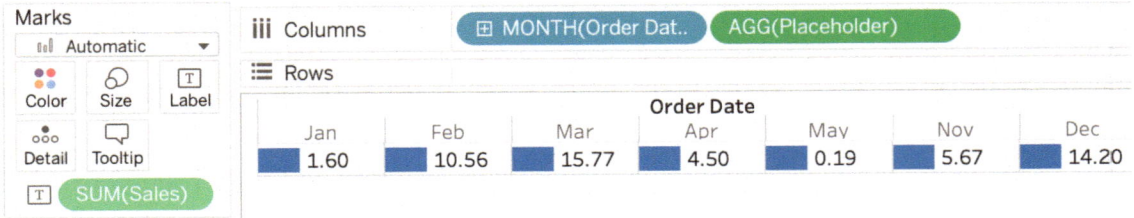

FIGURE 12.78

Turn off the Show Header.

FIGURE 12.79

Tip: *The chart will look strange if you forget to turn off the "Show Header."*

FIGURE 12.80

The Calculated field compare to last month.

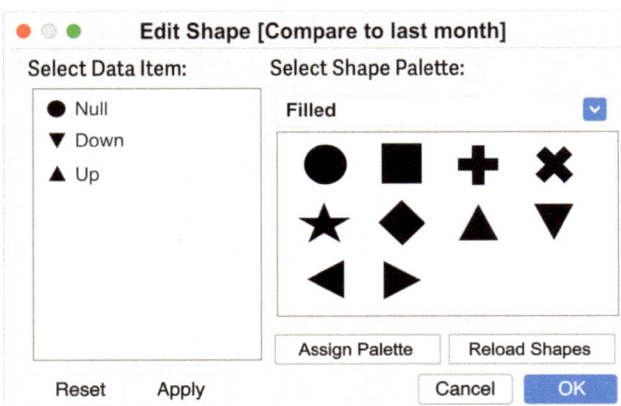

FIGURE 12.81

The Edit Shape dialog window.

- Diverging Quantitative Palettes (for continuous fields)
- Sequential Quantitative Palettes

Now, let's look at some interesting ways to use color in charts.

12.22.1 Title with Mark Colors

Figure 12.83 is a bullet graph from **Chapter 9**, where the title colors match the marks and the red reference line.

12.22.2 Match Label Colors to Bar Color

Tableau can match mark labels to bar colors, as shown in Figure 7.76. Select the *Label* tile and the double

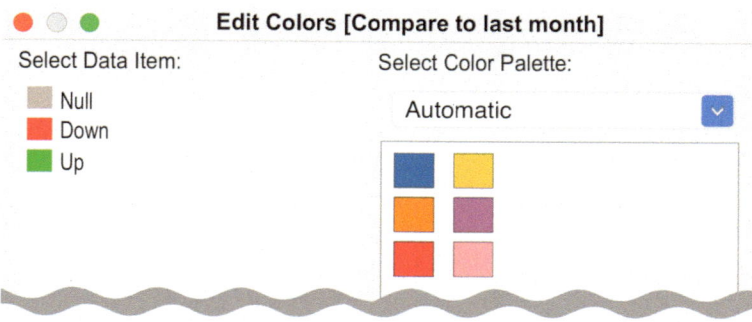

FIGURE 12.82
The **Edit Colors** dialog window.

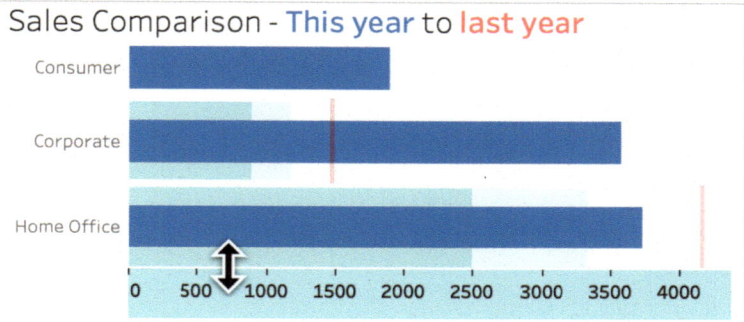

FIGURE 12.83
Title colors match marks and Reference Line.

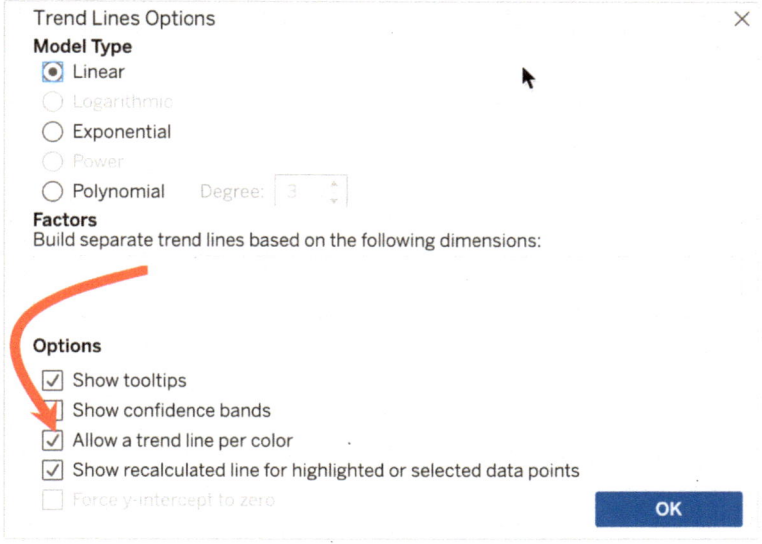

FIGURE 12.84
Trend Line Options.

arrow to the right of "**Font**" to open the *context menu* for the font. Click the "Match Mark Color" button.

12.22.3 Trend Line Color

To use a different color for a trend line, right-click the trend line and select "Edit All Trend Lines." In the "Trend Line Options" pop-up shown in Figure 12.84, at the bottom, uncheck "Allow a trend line per color."

12.22.4 Remove Vertical Lines from the Color Tile

Earlier, we looked at *Lines* in the **Format** control panel. The **Marks** card *Color* tile can also add vertical lines to the view. To remove lines, change the Opacity to 0% on the *Color* tile.

12.22.5 Color Not Applied

When you have a field on the *Color* tile and color is not applied, check if the **Mark Type** is "Shape." Select "Text" from the drop-down to change the **Mark Type** to "Text." After the change, you should see the colors.

If you use a calculated field to assign colors and change the logic in the calculated field, remove the field from the *Color* tile and add it back to see the new colors.

13

Labeling and Text

In this topic, we discuss

Mark Labels

Field Labels

Axis Titles

Headers

Worksheet Titles

Legends and Controls

Annotations

Placeholder Fields

Reference Line Labels

For this chapter, the topic of <u>labeling</u> encompasses mark labels, titles, annotations, legends, and other text elements. As you will see, small changes can bring charts to life. More than any other, this topic is an example of how the written word does not do justice to Tableau's nuanced features, so I use a gallery of screenshots rather than text alone.

There are a few out-of-the-box ideas for adding text to visualizations, such as placeholder fields or calculated fields for headings. Check out the chapters below to explore related topics involving text and labels.

- Captions (Comments in **Chapter 1**, *page 34*)
- Default Properties (**Chapters 4**, *page 76*)
- Create an Alias (**Chapter 2**, *page 42*)
- Text/Label Tile on the **Marks** card (**Chapter 5**, *page 129*)
- Headers (**Chapter 12**, *page 285*)
- Dashboard Container for Headings (**Chapter 14**, *page 316*)
- Background Images or Wallpaper (**Chapter 14**, *page 282*)
- Tooltips (**Chapter 15**, *page 360*)

13.1 Mark Labels

Mark labels display text with the value of a mark. In Figure 13.1, the marks are bars; in Figure 13.4, the marks are the shapes in a scatter plot. If you do not see "mark labels" in the view, on the **Analysis** menu, choose "Show Mark Labels," or double-click the *Label* tile on the **Marks** card and check "Show mark labels."

13.1.1 Stack Marks Off

In Figure 13.1, the red bars for [Price] are at the top of the bar. On the **Analysis** menu, select "Stack marks" and check "Off" to move the red marks to the bottom of the view, as shown in Figure 13.2.

13.1.2 Mark Labels and the Text Tile

The *Label* tile on the **Marks** card affects the appearance of labels on the chart even when there is no field on the *Label* tile, as shown in Figure 13.3. I changed the **Font** section below the **Text** box to use the "Tableau Book" font style. The size is 14 pt, and the color is orange. If no field exists on the *Text* tile, the **Text** box is an empty white box, and the ellipsis button is grayed out.

Add fields to the *Label* or *Text* tile on the **Marks** card for more text options. To change the text for the field, click the *Label* tile.

"Section 11.13.2 The Visualization Without LoD Calculations" on page 241 demonstrates how to add fields to the *Text* or *Label* property on the **Marks** card.

13.1.2.1 Always Show

"Section 3.7 Aggregation" on page 72 shows a scatter plot with no aggregation. In Figure 13.4, I want to add labels to this chart. First, I add the [Type] field to the *Label* tile on the **Marks** card.

I do not want the labels repeated for all the marks. When I click the *Label* tile on the **Marks** card and choose "Selected," all marks disappear from the view. To show one mark label, I right-click to select a mark in the view to open the *context menu*, as shown on the left in Figure 13.5. I select "Mark Label" and "Always Show" from the *context menu*. Now, one mark has the label "Tangerine." I repeat the steps to select an "Apple" mark and label that series of marks.

DOI: 10.1201/9781003566458-14

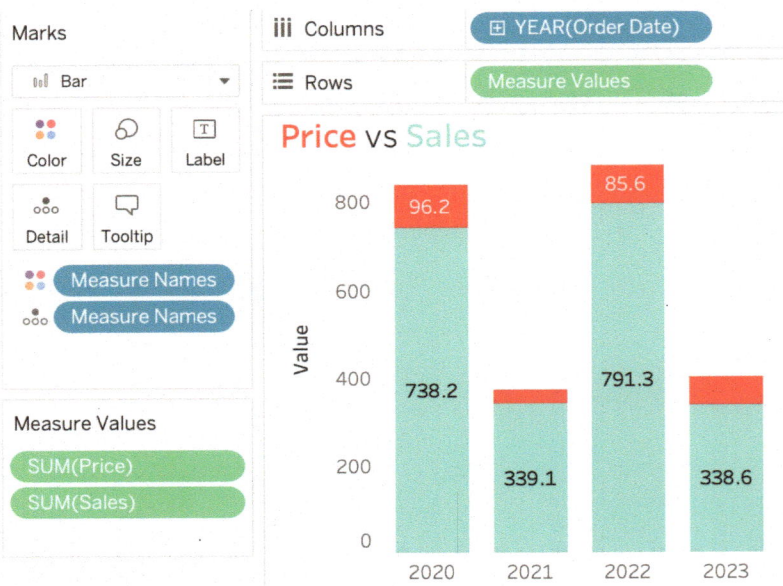

FIGURE 13.1
Mark Labels on bars.

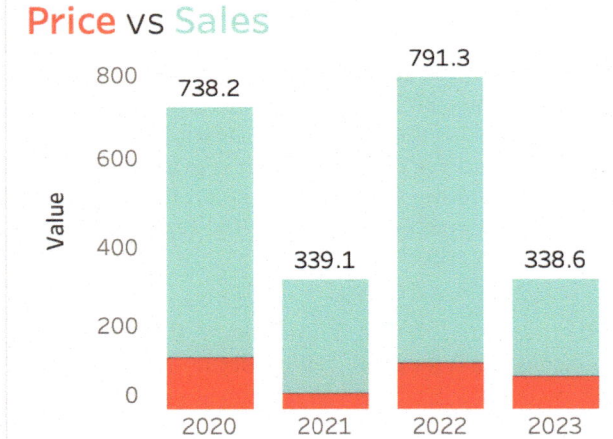

FIGURE 13.2
Stack Marks Off.

13.1.3 Move a Label

To move a label so it does not overlap other marks, click to select the label. The mouse changes to show the mark is selected, as shown in Figure 13.6, and you can drag the label to a new location.

13.1.4 Beginning and End of Line

Labeling both "Line Ends" highlights the change over time, as shown in Figure 13.7. Click the *Label* tile on the **Marks** card and then select the "Line Ends" button.

13.1.5 Move Headings to the Top

Occasionally, I like to move headings to the view's top instead of along the bottom. Select "Table Layout" on the **Analysis** menu. Under "Advanced," uncheck "Show innermost level at bottom of view when there is a vertical axis." *"Section 10.4.3 Slope Chart with a Rank Table Calculation" on page 215* also illustrates how to move headings.

13.1.6 Use Measure Names as Labels

Add the [Measure Names] field to the *Label* tile on the **Marks** card to use measure names as labels, as shown in Figure 13.8.

13.1.7 Reposition Mark Labels

Sometimes, you need to move a mark label. The *"Section 7.9.1 Trend Line Overlaps Mark Label" on page 157* example shows a trend line intersecting mark labels. Click the *mark label* and pause and then click-drag the mark label. If two labels are overlapping, double-click to select the mark.

13.1.7.1 Highlight Table – Mark Labels

A highlight table is a "Square" mark type with diverging colors. A highlight table is dependent on mark labels.

1. Connect to *Superstore* data and add the [Order Date] field to the **Columns** shelf.
2. Add the [Segment] field to the **Rows** shelf.

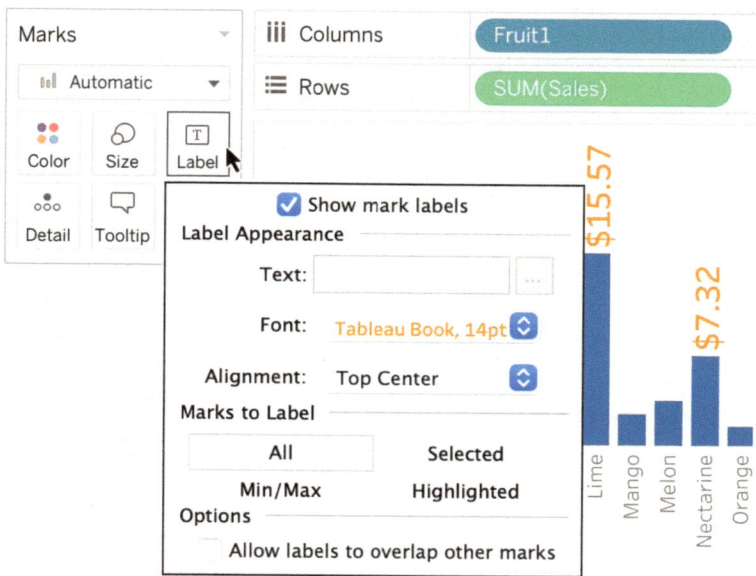

FIGURE 13.3
Empty Text box.

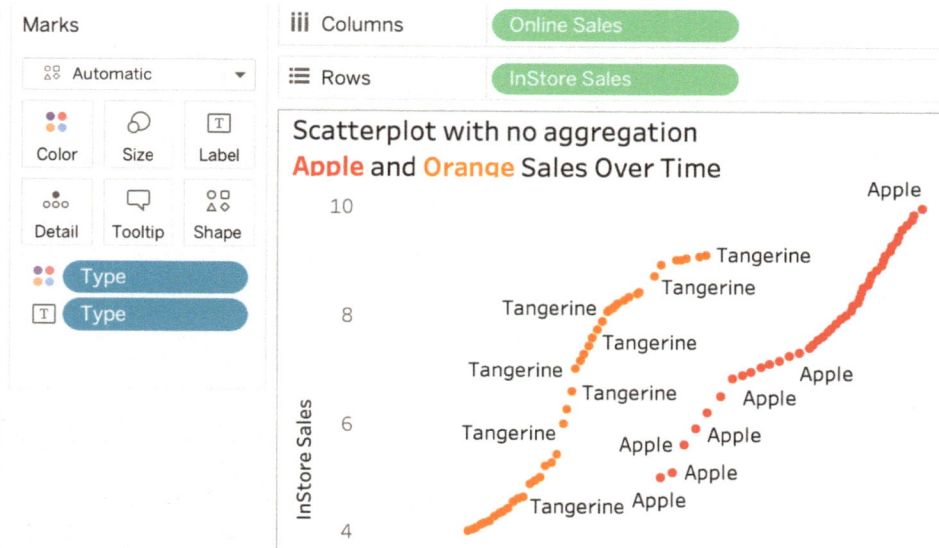

FIGURE 13.4
All marks.

3. Add the [Sales] field to the *Color* and *Label* tiles on the **Marks** card.

4. Select [Square] for the mark type from the drop-down menu on the **Marks** card.

5. On the **Analysis** menu, select "Show Mark Labels." (Figure 13.9)

For additional information on highlight tables, see these topics:

> https://public.tableau.com/views/Highlight Tables1070/HighlightTable?:language=en-US

&publish=yes&:display_count=n&:origin= viz_share_link

- *"Section 7.2.5 Square Mark Type" on page 125*
- *"Section 7.3.7 Highlight Table – Include Totals in Color" on page 143*

13.1.8 Toolbar Button

The **Show Mark Labels** button in the Toolbar also toggles mark label visibility.

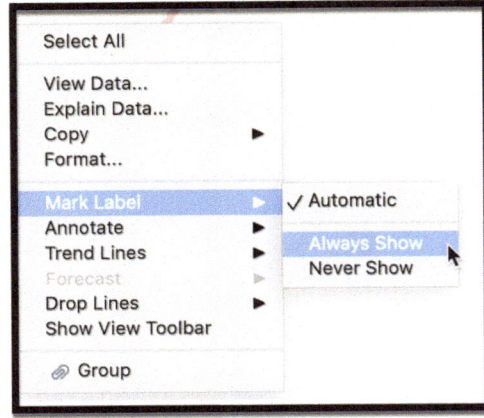

Scatterplot with no aggregation
Apple and **Orange** Sales Over Time

FIGURE 13.5
Always Show.

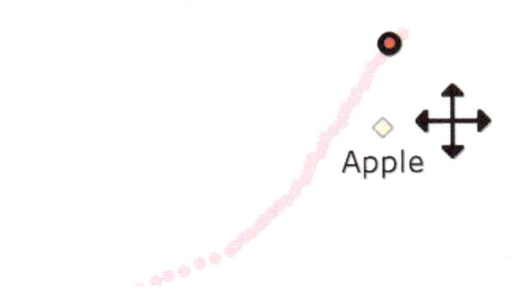

FIGURE 13.6
A selected mark.

FIGURE 13.7
Mark labels at Line Ends.

13.2 Axis Labels

"Figure 3.12 – A y-axis and an x-axis Chart" on page 63 demonstrates that Tableau creates axes for **continuous** fields on the **Rows** shelf or **Columns** shelf. In **Chapter 12**, we looked at formatting axes in *"Section 12.10 Axis" on page 275*. When working with **continuous** dates, edit the axis to change how months are displayed. In Figure 13.10, I changed the axis *Tick Marks*

tab in the **Edit Axis** pop-up window on the left. Right-click the axis at the bottom of the chart to open the **Edit Axis** window and select the *Tick Marks* tab.

Tableau 2023.1 added the ability to use dynamic fields in axis titles.

13.2.1 Format Axis

In addition to the axis settings, right-click the axis and choose "Format" to change axis formatting. The **Format** pane opens on the left. You can change date or number formats, the scale, font, alignment, and title on the *Axis* tab of the **Format** pane. Use the axis *context menu* setting "Clear Axis Range" to reset the axis range if needed.

13.2.2 Show or Hide Axis

You can hide or show an axis with the "Show Header" setting for a field on the **Rows** or **Columns** shelves. *"Section 6.5 Donut Chart" on page 112* illustrates how to hide an axis.

13.2.3 Independent Axis for Each Row

On the *General* tab of the **Edit Axis** window, select "Independent axis ranges for each row or column" to add independent axes, as shown in Figure 13.11.

Figure 13.12 shows the default, where all axes have the same range on the left. The right side is after the change.

13.2.4 Center Date Labels/Headers

In Figure 13.13, I cannot "center" labels under the bars because the [Order Date] field is **continuous**. When I right-click the field and change the field to **discrete**, Tableau adds headers instead of an axis.

FIGURE 13.8
Measure Names as Labels.

Highlight Table

Segment	Null	Order Date 2019	2020	2021	2022
Consumer	21	14,427	368		1,894
Corporate	200	3,150	61	1,483	3,572
Home Office	100		302	4,164	3,731

FIGURE 13.9
The Highlight.

In Figure 13.14, I right-click the month "Mar" on the x-axis, and the *context menu* has options to "Rotate Label" and "Show Header" because [Order Date] is **discrete**. If I choose "Format" from the *context menu* in Figure 13.14, I can edit the *Scale* to change the format for dates in the axis.

13.3 Field Labels

To show field labels, select "Table Layout" on the **Analysis** menu and then check "Show Field Labels for Rows." To hide field labels, right-click the field label on the canvas and check "Hide Field Labels for …" in the *context menu*, as shown in Figure 13.15. Note that this option is grayed out if you unchecked "Show Header" for the field.

When you choose "Format" from the field label's *context menu*, the **Format** pane opens on the left with options for font and shading, as shown in Figure 13.16. Scroll down to see all the settings. Field labels appear above the column header, as shown in the example, "A Heading for a Field on the 'Text' Tile" that follows. The beginning of **Chapter 12** has diagrams labeling the components of a visualization.

13.4 Headers

Tableau adds headers for **discrete** fields, as shown in the *"Section 3.5 Discrete vs. Continuous" on page 61* topic. We also looked at how to format column and row headings in the topic "Headers" in *"Section 12.17 Headers" on page 285*. While default heading names are usually okay, sometimes the headings need clarification.

13.4.1 Add Headers to Multiple Charts

In *"Section 6.3 Multiple Charts in One View" on page 105*, a placeholder field on the *Label* tile adds a layer for headings.

13.4.2 A Heading for a Field on the Text Tile

By default, there is no heading for a field on the *Text* tile on the **Marks** card, as shown in Figure 13.17.

To add a custom heading, create a calculated field and drag the new field to the **Rows** shelf or the

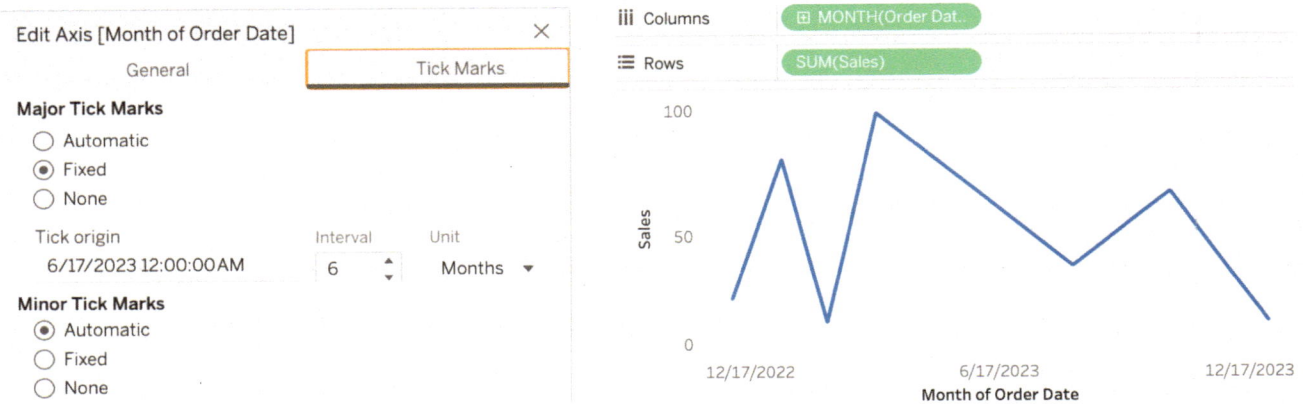

FIGURE 13.10
Month of Order Date.

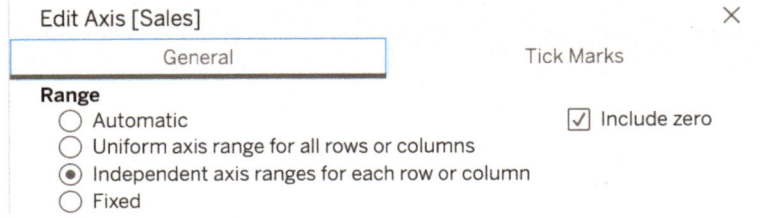

FIGURE 13.11
Independent axis setting.

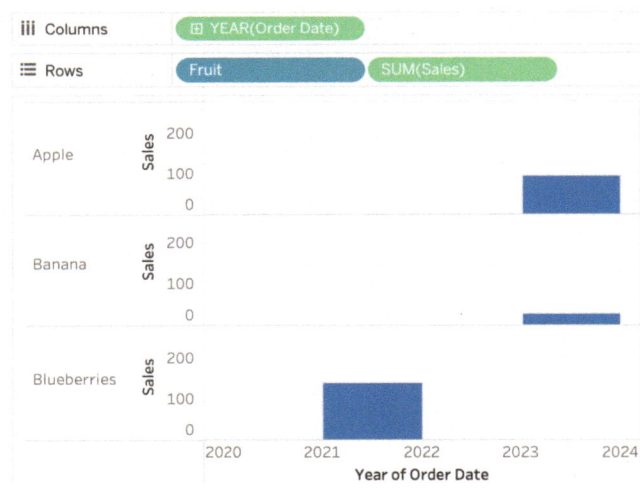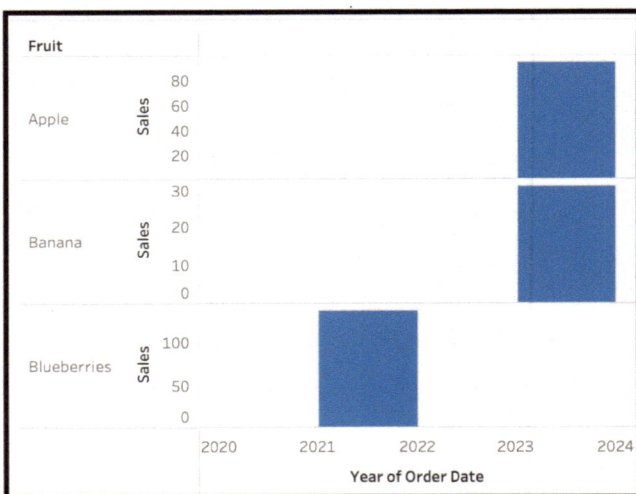

FIGURE 13.12
Independent axis example.

Column shelf. Next, in the view, right-click on the new field name, "Sales Heading," and select "Hide Field Labels for Columns," as shown in Figure 13.18. Right-click the field on the **Marks** card and choose "Format" to change the alignment to "Bottom" so the heading text is closer to the marks. Finally, I would adjust the column width.

13.4.3 Dashboard Container Only for Headings

When I want to rename my column headings or reuse aliases more than once, I create a container on my dashboard with a **text** object for each heading. A dashboard container with text objects for each heading provides flexibility for header names. *"Section 14.12.2 Dashboard Container for Headings" on page 316*

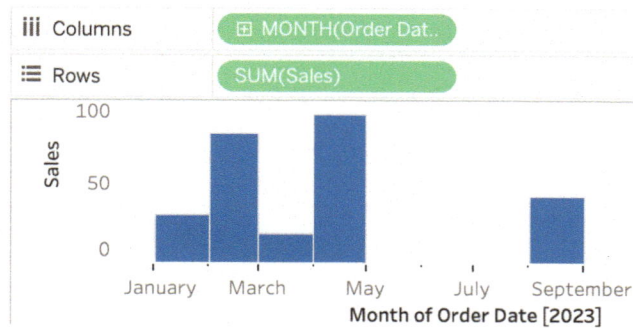

FIGURE 13.13
Continuous Date Axis.

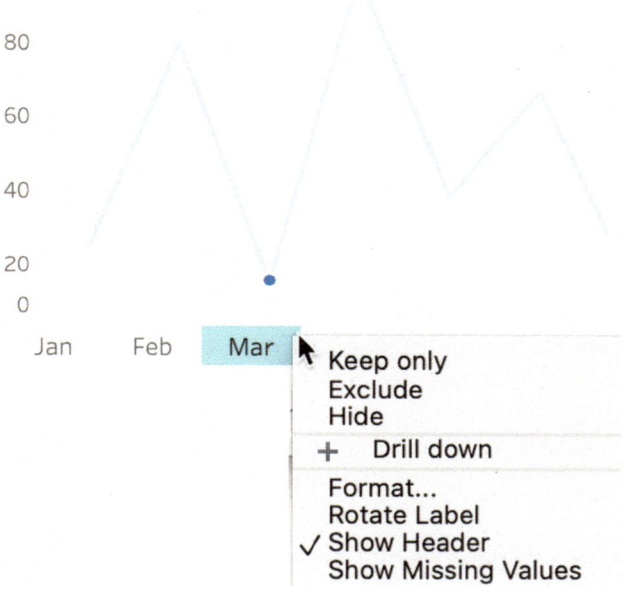

FIGURE 13.14
Rotate labels.

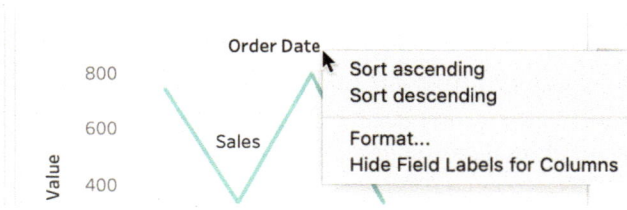

FIGURE 13.15
Hide field labels.

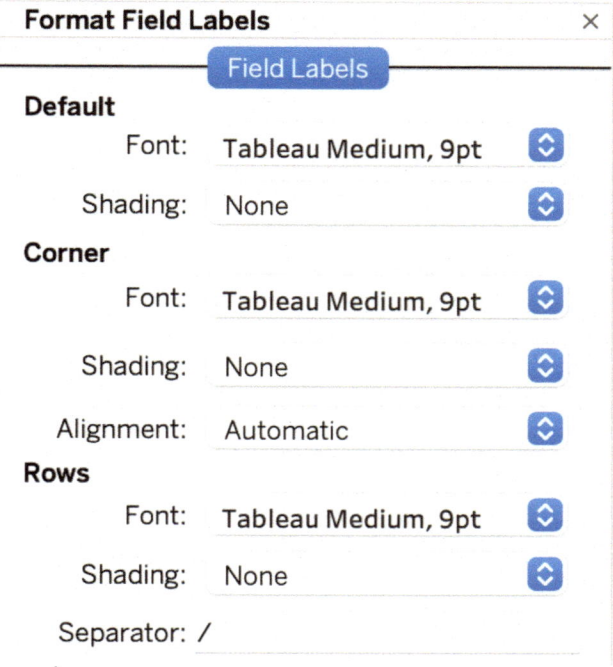

FIGURE 13.16
Format field labels.

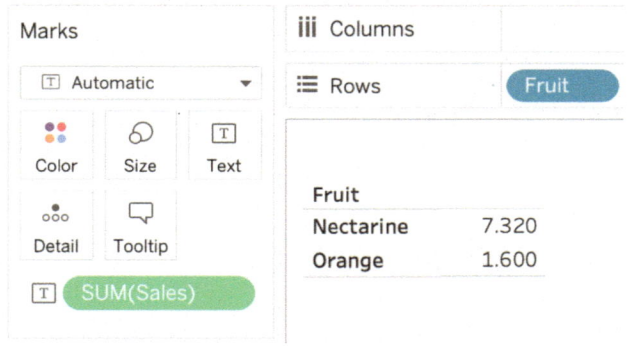

FIGURE 13.17
Heading for Text tile field.

walks through how to create this type of container. Because KPIs sometimes deal with the absence of data, *"Section 14.23 KPIs and BANs (Big Numbers)" on page 347* also explores headings for charts with no data.

13.5 Worksheet Titles

Double-click the title to open the **Edit Title** window. If the title is not showing, on the **Worksheet** menu, select "Show Title." The worksheet title appears at the top of the canvas, as shown in Figure 13.19. In *"Section 14.22 Titles When There Are No Rows of Data" on page 347*, we looked at how to make a worksheet title if a KPI chart has no rows after filtering. In addition to the **Chapter 12** topic, "Titles and Headings," *"Section 14.12.1 Include Field Data in the Dashboard Title"* is an interesting title. That example combines the *Text* tile on the **Marks** card and the worksheet

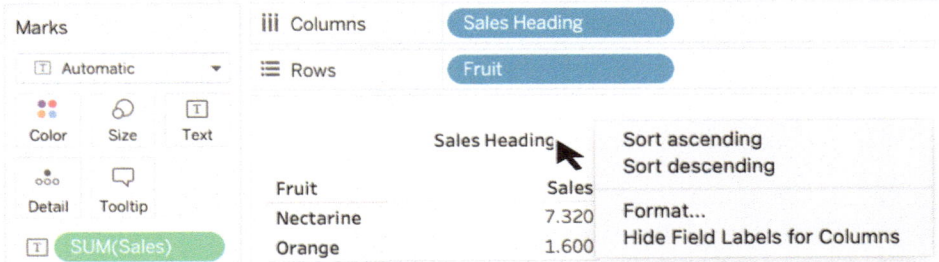

FIGURE 13.18
Hide Field Labels.

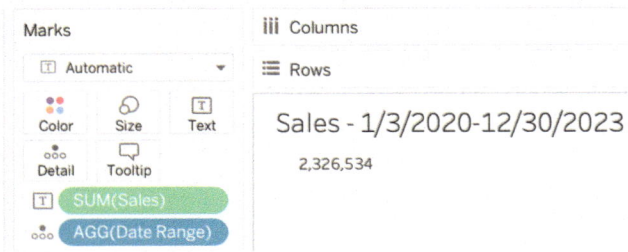

FIGURE 13.19
Worksheet titles.

title to add a dashboard title. *"Section 9.11 Avoid 'All' in a Date Title" on page 208* resolves the issue of multiple date values.

You must have a field on the *Text* tile to open the **Edit Label** window and edit the "Text" settings, as shown in Figure 13.20. In this example, I erased everything in the **Edit Label** text box.

13.5.1 Titles Including Field Data

In Figure 13.21, I added text and the [Date Range] field to the label.

13.6 Legends and Controls

To hide or show a legend, on the **Analysis** menu, select "Legends" and then select the shape, size, map, or color legend. Click-drag to reorder items in a **Shape** legend. When you change the color of the text title for a control or legend while working on a worksheet, you will see that change once you view a **Filter Control** or **Color Legend** on a dashboard. To set the default format for the workbook, on the **Format** menu, select "Filters," "Legends," "Highlighters," or "Parameters."

- *"Section 12.22.1 Title with Mark Colors" on page 288* adds legend colors as part of the title.

13.6.1 Edit Alias

You can assign aliases to **discrete** dimension values in a **Legend** when you right-click a value in the legend. You cannot create aliases for measures, dates, and **continuous** dimensions.

13.6.2 Legend Highlighting

You can highlight marks based on the legend value selected. The icon at the top of the **Legend** control indicates which mode you are using. You use one-way mode when the selected marks in the view control the highlighting. When selecting values in the **Legend** control highlighting, you are using two-way mode. For more information, see Tableau's online guide:

https://help.tableau.com/current/pro/desktop/en-us/actions_highlight_colorlegend.htm

13.6.3 Separate Color Legends

In Figure 13.22, there are two color legends with stepped color. To add separate color legends, right-click the [Measure Values] field on the *Color* tile of the **Marks** card and choose "Use Separate Legends."

13.6.4 Custom Color and Shape Legend (Diamond)

I am using yellow diamond shapes to mark the top three sales in this dual-axis chart. Earlier, we created several dual-axis charts in **Chapter 6**.

1. Create the chart as shown below, using a placeholder field [MIN(1)] to create a dual-axis. Ensure there are no fields on the **AGG(MIN(1))** layer on the **Marks** card (Figure 13.23).

2. The calculated field [Color Top 3] uses RANK to find the top three sales. In the following image, I have a calculated field called "Color Top 3" that uses Rank() to return two values.

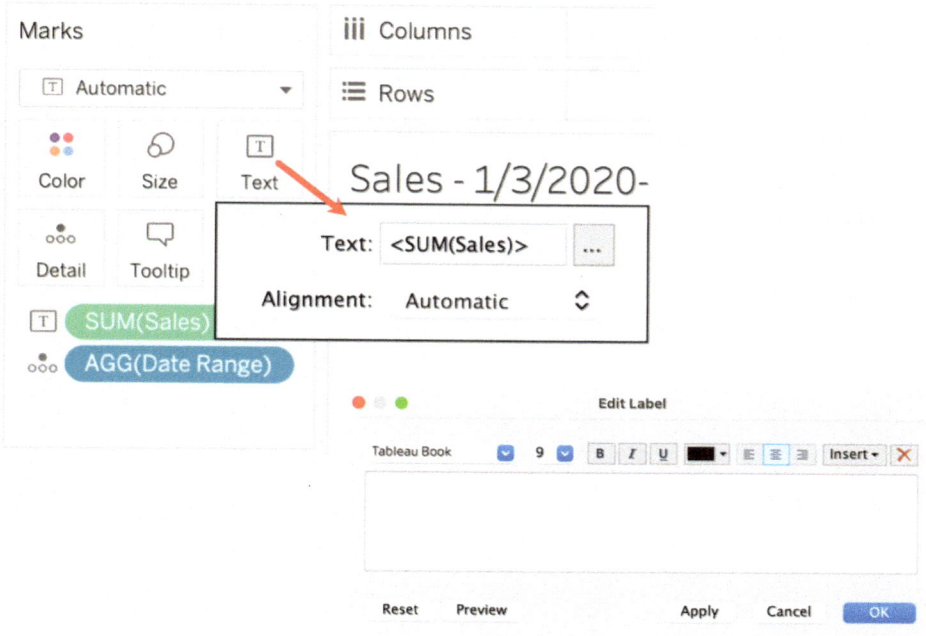

FIGURE 13.20
Erase all text in the Edit Label Box.

FIGURE 13.21
Edit label.

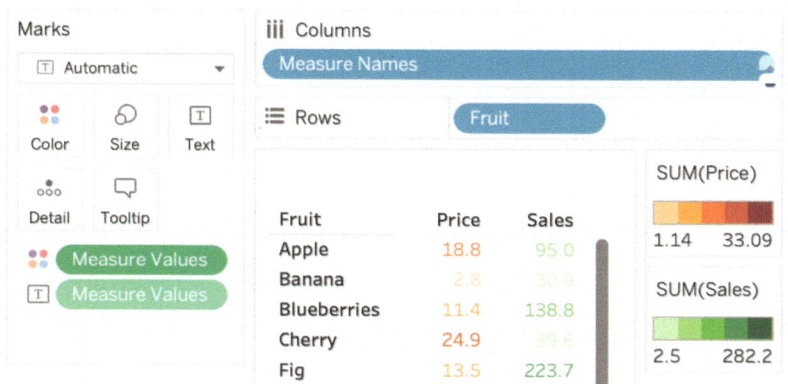

FIGURE 13.22
Stepped color and separate legends.

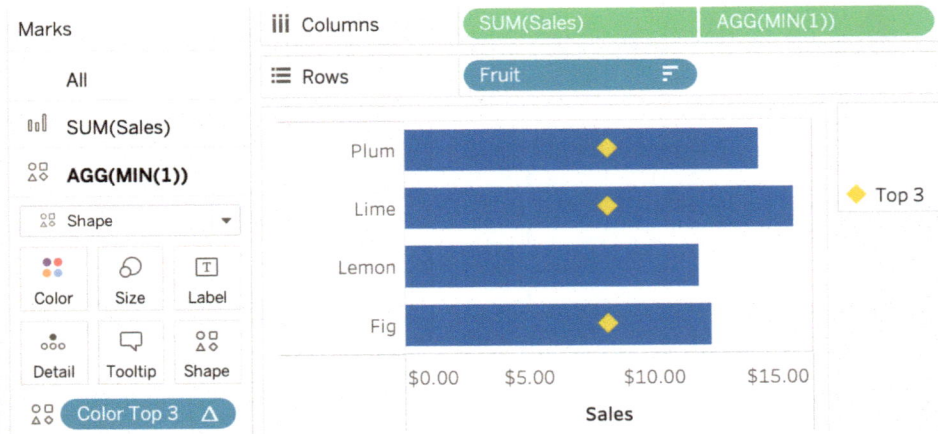

FIGURE 13.23
A bar chart with yellow diamonds.

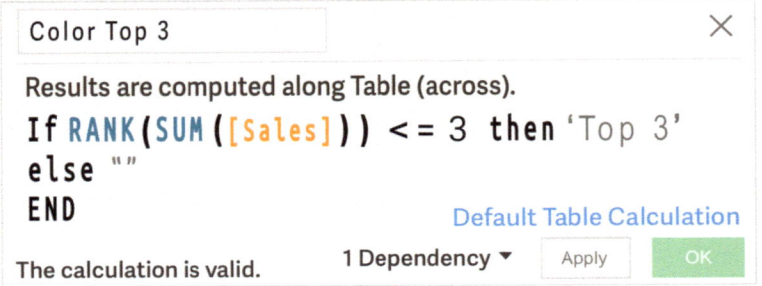

FIGURE 13.24
The calculated field color Top 3.

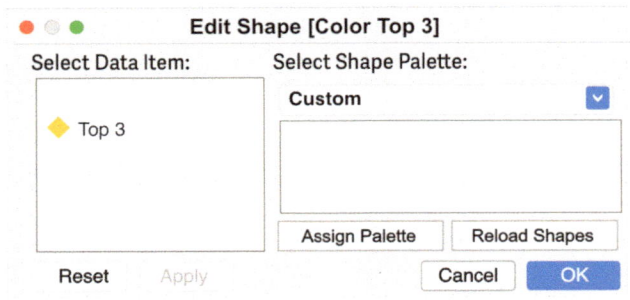

FIGURE 13.25
The Edit Shape dialog window.

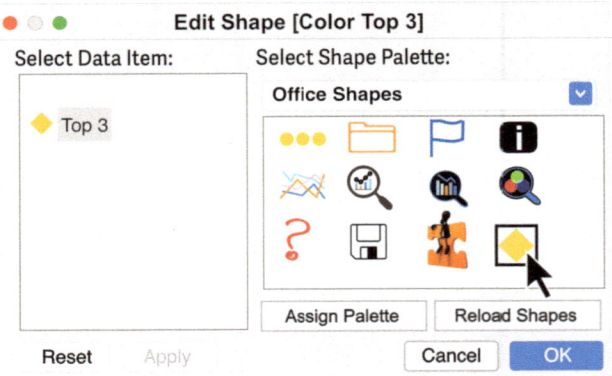

FIGURE 13.26
The Edit Shape dialog window.

This field is on both the *Color* and *Shape* tile on the **Marks** card (Figure 13.24).

3. Before you move forward with Step 3, look at the alternative version in Step 8. If you like Step 8 better, skip ahead to Step 7.

   For the second layer created by the [MIN(1)] placeholder field, I use a "Shape" mark type on the **Marks** card. The empty space is the first value on the left side of the **Edit Shape [Color Top 3]** window, and I have assigned a transparent custom shape. *"Section 7.2.7.1 Custom*

Shapes and Colors" on page 129 has more information about transparent shapes and a similar example of diamond shapes in a chart. Because the shape is transparent, in Step 6, I reordered the items in the **Shape Legend**, so the transparent shape is at the bottom (Figure 13.25).

4. Double-click the *Color* tile to assign a transparent color to the first value. Assign yellow to the "Top 3" value.

FIGURE 13.27
The calculated field Diamond Placement.

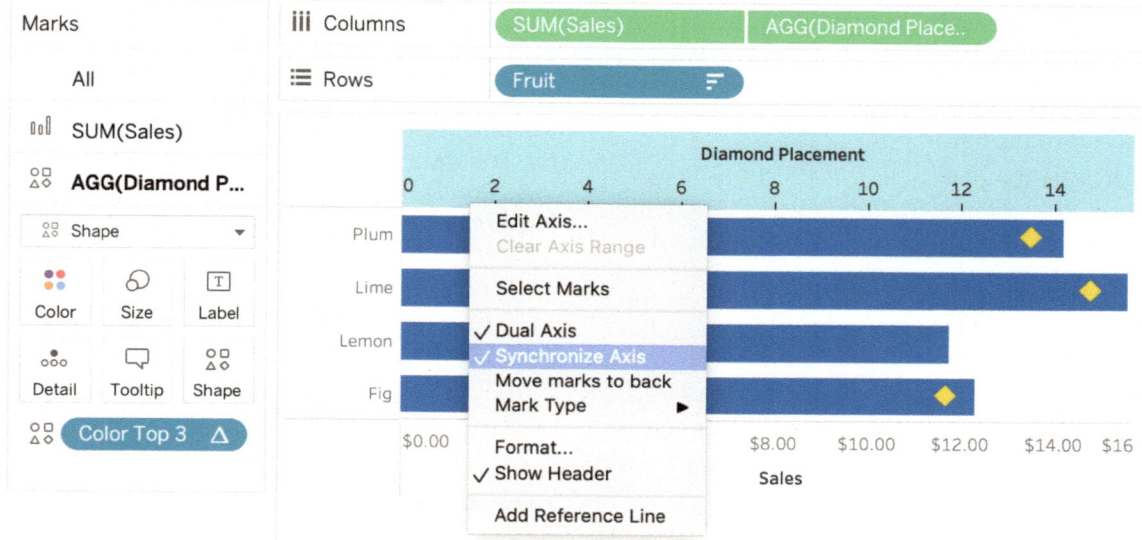

FIGURE 13.28
The Axis context menu.

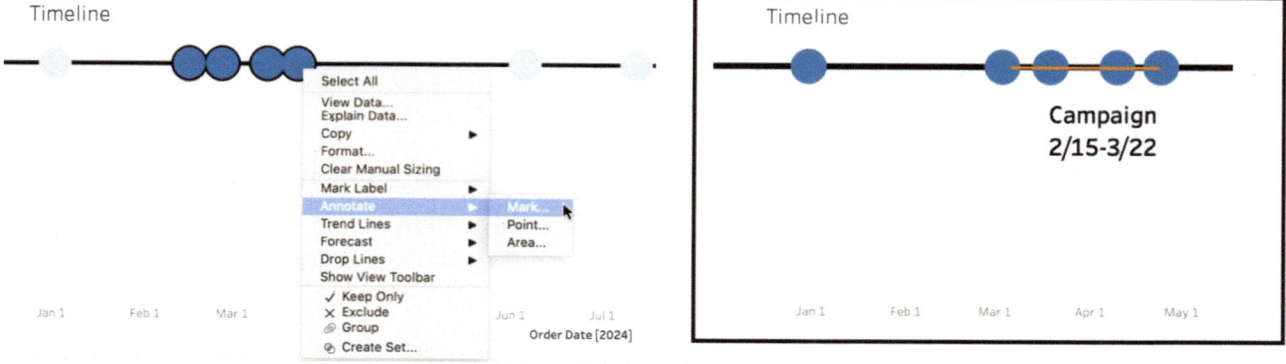

FIGURE 13.29
Annotate a mark.

5. I assigned a transparent shape to the first value, "", as shown Figure 13.26. For the second value, "Top 3," I assigned a custom shape I created: a yellow diamond. In this way, I apply both shape and color to the legend (Figure 13.26).

6. Because my custom "shape" has both the color and shape I want, I'd like to display the **Shape Legend Control** instead of the **Color Legend Control**. On the **Analysis** menu, I select "Legends" and then *Shape Legend*.

7. With the Rank() calculation, you see all values in the case of a tie. Edit the title of the **Color Legend** control to say something like, "*For ties, all tie values are shown.*" Also, click-drag the "Top 3" value so it is right under the title. If you do not want a title, right-click the drop-down arrow in the top-right corner of the **Shape Legend Control** and uncheck "Title."

8. Because I used MIN(1) as my placeholder, the diamond shape is at "1" on that axis. I want to change that because I want the shape to be placed near the end of the bar. I create a calculated field [Diamond Placement] to mirror my measure field. The new field has the same calculation and is multiplied by .95 to reduce the size slightly, so my shape will be just before the end of the bar (Figure 13.27).

9. Instead of the placeholder [MIN(1)] in Step 1, I add the calculated [Diamond Placement] field to create the dual-axis. Right-click the new field on the **Columns** shelf and choose dual-axis. Ensure there are no fields on the new layer **AGG(Diamond Placement)** on the **Marks** card.

10. Right-click the new *axis* at the top of the canvas and choose "Synchronize Axis." Finally, you could click on the new field and uncheck

"Show Header" to hide the second axis at the top of the canvas (Figure 13.28).

Tableau Public file: https://public.tableau.com/app/profile/cathy.y7960/viz/Top3diamondshapelegends1073/Dashboard1

13.7 Annotations

Annotations are attached to points, marks, or an area of the chart. After you select a mark, you can insert field data into the annotation comments. "*Section 7.2.8 Line Charts*" *on page 133* showed annotations with a slope chart. In Figure 13.29, I selected four marks on the timeline chart and added an annotation. To format the annotation, right-click the annotation on the canvas. Double-click the annotation to drag it to a new location, change the size, or edit it.

Tableau Public file:

https://public.tableau.com/app/profile/cathy.y7960/viz/annotatearea/Dashboard1US&:sid=&:display_count=n&:origin=viz_share_link

Figure 13.30 illustrates an Annotation Area.

13.8 Placeholder Fields

Placeholder fields on the **Columns** shelf or **Rows** shelf can add text in a vertical column or horizontal row, as shown in Figure 13.31.

Other examples using placeholder fields are in **Chapters 2, 4, 6, 9, and 12.**

13.9 Reference Line Labels

When configuring the labels for reference lines, you can customize the text and add field values, as shown in "*Section 7.8 Reference Lines*" *on page 152.*

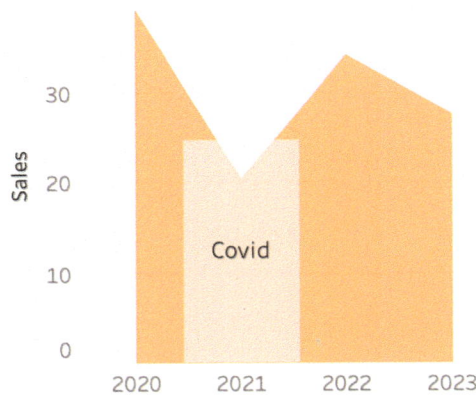

FIGURE 13.30
Annotate an Area.

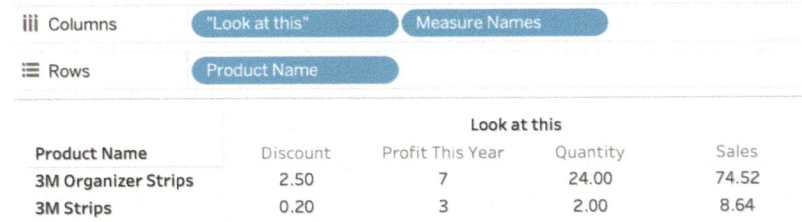

FIGURE 13.31
Placeholder field to add a label on the canvas.

14

Dashboards

Dashboards are comprised of containers and tiled areas. These areas contain objects like worksheets, text objects, and navigation buttons. You can adjust the height and width of objects and move them around the dashboard.

14.1 Create a Dashboard

To create a new dashboard, click the *New Dashboard* icon at the bottom of the view. Drag a worksheet from the **Dashboard** pane on the left onto the dashboard. In the middle of the **Dashboard** pane, the "Sheets" section lists all sheets in the workbook. Sheets used in the active dashboard have a slight blue check mark. You can also drag other objects at the bottom of the **Dashboard** pane onto the dashboard.

14.2 Dashboard Pane

The left side of the Tableau dashboard workspace is divided into a **Dashboard** pane or a **Layout** pane. The **Dashboard** pane has options for device layouts, the dashboard size, a section with the workbook's sheets, and a group of objects you can add to your dashboard at the bottom of the **Dashboard** pane.

14.2.1 Device Layout

Dashboard *layouts* are shown at the top of the **Dashboard** pane. Tableau creates a "Phone" layout under the "Default" layout. You must configure each layout separately, so if you do not intend to format the "Phone" layout, it is a good idea to right-click the layout and delete it. To remove the option from any new dashboard, uncheck the setting on the **Dashboard** menu called "Add Phone Layouts to New Dashboards."

14.2.2 Size

The "Size" setting on the **Dashboard** pane is the overall size of the dashboard, for example, "Desktop Browser" or "PowerPoint." Select a size based on how your users will use the dashboard. To size individual objects, use the **Layout** pane.

14.2.3 Sheets

The middle section of the **Dashboard** pane shows available sheets. You can drag sheets from the **Dashboard** pane onto the dashboard.

14.2.3.1 Swap Sheets

When you want to replace a dashboard sheet, select the sheet on the view or in the **Dashboard** pane. Sheets on the dashboard have a slight blue check mark, and the chosen sheet has a light gray background, as shown in Figure 14.1. In this example, I selected Sheet 1 and I am swapping it with Sheet 2. Move the mouse over the replacement sheet in the **Dashboard** pane (in this case, Sheet 2) until Tableau displays two small icons to the right of the sheet name. Click the double

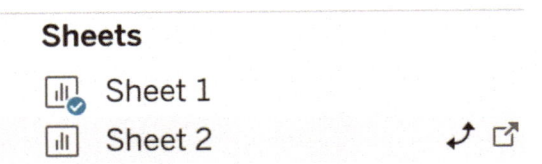

FIGURE 14.1
Selected sheet in the Dashboard pane.

arrow *Swap Sheets* button to replace or swap the sheet on the dashboard.

14.2.4 Objects

Near the bottom of the **Dashboard** pane, the "Objects" section lists various objects you can add to the dashboard. These objects vary based on your version of Tableau Desktop. Some of the objects I use most often are shown below. I like temporarily using the "Blank" object when laying out containers.

- Image
- Blank
- Web Page
- Navigation
- Download

14.2.5 Tiled and Floating

At the bottom of the **Dashboard** pane are two buttons for *Tiled* or *Floating*. *Tiled* objects are structured so that you may have several objects, including containers, on the same layer, and they fill the entire canvas. The dashboard size is always the same. *Floating* objects can be stacked on top of other objects in a layered effect, as shown in the example, *"Section 14.18 A Floating Container for Filters" on page 333*. Unlike tiled objects on a dashboard, you can control the order of stacked or floating objects. I'd recommend avoiding floating objects except for something like filter containers. We look at floating containers later in the "Containers" topic.

14.3 Layout Pane

Click the tab at the top of the panel on the left to switch to the **Layout** pane instead of the **Dashboard** pane. There are several sections on the **Layout** pane that control:

- Position and Size
- Borders Around Chart Elements

- Padding
- Item Hierarchy

14.3.1 Position and Size

For floating containers, you can adjust the position and size. The numbers represent pixels.

14.3.2 Background

Whenever you change a container to "Floating," Tableau changes the container opacity to transparent. To change the container background, click the background color tool in the middle of the **Layout** pane on the left and choose a color.

14.3.2.1 Background Image or Wallpaper

Tableau Public examples sometimes have a floating image as a background. I like to think of these images as "wallpaper" since they are merely graphics the author created for that particular dashboard. To personalize your dashboard with images, lay out your dashboard objects. Unlike tiled objects on a dashboard, you can control the order of floating objects.

14.3.2.2 Change a Floating Object Background Color

You can change background colors for worksheets when editing the worksheet or change dashboard objects using the **Layout** pane.

1. Select the dashboard object and select the **Layout** pane. In the *Background* section, choose "None."

2. Click anywhere within a worksheet and choose "Format." Select the *Shading* button and the *Sheet* tab. From the "Worksheet" drop-down menu, select "None." For additional details, see **Chapter 12** for more formatting options.

14.3.3 Item Hierarchy

Objects on the dashboard are listed in the **Item Hierarchy** section at the bottom of the **Layout** pane. In the **Item Hierarchy** section, expand the arrows to drill down into the hierarchy to see how objects are "nested" inside containers. A selected object has a light-shaded background in the **Item Hierarchy** section, indicating it is the selected object. When you right-click to select an object, the *context menu* opens with several options, as shown in Figure 14.2. To remove a container, right-click the container object in the Item Hierarchy to select the container and then choose "Remove Container" from the drop-down context menu.

14.3.4 Padding

In Figure 14.4, the dashboard **Layout** pane is on the left. The black area is the "Outer Padding," and the light blue area is the "Inner Padding." The blue border is between the outer padding and the inner padding. When you combine tiled objects and floating objects,

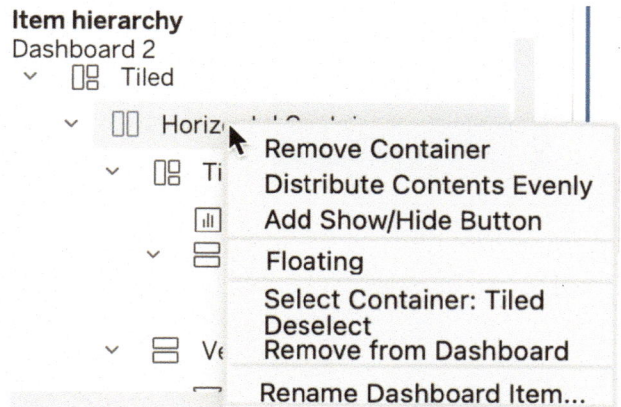

FIGURE 14.2
Object menu in Item Hierarchy.

FIGURE 14.3
Tip: *Padding is another way to center a text box for a column header.*

the floating objects are listed first in the **Item Hierarchy**. *"Section 14.4.5 Positioning Containers and Objects" on page 307* illustrates item hierarchies.

14.4 Containers

Horizontal and vertical container objects are a great way to organize your dashboard. Containers are either "tiled" or "floating." Tiled containers are on the same layer and automatically adjust size as you drag objects onto the dashboard. You will always have the same size dashboard, but the objects on the dashboard change height or width automatically to fit the dashboard. Floating containers are like sticky notes layered on the tiled layer, and you can reposition them anywhere on the dashboard and change the container size. This dashboard only has *tiled* objects in the bottom left in the **Layout** pane under the **Item hierarchy**, as shown in Figure 14.5.

In comparison, the objects in Figure 14.6 are inside a vertical container. On the left side, the **Layout** pane shows the new **Item hierarchy**.

When you select a container, a blue bounding box is displayed around its outside edges, as shown in Figure 14.13. The blue bounding box indicates a container into which you can drag objects. For example, you can drag objects like worksheets, text objects, or navigation buttons into the blue bounding box of the container.

"Section 14.18 A Floating Container for Filters" on page 333 demonstrates common container tasks. These are the relevant steps in that example.

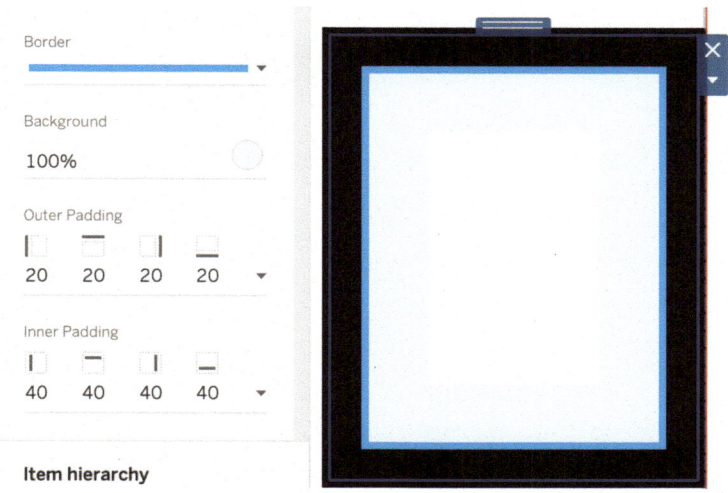

FIGURE 14.4
Dashboard Padding.

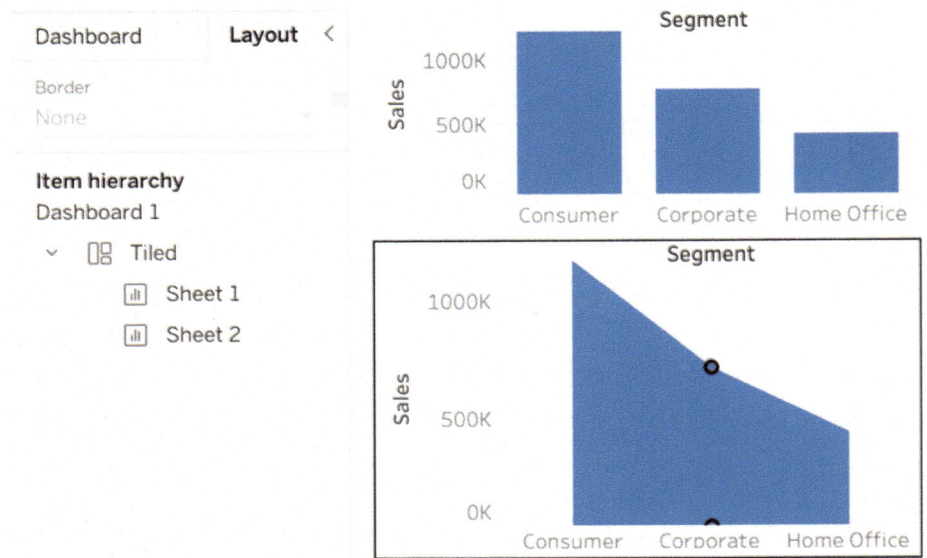

FIGURE 14.5
Tiled Dashboard objects.

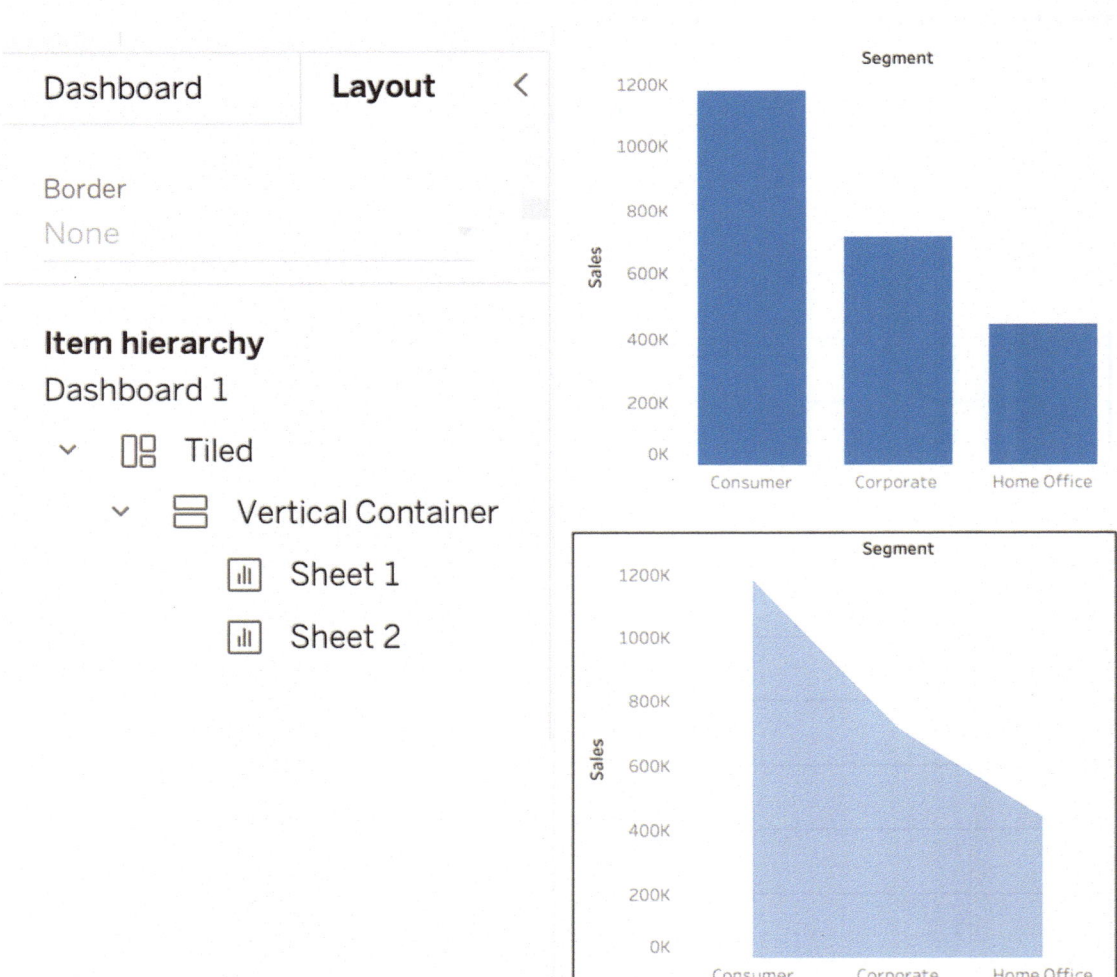

FIGURE 14.6
Objects inside a container.

Step 3: Rename the container.

Step 3: Change the container to a floating container.

Step 3: Set the background color of a container.

Step 4: Select a container.

Step 4: Rename a container.

Step 8: Change Floating Order.

Step 9: Add a Show/Hide Button to a Floating Container

14.4.1 Add a Container

To add a container, drag a horizontal or vertical *container* object from the "Objects" section at the bottom of the **Dashboard** pane onto the dashboard.

14.4.2 Add Objects to a Container

To add dashboard objects to a container, select the container, and then in the **Dashboard** pane, select the object and drag and drop the object into the container. A selected container has a blue bounding box around the edge. Be aware that the container may automatically resize after you drag an object into it.

14.4.3 Drag to Resize Containers, Sheets, and Objects

Select a container and drag the edge of the blue bounding box to resize the container. Drag the edge of the dark gray bounding box to resize a sheet or other object. *"Section 14.23 KPIs and BANs (Big Numbers)" on page 347* illustrates ways to resize objects in the topic "Size KPI Sheets and Containers." The topic "Object Menu" also outlines fit, height, and width settings.

> If you cannot resize a container object, check that the parent container is not using "Distribute Contents Evenly."

14.4.4 Select a Parent Container

To change to a **parent** container, select the object or container, then right-click the drop-down in the top right corner to open the *object menu*. Choose "Select a Container: *Container Name*" to move to the parent container and change the width.

14.4.5 Positioning Containers and Objects

I like to name my dashboard objects and containers so it's easy to find objects in the **Item Hierarchy** in the left pane. I find it easier to create a dashboard template and then add charts and update text. I uploaded this example in Figure 14.7 to Tableau Public as the "KPI Dashboard Template."

https://public.tableau.com/views/KPIDashboard Template_17053442999830/Template?:language= en-US&publish=yes&:display_count=n&:origin=viz_ share_link

If you want to add another filter control to an existing floating container, use Shift + Click to drag the new control into the floating container. When you create your first dashboard, placing objects inside containers can be a real challenge. My advice is to experiment with adding containers and objects; before long, you will be an expert.

- When adding objects to dashboard containers, I temporarily make the container larger. When selected, the container has a blue bounding box. Note that after you add one object to a container, the container may automatically resize.

- If you are unable to add a new object to a container, change the new object to "floating," then hold down the shift key and drag the floating object into the container. Also, select all objects in the Item Hierarchy and look for stray floating objects you can delete.

- Adding at least two "blanks" makes working with a new container easier. Adding objects *between two objects* is usually easier.

- When dragging objects into a container, drag the objects into the middle of the container, between two objects, or at the right edge of the container. If you pause moving the mouse, a light gray box appears, indicating where the object will be placed.

- If you cannot resize a container object, check that the parent container is not using "Distribute Contents Evenly." To change to a **parent** container, select the object or container, then right-click the drop-down arrow in the top right corner to open the *object menu*. Select the option "Select a Container: *Container Name*" to move to the parent container to change the width or height.

- When a container is nested within a parent container, and you cannot drag additional

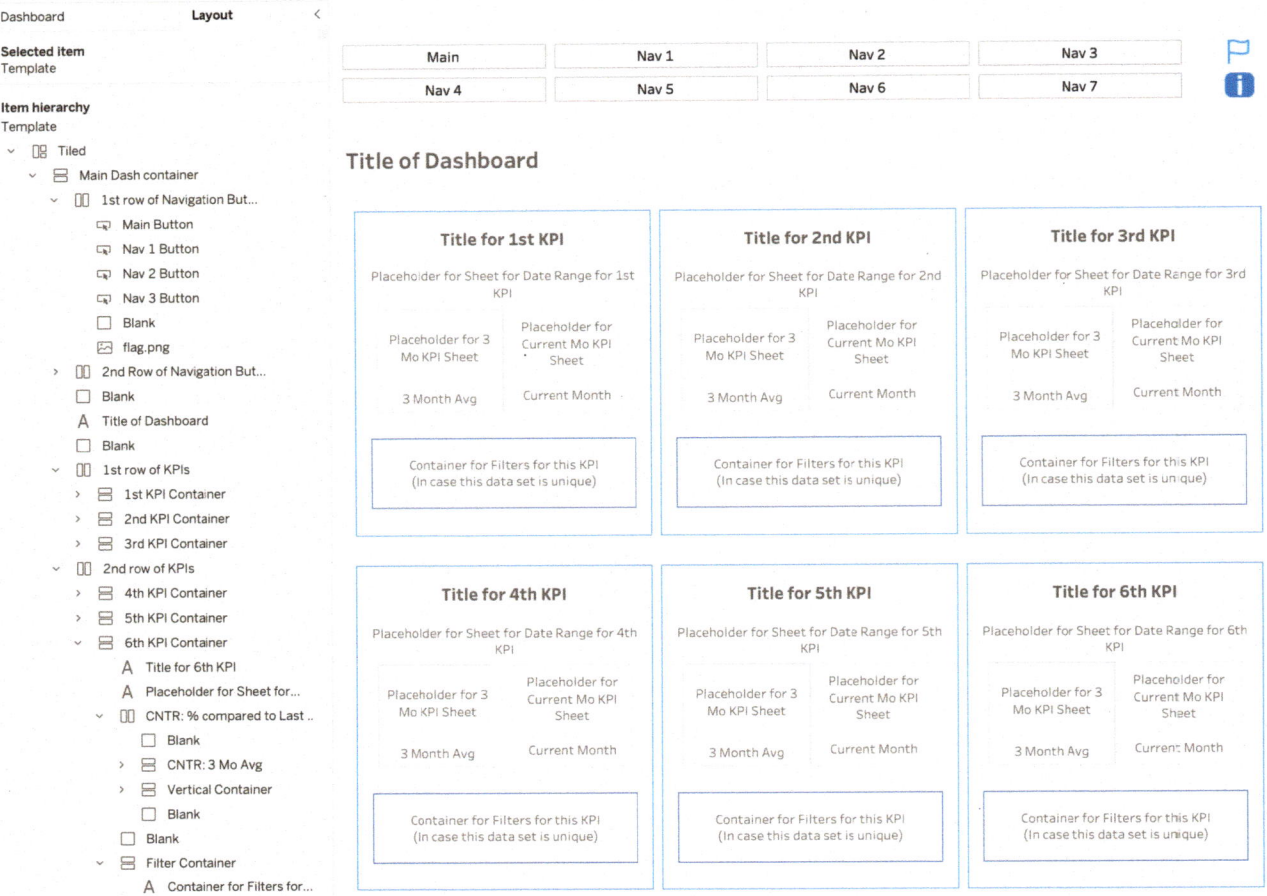

FIGURE 14.7
Dashboard KPI template.

objects into the main parent container, use the nested container's *object menu* to **resize** the nested container so it is half the size of the main parent container. Ideally, the parent container's blue bounding box will have an empty area indicated by diagonal blue lines.

- When a text object does not line up with a text value in a sheet, try changing the "Fit" for the sheet to "Entire View." You can also right-click the text object, choose "Format," and then adjust the alignment for the text object.

- Rearrange the object's position in relation to other objects once the object is inside the container.

- Remove blanks and resize the container to the final size after dragging sheets, images, and text objects where you want them.

14.5 Dashboard Objects

In addition to containers, blanks, and text objects, Tableau has several buttons that add interactivity to the dashboard.

Dashboard buttons are similar to menus in that they provide interactivity. Tableau has several button objects.

- Image Button
- Web Button
- Navigation Button
- Download Button

14.5.1 Image Button – URL or Email

While an image object might be a plain graphic, you can also choose to set up interactivity, as shown in Figure 14.8. Tableau accepts a wide range of image

FIGURE 14.8
Link to a Web Page URL.

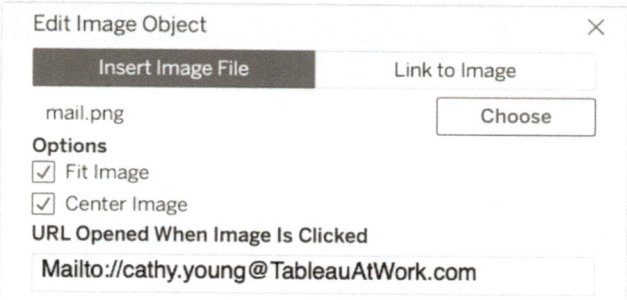

FIGURE 14.9
Link to an Email Address.

formats. My favorite images are vector *.svg files because of their quality and resolution. If I'm using a background color, I also like objects that support transparency. For example, if I have a circle image, transparency means there is no white background around the circle.

While I haven't tried all of the URI schemes from RFC 1738, I have used mailto://, as shown in Figure 14.9, to send emails. Some interesting articles on the web discuss using other URI schemes with Tableau, such as instant messaging.

14.5.2 Web Page Button

The web page button is similar to an image button, except it is merely a link.

14.5.3 Menus from Buttons

In a Tableau dashboard, when adding "Objects" from the **Dashboard** panel, you may have noticed there is no "Menu" object. The dashboard buttons for "Navigation" and "Images" are similar to a menu in that they provide interactivity. In later examples, I use floating containers with worksheets and parameters to create the appearance of a menu. "Navigation" buttons, as shown in Figure 14.10, move to other dashboards or worksheets.

14.5.4 Download Button

The "Download" button in Figure 14.11 exports data to several formats, including PDF and PowerPoint.

14.5.5 Copy a Dashboard Object

Tableau version 2021.4 and later allow you to copy some dashboard objects within the same dashboard or a different dashboard. However, you won't always see the copy option because Tableau won't copy an object tied to a specific worksheet. Creating a template of containers, blanks, and text objects is a great way to experiment with copying dashboard objects.

To copy an object, select it on the dashboard or from the **Layout** pane: **Item Hierarchy** section. In Figure 14.12, I click the top right corner of a container's bounding box to open the *object menu* and select Copy Dashboard Item. You can also right-click the object in the *Item Hierarchy* section to copy it. Move to the dashboard location where you want to paste the object, and from the **File** menu, select "Paste." After pasting, you can open the *object menu* to change from **Floating** to **Tiled** or other options.

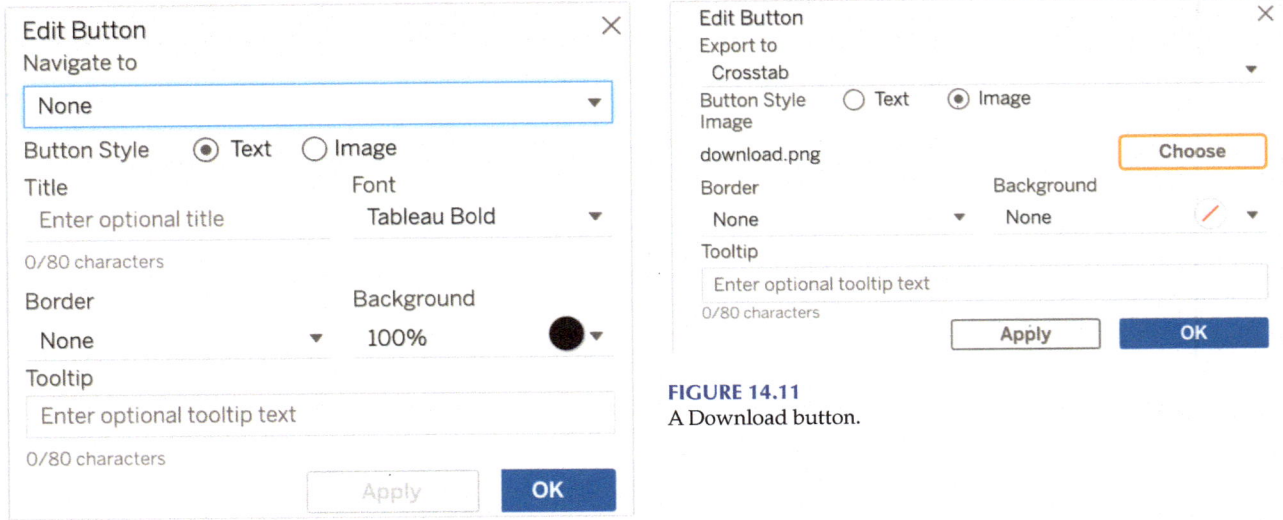

FIGURE 14.10
Navigation button.

FIGURE 14.11
A Download button.

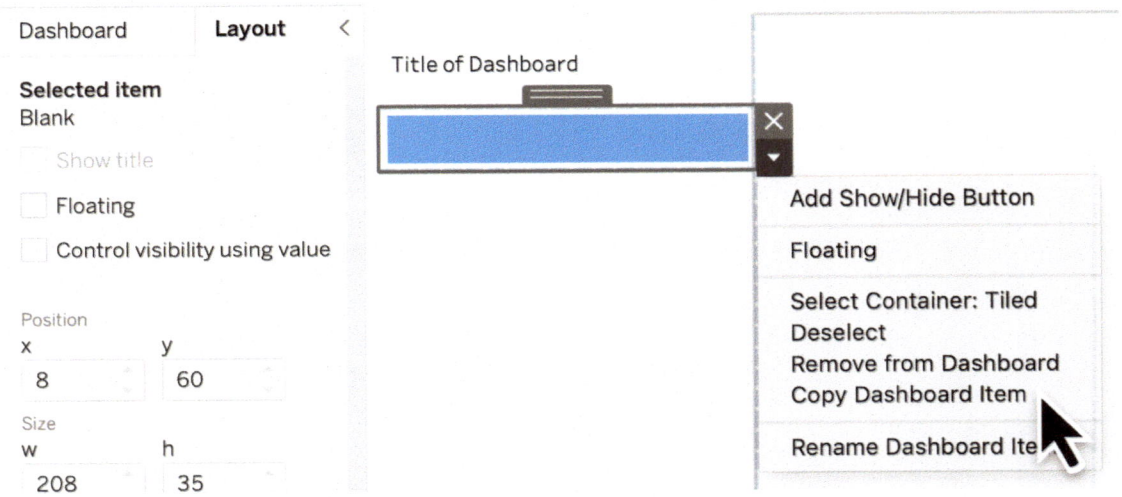

FIGURE 14.12
Copy a Dashboard item.

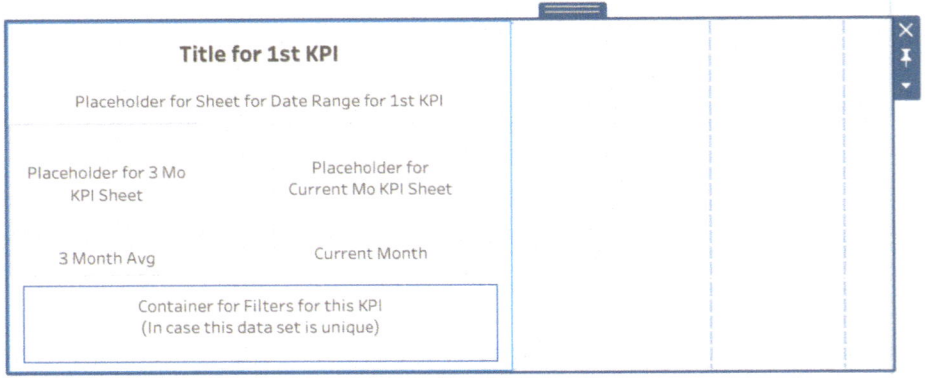

FIGURE 14.13
Select the container.

In Figure 14.13, I have two blanks on the right side of a container. Since the selected object is a container, the bounding box around the outside is blue.

Move to the dashboard location where you want to paste the object, and from the **File** menu, select "Paste." In the example above, I have two blanks. After pasting, you can open the new item's *object menu* to change from "Floating" to "Tiled" or other options.

14.6 Object Menu

When you select an object like a sheet, navigation button, image button, or text object, a dark gray bounding box indicates the selected object. There are buttons in the top-right corner and a drop-down menu. A container has a blue bounding box with the same buttons in the top-right corner. Click the drop-down arrow to open the *object menu* shown in Figure 14.14. The options vary depending on whether you selected an object or container and may include these tasks.

- Distribute Contents Evenly.
- Change to Floating (or back to Tiled.)
- Fix or Edit the Width or Height.
- Select a Parent Container with "Select a Container: *container name*."
- Copy or Rename the Dashboard Item.

- For Floating Containers: Add a Show/Hide Button.
- For Floating Containers: Change the Floating Order.

14.6.1 Fit

When you select worksheets and objects, the dark gray bounding box appears with a drop-down arrow to open the *object menu* in the top right corner. "Fit Width" is under "More Options" on the *object menu*. Also, in the toolbar area at the top of the screen, you can select "Fit" options like:

- Standard
- Fit Width
- Fit Height
- Entire View

14.6.1.1 Align Two Charts with Fit Width

When two charts on the dashboard have very different sizes, I like to adjust the layout to align them.

1. In this example, the bar chart and area chart are different sizes (Figure 14.15).
2. Select each chart and choose "Fit Width" from the toolbar drop-down at the top of the workspace (Figure 14.16).

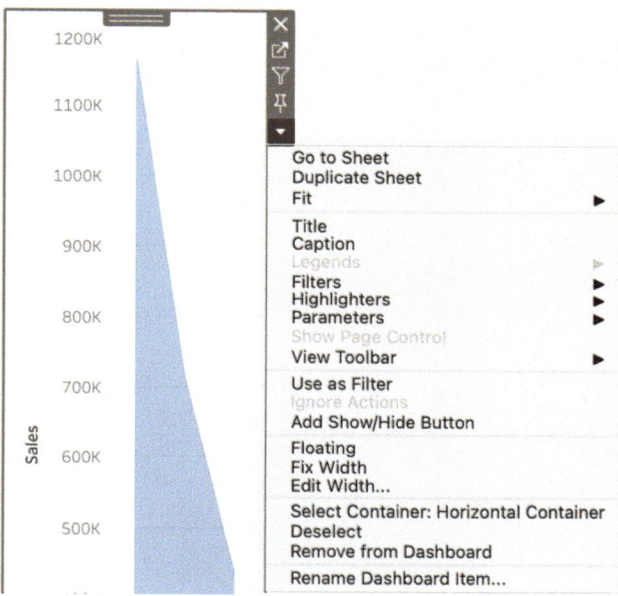

FIGURE 14.14
Object menu.

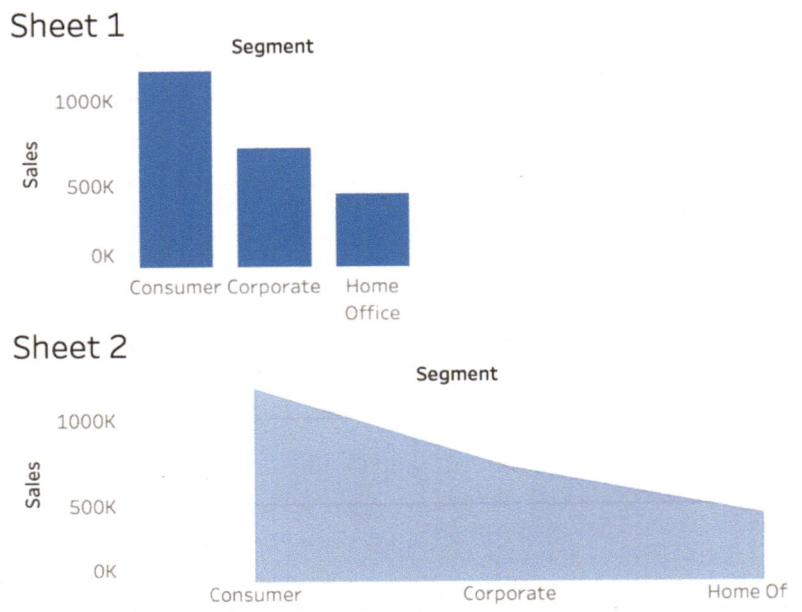

FIGURE 14.15
A dashboard with a Bar Chart and an Area Chart.

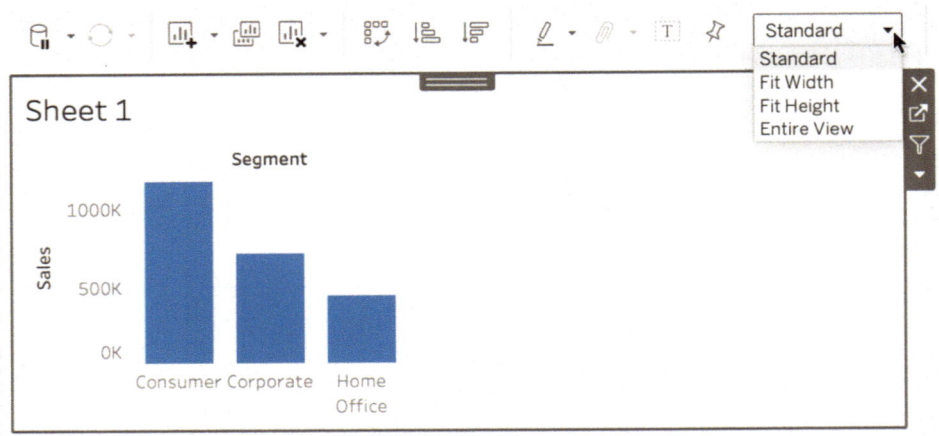

FIGURE 14.16
The Toolbar with the Fit Drop-Down menu.

3. Drag a "Blank" object to the right side of the dashboard. A dark gray bounding box appears around it (Figure 14.17).

14.6.2 Caption

When viewing a worksheet, the **Worksheet** menu can turn on captions. Tableau adds "Caption" as a title for the caption panel. However, when you turn on a worksheet's caption on a dashboard, the title "Caption" is not shown.

14.6.3 Size: Edit Height or Width

As you layout your dashboard objects, you can adjust the size of containers in various ways.

Depending on whether a container is horizontal or vertical, you see either "Edit Height" or "Edit Width."

When a vertical container is nested inside a horizontal container, you can move to the parent container to edit height or width. To change to a **parent** container, select the object or container, then right-click to open the container's *object menu* and select the option "Select a Container: *Container Name*" to move to the parent container to change the width or height.

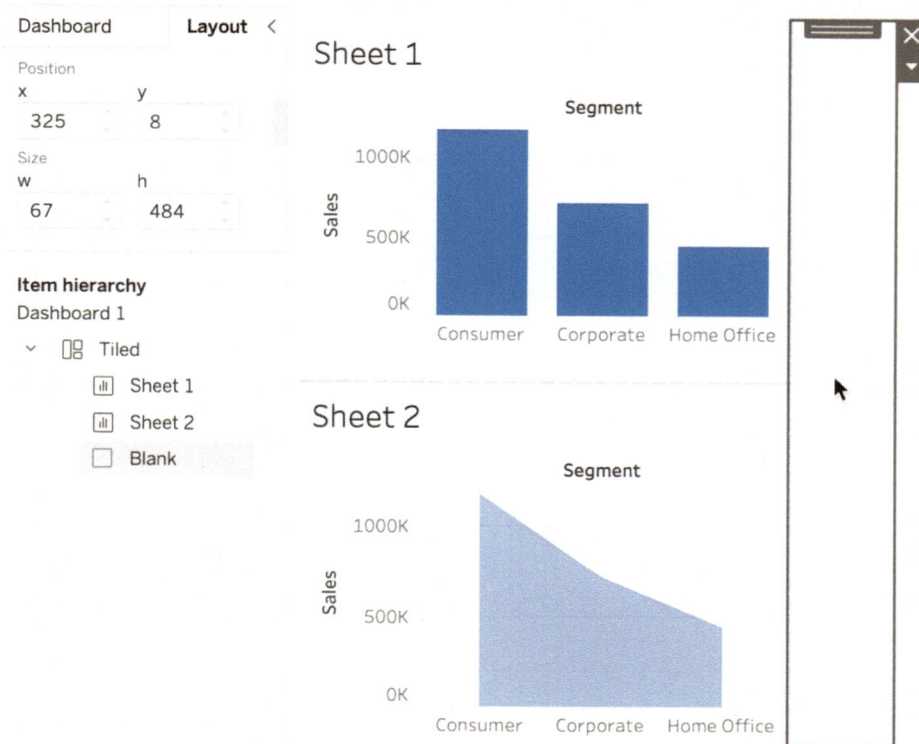

FIGURE 14.17
A blank object selected on a dashboard.

Sometimes, you will notice objects (like other nested containers or sheets) that do not fill the entire container, and there is a gap at the bottom (or right edge) with blue diagonal lines. Select "Fixed Height," and then you can enter a specific height size so it fits the entire container.

Finally, if a worksheet has no rows of data, select the sheet on the dashboard and click the drop-down arrow to open the sheet's *context menu* to edit the height. Editing the height is useful when you have a row of KPI charts you are trying to align. If you aren't sure which object is selected, the **Dashboard** pane on the left lightly shades the background of the selected object.

14.6.4 Align Sheets (Height)

If you struggle to align KPIs on a dashboard, ensure you have the same number of fields on the **Columns** shelf, **Rows** shelf, and *Text* tile on the **Marks** card. Check the overall "Alignment" for the *Text* tile and the *Label* alignment. Finally, on the **Format** menu, make sure the fields have the same alignment.

14.6.5 Distribute Contents Evenly

The container *object menu* has an option to "Distribute Contents Evenly," which is ideal for sizing navigation buttons. If you cannot resize an object, check that the parent container is not using "Distribute Contents Evenly." To change to a **parent** container, select the object or container, then right-click to open the *object menu* and select the option "Select a Container: *Container Name*" to move to the parent container.

14.6.6 Floating Container: Show/Hide Button

Only floating containers have a *Show/Hide* button. Select "Floating" in the **Dashboard** pane on the left when creating a new container. You can also change a tiled container into a floating container at any time.

A floating container with a Show/Hide button allows you to hide the container when not in use, freeing up valuable real estate. You can add an image and descriptive text to the button. Later in this chapter, we use a *Show/Hide* button in *"Section 14.18 A Floating Container for Filters"* on page 333.

14.6.7 Reorder Objects in a Container

Click to select an object, then drag to reorder objects within a container.

14.6.8 Floating Order

Select the floating container and click the drop-down arrow in the top right corner to open the *object menu*.

Select *Floating Order* and select the option to move the container to the front or back.

14.6.9 Select Parent Container

When the object is inside another container, there is a choice near the bottom of the *object menu* to select the parent container. To change to a **parent** container, select the object or container, then right-click to open the *object menu* and select the option "Select a Container: *Container Name*" to move to the parent container.

14.7 Filters

The *object menu* for worksheets on dashboards allows you to display **Filter Controls** for that worksheet. In the "Actions" section that follows, the example, "Pop-out Chart," uses a *Filter Action* to show and hide a worksheet.

Once you add a worksheet to your dashboard, you can display **Filter Controls**. For example, if you have a simple dashboard with a "Sales" worksheet, follow these steps to add a **Filter Control**.

1. Click the "Sales" worksheet on the dashboard.

   A dark bounding box indicates the "Sales" sheet is selected.

2. In the top right corner of the bounding box, click the drop-down arrow to open the *object menu*.

3. Select "Filters" and select a filter from the list. Tableau adds a **Filter Control** to a new container on the dashboard.

14.7.1 Identifying Particular Worksheet Filters

Knowing which worksheet the filter is from can be confusing, especially if your dashboard uses multiple data sources. Select the filter control on the dashboard and right-click the filter control to open the filter's *object menu*. Choose "Apply to Worksheets" to view worksheets with the filter.

14.7.2 Format a Filter Control Title

After you add a filter to the dashboard, the **Format Control** *object menu* will have a choice to format the title. To set the default format for the workbook, on the **Format** menu, select "Filters."

Note that if you change the formatting for a **Filter Control's** title color while working on a worksheet, you won't see that change until you view the **Filter Control** on a dashboard.

14.7.3 Apply Filter to all Data Sources

Apply a dashboard filter to all data sources, as shown in *"Section 8.4 Filter Actions" on page 161*. Select a sheet on the dashboard, and in the top right corner of the bounding box, click the drop-down arrow to select the **Filter** icon. An active filter has a solid **Filter** icon. Click the drop-down arrow to open the *context menu*, then select "Use as Filter." Tableau automatically generates a filter action, as shown in Figure 12.14.

14.7.4 Filter Dashboard Sheets When Data Points Are Selected

You can also use "filter actions" on a dashboard so that when a user selects data points in one view, it filters other views on the same dashboard. To quickly create a dashboard filter action, choose a sheet on the dashboard and click the drop-down arrow to open the *context menu*. Select "Use as Filter." To edit the new filter action on the **Dashboard** menu, select "Actions." The new action *Filter 1 (Generated)* is added to the list of available actions, as shown in Figure 14.18.

14.7.5 Apply Filter to All Worksheets on Dash

From the **Filter Control** drop-down *object menu*, select "Apply to Worksheets" then "Selected Worksheets…" to open the dialog box in Figure 14.19. In the bottom left corner, the button "All on dashboard" is a quick way to apply filters to dashboard worksheets. When the filter applies to multiple data sources, the filter icon appears to be filled in.

14.8 Legend

Once you add a worksheet to your dashboard, you can display a color, map, shape, or size **Legend**.

To set the default format for legends in the workbook, on the **Format** menu, select "Legends."

1. Click the "Sales" worksheet on the dashboard.

   A dark bounding box indicates the "Sales" sheet is selected.

2. In the top right corner of the bounding box, click the drop-down arrow to open the *context menu*.

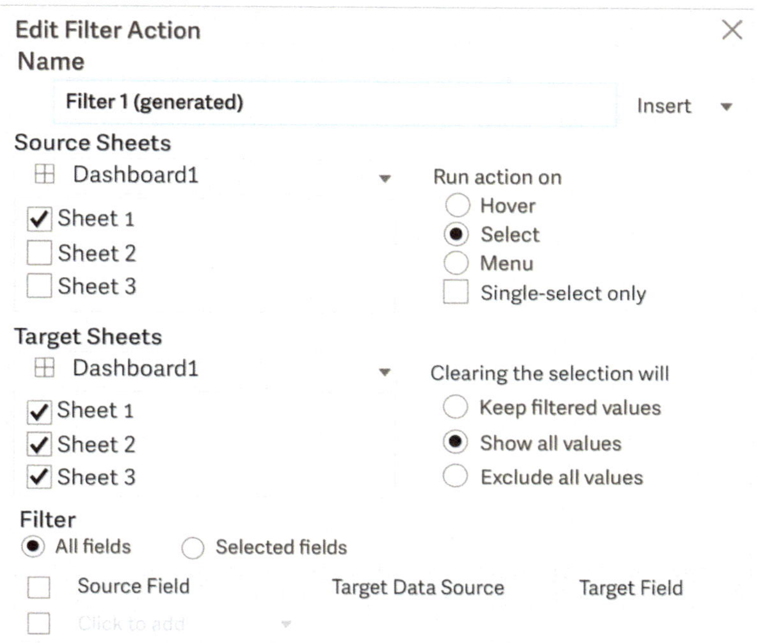

FIGURE 14.18
Filter Action.

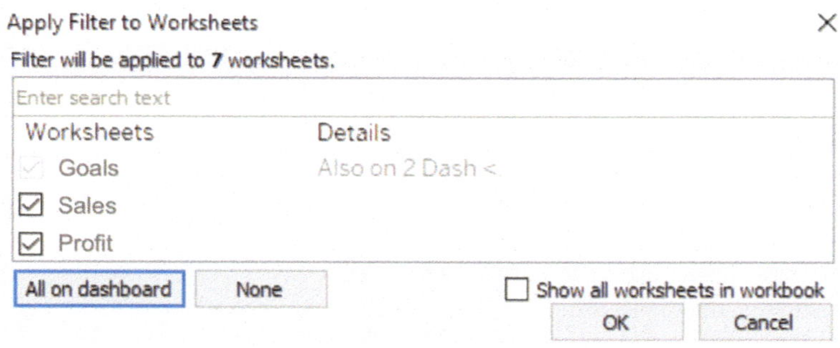

FIGURE 14.19
Apply filter to worksheets.

3. Select "Legends" and then "Color Legends." A **Color Legend** is added to the dashboard on the right side in a new "Vertical" container.

   Note, if you change the color of the text title for a **Color Legend** or **Parameter Control** while working on a worksheet, you won't see the change until you view the **control** or **legend** on a dashboard.

14.9 Parameter Controls

You can add parameter controls once you add a worksheet to your dashboard. For example, if you have a simple dashboard with a "Sales" worksheet, follow these steps to display a **Parameter Control**. To set the default format for parameter controls for the workbook, on the **Format** menu, select "Parameters."

1. Click the "Sales" worksheet on the dashboard.

   A dark bounding box indicates the "Sales" sheet is selected.

2. In the top right corner of the bounding box, click the drop-down arrow to open the *context menu*.

3. Select "Parameters" and select a parameter from the list. Tableau adds a **Parameter Control** to a new container on the dashboard.

14.10 Dashboard Menu

While I mainly use the **Dashboard** menu to create dashboard actions, the menu includes other options for formatting, showing a grid, or exporting the dashboard as an image, as shown in Figure 14.20.

14.10.1 Align Items with a Grid

Display the grid to make it easier to size and align objects properly. On the **Dashboard** menu, select "Show Grid" or "Grid Options."

14.11 Actions

While we look at actions in **Chapter 15**, I included these examples of dashboard actions later in this chapter.

- Reset All Filters Button
- Sheet Selection Menu
- Pop-out Chart
- Filter Dashboard Sheets When Data Points Are Selected

14.12 Titles and Headings

The **Dashboard** menu does have an option to show a dashboard title. Still, I often want additional data in

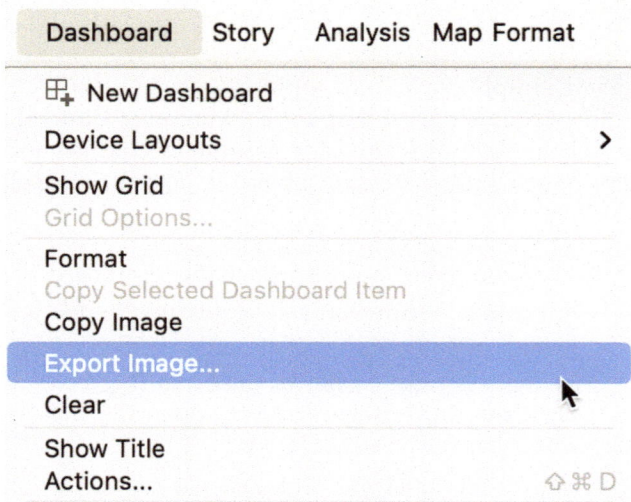

FIGURE 14.20
The Dashboard menu.

my titles in the context of a particular worksheet. Let's look at ways to enhance dashboard titles and make the dashboard cleaner.

14.12.1 Include Field Data in the Dashboard Title

For dashboard titles, I often create a worksheet with only a title. Because Tableau must have at least one row of data to render a chart, I want the number of rows in the bottom left corner of the view to indicate the number of rows is at least one.

1. I added a measure field to the *Text* tile on the **Marks** card for my title so the view has data.
2. I then remove all text and fields in the Text tile's **Text Editor**. I also change the *Color* tile opacity to 0%.
3. I add my title fields to the *Details* tile on the **Marks** card and edit the worksheet **Title**. In this way, Tableau creates a chart with a title.
4. I like to control background colors on my dashboard, so I also use the **Format** pane to change the worksheet shading to "None."

In *"Section 4.2.5 No Data" on page 76*, we looked at creating a worksheet title if a KPI chart has no rows. *"Section 12.15.3 Worksheet Title and Caption" on page 283* also has some ideas for creating titles.

14.12.2 Dashboard Container for Headings

When I want to rename my column headings or reuse aliases more than once, I create a container on my dashboard with a **text** object for each row or column heading. A dashboard container with text objects for each heading provides flexibility for header names. Because KPIs sometimes deal with the absence of data, later, we explore headings for charts with no data in the topic, "KPIs and BANs."

1. Create a calculated field called [Country Header] and add the field to the **Rows** shelf.
2. Hide the field label for the [Country Header] field. Right-click the field name and choose "Hide Field Labels for Rows" (Figure 14.21).
3. Right-click the field [Country Header] and select "Format" to change the alignment to "bottom."

14.13 Aligning KPIs on a Dashboard

If you need to vertically align KPI worksheets on the dashboard, ensure you have the same number of fields

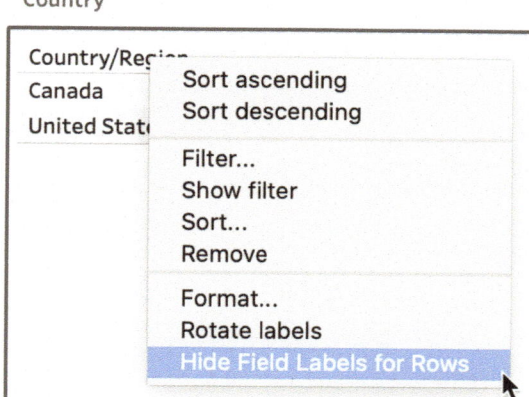

FIGURE 14.21
The Object menu with hide field labels for Rows selected.

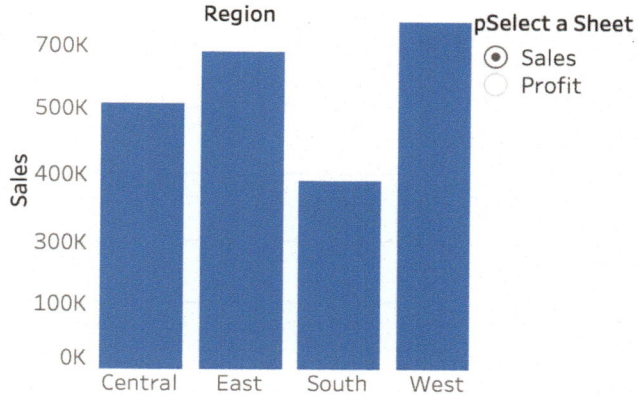

FIGURE 14.22
Sheet selection dashboard.

on the **Columns** shelf, **Rows** shelf, and *Text* tile on the **Marks** card. Check the overall "Alignment" for the *Text* tile and the *Label* alignment, and also check that there are no blank rows in the *Label*. Finally, on the **Format** menu, make sure the fields are all aligned the same.

14.14 Dashboard Sheet Selection Menu

In this Tableau dashboard example, a parameter called [pSelect a Sheet] moves between two floating sheets on the dashboard. A calculated field on each worksheet on the **Filter** shelf is critical to this implementation.

The link to the Tableau Public file is at the end of the exercise, along with a checklist of the elements and settings in the example.

14.14.1 Preview – The Finished Dashboard

The dashboard has two views on top of each other; when the parameter changes, the dashboard changes between the "Sales" view and the "Profit" view (Figure 14.22).

14.14.2 Create the Visualization

1. Create two worksheets, **Sales** and **Profit**, using the *Sample Superstore* data source, as shown at the end of this exercise.

2. Create a parameter called [pSelect a Sheet]. At the top of the **Data** pane on the left, click the drop-down arrow to open the *object menu* and select "Create Parameter." (Figure 14.23)

3. Create a calculated field called [Sheet Calc], as shown below. At the top of the **Data** pane on

the left, click the drop-down arrow to open the *object menu* and select "Create Calculated Field…" (Figure 14.24)

4. Drag the new field [Sheet Calc] to the **Filters** shelf on the **Sales** worksheet. Select *Custom value list*, click within the yellow bar, and type "Sales" (Figure 14.25).

   After typing "Sales" in the yellow bar, click the small plus symbol on the right, as shown below (Figure 14.26).

   The list box should only show "Sales." Click OK.

   The **Filter** reflects the *Custom value list* of "Sales," as shown below (Figure 14.27).

5. While still on the **Sales** worksheet, click the parameter in the bottom left corner of the **Data** pane and select "Show Parameter."

6. Repeat step 4 for the **Profit** worksheet. Drag the new field [Sheet Calc] to the **Filters** shelf on the

   Profit worksheet. Click within the yellow bar and type "Profit."Both worksheets use the field [Sheet Calc] as a filter, but the *Custom value list* is specific to each worksheet (Figure 14.28).

7. On the **Profit** worksheet, click on the parameter and select "Show Parameter" at the bottom left corner.

8. Create a dashboard and click on "Floating" in the **Dashboard** pane on the left. Drag both worksheets onto the dashboard so they float on top of each other (Figure 14.29).

9. Click the drop-down arrow for the worksheet to open the *object menu* and uncheck "Title." Also, click "Parameters" from the *object menu*

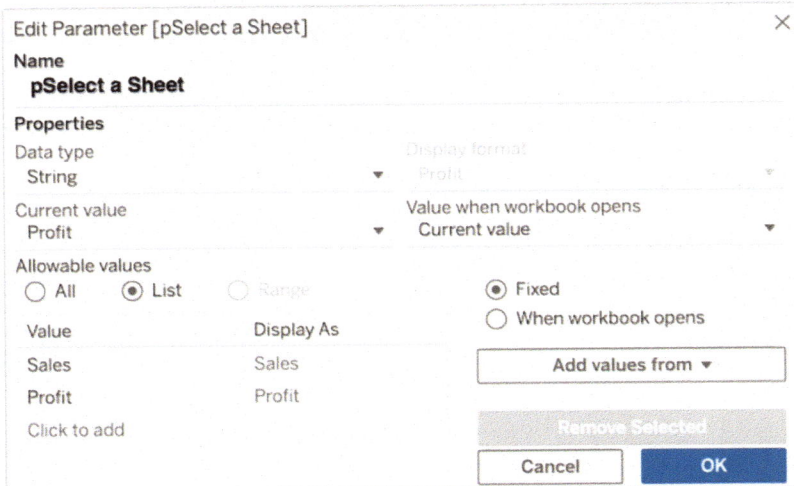

FIGURE 14.23
The Edit parameter window.

FIGURE 14.24
A calculated field with a parameter expression.

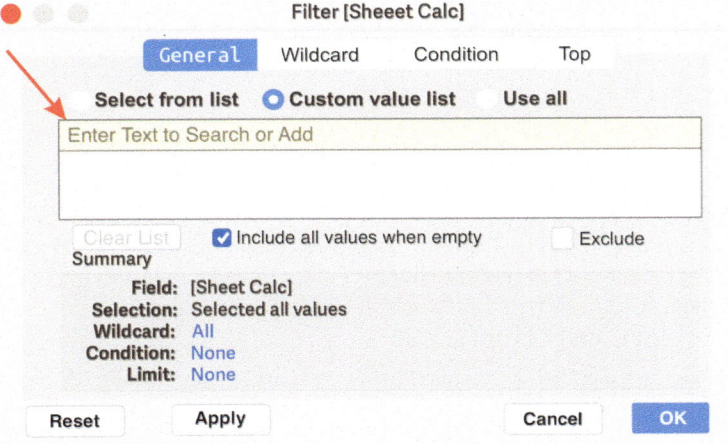

FIGURE 14.25
The Custom value list Filter option.

and select the new parameter "pSelect a Sheet" to display the **Parameter** control.

14.14.3 Testing

On the dashboard, click the Parameter Control to switch between worksheets.

Tableau Public file:

https://public.tableau.com/views/Sheet
SelectionDashMenus1049/Dashboard1?:
language=en-US&:sid=&:display_count=n&:
origin=viz_share_link

https://youtu.be/9FNCoxRqX5s

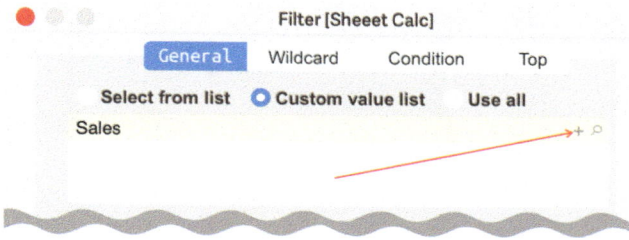

FIGURE 14.26
Click the plus symbol to Add the text.

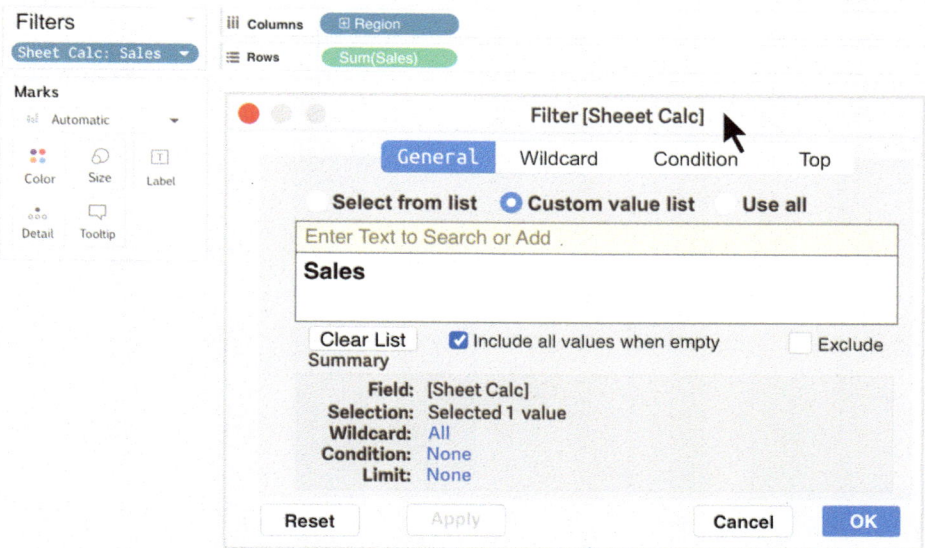

FIGURE 14.27
The completed Sales filter.

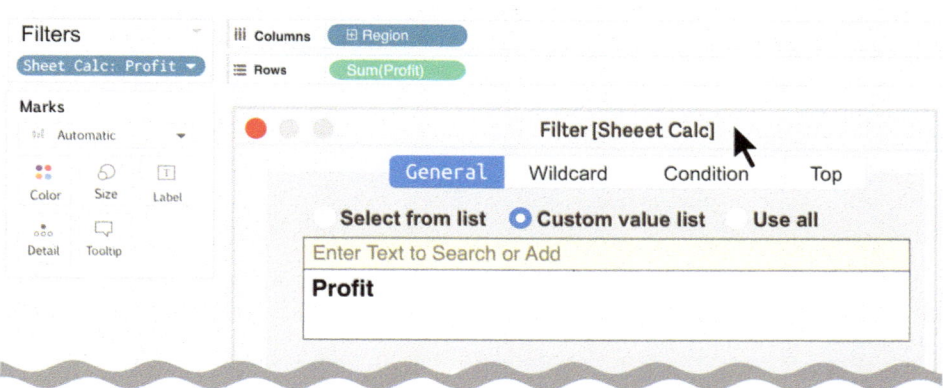

FIGURE 14.28
The Completed Profit filter.

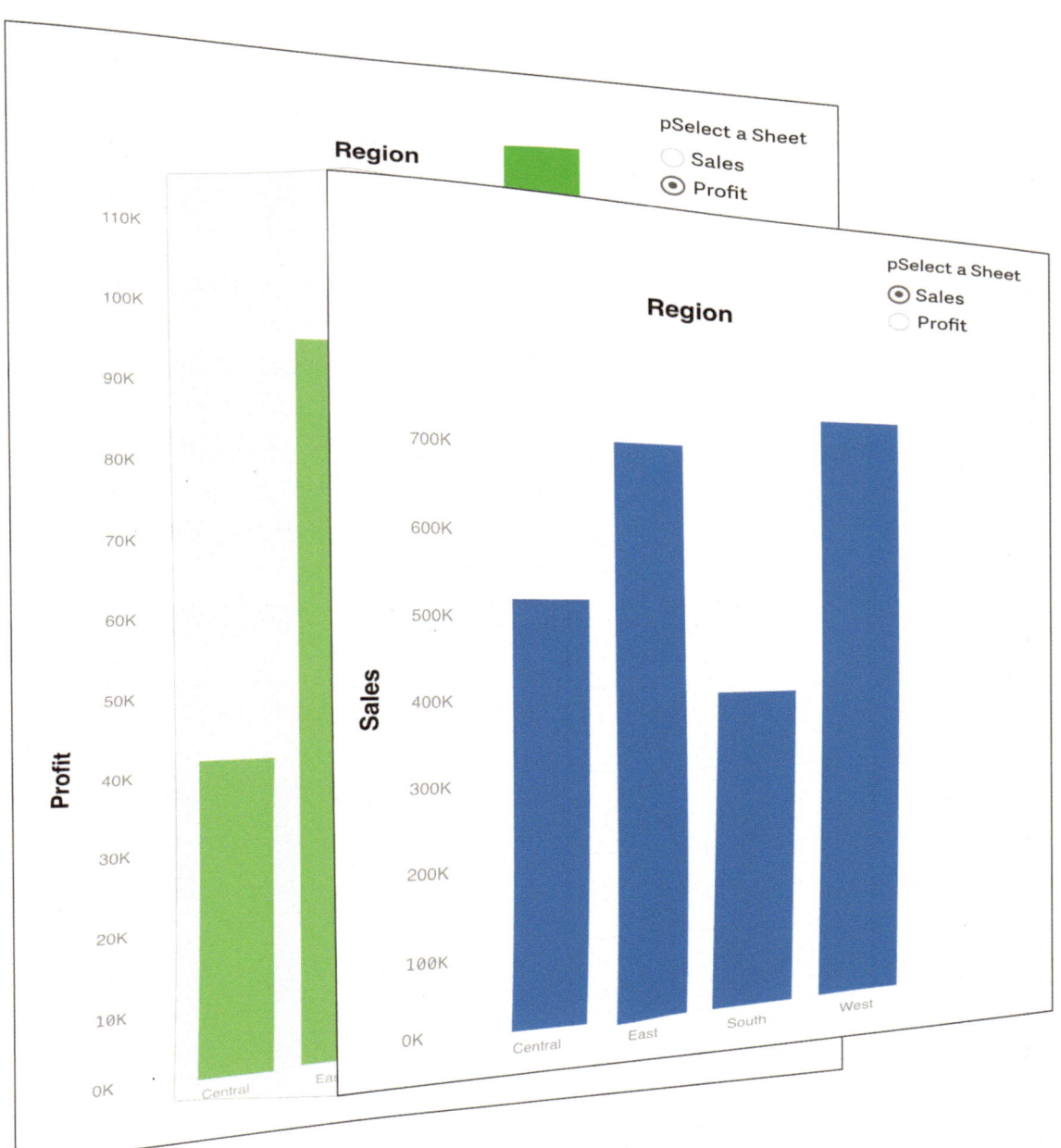

FIGURE 14.29
Two Floating Charts on a dashboard.

14.14.4 Worksheets and Dashboard

This workbook has two worksheets. Each has the [Sheet Calc] field on the **Filters** shelf, and each filter is unique to that worksheet (Figures 14.30 and 14.31).

- Profit
- Sales

14.14.5 Data and Fields

This workbook is based on the *Sample Superstore* data source and includes these fields.

- Region
- Profit
- Sales
- Sheet Calc

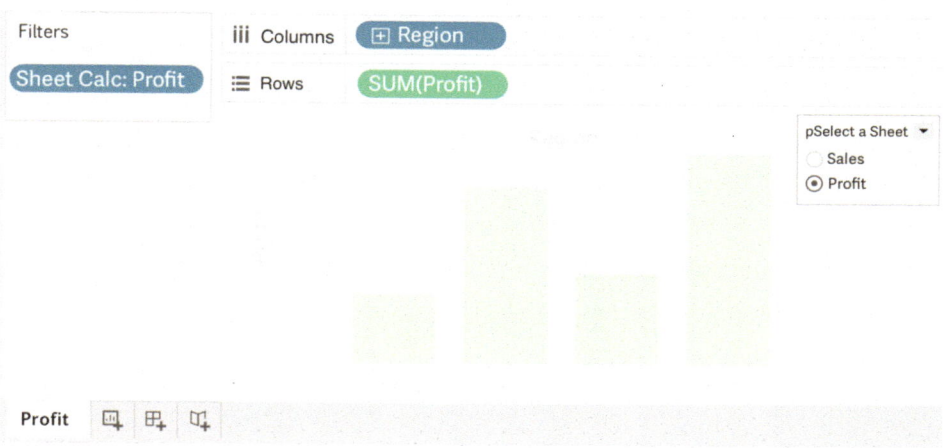

FIGURE 14.30
The Profit worksheet.

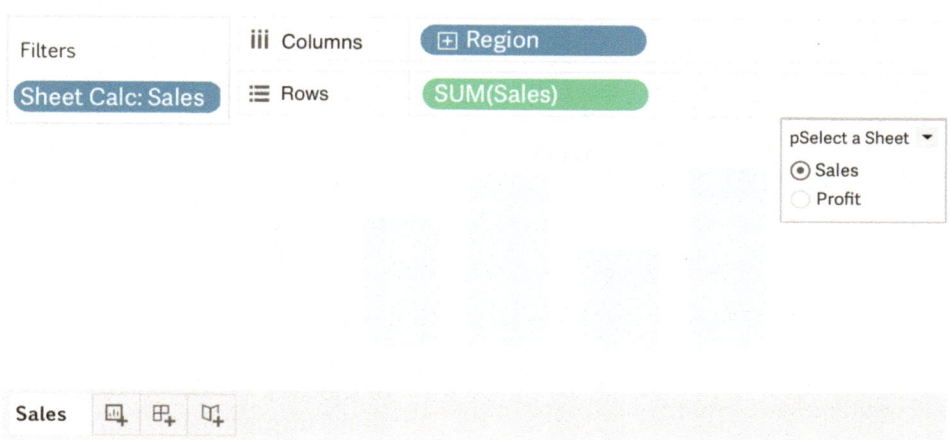

FIGURE 14.31
The Sales worksheet.

14.14.6 Calculated Fields

There is one calculated field, [Sheet Calc], on the **Filters** shelf of both worksheets.

14.14.7 Components or Elements

- Columns Shelf
- Rows Shelf
- Parameter
- Parameter Control
- Filters Shelf

14.14.8 Columns Shelf

The [Region] field is on the **Columns** shelf on both worksheets.

14.14.9 Rows Shelf

The [Profit] field is on the **Rows** shelf on the "Profit" worksheet. Likewise, the [Sales] field is on the **Rows** shelf on the "Sales" worksheet.

14.14.10 Parameter

There is one parameter in this workbook called "pSelect a Sheet."

14.14.11 Parameter Control

Both worksheets show the **Parameter Control** that switches between the worksheets.

14.14.12 Filters Shelf

The [Sheet Calc] field is on the **Filters** shelf of each worksheet, and there is a *Custom Value List* for the filter.

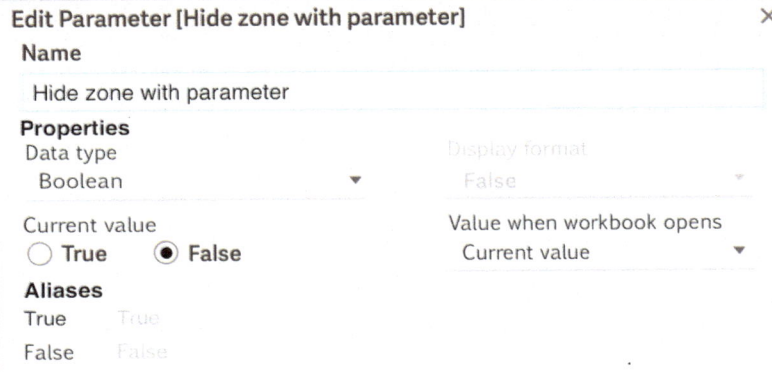

FIGURE 14.32
Editing the Parameter.

FIGURE 14.33
The Calc Field with the TRUE expression.

14.14.12.1 *Profit Worksheet Filter*

The *Custom Value List* filters to "Profit."

Sheet Calc: Profit

14.14.12.2 *Sales Worksheet Filter*

The *"Custom Value List* filters to "Sales."

Sheet Calc: Sales

14.15 Dynamic Zone Visibility

Tableau 2023 and later has a dashboard setting for dynamic zone visibility (DZV). In this example, we create a parameter, a calculated field, and a parameter action. Finally, we use the new "Control visibility using value" dashboard setting on the **Layout** pane.

1. Create a parameter called "Hide zone with parameter." (Figure 14.32)
2. Create a calculated field for each parameter value. The field must be a Boolean type (Figure 14.33).

3. Add the "Sales by Category" sheet to a new dashboard. Add the second sheet, "SubCategory Sales," on the right side of the dashboard.
4. On the dashboard, select the first worksheet, "Sales by Category," and click the drop-down arrow to open the *context menu*. Select "Use as Filter." This step is optional (Figure 14.34).
5. On the dashboard **Layout** pane, check the box for "Control visibility using value…" and choose the calculated field, "Hide zone with parameter." (Figure 14.35)
6. Show the **Parameter Control** or add a parameter action to the dashboard.
7. Create a dashboard action to "Change Parameter." (Figure 14.36)
8. At this point, the dashboard has two actions (Figure 14.37).

14.15.1 Testing

In the "Hide zone" with **Parameter Control**, select "False" from the drop-down list. The dashboard displays one chart (Figure 14.38).

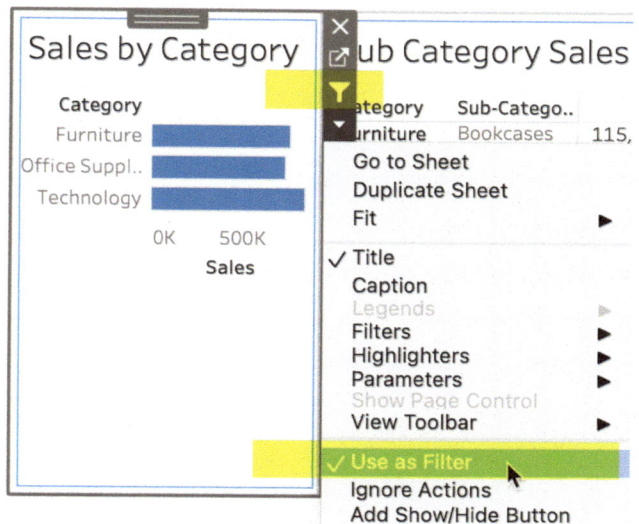

FIGURE 14.34
The Worksheet Context menu on a dashboard.

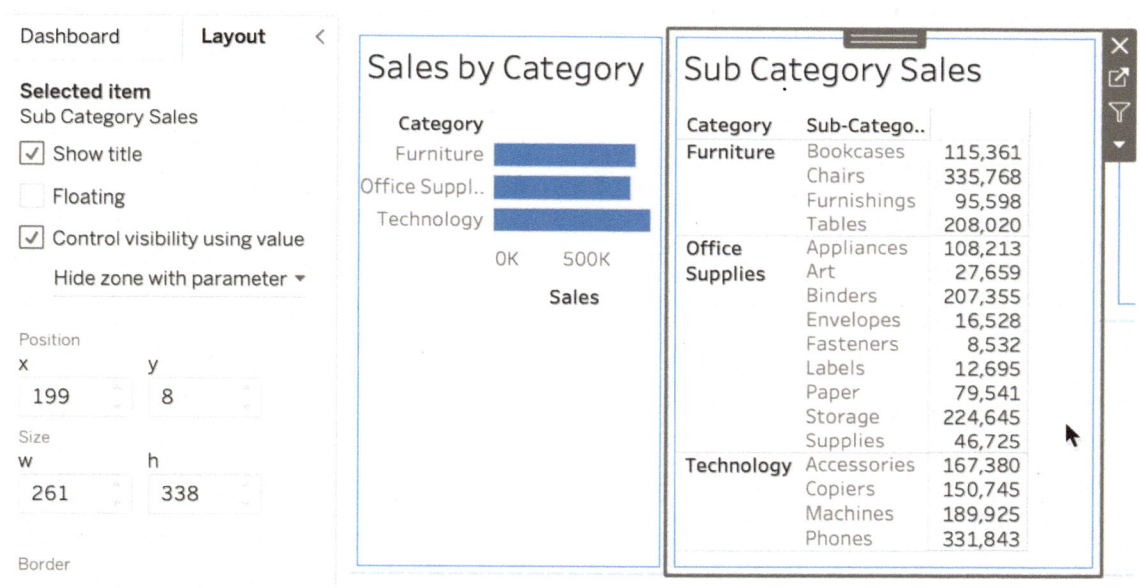

FIGURE 14.35
On the dashboard the Chart on the Right Is Selected

Change the parameter to "True." The dashboard displays both charts. To test filtering, click a bar in the "Sales by Category" chart on the left. The second chart, "SubCategory Sales," is filtered (Figure 14.39).

14.16 Horizontal Radial Buttons to Change Filters

In this example, radial buttons at the top of the dashboard indicate the selected filter. The buttons are really

marks on the **Buttons** worksheet. A calculated field links a parameter to values in the [Region] field. When the parameter matches a region, there is a check mark shape. There are two worksheets in this example:

- Sales
- Buttons

Tableau Public file:

https://public.tableau.com/shared/DY32RZKTK?:display_count=n&:origin=viz_share_link

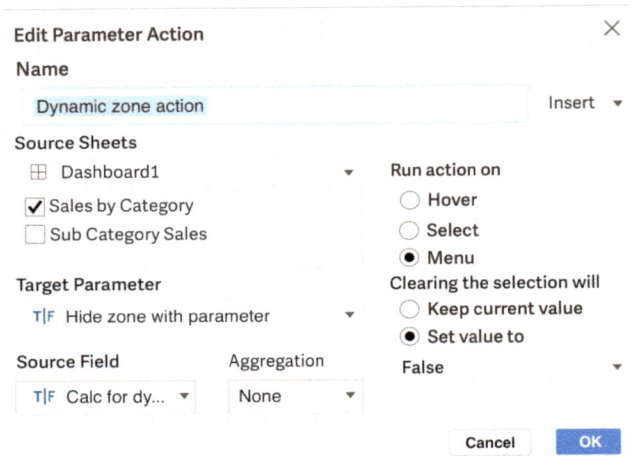

FIGURE 14.36
Create a Parameter Dashboard action.

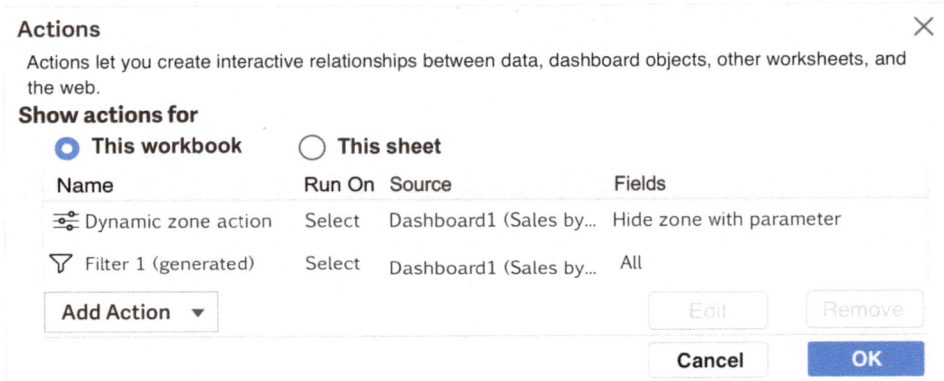

FIGURE 14.37
The Actions Window for the dashboard.

FIGURE 14.38
Sales by Category worksheet.

FIGURE 14.39
SubCategory Sales Worksheet

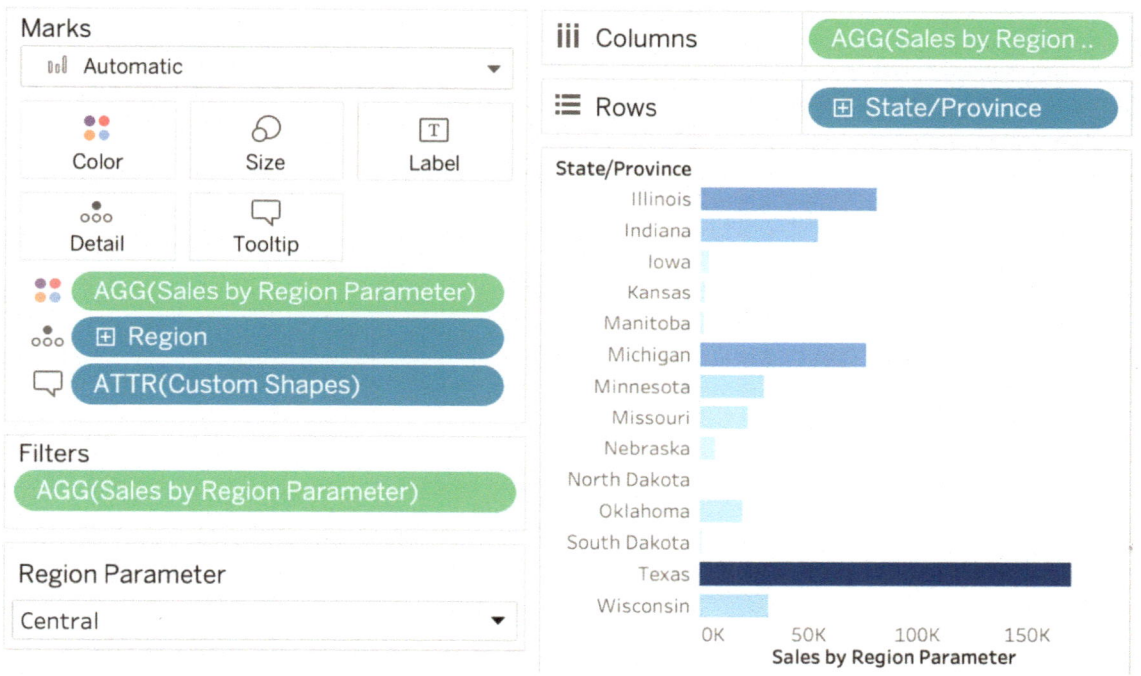

FIGURE 14.40
The Sales Worksheet.

1. This "Sales" worksheet uses the *Sample Superstore* data source and has the [Region] field on the *Detail* tile of the **Marks** card so that I can use the data in the calculated field [Sales by Region Parameter] (Figure 14.40).

2. Create a calculated field [Custom Shapes] that references the parameter (Figure 14.41).

Let's break down the logic in this calculated field. The first part of the expression tests whether the parameter value equals [Region] and returns "false" or "true."

```
[Region Parameter] = [Region]
```

To illustrate this logic, I created a [test] field with the same expression. In the **Data** pane, Tableau adds the icon **=T | F**, indicating this is a Boolean value (Figure 14.42).

For my [Custom Shapes] calculated field, adding the **Str()** function converts the return value to a string so that the expression returns "f" or "t."

```
Str([Region Parameter] = [Region])
```

The last part of the expression concatenates or adds the [Region] value to the string.

```
+ + [Region]
```

FIGURE 14.41
The Custom Shapes calculated field.

FIGURE 14.42
The calculated Field Test.

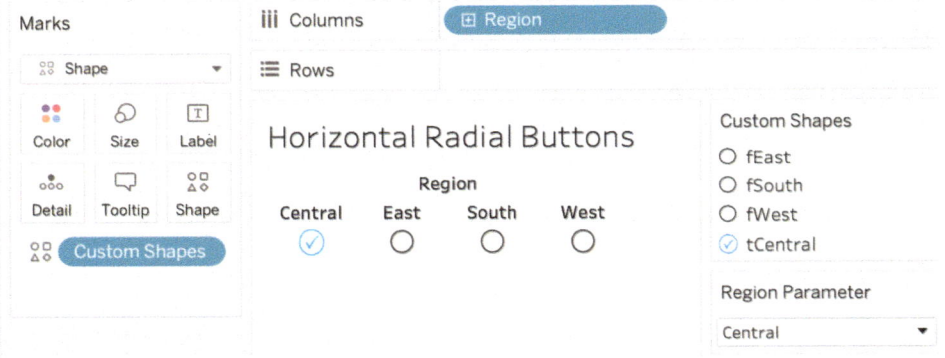

FIGURE 14.43
The Buttons worksheet.

The final expression is shown below.

> Str([Region Parameter] = [Region])+ [Region]

When the parameter value equals the [Region] value, the calculated field returns "t" plus the [Region] value. The other values return "f" plus the [Region] value. When the parameter value is *Central,* the calculation field returns these four values:

fEast

fSouth

fWest

tCentral

3. The next step is to assign a shape to these four values on a new "Buttons" worksheet. Create the **Buttons** worksheet with a "Shape" mark type. Tableau adds a *Shape* tile to the **Marks** card. Add [Region] to the **Columns** shelf and [Custom Shapes] to the *Shape* tile of the **Marks** card (Figure 14.43).

4. On the **Buttons** worksheet, double-click the *Tooltip* tile on the **Marks** card and uncheck "Show Tooltips."

5. Create a parameter [Region Parameter] (Figure 14.44). Select the parameter in the **Data** pane on the left and choose "Show Parameter" to display the **Parameter Control**.

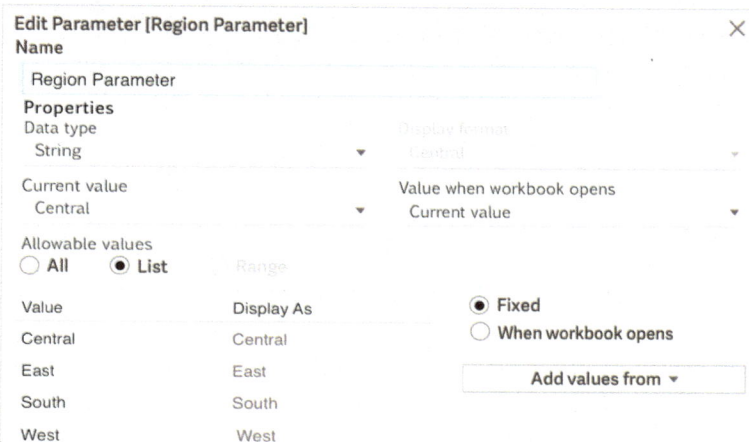

FIGURE 14.44
The Region parameter.

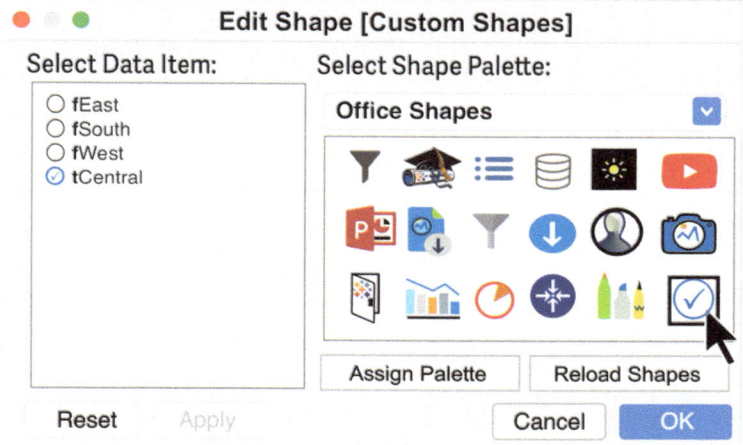

FIGURE 14.45
Editing shapes.

Next, we assign shapes to our parameter values (Figure 14.45).

6. My check box shape is blue, and I'd like the other shapes to be black. On the **Marks** card, click the *Color* tile and choose black as the default color.

7. On the **Buttons** worksheet, assign shapes to the four values. In Step 3, the *Region Parameter* is "Central," so I assign the check mark shape to the value **tCentral** and a circle shape to the fEast, fSouth, and fWest values.

   Click on the *Shape* tile on the **Marks** card to open the **Edit Shape** dialog window. In the left pane, select the "tCentral" value. In the right pane, select the check mark shape. I added this custom shape to the *Office Shapes* folder, as shown in *"Section 7.2.7.1*

Custom Shapes and Colors" on page 129 (Figure 14.45).

8. We need to repeat Step 6 for the other parameter values. On the "Buttons" worksheet, change the parameter value to "South." Notice the shapes are still the default values (Figure 14.46).

   Repeat Step 6, selecting the "tSouth" value in the left pane of the **Edit Shape** dialog window and assigning the check mark shape. Assign a circle shape to the other values. Select the other two parameter values and assign shapes.

9. I want to adjust the formatting because I want the "Buttons" worksheet to mimic buttons. Right-click anywhere on the view and select "Format." In the left **Format Borders** pane, scroll down to **Row Divider** and change *Pane* to "None."

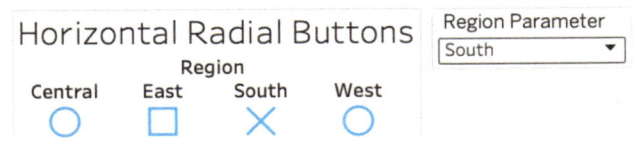

FIGURE 14.46
The Region Parameter Control.

> **Sales by Region Parameter**   ✕
>
> **If** `Attr`(`[Region Parameter]`) = `Attr`(`[Region]`)
> **then** `SUM`(`[Sales]`)
> **END**
>
> The calculation is valid.   2 Dependencies ▾   Apply   OK

FIGURE 14.47
The calculated field sales by Region Parameter.

If you use a background color on the dashboard, select the shading tool at the top of the **Format Borders** pane and select the *Sheet* tab – the pane's heading changes to **Format Shading**. Use the drop-down arrow to change the "Worksheet" shading to "None."

10. We need a new calculation field called [Sales by Region Parameter], as shown in Figure 14.47, to tie the parameter to the worksheet data. Add this field to the *Color* tile of the **Marks** card, the **Filters** shelf, and the **Columns** shelf on the **Sales** worksheet.

    You may wonder why the field is on the **Filters** shelf. Suppose [Sales by Region Parameter] is not on the **Filters** shelf. In that case, you see *all* the state names and only [Sales] for the selected region, for example, southern states.

11. Create a dashboard and add the **Buttons** worksheet at the top of the dashboard. Right-click the title and select "Hide title." When you add the "Buttons" worksheet, Tableau also adds the **Parameter Control**.

    If you do not see the **Parameter Control**, select the "Buttons" worksheet to display a dark bounding box around "Buttons," click the drop-down arrow to open the worksheet's *context menu*. To display the **Parameter Control**, select "Parameters" and then select the "Region Parameter."

12. While "Buttons" is selected, in the toolbar at the top of the dashboard, choose "Fit" and select "Fit Width" from the drop-down menu. Click [Region] in the top area and choose "Hide Field Labels for Columns."

13. Add the "Sales" worksheet below the "Buttons" worksheet on the dashboard. The dashboard is shown below (Figure 14.48).

14.16.1 Testing

Click the drop-down arrow in the [Region] **Parameter Control** and select another region. The dashboard shows those values.

If you are curious about what the test for a match between a parameter and a field value is doing, add the calculation *Str([Region Parameter] = [Region])* to the *Text* tile of the **Marks** card on a new sheet so that the view shows "f" and "t" for false and true. The expression is Boolean and returns 0 or 1, or false or true (Figure 14.49).

14.17 Horizontal Radial Buttons to Switch Sheets

If you aren't opposed to floating objects on your dashboard, you can combine the two examples below. In this exercise, a new dashboard has a worksheet with horizontal radial buttons to switch between the "Managers" and "Regions" worksheets.

"Horizontal Radial Buttons to Change Filters"

"Dashboard Sheet Selection Menu"

Tableau Public file:

https://public.tableau.com/shared/GK9CS7RN4?:display_count=n&:origin=viz_share_link

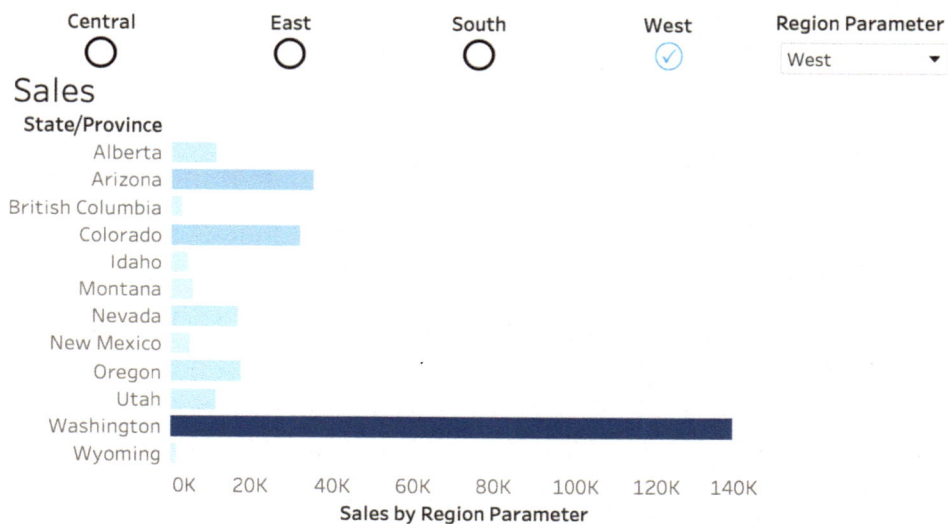

FIGURE 14.48
The dashboard with the sales chart below and the Buttons worksheet above.

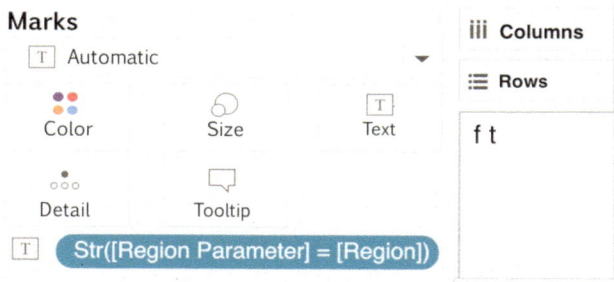

FIGURE 14.49
The String values.

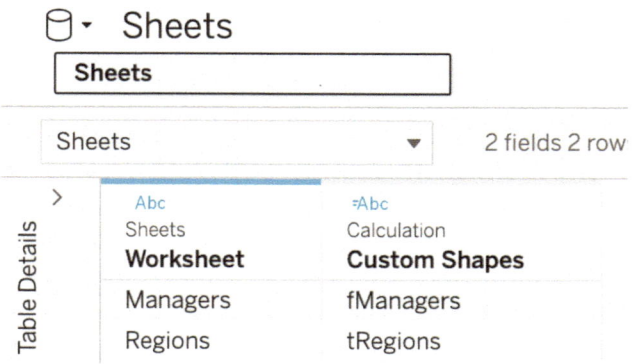

FIGURE 14.50
The sheets data source table.

1. For my worksheet names, I added a worksheet to my Excel file to create a simple data source, "Sheets," as shown below. This data is unrelated to the primary data source and is only used by Tableau internally (Figure 14.50).

2. The **Buttons** worksheet uses a calculated field called [Custom Shapes] to create a string. The first part of the expression returns "t" or "f," and then the right side of the expression, "+ [Worksheet]," combines the string with the [Worksheet] (Figure 14.51).

FIGURE 14.51
The calculated field Custom Shapes.

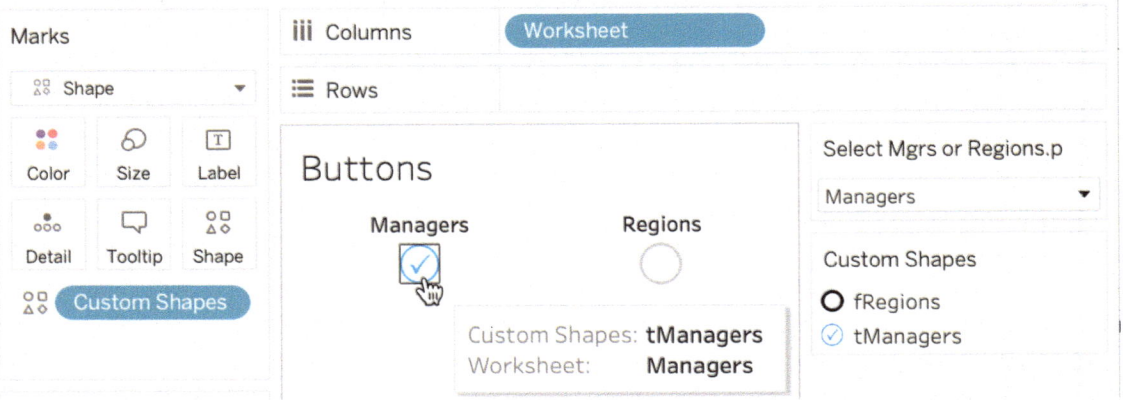

FIGURE 14.52
The Parameter Control on the Right.

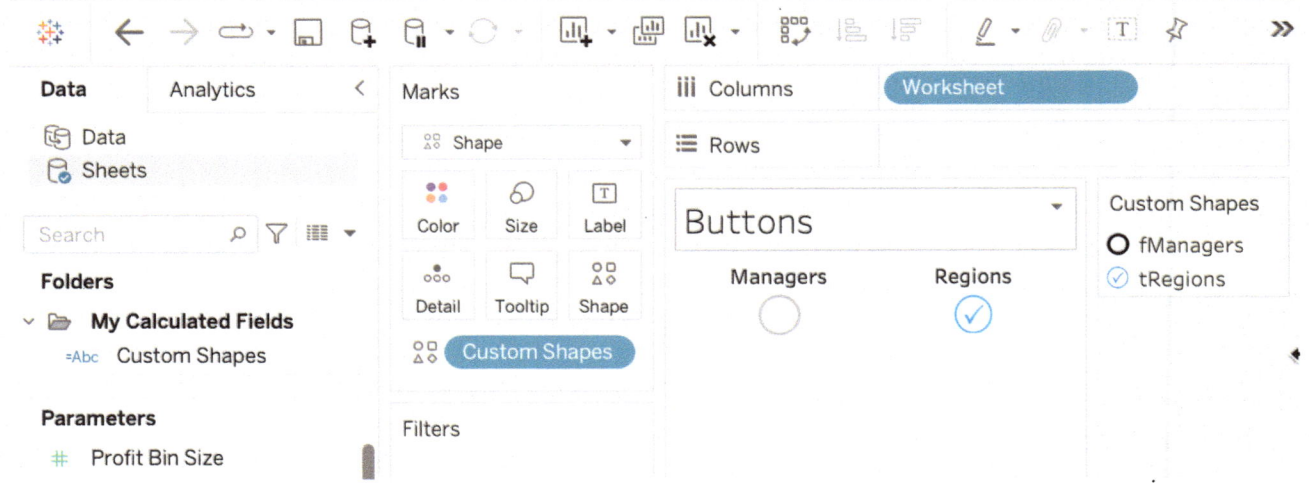

FIGURE 14.53
The Buttons worksheet.

To illustrate this behavior, I temporarily display the "Managers" **Parameter Control**. The [Custom Shapes] field has a value of tManagers because "Managers" is selected in the **Parameter Control** drop-down list on the right (Figure 14.52).

3. In the worksheet **Buttons** below, the **Shape** control is on the right, the [Worksheet] field is on the **Columns** shelf, and the [Custom Shapes] field is on the *Shape* tile on the **Marks** card. In the top left corner of the **Data** pane, the "Sheets" data source is selected (Figure 14.53).

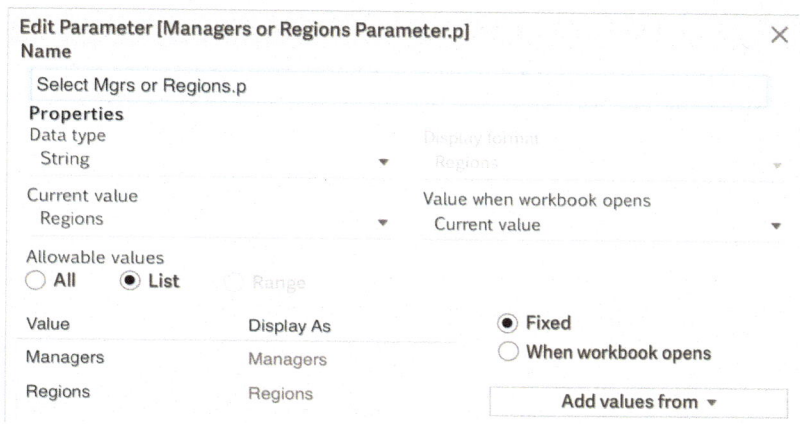

FIGURE 14.54
The edit parameter Dialog Box.

FIGURE 14.55
The calculated field Select Sheet.

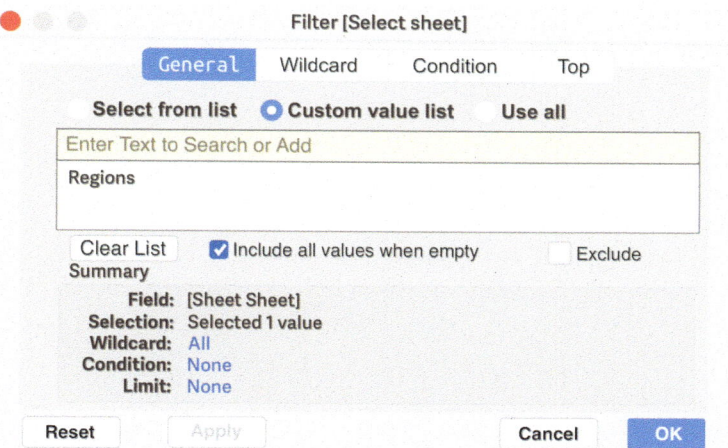

FIGURE 14.56
The filter Dialog Box.

4. The parameter has the names of the worksheets: Regions and Managers (Figure 14.54).

5. The "Regions" and "Managers" worksheets both have this [Select Sheet] field on the **Filters** shelf (Figure 14.55).

6. The steps to create a *Custom value list filter* are shown in the previous "Dashboard Sheet Selection Menu" example. In the following image, the *Custom value* in the [Select Sheet] filter is "Regions," whereas the [Select Sheet] filter is on the Regions worksheet (Figure 14.56).

7. The **Region** worksheet with the [Select Sheet] filter is below (Figure 14.57).

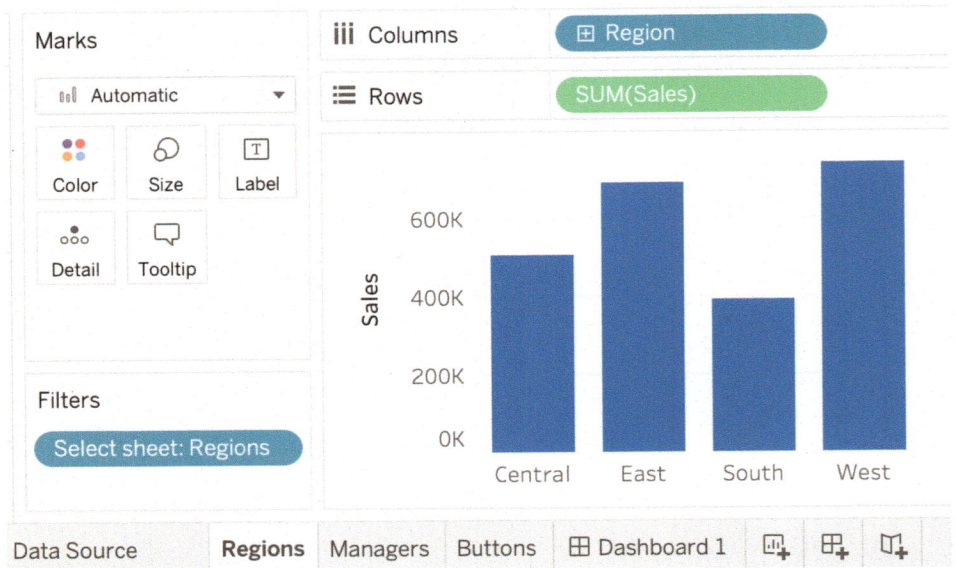

FIGURE 14.57
The Regions Worksheet.

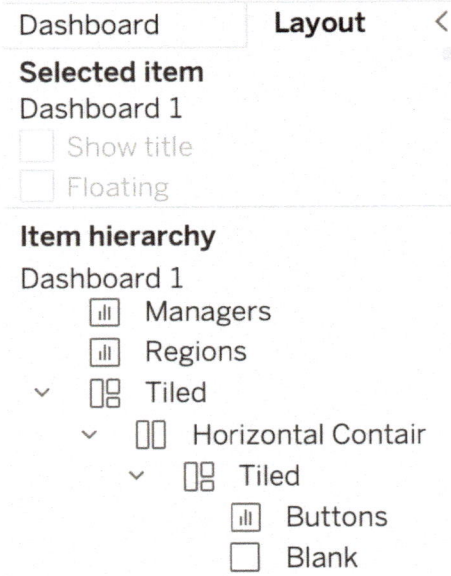

FIGURE 14.58
The Layout pane.

8. The final step is to create a dashboard with the button sheet at the top and two worksheets, **Regions** and **Managers** as "floating" objects. Hide the title of each worksheet.

This combination of floating and tiled objects is shown in the **Item Hierarchy** of the **Layout** pane on the left side of the dashboard. In the following image, the "Managers" worksheet is floating over the "Regions" worksheet and the "Tiled" objects are below that (Figures 14.58 and 14.59).

If you add worksheet shading, you can clearly see how the objects are stacked on each other. In the following image, I added yellow shading to the tiled object.

When I click the *Managers* radial button, the **Managers** worksheet is shown below the Buttons worksheet (Figure 14.60).

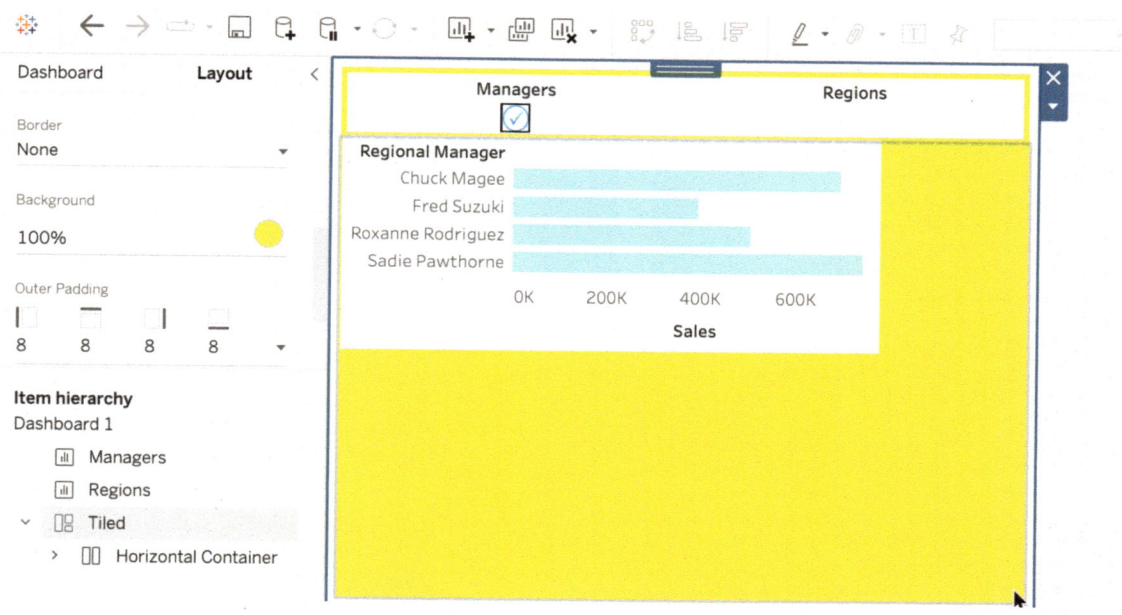

FIGURE 14.59
The Objects on the dashboard.

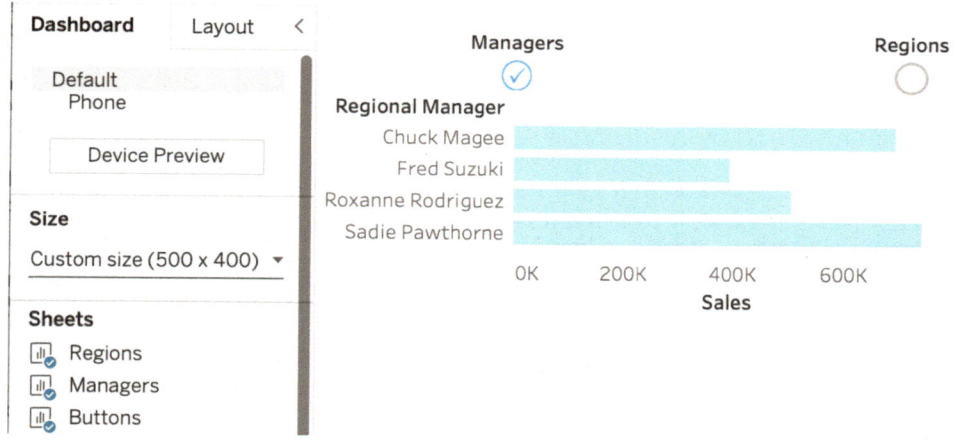

FIGURE 14.60
The Managers worksheet at the top of the dashboard.

9. In the following image, the **Regions** radial button is selected and the Regions worksheet is visible (Figure 14.61).

14.18 A Floating Container for Filters

A floating container with a button is handy for a busy dashboard. I didn't quite grasp the concept the first time I saw this in action, so this example includes many screenshots to walk you through the process.

14.18.1 Introduction

This dashboard has two filter controls I want to hide when not in use to allow more room for my visualization. I have one worksheet, "Sales." The filter controls are in a floating container. To demonstrate interactivity when the filter container is visible, I added a yellow background so you can easily see it overlays the "Sales" visualization. The "Filters" container overlaps the "Sales" worksheet so that the floating "Filters" container object is on top of the underlying "Sales" visualization. The "Filters" container is similar to a sticky note on top of a piece of paper. If you remove the sticky note, you can see the chart underneath.

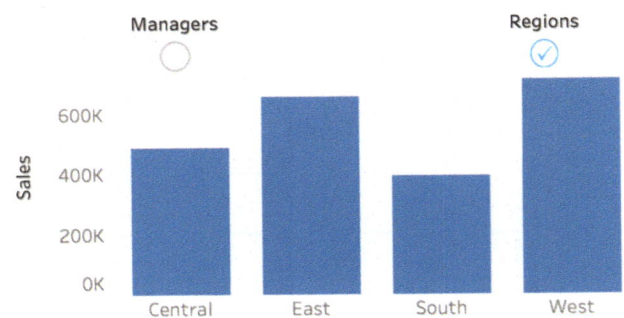

FIGURE 14.61
The Regions worksheet.

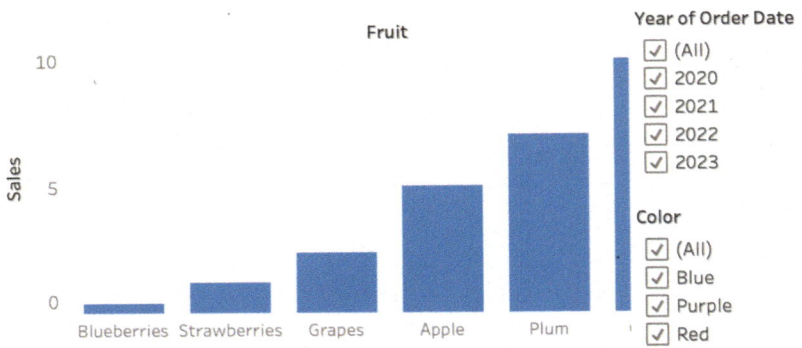

FIGURE 14.62
The Sales worksheet

The container has a *Show/Hide* button to toggle visibility. You can add text, images, or tooltips to a button. I use a funnel image as a visual clue for a user to click the icon to show the container. When the container is open, clicking a "Hide" icon, "X," toggles visibility and hides the container. The link to the Tableau Public file is at the end of the exercise, along with a checklist of the elements and settings in the example.

> Only a floating container has a "Show-Hide" button.

14.18.2 Preview – The Finished Dashboard

First, I'd like to show you the "Sales" chart with the two filters on the right (Figure 14.62).

The following image is the finished dashboard. The yellow floating container on the right has two filter controls. You would probably want to shade this container with white, but here, I use yellow so you can see the stacked effect. The "X" image is a button to control the visibility of the yellow filter container. The yellow container partially hides the chart underneath (Figure 14.63).

14.18.2.1 *Hide the Filters Container*

When the filter container is closed, the button is a small funnel icon in the top right area. It indicates there is a filter container, as shown below. When a user clicks the icon, the yellow container with filters is visible (Figure 14.64).

The button is a separate object; you can move the funnel anywhere on the dashboard.

14.18.3 Create the Visualization

1. Create a simple "Sales" sheet and a new dashboard.

   At the bottom of the view, click the *New Dashboard* icon. Drag the worksheet "Sales" from the left-hand **Dashboard** pane onto the dashboard. The "Sheets" list is in the middle of the **Dashboard** pane.

2. Add the filters to the dashboard. Click the "Sales" worksheet on the dashboard. A dark bounding box indicates the "Sales" sheet is selected. Click the drop-down arrow to open the *object menu* in the top right corner of the worksheet's bounding box. Select "Filters"

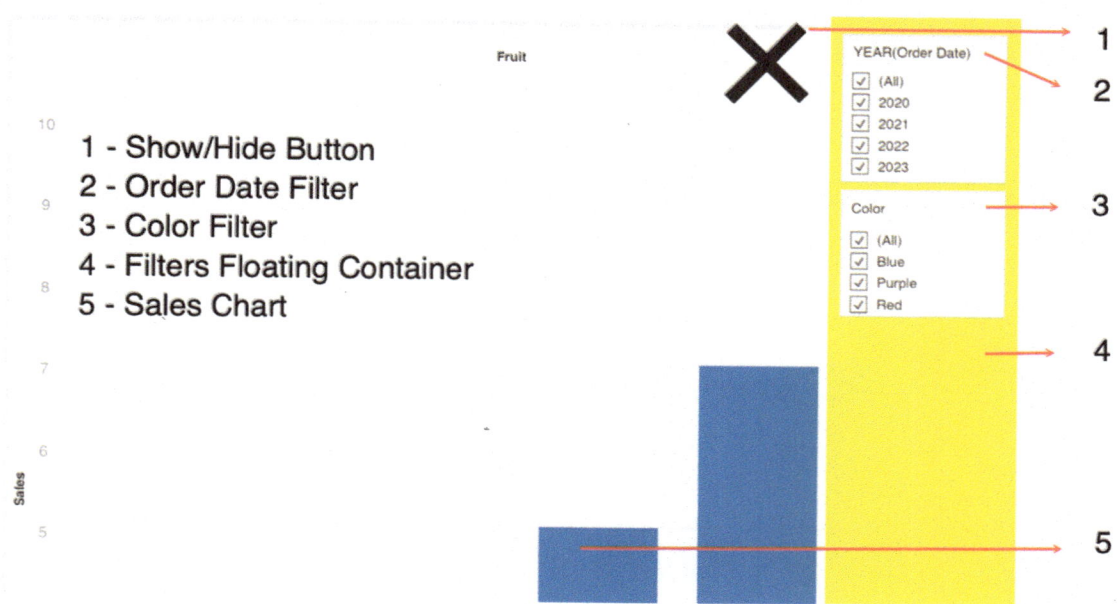

1 - Show/Hide Button
2 - Order Date Filter
3 - Color Filter
4 - Filters Floating Container
5 - Sales Chart

FIGURE 14.63
The labeled finished dashboard.

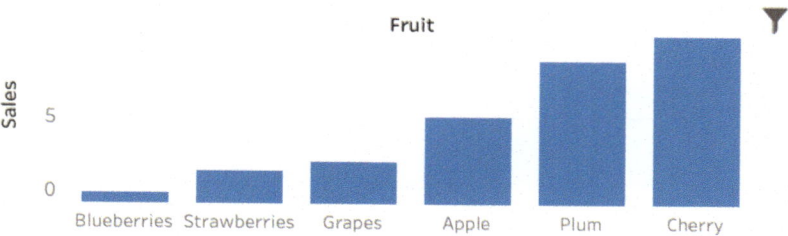

FIGURE 14.64
The Filters Container is hidden.

and click on "Color." A **Filter Control** for the [Color] field is added to the dashboard on the right side in a new "Vertical" container.

Repeat the steps to add a filter for [Year of Order Date]. Note that both **Filter Controls** are in the same new vertical container.

3. Next, I want to rename the new vertical container, resize it, change it to floating, and set a yellow background color. To select the vertical container, click anywhere in either **Filter Control** on the right.

Click the drop-down arrow to open the *object menu*. Near the bottom of the *object menu*, choose "Floating." You should see the two filter controls inside this container (Figure 14.65).

4. A blue bounding box around the vertical container indicates it is selected. Also, in the left **Layout** pane at the bottom, the vertical container is shaded in the *Item Hierarchy* section,

indicating this is the selected object. Right-click "Vertical Container," choose "Rename Dashboard Item," and type "Filters." Click the tab in the top left corner to switch to the **Layout** pane instead of the **Dashboard** pane (Figure 14.66).

5. Drag the edges of the bounding box on the dashboard to resize the container.

6. In the top right corner of the bounding box around the "Filters" container, click the drop-down arrow to open the *object menu* and select "Floating." (Figure 14.67)

The transparent "Vertical" container floats above the main chart in the top right corner, as shown below (Figure 14.68).

7. Whenever you change a container to "Floating," Tableau changes its opacity to transparent. I want the container's background color to be yellow for demonstration

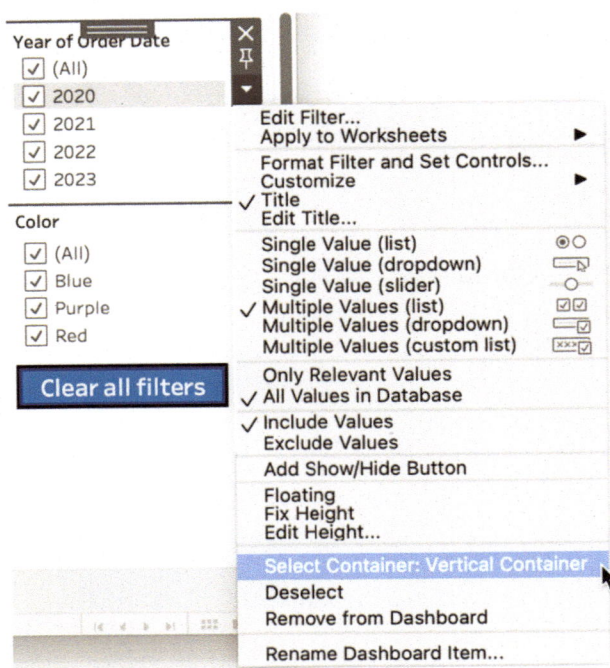

FIGURE 14.65
The Object Menu for a Dashboard worksheet object.

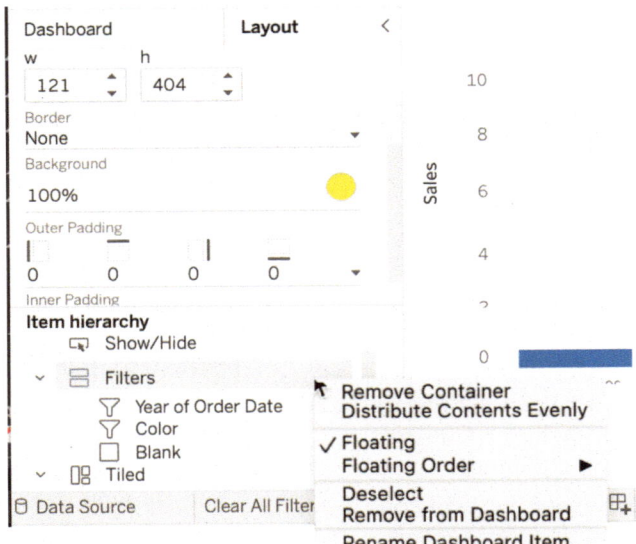

FIGURE 14.66
The Filters Container selected in the Item Hierarchy.

purposes. To do so, click the background color tool in the middle of the **Layout** pane on the left and choose a yellow color.

8. To add the *Show/Hide* button to the dashboard with the container selected, click the drop-down arrow to open the Container's *object menu*. Select "Add Show/Hide Button." In

this example, I use the default "X" image indicating the container is open or shown. Because the button is a separate floating object, you can drag it anywhere on the dashboard (Figure 14.69).

9. You can use the Show/Hide button's *object menu* to change the *Floating Order* to bring the

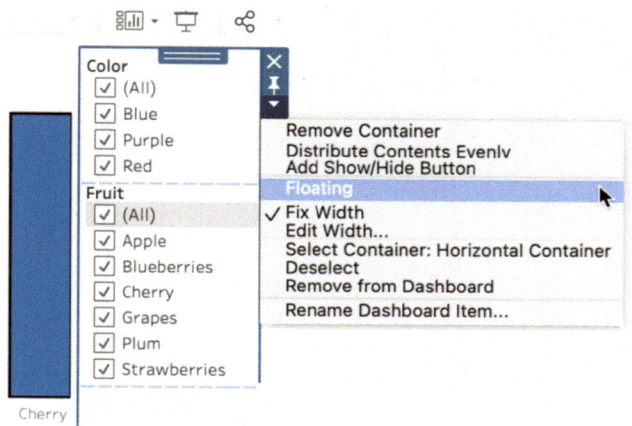

FIGURE 14.67
A Blue Bounding Box Around the Floating Container.

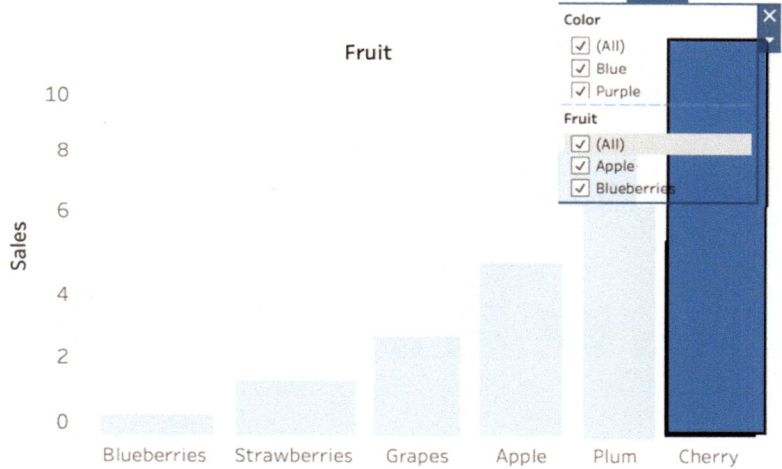

FIGURE 14.68
The floating container on the right.

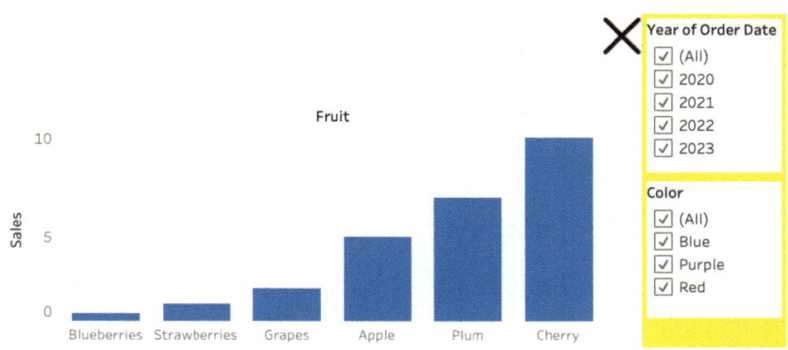

FIGURE 14.69
The Dashboard with the floating container.

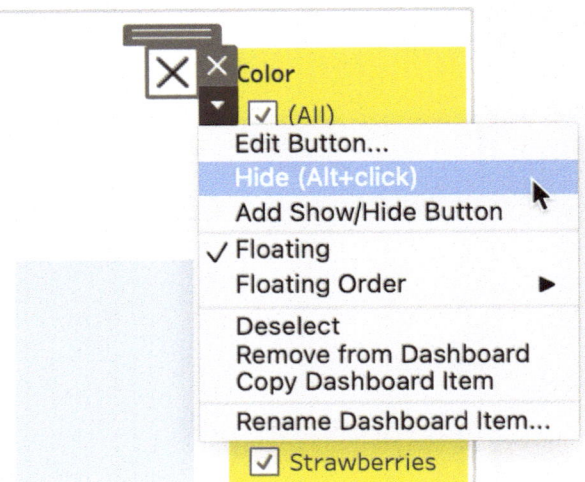

FIGURE 14.70
The context menu for the Show/Hide Button.

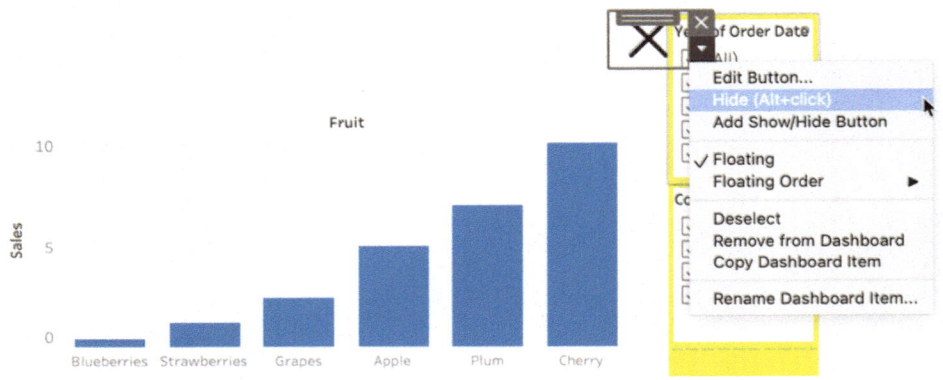

FIGURE 14.71
Hide the filter container.

button to the front of the page. The button is a separate object from the "Filters" container (Figure 14.70).

14.18.4 Testing

Anyone who views the dashboard on a Tableau server can click the button icon to toggle visibility. In Tableau Desktop, switch to *Presentation Mode* on the **Window** menu to see the functionality. On a Windows machine, Alt-click toggles visibility or Option-click in MacOS. You can also use the drop-down *object menu* for the button to switch between "Show" and "Hide." (Figure 14.71)

Tableau Public file:

```
https://public.tableau.com/views/
DashboardContainerforFilterss1045_
16931630475220/Dashboard?:language=
en-US&:sid=&:redirect=auth&:
display_count=n&:origin=viz_share_link
```

14.18.5 Worksheet and Dashboard

There is one dashboard and one worksheet in this workbook: Sales.

14.18.6 Data and Fields

This chart utilizes these fields.

- Order Date
- Color
- Fruit
- Sales

The **[Order Date]** field is on the **Filters** shelf. I chose the *Date Level* "Date Part" of "Year." A "Date Part" is **discrete**, so individual years are shown in the **Filter Control**.

The **[Color]** field is a **discrete** dimension with a "String" data type. [Color] is on the **Filters** shelf, and because I checked "Show Filter" from the drop-down *object menu*, the **Filter Control** is now on the right side of the view. As expected, the field has a blue background or "pill" because it is **discrete**.

The **[Fruit]** field is a **discrete** dimension with a "String" data type, and it is also on the **Filters** shelf. As expected, the field has a blue background or "pill" because it is **discrete**.

The data type for **[Sales]** is a "Number (decimal)." In this view, [Sales] is a **continuous** field on the **Rows** shelf. Because it is a **continuous** field, it creates a vertical y-axis on the view.

14.18.7 Components or Elements

In addition to the calculated field, this view has several elements.

- Rows Shelf
- Columns Shelf
- Filters Shelf
- Filter Controls
- Floating Dashboard Container with a Show/ Hide Button

14.18.8 Rows Shelf

The aggregated field [SUM(Sales)] is on the **Rows** shelf, creating a vertical y-axis for values.

14.18.9 Columns Shelf

Looking back at the "Sales" worksheet, notice the [Fruit] field is on the **Columns** shelf. Because [Fruit] is **discrete**, Tableau adds headers to the view; in this case, column headings are at the bottom of the chart because [Fruit] is on the **Columns** shelf.

14.18.10 Filters Shelf

The **discrete** [Order Date] dimension field and the dimension field [Color] are on the **Filters** shelf. When you drag the [Order Date] field onto the **Filters** shelf, choose the date part "Year" from the date field's *context menu*.

If you aren't sure what date level you selected, click the drop-down arrow of the [Order Date] field on the **Filters** shelf to open the date field's *context menu*. The items in the middle section of the *context menu* are divided by a line. The top part has *Date Part* levels,

which is what we want. The bottom part is the actual *Date Values*.

14.18.11 Filter Controls

To display the **Filter Control** for both the [Color] and [Order Date] fields, click the drop-down arrow on the [Order Date] field in the **Filters** shelf. Check "Show Filter" from the drop-down *object menu* to display the **Filter Control** on the right side of the view (and the dashboard). Repeat these steps for the [Color] field.

14.18.12 Dashboard Container and Show/ Hide Button

When I add the two **Filter Controls** to the dashboard, Tableau automatically creates a new container for the filters. I renamed this container "Filters" and made it a floating container. I also resized the "Filters" container to partially hide the chart underneath, as shown in Figure 14.72.

Earlier, I said the "Filters" container is similar to a sticky note on top of a piece of paper. If you remove the sticky note, you can see the chart underneath. In the following image, I rotated the chart to give a 3-D dashboard perspective so you can see the filter controls inside the container. When the yellow "Filters" container is active, the button image is an "X." The image changes to a **Funnel** when you hide the "Filters" container. During testing, while in "Presentation" mode, click the button to show or hide the container (Figure 14.69).

14.18.13 Formatting

The only special formatting is that the container has shading.

14.19 A Reset All Filters Button

This example from Tableau's site is a great solution if you have views with the same filter fields. At the end of the exercise, there is a link to the Tableau Public file and a checklist of the elements and settings.

14.19.1 Introduction

Expanding on the previous example, I created a worksheet that only has the text "Clear all filters." After I add the worksheet to the dashboard, I use formatting so that it looks like a button. When a user clicks the worksheet, a dashboard filter action runs to reset all filters.

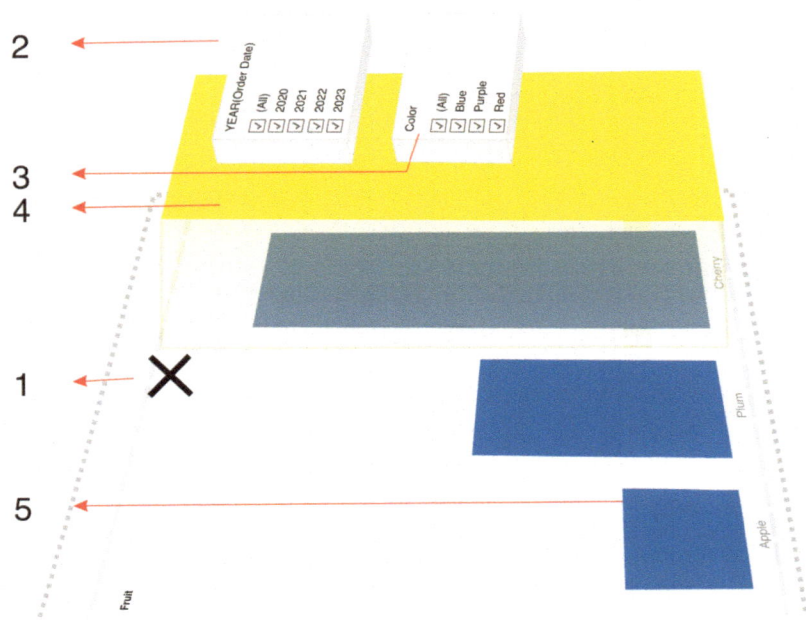

FIGURE 14.72
The dashboard objects.

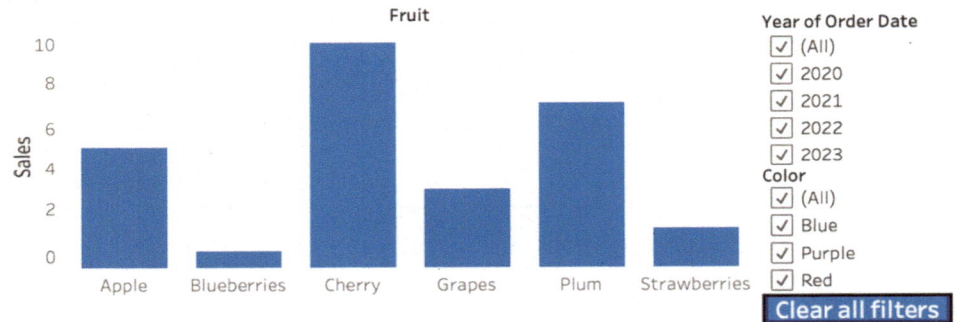

FIGURE 14.73
The dashboard with a Clear all filters button.

14.19.2 Preview – The Finished Dashboard

My dashboard has two worksheets. The "Sales" worksheet is on the left side, and a floating container is on the right side of the dashboard. The floating container has two **filter controls** at the top. The second worksheet, "Clear all filters," is inside the "filters" container at the bottom (Figure 14.73).

14.19.3 Create the Visualization

1. Create a "Sales" worksheet and add fields.

- Add Year of [Sales] to the **Rows** shelf.
- Add [Fruit] to the **Columns** shelf.

2. Add [Order Date] to the **Filters** shelf. For the [Order Date] field, I choose the Date Level "Date Part" of "Year." A "Date Part" is **discrete**, so individual years are shown in the **Filter Control**.

   Also, add the [Color] dimension field to the **Filter** shelf.

3. Click the drop-down arrow on each field on the **Filter** shelf and check "Show filter" to display the filter controls.

4. Create a *calculated field* called [Select all Filters]. The formula is text that says, "Select all Filters."

5. Create another worksheet called **Select all Filters**.

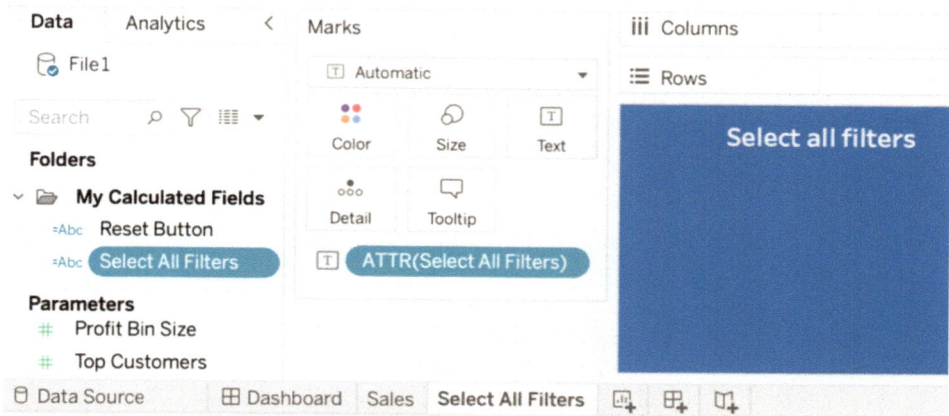

FIGURE 14.74
The Select All Filters worksheet.

- Add the new calculation [Select all Filters] field to the *Text* tile on the **Marks** card.

- On the toolbar, click the drop-down arrow on the "Fit" tool to select "Fit Width." This setting ensures the worksheet looks like a button on the dashboard.

- Click on the "Text" tool on the **Marks** card and change the alignment to "Bottom Center."

- Change the worksheet *shading* for the **Select All Filters** worksheet so the background looks like a button. On the **Format** menu, select "Shading" and choose a color. This formatting will give the appearance of a button on the dashboard (Figure 14.74).

6. Create a dashboard.

- Drag the "Sales" worksheet onto the new dashboard.

- Both **filter controls** should be visible on the right side of the dashboard. If you do not see the **filter controls**, click on the "Sales" worksheet. A dark bounding box outlines the worksheet, with several icons in the top right corner. Click the drop-down arrow in the top right corner and choose "Filters." Check both filters:

  - Color
  - Year of Order Date

  Tableau creates a new tiled vertical container for the filters. In the **Filter controls** on the dashboard, ensure *all items are checked* in both **filter controls**, as shown in Step 9.

7. Next, I want to rename the new vertical container, change the container to floating, and set a background color.

- To select the vertical container, click anywhere in either **Filter Control** on the right. Click the drop-down arrow to open the **Filter Control's** *object menu* and select the parent container.

- Click the drop-down arrow to open the container's *object menu*. Near the bottom of the *object menu*, choose "Floating." You should see the two **filter controls** inside this container.

- While the container is still selected, use the *object menu* to rename it "Filters." (Figure 14.75)

8. A blue bounding box around the vertical container indicates that it is selected. Also, in the left **Layout** pane at the bottom, the vertical container is shaded in the *Item Hierarchy* section, indicating that it is the selected object. Right-click "Vertical Container," choose "Rename Dashboard Item," and type "Filters."

9. Drag the "**Select all Filters**" worksheet onto the dashboard under the two **Filter Controls** in the "Filters" container on the right.

   It is a little hard to see, but in the **Dashboard** pane on the left, in the **Sheets** section, **Select All Filters** has a light gray background indicating that the sheet is selected. The dashboard view has a gray bounding box around the sheet.

   In the toolbar at the top of the workspace, select "Fit Width."

10. The last step is to create a dashboard "Filter" action so that when a user selects the **Select All Filters** worksheet in the dashboard, filters update and "Show all Values."

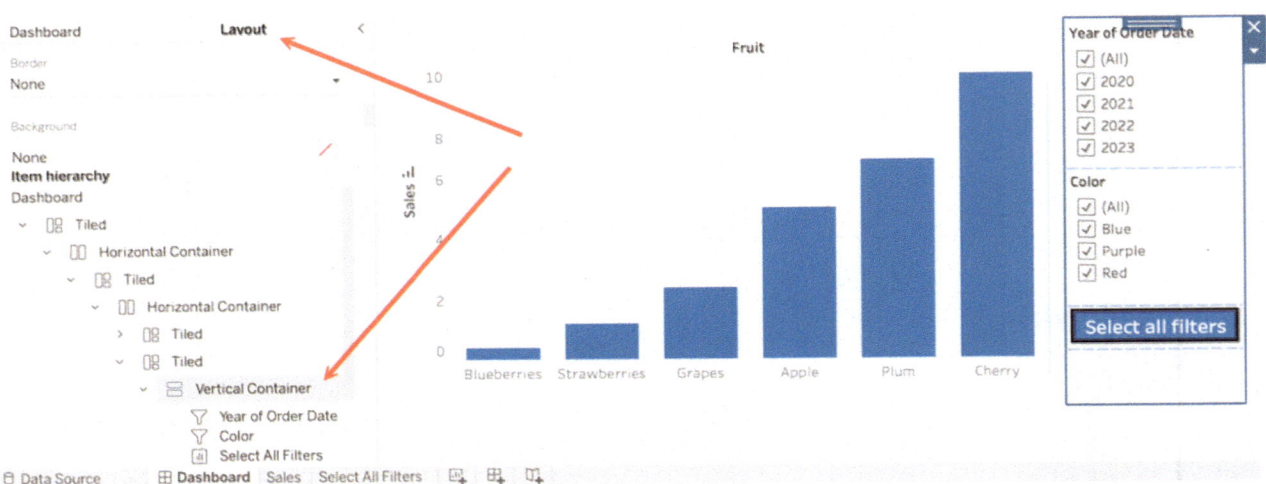

FIGURE 14.75

The Filters Container with a blue bounding box.

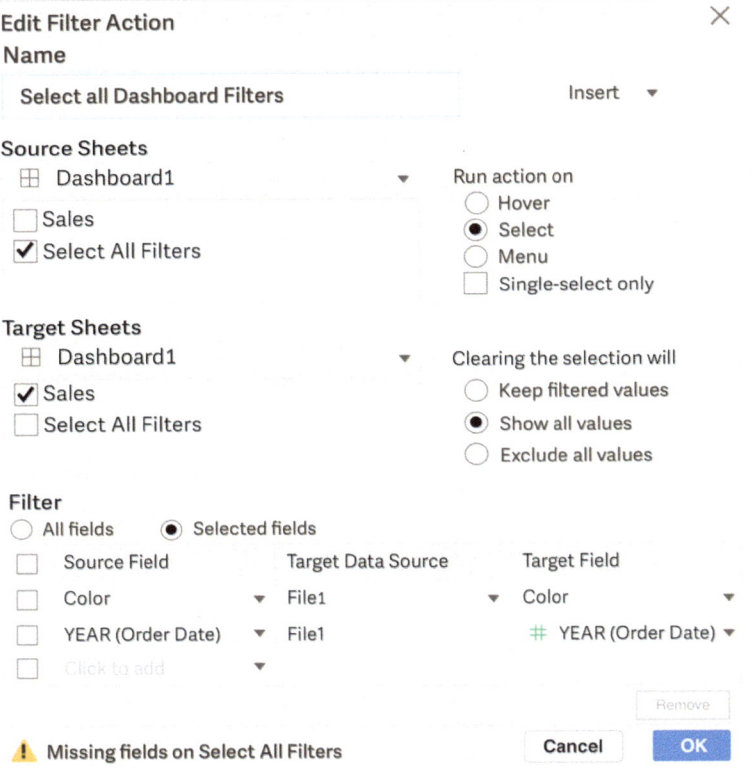

FIGURE 14.76

The Edit Filter Action Dialog Window.

- On the **Dashboard** menu, select "Actions…"
- In the bottom left corner of the **Actions Dialog Window**, select "Add Action" and click on "Filter." (Figure 14.76)

Name this action: "Select All Dashboard Filters." In the "Edit Filter Action" screen, configure these settings.

* Source sheets: "Select All Filters"
* Run action on: Select
* Target sheet: Only check the "Sales" worksheet
* Clearing the selection will "Show all values"
* Target filters: [Color] and [YEAR(Order date)]. These are the same fields as step two – the **Filter** shelf

* Ignore the message in the bottom left, "Missing fields on Select All Filters."

14.19.4 Testing

Anyone who views the dashboard on a server can select the new **Select all Filters** worksheet to toggle visibility. Switch to *Presentation Mode* on the **Window** menu to see the functionality within Tableau Desktop. On a Windows machine, Alt-click toggles visibility or Option-click in MacOS.

Tableau Public file:

https://public.tableau.com/views/s1044Clear AllFiltersv2/Dashboard?:language=en-US& publish=yes&:sid=&:display_count=n&:origin= viz_share_link

14.19.5 Worksheets

There are two worksheets in this workbook.

* Select All Filters
* Sales

14.19.5.1 Select All Filters Worksheet

The **Select All Filters** worksheet has one field on the *Text* tile on the **Marks** card, as shown in Step 5. This worksheet is in a floating "Filters" container on the dashboard and has been resized to be the size of a button. A dashboard action with the setting "Select all filters" resets filter choices whenever a user clicks on this worksheet.

> Suppose there are multiple worksheets on the dashboard. For the "Select all filters" filter action to work correctly, all worksheets must have the same filter fields in common.

14.20 A Floating Dashboard Container

The "Filters" container is floating and has a Show/Hide button.

14.20.1 Rows Shelf

The aggregated field [SUM(Sales)] is on the **Rows** shelf of the "Sales" worksheet. Because it is **continuous**, it creates a vertical y-axis for values.

14.20.2 Columns Shelf

Looking back at the "Sales" worksheet image, notice the [Fruit] field is on the **Columns** shelf. Headings are added to the view because [Fruit] is discrete. In this case, column headings are added to the bottom of the chart because [Fruit] is on the **Columns** shelf.

14.20.3 Filters Shelf

The **discrete** [YEAR(Order Date)] dimension field and the dimension [Color] field are both on the **Filters** shelf of the "Sales" worksheet.

14.20.4 Filter Controls

To display the **Filter Control** for the [Color] and [Order Date] fields, click the drop-down arrow for each field on the **Filters** shelf to open the field's *context menu*. Check "Show Filter" from the field's *context menu* to display the **Filter Control** on the right side of the view.

14.20.5 Filters Action

As outlined in Step 10, I created a filter action, "Select All Dashboard Filters," to reset all filters.

14.20.6 Formatting

The dashboard floating container has shading and is sized to lay over the "Sales" chart. The "Select all Filters" worksheet is also set to "Fit Width."

14.21 A Pop-Out Chart (Filter Action)

This example has two charts on a dashboard, and both are set to fit the entire view. When you click a mark in "Chart 1," Tableau displays the second chart, "Pop-out Chart 2," filtered by the selected mark from "Chart 1." A Tableau "Filter Action" hides the second chart until a user selects a mark in "Chart 1."

The link to the Tableau Public file is at the end of the exercise, along with a checklist of the elements and settings in the example.

FIGURE 14.77

Tip: *Click and drag the Filter controls to move the control to a different area of the view.*

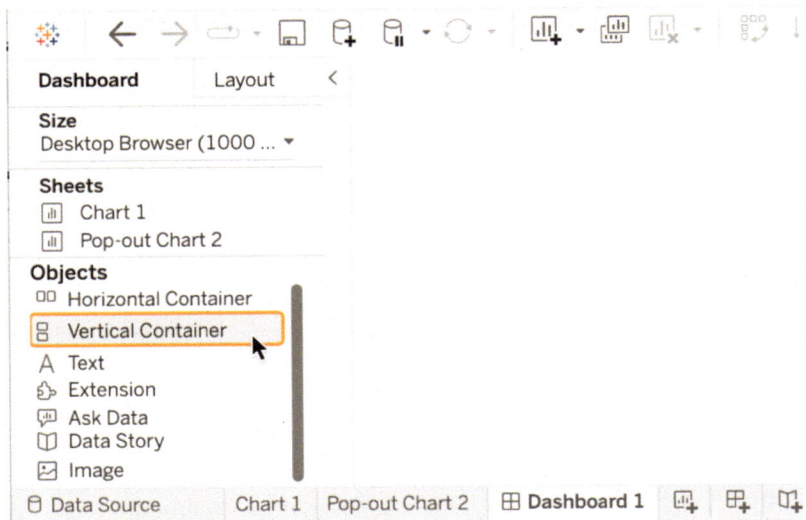

FIGURE 14.78
The Dashboard pane with the section for objects.

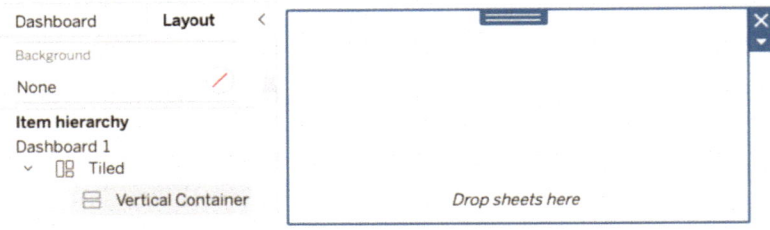

FIGURE 14.79
A Blue Bounding Box Around the Vertical Container.

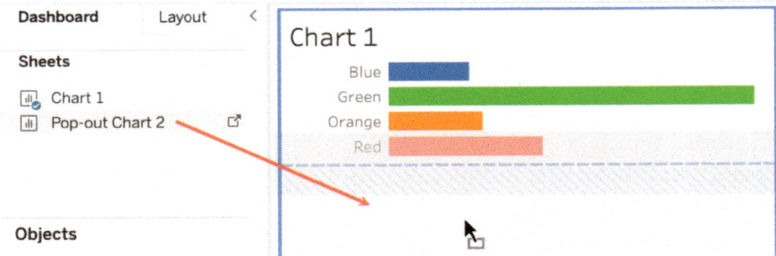

FIGURE 14.80
The Chart on the Dashboard.

14.21.1 Create the Visualization

1. Connect to a data source and create two charts. I have already created two charts for my example.

2. Create a new dashboard and add a vertical container to the dashboard (Figure 14.78).

3. Drag a tiled vertical container from the **Dashboard** pane onto the dashboard. By default, "Tiled" is selected. Do not use

"Floating." A blue bounding box indicates the container is selected. On the **Layout** pane on the left, the name "Vertical Container" is lightly shaded to indicate the selected container (Figure 14.79).

4. With the vertical container selected, drag and drop "Chart 1" from the **Dashboard** pane on the left into the vertical container.

5. Drag and drop "Pop-out Chart 2" into the bottom of the **same** vertical container (Figure 14.80).

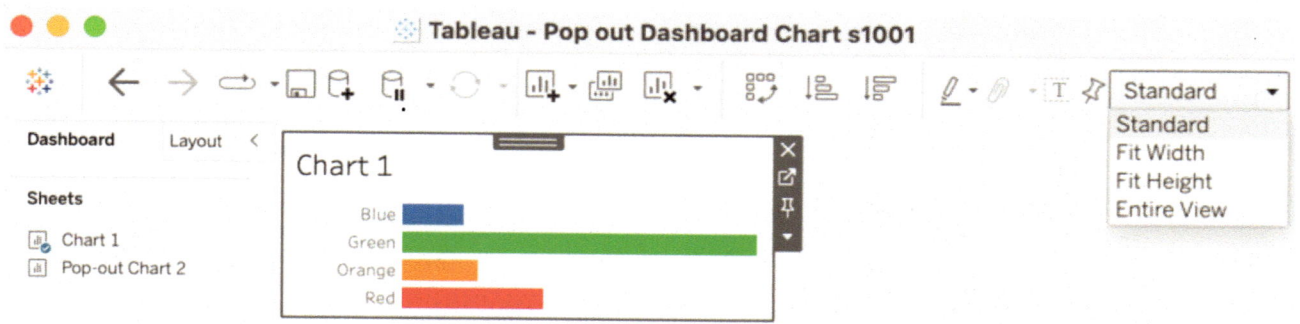

FIGURE 14.81
The Toolbar with the Drop-Down Fit Menu.

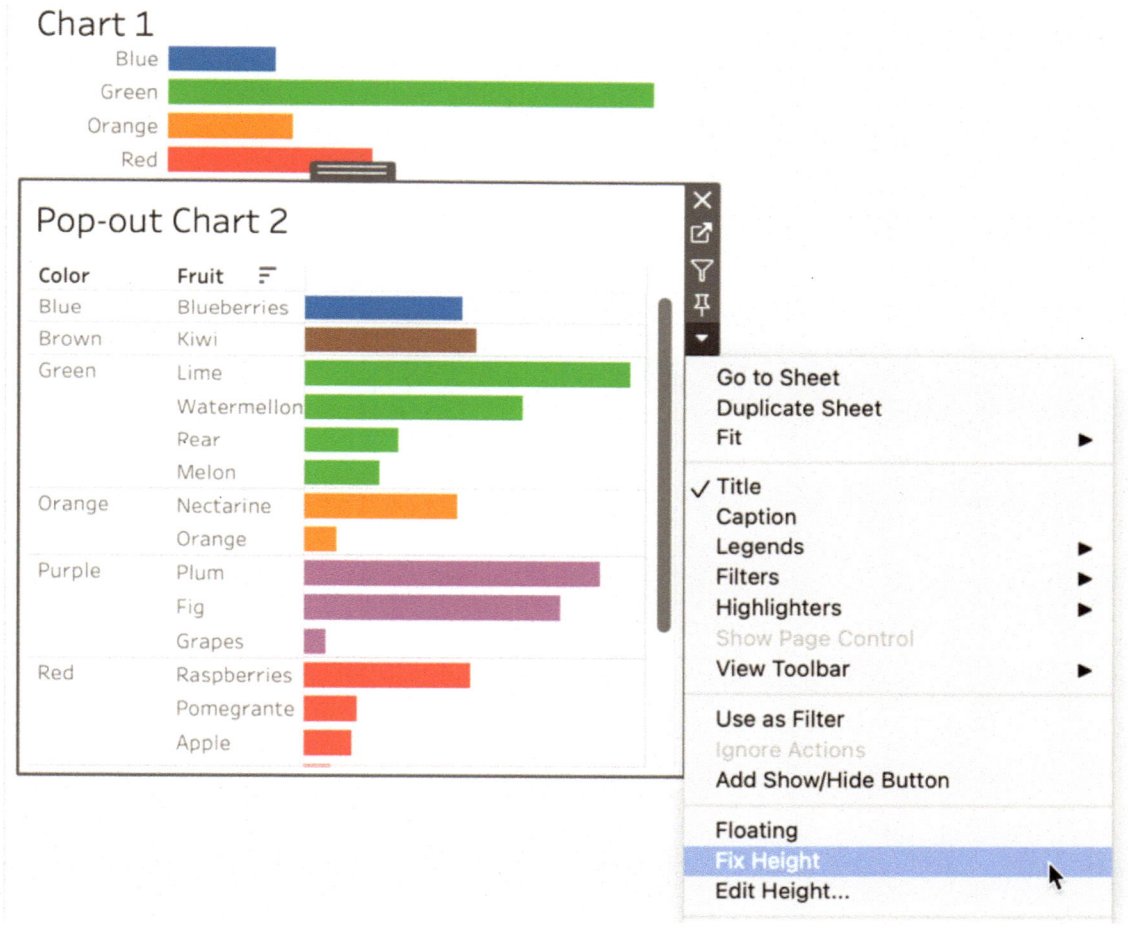

FIGURE 14.82
The Fix Height Choice for a Worksheet Object.

6. In the **Toolbar** at the top of the view, use the drop-down menu to change the **fit** for Chart 1 to "Entire View." (Figure 14.81)

7. Click inside the "Pop-out Chart 2" to select the chart. Tableau displays a dark gray bounding box with icons in the top right corner, as shown below. Click the down arrow to open the *object menu*.

Uncheck "Title" and "Fix Height." *This is a critical step*. The **fit** for both worksheets is *Entire View* (Figure 14.82).

8. To create the "Filter" action, open the **Dashboard** menu at the top of the view and choose "Actions…" In the bottom left corner of the dialog window, click the drop-down arrow by "Add Action" and select "Filter…" (Figure 14.83)

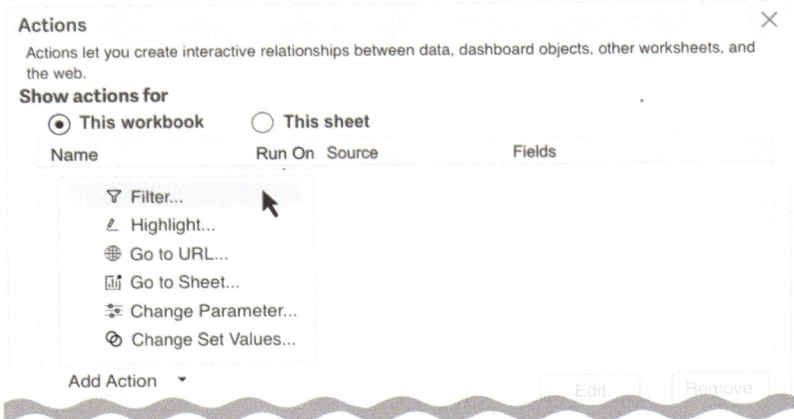

FIGURE 14.83
The Add Action drop-down menu.

Edit Filter Action

Name

Filter Pop-out Chart2   Insert ▼

Source Sheets
⊞ Dashboard1   ▼   **Run action on**
☑ Chart 1   ○ Hover
☐ Pop-out Chart 2   ● Select
                                                                        ○ Menu
                                                                        ☐ Single-select only

Target Sheets
⊞ Dashboard1   ▼   **Clearing the selection will**
☐ Chart 1   ○ Keep filtered values
☑ Pop-out Chart 2   ○ Show all values
                                                                        ● Exclude all values

Filter
● All fields   ○ Selected fields
☐   Source Field   Target Data Source   Target Field
☐   Click to add   ▼

                                                                        Remove

                                                Cancel   OK

FIGURE 14.84
The Edit Filter Action Dialog window.

9. Set up the action as shown in Figure 14.84.

Both charts are on the dashboard; you are ready to test and activate the action.

14.21.2 Testing

Click a mark (bar) in "Chart 1," and Tableau filters and displays the second chart, "Pop-out Chart 2," based on the selected mark. Press "ESC" or click within "Chart 1" again to clear the selection. Tableau hides "Pop-out Chart 2" because the filter action is configured to "Exclude all values" when the selection is cleared. Repeat step 1, selecting a different mark in "Chart 1."

Tableau Public

https://public.tableau.com/views/SheetSelection DashMenus1049/Dashboard1?:language=en-US& publish=yes&:display_count=n&:origin= viz_share_link

This second example of a tree map chart also illustrates a pop-out chart.

https://public.tableau.com/views/Popout DashboardCharts1001/Dashboard1?:language=en-US&:sid=&:redirect=auth&:display_count=n&:origin=viz_share_link

14.21.3 Worksheets

There are two worksheets in this workbook: Chart 1 and Pop-out Chart 2.

14.21.4 Dashboard

There is one dashboard with a vertical container. The vertical container has two charts with a Fit of "Entire View."

14.21.4.1 Vertical Container: Chart 1

Fit: Entire View
  Uncheck "Title" so the title is not visible

14.21.4.2 Vertical Container: Pop-Out Chart 2

Fit: Entire View
  Uncheck "Title" so the title is not shown
  Uncheck "Fix Height"

14.21.5 Filter Action

The dashboard has a filter action with these settings.

Setting	Value
Name	Filter Pop-out Chart2
Source Sheets	Chart 1
Run action on	Select
Target Sheets	Pop-out Chart 2
Clearing the selection will	Exclude all values
Filter	All Fields

14.22 Titles When There Are No Rows of Data

When KPIs track metrics like failures over 12 months, the lack of data is an improvement. The absence of data can be challenging in Tableau. We looked at this situation in *"Section 4.2.5 No Data" on page 76.* Tableau displays a row count in the bottom left corner of the screen. If there are no rows of data, Tableau does not create a chart. For example, let's say you are working on a KPI for the current month, and there is no data for the last two months. I cannot use current report data for a report date heading because there is no data.

As a workaround, I can add a measure to the *Text* tile on the **Marks** card so Tableau has at least one row of data to create a chart. Since I only want to see data for the current month, I remove all text from the **Text Editor**. Tableau creates a blank chart with a title. I then add a calculated field to retrieve last month's date on the *Detail* tile on the **Marks** card. The only thing on the visualization is the date field in the title. While the date is not linked to chart data, that is OK in this instance.

14.23 KPIs and BANs (Big Numbers)

KPIs and BANs are unique because they show a summary number, an icon, or a small indicator comparing the KPI to another metric. A KPI is a key progress indicator, and a BAN refers to big numbers. When combined with comparison metrics, the visual analysis is obvious. A metric to display a percentage of the whole would use a *Level of Detail* expression and a *Table Calculation*. Often, KPI's use a "Shape" mark type, and the color has 0% opacity. Throughout this example, I call out elements we've looked at in previous chapters, like shapes and colored arrows. I want to compare the current year's profit to last year's and add a colored arrow (shape) to highlight whether the profit is up or down. I illustrate two ways to add arrows: using a shape chart or a custom number format. Tableau Online also has an example of KPIs.

The first section of this example creates a KPI worksheet to show unprofitable products. For colored arrows indicating whether the count of unprofitable products is going up or down compared to last year, I create a calculated field with the Lookup() function that returns only the most recent value. *"Section 12.21 Arrows Comparing Two Values" on page 287* is similar.

During development, I want to see data for every year so I can assign shapes and colors to all possible values. In the last step, I used a table calculation filter to hide all data except the current months; this is similar to the example in *"Section 8.7.2 Filter the View, Not the Underlying Data" on page 169.* The link to the Tableau Public file is at the end of the exercise, along with a checklist of the elements and settings in the example.

14.23.1 Create the Visualization

1. After connecting the Sample Superstore data source, create a calculated field called [compare to last year], as shown below (Figure 14.85).

2. Add the new table calculation field [compare to last year] to the *Text* tile of the **Marks** card.

3. Drag the Tableau generated field [ORDER(Count)] onto the *Label* tile of the **Marks** card. The field is renamed CNT(ORDER) (Figure 14.86).

4. Double-click the *Label* tile and select the ellipsis (three dots) to edit the text. Remove the [Compare to Last Year] field and adjust the size of the remaining <CNT(ORDER)> field, as shown below (Figure 14.87).

5. Change the "Mark" type to "Shape." On the **Marks** card, click the drop-down arrow to select "Shape."

6. Select the *Size* tool on the **Marks** card to adjust the shape size.

7. Add the field [compare to last year] to the *Color* and *Shape* tiles on the **Marks** card (Figure 14.88).

8. Double-click the *Color* tile to edit the colors assigned to shapes. In the "Edit Colors" dialog window, select "Down" in the left pane. In the right pane, use the drop-down arrow to choose a "Color" palette. Underneath the palette drop-down, select a green color.

9. To assign colors and shapes to all possible values, adjust filters or add fields to the view. Because I want to compare year-over-year values, I temporarily added the [Order Date] field to the **Rows** shelf.

If you do not see a choice for "Up," remove the field [compare to last year] from the *Color* tile, adjust filters, or add fields so you see all possible values, and then add the field [compare to last year] back to the *Color* tile.

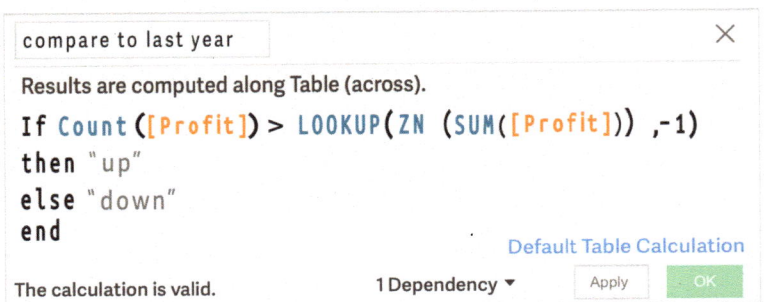

FIGURE 14.85
The Calculated Field Compare to last year.

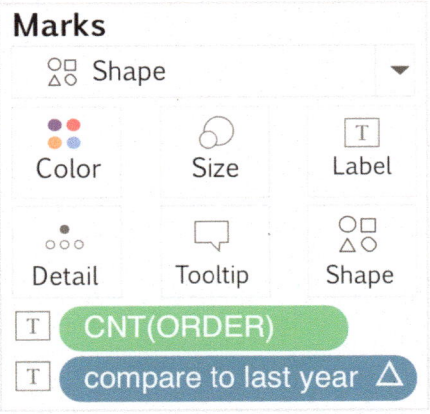

FIGURE 14.86
The Marks card with the CNT(ORDER) field.

FIGURE 14.87
The Edit Label dialog box.

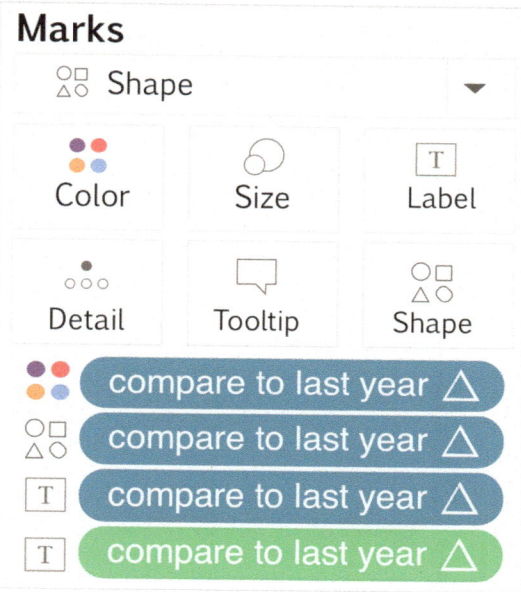

FIGURE 14.88
The Marks card with fields on Color, Shape, and Text Tiles.

FIGURE 14.89
The placeholder field on the Columns shelf.

10. Add a placeholder field to the **Columns** shelf to aid in the next step, where we format the alignment (Figure 14.89).

11. At this point, the shape and numbers overlap. To make room for the shape, click the *Label* tile on the **Marks** card. In the middle of the pop-up window, set the alignment to "Left." (Figure 14.90)

12. You can also adjust the width of the chart. In this example, I have four rows of marks. Hover over the right edge of the chart until a double arrow appears, then click-drag to resize the width, as shown below (Figure 14.91).

The chart shows several years of data and I only want to see unprofitable data, I create a set filter as shown in Step 13. I like sets for filtering because they are applied early in the Tableau *Order of Operations*. **Chapter 8** on *"Section 8.1 Filter Logic and the Order of Operations" on page 158* has more information on the *Order of Operations*.

13. Create a [Product Name Set Unprofitable] set with the below *Condition*. In the **Data** pane, right-click the [Product Name] field and choose "Create->Set…" (Figure 14.92)

14. Add the set [Product Name Set Unprofitable] to the **Filter** shelf and select "In," as shown below (Figure 14.93).

If you do not see the *In/Out* filter options, right-click the field on the **Filters** shelf and

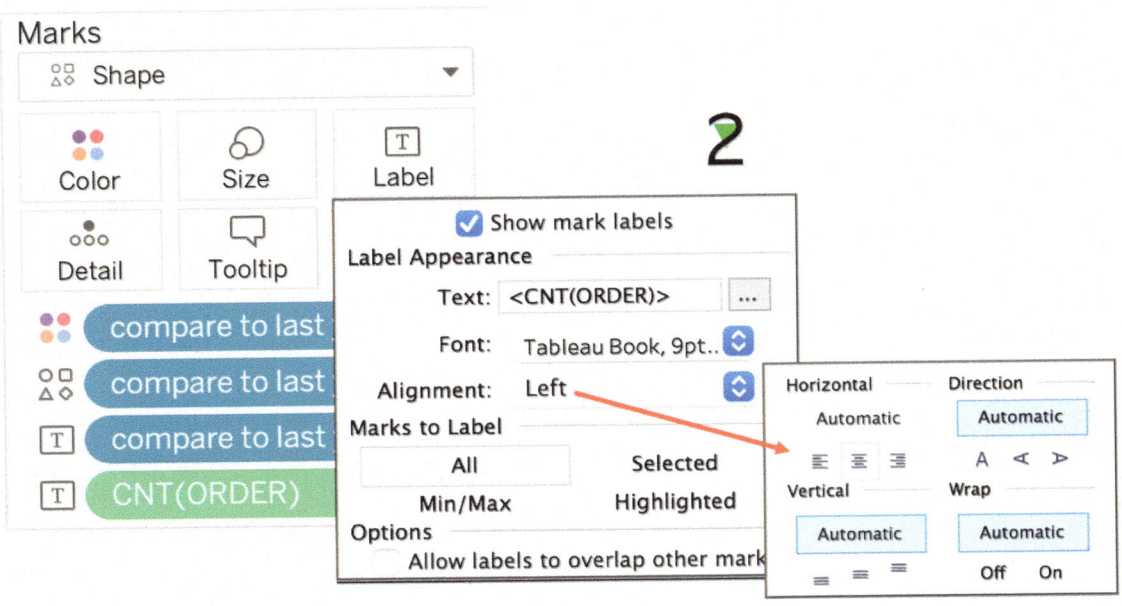

FIGURE 14.90
The Edit Label dialog boxes.

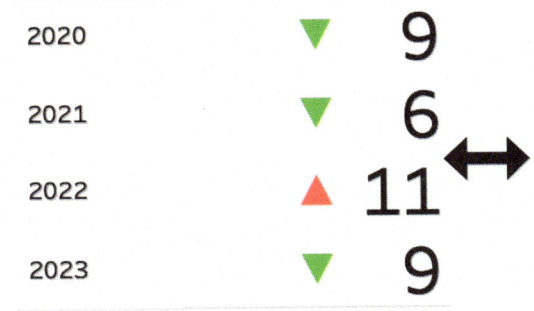

FIGURE 14.91
Resize the chart with the black double arrow.

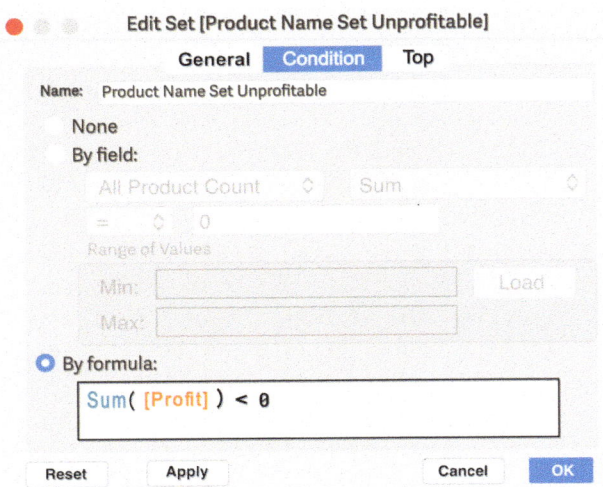

FIGURE 14.92
The Edit Set dialog box.

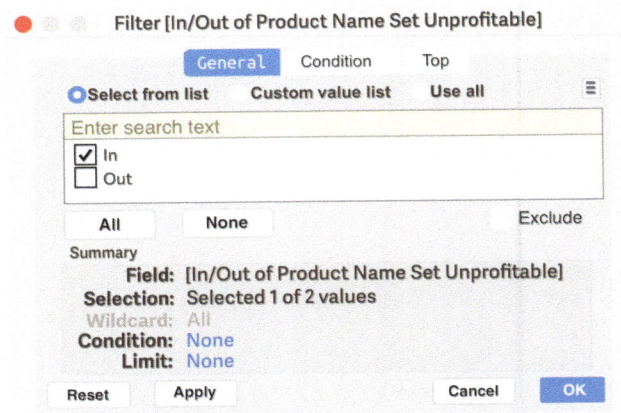

FIGURE 14.93
Filter In/Out of set.

select "Show In/Out of Set." (Figures 14.94 and 14.95)

15. I want to filter this KPI to only the current year, so I created a new calculated field, [Date Lookup Filter]. In the **Data** pane on the left, click the drop-down arrow to open the *object menu* and select "Create Calculated Field." In the calculation editor, enter the formula shown below (Figure 14.96).

"Section 8.7.2 Filter the View, Not the Underlying Data" on page 169 illustrates the use of a table calculation in this way. You may recall from **Chapter 10** that a table calculation filter affects the view but does not affect the underlying data.

16. Drag the new [Date Lookup Filter] field to the **Filters** shelf (Figure 14.97).

14.23.2 Display Only Shapes

In Step 12, drag the field [CNT(Order)] field from the *Text* tile to the *Detail* tile if you only want to see the shapes, as shown below (Figure 14.98).

14.23.3 Size KPIs Sheets and Containers

Once the basic KPI chart is created, I need to adjust worksheet elements and the dashboard container. When adding objects to dashboard containers, I

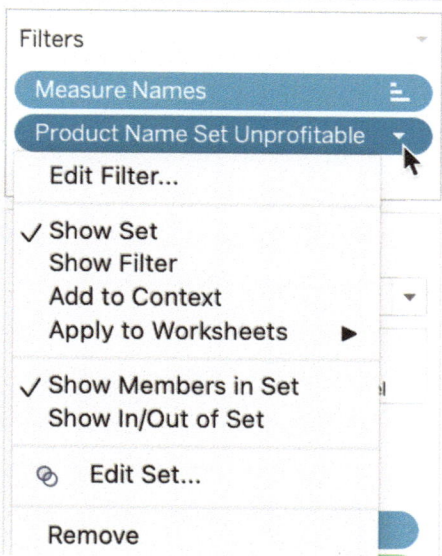

FIGURE 14.94
The context Filter with show In/Out of set.

FIGURE 14.95
The Filters shelf.

temporarily make the container larger. I have also found that adding at least two "blanks" makes working with a new container easier. When dragging objects into a container, it is easier to drag them into the middle of the container or between two blanks. I rearrange the object's position once it is inside the container. Once I have dragged my sheets, images, or text objects where I want them, I remove the blanks and resize the container to the final size.

When adjusting the KPI containers to line up properly, try a combination of settings to find the right ones for your dashboard.

- On the worksheet **Format** menu, select "Cell Size" and then "Text Cell." A text cell has an aspect ratio of 3:1, and a "Square Cell" has an aspect ratio of 1:1.
- On the *Label* tile of the **Marks** card, select "Alignment: Middle Center."
- On the dashboard, select the container and right-click to open its *object menu*. Depending on the type of container, choose "Edit Height" or "Edit Width."
- On the dashboard, select the object (like a sheet), and from the *object menu*, select "More Options." Choose "Edit Height" or "Edit Width."
- Move the mouse to the edge of the chart until a double arrow is displayed, and then click and drag to resize the chart.
- In the earlier topic, "Align Sheets (Height)," we looked at items that may affect sheet alignment.
- On all KPI worksheets, ensure you have the same number of fields on the **Columns** shelf, **Rows** shelf, and *Text* tile on the **Marks** card.
- Check the overall "Alignment" for the *Text* tile and the *Label* alignment.
- On the **Format** menu, ensure all fields have the same alignment.
- When you select worksheets and objects, the dark gray bounding box appears with the drop-down arrow in the top right corner to

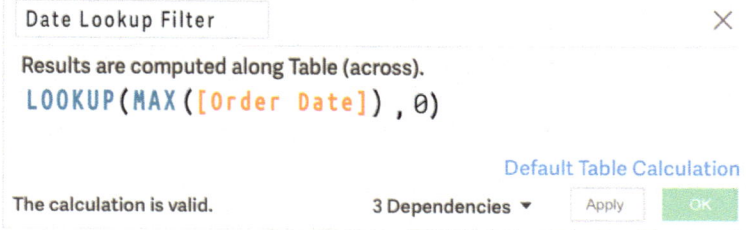

FIGURE 14.96
The Calculated Field Date Lookup Filter.

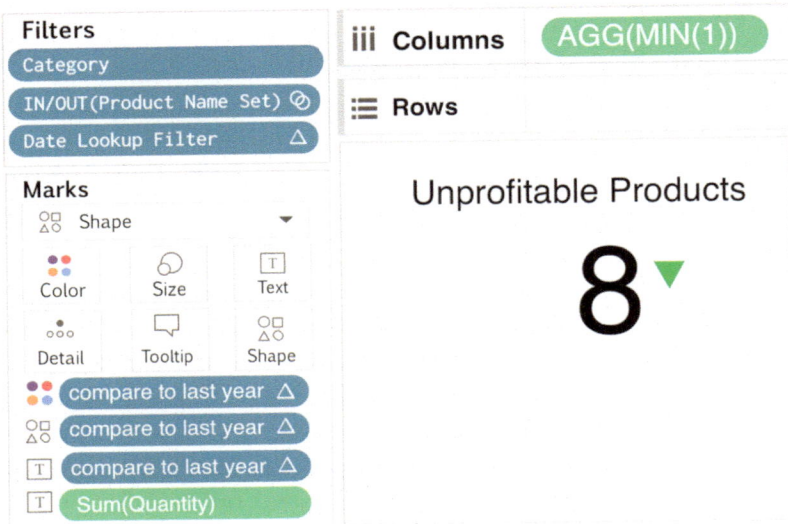

FIGURE 14.97
The Filters shelf with the date lookup Filter field.

FIGURE 14.98
Shape chart.

open the *object menu*. "Fit Width" is under "More Options" on the *object menu*. Also, in the toolbar area at the top of the Tableau workspace, you can select "Fit" options.

- Create a new placeholder field [MAX(2)] on the **Rows** shelf. Right-click on the new vertical axis and select "Edit Axis." Change the "Range" to **Fixed** with a *Fixed Start* of 1 and a *Fixed End* of 3.

14.23.4 Arrows from Number Format

Instead of using "Shape" for the mark type in the previous example, I can create a separate worksheet and use the field's "Default Properties" to add shapes to the **Number Format**. *"Section 12.11.6 Number Format:*

Custom Arrows" on page 278 illustrates adding shapes to "Default Properties."

Tableau Public file:

```
https://public.tableau.com/views/
KPIDashboardTemplate_17053442999830/
Template?:language=en-US&:sid=&:display_
count=n&:origin=viz_share_link
```

14.23.5 Data and Fields

This workbook is based on the *Sample Superstore* data source and includes these chart fields.

- CNT(ORDER)
- Category
- Order Date

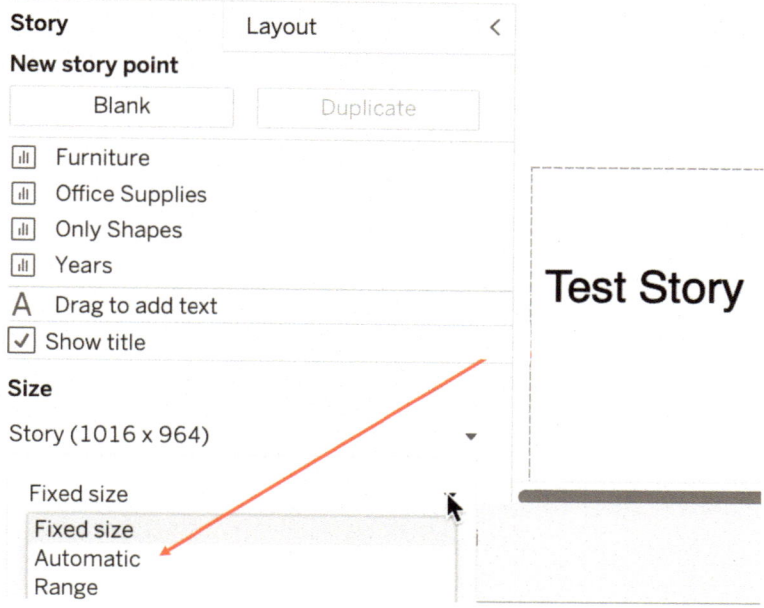

FIGURE 14.99
Size the Story.

14.23.6 Calculated Fields

- [compare to last year] uses the Lookup() function.
- [MIN(2)] is a placeholder field to add another layer to the **Marks** card.
- The [Date Lookup Filter] field is a table calculation because I want to filter the view and still have all the data I need to compare years.

14.23.7 Rows and Columns Shelves

[MIN(2)] is a placeholder field on the **Columns** shelf. During development, [MONTH(Order Date)] is on the **Rows** shelf to validate calculations.

14.23.8 Set

Add the set [Product Name Set Unprofitable] to the **Filter** shelf and select "In."

14.23.9 Marks

1. Select "Shape" from the drop-down on the **Marks** card. Adjust the size of the arrow shapes as needed.
2. Text alignment: left.
3. Add [Compare to Last Year] to *Color* on the **Marks** card.

14.23.10 Filters Shelf

Add the [Date Lookup Filter] table calculation field to the **Filters** shelf. Also, add the set [Product Name Set Unprofitable] to the **Filters** shelf and select "In."

14.24 Stories

Stories are a way to tailor visualizations to particular needs. For example, add a worksheet or dashboard to a story and change the filter to the first supervisor. Add another story point and repeat the steps, but filter to the second supervisor. Stories are an excellent way to arrange or export data pre-filtered for a particular group.

The navigator buttons are at the top of the story window. In Tableau Desktop, you can click-drag to resize the buttons.

14.24.1 Size Options

There are options for stories like "Automatic," where the screen adjusts to any screen automatically, although that can impact performance (Figure 14.99).

When you use a dashboard in a story, on the dashboard's **Layout** pane, you can choose to fit the dashboard size to the story. Because I have a story called "Test Story" in the dashboard's **Size** drop-down,

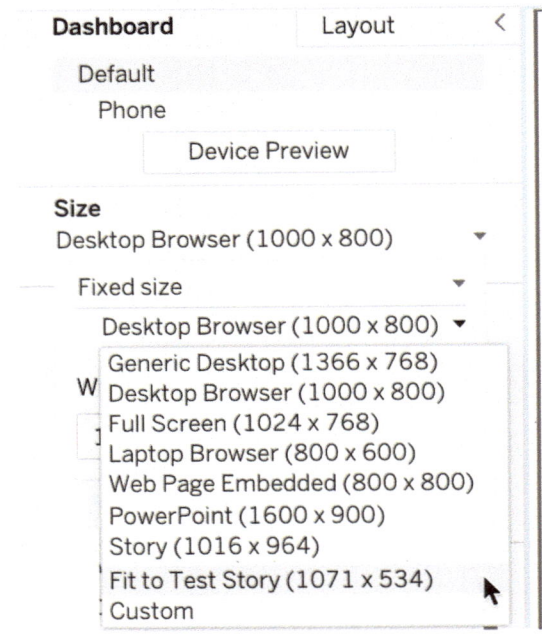

FIGURE 14.100
Size options.

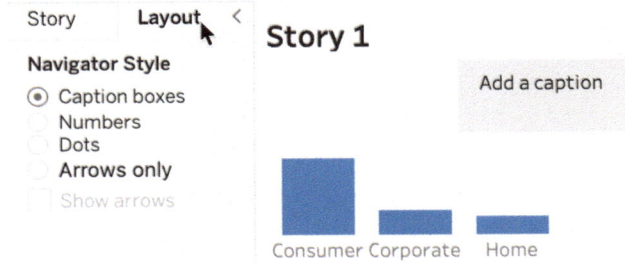

FIGURE 14.101
The Layout pane.

Tableau adds a choice to "Fit to Test Story," as shown below (Figure 14.100).

14.24.2 Layout Pane

The "Navigator Style" of the **Layout** pane for a story controls the appearance of the caption boxes at the top of the story window, as shown below. In this case, there is a gray box with the phrase "Add a caption." In Tableau Desktop, you can click-drag to resize the navigator buttons (Figure 14.101).

14.24.3 Title

To show or hide the worksheet's "Title," on the **Story** menu, check "Show Title." You can also toggle the "Show title" option in the left **Story** pane.

14.24.4 Add Text

The option "Drag to add text" in the **Story** pane on the left adds a text object to the story. Click-drag to add a text object to the story (Figure 14.102).

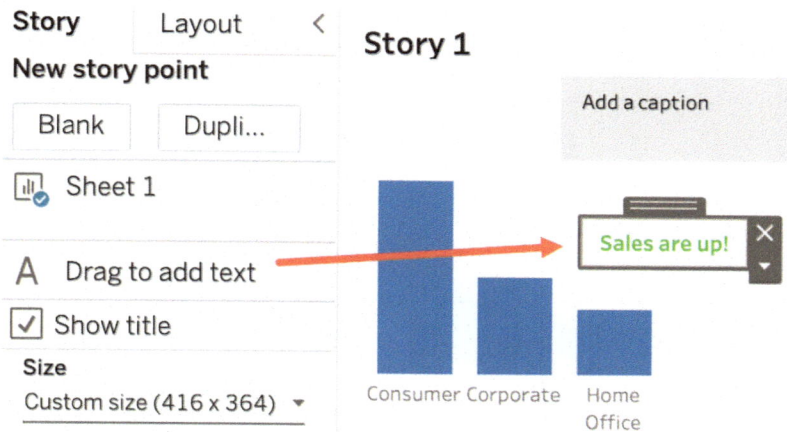

FIGURE 14.102
A Story text object.

15

Interactivity

In this topic, we discuss

Actions
Tooltips
Parameters
Highlighting
Hierarchies

This chapter explores ways to introduce interactivity to Tableau worksheets and dashboards. Users can interact directly with Tableau when they open Tableau files in Tableau Desktop or from a Tableau server. If you cannot access a Tableau server, check out Tableau Public.

15.1 Actions

Tableau actions change the view or navigate to other locations and are available for dashboards and worksheets. As we walk through this overview of actions, I showcase the in-depth examples from other chapters. When adding actions, the drop-down list box has these choices (Figures 15.1–15.6):

15.1.1 Run Action On

When configuring actions, you must specify when to activate the action. There are three choices for the **Run action on** setting, as shown below. The action examples that follow demonstrate each setting.

- Hover
- Select
- Menu

I use *Hover* in a "Go to URL Action." *Hover* is also a good choice for "Highlight actions." The "Email Link" and "Drill Down with a Set Action" topics that follow both use *Select* for the **Run action on** setting. With the *Menu* setting, a user must click to activate the action, which is perfect for a tooltip, as shown in the topics "Go to Sheet Action" or "Open Other Worksheet From Within a Tooltip."

15.1.2 Filter Action

In previous chapters, these examples used filter actions.

"Section 8.4 Filter Actions" on page 161

"Section 14.7.4 Filter Dashboard Sheets When Data Points are Selected" on page 314

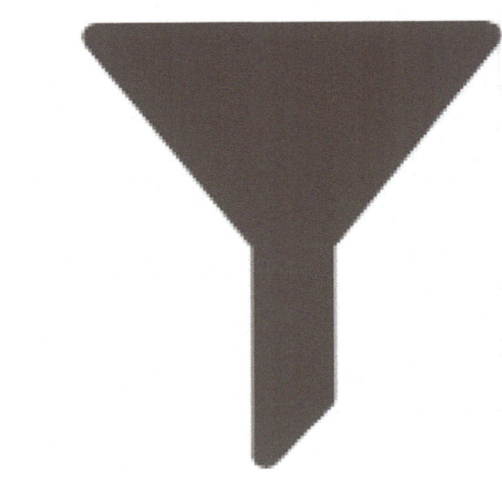

FIGURE 15.1
Filter.

FIGURE 15.2
Highlight.

FIGURE 15.3
Go to URL.

FIGURE 15.4
Go to Sheet.

FIGURE 15.5
Change Parameter.

FIGURE 15.6
Change Set Members.

DOI: 10.1201/9781003566458-16

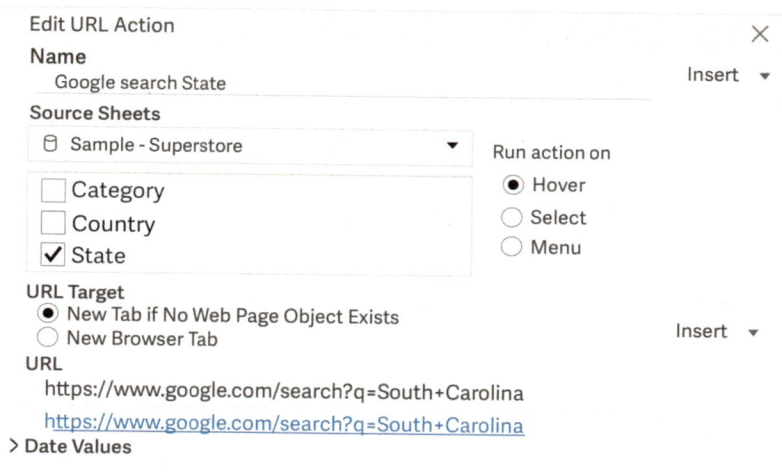

FIGURE 15.7
URL action.

FIGURE 15.8
Insert a field into the URL action.

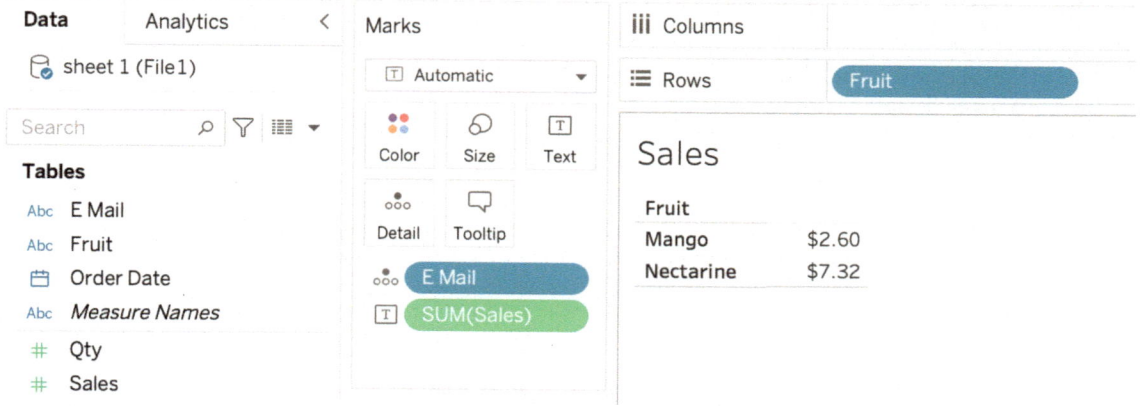

FIGURE 15.9
Worksheet with Email field.

"Section 14.19 A Reset All Filters Button" on page 339

"Section 14.21 A Pop-Out Chart (Filter Action)" on page 343

15.1.3 Highlight Action

When I have two worksheets on a dashboard, I like highlight actions when I *hover* over a mark in the first worksheet. Tableau highlights related marks in other worksheets. You can apply highlighting to selected fields, "dates and times," or all fields.

15.1.4 Go to URL Action

A Tableau **URL Action** is a hyperlink to a resource outside of Tableau. In Figure 15.7, I have a universal resource locator (URL) to Google where I was searching for the state "South Carolina." To test a URL action, click the blue link below the URL in the **Edit URL Action** window.

To include field data, click the drop-down arrow in the bottom right corner by "Insert" and select a field. In Figure 15.8, I inserted the [State/Province] field into my URL path. A naming convention that utilizes valid URL characters is important if you plan to create URL links. See the RFC 3986 (Uniform Resource Identifier (URI): Generic Syntax) and URI schemes from RFC 1738. RFCs govern standards used across the Internet.

*If the fields referenced in the action are not already in the view, add them to the Detail tile on the **Marks** card. Otherwise, the link won't display in the visualization, even if it functions when you test the link in the **Edit URL Action** window.*

15.1.4.1 *Link to Tableau Server Dashboards and Worksheets*

When you think of a URL, you probably think of a hyperlink to a website like http://www.tableau.com. However, **URL Actions** can also link to dashboards and worksheets published to a Tableau Server.

15.1.4.2 *Email (URL Link)*

One of my favorite Tableau **URL Actions** is to send an email. *"Section 15.1.4.2 Email (URL Link)" on page 358* demonstrates email syntax. In the following example, I create a worksheet and add the fields, as shown in Figure 15.9. I have a field [E Mail] with email addresses. Because I use the [E Mail] field in the URL action, I add the field to the *Detail* tile on the **Marks** card.

Create a URL action using the *mailto* syntax, as shown in Figure 15.10.

15.1.5 Go to Sheet Action with a Tooltip

The **Go to Sheet** action opens another worksheet when you *hover*, *select*, or choose a *menu* item in a tooltip. I like to use this action in tooltips to open another chart with more details.

1. Create a worksheet action "Go to Sheet - State." On the **Worksheet** menu, select "Actions" and choose "Go to Sheet" from the "Add Action" button in the bottom left corner. The **Add Go to Sheet Action** window opens, as shown below (Figure 15.11).

2. Insert a sheet in the tooltip. In the following image, I used the drop-down "Insert" menu in the top right corner to add the "State" sheet to my tooltip. I did not change the default

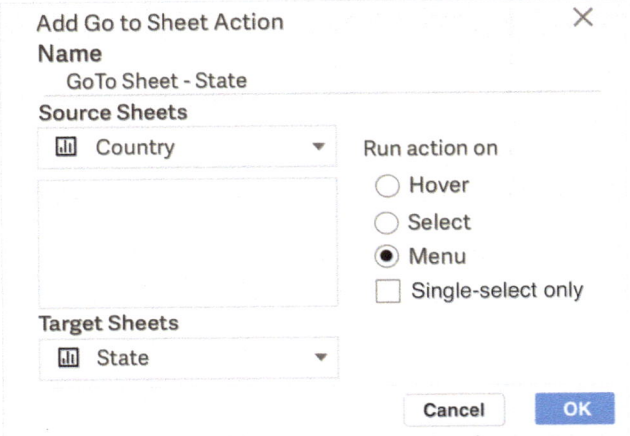

FIGURE 15.11
The Add Go to Sheet Action dialog window.

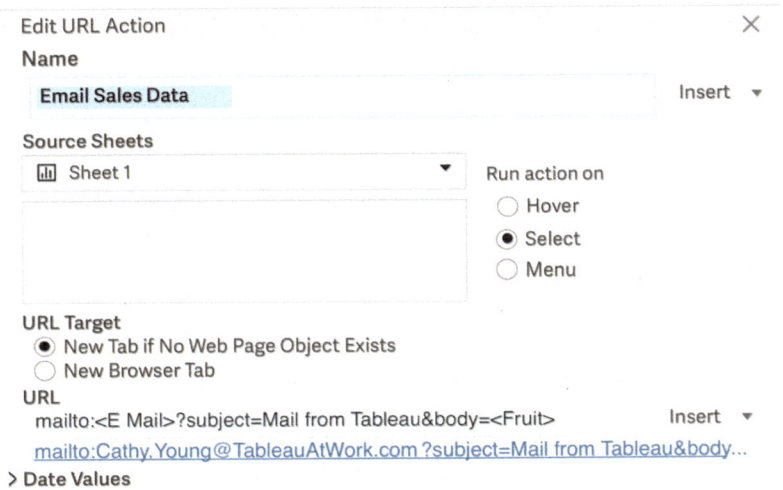

FIGURE 15.10
The Mail Message Field.

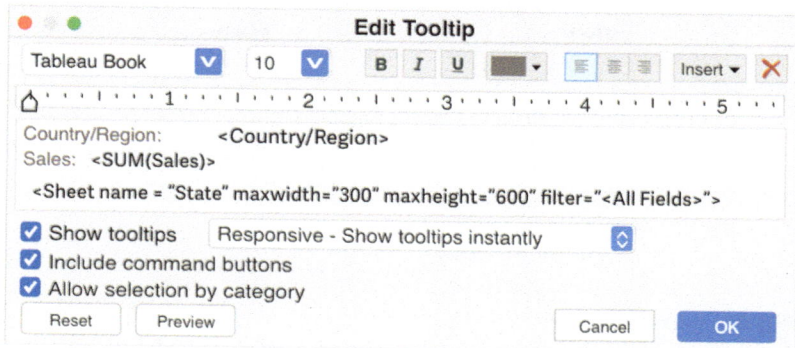

FIGURE 15.12
The Edit Tooltip window.

FIGURE 15.13
A tooltip with the Go to Sheet Link at the bottom.

values but could adjust the *maxwidth* and *maxheight* settings if the sheet was too large (Figure 15.12).

When a user opens a tooltip and pauses for a few seconds, the **Go to Sheet - State** link appears at the bottom of the tooltip, as shown below (Figure 15.13).

15.1.6 Change Parameter Action

"Section 8.14 Hover to Choose a Field for Sorting" on page 181 uses a parameter action for sorting. We look at many parameter actions for changing sheets and dynamically selecting dimensions or measures in more detail later in the topic *"Section 15.4 Parameters" on page 368*.

15.1.7 Change Set Action

When you want your audience to update the view by changing set members, use the **Change Set Values** action. The following example uses a set action to drill down into a hierarchy. *"Section 8.13 Click Data Points to Sort with a Set" on page 175* also uses a set action.

15.1.8 Drill Down with a Set Action

In this example, we:

- Create a set and display the **Set Control**.
- Assign arrows to the **Set Control** values: In and Out.
- Create a **Change Set Values** action.
- Create two calculated fields.

The link to the Tableau Public file is at the end of the exercise.

1. Create a set [Selected Category Set] based on the first field you want to drill down into, in this case, [Category]. In the **Data** pane, right-click the [Category] field to open the field's drop-down *context menu* and select "Create, Set…" Select the set in the **Data** pane and choose "Show set" in the set's *context menu* to show the **Set Control**, so we can use the set control to test during step 7 (Figure 15.14).

2. Create a calculated [Category copy] field equal to [Category].

3. Create a [SubCategory] calculated field to display the subcategory when the category set matches, as shown below (Figure 15.15).

4. Add [Selected Category Set], [Category copy], and [SubCategory] to the **Rows** shelf.

5. Right-click "In" on the left side of the canvas and select "Edit Alias…" from the *context*

menu. Tableau adds a blue highlight on the left, as shown below (Figure 15.16).

Select "Edit Alias…" to change the alias to a down arrow (Figure 15.17).

"Section 12.11.6 Number Format: Custom Arrows" on page 278 shows how to add ASCII symbols to Tableau dialogs.

6. Repeat Step 5, selecting "Out" on the canvas and changing the alias to the right arrow.

7. On the **Worksheet** menu, select "Actions" and then click the "Add Actions" button in the bottom left corner of the **Actions** window to open the **Edit Set Action** dialog window. Name the new action "Category Set Action," and for the **Run action on**, choose *Select*. Choose the options as shown below (Figure 15.18).

To test the action, use the **Set Control** on the right side of the view to select different categories (Figure 15.19).

Tableau Public file:

https://public.tableau.com/views/Drill downwithSetActionss1085/Dashboard?: language=en-US&publish=yes&:sid=&: display_count=n&:origin=viz_share_link

15.2 Tooltips

Tableau <u>Tooltips</u> appear when a user moves the mouse over a *mark* in the view. When combined with actions, you can include these elements in your tooltip:

- Email
- URL
- Create a Visualization Inside the Tooltip
- Open Other Worksheets or Dashboards

FIGURE 15.14
The Edit Set dialog window.

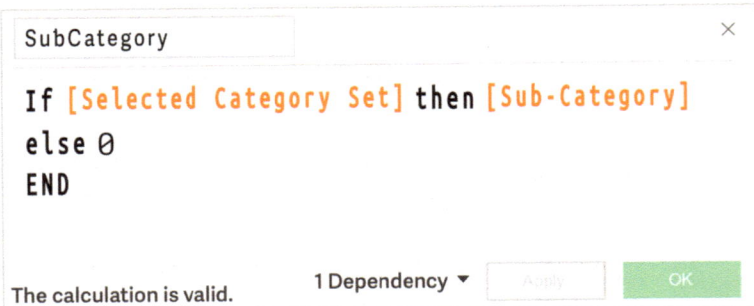

FIGURE 15.15
The calculated field SubCategory.

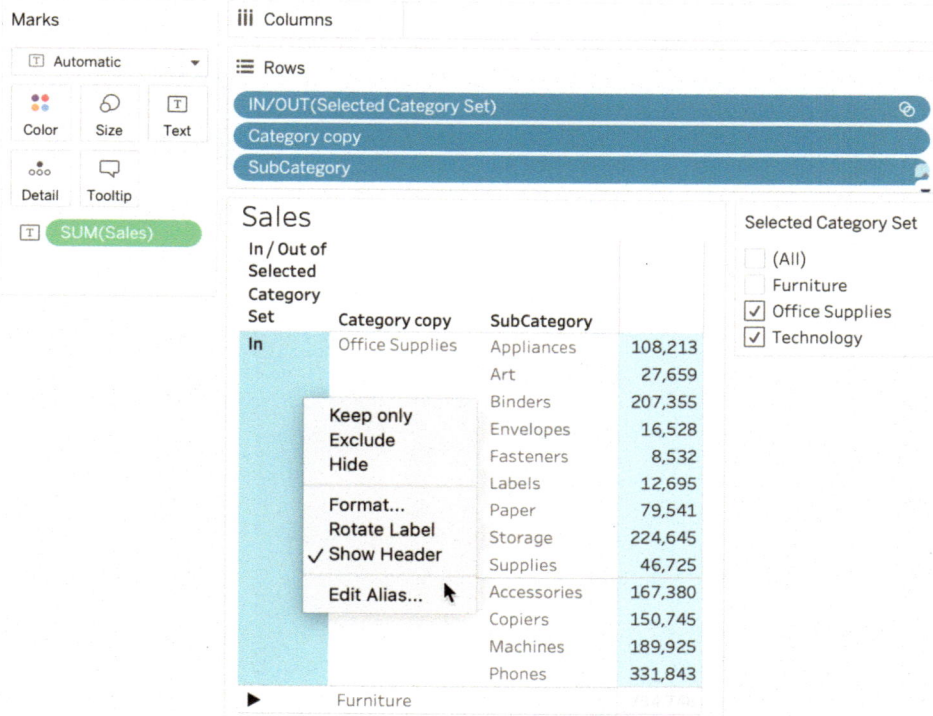

FIGURE 15.16
Editing the "In" Alias.

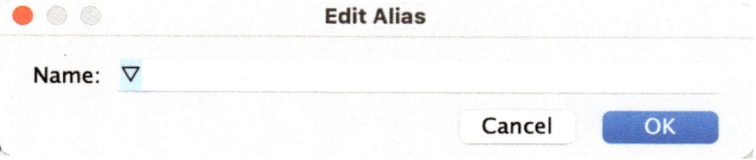

FIGURE 15.17
The Edit Alias dialog window.

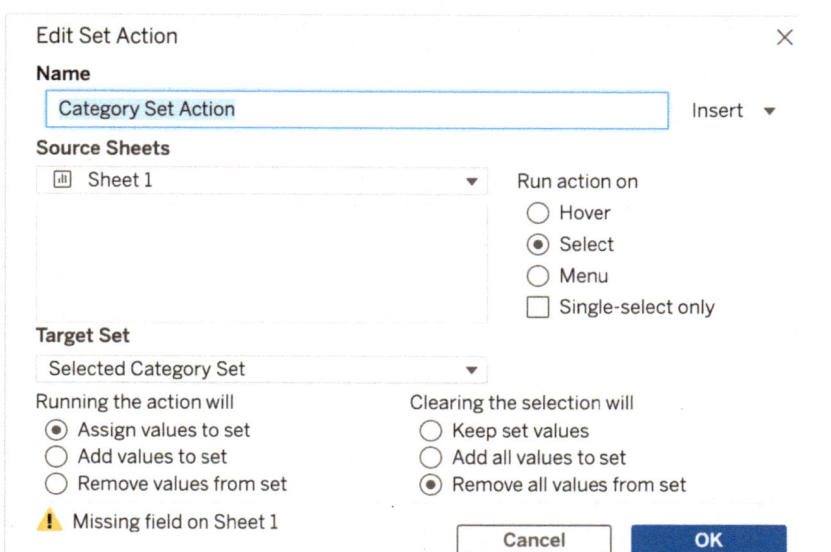

FIGURE 15.18
The Edit Set Action window.

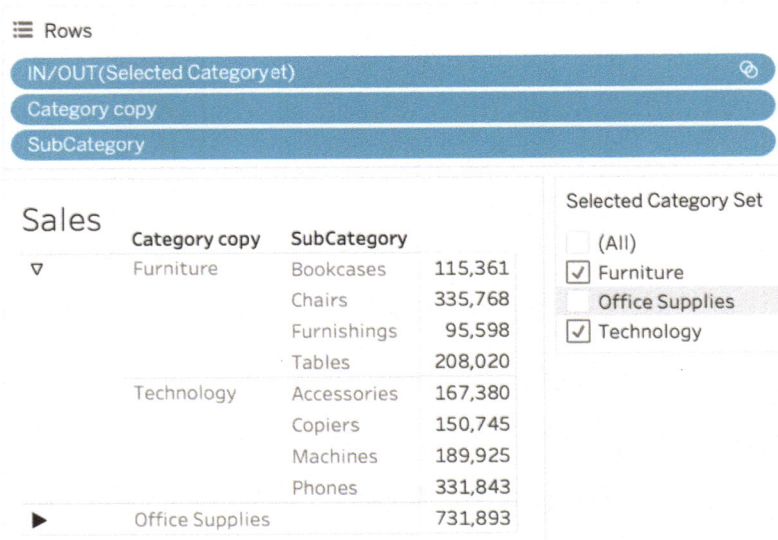

FIGURE 15.19
The Set Control on the right side of the view.

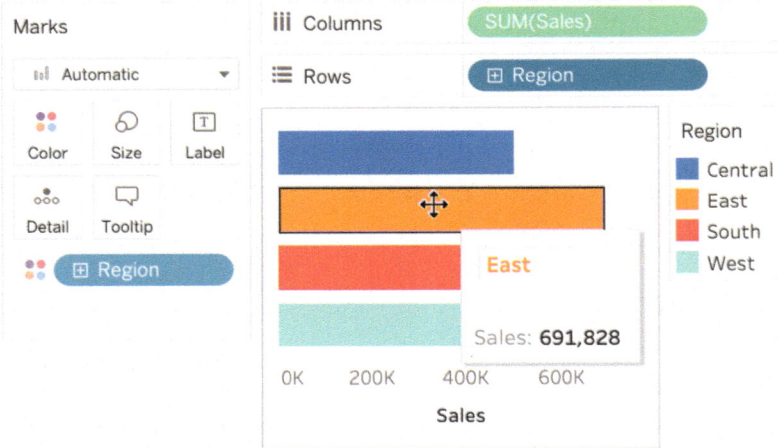

FIGURE 15.20
Color legend in Tooltip.

An interesting alternative to a **Legend Control** is a color legend inside a tooltip. In Figure 15.20, I have a separate worksheet with the color legend.

15.2.1 Edit Tooltip

Click the *Tooltip* tile in the **Marks** card to open the **Edit Tooltip** dialog window. In the bottom left corner of the window, there are three options.

- Show tooltips
- Include command buttons
- Allow selection by category

The option "Allow selection by category" selects marks in a view that has the same value when you click a discrete field in a tooltip.

15.2.2 Tooltip Command Buttons

The command buttons in Figure 15.28 include these options (Figures 15.22 through 15.27).

15.2.3 Field Not Showing in Tooltip

When you have a dual-axes chart and fields on the tooltip are not displayed properly, try adding both axis fields to the tooltips and reset both tooltips.

FIGURE 15.21
Warning: *If the tooltip text does not align as expected, click "Reset" in the bottom left corner of the* **Edit Tooltip** *dialog window.*

✓

FIGURE 15.22
Keep only.

⊘

FIGURE 15.23
Exclude.

🖇

FIGURE 15.24
Group.

💡

FIGURE 15.25
Explain data.

⊗

FIGURE 15.26
Create set.

☰

FIGURE 15.27
View data.

15.2.4 Unhide Tooltip Worksheet

If you've hidden a worksheet that is embedded inside a **Tooltip**, go to the *main* worksheet, right-click the worksheet name in the tabs along the bottom of the workspace, and choose "Unhide."

15.2.5 Insert a Chart Inside the Tooltip

To add a chart inside a tooltip, click the *Tooltip* tile on the **Marks** card. Then click the "Insert" drop-down and select *Sheets*, as shown in Figure 15.30.

An asterisk in a **Tooltip** indicates multiple rows. To view more detail, insert another visualization inside the tooltip, as shown in Figure 15.31. At the bottom of this tooltip, a banner says, "View is too large to show." You can adjust the tooltip *maxwidth* and *max-height* size as shown earlier in the example, "Go to Sheet Action."

15.2.6 Email from within a Tooltip

When you think of a URL, you probably think of a link to a website like http://www.tableau.com. Emails and other default types also fall within the confines of a URL. This example uses a URL Action with a calculated field that creates the **mailto** link. This syntax is similar to the earlier email action.

15.2.7 Open Other Worksheet from within a Tooltip

In the earlier topic, "Actions," we looked at the "Go To Sheet" action to open another worksheet.

1. Connect to a data source and create two worksheets, "Sheet 1" and "Sheet 2." Add [Category] and [Sales] to the view.
2. Create a "Go To Sheet" action for "Sheet 1." On the **Worksheet** menu, select *Actions* and choose "Go to Sheet" from the drop-down list. The **Edit Go to Sheet Action** dialog window opens, as shown below (Figure 15.32).
3. For the setting "Run action on," choose *Menu* (this step is critical).
4. To test the action, on Sheet 1, hover over a mark to open the tooltip. If you don't see the link to Sheet 2 in the tooltip, click once, and you should see the link at the bottom of the tooltip, as shown below (Figure 15.33).

15.3 Highlighting

Tableau's <u>highlighting behavior</u> has several configuration options.

- Disable Workbook Highlighting
- Disable Sheet Highlighting
- All Fields
- Dates and Times
- Selected Field(s)

  Select the fields you want to use for highlighting and choose one of the following options:

- **All Fields** – Marks in the target sheet are highlighted when they match the marks selected in the source sheet. All fields are considered when determining a match.

- **Dates and Times** – Marks in the target sheet are highlighted when their date and time match the marks selected in the source sheet. The source and target worksheets can only have *one date field each*; however, the fields can have different names.

- **Selected Fields** – Marks in the target sheet are highlighted based on selected fields. For example, highlighting using the [Ship Mode]

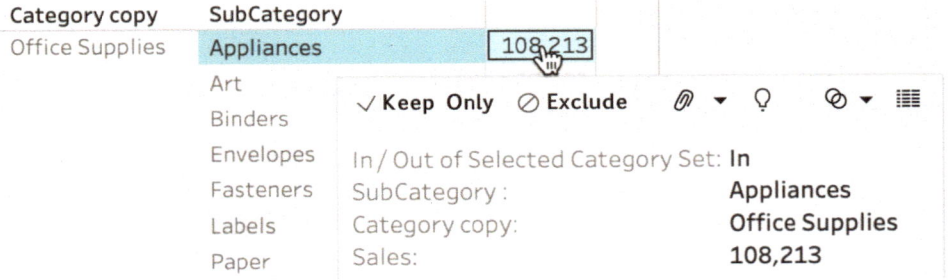

FIGURE 15.28
Tooltip with command buttons.

FIGURE 15.29
Tip: *You can hide command buttons to avoid confusing users. Click the Tooltip tile in the Marks card and uncheck "Include command buttons" in the bottom left corner of the Edit Tooltip dialog window.*

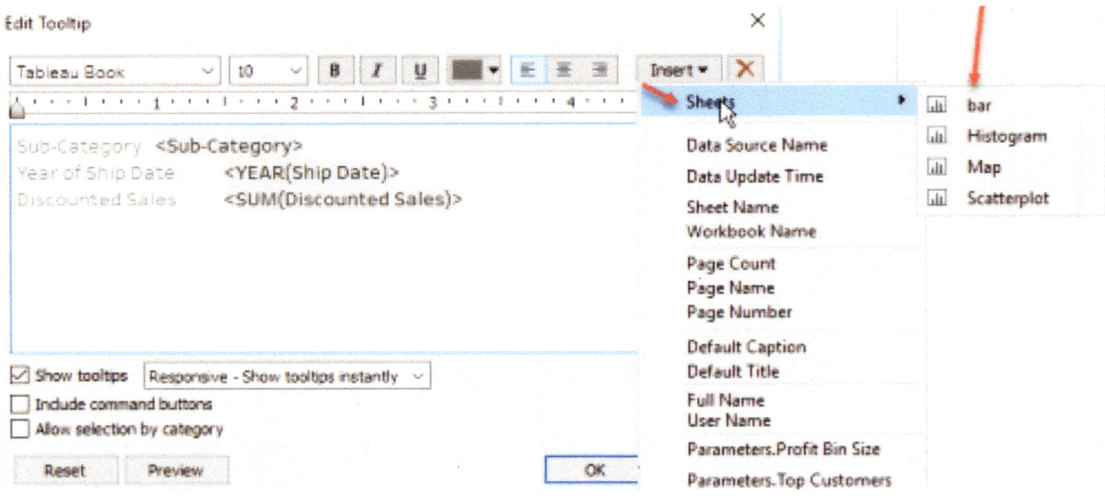

FIGURE 15.30
Insert a sheet into the Tooltip.

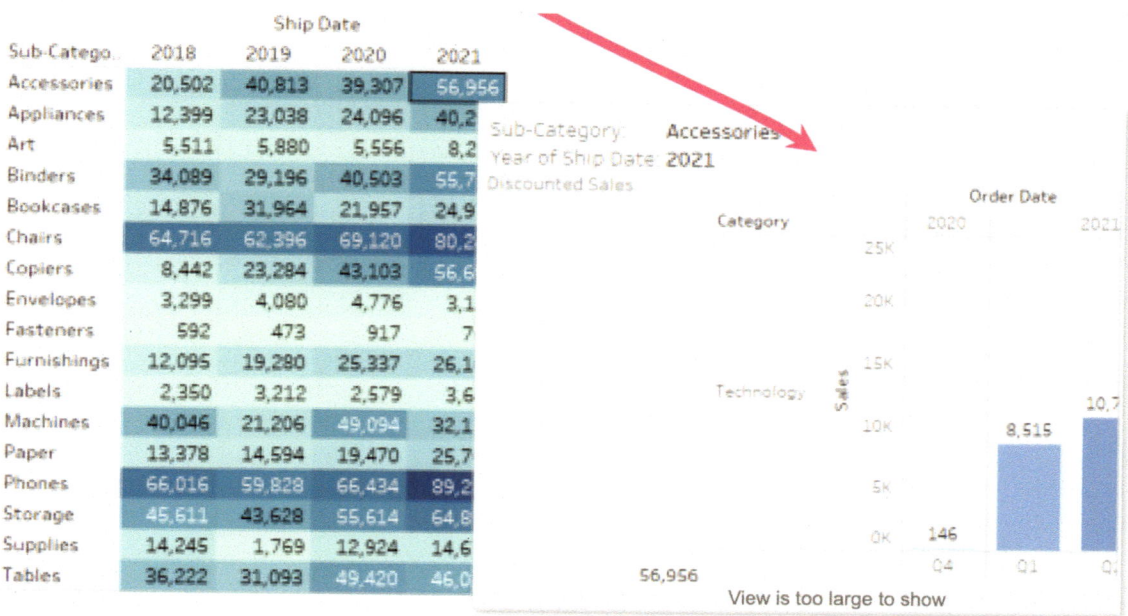

FIGURE 15.31
Tooltip with a view.

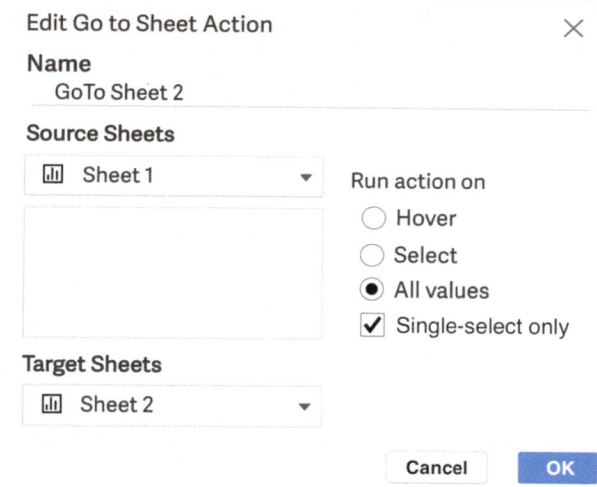

FIGURE 15.32
The **Edit Go to Sheet Action** dialog.

field will result in an action highlighting all marks in the target sheet with the same [Ship Mode] as the selected mark in the source sheet.

15.3.1 Toolbar: Highlight

When you click to select a mark on the visualization, Tableau's default behavior highlights the mark and changes all other marks to gray. To turn this behavior off, follow the steps in the "Calculation Field to Turn Off Highlighting" topic that follows.

"Section 8.13 Click Data Points to Sort with a Set" on page 175 and *"Section 10.4.3 Slope Chart with a Rank Table Calculation" on page 215* illustrate how to show the highlighter and display the **Highlight** control.

15.3.2 Choose Highlight Fields

The <u>Highlight</u> tool in the toolbar at the top of the workspace allows you to choose which fields are highlighted when a user selects a mark. Because I selected [Qty] in the example in Figure 15.34, when I click a mark that is "2" in the [Qty] field, all marks with a "2" are highlighted.

Next, I filter by a particular field. In Figure 15.35, I selected the [Preferences] field on the **Rows** shelf. I clicked the drop-down arrow to open the field's *context menu* and selected "Show Highlighter." I then selected the highlighter tool in the toolbar; it shows that [Preferences] is selected.

I selected "8" in the view's first row of the *Oct* column. In Figure 15.36, the mark is highlighted in yellow. Because I configured highlighting to use the [Preferences] field in this example, Tableau highlights other values that match the [Preferences] value for that row, in this case, "OK if ripe."

15.3.3 Calculation Field to Turn Off Highlighting

"Section 8.13 Click Data Points to Sort with a Set" on page 175 changes highlighting. In the last step, I set the highlighting tool to highlight with the calculated field

FIGURE 15.33
The Tooltip with the GoTo Sheet 2 at the bottom.

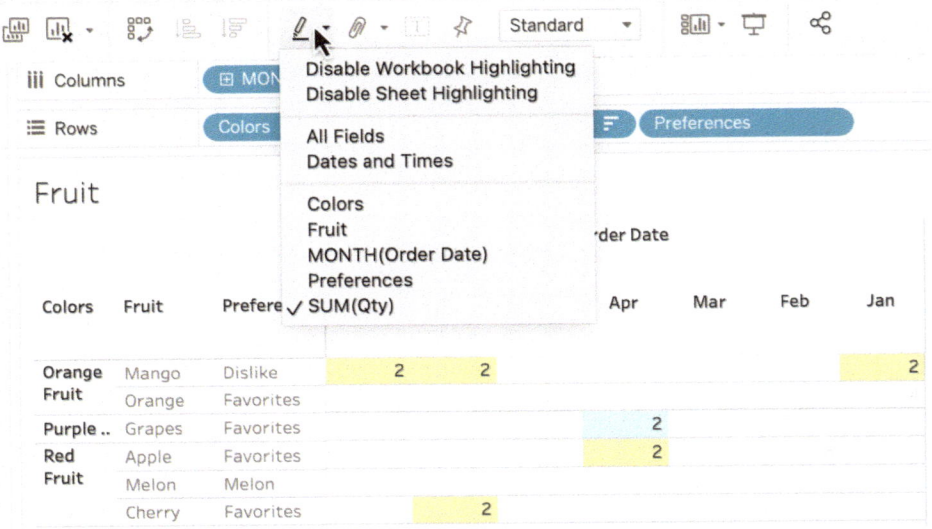

FIGURE 15.34
The Highlight tool.

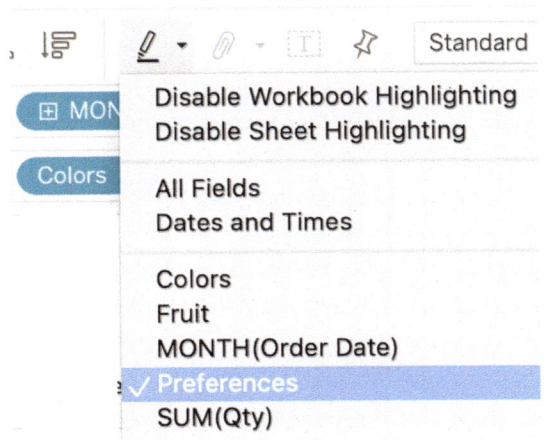

FIGURE 15.35
The Preferences field is selected.

[Calc to turn off highlighting], effectively turning off highlighting.

This calculated field [Calc to turn off highlighting] in Figure 15.37 is a placeholder field that I use to adjust highlighting. The value of a placeholder field can be anything. I add the calculated field [Calc to turn off highlighting] to the **Marks** card on the *Details* tile, as shown in Figure 15.38.

On the **Toolbar**, select the highlight tool and open the *context menu*. Select the field [Calc to turn off highlighting], as shown in Figure 15.39.

15.3.4 Legend Highlighting

You can highlight marks based on the members selected in the **Legend Control**. The icon at the top of

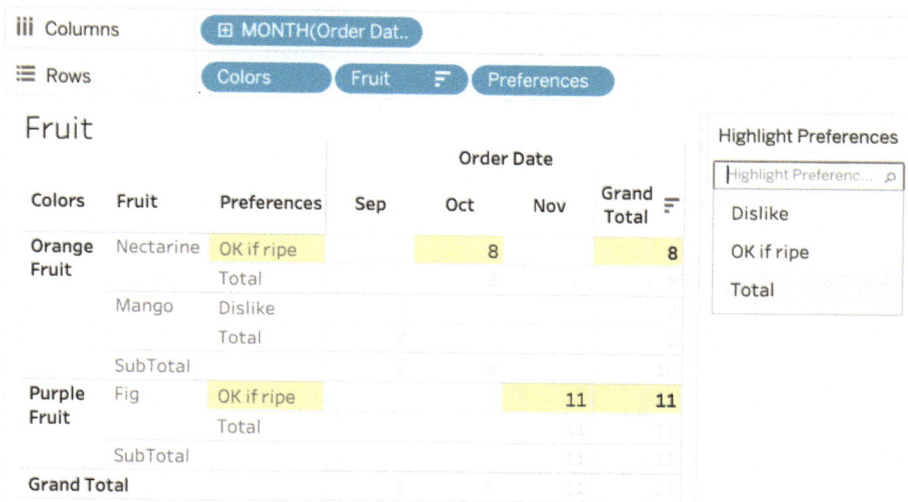

FIGURE 15.36
The Highlight control.

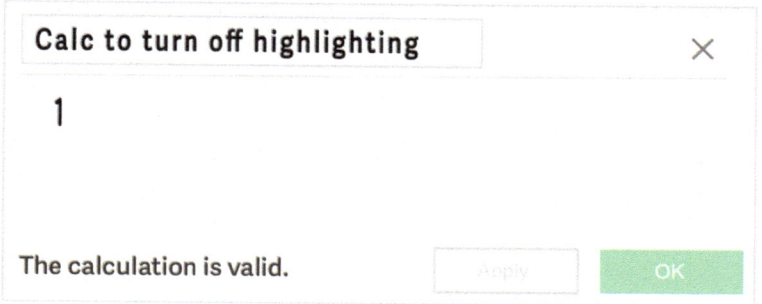

FIGURE 15.37
The [Calc to turn off highlighting] Field.

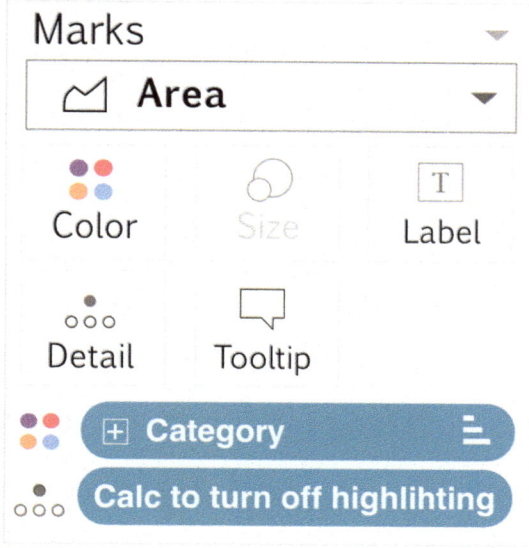

FIGURE 15.38
Detail tile.

FIGURE 15.39
Highlight tool.

the control indicates which mode you are using. With "one-way highlighting," the selected marks in the view control the highlighting, and with "two-way highlighting," the selected values in the **Legend Control** set highlighting. For more information, see Tableau's online guide:

> https://help.tableau.com/current/pro/desktop/en-us/actions_highlight_color legend.htm

15.4 Parameters

Parameters are placeholder variables that replace constants. The beauty of parameters is that they are available to all worksheets or dashboards, even across data sources. So, if someone picks a date range on one dashboard, it applies to all. Parameters allow viewers to explore with filter values or reference lines when combined with calculated fields. Earlier, we looked at these examples that used parameters.

"Section 7.8.1 Reference Line with Shading" on page 153

"Section 8.7.1 Filter to Dynamic Range & Top N" on page 168

"Section 8.5.9 Filtering with Parameters" on page 167

"Section 9.13 Date Parameter in Axis Label" on page 208

"Section 14.14 Dashboard Sheet Selection Menu" on page 317

"Section 14.16 Horizontal Radial Buttons to Change Filters" on page 323

"Section 14.17 Horizontal Radial Buttons to Switch Sheets" on page 328

When hiding unused files, Tableau does not consider fields used to populate parameters, as shown in *"Section 9.11 Avoid 'All' in a Date Title" on page 208*.

15.4.1 Create Parameter

To create a new parameter, click the drop-down arrow at the top of the **Data** pane. Parameters are shown in the **Parameters** section at the bottom of the **Data** pane.

When populating your list of "choices" for your parameter, you can use field data and even load that data as the workbook opens. In the case of dates, I like to give my audience the ability to choose their start and end dates based on the values in the data source. So, for example, I choose "Range of Values Fixed," then say "Set Values from," and choose the field [Order Date]. Now, only relevant dates are included in the parameter, which is fantastic.

15.4.2 Populate with the Latest Date

In Figure 15.40, I use the field [Data Update Date Time] to populate the default parameter value when the workbook opens.

The [Latest Date] field in Figure 15.41 returns the maximum [Data Update Date Parameter].

15.4.3 Filter with Parameter

Often, I'll create a [Start Date] and [End Date] parameter so my audience can choose dates for filters. I

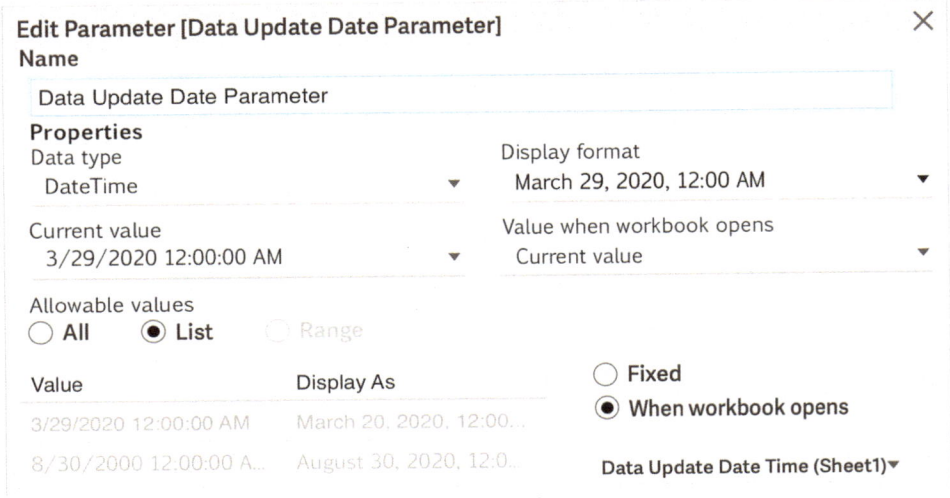

FIGURE 15.40
Data Update Date parameter.

added a calculated field to the Filter shelf that has logic to compare a date field to parameters.

15.4.4 Parameter Control

To display a **Parameter Control** on a worksheet, right-click the parameter name at the bottom of the **Data** pane and select "Show Parameter." Select a worksheet object on a dashboard so that a dark gray bounding box is displayed around the sheet. In the top right corner of the bounding box, click the drop-down arrow to open the *object menu*. Select "Parameters" and then select one of the parameters from the list.

> Suppose you change the color of the text title for a **Filter Control** or **Parameter Control** while working on a worksheet. In that case, you only see that change once you view the **Filter Control** or **Parameter Control** on a dashboard.

15.5 Switch between Measures with Parameters

Create a parameter and calculated field to let users choose which measure (field) to display in the chart. There is no parameter action on this chart. Instead, when a user selects the measure name in the **Parameter Control**, a calculated field on the **Columns** shelf displays the selected field data.

In this example, we'll switch between sales and profit with a dynamic measure. If you need different types of formatting, such as percentage and currency, add characters to the calculation field in addition to the parameter logic. This chart also has a diverging color palette showing the positive and negative

numbers. The link to the Tableau Public file is at the end of the exercise, along with a checklist of the elements and settings in the example.

15.5.1 Create the Visualization

1. After connecting to a data source, click the drop-down arrow at the top of the **Data** pane to create a parameter.

2. Right-click the parameter at the bottom of the **Data** pane and select "Show Parameter." The **Parameter Control** appears on the right (Figure 15.42). By right-clicking the drop-down arrow on the right, you can edit the title and change the appearance of the control.

3. Create the calculated field (after creating the new parameter). At the top of the **Data** pane, use the drop-down arrow to select "Create Calculated Field." Name the field [Sales or Profit.calc], as shown in Figure 15.43.

4. Add the new calculated field to the **Columns** shelf.

5. Add the calculated field to *Color* on the **Marks** card, as shown in Figure 15.44.

6. Click the *Color* tile on the **Marks** card to open the "Edit Colors" dialog. Check *Stepped Color* and use the arrows to change the "Steps" value to 2, as shown in Figure 15.45.

7. If you like, customize the title to include the parameter so the title has either *Sales* or *Profit*.

15.5.2 Testing

Click within the **Parameter Control** on the right to switch between measures. When "Profit" is selected,

FIGURE 15.41
The Latest Date field.

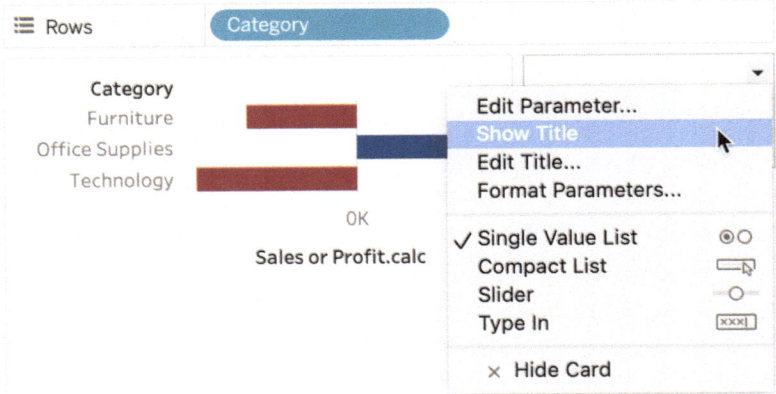

FIGURE 15.42
The Parameter Control context menu.

FIGURE 15.43
The Calculated field sales or Profit calc.

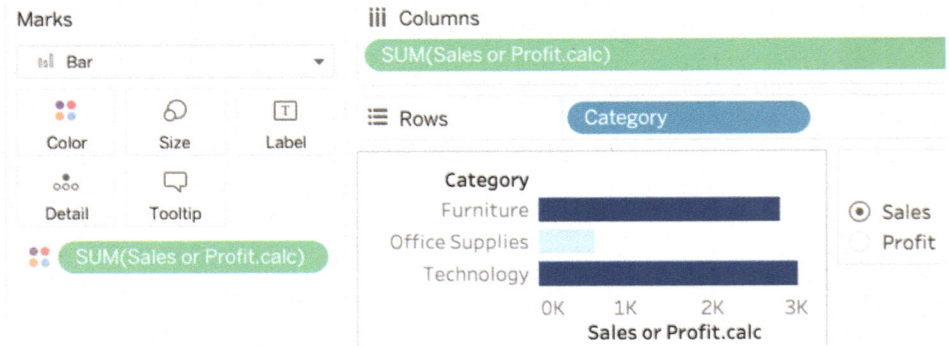

FIGURE 15.44
The new field on the Marks card on the Left.

marks are encoded with positive and negative colors, as shown in Figure 15.46.

Tableau Public file:

```
https://public.tableau.com/views/
SwitchBetweenMeasuress1058/Sheet1?:
language=en-US&:display_count=n&:origin=
viz_share_link
```

15.5.3 Data and Fields

For this visualization, in addition to the [Category] field, I use the [Sales] and [Profit] fields.

Category

Sales

Profit

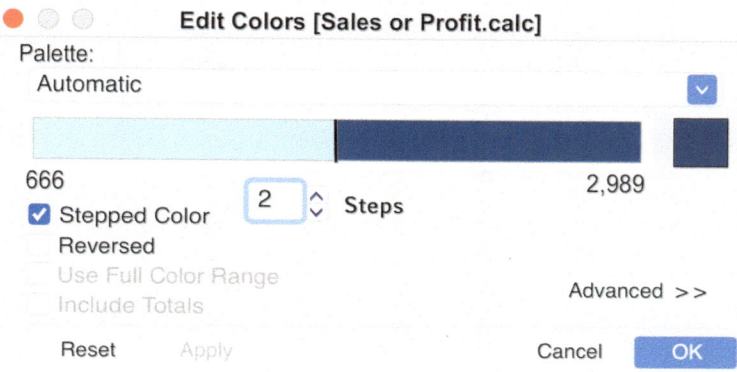

FIGURE 15.45
The Edit Colors dialog window.

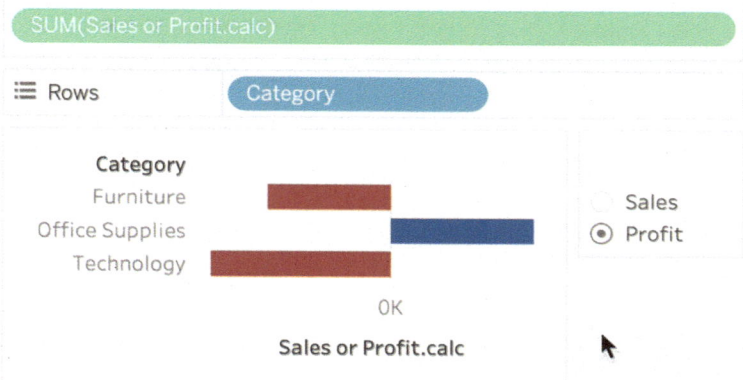

FIGURE 15.46
The Parameter Control on the right.

15.5.3.1 Calculated Field

The calculated field logic uses a parameter, so I *create the parameter first*.

> Sales or Profit.calc

15.5.4 Columns Shelf

The **Columns** shelf has the new calculation field, [Sales or Profit.calc].

15.5.5 Rows Shelf

The [Category] field is on the **Rows** shelf.

15.5.6 The Parameter and a Parameter Control

This example has a parameter, [Sales or Profit.p]. Users can click the **Parameter Control** to switch between measure fields.

> Sales or Profit.p

15.5.7 Marks Card: Color Tile

The values in my data set include negative and positive numbers for the [Profit] field, so I use a diverging color palette with two steps for the *Stepped Color*.

15.6 Switch between Aggregation: Sum and %

Using parameters to change aggregations and calculated fields is similar to the previous example, "Switch Between Measures." In Figure 15.47, the parameter control "Select Aggregation" is on the right side of the view.

In Figure 15.48, I have one calculated field that uses a case statement to return a sum or percentage calculation based on the selected parameter, "Select

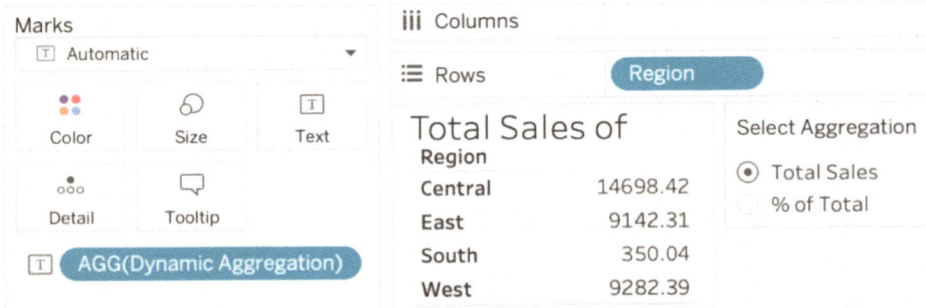

FIGURE 15.47
Select Aggregation Parameter Control on the Right Side.

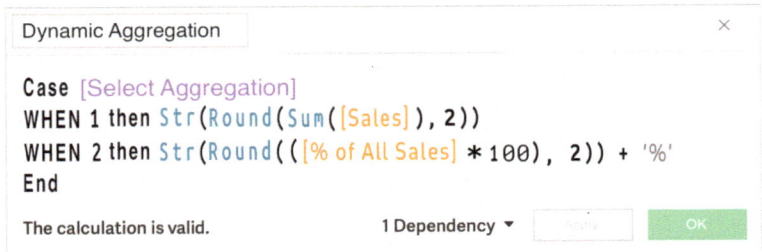

FIGURE 15.48
Dynamic Aggregation Field.

Aggregation." I've also included formatting in the expression. Customize the title to include the parameter so the title has either a *sum* or *percentage*.

Tableau Public file:

https://public.tableau.com/views/Switch BetweenAggregationsSumands1059/Sheet1?: language=en-US&:display_count=n&:origin= viz_share_link

15.6.1 Switch Between Dimensions

This example uses a parameter to filter dimension values along the same lines as the previous parameter examples. I am not using the **Filter** shelf. Instead, I created a [Yellow Fruit Group] based on the [Fruit] field. The **Parameter Control** for [What do you want to see.p] allows my audience to switch between the [Fruit] dimension, which is all fruit, and the group. A calculated field [calc to pick field] on the **Rows** shelf switches between the field and group, as shown in Figure 15.49.

The calculated field [calc to pick field] in Figure 15.50 selects the field or group. In **Chapter 8**, we looked at another dimension filter in *"Section 8.5.2 Dimension Filters" on page 164*. Customize the title to include the parameter so the title has either *fruit* or *yellow fruit*.

Tableau Public file:

https://public.tableau.com/views/Parameter tofilterdimensionss1039/Sheet1?:language=en-US&publish=yes&:display_count=n&:origin= viz_share_link

15.7 Hierarchies

Create **Hierarchies** to organize related dimension fields, as shown in Figure 15.51. Hierarchies allow users to drill down to a different level of detail. When we created a chart in **Chapter 5**, we looked at two ways to drill down into hierarchies. Earlier, the "Drill Down with a Set Action" example used a set action to display a hierarchy with arrow indicators. *"Section 7.2.6.1 Bullet Graph" on page 127* also uses a hierarchy.

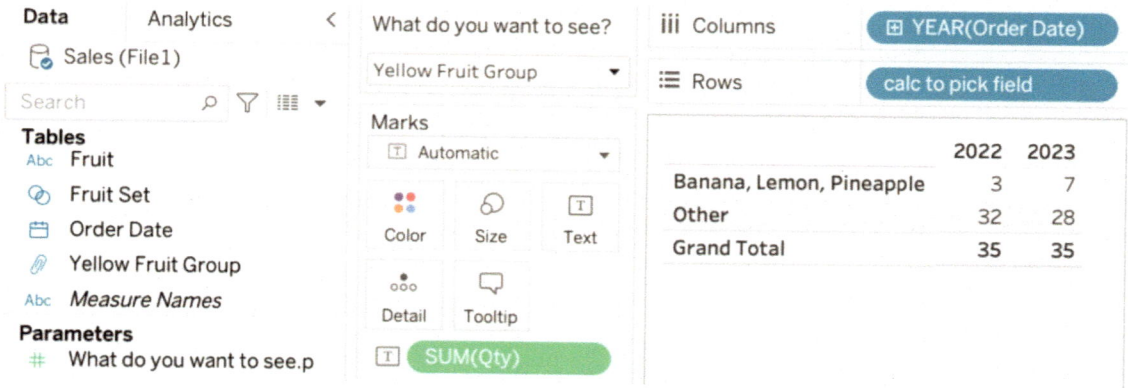

FIGURE 15.49
The "What do you want to see" Parameter.

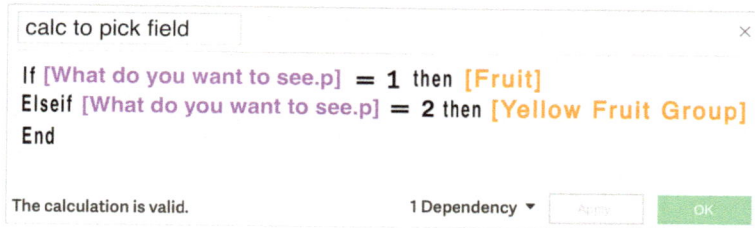

FIGURE 15.50
Calculated field.

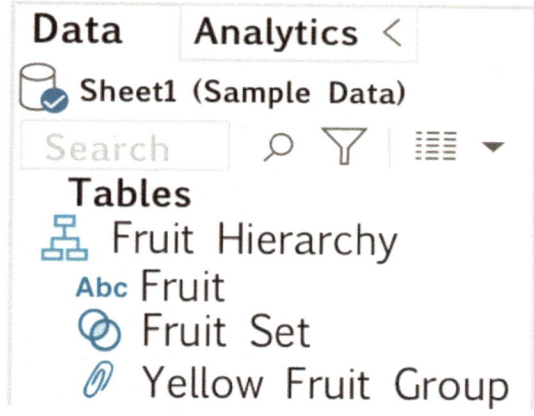

FIGURE 15.51
The Fruit hierarchy.

FIGURE 15.52
Tip: *Add instructions in the worksheet title for the audience to expand the hierarchy.*

Index

Pages in *italics* refer to figures.